Old English Word List

A Brief Glossary of 15,000 Old English Words

Matthew Leigh Embleton

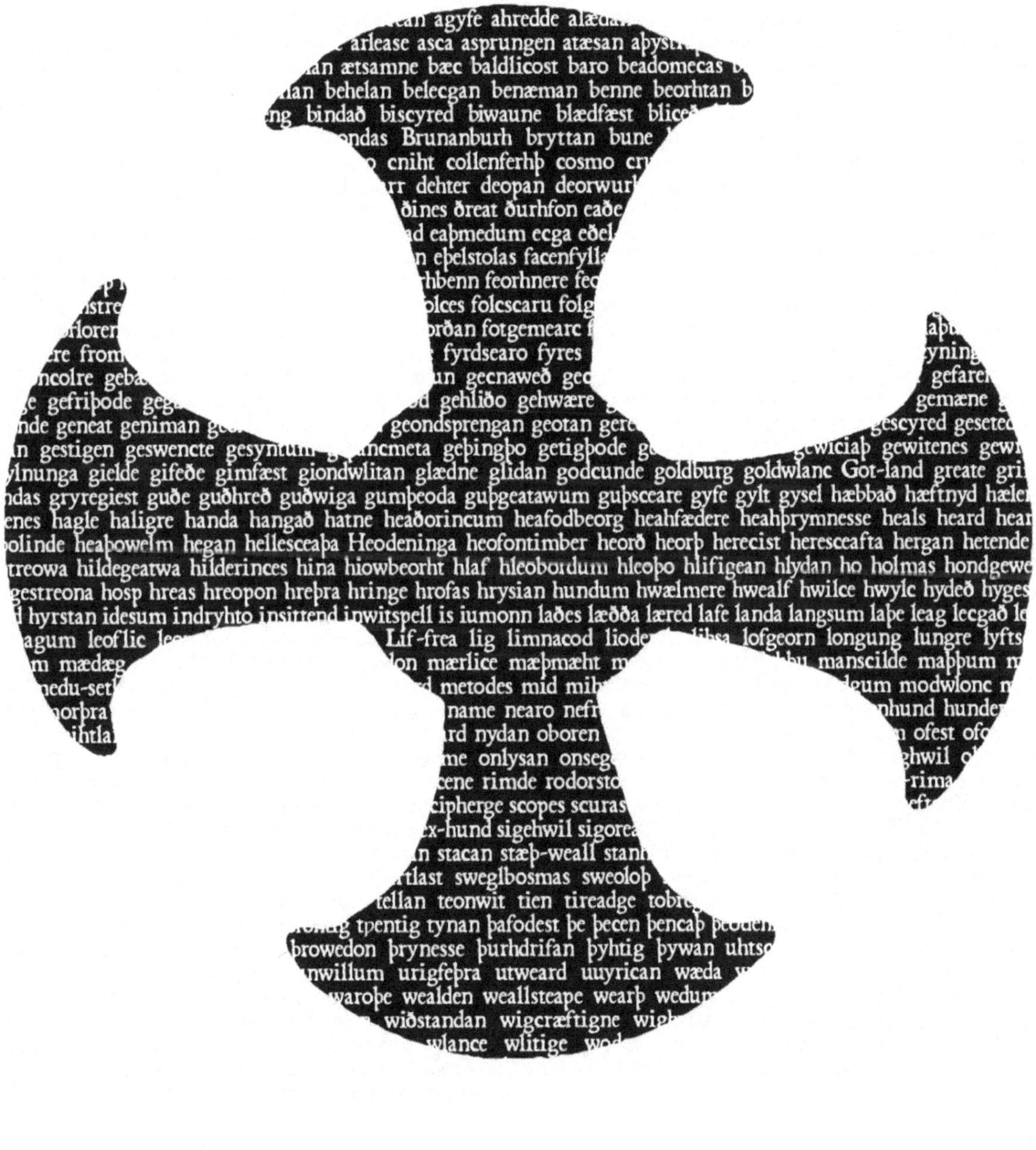

Copyright ©2022 Matthew Leigh Embleton. All rights reserved.

Old English Word List

Notes on the Language 1
   The Evolution of the Alphabet 1
   The Anglo-Saxon Futhorc..1
   The Old English Latin Alphabet 2
   Articles: this (*þes*) 2
   Demonstratives: that (*se*) 2
   Personal Pronouns: I, you, he / she / it, we, you, they 2
   Interogative Pronouns: who (*hwa*) and what (*hwæt*) 3
   The Verb to be 3
   Numbers 4
   One, Two and Three..4
   Cardinal Numbers...4
   Ordinal Numbers 5
Word List (*Ænglisc* to English) 7
Word List (English to *Ænglisc*) 277

Cover: Old English words laid over an outline of an Anglo-Saxon cross, author's design.

Acknowledgments

I have long been fascinated by languages and history, and I am very grateful to the special people in my life who have supported and encouraged me in my work. Thank you for believing in me. You know who you are.

Introduction

Old English (Ænglisc) is the earliest recorded form of the English language. It was brought to Britain by Anglo-Saxon settlers in the mid-5th century. The first literary works in Old English date from the mid 7th century. Spelling was not standardised but varied by region and dialect over time.

This book contains a list of over 15,000 Old English words translated into English.

Also included are notes on alphabet, grammar, numbers, and a list of over 7,000 English words translated into Old English.

This book is designed to be of use and interest to anyone with a passion for the Old English language, Anglo-Saxon history, or languages and history in general.

Notes on the Language

The Evolution of the Alphabet

When the Anglo-Saxons began settling England in the 5th century CE, they used runes as their writing system or alphabet. The word 'alphabet' itself comes from the Greek *'alpha'* + *'beta'*, the first two letters in the sequence. Likewise, the runic alphabets are referred to as *'futharks'* in the same way, because of the first six letters in the sequence *'F', 'U', 'Þ', 'A', 'R', 'K'*.

The Anglo-Saxons adapted the original Common Germanic runes or Elder Futhark into what would become known as the *Futhorc* or 'Anglo-Saxon Futhorc', sometimes referred to as 'Anglo-Frisian'. With the gradual Christianisation of Anglo-Saxon England came the introduction of the Old English version of the Latin Alphabet, known as the *'Læden stæf-rof'* (Latin stave-set). The following letters were borrowed from the Anglo-Saxon Futhorc:

- Þ þ — *'thurisaz'* or *'thorn'* which represents the unvoiced 'th' sound as in 'think', later replaced by 'th'.
- Ƿ ƿ — *'wynn'* which represents the /w/ sound as in 'water', later replaced by 'w'.

The following letters were adapted from the Latin Alphabet:

- Ð ð — *'thæt'*, *'eth'*, or *'edh'* which represents the voiced 'th' sound as in 'the', which was later replaced by 'th' or 'd'.
- Æ æ — *'aesc'* or *'ash'* representing the Latin diphthong or 'gliding vowel' of 'a'+'e'.

Also used was:

- ⁊ — representing 'and' which is similar in appearance to the number seven but sitting lower down in the script stave, which was later replaced by the latin ligature *'et'* and later *'and per se and'* or *'ampersand'* '&'.
- Þ̵ þ̵ — 'thorn with a stroke' which represents the word *'þæt'* or *'that'*.

These extra letters started to fall out of use after the Norman Conquest of England in 1066, but continued to be used in dialects of Middle English outside of London and the South-East of England as late as the end of the 14th century and beyond. One example of this is the original manuscript of 'Sir Gawain and the Green Knight' in the North West Midland dialect.

The Anglo-Saxon Futhorc

	Rune	Name	Sound		Rune	Name	Sound		Rune	Name	Sound
1	ᚠ	Feoh	/F/, [V]	12	ᛄ	Ger	/J/	23	ᛟ	Eðel	/Ø/, /Ø:/
2	ᚢ	Ur	/U/, /U:/	13	ᛇ	Eoh	/I:/? /X/, [Ç]	24	ᛗ	Dæg	/D/
3	ᚦ	Þorn	/Θ/, [Ð]	14	ᛈ	Peorð	/P/	25	ᚪ	Ac	/a/, /a:/
4	ᚩ	Os	/O/, /O:/	15	ᛉ	Eolhx	/KS/	26	ᚫ	Æsc	/Æ/, /Æ:/
5	ᚱ	Rad	/R/	16	ᛋ	Sigel	/S/, [Z]	27	ᚣ	Yr	/Y/, /Y:/
6	ᚳ	Cen	/K/, /Ki/, /TΣ/	17	ᛏ	Ti, tir	/T/	28	✳	Ior	/IO/?, /I:O:/?
7	ᚷ	Gyfu	/g/, [ɣ], /gʲ/), /J/, /X/?, /Gi/	18	ᛒ	Beorc	/B/	29	ᛠ	Ear	/Æa/, /Æ:a/

1

	Rune	Name	Sound		Rune	Name	Sound		Rune	Name	Sound
8	ᚹ	Ƿynn	/W/	19	ᛖ	Eh	/E/, /E:/	30	ᛣ	Calc	/K/
9	ᚺ	Hægl	/H/, /X/, [ç]	20	ᛗ	Mann	/M/	31	ᛤ ᛥ	Gar, Gungnir	/K/G/, [ɣ]
10	ᚾ	Nyd	/N/	21	ᛚ	Lagu	/L/	32	ᛢ	Cweorð	/K/KW
11	ᛁ	Is	/I/, /I:/	22	ᛜ ᛝ	Ing	/ŋG/, /ŋ/	33	ᛪ	Stan	/ST/

The Old English Latin Alphabet

	Letter	Sound		Letter	Sound		Letter	Sound
1	A / a	[ɑ, ɑ:]	9	G ᵹ / g ᵹ	[g, ɣ, j, dʒ]	17	R / r	[ɹ]
2	Æ / æ	[æ, æ:]	10	H / h	[h, ç, x]	18	S ſ / s ſ	[s, z]
3	B / b	[b]	11	I / i	[i]	19	T / t	[t]
4	C / c	[k, t͡ʃ]	12	L / l	[l]	20	Þ / þ	[θ, ð]
5	D / d	[d]	13	M / m	[m]	21	U / u	[u]
6	Ð / ð	[θ, ð]	14	N / n	[n]	22	Ƿ / ƿ	[w]
7	E / e	[e, e:]	15	O / o	[o, o:]	23	X / x	[ks, xs, çs]
8	F / f	[f, v, f:]	16	P / p	[p]	24	Y / y	[y, y:]

Articles: this (þes)

this	Singular			Plural
	Masculine	Neuter	Feminine	
Nominative	þes	þis	þeos	þas
Accusative	þisne	þis	þas	þas
Genitive	þisses	þisses	þisse	þissa
Dative	þissum	þissum	þisse	þissum
Instrumental	þys	þys	þisse	þissum

Demonstratives: that (se)

that	Singular			Plural
	Masculine	Neuter	Feminine	
Nominative	se	þæt	seo	þa
Accusative	þone	þæt	þa	þa
Genitive	þæs	þæs	þære	þara
Dative	þam	þam	þære	þam
Instrumental	þon, þy	þon, þy	þære	þam

Personal Pronouns: I, you, he / she / it, we, you, they

1st Person	Singular		Dual		Plural	
Nominative	I	ic	we (two)	wit	we	we

Accusative	me	*mec*	us (two)	*unc*	us	*us*
Dative	me	*me*	us (two)	*unc*	us	*us*
Genitive	mine	*min*	our (two)	*uncer*	our	*ure*

2nd Person	Singular		Dual		Plural	
Nominative	you	*þu*	you (two)	*git*	you (plural)	*ge*
Accusative	you	*þe*	you (two)	*inc*	you (plural)	*eow*
Dative	you	*þe*	you (two)	*inc*	you (plural)	*eow*
Genitive	your	*þin*	your (two)	*incer*	your (plural)	*eower*

3rd person	Singular						Plural	
	Masculine		Neuter		Feminine			
Nominative	he	he	it	hit	she	heo	they	hie
Accusative	he	hine	it	hit	she	hie	they	hie
Dative	him	him	it	him	her	hire	them	him
Genitive	his	his	its	his	hers	hire	their	heora

Interogative Pronouns: who (*hwa*) and what (*hwæt*)

	who	what
Nominative	*hwa*	*hwæt*
Accusative	*hwone*	*hwæt*
Genitive	*hwæs*	*hwæs*
Dative	*hwam*	*hwam*
Instrumental	*hwon, hwy*	*hwon, hwy*

The Verb to be

Infinitive				be	*beon*	*wesan*
				to be	*to beonne*	*to wesanne*
Participle	Present			being	*beonde*	*wesende*
	Past			been	*(ge)beon*	*(ge)wesan*
Indicative	Present	Singular	1st person	I am	*beo*	*eom*
			2nd person	you are	*bist*	*eart*
			3rd person	he / she / it is	*biþ*	*is*
		Plural		we / you / they are	*beoþ*	*sind*
	Past	Singular	1st person	I was	*wæs*	*wæs*
			2nd person	you were	*wære*	*wære*
			3rd person	he / she / it was	*wæs*	*wæs*
		Plural		we / you / they were	*wæron*	*wæron*
Subjunctive	Present	Singular		be	*beo*	*sie*
		Plural		be	*beon*	*sien*
	Past	Singular		were	*wære*	*wære*
		Plural		were	*wæren*	*wæren*
Imperative		Singular		be	*beo*	*wes*
		Plural		be	*beoþ*	*wesaþ*

Some of the above word forms can be recognised via their Early Modern English and Modern English counterparts:

Ænglisc	Early Modern English	Modern English
ge	ye	you (plural)
hæfþ, hafaþ	hath, haveth	have, has, had
ic eom	I am	I am
ic wæs	I was	I was
min	mine	mine
þin	thine	your
þu	thou	you
þu eart	thou art	you are

Numbers

One, Two and Three

One	masculine	feminine	neuter
nominative	*an*	*an*	*an*
accusative	*an-ne*	*an-e*	*an*
genitive	*an-es*	*an-re*	*an-es*
dative	*an-um*	*anre*	*an-um*
instrumental	*an-e*	*an-re*	*an-e*

Two	masculine	feminine	neuter
nominative	*tpegen*	*tpa*	*tpa, tu*
accusative	*tpegen*	*tpa*	*tpa, tu*
genitive	*tpega*	*tpega*	*tpega*
dative	*tpam*	*tpam*	*tpam*
instrumental	*tpam*	*tpam*	*tpam*

Three	masculine	feminine	neuter
nominative	*þri*	*þreo*	*þreo*
accusative	*þri*	*þreo*	*þreo*
genitive	*þreora*	*þreora*	*þreora*
dative	*þrim*	*þrim*	*þrim*
instrumental	*þrim*	*þrim*	*þrim*

Cardinal Numbers

1	one	*an*
2	two	*tpegen*
3	three	*þri*
4	four	*feoper*
5	five	*fif*
6	six	*siex*
7	seven	*seofon*
8	eight	*eahta*
9	nine	*nigon*

10	ten	*tien*
11	eleven	*endleofan*
12	twelve	*tpelf*
13	thirteen	*þreotine*
14	fourteen	*feopertine*
15	fifteen	*fiftine*
16	sixteen	*siextine*
17	seventeen	*seofontine*
18	eighteen	*eahtatine*
19	nineteen	*nigontine*
20	twenty	*tpentig*
21	twenty one	*an and tpentig*
22	twenty two	*tpegen and tpentig*
23	twenty three	*þri and tpentig*
30	thirty	*þritig*
31	thirty one	*an and þritig*
32	thirty two	*tpegen and þritig*
33	thirty three	*þri and þritig*
40	forty	*feopertig*
41	forty one	*an and feopertig*
42	forty two	*tpegen and feopertig*
43	forty three	*þri and feopertig*
50	fifty	*fiftig*
60	sixty	*sixtig*
70	seventy	*hundseofontig*
80	eighty	*hundeahtatig*
90	ninety	*hundnigontig*
100	a hundred	*hundteontig*
110	a hundred and ten	*hundendleftig*
120	a hundred and twenty	*hundtpelftig*
200	two hundred	*tpa*
300	three hundred	*þreo*
1000	a thousand	*þusend*
2000	two thousand	*tpa þusend*
3000	three thousand	*þreo þusend*

Ordinal Numbers

1	first	*forma*
2	second	*oþer*
3	third	*þridda*
4	fourth	*feorþa*
5	fifth	*fifta*
6	sixth	*sixta*
7	seventh	*seofoþa*
8	eighth	*eahtoþa*

9	ninth	*nigoþa*
10	tenth	*teoþa*
11	eleventh	*endlefta*
12	twelfth	*twelfta*
13	thirteenth	*þreotteoþa*
14	fourteenth	*feowerteoþa*
15	fifteenth	*fifteoþa*
16	sixteenth	*sixteoþa*
17	seventeenth	*seofonteoþa*
18	eighteenth	*eahtateoþa*
19	nineteenth	*nigonteoþa*
20	twentieth	*twentigoþa*
21	twenty first	*an and twentigoþa*
22	twenty second	*twa and twentigoþa*
23	twenty third	*þreo and twentigoþa*
30	thirtieth	*þritigoþa*
31	thirty first	*an and þritigoþa*
32	thirty second	*twa and þritigoþa*
33	thirty third	*þreo and þritigoþa*
40	fortieth	*feowertigoþa*
41	forty first	*an and feowertigoþa*
42	forty second	*twa and feowertigoþa*
43	forty third	*þreo and feowertigoþa*
50	fiftieth	*fiftigoþa*
60	sixtieth	*sixtigoþa*
70	seventieth	*hundseofontigoþa*
80	eightieth	*hundeahtatigoþa*
90	ninetieth	*hundnigontigoþa*
100	hundredth	*hundteontigoþa*
101	hundred and first	*hundteontigoþa and forma*

Word List (*Ænglisc* to English)

Ænglisc	English	*Ænglisc*	English
7, 7		*abræd*	draw, draw-a-sword, remove, take-away, withdraw
7	and	*abrægd*	draw, draw-a-sword, remove, take-away, withdraw
7sware	answer		
A, a		*Abrame*	Abraham (name)
		abreat	destroy, kill
a	a, ages, all, always, bake, destroy, eternally, ever, from, from (Latin)	*abrecan*	break, destroy, violate
		abredwade	destroy, kill
		abredwian	kill
aæðan	destroy	*abregd*	draw, draw-a-sword, remove, take-away, withdraw
aæþan	destroy		
ab	from (Latin)		
abacæ	bake	*abregdan*	draw, draw-a-sword, remove, take-away, withdraw
abacan	bake		
abal	might, power		
abbod	abbot	*abregde*	draw, draw-a-sword, remove, take-away, withdraw
abbude	abbot		
abead	admonish, announce, bid, command, offer, provide, summon		
		abreoðan	destroyed, fail, perish
		abreoðe	destroyed, fail, perish
abeag	bend, bow, incline, rings	*abreot*	destroy, kill
abealch	anger, enrage, offend	*abreotan*	destroy, kill
		abreoten	destroy, kill
abelgan	anger, angry, enrage, enraged, offend	*abreoþan*	destroyed, fail, perish
		abreoþe	destroyed, fail, perish
abeod	admonish, command, offer, provide, summon	*abrocen*	break, broken, destroy, violate
abeodan	admonish, announce, bid, command, offer, provide, summon	*abrocene*	break, destroy, violate
		abroden	draw, draw-a-sword, remove, take-away, withdraw
abidan	abide, await		
abiddan	ask, obtain, pray	*abroten*	destroy, kill
aboden	announce, bid	*abrugdon*	draw, draw-a-sword, remove, take-away, withdraw
abolescit	fades-away (Latin)		
abolgen	anger, angry, enrage, enraged, offend	*abscondita*	was-hidden (Latin)

Word List (*Ænglisc* to English)

Ænglisc	English	*Ænglisc*	English
abude	admonish, command, offer, provide, summon	acwyþ	banish, reject, say, speak
abudon	announce, bid	acyþan	make-known, proclaim
abugan	bend, bow, incline	ad	fire, pyre
abutan	about, around	að	oath
ac	and, bear, but, give-birth-to, however, nevertheless, never-the-less, so, yet	aða	oath
		adælan	divide, separate
		adæled	divide, separate
		adælede	divide, separate
acende	bear, begot, give-birth-to	aðas	oath
		ade	fire, pyre
acennan	bear, bring-forth, give-birth-to	aðe	oath
		Aðeluuold	Æthelwold (name)
acenned	bear, born, give-birth-to	Aðelwold	Æthelwold (name), judge
acigan	call	ademan	judge
acigde	call	ademest	judge
aclænsian cleanse	call	adfære	funeral-procession, funeral-pyre, path-to-the-pyre
acol	alarmed, dismayed, timid		
acolað	grows-cold	adfaru	funeral-pyre
acolaþ	grows-cold	adl	disease, sickness
acsian	ask, deserve, seek	adlegan	sick, suffering
actreo	oak, the-oak	adlig	sick, suffering
acuman	come	adligum	sick, suffering
acumen	come	ado	put
acwæð	banish, reject, say, speak	aðohte	consider, contrive, intend, think
acwæþ	banish, reject, say, speak	adon	put
		aðor	either
acwealde	destroy, kill, killed	adræfed	driven-away
acweccan	brandish, quiver, shake	adraf	drive-away, drove-away
acweðan	banish, reject, say, speak	adreogan	endure
		adrifan	drive-away
acweht	brandish, quiver, shake	adrifen	drive-away
		adrifest	drive-away
acwehte	brandish, quiver, shake	aðsweord	oath, oath-sworn, sworn-oath
acwellan	destroy, kill	aðum	oath
acweþan	banish, reject, say, speak	aðumsweoras	son-in-law-and-father-in-law
acwið	banish, reject, say, speak	aðumsweran	son-in-law-and-father-in-law
acwiþ	banish, reject, say, speak	adwæsce	quenched
		aðystrað	grows-dark, law
acwyð	banish, reject, say, speak	aeðða	excellent, or

Word List (*Ænglisc* to English)

Ænglisc	English
aelda	elders, elders', fire, men
aelicce	ash-woods, battle
aerendfaest	errand, mission
aergewin	former-struggle
aerist	building, first
aeþþa	excellent, or
afanda	find-out, test, try
afandian	find-out, test, try
afaran	offspring, travelled
afeallan	fall
afeallen	fall
afedan	beget, bring-forth, feed, produce
afeded	beget, bring-forth, produce
afera	depart, descendant, heir, heir-of, son
aferian	depart, withdraw
aferige	depart, withdraw
afligde	drive-out, expel
aflygan	drive-out, expel
aflygde	drive-out, expel
aflyman	drive-away, put-to-flight
aflymde	drive-away, put-to-flight
afor	bitter, fierce, harsh
aforan	descendant, heir, son
afylgde	persecute, pursue
afylgean	persecute, pursue
afyllan	fill
afylled	cast-down, fill
afyrhtan	frighten
afyrhte	frighten
afyrran	take-away
afyrred	take-away
afysan	drive-away, urge-on
afysed	drive-away, urge-on
agalan	sing, sing-out
agan	achieve, control, end, have, own, pass-away, possess, rule, to-hold
a-gan	away-go, occur, pass
agangan	go, go-by, happen, pass
agangen	go, go-by, happen, pass
age	have-control, own, possess, rule
ageaf	give, give-up, grant, relinquish
ageafe	give, give-up, grant, relinquish
ageafon	give, give-up, grant, relinquish
ageald	offer, yield
ageat	deprive, pout-out, shed
agen	have-control, own, possess, proper, rule
agend	owner, ruler
agendes	owner
agendfrea	owner, possessing-lord
agendfrean	owner, possessing-lord
agene	own, proper
agenes	own, proper
agenre	own, proper
agenum	own, proper
ageotan	deprive, pour-out, shed
agetan	destroy
ageted	destroyed
agiefan	give, give-up, grant, relinquish
agieldan	offer, yield
agif	give, give-up, grant, relinquish
agifan	give, give-up, grant, relinquish
agifen	give, give-up, grant, relinquish
aglæacan	fierce-fighter, terrible-attacker
aglæca	combatant, fierce-fighter, monster, terrible-attacker, the-terrible-one

Word List (*Ænglisc* to English)

Ænglisc	English	*Ænglisc*	English
aglæcan	fierce-fighter, terrible-attacker, the-attacker	*ahloh*	exult, laugh-at
		ahof	achieve, exalt, lift, lift-up, maintain, raise, raise-up
aglæcean	fierce-fighter, terrible-attacker	*ahofe*	raised
aglæcwif	attacking-woman, fierce	*ahofon*	achieve, exalt, lift, lift-up, maintain, raise, raise-up
agnian	acquire, dedicate, obtain, own	*ahon*	hang, suspend
agnum	own, proper	*ahongen*	hang, suspend
agol	sing, sing-out	*ahrædde*	rescue, save
agon	have, have-control, own, possess, rule	*ahreddan*	rescue, save
		ahredde	rescue, save
agongen	go, go-by, happen, pass	*ahreddest*	rescue, save
		ahreded	rescue, save
agoten	pour-out, shed	*ahsian*	ask, deserve, seek
agotene	deprive, pour-out, shed	*ahsode*	ask, deserve, seek
		ahsodon	ask, deserve, seek
agrafan	carve, engrave	*aht*	anything, at-all, nothing, something
agrof	carve, carved, engrave	*Ahte*	had, have, have-control, own, possess, rule, ruled
agyfe	give, give-up, grant, relinquish		
agyfen	give, give-up, grant, relinquish	*ahton*	have-control, own, possess, rule
ah	have, have-control, own, possess, rule	*ahudan*	plunder
		ahuðan	plunder
ahæfen	achieve, exalt, lift, maintain, raise-up	*ahuþan*	plunder
		ahwæðer	either
ahafen	achieve, exalt, lift, lift-up, maintain, raise, raise-up	*ahwær*	anywhere
		ahwæþer	either
		ahwearf	turn-aside-from, turn-away
ahangen	hang, suspend		
aheawan	cut-down	*ahweorfan*	turn-aside-from, turn-away
aheawen	cut-down		
ahebban	achieve, exalt, lift, lift-up, maintain, raise, raise-up	*ahwet*	reject
		ahwettan	reject
		ahwurfon	turn-aside-from, turn-away
aheng	hang, suspend		
ahengon	hung-up	*ahycgan*	consider, devise
aherian	praise	*ahyrdan*	harden
ahicgan	consider, devise	*ahyrded*	harden
ahiþan	destroy, devour	*airnan*	pass-away, run-out
ahlæcan	fierce-fighter, terrible-attacker	*akende*	brought-forth
		alaðað	becomes-loathed
ahleapan	leap-up	*alaðaþ*	becomes-loathed, lead
ahleop	leap-up		
ahliehhan	exult, laugh-at	*alædan*	lead
ahlog	exult, laugh-at	*alædde*	lead

Word List (Ænglisc to English)

Ænglisc	English	Ænglisc	English
alæde	lead	alecgan	abandon, conquer, lay, lay-down, put-down, relinquish
alæg	cease, fail		
alætan	forgive, give-up, pardon, relinquish	alecgean	abandon, conquer, lay, lay-down, put-down, relinquish
alæte	forgive, give-up, pardon, relinquish		
alamp	come-to-be, happen	alede	abandon, conquer, lay, lay-down, put-down, relinquish
alaþaþ	becomes-loathed, lead		
aldor	elder, eternity, king, life, lord, prince, superior	aledon	abandon, conquer, lay, lay-down, put-down, relinquish
aldorbana	killer, murderer	alegde	abandon, conquer, lay, lay-down, put-down, relinquish
aldorbanan	killer, murderer		
aldorbealu	death-danger, life-destruction		
aldorceare	great-sorrow	alegdon	abandon, conquer, lay, lay-down, put-down, relinquish
aldorcearu	great-sorrow		
aldordæg	life-day	aleh	fail-to-fulfil
aldordagum	life-day	aleoðode	remove, separate
aldordema	lord, magistrate	aleogan	fail-to-fulfil
aldorduguð	leading-warriors, nobility	aleoþian	remove, separate
		aleoþode	remove, separate
aldorduguðe	leading-warriors, nobility	ales	all
		alesan	pick, select
aldorduguþ	leading-warriors, nobility	alesen	pick, select
		alicgan	cease, fail
aldorduguþe	leading-warriors, nobility	alicgean	cease, fail
		alimpan	befall, come-to-be, come-to-pass, happen
aldorgedal	death		
aldorleas	dead, leaderless, lifeless		
		allmectig	all-ruler, almighty
aldorlease	leaderless	allwalda	all-ruler
aldorleasne	dead, leaderless, lifeless	allwihta	all-creatures
		also	as, likewise
aldornere	life-saving, safety, salvation	alswa	as
		alumpen	come-to-be, happen
aldorneru	life-saving, safety, salvation	alwalda	all-ruler
		alwaldan	all-ruler
aldorþegn	chieftain, important-noble, thegn	alwaldend	all-ruler
		alwealdan	all-ruler
aldorwisa	chief, leader	alwihta	all-creatures
aldre	elder, eternity, king, life, lord, prince, superior	alyfan	allow, entrust, grant, permit
		alyfde	allow, entrust, grant
aldres	eternity, life	alyfed	allow, entrust, grant
aldrum	eternity, life	alynnan	deliver, release
		alysan	loosen, take-off-armour

11

Word List (*Ænglisc* to English)

Ænglisc	English
alysde	released
alysed	loosen, take-off-armour
ambyht	command, service
ambyhto	command, service
ambyhtsecg	servant
ambyr	fair, favourable
ameldian	betray, denounce, make-known, reveal
ameldod	betray, denounce, make-known, reveal
amen	amen, disable
amor	love (Latin)
amyrde	disable, hinder, prevent
amyrran	disable, hinder, prevent, wound
amyrred	disable, hinder, prevent
an	1, 1 (accusative neuter), 1 (nominative feminine), 1 (nominative masculine), 1 (nominative neuter), a, about, allow, alone, an, grant, in, into, like, offer, on, one, one (accusative neuter), one (nominative feminine), one (nominative masculine), one (nominative neuter), onto, single, wish
an and feowertig	41, forty one
an and feopertig	41, forty one
an and feowertigoþa	forty first
an and fiftig	51, fifty one
an and fiftigoþa	fifty first
an and hundeahtatig	81, eighty one
an and hundeahtatigoþa	eighty first
an and hundendleftig	111, a hundred and eleven
an and hundnigontig	91, ninety one
an and hundnigontigoþa	ninety first
an and hundseofontig	71, seventy one
an and hundseofontigoþa	seventy first
an and hundteontig	101, a hundred and one
an and sixtig	61, sixty one
an and sixtigoþa	sixty first
an and þritig	31, thirty one
an and þritigoþa	thirty first
an and twentig	21, twenty one
an and tpentig	21, twenty one
an and twentigoþa	twenty first
ana	alone, one, retainer
anbre	bucket
anbyhtscealc	retainer, servant
anbyhtscealcas	retainer, servant
ancor	anchor
ancre	anchor
and	and, anger
anda	anger, hostility, injury, malice, vexation
andæg	one-day-long
andægne	one-day-long
andan	anger, injury, perceptible-sign, vexation
andette	confess
andgiettacen	perceptible-sign
andgit	knowledge, meaning, perception, sense, understanding
andlang	accompanying, entire, extended
andlean	retaliation, revenge
andlifen	food, nourishment, wages
andlifne	food, nourishment, wages
andlong	accompanying, entire, extended
andlongne	accompanying, entire, extended
andraedan	dread, fear

Word List (*Ænglisc* to English)

Ænglisc	English	*Ænglisc*	English
andrysne	awe-inspiring, fearful, terrible, venerable	an-es	1 (genitive masculine), 1 (genitive neuter), one (genitive masculine), one (genitive neuter)
andrysnum	awe-inspiring, fearful, terrible, venerable		
andsaca	adversary, enemy	anew	time, turn
andsacum	enemy	anfeald	one-fold, plain, simple, uncomplicated
andsund	healthy, sound, uninjured, whole		
andsware	answer, reply	anfealdne	plain, simple, uncomplicated
andswarede	answer, reply		
andswaredon	answer, reply	anfenge	accept, receive, take, take-up
andswarian	answer, reply, respond		
		anfloga	solitary-flier
andswarod	answer, respond	anforht	frightened
andswarode	answer, reply, respond	anforlætan	abandon, lose, relinquish
andswarodon	answer, reply	anforleten	abandon, lose, relinquish
andswaru	answer, reply, response	anga	only
andwærden	opposite, present	angan	attempt, begin, only, try, undertake
andweard	opposite, present		
andweardan	opposite, present	angeald	atone-for, be-punished-for, pay-for
andweardne	opposite, present		
andweorc	matter, substance		
andwig	resistance, retaliation	angeat	perceive, understand
andwlita	countenance, face	angel	hook
andwlitan	countenance, face	Angel-cynn	Angle-kin
andwyrdan	answer	angenga	alone-walker, solitary-one
andwyrde	answer, reply		
ane	alone, one	angengea	alone-walker, solitary-one
an-e	1 (accusative feminine), 1 (instrumental masculine), 1 (instrumental neuter), one (accusative feminine), one (instrumental masculine), one (instrumental neuter)	angin	action, beginning, enterprise, one-step
		anginn	beginning
		angla	angels
		Anglo-Saxon	English (name)
		angolsexna	of-the-Anglo-Saxons
		anhaga	exile, hermit, one-who-dwells-alone, recluse, solitary-dweller, solitary-one, wanderer
anegum	any	anhar	very-grey-haired
anes	a, alone, one, time	anhogan	hermit, recluse, solitary-dweller

Word List (*Ænglisc* to English)

Ænglisc	English	*Ænglisc*	English
anhydig	brave, firm, resolute, strong-minded	an-re	1 (genitive feminine), 1 (instrumental feminine), one (genitive feminine), one (instrumental feminine)
aninga	certainly, entirely, immediately, must-do, right-away		
Anlaf	Anlaf (name)		
Anlafe	Anlaf (name)		
Anlafes	Anlaf's (name)	ansien	beauty, face, figure, sight
anleofan	food		
anlicnes	appearance, form, image, likeness, resemblance	anstapan	land-wanderer
		ansund	healthy, sound, uninjured, whole
anlicnesse	appearance, form, likeness, resemblance	ansyn	beauty, face, figure, sight
		ansyne	beauty, face, figure, sight
anlycnysse	appearance, form, likeness, resemblance	antid	the-same-time
		antwig	resistance, retaliation
anmod	resolute, single-minded, unanimous, united	anum	alone, one
		an-um	1 (dative masculine), 1 (dative neuter), one (dative masculine), one (dative neuter)
anmode	resolute, single-minded, unanimous, united		
anmodlice	resolutely		
ann	bestow, grant	anunga	certainly, entirely, immediately, right-away
Annan	Anna (name)		
anne	alone, one		
an-ne	1 (accusative masculine), one (accusative masculine)	anwalda	sole-ruler
		anwaldan	sole-ruler
		anwealda	ruler, sole-ruler
		anyman	away
annesse	alone	apostol	apostle
anon	alone	apostoles	apostle
anpaðas	narrow-path	ar	copper, dignity, favour, honour, mercy, messenger, oar, prosperity, respect, virtue
anpæð	narrow-path		
anpæþ	narrow-path		
anpaþas	narrow-path		
anra	alone, one		
anræd	determined, resolute	ara	dignity, honour, mercy, prosperity, respect, virtue
anre	1 (dative feminine), alone, one, one (dative feminine)		
		arað	honour, respect
		aræd	arranged, decided, determined, inexorable
		aræman	lift, raise-up, stand-up

Word List (*Ænglisc* to English)

Ænglisc	English	*Ænglisc*	English
aræmde	lift, raise-up, stand-up	arleas	base, dishonourable, humiliated, sinful, sinner, wicked, without-honour
arær	raise-up		
aræran	lift-up, raise		
arærde	lift-up, raise		
arærdon	lift-up, raise	arlease	humiliated, sinful, sinner, without-honour
aræred	dignity, lift-up, raise		
aran	dignity, honour, mercy, prosperity, respect, virtue	arleasra	humiliated, sinful, sinner, without-honour
aras	arise, arose, messenger	arlice	honourably, kindly
araþ	honour, respect	arlicne	honourably
ardlice	quickly	arn	hasten, move-quickly, run
ardor	heat (Latin)		
are	dignity, grace, honour, mercy, prosperity, respect, virtue	arna	dignity, honour, mercy, prosperity, respect, virtue
		arod	bold, ready
areafian	carry-off, take-away	arra	dignity, honour, mercy, prosperity, respect, virtue
areafod	carry-off, take-away		
areccan	reckon		
areccean	declare	arstaf	benefit, kindness, support
arena	dignity, honour, mercy, prosperity, respect, virtue	arstafum	benefit, kindness, support
ares	messenger	arum	dignity, honour, mercy, prosperity, respect, virtue
aretan	encourage, gladden		
areted	encourage, gladden		
arette	cheered	arweorðian	honour
arfæst	honourable, pious, righteous, virtuous	arweorþe	honourable
		arweorþian	honour
arfæstan	honourable, pious, righteous, virtuous	arwurðlice	reverently, with-honour
arfæste	honourable, pious, righteous, virtuous	arwurðnys	honour, reverence
		arwurðnysse	honour, reverence
arfestnesse	mercifulness	arwurðode	honour
arhwate	eager	arwurþlice	reverently, with-honour
arian	honour, respect		
ariht	properly	arwurþnys	honour, reverence
arim	recite	arwurþnysse	honour, reverence
ariman	recite	arwurþode	honour
arinnan	expire, run-out	asæcgan	speak
aris	arise	asæde	declare, explain
arisað	arise, arises	asægd	relate, say
arisan	arise	asægde	relate, say
arisaþ	arise	asælan	bind-with-fetters, constrain, oppress
arisen	arise		
arison	arise	asca	ash-tree, ship, spear

Word List (*Ænglisc* to English)

Ænglisc	English	*Ænglisc*	English
asceacan	brandish, shake	astreccan	extend, lie-down, prostrate, reach-out, stretch-out
asceaf	drive-out, expel, remove		
asceoc	brandish, shake	astrece	extend, lie-down, prostrate, reach-out, stretch-out
ascian	ask, discover, find-out		
ascufan	drive-out, expel, remove	astreht	extend, lie-down, prostrate, reach-out, stretch-out
asealcan	slacken, weaken		
asecgan	declare, explain, relate, say, tell	astrienan	beget, give-birth-to
		astrynde	beget, give-birth-to
asendan	send, send-forth	astypan	deprivation?
asende	send, send-forth	astypednes	deprivation?
asendest	send, send-forth	astyred	excite, move, stir-up
asendne	sent-forth	astyrian	excite, move, remove, stir-up, to-move
aseted	appoint, place, set		
asettan	appoint, place, set		
asette	appoint, place, set	asungen	chant, sing
asetton	appoint, place, set	aswamað	cease, grow-dark
asingan	chant, sing	aswamaþ	cease, grow-dark
asinge	chant, sing	aswamian	cease, grow-dark
aslupan	disappear, slip-away-from	aswefan	kill, put-to-sleep
		aswefede	kill, put-to-sleep
asmiðigen	construct, smith	asyndrod	asunder
asmiþigen	construct, smith	atæsan	injure, wound
asmiþod	construct, smith	atæsed	injure, torn, wound
asolað	grows-dirty	ateah	deal-with, dispose-of, journey, remove, take-away
asolaþ	grows-dirty		
aspaw	vomit		
aspiwan	vomit	atelic	dreadful, horrible, terrifying
aspringan	arise, spring-up		
asprungen	arise, spring-up	atemian	tame
astag	arise, become-proud, mount, rise	ateon	deal-with, dispose-of, draw, journey, remove, take-away, unsheathe
astah	arise, become-proud, mount, rise		
astandan	stand-up	atertan	poison-twig
asteah	arise, become-proud, mount, rise	atertanum	poison-twig
		aþ	oath
astelidæ	arise, established	aþa	oath
astigan	arise, become-proud, mount, rise	aþas	oath
		aþe	oath
astigeð	arise, become-proud, mount, rise	aþecgan	serve-food, to-kill?
		Aþeluuold	Æthelwold (name)
astigeþ	arise, become-proud, mount, rise	Aþelwold	Æthelwold (name), judge
astod	stand-up	aþencan	consider, contrive, intend, think
astondeð	standing		
		aþenedon	extend, stretch-out

Word List (*Ænglisc* to English)

Ænglisc	English
aþenian	extend, stretch-out
aþohte	consider, contrive, intend, think
aþringan	push, shove
aþrong	push, rushing, shove
aþsweord	oath, oath-sworn, sworn-oath
aþum	oath
aþumsweoras	son-in-law-and-father-in-law
aþumsweran	son-in-law-and-father-in-law
aþwean	cleanse, wash
aþwoh	cleanse, wash
aþystraþ	grows-dark, law
atol	dire, hateful, horrible, repulsive, terrible
atolan	horrible, terrible
atole	horrible, terrible
atolne	horrible, terrible
attack	attack
attor	poison, venom
attorsceaða	poisonous-enemy
attorsceaðan	poisonous-enemy
attorsceaþa	poisonous-enemy
attorsceaþan	poisonous, poisonous-enemy
attres	poison
auctor	author (Latin)
aurnen	expire, pass-away, run-out
awa	eternally, for-ever
awacan	arise, awake, be-born, begin
awæcniað	arise, descend
awæcnian	arise, descend
awæcniaþ	arise, descend
awægan	cancel-out, destroy
awage	away
aweahte	arouse, awake, beget, raise-up
aweaxan	grow
aweccan	arouse, awake, beget, raise-up
aweg	away
awehte	arouse, awake, beget, raise-up
awend	change, convert, pervert
awendan	change, convert, pervert
awende	change, convert, pervert
aweorpan	cast-down, cast-out, reject
aweox	anything, grow, growing
awiht	anything, at-all, nothing, something
awoc	arise, awake, be-born, begin
awocon	arise, awake, be-born, begin
aworpene	cast-down, cast-out, reject
awox	grow
awræc	narrate, say, tell
awræce	avenge, punish
awrecan	avenge, narrate, punish, say, tell
awritan	inscribe, write
awrite	inscribe, write
awuht	anything, at-all, nothing, something
awyrdan	destroyed, doomed
awyrded	destroyed, doomed
awyrgan	curse, outlaw
awyrgda	cursed-one, the-cursed-one, the-devil
awyrged	curse, outlaw
axan	ash, cinder
axe	ash, cinder
axian	ask, discover, find-out
axoden	ask, discover, find-out
axude	ask, discover, find-out

Æ, æ

Ænglisc	English
æ	law
æce	eternal
æcer	acre, cultivated-field, field

Word List (*Ænglisc* to English)

Ænglisc	English	*Ænglisc*	English
æcera	acre, field	æfenne	evening
æceras	acre, field	æfenræst	evening-rest
æðela	excellent, man, noble, person	æfenræste	evening-rest
æðelan	excellent, man, noble, person	æfenscima	evening-glow, evening-light
æðelboren	noble-born	æfenspræc	evening-speech
æðelborennis	noble-born	æfenspræce	evening-speech
æðele	excellent, man, nobility, noble, person	æfentid	evening
		æfentide	evening
		æfestra	envy
æðeling	noble, noble-descendant, nobleman, prince	æfnan	carry-out, construct
		æfnde	carry-out, construct
		æfre	always, ever, every, forever
æðelinga	noble, prince	æfst	hatred, malice, rivalry, spite
æðelingas	noble, prince		
æðelinge	noble, prince	æfstum	hatred, malice, rivalry, spite
æðelinges	noble, prince		
æðelo	excellent, man, nature, nobility, noble, noble-race, origin, person, talent	æftan	behind
		æfter	according-to, after, afterwards, along, amid, among, for, next, second, then, through, to
æðelu	descent, lineage		
æðelum	excellent, man, nature, nobility, noble, noble-one, origin, person, talent	æftera	next, second
		æftercweþend	after-speaking, eulogy
		æftercweþendra	after-speaking, eulogy
æðm	breath		
æðme	breath	æfterfylgan	follow, to-come-after
ædra	artery, spring, stream, vein	æfterlean	recompense, retribution, reward
ædre	artery, channel, immediately, soon, spring, stream, vein	æfþanc	injury, insult, malice
		æfþancum	injury, insult, malice
		æfþonca	injury, insult, malice
ædrum	artery, immediately, soon, spring, stream, vein	æfþoncan	injury, insult, malice
		æfþunca	irritant, repugnant, repugnant-thing
æfæst	faultless, law-abiding, pious, righteous		
		æftre	next, second
		æfyn	evening
æfæste	faultless, law-abiding, righteous	æghuuæt	everything
		æghwa	each, everyone, everything
æfðoncan	injury, insult, malice		
æfen	evening	æghwæðer	both, each, either
æfengrom	hostile	æg-hwæðer	both...and
æfenleoð	evening-song	æghwæðre	both, each, either
æfenleoht	evening-light, evening-song	æghwæðres	both, each, either
		æghwæðrum	both, each, either
æfenleoþ	evening-song	æghwæm	each, everyone

18

Word List (*Ænglisc* to English)

Ænglisc	English	*Ænglisc*	English
æghwær	everywhere	ælcum	each
æghwæs	each, each-thing, entirely, everyone, of-which	æld	fire
		ældo	age
		æled	fire
æghwæt	both, everything	æledleoma	fire-lit, torch
æghwæþer	both, each, either	æledleoman	fire-lit, torch
æg-hwæþer	both...and	ælf	elf, fairy, goblin
æghwæþre	both, each, either	ælfheres	Aelfhere's (name)
æghwæþres	both, each, either	Ælfred	Alfred (name)
æghwæþrum	both, each, either	Ælfrices	Ælfric (name), Ælfric's (name), fairy-bright
æghwam	altogether		
æghwilc	all, each, every		
æghwilcne	each	ælfsciene	fairy-bright, very-beautiful
æghwylc	each		
æghwylcne	each	ælfscieno	fairy-bright, very-beautiful
æghwylcum	each		
æglæca	fierce-fighter, terrible-attacker	ælfscinu	fairy-bright, very-beautiful
ægnian	acquire, dedicate, obtain, own	ælfscyne	beautiful-as-a-fairy
		ælfylce	foreign-army
ægþer	both, each, either	ælfylcum	foreign-army
ægweard	shore-watch	ælgrene	all-green, very-green
ægwearde	shore-watch, watch-over-the-shore		
		ællmihtig	almighty
æht	lands, livestock, possession, possessions, property	ælmehtig	almighty
		ælmesmann	almsman, beggar
		ælmesmannum	almsman, beggar
		ælmessan	alms
æhta	livestock, possession, property	ælmihtegan	almighty
		ælmihtgian	almighty
		ælmihtig	almighty
æhte	livestock, possession, property	ælmihtiga	almighty, god
		ælmihtigan	almighty
		ælmihtiges	almighty
æhtnyss	persecution	ælmihtigne	almighty
æhtnyssa	persecution	ælmyssan	alms, charity
æhtum	livestock, possession, property	ælmysse	alms, charity
		æltimbred	all-timbered
		ælwiht	alien-being
æl	eel	ælwihta	alien-being
æla	oh	æmettig	empty
ælað	kindle, kindling, light	æminde	forgetfulness
ælan	kindle, light	æne	any, at-once, none, once, only
ælaþ	kindle, light		
ælc	all, any, each, every	ænegum	any, none, only
ælcere	each	ænga	confined, cramped, narrow
ælces	each		
ælcon	each	ænge	confined, cramped, narrow
ælcre	each		

Word List (*Ænglisc* to English)

Ænglisc	English
ænges	any
ænglum	the-angels
ængum	any, none, only
ænig	any
ænige	any
æniges	any
ænigne	any
ænigra	any
ænigre	any
ænigum	any
ænlic	beautiful, incomparable, only, peerless
ænlice	singularly
ænlicra	one-like
ænlicu	beautiful, incomparable, peerless
ænne	alone, one
ænyg	any
æple	apple, fruit
æppel	apple, fruit
æppelfealo	apple-dark
æppelfealowe	apple-dark
æppelfealuwe	apple-dark
ær	before, brass, bronze, dawn, earlier, earlier-born, ere, formerly, previously, yet
æra	the-sea
ærboren	earlier-born
ærdæg	dawn, daybreak, earlier-day, previous-time
ærdæge	dawn, daybreak, earlier-day, previous-time
ærdagum	dawn, daybreak, days-of-old, earlier-day, former-days, previous-time
ærðon	before
ærenda	errand, message
ærende	errand, message
ærendgast	angel, messenger-spirit
ærendian	errand, message-carrying
ærendraca	messenger
ærendreca	messenger
ærendrecan	messenger
ærendsecg	messenger
ærest	first, resurrection
æresta	first
ærfæder	ancestor, father-before-him, forefather, old-father
ærgestreon	ancient-treasure, former-treasure
ærgeweorc	ancient-treasure, former-work, work-of-former-times
ærgewinn	ancient-hostility
ærglad	former-grace
ærglade	former-grace
ærgod	former-good, good-from-old-times, good-in-former-times, proven-good-because-of-age
ærn	building
ærnan	gallop, run
ærndon	gallop, run
ærnes	building
ærnum	bronze
æror	before, earlier, first, formerly
ærost	first
ærra	former
ærran	earlier, former
ærsceaft	creation
ærþan	before
ærþon	before
ærur	before, earlier, formerly
ærwelan	ancient-riches
æs	food
æsæled	constrain, fetter-bound, oppress
æsc	ash-tree, boat, ship, spear
æsca	ash-tree, ship, spear
æscberend	ash-bearer, spear-bearer, warrior
æscberendra	ash-bearer, spear-bearer, warrior
æschere	ash-army

Word List (*Ænglisc* to English)

Ænglisc	English	Ænglisc	English
æscholt	ash-wood	ætgædre	together
æscplega	ash-wood, battle, spear-fight, spear-sport	ætgiefan	nourisher, provider
		ætgifa	nourisher, provider
		æt-gifa	food-giver
æscplegan	ash-wood, battle, spear-sport	ætgifan	give, nourisher, provide, provider
æscrof	ash-wood, battle-brave, brave-in-battle, spear-brave	ætgræpe	grappling-with, grasping
		æþela	excellent, man, noble, person
æscrofe	ash-wood, battle-brave, spear-brave	æþelan	excellent, man, noble, noble-descendant, person
æscþræcu	ash-woods, battle		
æscþraelicce	ash-woods, battle		
æsctir	ash-wood, battle-glory, spear, victory	æþelboren	noble-born
		æþelborennis	noble-born
æscum	ash-tree, ship, spear	æþelborennyss	noble-birth
æscwiga	ash-warrior	æþele	a-noble, atheling, excellent, man, nature, nobility, noble, noble-descendant, origin, person, talent
æse	food		
æses	food		
æstel	pointer		
æt	against, at, by, eat, food, from, in, near, of, yet		
		æþelicra	excellent
ætæwde	appear, display, reveal	æþeling	atheling, noble, noble-descendant, nobleman, prince
ætbær	bring, bring-to, carry, carry-away, carry-up-to, give	æþelinga	noble, prince
		æþelingas	noble, prince
ætbæron	bring, bring-to, carry, carry-away, carry-up-to, give	æþelinge	noble, prince
		æþelinges	noble, prince
		æþellingum	noble, noble-descendant, prince
ætberan	bring, bring-to, carry, carry-away, carry-up-to, give	æþelne	nobler
		æþelo	descent, excellent, lineage, man, nature, nobility, noble, noble-lineage, noble-race, origin, person, talent
æte	eat, food		
æteowan	appear, display, reveal		
æteowde	appear, display, reveal		
æterna	eternal (Latin)	Æþelrædes	Aethelred's (name)
ætes	food	æþelstan	Athelstan (name)
ætfealh	hold-firmly	æþelu	descent, excellent, lineage, man, nature, nobility, noble, noble-descendant, nobly, origin, person, talent
ætfeohtan	fight-against		
ætfeolan	hold-firmly		
ætferede	carry-off, carry-off-from		
ætferian	carry-off		
ætforan	before, in-front-of		
ætgædere	together		

Word List (*Ænglisc* to English)

Ænglisc	English	*Ænglisc*	English
æþelum	excellent, man, nature, nobility, noble, noble-one, origin, person, talent	bad	await, bide, continue, endure, expect, live, remain, stay, wait
Æþlmær	Æthelmaer (name), touch	bæc	back
		bæc-bord	larboard, port-side
æþm	breath	bæcere	baker
æþme	breath	bæd	ask, beseech, bid, pray, urge
æthran	touch		
æthrinan	touch	bæð	bath
æthwearf	go-to, return	bædan	dispatch, impel, urge
æthweorfan	go-to, return		
ætlan	intended	bædde	dispatch, impel, urge
ætrihte	immediately		
ætsamne	together	bædon	ask, beseech, bid, pray, urge
ætsomne	at-once, together, united		
		bæðweg	bath-road, sea
ætspranc	spurt-out	bæl	fire, flame, funeral-pyre, pyre
ætspringan	spurt-out		
ætstaeppan	step-towards, up-to	bælc	arrogance, pride
ætstandan	remain-standing, stand-still, stop	bæle	fire, flame, pyre
		bælfyr	pyre, sacrificial-fire
ætstealle	waypoint	bælstede	pyre-stood
ætstod	remain-standing, stand-still, stop	bælwudu	pyre-wood
		bær	bare, bear, bore, carry, give-birth-to, litter, naked, stretcher
ætstop	step-towards, up-to		
ætterne	deadly, poisoned		
ættren	deadly, poisoned		
ættrynne	deadly, poisoned	bæran	bear, behave, carry, give-birth-to
ætwæg	carry-away		
ætwand	escape	bære	bear
ætwegan	carry-away	bærnan	burn, cause-to-be-burned
ætwindan	escape		
ætwist	food, sustenance	bæron	bear, carry, give-birth-to
ætwitan	blame, reproach		
ætwiton	blame, reproach	bærst	break, burst
ætywan	appear, display, reveal, to-show	bætan	to-bridle, to-halter
		bæþ	bath
ætywe	revealing	bæþweg	bath-road, sea
ætywed	manifest, revealed	bald	bold, brave
æwela	ancient-riches	baldlice	boldly, bravely
æwiscmod	ashamed, disgraced	bald-lice	boldly
æwiscmode	disgraced-in-mind	baldlicost	boldly, bravely
		baldor	lord
		balwon	evil, miserable

B, b

Ænglisc	English
ba	both
bam	both
ban	bone, tooth
bana	bane, killer, slayer
banan	killer

22

Word List (*Ænglisc* to English)

Ænglisc	English
bancofa	body, bone-chamber
bancofan	body, bone-chamber
bane	bone, tooth
banena	killer
banfæt	body
banfag	decorated-with-bone
banfatu	body
banhelm	bone-helm
banhring	bone-ring, vertebra
banhringas	bone-ring, vertebra
banhus	body, bone-house
banleas	boneless
banlease	boneless
banloca	body, bone-enclosure, muscle, muscles, the-body
banlocan	muscle, the-body
bannan	command, order
banum	bone, tooth
bar	boar
bare	bare, naked
barnum	bare, children
baro	bare, naked
baru	bare, naked
basnedon	await, expect
basnian	await, expect
bat	bite, boat, ship
bates	a-boat, boat, ship
baþian	bathe
baþu	bath
batweard	boat-guardian, ship-guardian
batwearde	boat-guardian, ship-guardian
be	about, at, be, because-of, beside, by, by-means-of, concerning, near, nearby, north-of, regarding, with
be norðan	north-of
be norþan	north-of
beacen	beacon, monument, portent, sign
beacna	monument, portent, sign
beacne	monument, portent, sign
beacnian	point-out, show
beacnum	monument, portent, sign
bead	announce, bid, command, give, grant, make-known, offer, proclaim
beadogrima	battle-mask, faceplate, war-helmet
beadogriman	battle-mask, faceplate, war-helmet
beadohata	battle-proclaimer
Beadohilde	Beadohild (name)
beadohrægl	battle-garment
beadoleoma	battle-gleam, battle-light, sword
beadomecas	battle-sword
beadomece	battle-sword
beadorinc	warrior
beadorinca	warrior
beadowe	battle, war
beadu	battle, war
beaducafa	brave-in-battle
beadufolm	fighting-hand
beadufolme	fighting-hand
beadulac	battle-play
beadulace	battle-play
beaduræs	attack, battle-onslaught
beadurinc	warrior
beadurof	bold, bold-in-battle, brave-in-battle, heroic
beadurofes	brave-in-battle
beadurun	fighting-speech, verbal-attack
beadurune	fighting-speech, verbal-attack
beaduscearp	battle-sharp
beaduscrud	battle-clothing, mail-coat
beaduscruda	battle-clothing, mail-coat
beaduserce	battle-coat
beadusercean	battle-coat
beaduwe	battle, war
beaduweorc	battle-work, martial-deed

Word List (Ænglisc to English)

Ænglisc	English
beaduweorca	war-working
beaduweorces	battle-work, martial-deed
beadwa	battle, war
beadwe	battle, war
beæftan	behind
beag	armlet, bent, circle, circular-ornament, crown, ring, treasures, wealth
beaga	armlet, circle, ring, rings, treasures, wealth
beagas	armlet, circle, ring, rings, treasures, wealth
beage	armlet, circle, ring, treasures, wealth
beages	armlet, circle, ring, treasures, wealth
beaggyfa	lord, ring-giver
beaggyfan	lord, ring-giver
beaggyfu	generosity, ring-giving
beaghord	ring-hoard, treasure
beaghroden	bejewelled, decorated-with-treasure
beagum	armlet, circle, ring, rings, treasures, wealth
beah	armlet, bow, circle, lie-down, of-a-dragon-coil, rest-inactive, ring, sit-down, stoop, submit, treasures, turn-away, wealth
beahðege	ring-receiving, treasure-receiving
beahðegu	ring-receiving, treasure-receiving
beahgifa	lord, ring-giver, ring-giving
beahgifan	lord, ring-giver
beahgife	ring-giving
beahgyfa	reward-giver
beahhord	treasure-hoard
beahhorda	treasure-hoard
beahhordes	treasure-hoard
beahhordum	treasure-hoard
beahhroden	bejewelled, decorated-with-treasure
beahhrodene	bejewelled, decorated-with-treasure
beahsele	ring--giving-hall
beahþege	ring-receiving, treasure-receiving
beahþegu	ring-receiving, treasure-receiving
beahwriða	circlet, ring, torque
beahwriðan	circlet, ring, torque
beahwriþa	circlet, ring, torque
beahwriþan	circlet, ring, torque
beald	bold, brave
bealde	bold, brave
bealdian	be-bold, be-brave
bealdode	be-bold, be-brave
bealdor	lord
bealewa	destruction, evil, misery
bealo	evil, harm, injury
bealocwealm	evil-death
bealofull	evil-full
bealofulla	evil-full
bealofullan	evil-full
bealohycgend	intending-evil-or-destruction
bealohycgendra	intending-evil-or-destruction
bealohydig	intending-evil-or-destruction
bealonið	evil-affliction
bealoniðe	evil-affliction
bealoniþ	evil-affliction
bealoniþe	evil-affliction
bealosiþ	harmful-or-evil-experience
bealu	destruction, enmity, evil, harm, injury, miserable, misery
bealubenn	serious-wound
bealuhygdig	hostile, intending-evil
bealu-sið	calamity, harm-journey, peril

Word List (Ænglisc to English)

Ænglisc	English	Ænglisc	English
bealusiþ	bitter-experience, painful-journey	bearnum	child, children, grove, offspring, son, sons, wood
bealu-siþ	calamity, harm-journey, peril	bearo	grove, wood
bealuwa	destruction, evil, misery	bearowe	the-woods
bealuwara	dwellers-in-iniquity, evil-doers	bearu	grove, wood
bealuwaras	dwellers-in-iniquity, evil-doers	bearwas	grove, wood
bealwa	destruction, evil, harm, injury, misery	bearwe	grove, the-boughs, wood
bealwe	evil, harm, injury	beatað	beat, pound, strike-against
bealwes	evil, harm, injury	beatan	beat, pound, strike, strike-against
beam	beam, beam-of-light, cross, timber, tree	beataþ	beat, pound, strike-against
beama	beam, beam-of-light, cross, timber, tree	beateð	beat, pound, strike-against
beaman	beam, beam-of-light, cross, timber, tree	beaten	beat, pound, strike
beamas	beam, beam-of-light, cross, timber, tree	beateþ	beat, pound, strike-against
beame	beam, beam-of-light, cross, timber, tree	bebead	bid, command, commanded, commit, dedicate, entrust, instruct
beames	beam, beam-of-light, cross, timber, tree	bebeod	command, commit, dedicate, entrust, instruct
beamsceade	protecting-trees, three-shadow	bebeodan	command, commit, dedicate, entrust, instruct
beamsceadu	protecting-trees, three-shadow		
beamtelg	tree-dye	bebeode	command
beamtelge	tree-dye	bebeorgan	protect, shield
bearh	preserve, save	bebeorh	protect, shield
bearhtm	brightness, din	bebicgan	sell, trade
bearhtme	brightness, din	bebicge	sell, trade
bearm	bosom, lap, ship-hold, stomach	bebod	command, commandment
bearme	bosom, lap, ship-hold, stomach	beboden	command, instruct
bearmum	bosom, lap, ship-hold, stomach	bebodu	command, commandment
		bebohte	sell
bearn	child, children, occur, offspring, son, with-child	bebudon	command, instruct
		bebugan	encircle, surround
		bebugeð	encircle, surround
bearna	child, children's, offspring, of-men	bebugeþ	encircle, surround
		bec	book, books
bearne	child, offspring	because	because
bearnes	child, offspring	becearf	cut-off
bearngebyrdo	child-bearing	beceorfan	cut-off

Word List (Ænglisc to English)

Ænglisc	English
beclypan	embrace, hug
beclypte	embrace, hug
becn	beacon, monument, portent, sign
becom	arrive, befall, come, happen
becoman	arrive, became, befall, come, happen
becomon	arrive, befall, come, happen
becuman	arrive, befall, come, happen
becwom	arrive, befall, come, happen
bed	bed, garden-bed
bedælan	deprive, release
bedæled	deprive
bedd	bed, garden-bed
bedde	bed, garden-bed
beddes	bed, garden-bed
beddrest	bed
beddreste	bed
beddum	bed, garden-bed
bedealf	bury
bedelfan	bury
beden	beseech, bid, urge
bediglan	conceal
bedraf	cover, drive-away, drive-out, spatter
bedragan	draw, entice, lure
bedreas	bereave, deprive-of
bedreosan	bereave, deprive, deprive-of, fall, perish-with
bedrest	bed
bedreste	bed
bedrifan	cover, drive-away, drive-out, spatter
bedrifenne	cover, drive-away, drive-out, spatter
bedrog	draw, entice, lure
bedroren	bereave, deprive, deprive-of, fall, perish-with
bedrorene	deprive, fall, perish-with
bedruron	bereave, deprive-of
bedyrnan	conceal
bedyrnded	conceal
bedyrndon	conceal
bedyrned	conceal
befælled	befall, felled
befæstan	commit, entrust, fasten, imprison
befæste	commit, entrust, fasten, imprison
befangen	clasp, ensnare, lay-hold-of, seize, surround
befealdan	clasp, envelope, fold
befealdest	clasp, envelope, fold
befeallan	bereave, deprive, fall
befeallen	bereave, deprive, fall
befeallene	bereave, deprive, fall
befeng	beheld
befleon	flee-from
beflowan	flow-about
beflowen	flow-about, flows-about
befon	clasp, ensnare, lay-hold-of, seize, surround
befongen	clasp, ensnare, lay-hold-of, seize, surround
beforan	before, in-front, in-front-of, in-presence-of, in-the-lead
befyllan	befall, felled
befylled	befall, felled
beg	treasure
bega	both, ring
begale	recite
began	began, begin
begang	expanse, extent
begann	begin
begas	armlet, circle, ring, treasures, wealth
begea	both
begeall	scream, screech, yell

Word List (*Ænglisc* to English)

Ænglisc	English
begeat	acquire, befall, get, overcome, take, taking
begeatan	to-get
begeate	acquire, befall, get, overcome, take
begeaton	acquire, befall, get, overcome, take
begen	both
begeondan	beyond
begeotan	cover, drench, drip-over
beget	acquire, befall, get, overcome, take
begiellan	scream, screech, yell
begietan	acquire, befall, get, overcome, take, to-acquire
begieten	acquire, get
beginnan	begin
begnornian	lament, mourn
begnornod	lament, mourn
begnornode	lament, mourn
begnornodon	lament, mourn
begollen	scream, screech, yell
begong	expanse, extent
begoten	cover, drench, drip-over
begra	both
begrindan	deprive, grind-away
begrindeð	deprive, grind-away
begrindeþ	deprive, grind-away
begrornian	mourn-about
begrunden	deprive, grind-away
begullon	scream, screech, yell
begylpan	boast-about
begytan	acquire, befall, get, overcome, take
behabban	detain, have
behæfdon	detain, have
behð	evidence, sign
behðe	evidence, sign
beheafdian	behead, decapitate
beheafdod	behead
behealdan	behold, gaze-upon, have, possess
behelan	cover, hide
beheng	hang-round
behengon	hang-round
beheold	behold, gaze-upon, have, possess
beheoldon	behold, gaze-upon, have, possess
beheowan	cut-off, cut-off-from, deprive-of
beheowe	cut-off, cut-off-from, deprive-of
behindan	behind
behofað	have-need-of
behofaþ	have-need-of
behofian	have-need-of
beholen	cover, hide
behon	hang, hang-round
behongen	hang-round
behreosan	cover, fall-upon
behreowsian	repent
behriman	frost-over
behrimed	frost-over
behþ	evidence, sign
behþe	evidence, sign
beirnan	occur
bel	fire, flame, pyre
beladian	exculpate, vindicate
belamp	befall, happen
beleac	close, enclose, lock, lock-up, protect, shut
belean	dissuade-from
beleas	be-deprived-of, lose
belecgan	cover
belegde	be-deprived-of, cover, covered
beleosan	be-deprived-of, lose
belgan	angry, cause-anger-in, enrage, enraged-from
belicgan	lie-about, surround
belið	lie-about, surround
beliðan	deprive-of
belidenne	deprive-of
beligeð	lie-about, surround
beligeþ	lie-about, surround
belimpan	befall, happen
belisnod	castrated-man, eunuch

Word List (*Ænglisc* to English)

Ænglisc	English	*Ænglisc*	English
belisnode	castrated-man, eunuch	beneoteð	deprive-of
		beneoteþ	deprive-of
beliþ	lie-about, surround	bengeat	wound-opening
beliþan	deprive-of	bengeato	wound-opening
belocen	close, lock, shut	beniman	assume, deprive, take
belocun	locked		
beloren	be-deprived-of, lose	benn	wound
belorene	be-deprived-of, lose	benne	wound
belucan	close, enclose, lock, lock-up, protect, shut	bennum	wound
		benumen	assume, deprive, take
beluce	enclose, fasten	beo	be, to-be
belucon	close, lock, shut	beoð	announce, be, being, shall-be, to-be
bemearn	lament, mourn-about		
bemum	trumpet	beodan	announce, await, bid, command, continue, endure, expect, give, grant, live, make-known, offer, proclaim, stay, wait
bemurnan	lament, mourn-about		
ben	petition, request		
bena	ask, request, to-petition		
benæman	deprive-of, take-away		
		beodeð	announce, give, grant, make-known, offer, proclaim
benam	assume, deprive, take		
benan	ask, request, to-petition	beodeþ	announce, give, grant, make-known, offer, proclaim
benc	bench		
bence	bench	beodgeneat	table-companion
bencsittende	bench-sitters, courtiers, warriors	beodgeneatas	table-companion
		beodgereordu	food, meals
bencsittendum	bench-sitters, courtiers, warriors	beoducaf	brave-in-battle
		beon	be, become, bees, being, exist, to-be
bencsweg	bench-sound, merriment		
		beor	beer
bencþelu	bench-floor	beore	beer
bencum	bench	beorg	barrow, hill, mound, mountain, tumulus
bend	band, bond, fetter		
bende	bound	beorgan	defend, preserve, protect, save
bendum	band, bond, fetter		
bene	petition, request	beorgas	barrow, hill, mountain, tumulus
beneah	enjoy, possess, possesses		
		beorge	barrow, hill, mountain, tumulus
benedicite	bless		
benemde	declare, name, say	beorges	barrow, hill, mountain, tumulus
benemdon	declare, name, say		
benemnan	declare, name, say	beorgum	barrow, hill, mounds, mountain, tumulus
beneotan	deprive-of		
beneote	deprive-of		

Word List (*Ænglisc* to English)

Ænglisc	English
beorh	barrow, embankment, hill, mountain, tumulus
beorhhleoþum	mountain-slope
beorhhlið	mountain-slope
beorhhliþ	mountain-slope
beorht	bright, clear, light, pure
beorhta	bright, clear, light, pure
beorhtan	bright, clear, light, pure
beorhtblowan	blossom-brightly
beorhtblowende	blossom-brightly
beorhte	become-bright, bright, brightly, clear, light, pure
beorhtian	become-bright
beorhtne	bright, clear, light, pure
beorhtode	become-bright
beorhtost	bright, clear, light, pure
beorhtra	bright, brighter, clear, light, pure
beorhtre	bright, clear, light, pure
beorhtum	bright, clear, light, pure
beorma	barm, sourdough-starter, yeast-foam-from-beer
beorman	barm, sourdough-starter, yeast-foam-from-beer
beorn	burn, burned, man, men, nobleman, warrior
beorna	man, warriors
beornas	man
beorncyning	warrior-king
beorne	man
beornes	man
beornþreat	band-of-men
beornum	man
beorscealc	beer-man, drinker, reveller
beorscealca	beer-man, drinker, reveller
beorsele	beer-hall
beorþege	beer-drinking
beorþegu	beer-drinking
beot	beat, boast, pound, strike, vow
beotan	beat, pound, strike-against
beotedan	boast, vow, vowed
beoþ	announce, be, shall-be, to-be
beotian	boast, vow
beotode	boast, vow
beoton	beat, pound, strike
beotword	boasting-word, vow, vowing
beotwordum	boasting-word, vow, vowing
Beo-wulf	bear, bee-wolf
bepæcan	deceive, seduce
bepæceð	deceive, seduce
bepæceþ	deceive, seduce
Bera	bear
berað	bear, carry, give-birth-to
berædan	to-determine-by-discussion
beræddon	over-ride
beran	bear, carry, give-birth-to
beraþ	bear, carry, give-birth-to
bere	bear, carry, give-birth-to
bereafan	deprive
bereafian	bereave, deprive
bereafod	bereft, without
bereð	bear, carry, give-birth-to
beredon	clear, make-bare
beren	bear, carry, give-birth-to
berenedon	carry-out, commit
berenian	carry-out, commit
bereofan	deprive
bereþ	bear, carry, give-birth-to
berewæstm	barley-crop
berewæstma	barley-crop
berhge	hill

Word List (Ænglisc to English)

Ænglisc	English	Ænglisc	English
berian	clear, make-bare	besmiþod	construct, make-by-craftsmanship
berofan	deprive		
berofen	bereft, deprive	besnyðede	deprive-of, rob
berofene	deprive	besnyðian	deprive-of, rob
beron	bear, carry, give-birth-to	besnyþede	deprive-of, rob
		besnyþian	deprive-of, rob
beroþor	break, brother	bestandan	stand-about, stand-on-either-side-of
berstan	break, burst		
besæt	encircle, surround	besteman	moisten, wet
besceawian	care-about, consider, look-about	bestemed	moisten, stand-about, wet
bescierian	deprive-of, separate-from	bestodon	stand-about, stand-on-either-side-of
bescufan	shove, throw, thrust	bestrudan	plunder, rob
bescyrede	deprive-of, separate-from	bestrudon	plunder, rob
		bestyman	moisten, wet
beseah	look-around, look-at, see	bestymed	moisten, wet
		besuncen	sink
beseald	cover, surround	beswac	betray, deceive
besellan	cover, surround	beswælan	burn
besencan	drown, sink, submerge	beswæled	burn
		beswicað	betray, deceive
besenceð	drown, sink, submerge	beswican	betray, deceive, deceived, ensnare
besenceþ	drown, sink, submerge	beswicaþ	betray, betrays, deceive
beseo	look-around, look-at, see, seen	beswicen	betray, deceive, deceived
beseon	look-around, look-at, see	beswicene	betray, deceive
		beswyled	drench, flood
besettan	ornament	beswylian	drench, flood
besette	ornament	besyred	ensnare, entrap, trick
besincan	sink		
besittan	encircle, surround	besyrwan	ensnare, entrap, trick
beslægene	cut-off, deprive-by-striking, smite, strike, take-away	bet	better
		betæcan	commend, entrust
beslagen	inflicted	betæhte	commend, entrust
beslean	cut-off, deprive-by-striking, smite, strike, take-away	betan	amend, compensate, increase, restore
besloh	cut-off, deprive-by-striking, smite, strike, take-away	bete	amend, compensate, increase, restore
besmitan	defile, pollute	betend	repairers
besmiten	defile, pollute	betera	a-better, a-superior
besmiþian	construct, make-by-craftsmanship	beteran	a-better, a-superior, better
		betere	a-better, a-superior

Word List (Ænglisc to English)

Ænglisc	English	Ænglisc	English
betest	a-better, a-superior	beweredon	protect
beþeahte	conceal, cover, surround	bewerian	protect
beþeahton	conceal, cover, surround	bewindað	consider, enwreathe, revolve, surround
beþeccan	conceal, cover, surround	bewindan	consider, enwreathe, revolve, surround
beþenede	cover, stretch-over	bewindaþ	consider, enwreathe, revolve, surround
beþenian	cover, stretch-over		
Bethleem	Bethlehem (place)		
Bethlem	Bethlehem (place)		
betimbran	build, construct	bewitiað	attend-to, look-after, observe
betimbred	build, construct		
betimbrede	build, construct	bewitian	attend-to, look-after, observe
betimbredon	build		
betimbrian	build	bewitiaþ	attend-to, look-after, observe
betlic	excellent		
betost	a-better, a-superior	bewitigað	attend-to, look-after, observe
betst	a-better, a-superior		
betsta	a-better, a-superior	bewitigaþ	attend-to, look-after, observe
betstan	a-better, a-superior		
betste	a-better, a-superior	bewlat	look-about
betuh	between, betwixt	bewlitan	look-about
betux	between	beworht	construct, cover, work
betweonan	between		
betweox	between	beworhte	construct, cover, work
beutan	outside		
bewægnan	offer	beworhton	build-around
bewægned	offer	beworpen	cast, surround, throw
bewand	consider, enwreathe, revolve, surround	bewreon	conceal, cover, enclose, hide, protect, wrap-up
bewarigan	protect		
bewawan	of-wind-to-blow-around	bewrigen	cover, enclose, hide, protect, wrap-up
beweaxan	grow-around, grow-over	bewrigene	cover, enclose, hide, protect, wrap-up
beweaxne	grow-around, grow-over, overgrown	bewrigenum	cover, enclose, hide, protect, wrap-up
bewegan	cover	bewunden	consider, enwreathe, revolve, surround
bewegen	cover		
bewenede	entertain		
bewennan	entertain	bewyrcan	build-around, construct, cover, work
beweorpan	cast, surround, throw		
beweotede	attend-to, look-after, observe		
beweotode	attend-to, look-after, observe		

Word List (*Ænglisc* to English)

Ænglisc	English
bi	about, because-of, beside, buy, by, by-means-of, for, nearby, regarding, with
biblos	the-book (Latin)
bibugeð	avoiding
bicgan	buy, get, get-in-exchange
bid	standstill
bið	be, being, deprive, release, to-be
bidað	awaiting
bidælde	deprive, release
bidæled	bereft, deprive, release
bidan	await, bide, continue, endure, expect, experience, live, remain, stay, wait
biddan	ask, beseech, bid, pray, urge
bidde	ask, pray
biddu	bid
bideð	await, continue, endure, expect, live, stay, wait
biden	bide, endure, remain
bideþ	await, continue, endure, expect, live, stay, wait
bidon	await, bide, continue, endure, expect, live, remain, stay, wait
bidroren	deprive, fall, perish-with
bidrorene	deprive, fall, perish-with
bifæstan	commit, entrust, fasten, imprison
bifæste&th	commit, entrust, fasten, imprison
bifæsteð	by-fastened
bifian	quake, shake, shiver
bifiende	quake, shake, shiver
bifode	quake, shake, shiver
bifongen	clasp, ensnare, lay-hold-of, seize, surround
biforan	before, in-front-of, in-the-lead
big	about, because-of, beside, by, by-means-of, nearby, regarding, with
bigang	expanse, extent
bigeal	yell-about
bigeat	acquire, befall, get, overcome, take
bigeng	observance, practice, worship
bigengum	observance, practice, worship
bigong	worship
bigstandað	stand-by, support
bigstandan	stand-by, support
bigstandaþ	stand-by, support
bigyllan	yell-about
bihlemman	crash-together
bihlemmeð	crash-together
bihlemmeþ	crash-together
bihongen	hang
bihrorene	cover, deprive-of-by-falling-off, fall-upon
bil	sword
bilecgað	cover
bilecgaþ	cover
bilegde	cover
bilewit	sincere
bilgeslehtes	sword-slaying
bill	sword
billa	sword
bille	sword
billes	sword
billum	sword
bilwit	gracious, merciful
bimurneð	lament, mourn-about
bimurneþ	lament, mourn-about
bind	bind
bindað	bind
bindan	bind, tie
bindaþ	bind
binde	bind

Word List (Ænglisc to English)

Ænglisc	English
bindeð	bind
bindeþ	bind
bineat	deprive-of
binnan	within
binom	assume, deprive, deprived, take
bio	to-be
bioð	be, to-be
biodan	announce, give, grant, make-known, offer, proclaim
biorgas	barrow, hill, mountain, tumulus
biorges	barrow, hill, mountain, tumulus
biorh	barrow, hill, mountain, tumulus
biorn	man
biorna	man
biorsele	beer-hall
bioþ	to-be
bireafod	deprived-of, without
bireð	bear, carry, give-birth-to
bireþ	bear, carry, give-birth-to
birgenne	burial-site, grave
bisceawað	care-about, consider, look-about
bisceawaþ	care-about, consider, look-about
bisceop	bishop, prelate
bisceope	bishop
biscyred	deprive-of, separate-from
bisen	command, example, form, pattern, rule
bisenceð	be-sinking
bisgian	occupy, trouble
bisgo	affliction, busy, care, trouble
bisgodon	occupy, trouble
bisgu	occupation
bisgum	affliction, busy, care, trouble
bisigu	affliction, busy, care, trouble
bismorlic	degrading, shameful
bismorlicum	degrading, shameful
bisne	command, example, form, pattern, rule
bist	be, to-be
bit	bite
bitan	bite
bite	bite, cut
biter	bitter, bitterness, harsh
biteran	bitter, harsh
bitere	bitter, harsh
biteres	bitter, harsh
biþ	be, being, conceal, deprive, release, to-be
biþeaht	bitter, conceal, cover, covered, surround, surrounded
biþeahte	covered
bitre	bitter, bitterly, bitterness, harsh, sharp
bitres	bitter, bitterness, harsh
bitresta	bitter, harsh
bitter	bitter, harsh
biwaune	of-wind-to-blow-around
biwenede	entertain
biwergan	protect
biworpen	cast, surround, throw
biwrah	conceal, cover, enclose, hide, protect, wrap-up
biwrigen	conceal, cover
biwrigon	conceal, cover
biwunden	consider, curved, enwreathe, revolve, surround
blac	ashy, black, bright, dark, pale, pallid, white
blaca	black, dark
blacað	become-pale
blacaþ	become-pale
blace	black, dark
blachleor	pale-faced
blacian	become-pale

Word List (*Ænglisc* to English)

Ænglisc	English	*Ænglisc*	English
blacne	ashy, pale, pallid, white	*bletsunge*	blessing, grace
blacum	black, dark	*blican*	gleam, shine, sparkle
blado	branch, fruit, sprig	*blicð*	gleam, shine, sparkle
blæc	black, dark	*bliceð*	shining
blæd	blade, blossoming, branch, breath, fruit, glory, leaf, life, spirit, splendour, sprig	*blicon*	gleam, shine, sparkle
		blicþ	gleam, shine, sparkle
blæda	branch, fruit, sprig	*blið*	joyous, pleasant
blædæ	branch, fruit, sprig	*bliðe*	joyous, pleasant
blædagande	glorious, victorious	*bliðemod*	joyous-minded
blæddæg	glorious-day	*bliðheort*	glad-hearted
blæddaga	glorious-day	*bliðne*	joyous, pleasant
blæde	glory, splendour	*bliðu*	blithe
blædes	glory, splendour	*blind*	blind, lightless
blædfæst	famous, glorious	*blindne*	blinded
blædfæstne	famous, glorious	*blindum*	blind, lightless
blædu	branch, fruit, sprig	*blis*	bliss, joy
blædum	blossoms	*bliss*	bliss, happiness, joy
blæst	blowing, breeze, wind	*blisse*	bliss, joy
blætsiað	blessing	*blissian*	become-happy, delight, get-drunk, have-fun, make-happy
blanca	white-horse		
blancum	white-horse		
bland	blending, confusion, mixture	*blissigende*	become-happy, delight, get-drunk, have-fun, make-happy
blandenfeax	blond-hair		
blatan	darken, livid, pale		
blatende	darken, livid, pale		
blawan	blow	*blission*	bliss
bleate	miserably, wretchedly	*bliþ*	joyous, pleasant
		bliþe	joy, joyful, joyous, pleasant
bledum	glory, splendour		
blende	blinded	*bliþemod*	joyous-minded
bleo	colour	*bliþheort*	glad-hearted
bleobord	chessboard, coloured-board, game-board, gaming-table	*bliþne*	joyous, pleasant
		bliþra	joyous, pleasant
		blod	blood
		blode	blood, bloodied, blood-stained
bleobordes	chessboard, coloured-board, game-board, gaming-table	*blodfag*	blood-stained, bloody
		blodge	bloody
bleom	colour	*blodgyte*	bloodshed
bleos	colour	*blodig*	bloody
bletsian	bless	*blodigan*	bloody
bletsung	blessing, grace	*blodige*	bloody
bletsunga	blessing, grace		

Word List (Ænglisc to English)

Ænglisc	English	Ænglisc	English
blodigian	bloody, make-bloody	bogum	arm, bough, shoulder
blodigne	bloody	bolca	gangplank
blodigtoð	bloody-toothed	bolcan	gangplank
blodigtoþ	bloody-toothed	bold	building, house, residence
blodreow	bloody-and-fierce, cruel	bolda	building, house, residence
blondenfeax	grey-hair, mixed-hair-colour	boldagend	building-owner, householder
blondenfeaxe	grey-hair, mixed-hair-colour	boldagendra	building-owner, householder
blondenfeaxum	grey-hair, mixed-hair-colour	bolgenmod	angry, enraged
blondenfexa	grey-hair, mixed-hair-colour	bolla	bowl, drinking-cup
		bollan	bowl, drinking-cup
blostm	blossom	bolster	pillow
blostmum	blossom, blossoming	bolstrum	pillow
		bona	killer
blotan	offer-in-sacrifice	bonan	killer
blowan	bloom	bond	bind, tie
blysse	bliss, joy	bongar	murderous-spear
boc	book	bonus	a-good
boca	of-books	bord	board, shield, ship-deck, ship-hold, ship-side
boceras	scholar, scribe, writer		
bocere	scholar, scribe, writer	borda	board, shield, ship-deck, ship-hold, ship-side
boda	herald, messenger		
bodan	herald, messenger	bordes	board, shield, ship-deck, ship-hold, ship-side
bodedan	declared		
bodedon	foretell, preach, proclaim, tell	bordhæbbende	shield-owning-persons, warriors
boden	announce, bid, command, give, grant, make-known, offer, proclaim	bordhreoða	battle-row, shield-row
		bordhreoþa	battle-row, shield-row
bodian	foretell, preach, proclaim, tell	bordrand	shield
bodig	body	bordum	board, shield, ship-deck, ship-hold, ship-side
bodode	foretell, preach, proclaim, tell		
bodscipe	commandment, message	bordweal	shield-wall
		bordweall	shield-wall
boethia	Boethius (name)	bordwudu	wooden-shield
bog	arm, bough, shoulder	boren	bear, born, carry
		borian	bore, drill-a-hole
boga	bow	borige	bore, drill-a-hole
bogan	bow	born	burn, burned

Word List (Ænglisc to English)

Ænglisc	English	Ænglisc	English
bosm	bosom, breast, ship-hold	bræd	draw-a-sword, feign, mail-coat-rings, move, pretend, swing, weave
bosme	bosom, breast, ship-hold		
bot	better, compensation, remedy	brædan	spread-out
		brægd	draw-a-sword, feign, mail-coat-rings, move, pretend, swing, weave
bote	compensation, remedy		
botl	building, house, residence	brand	burning, fire, flame, glowing-coal, sword
botle	building, house, residence	breac	benefit-from, enjoy, use
botlgestreon	household-treasure	breahtm	noise, revelry
botlgestreona	household-treasure	breahtma	noise, revelry
botlgestreonum	household-treasure	breat	break, kill
botlwela	prosperous-dwelling	brecað	break, burst, destroy, of-curiosity, torment, transgress-a-commandment
botm	bottom		
botme	bottom		
brad	broad, extensive, open, wide	brecan	break, burst, destroy, of-curiosity, torment, transgress-a-commandment
brada	broad		
bradan	broad, extensive, wide		
brade	broad, broadly, extensive, wide, widely	brecaþ	break, burst, destroy, of-curiosity, torment, transgress-a-commandment
bradnæ	broad, extensive, wide		
		brecð	grief
bradre	broad, extensive, wide	brecða	grief
		brecþ	grief
bradswurd	broadsword	brecþa	grief
bradswyrd	broadsword	bregdan	draw-a-sword, feign, mail-coat-rings, move, pretend, swing, weave
bræc	benefit-from, break, burst, destroy, enjoy, of-curiosity, torment, transgress-a-commandment, use		
		bregde	draw-a-sword, feign, mail-coat-rings, move, pretend, swing, weave
bræce	break, burst, destroy, of-curiosity, torment, transgress-a-commandment		
		bregdende	shimmered
		bregdon	draw-a-sword, feign, mail-coat-rings, move, pretend, swing, weave
bræcon	break, burst, destroy, of-curiosity, torment, transgress-a-commandment		
		brego	lord, ruler, the-lord
		bregorice	kingdom
		bregorices	kingdom
		bregorof	lordly, noble

Word List (*Ænglisc* to English)

Ænglisc	English	*Ænglisc*	English
bregostol	lordly-seat	*breostwylm*	breast-surge, emotion
bregoweard	king, ruler		
bregowearda	king, ruler	*breotan*	break, kill
bregoweardas	king, ruler	*brer*	bramble, brier
bregu	ruled	*brerd*	border, edge, rim
brema	glorious, honoured, noble	*brerum*	bramble, briars, brier
breman	glorious, honoured, noble	*bresne*	strong
		bretene	Britain (place)
brember	blackberry-bush, bramble, briar	*breþer*	brother
		bricg	bridge, causeway
brembrum	blackberry-bush, bramble, briar	*bricge*	bridge, causeway
		bricgweard	bridge-guard, bridge-keeper
breme	famous, glorious, honoured, noble, renowned	*bricgweardas*	bridge-guard, bridge-keeper
		brigda	brighter
brenting	ship	*Brim*	briny-deep, sea, water
brentingas	ship		
breost	breast, chest, heart	*brimclif*	sea-cliff
breosta	breast, chest, heart	*brimclifu*	sea-cliff
breostceare	breast-care, misery	*brimes*	sea, water
breostcearu	breast-care, misery	*brimfuglas*	seabird
breost-cearu	anxiety, heart-care	*brimfugol*	seabird
breostcofa	breast, chest, the-chest	*brimhlæst*	fish, sea-burden
		brimhlæste	fish, sea-burden
breost-cofa	affections, heart	*brimlad*	sea-journey
breostcofan	breast, breast-chamber, chest, the-chest	*brim-lad*	path-of-the-sea, sea-lane
		brimlade	sea-journey
breostgehygd	inner-thought	*brimliðend*	sailor
breostgehygdum	inner-thought	*brimliðende*	sailor
breostgewædu	mail-coat	*brimliþend*	sailor
breosthord	breast-hoard, mind, thought	*brimliþende*	sailor
		brimliþendra	sailor
breostnet	breast-net, mail-coat	*brim-man*	sailor, sea-man
breostum	bosom, breast, chest, heart	*brimmann*	sailor, seaman
		brimmanna	sailor, seaman
breostweorðung	armour, breast-adornment, mail-coat, weapons	*brimmen*	sailor, seaman
		brimstream	ocean-stream, sea-current
breostweorðunge	armour, breast-adornment, mail-coat, weapons	*brimstreamas*	sea-current
		brimu	sea, water
breostweorþung	armour, breast-adornment, mail-coat, weapons	*brimwisa*	sea-leader
		brimwisan	sea-leader
		brimwylf	female-sea-wolf
breostweorþunge	armour, breast-adornment, mail-coat, weapons	*brimwylm*	surging-sea, water
		bringað	bring
		bringan	bring

Word List (*Ænglisc* to English)

Ænglisc	English
bringaþ	bring
bringe	bring
bringeð	bring, brings
bringeþ	bring
brittade	dispense, divide
brittian	dispense, divide
broc	affliction, brook, disease, sickness
broce	affliction, brook, disease, sickness
brocen	break, burst, destroy, of-curiosity, torment, transgress-a-commandment
brocian	afflict
broden	draw-a-sword, feign, mail-coat-rings, move, pretend, swing, weave
brodenmæl	braided-sword
broðer	brother
broðor	brother
broðorcwealm	fratricide
broðorcwealmes	fratricide
broðorgyld	brother-gold, brother-payment, compensation, recompense
broðru	brother
broðrum	brother
broga	danger, dread, terror
brogan	dread, terror
brogdenmæl	braided-sword
brogdne	draw-a-sword, feign, mail-coat-rings, move, pretend, swing, weave
broht	bring
brohtan	bring
brohte	bring, brought
brohþrea	dreadful-calamity
brohton	bring
brond	burning-wood, fire, flame, glowing-coal, sword
bronda	burning-wood, fire, flame, glowing-coal, sword
brondas	burning-wood, fire, flame, glowing-coal, sword
bronde	burning-wood, fire, flame, glowing-coal, sword
bront	high, steep
brontne	high, steep
brosnað	decay, decays
brosnade	decayed
brosnaþ	decay
brosnian	decay
brosnung	corruption, decay
broþer	brother
broþor	brother
broþorcwealm	fratricide
broþorcwealmes	fratricide
broþorgyld	brother-gold, brother-payment, compensation, recompense
broþra	brother, brother's
broþru	brother
broþrum	brother
bruc	benefit-from, enjoy, use
brucað	benefit-from, enjoy, use
brucan	benefit-from, enjoy, enjoyed, use
brucaþ	benefit-from, enjoy, use
bruce	benefit-from, enjoy, use
bruceð	benefit-from, enjoy, use
bruceþ	benefit-from, enjoy, use
brudon	draw-a-sword, feign, mail-coat-rings, move, pretend, swing, weave
brugdon	draw-a-sword, feign, mail-coat-rings, move, pretend, swing, weave
brun	black, bright, brown, dark, lustrous, purple, red

Word List (*Ænglisc* to English)

Ænglisc	English	*Ænglisc*	English
Brunanburh	Brunanburh (place)	*buan*	dwell, live, settle
brune	bright, brown, dark, lustrous	*buaþ*	dwell, live, settle
brunecg	bright-edged	*bude*	announce, dwell, give, grant, live, make-known, offer, proclaim
brunfag	brightly-decorated		
brunfagne	brightly-decorated		
brungen	bring	*budon*	announce, bid, command, give, grant, make-known, offer, proclaim
brunne	bright, brown, dark, lustrous		
bryd	bride, wife		
bryda	bride, wife	*buend*	dweller, inhabitant
brydbur	marital-bedroom	*buendra*	dweller, inhabitant
brydbure	marital-bedroom	*bufan*	above, on, on-top-of, over
bryde	bride, wife		
brymu	sea, water	*bufolc*	inhabiting-people, nation
bryne	burning, fire		
brynegield	burnt-offering	*bugan*	bow, dwell, dwell-in, lie-down, live, of-a-dragon-coil, rest-inactive, settle, sit-down, stoop, submit, turn-away
brynegielde	burnt-offering		
bryneleoma	burning-gleam		
brynewylm	burning-flame		
brynewylmum	burning-flame		
brytencyning	great-king, powerful-king		
brytencyninges	great-king, powerful-king	*bugeð*	bow, lie-down, of-a-dragon-coil, rest-inactive, sit-down, stoop, submit, turn-away
Brytene	Britain, Britain (place)		
brytnade	dispense, give-out	*bugeþ*	bow, lie-down, of-a-dragon-coil, rest-inactive, sit-down, stoop, submit, turn-away
brytnian	dispense, give-out		
brytta	dispenser, distributor, giver, lord, one-who-hands-out		
bryttað	distribute, divide, enjoy, share, use	*bugon*	bow, lie-down, of-a-dragon-coil, rest-inactive, sit-down, stoop, submit, turn-away
bryttade	distribute, divide, enjoy, share, use		
bryttan	dispenser, giver, lord	*bun*	dwell, live, settle
		bunan	beaker, cup
bryttaþ	distribute, divide, enjoy, share, use	*bunden*	bind, tie
		bundenheord	having-bound-hair
bryttedon	distribute, divide, enjoy, share, use	*bundenheorde*	having-bound-hair
		bundenne	bind
bryttian	distribute, divide, enjoy, share, use	*bundenstefna*	bound-prow, bound-stave
bryttigin	distribute, divide, enjoy, share, use	*bundon*	bind, tie
		bune	beaker, cup
bu	both	*buon*	dwell, live, settle
buað	dwell, live, settle		

Word List (*Ænglisc* to English)

Ænglisc	English	*Ænglisc*	English
bur	bedroom, cottage, women's-apartment	burhwela	city-riches, fort-or-castle
bure	bedroom, cottage, women's-apartment	burhwelan	city-riches, fort-or-castle
burg	castle, city, dwelling, enclosure, fort, stronghold, town	burnan	stream
		burne	stream
		burnon	burn, burned
burga	boroughs, castle, dwelling, fort, preserve, town	burnsele	bathhouses
		burston	break, broken, burst
		burþen	chamberlain, steward
burgan	preserve, save		
burgeteld	sleeping-tent	burþene	chamberlain, steward
burgetelde	sleeping-tent		
burgeteldes	sleeping-tent	buruhðelu	burgh-floor
burgleoda	citizen, city-dweller	burum	bedroom, cottage, women's-apartment
burgon	preserve, save		
burgræced	wall-buildings	buta	outside
burgsalum	castle-halls	butan	but, butter, except, unless, without
burgsittendra	city-dwellers		
burgsteall	city-place	bute	unless
burgstede	city-place	buteran	butter
burgtun	walled-town	butere	butter
burgtunas	city-walls, walled-town	buton	but, except, except-for, unless, without
burgum	castle, cities, citizens, dwelling, fort, town	butu	both
		bycgan	buy, get, get-in-exchange
burgwara	citizens, city-dwellers	byð	be, is, to-be, trembling
burh	castle, dwelling, enclosure, fort, stronghold, town	bydde	ask
		byfigynde	debase, trembling
		bygan	debase, lower, pull-down
burhfæsten	castle, fort, fortress		
burhgeat	city-gate	byht	dwelling
burhgeate	city-gate	byldan	cheer, encourage, to-embolden
burhleod	citizen, city-dweller		
burhleodum	citizen, city-dweller	bylde	cheer, encourage, to-embolden
burhloca	fortress, walled-town		
burhlocan	fortress, walled-town	bylded	cheer, encourage
burhsittende	city-dwellers	byman	trumpet
burhsittendum	city-dwellers	byme	trumpet
burhstede	castle, city, fort	byn	inhabited, occupied
burhwara	citizens, city-dwellers	byne	dwell, live
		byras	child, son
burhwaras	citizens, city-dwellers	byre	child, opportunity, son, time
burhwarena	citizens, city-dwellers	byreð	bear, born, carry, give-birth-to
		byrelas	serving-person

Word List (Ænglisc to English)

Ænglisc	English
byrele	serving-person
byreles	serving-person
byreþ	bear, born, carry, give-birth-to
byrgan	bury, eat, taste
byrgde	eat, taste
byrgean	eat, taste
byrgen	grave
byrgenne	burial-mound, grave
byrhtan	bright, clear, light, pure
byrig	castle, city, dwelling, fort, town
byrigde	buried, eat, taste
byrige	eat, taste
byrnað	burning
byrnan	burn, burned, corselet, mail-coat
byrne	corselet, mail-coat, mail-shirt
byrnende	burn, burned, burning, corselet, glowing
byrnhom	corselet, mail-coat
byrnhomas	corselet, mail-coat
byrnhomon	armour
byrnum	corselet, mail-coat
byrnwiga	mail-shirted-warrior
byrnwigena	mail-shirted-warrior
byrnwiggend	mail-shirted-warrior
byrnwiggende	mail-shirted-warrior
byscop	a-bishop
bysen	command, model, rule
bysene	command, model, rule
bysgað	occupy, trouble, troubles
bysgaþ	occupy, trouble
bysig	busy
bysige	busy
bysigu	affliction, busy, care, trouble
bysigum	affliction, busy, care, trouble
bysmeredon	degrade, dishonour, mock, revile
bysmerian	degrade, dishonour, mock, revile
bysmerlice	contemptuously
bysmor	disgrace, insult, mockery, shame
bysmorful	shameful
bysmorfullum	shameful
bysna	command, model, rule
bysnian	instruct-by-example, set-an-example
byþ	be, to-be, trembling
bytlian	build
bywan	polish

C, c

Ænglisc	English
caf	bold, quick, vigorous
caflice	boldly, vigorously
cafne	bold, quick, vigorous
cald	cold
caldast	cold
calde	cold
caldum	cold
camp	battle
campað	fights-for
campe	battle
campstede	battlefield
can	be-able-to, can, know
candel	candle
cann	be-able-to, can, know, know-how-to
canst	be-able-to, can, know
carfulnys	care, carefulness
carfulnysse	care, carefulness
carleas	careless, without-pity
carleasan	careless, without-pity
Carnis	flesh (Latin)
caseras	emperor
casere	emperor
catholicam	catholic (Latin)
CCC	three-hundred
ceafl	jaw, jaws, mouth
ceald	cold
cealde	cold
cealdost	cold, coldest
cealdum	cold

Word List (*Ænglisc* to English)

Ænglisc	English
ceallian	call, shout
ceap	acquisition, bargain, cattle, goods, property
ceapa	cattle
ceapas	acquisition, bargain, cattle, goods, property
ceape	acquisition, bargain, cattle, goods, property
ceapian	buy
cear	care, sorrow
ceara	anxious, be-sorrowful, take-trouble, worry
cearað	anxious, be-sorrowful, take-trouble, worry
cearaþ	anxious, be-sorrowful, take-trouble, worry
ceare	care, sorrow
cearian	anxious, be-sorrowful, take-trouble, worry
cearo	care, sorrow
cearseld	care-house, miserable-residence
cear-seld	care-place, place-of-sorrow
cearselda	care-house, miserable-residence
cearsið	sad-experience, sorrowful-expedition
cearsiðum	sad-experience, sorrowful-expedition
cearsiþ	sad-experience, sorrowful-expedition
cearsiþum	sad-experience, sorrowful-expedition
cearsorg	misery
cearsorge	misery
cearu	care, grief, sorrow
cearum	care, sorrow
cearwælm	current-flame, sorrow-flame, surge
cearwælmum	current-flame, sorrow-flame, surge
cearwylm	current-flame, sorrow-flame, surge
cearwylmas	current-flame, sorrow-flame, surge
ceas	chose
ceaster	castle, fort, town
ceasterbuend	castle-dweller, city-dweller
ceasterbuendum	castle-dweller, city-dweller
ceastra	castle, cities, fort, town
ceastre	castle, fort, fortress, town
ceastrum	castle, cities, fort, town
cellod	shield
cempa	champion, fighter, warrior
cempan	champion, company, fighter
cen	declare, show
cende	bear, bore, give-birth-to, give-names-to
cenðu	bravery
cene	bold, brave, bravely, fierce
cennað	bear, give-birth-to, give-names-to
cennan	bear, beget, breeding, bring-forth, conceive, declare, give-birth-to, give-names-to, show
cennaþ	bear, give-birth-to, give-names-to
cenned	bear, beget, bring-forth, conceive, give-birth-to, give-names-to, name-given
cennede	beget, bring-forth, conceive
cenoste	brave, fierce
cenra	brave, fierce
cenre	brave, fierce
cenþu	bravery

Word List (*Ænglisc* to English)

Ænglisc	English	*Ænglisc*	English
cenum	brave	*cirman*	call, cry-out, make-a-noise
ceol	ship		
ceolas	ship	*cista*	choice, excellence, hand-picked, military-company, the-best
ceole	ship		
ceoles	ship		
ceolþel	ship-board		
ceolþele	ship-board, ship's-deck	*clað*	cloth
		clæne	clean, innocent, pure
ceorfan	carve, cut-out		
ceorl	free-man, man	*clænnys*	innocence, purity, virginity
ceorlas	free-man, man		
ceorle	free-man, man	*clænnysse*	innocence, purity, virginity
ceorles	free-man, man		
ceosan	accept, choose, seek-out, select	*clænre*	cleansed
		clammum	bond, fetter, grasp, grip
cepan	receive, seek-after		
cepemann	merchant	*claþ*	cloth
cepemannum	merchant, merchants	*claþe*	cloth
		clea	claw
Christi	of-Christ (Latin)	*cleofan*	cleave, split
Christum	Christ (name) (Latin)	*cleofiað*	adhere, be-attached, cleaved
cicen	chicken		
cide	chide	*cleofian*	adhere, be-attached
cierr	occasion, time, turn	*cleofiaþ*	adhere, be-attached
cigan	call, summon	*cleopað*	call, cry-out, speak
cigde	call, summon	*cleopaþ*	call, cry-out, speak
cigean	call, summon	*cleopian*	call, cry-out, speak
cigeð	call, summon	*clibbor*	clinging
cigeþ	call, summon	*clif*	cliff
cild	child	*clifu*	cliff
cilde	child	*clifum*	cliff
cildes	child, child's	*clinge*	shrink
cildisc	child-like	*clipian*	call
cime	arrival, coming	*clipige*	invoke
cinberg	chin-protector	*clom*	bond, fetter, grasp
cinberge	chin-protector	*clomm*	bond, fetter, grasp, grip
cinges	the-king's		
cining	king	*clommas*	bond, fetter, grasp, grip
cinne	family, kind, manners, offspring, propriety, race, sort		
		clomme	bond, fetter, grasp, grip
ciosan	accept, choose, seek-out, select	*clommum*	bond, fetter, grasp, grip
circean	church	*cludig*	rocky
circinde	roaring	*clufan*	cleaved
cirdon	change, convert, turn, turn-back	*clufon*	cleave, split
		clustor	barrier, enclosure
cirice	church	*clustro*	barrier, enclosure
cirm	cry, roar, tumult	*clypian*	call, cry-out, speak

Word List (*Ænglisc* to English)

Ænglisc	English	*Ænglisc*	English
clypode	call, cry-out, speak	*cnossian*	crash, dash, drive, pitch, toss
clyppað	clasp, embrace, surround	*cnossod*	drive, pitch
clyppan	clasp, embrace, surround	*cnossode*	drive, pitch
clyppaþ	clasp, embrace, surround	*cnyhtum*	boy, knight, servant, soldier, youth
clyppe	clasp, embrace, surround	*cnysed*	beat, strike
clypte	clasp, embrace, surround	*cnysedan*	crash-against, dash-against, toss
cnawan	find-out, know, perceive, recognize	*cnysede*	beat, strike
cnea	generations	*cnyssað*	crash-against, dash-against, toss
cnear	small-ship	*cnyssan*	ailment, beat, crash-against, dash-against, drive, strike, toss
cnedan	kneed		
cneo	knee		
cneomæg	descendent, male-kinsman	*cnyssaþ*	crash-against, dash-against, toss
cneomægum	ancestors	*coðu*	ailment, disease, sickness
cneomagum	descendent, male-kinsman	*cofa*	cave, chamber, closet, room
cneorim	descendants, population, progeny	*cofan*	cave, chamber, closet, room
cneoris	family, posterity	*cohhetan*	cough?-clear-one's-throat?
cneorisn	family, posterity		
cneoriss	family, posterity	*col*	become-cold, coal, cold, cool, not-painful
cneorissa	family, posterity		
cneorisse	family, posterity		
cneorissum	family, posterity	*colian*	become-cold, cool
cneowmæg	ancestor, male-descendant, relation	*collenferð*	brave, proud
		collenferhð	brave, proud
cneowmægas	ancestor, male-descendant, relation	*collenferhðe*	brave, proud
		collenferhþ	brave, proud
cneowmagas	ancestor, male-descendant, relation	*collenferhþe*	brave, proud
		collenferþ	brave, proud
cneowrim	descendants, population, progeny	*collenferþe*	brave, proud, the-brave
cniht	boy, knight, servant, soldier, youth	*colode*	become-cold, cool
		colran	cold, cool, not-painful
cnihtas	boy, knight, servant, soldier, youth	*com*	arrive, came, come
cnihtum	boy, knight, servant, soldier, youth	*coman*	arrive, come
		come	arrive, come
cnihtwesende	being-a-boy	*cometa*	Cometa (name)
cnosl	family, kin	*communionem*	communion (Latin)
cnosle	family, kin	*comon*	arrive, came, come
cnossað	crash, dash, toss	*comp*	battle
cnossaþ	crash, dash, toss	*compe*	battle

Word List (Ænglisc to English)

Ænglisc	English
compwig	battle, war
compwige	battle, war
con	be-able-to, can, know
condel	candle
const	be-able-to, can, know
corðor	multitude, troop
corðre	multitude, troop
corðrum	multitude, troop
corn	corn, grain, seed, wheat
corna	corn, grain, seed, wheat
corþor	multitude, troop
corþre	multitude, troop
corþrum	multitude, troop
cosmo	the-world
cost	excellent, proven
costigan	tempt, try
costode	tempt, try
Costontinus	Costontinus (name)
costunga	temptation
coþu	ailment, disease, sickness
coþum	ailment, disease, sickness
cræft	skill, strength, virtue
cræfta	skill, strength
cræftas	skill, strength
cræfte	cunning, skill, strength
cræftgleawe	science-learned
cræftig	craftily, crafty, skilful, skilled, strong
cræftum	skill, strength
cread	pressed
Credo	I-believe (Latin)
crescite	grow, increase
crincgan	fall-in-battle
cringan	cringe, die, fall, fall-in-battle, perish, yield
Crist	Christ (name)
Criste	Christ (name), cringe
cristene	Christian
Cristes	Christ's (name), of-Christ (name)
crong	cringe, die, yield
crucem	the-cross (Latin)
cruncon	fall-in-battle
crunge	fall-in-battle
crungen	cringe, die, yield
crungon	cringe, die, fall-in-battle, fell-in-battle, yield
crungun	perished
crux	cross, cross (Latin)
cu	cow
cucra	alive, living
cuð	certain, clear, known, manifest
cuðe	be-able-to, can, certain, clear, know, know-how-to, known, manifest
cuðes	certain, clear, known, manifest
cuðlice	clearly, openly
cuðlicor	openly
cuðon	be-able-to, can, know
cuðra	certain, clear, known, manifest
culufran	dove
culufre	dove
cum	with (Latin)
cuma	guest, new-arrival, stranger
cumað	arrive, come, coming
cuman	arrive, come, guest, new-arrival, stranger
cumaþ	arrive, come
cumbles	banner, standard
cumblum	banner, standard
cumbol	banner, standard
cumbolgehnastes	banner-conflict
cumbolwiga	banner-warrior
cumbolwigan	banner-warrior
cume	arrive, come
cumen	arrive, come, coming
cumene	arrive, come
cumenra	arrive, come
cunnað	explore, find-out, try-out

Word List (Ænglisc to English)

Ænglisc	English	Ænglisc	English
cunnade	explore, find-out, knew, try-out	cwalm	death, murder, pain, torment
cunnan	be-able-to, can, know, know-how-to	cwanian	bemoan, complain-about, lament
cunnaþ	explore, find-out, try-out	cwealdest	kill, murder
cunne	be-able-to, can, know	cwealm	death, murder, pain, torment
cunnedon	explore, find-out, try-out	cwealmbealu	capital-crime, mortal-evil
cunnian	experience, explore, find-out, seek, try-out	cwealmcuma	murderous-visitor, one-come-to-do-murder
cunnige	explore, find-out, try-out	cwealmcuman	murderous-visitor, one-come-to-do-murder
cunnod	experience, explore, seek	cwealmdreor	death-blood
cunnode	experience, explore, find-out, seek, try-out	cwealme	death, murder, pain, torment
cunnon	be-able-to, can, know, know-how-to	cwealmes	death, murder, pain, torment
cure	accept, choose, seek-out, select	cwealmþrea	deadly-calamity
		cweartern	prison
curfon	carve, cut-out	cwearterne	prison
curon	accept, choose, seek-out, select	cweccan	shake, vibrate
		cweð	say
cusc	pure, virtuous	cweðan	say, speak
cuscne	pure, virtuous	cweðaþ	say
cuþ	certain, clear, known, known-to, manifest	cweðe	say
		cweden	say, speak
cuþe	be-able-to, can, certain, clear, know, know-how-to, known, manifest	cwehte	shake, vibrate
		cwellan	kill, murder
		cwellendum	a-killing-one, kill, murder
cuþes	certain, clear, known, manifest	cweman	gratify, please, serve
		cwen	consort, princess, queen, wife, woman
cuþlice	openly	cwenlic	appropriate-for-a-queen, queenly
cuþlicor	openly		
cuþon	be-able-to, can, know	cwet	saying
		cweþ	said, say
cuþra	certain, clear, known, manifest	cweþað	speak-out
		cweþan	say, speak
cwæð	said, say, speak, speaks	cweþaþ	say
		cweþe	quote, say
		cwic	alive, living, quick
cwædon	say, speak	cwican	alive, living
cwæþ	say, speak		

46

Word List (Ænglisc to English)

Ænglisc	English	Ænglisc	English
cwicbeam	mountain-ash, quick-beam, service-tree, spear	cyð	make-known, reveal, say, tell
cwicbeame	mountain-ash, quick-beam, service-tree, spear	cyðað	make-known, reveal, say, tell
		cyðan	make-known, reveal, say, tell
cwice	alive, living	cyðaþ	proclaimed
cwicera	alive, living	cyðð	home, kindred, kith, native-land
cwices	alive, living		
cwiclifigende	living	cydde	make-known, reveal, say, tell
cwiclifigendra	living		
cwicne	alive, living	cyðde	make-known, reveal, say, tell
cwico	alive, living		
cwicra	alive, living	cyððe	home, kindred, kith, native-land
cwicsusl	hell, living-torment		
cwicsusle	hell, living-torment	cyddest	proclaims
cwið	say	cyðdon	make-known, reveal, say, tell
cwiðan	accuse, bewail, lament, mourn		
		cyðed	make-known, reveal
cwiðdon	bewail, mourn	cygan	call, name, speak, summon
cwide	speech, utterance		
cwiðe	accuse, bewail, lament	cygde	call, name, speak, summon
cwiðed	accuse, bewail, lament	cymð	arrive, come
		cyme	arrival, arrive, come, coming
cwidegiedd	song, story		
cwidegiedda	song, story	cymeð	arrive, come, comes
cwidol	nattering	cymen	arrive, come
cwild	disease, pestilence, plague	cymest	arrive, come
		cymeþ	arrive, come
cwiþ	say	cymlice	beautifully, nobly, splendidly
cwiþan	accuse, bewail, lament, mourn		
		cymlicor	beautifully, nobly, splendidly
cwiþdon	bewail, mourn		
cwiþe	accuse, bewail, lament	cymþ	arrive, come
		cyn	family, kind, manners, offspring, propriety, race, sort
cwiþed	accuse, bewail, lament		
cwom	arrive, come		
cwoman	arrive, came, come	cynd	nature, property, quality
cwome	arrive, come	cynde	nature, property, quality
cwomon	arrive, come		
cwucra	revive	cynebearn	national, tribal-offspring
cwyð	say, saying		
cwyde	saying, speech, utterance, word	cynebearna	national, tribal-offspring
cwyldrof	brave-in-killing, renowned-for-killing	cynedom	kingdom
		cynegod	noble
cwyþ	say, saying	cynegode	noble

Word List (*Ænglisc* to English)

Ænglisc	English	*Ænglisc*	English
cynegodum	noble	cyrtenu	beautiful, elegant, neat
cynelic	kingly		
cynerice	kingdom	cyse	cheese
cynerices	kingdom	cyssan	kiss
cynerof	kingly-brave, renowned	cysse	kiss
		cyst	choice, excellence, hand-picked, military-company, no-good, the-best
cynerofe	kingly-brave, renowned		
cynestolum	king's-seat		
Cyneweard	Cyneweard (name)	cystleas	no-good, worthless
cyniges	king	cystleasa	no-good, worthless
cynincg	king	cyston	kiss
Cyning	a-king, king, the-king	cystum	choice, excellence, hand-picked, military-company, the-best
cyninga	king		
cyningas	king, kings		
cyningbald	kingly-brave, royally-brave	cyþ	make-known, reveal, say, tell
cyningbalde	kingly-brave, royally-brave	cyþað	make-known
		cyþan	inform, make-known, reveal, say, tell
cyningc	of-kings		
cyninge	king		
cyninges	king	cyþaþ	make-known, reveal, say, tell
cyningwuldor	glorious-king		
cynn	a-kind-of, family, kind, kindred, kinds, manners, offspring, propriety, race, sort	cyþde	make-known, reveal, say, tell
		cyþdon	make-known, reveal, say, tell
cynna	family, kind, manners, offspring, propriety, race, sort	cyþed	make-known, reveal
		cyþþ	home, kindred, kith, native-land
cynne	family, kind, manners, offspring, propriety, race, sort	cyþþe	home, kindred, kith, native-land

D, d

Ænglisc	English
cynnes	family, kind, kindred, manners, offspring, propriety, race, sort
dæd	action, deed
dæda	action, brave-in-deeds, deed, deeds
cynren	a-brood
cyrcan	church
cyrican	church
dædcene	brave-in-deeds
cyrm	cry, roar, tumult
dæde	action, deed
cyrran	change, convert, turn, turn-back
dædfruma	deed-doer
dædfruman	deed-doer
cyrreð	change, convert, turn, turn-back
dædhata	deadly, deed-hater, enemy, hostile-attacker-literally
cyrreþ	change, convert, turn, turn-back
dædlean	retribution-for-deeds-done
cyrten	beautiful, elegant, neat

Word List (*Ænglisc* to English)

Ænglisc	English	*Ænglisc*	English
dædon	act, cause, do, make, perform, put, take	dælde	allot, deal-in, divide, engage-in, share, share-in
dædrof	deeds, good-renowned	dældon	allot, deal-in, divide, engage-in, share, share-in
dædum	action, deed, deeds		
dæg	day, days, of-the-day, the-day	dæle	allot, deal-in, divide, division, engage-in, lot, part, piece, portion, separation, share, share-in
dæge	day		
dæges	day		
dæghwil	day-while		
dægred	dawn	dæleð	allot, deal-in, divide, engage-in, share, shared, share-in
dægrim	day-number, numbered-day		
dægrime	day-number, numbered-day	dælest	share
		dæleþ	allot, deal-in, divide, engage-in, share, share-in
dægrimes	day-number, numbered-day		
dægtid	day-time, period	dælon	allot, deal-in, divide, engage-in, share, share-in
dægweorc	day's-work		
dægweorce	day's-work		
dægweorces	day's-work	Dæne	Danes (name)
dægwilla	desired-day, joyous-day	dænnede	darkened
		dærede	harm, injure
dægwillan	desired-day, joyous-day	daga	day, days
		dagað	dawn
dæhter	daughter	dagas	day, days
dæhwila	day-while	dagaz	a-breakthrough
dæiges	by-days, day	dagian	become-day, dawn
dæl	abyss, division, lot, part, part-of, piece, portion, separation, share, share-of, valley	dagige	become-day, dawn
		dagum	day, days
		dala	abyss, valley
		dalo	abyss, valley
		darada	spear
dælað	allot, deal-in, divide, engage-in, share, share-in	dareðlacende	spear-brandishing
		dareðum	spear
		dareþum	spear
dælan	allot, deal-in, dealing, divide, engage-in, share, share-in	daroð	spear
		daroþ	spear
		Dauit	David (name)
		dead	dead
dælas	division, lot, part, piece, portion, separation, share	deað	death, died
		deaðbeam	death-beam, death-tree
dælaþ	allot, deal-in, divide, engage-in, share, share-in	deaðbeames	death-beam, death-tree
		deaðbedd	death-bed
		deaðbedde	death-bed
		deaðcwalu	death

Word List (Ænglisc to English)

Ænglisc	English
deaðcwalum	death
deaðcwealm	painful-or-violent-death
deaðdæg	death-day
deaðdæge	death-day
deaðdege	dead, death-day
deade	dead
deaðe	death
deaðes	death
deaðfæge	doomed-to-die
deadne	dead
deadra	the-dead
deaðscua	death-shadow
deaðsele	death-hall
deadum	dead
deaðwerig	dead-incapacitated-by-death
deaðwerigne	dead-incapacitated-by-death
deagan	die?-conceal-oneself?
deah	be-good, good, look-after, strong
deal	magnificent, proud
deall	magnificent, proud
dealle	magnificent, proud
dealne	magnificent, proud
dear	dare
dearnenga	in-secret, insidiously, privately
dearnunga	in-secret, insidiously, privately
dearnunge	in-secret, insidiously, privately
dearr	dare
dearst	dare
deaþ	death
deaþbeam	death-beam, death-tree
deaþbeames	death-beam, death-tree
deaþbedd	death-bed
deaþbedde	death-bed
deaþcwalu	death
deaþcwalum	death
deaþcwealm	painful-or-violent-death
deaþdæg	death-day
deaþdæge	death-day
deaþdege	dead, death-day
deaþe	death, deathly-home
deaþes	death
deaþfæge	doomed-to-die
deaþscua	death-shadow
deaþsele	death-hall
deaþwerig	dead-incapacitated-by-death
deaþwerigne	dead-incapacitated-by-death
deaþwic	deathly-home, death-place
deawigfeðera	having-dewy-plumage
deawigfeðere	having-dewy-plumage
deawigfeþera	having-dewy-plumage
deawigfeþere	having-dewy-plumage
deð	act, cause, do, make, perform, put, take
dege	avail
dehter	daughter
dema	judge, ruler
demað	judge, praise
deman	deem, judge, praise, ruler
demaþ	judge, praise
demde	deem, judge, praise
demdon	judge, praise
deme	judge, praise
demed	deem, deemed, judge, praise
demend	judge, judging
dena	valley
Dene	the-Danes
denn	den
dennes	den
denu	valley
deoð	death
deoðdaege	death-day, nation
deofla	devil
deofle	devil
deofles	devil, devil's
deoflum	devil, the-devil
deofol	devil
deofolcund	devilish, fiendish

Word List (*Ænglisc* to English)

Ænglisc	English	*Ænglisc*	English
deofolcunda	devilish, fiendish	deþ	act, cause, do, make, perform, put, take
deog	die?-conceal-oneself?		
deogol	hidden, mysterious, secret	deum	God (Latin)
		die	day (Latin)
deop	abyss, deep, depth, profound, the-depths	Difelin	Dublin
		digle	secret-place
		digol	dark, secret
deopan	deep, profound, the-depths	digolnes	secret
		digolnesse	secret
deope	completely, deeply	digolnysse	secret
deopnesse	deepness	dihtig	strong
deor	animal, animals, beast, brave, daring, Deor (name), valiant, wild-animal	dim	dark, dim, gloomy
		dimman	dark, dim, gloomy
		dimme	dark, dim, gloomy
		dinamis	powerful (Latin)
deora	beasts, dear	Dinges	Irish
Deoraby	Derby (place)	diope	completely, deeply
deoran	beloved, dear	dior	brave, daring
deorc	dark, gloomy	diore	beloved, dear
deorcan	dark, gloomy	disc	dish
deorce	dark, gloomy	discas	dish
deorcum	dark, gloomy	do	act, cause, do, make, perform, put, take
deore	beloved, brave, daring, dear		
deoreðsceaft	spear-shaft	doð	act, cause, do, make, perform, put, take
deoreðsceaftum	spear-shaft		
deores	beast		
deorestan	beloved, dear	doemed	deemed
deoreþsceaft	spear-shaft	doemid	day, deemed
deoreþsceaftum	spear-shaft	dogera	day
deorlic	bold, brave, daring	dogor	day
deorlice	bold, brave, daring	dogora	day
deormod	brave, brave-minded	dogore	day
deorost	dearest	dogores	day
deorre	beloved, dear	dogorgerim	day-count
deorum	brave, daring	dogorgerimes	day-count
deorwurðan	precious, venerated	dogra	day
deorwurðe	precious, venerated	dogrum	day
deorwurþan	precious, venerated	dohte	be-good, good, look-after, strong
deorwurþe	precious, venerated		
deoþ	death	dohter	daughter
deoþdaege	death-day, nation	dohtest	be-good, good, look-after, strong
deposit	lodge, place		
depravedly	crooked, depraved, perverse	dohtor	daughter
		dohtra	daughter
derede	harm, injure	dohtrum	daughter
derian	harm, injure	dol	folly, foolish
		dole	folly, foolish

Word List (Ænglisc to English)

Ænglisc	English
dolg	scar, sore, wound
dolgilp	foolish-boast
dolgilpe	foolish-boast
dolhwund	wounded
dollic	daring, foolish, rash
dollice	foolishly, rashly
dollicra	daring, foolish, rash
dolsceaða	wounding-enemy
dolsceaðan	wounding-enemy
dolsceaþa	wounding-enemy
dolsceaþan	wounding-enemy
dom	decision, doom, glory, honour, judgement, justice, majesty, might
doma	deeming
domas	glory, honour, judgement, justice, majesty, might
dome	glory, honour, judgement, justice, majesty, might
domę	glorious, glory
domeadig	glorious, mighty
domes	doom, glory, honour, house, judgement, justice, majesty, might
domfæst	honourable, righteous
domfæstne	judgement-firm
domgeorn	eager-for-good-judgement, fame-seeking
dom-georn	glory-desirous
domgeorne	eager-for-good-judgement, fame-seeking
dominum	lord (Latin)
domleas	ignominious, without-glory
domleasan	ignominious, without-glory
domlice	gloriously, justly
don	act, cause, do, make, perform, put, take
Dor	The-Dore (place)
dorste	dare
dorston	dare
doþ	act, cause, do, make, perform, put, take
draca	dragon
dracan	dragon, the-dragon
draf	drive, launch, sail
dranc	drink
dreag	do, endure, endured, experience, fulfil, perform, suffer
dreah	do, endure, experience, fulfil, perform, suffer
dream	delight, gladness, joy, joys, melody, music, rejoicing
dreama	dreams, gladness, joy, melody, music, rejoicing
dreamas	dreams, gladness, joy, joys, melody, music, rejoicing
dreame	gladness, joy, melody, music, rejoicing
dreames	gladness, joy, melody, music, rejoicing
dreamhabbende	happy, joyful, rejoicing
dreamhabbendra	happy, joyful, rejoicing
dreamhealdende	joyful
dreamleas	without-joy
dreamum	gladness, joy, melody, music, rejoicing
dreccan	afflict, harass, oppress, torment
dreceð	afflict, oppress, torment
dreceþ	afflict, oppress, torment
drefan	afflict, beset, stir-up, trouble
drefde	afflict, beset, stir-up, trouble

Word List (Ænglisc to English)

Ænglisc	English	Ænglisc	English
drefeð	vexed	dreoseð	fail, fall, perish
dreht	afflict, harass	dreoseþ	fail, fall, perish
drehte	afflict, harass, oppress, torment	drep	afflict, strike
		drepan	afflict, strike
drenc	drinking, drowning	drepe	blow, stroke
drencan	cause-to-drink, drown	drepen	afflict, strike
		drifað	drive, launch, sail
drence	drinking, drowning	drifan	drive, launch, sail
drenceflod	drowning, flood	drifaþ	drive, launch, sail
drencte	cause-to-drink, drown	drife	drive, launch, sail
		drige	dry
dreng	warrior	driht	company, multitude, nation, people
drenga	warrior		
dreogað	do, endure, experience, fulfil, perform, suffer	drihta	company, multitude, nation, people
		drihten	lord, lord-of, prince, ruler, the-Lord
dreogan	do, endure, experience, fulfil, perform, suffer	drihtenes	prince, ruler, the-Lord
		drihtenhold	faithful-or-obedient-to-the-Lord
dreogaþ	do, endure, experience, fulfil, perform, suffer	drihtfolc	nation, people, troop
		drihtfolca	nation, people, troop
dreogeð	do, endure, enduring, experience, fulfil, perform, suffer, suffers	drihtgesiða	associates
		drihtguma	man, retainer
		drihtguman	man, retainer
		drihtlecu	splendid
dreogeþ	do, endure, enduring, experience, fulfil, perform, suffer	drihtlic	splendid
		drihtlice	lordly, nobly, splendid
		drihtlicu	splendid
dreoh	do, endure, experience, fulfil, perform, suffer	drihtna	prince, ruler, the-Lord
		drihtne	corpse, lord, prince, ruler, the-Lord
dreor	blood, dripping-blood, gore	drihtnes	lord, prince, ruler, the-Lord, the-lord's
dreore	blood, gore		
dreorfah	blood-stained, splashed-with-blood	drihtneum	corpse
		drihtscipe	dignity, lordship, majesty, noble-action
dreorgiað	failing		
dreorig	bloody, drearily, dreary, sad, sadly	drihtscipes	dignity, lordship, noble-action
dreorighleor	sad-faced	drihtscype	dignity, lordship, noble-action
dreorigmod	sad-minded		
dreorigne	bloody, dreary, sad	drihtsele	noble-hall
dreorlicre	bloodier	drihtwer	man, nation-member
dreorsele	dreary-hall, dreary-hall?-bloody-hall?		
dreosan	fail, fall, perish		

Word List (*Ænglisc* to English)

Ænglisc	English	*Ænglisc*	English
drihtwera	man, nation-member	drusade	become-calm, subside
drihtweras	man, nation-member	drusian	become-calm, subside
drinc	beverage, drink, drinking	dry	magician, sorcerer, sorcery
drincan	drink	dryctin	lord, mighty
drincend	drinker	dryge	dry
drincendra	drinker	dryht	men, nation, people
drincfaet	ornamented-drinking-cup	dryhta	of-men
		dryhtbearn	lordly-scion, prince
driorig	bloody, dreary, sad	dryhten	lord, nation-people, prince, ruler, the-Lord
driorigne	bloody, dreary, sad		
drogen	endure, suffer		
drohtað	employment, living, plight, way-of-life	dryhtfolc	nation-people
		dryhtfolca	nation-people
drohtaþ	employment, living, plight, way-of-life	dryhtguma	man, retainer
		dryhtguman	man, retainer
drohtende	act, behave, behaves	dryhtgumum	man, retainer
		dryhtlic	splendid
drohtian	act, behave	dryhtlicestum	splendid
drohtnian	monastic-life, way-of-life	dryhtmaðm	noble-treasure
		dryhtmaðma	noble-treasure
drohtnode	monastic-life, way-of-life	dryhtmaþm	noble-treasure
		dryhtmaþma	noble-treasure
drohtnung	monastic-life, monastic-rule, way-of-life	dryhtna	of-lords, prince, ruler, the-Lord
		dryhtne	lord, prince, ruler, the-Lord
drohtnunge	monastic-life, monastic-rule, way-of-life	dryhtnes	prince, ruler, the-Lord
drohtoð	employment, living, plight, way-of-life	dryhtscipe	valour
drohtoþ	employment, living, plight, way-of-life	dryhtscype	dignity, lordship, noble-action
		dryhtsele	noble-hall
dropen	afflict, strike	dryhtsibb	peace
druge	do, endure, experience, fulfil, perform, suffer	dryhtsibbe	peace
		dryhtum	men, nation, people
		dryman	enjoy-oneself, rejoice
drugon	do, endure, experience, fulfil, perform, suffer	drymdon	enjoy-oneself, rejoice
druncen	drunk	dryncfæt	cup, drinking-vessel
druncmennen	drunken-female-slave	drype	drip
		dryppan?	drip
druncne	drunk	dryum	magician, sorcerer, sorcery
druncnum	drunken		
druncon	drunken	dufan	sink-in

Word List (*Ænglisc* to English)

Ænglisc	English	*Ænglisc*	English
dugan	be-good, be-of-use, good, look-after, strong	dugeþe	company, excellence, glory, host, majesty-people, multitude, nobles, often-in-contrast-with, property, riches, the-older, tried-retainers, virtue
duge	be-good, good, look-after, strong		
dugeða	company, excellence, glory, host, majesty-people, multitude, nobles, often-in-contrast-with, property, riches, the-older, tried-retainers, virtue	dugeþum	company, excellence, glory, host, majesty-people, multitude, nobles, often-in-contrast-with, property, riches, the-older, tried-retainers, virtue
dugeðe	company, excellence, glory, host, majesty-people, multitude, nobles, often-in-contrast-with, property, riches, the-older, tried-retainers, virtue	dugoða	company, excellence, glory, host, majesty-people, multitude, nobles, often-in-contrast-with, property, riches, the-older, tried-retainers, virtue
dugeðum	company, excellence, glory, host, majesty-people, multitude, nobles, often-in-contrast-with, property, riches, the-older, tried-retainers, virtue	dugoðe	company, excellence, glory, host, majesty-people, multitude, nobles, often-in-contrast-with, property, riches, the-older, tried-retainers, virtue
dugeþa	company, excellence, glory, host, majesty-people, multitude, nobles, often-in-contrast-with, property, riches, the-older, tried-retainers, virtue, virtues	dugoþa	company, excellence, glory, host, majesty-people, multitude, nobles, often-in-contrast-with, property, riches, the-older, tried-retainers, virtue

Word List (*Ænglisc* to English)

Ænglisc	English	*Ænglisc*	English
dugoþe	company, excellence, glory, host, majesty-people, multitude, nobles, often-in-contrast-with, property, riches, the-older, tried-retainers, virtue	*duguþ*	body-of-retainers, company, excellence, glory, host, majesty-people, mature-men, multitude, nobles, often-in-contrast-with, property, riches, the-older, tried-retainers, troop-of-seasoned-retainers, virtue
duguð	body-of-retainers, company, excellence, glory, host, majesty-people, multitude, nobles, often-in-contrast-with, property, riches, the-older, tried-retainers, virtue	*duguþa*	company, excellence, glory, host, majesty-people, multitude, nobles, often-in-contrast-with, property, riches, the-older, tried-retainers, virtue
duguða	company, excellence, glory, host, majesty-people, multitude, nobles, often-in-contrast-with, property, riches, the-older, tried-retainers, virtue	*duguþe*	company, excellence, glory, goods, host, majesty-people, multitude, nobles, often-in-contrast-with, property, riches, the-older, tried-retainers, virtue
duguðe	company, excellence, glory, goods, host, majesty-people, multitude, nobles, often-in-contrast-with, property, riches, the-older, tried-retainers, virtue	*duguþum*	company, excellence, glory, host, majesty-people, multitude, nobles, often-in-contrast-with, property, riches, the-older, tried-retainers, virtue
duguðum	company, excellence, glory, host, majesty-people, multitude, nobles, often-in-contrast-with, property, riches, the-older, tried-retainers, virtue	*dumb*	dumb, silent
		dun	mountain
		duna	mountain, mountains
		dune	mountain, mountains
		dunscrafum	hill-caves, mountain-cave
		dunum	mountain

Word List (*Ænglisc* to English)

Ænglisc	English
dura	the-door
durran	dare
durre	dare
durron	dare
duru	door
durum	door
dust	dust
duste	dust
dweleð	hinder, hindered, restrain
dweleþ	hinder, restrain
dwellan	hinder, restrain
dweores	convulsive-fever, dwarf
dweorh	convulsive-fever, dwarf
dyde	act, cause, did, do, make, perform, put, take
dydest	act, cause, deed, do, make, perform, put, take
dydon	act, cause, do, make, perform, put, take
dyfan	dip, immerse
dyfde	dip, immerse
dygel	hidden, mysterious, secret
dygle	secret
dyhttig	strong
dynedan	make-a-din, resound
dynede	make-a-din, resound, resounded
dynian	make-a-din, resound
dyran	hold-dear
dyre	beloved, conceal, dear, dear-to
dyrnan	conceal, deceitful, evil, secret
dyrnde	conceal
dyrne	beloved, dear, deceitful, deep, evil, secret, secretly
dyrnne	beloved, dear
dyrnra	deceitful, evil, secret
dyrnum	deceitful, evil, secret
dyrre	dare
dyrsian	glorify, honour
dyrstig	brave
dyrum	beloved, dear
dysig	foolish

Ð, ð

Ænglisc	English
ða	as, being-the-case, that, that-in, the, them, then, they, those, thus, when, where, which
ðæm	that-in, the, there, those
ðær	that-in, there, wherein-such-a-case-where
ðæra	that, those
ðære	that, that-in, the, there, those
ðæron	in-it, therein, thereon
ðæs	that-in, the, these, this, those
ðæt	he, it, she, so-that, that, the, which, who
ðafian	agree-to, consent
ðah	endure, prosper, thrive
ðam	that, that-in, the, those
ðan	the
ðanc	agree-to, consent, grace, mercy, thanks
ðane	the
ðanon	from-there, thence
ðar	there, wherein-such-a-case-where
ðara	that-in, the, those
ðas	these, this
ðe	as, dead, death, ever, that, that-in, the, thee, those, thou, to, to-thee, to-you, which, who, you, yourself
ðeah	although, nevertheless, though
ðeah ðe	although, even-if

Word List (Ænglisc to English)

Ænglisc	English	Ænglisc	English
ðeaht	conceal, cover	ðicce	closely, thickly
ðeahte	conceal, cover	ðicgean	accept, eat, partake-of, receive
ðearf	have-occasion-to, need, needs, requirement	ðigen	prosper, thrive
		ðigon	prosper, thrive
ðearfe	need	ðin	thou, you, your
ðeaw	custom, habit	ðine	yours
ðeawum	custom, habit, manner, virtue	ðines	your
		ðing	assembly, circumstance, contest, meeting, thing
ðec	thou, you		
ðeccan	conceal, cover		
ðegenlice	nobly		
ðegn	man, minister, nobleman, officer, retainer, servant, thane	ðinga	assembly, circumstance, contest, meeting, thing
ðegna	man, minister, nobleman, officer, retainer, servant, thane	ðinges	assembly, circumstance, contest, meeting, thing
ðegnas	man, minister, nobleman, officer, retainer, servant, thane	ðinne	thou, you, your
		ðinra	thou, you
		ðinre	your
		ðinum	your
ðeh	although, nevertheless	ðiodcyning	people-king
		ðis	dish, these, this
ðencan	intend, resolve, think	ðisne	these
ðenden	as-long-as, while	ðisse	these, this
ðeod	nation, people	ðisses	these, this
ðeoda	nation, people	ðoht	intend, resolve, think
ðeodcyning	people-king	ðohte	intend, resolve, think
ðeod-cyning	people-king	ðolad	endure, hold-out
ðeode	nation, people	ðolade	endure, hold-out
ðeoden	king, lord	ðolian	endure, hold-out
ðeodenleas	lord-less	ðoliaþ	allow, endure, forgo, lose, suffer
ðeodenlease	lord-less		
ðeodkyning	people-king	ðolode	allow, endure, forgo, lose, suffer
ðeodne	king, lord		
ðeodnes	king, lord	ðon	from-there, than, that-in, the, those
ðeodric	Theodric (name)		
ðeodsceaða	national-enemy, people-destroyer	ðonan	from-there, thence
		ðonne	from-there, than, that, then, thence, when
ðeon	endure, prosper, thrive		
ðeos	death-day, this	ðonon	from-there, thence
ðeowa	held-dear	ðonosnottorra	have-occasion-to, thought-wiser
ðeowian	serve		
ðes	these, this	ðorfte	have-occasion-to, need
ði	your		

Word List (*Ænglisc* to English)

Ænglisc	English
ðrean	afflict
ðreat	band, troop
ðreatum	company, troop
ðriddan	third
ðrinesse	yours
ðriostre	falling
ðrist	audacious, bold, shameless
ðriste	audacious, bold, shameless
ðrittiges	thirty
ðrowad	endure, suffer
ðrowade	endure, suffer
ðrowian	endure, suffer
ðrowode	endure, suffer
ðrowunga	suffering
ðry	three
ðryðlic	mighty, powerful
ðryðswyð	strong-and-powerful, very-mighty
ðrym	force, glory, host, majesty, power, troop
ðrymme	people
ðrymmum	mightily
ðrynes	trinity
ðrynesse	trinity
ðrysman	become-dark, become-smoky
ðrysmaþ	become-dark, become-smoky
ðrybærn	hall, majestic-building
ðu	thee, thou, you
ðuhte	appear, seem, think
ðurh	by-means-of, for-the-sake-of, in, through
ðurhfon	get-through, penetrate
ðurhwadan	penetrate, pierce
ðurhwaden	penetrate, pierce
ðurhwod	go-through, penetrate, pierce
ðurhwodon	penetrate, pierce
ðwoh	cleanse, wash
ðy	it, that, therefore
ðyle	orator, spokesman
ðyn	your
ðyncan	appear, seem, think
ðyrel	shot-through
ðys	these, this
ðysne	these, this
ðysse	these, this
ðyssum	these, this
ðysum	these, this

E, e

Ænglisc	English
e	e
ea	also, river
eac	also, another, besides, each, even, every, in-addition-to, moreover, reinforcement
eaca	reinforcement, reinforcing-troop
eacen	augmented, endowed, huge, increased, numerous, pregnant
eacencræftig	strong
eacne	augmented, endowed, huge, increased, numerous, pregnant
eacnian	become-pregnant, bring-forth, conceive
eacniendra	become-pregnant, bring-forth, conceive
eacnum	augmented, endowed, huge, increased, numerous, pregnant
ead	happiness, property, prosperity, riches
eaðe	clearly, easily, easy, pleasant
eadega	blessed, happy, prosperous
eades	happiness, prosperity, riches
eaðfynde	easily-found
eadga	blessed, happy, prosperous
Eadgar	Edgar, Edgar (name)

Word List (*Ænglisc* to English)

Ænglisc	English	*Ænglisc*	English
eadge	blessed, happy, prosperous	*eaforan*	descendant, heir, son
eadgestreonum	heirloom, old-treasure	*eaforheafodsegn*	banner, boar's-head-banner, boar's-head-sign, boar's-head-symbol
eadhreðig	blessed, happy		
eadhreðige	blessed, happy		
eadhreþig	blessed, happy	*eaforum*	descendant, heir, son
eadhreþige	blessed, happy		
eadig	blessed, happy, prosperous	*eafoþ*	might, strength
		eafoþes	might, strength
eadigan	blessed, happy, prosperous	*eafrum*	descendant, heir, son
eadiges	prosperous	*eagan*	eye
eadiglice	happily, prosperously	*eage*	eye
		eagena	eye
eadignes	blessedness	*eagorstream*	ocean-current
eadignesse	blessedness	*eagor-stream*	current, sea-stream
eadlean	punishment, recompense, reward	*eagum*	eye, eyes
		Eaha	Eaha (name)
eadleane	punishment, recompense, reward	*eahta*	8, eight
		eahta and feowertig	48, forty eight
eaðmede	humble	*eahta and feopertig*	48, forty eight
eaðmedu	humility, reverence	*eahta and feowertigoþa*	forty eighth
eaðmedum	humility, reverence		
eaðmod	humble, obedient, submissive	*eahta and fiftig*	58, fifty eight
		eahta and fiftigoþa	fifty eighth
eadmoda	humble	*eahta and hundeahtatig*	88, eighty eight
eadmodlice	humbly		
eadmodnes	humility	*eahta and hundeahtatigoþa*	eighty eighth
eadmodnesse	humility		
Eadmund	Eadmund (name), Edmund (name)	*eahta and hundendleftig*	118, a hundred and eighteen
eaðost	easily	*eahta and hundnigontig*	98, ninety eight
Eadweard	Edward (name)		
Eadweardes	Edward (name), Edward's (name)	*eahta and hundnigontigoþa*	ninety eighth
eadwela	prosperity, riches	*eahta and hundseofontig*	78, seventy eight
eadwelan	prosperity, riches		
eafera	descendant, heir, son	*eahta and hundseofontigoþa*	seventy eighth
eaferan	descendant, heir, son	*eahta and hundteontig*	108, a hundred and eight
eaferum	descendant, heir, son	*eahta and sixtig*	68, sixty eight
		eahta and sixtigoþa	sixty eighth
eafeþum	might, strength	*eahta and þritig*	38, thirty eight
eafoð	might, strength	*eahta and þritigoþa*	thirty eighth
eafora	descendant, heir, son	*eahta and twentig*	28, twenty eight
		eahta and tpentig	28, twenty eight

Word List (*Ænglisc* to English)

Ænglisc	English	*Ænglisc*	English
eahta and twentigoþa	twenty eighth	ealdgesiþ	old-retainer, seasoned-warrior
eahtahund	eight-hundred	ealdgesiþas	old-retainer, seasoned-warrior
eahtateoþa	eighteenth	ealdgestreon	heirloom, old-treasure
eahtatine	18, eighteen	ealdgestreona	heirloom, old-treasure
eahteðan	eighth	ealdgewin	heirloom, old-treasure
eahtedon	consider, deliberate-upon, discuss, mention, praise	ealdgewinna	old-enemy
eahtian	consider, deliberate-upon, discuss, esteem, mention, praise	ealdgewyrht	former-transgression
eahtod	esteem, praise	ealdgewyrhtum	former-transgression
eahtodan	consider, deliberate-upon, discuss, mention, praise	ealdhettende	old-enemies
		ealdhlaford	long-time-lord, old-lord
eahtode	consider, deliberate-upon, discuss, esteem, mention, praise	ealdhlafordes	long-time-lord, old-lord
		ealdian	age, grow-old
eahtoþa	eighth	ealdne	old
eal	alas!, all, easily, entirely, indeed	ealdor	age, a-prince, elder, eternity, king, leader, life, lord, lordship, parent, prince, prince-of, superior, the-elder
eala	alas!, woe!		
eald	old		
ealda	elders, old		
ealdað	age, grow-old		
ealdafæder	grandfather	ealdordom	lordship
ealdan	old	ealdorduguð	leadership
ealdaþ	age, grow-old	ealdorduguðe	leadership
ealde	elder, old	ealdorduguþ	leadership
ealdelm	Aldhelm (name)	ealdorduguþe	leadership
ealderdagum	life-day	ealdorgedal	death
ealdes	long-ago, old	ealdorgewinna	deadly-enemy, enemy-to-the-death
ealdfæder	ancestor, forefather, honoured-father	ealdorlangne	lifelong
ealdfeond	old-enemy	ealdorleas	dead, lifeless
ealdfeondum	old-enemy	ealdorleasne	dead, lifeless
ealdgeniðla	old-enemy	ealdorman	ealdorman, noble
ealdgeniðlan	old-enemy	ealdormann	ealdorman, noble
ealdgeniþla	old-enemy	ealdor-monn	nobleman, older-man
ealdgeniþlan	old-enemy		
ealdgesegen	old-story	ealdorþegn	general, leading-officer
ealdgesegena	old-story		
ealdgesið	old-retainer, seasoned-warrior	ealdorþegnum	general, leading-officer
ealdgesiðas	old-retainer, seasoned-warrior		

Word List (Ænglisc to English)

Ænglisc	English
ealdre	elder, eternity, king, life, lord, prince, superior
ealdres	elder, eternity, king, life, lord, prince, superior
ealdum	old
ealfela	very-many
ealgearo	all-ready, complete
ealgian	avenge, defend, protect
ealgode	avenge, defend, protect
ealgodon	defend
ealgylden	all-golden, completely-gilded
eall	all, easily, entirely, indeed
ealle	all, completely, entirely
eallenga	completely, entirely
ealles	all, all-ready, complete, entirely, every
eallgearo	all-ready, complete
eallgylden	all-golden, entirely-gilt
eallinga	completely, entirely
ealliren	all-iron
eallirenne	all-iron
eallon	entirely
eallra	all
eallum	all, entirely
eallunga	altogether
eallwealda	all-ruler, the-Lord
eallwihta	all-creatures
ealne	ale-bench, all
ealneg	always
ealobenc	ale-bench
ealobence	ale-bench
ealodrincend	ale-drinker
ealodrincende	ale-drinker
ealogal	drunk-on-ale
ealogalra	drunk-on-ale
ealond	island
ealonde	island
ealowæg	ale-beaker
ealowæge	ale-beaker
ealowosa	garrulous-drunk
ealowosan	garrulous-drunk
ealra	all, altogether, every, of-all, sometimes-used-in-all
ealre	all, altogether, sometimes-used-in-all
ealteawne	all-good
ealubence	ale-bench
ealuscerwen	ale-depriving, ale-dispensing
ealuwæg	ale-beaker
ealuwæge	ale-beaker
eam	usually-maternal-uncle
eame	usually-maternal-uncle
ear	earth
earc	ark, chest, coffer, the-Ark
earce	chest, coffer, the-Ark
eard	country, home, homeland, homesteads, land, region
earda	country, homeland, land, region
eardas	country, earth, homeland, land, region
eardast	dwell
earde	country, homeland, land, region
eardes	country, homeland, land, region
eardfæst	established, settled
eardgeard	dwelling-place, land
eardian	dwell, dwell-in, live, occupy
eardigean	dwell-in, live, occupy
eardlufan	beloved-land
eardlufe	beloved-land
eardod	dwell, live
eardode	dwell, dwell-in, live, occupy
eardodon	dwell-in, live, occupy
eardstapa	traveller

Word List (*Ænglisc* to English)

Ænglisc	English
eard-stapa	earth-stepper, wanderer
eardwica	dwelling-place
eare	ear
earfeðe	hardship, suffering
earfeðmæcg	miserable-person
earfeðmæcgum	miserable-person
earfeðu	difficulty, hardship, trouble
earfeþa	difficulty, hardship, trouble
earfeþe	hardship, suffering
earfeþmæcg	miserable-person
earfeþmæcgum	miserable-person
earfeþo	difficulty, hardship, trouble
earfeþu	difficulty, hardship, trouble
earfoða	difficulty, hardship, trouble, troubles
earfoðhwil	hardship-while, trouble-while
earfoð-hwil	hardship-time
earfoðhwile	hardship-while, trouble-while
earfoðlic	difficult, hard, miserable
earfoðlice	miserably, with-difficulty-or-hardship
earfoðsið	hardship-since, miserable-journey, trouble-since
earfoðsiða	hardship-since, miserable-journey, trouble-since
earfoðsiþ	hardship-since, miserable-journey, trouble-since
earfoðþrag	trouble-time
earfoðþrage	hardship-time
earfoþ	hardship, work
earfoþa	difficulty, hardship, misery, trouble, troubles
earfoþe	difficulty, hardship, trouble
earfoþhwil	hardship-while, trouble-while
earfoþ-hwil	hardship-time
earfoþhwile	hardship-while, trouble-while
earfoþlic	difficult, hard, miserable
earfoþlice	miserably, with-difficulty-or-hardship
earfoþsiþ	hardship-since, miserable-journey, trouble-since
earfoþsiþa	hardship-since, miserable-journey, trouble-since
earfoþþrag	trouble-time
earfoþþrage	hardship-time
earg	cowardly, wretched
earges	cowardly, wretched
eargra	cowardly, wretched
earh	cowardly, wretched
earm	arm, lonely, miserable, poor
earmbeag	arm-ring, bracelet
earmbeaga	arm-ring, bracelet
earmcearig	miserable
earm-cearig	miserable, wretched-caring
earme	arm, badly, miserable, miserably, poor
earming	miserable
earminge	commiseration
earmlic	miserable
earmlice	miserably
earmne	miserable, poor
earmon	arm
earmra	miserable, poor
earmran	miserable, poor
earmre	miserable, poor
earmread	arm-ornament, bracelet
earmreade	arm-ornament, bracelet
earmsceapen	vile, wretched
earmum	arm
earn	eagle, osprey, sea-eagle
earna	deserving, earn, merit
earne	eagle, osprey, sea-eagle

Word List (Ænglisc to English)

Ænglisc	English
earnes	eagle's, the-eagle's
earnian	deserving, earn, earning, merit, to-be
eart	are, be, east, to-be
east	east, from-the-east
eastan	from-the-east
easteð	river-bank, shore
easteðe	river-bank, shore
easten	from-the-east
easterne	eastern
easteþ	river-bank, shore
easteþe	river-bank, shore
eastland	eastern-land
eastlandum	eastern-land
eaststream	eastern-river
eaststreamas	eastern-river
eastweard	eastward
east-weard	eastward
eaþe	easily, easy, pleasant
eaþfynde	easily-found
eaþmedu	humility, reverence
eaþmedum	humility, reverence
eaþmod	humble, obedient, submissive
eaþost	easily
eatol	horrible, terrible
eatolne	horrible, terrible
eaweð	appear, present, reveal, show
eaweþ	appear, present, reveal, show
eaxl	shoulder
eaxle	shoulder
eaxlgespann	cross-beam, shoulder-fastening
eaxlgespanne	cross-beam, shoulder-fastening
eaxlgestealla	close-companion, shoulder
eaxlgesteallan	close-companion, shoulder
eaxlum	shoulder
ebba	ebb
ebbade	ebb, subside
ebban	ebb
ebbian	ebb, subside
ec	also, eternal, though
eca	eternal
ecan	augment, eternal, grow, increase, reinforcement, reinforcing-troop
ecclesiam	church (Latin)
ece	eternal, eternally, everlasting
ecea	eternal
ecean	eternal
eces	eternal
ecg	blade, edge, sword, the-blade
ecga	blade, edge, sword
ecgbana	sword-killer
ecgbanan	sword-killer
ecgclif	shoreline-cliff
ecge	blade, edge, sword
ecghete	enmity, sword-hate
ecgplega	edge-play, edge-sport, sword-play
ecgplegan	edge-play, edge-sport, sword-play
ecgþracu	attack, edge-rush, sword-rush
ecgþræce	attack, edge-rush, sword-rush
ecgum	blade, edge, sword
ecgwal	corpse-pile, edge-wall
ecgwale	corpse-pile, edge-wall
eci	augmented, eternal
ecne	augmented, endowed, eternal, huge, increased, numerous, pregnant
ecnis	eternity
ecnisse	eternity
ecum	eternal
eðbegete	easily-gotten
eðe	easy, pleasant
eðel	country, home, homeland, native-land
eðeldream	homeland-joy
eðeldreamas	homeland-joy
eðelðrym	native-power, noble-power
eðeleard	native-land

Word List (*Ænglisc* to English)

Ænglisc	English	*Ænglisc*	English
eðeleardum	native-land	*edrum*	artery, stream, vein-spring
eðelland	native-land		
eðel-land	native-land	*eðulstæfe*	child, heir
eðelleas	exiled, homeless	*edwendan*	change, reverse
eðelleasum	exiled, homeless	*edwenden*	change, reversal
eðelmearc	country, nation	*edwihtan*	anything, something
eðelmearce	country, nation	*edwihte*	anything, something
eðelriht	right-to-a-native-land	*edwit*	reproach, shame
		edwitlif	shameful-life
eðelrihtes	right-to-a-native-land	*edwitscype*	disgrace
		edwylm	surging-fire
eðelseld	noble-settlement	*edwylme*	surging-fire
eðelsetl	noble-settlement	*edygled*	the-country
eðelstaðol	secure-homeland	*eðyl*	country, native-land
eðelstaðolas	secure-homeland	*eðylstæf*	child, heir
eðelstæf	child, heir	*eðyltyrf*	homeland, native-soil
eðelstol	capital-city, high-place, national-fortress, noble-place	*efeneadig*	equally-blessed
		efenlæcan	be-like, emulate, equal, match
eðelstow	homeland, native-place	*efenlang*	just-as-long, of-the-same-length
eðelstowe	homeland, native-place	*efnan*	carry-out, construct
eðelturf	homeland, native-soil	*efnde*	carry-out, construct
		efne	carry-out, construct, even, exactly, just, shave
eðeltyrf	noble-soil		
eðelweardas	king, noble-guardian		
eðelwyn	noble-delight, noble-land	*efsian*	shave, shear
		efstan	go-quickly, hurry
ederas	building, enclosure, lord, protector	*efste*	go-quickly, hurry
		efston	go-quickly, hurry
eðest	noblest	*eft*	after, afterward, afterwards, again, back, in-answer, in-turn, return, thereupon
eðgesyne	easily-seen, plentiful		
edhwyrft	reversal		
eðle	country, homeland, native-land, punishment		
		eftcyme	return
edlean	punishment, recompense, reward	*eftcymes*	return
		efter	after, return-journey
edleane	punishment, recompense, reward	*eftsið*	return-journey, subsequent-journey
eðles	land	*eftsiðas*	return-journey, subsequent-journey
edmod	obedient		
edmodne	obedient	*eftsiðes*	return-journey, subsequent-journey
edneowe	continual, renewed		
edor	building, enclosure, lord, protector	*eftsiþ*	return-journey, subsequent-journey
edoras	building, enclosure, lord, protector	*eftsiþas*	return-journey, subsequent-journey

Word List (*Ænglisc* to English)

Ænglisc	English	*Ænglisc*	English
eftsiþes	return-journey, subsequent-journey	*ehtnys*	attack, harassment, persecution
egbuendra	island-dwelling	*ehtnysse*	attack, harassment, persecution
ege	fear	*ehton*	attack, harass, persecute
egesa	awe, fear, horror, peril	*eiglande*	island
egesan	awe, fear, horror, peril	*eius*	yours (Latin)
egesful	awe-inspiring, terrible	*elde*	men
egesfull	awe-inspiring, terrible	*elðeod*	foreigners, foreign-nation
egesian	frighten, intimidate	*elðeoda*	foreigners, foreign-nation
egeslic	frightening, horrid	*elðeodig*	alien, foreign, strange
egeslican	frightening, horrid		
egesum	awe, fear, horror, peril	*elðeodigra*	foreign
		eldo	age, old-age
eghwam	everything	*eldum*	men
eglan	afflict, trouble	*ele*	oil
egle	horrible	*elebeam*	olive-tree
eglond	island	*elebeames*	olive-tree
eglu	horrible	*Eligbyrig*	Ely-in-the-Fens (place)
egorhere	flood, wave-battalion		
egorstream	flood-current	*Elizabet*	Elizabeth (name)
egorstreamas	flood-current	*elland*	foreign-land
egsa	awe, fear, horror, peril, terrifying	*ellðeodigra*	foreign
		ellen	courage, nobility, strength, valour
egsan	awe, fear, horror, peril	*ellendæd*	valour-deed
egsian	terrify	*ellendæda*	valour-deed
egsod	terrify	*ellendædum*	valour-deed
egsode	frighten, intimidate, terrify	*ellenlice*	bravely, valiantly
		ellenmærðum	valorous, valour
egstream	current, river, stream	*ellenmærþu*	valorous, valour
		ellenmærþum	valorous, valour
egstreamum	current, river, stream	*ellenrof*	courageous, noble
		ellenrofe	courageous, noble
eht	keep	*ellenrofum*	courageous, noble
ehtan	attack, harass, persecute	*ellenþrist*	bold, daring, heroic
		ellenþriste	bold, daring, heroic
ehteð	pursuing	*ellenweorc*	courage-work
ehtende	attack, harass, persecute	*ellen-weorc*	work-of-courage
		ellenweorca	courage-work
ehtigað	consider, deliberate-upon, discuss, mention, praise	*elles*	anything-else, besides, else, otherwise
ehtigaþ	consider, deliberate-upon, discuss, mention, praise	*ellor*	another, elsewhere
		ellorfus	eager, elsewhere
		ellorfuse	eager, elsewhere

Word List (*Ænglisc* to English)

Ænglisc	English	*Ænglisc*	English
ellorgæst	alien-spirit, ghost-from-elsewhere	endelaf	final-remains, last-survivor
ellorgast	alien-spirit, ghost-from-elsewhere	endelean	final-reward
		endeleas	endless
ellorsið	death, journey-elsewhere	endesæta	boundary-watcher, coast-guard
ellorsiþ	death, journey-elsewhere	endestæf	end
		endian	agreement, end, stop
ellþeodig	foreign		
ellþeodigne	foreign	endlefta	eleventh
ellþeodigra	foreign	endleofan	11, eleven
eln	ell, fore-arm, measure	enge	confined, cramped, narrow
elna	ell, fore-arm, measure	engel	angel
		engelcynn	angel-kin, Angle-kin
elne	courage, nobility, valour	engelcynna	angel-kin, Angle-kin
elnes	courage, nobility, valour	engla	angel, angelic, angels, English (name), of-angels, of-the-Angles, the-English
elngemet	measured-cubit, measured-ell		
elngemeta	measured-cubit, measured-ell	englas	angel, angels
		engle	angel, Angles
elnian	grow-strong	engles	angel
elniendra	grow-strong	englum	angel, angels, the-angels
elra	another		
elran	another	engyl	angel
elþeod	foreigners, foreign-nation	enne	a
		ent	giant
elþeoda	foreigners, foreign-nation	enta	giant, giants, giants'
		entisc	giant-made, gigantic, troll-made
elþeode	foreigners, foreign-nation, strangers	entiscne	giant-made, gigantic, troll-made
elþeodig	alien, foreign, strange	eode	acquire, carry-out, go, observe, overrun, take-place
elþeodige	foreign		
elþeodigra	foreign		
embe	about, after, around	eoderas	building, enclosure, lord, protector
emne	exactly, just		
emnlange	along	eodon	acquire, carry-out, go, observe, overrun, take-place
encratea	power-inside		
end	and, end		
ende	an-end, end, to-the-end	eodor	building, enclosure, lord, protector
endebyrdnes	order, sequence	eodur	building, enclosure, lord, protector
endedæg	death-day, final-day		
endedogor	death-day, final-day	eofer	wild-boar, wild-boar-banner, wild-boar-sign
endedogores	death-day, final-day		

Word List (Ænglisc to English)

Ænglisc	English	Ænglisc	English
eoferas	wild-boar, wild-boar-banner, wild-boar-sign	eorðscrafa	cave, grave
		eorðscrafu	cave, earth's-chest, grave
eoferholt	boar-decorated-spear	eorðsele	earth-dwelling, earth-hall
eoferspreot	boar-spear	eorðweall	dyke, earthwork
eoferspreotum	boar-spear	eorðweg	earthly-road-or-path
eofoð	might, strength	eorðwege	earthly-road-or-path
eofoðo	might, strength	eorðwela	earthly-possession
eofor	boar	eorðwelan	earthly-possession
eoforlic	boar-image	eored	company, troop
eofoþ	might, strength	eoredcystum	military-troop
eofoþo	might, strength	eoredgeatwe	military-equipment
eoh	horse	eorl	earl, leader, man, noble, nobleman, warrior
eolet	voyage-?		
eoletes	voyage-?		
eom	am, I-am, precious-stone, to-be	eorla	earls, leader, man, nobleman, nobles, the-earl, warrior
eonene	pass		
eorcanstan	precious-stones	eorlas	earls, leader, man, men, nobleman, warrior, warriors
eorclanstan	precious-stone		
eorclanstanas	precious-stone		
eorð	earth	eorle	earl, leader, man, men, nobleman, the-earl, warrior
eorðan	earth, earth-dweller, earthly, earth's, elders', human, the-earth		
		eorles	leader, man, nobleman, warrior
eorðbuend	earth-dweller, human	eorlgestreon	nobleman's-treasure
		eorlgestreona	an-earl's-treasures, nobleman's-treasure
eorðbuende	earth-dweller, earth-dwellers, human	eorlgewæde	noble-clothing
eorðbuendra	earth-dweller, earth-dwellers, human	eorlgewædum	noble-clothing
		eorlic	noble
eorðbuendum	earth-dweller, earth-dwellers, human	eorlscipe	bravery, heroic-deeds, nobility
eorðbugende	earth-dwellers	eorlscype	bravery, nobility
eorðcund	earthly	eorlum	leader, man, nobleman, warrior
eorðcunde	earthly		
eorðcyning	earthly-king	eorlweorod	men-troop
eorðcyninges	earthly-king	Eormanrices	Ermanaric's (name)
eorðdraca	earth--dwelling-dragon	eormencynn	all-mankind, mankind
eorðe	earth, earth-building	eormencynnes	all-mankind, mankind
eorðgrap	earth		
eorðreced	earth-building, subterranean-building	eormengrund	the-vast-earth
		eormenlaf	great-treasure, vast-heritage
eorðscræf	cave, grave	eormenlafe	great-treasure, vast-heritage
eorðscræfe	a-cave		

Word List (*Ænglisc* to English)

Ænglisc	English	*Ænglisc*	English
eornoste	courageously, firmly, resolutely	eotonweard	watch-against-giants-or-trolls
eorodcistum	the-troops	eow	acquire, you, you (plural)
eorp	dark		
eorres	angry	eowde	acquire, carry-out, go, observe, overrun, take-place
eorþ	earth		
eorþan	a-surrounding-earth-work, earth, earth-dweller, earth-kingdom, elders', human, the-earth	eowdon	appear, present, reveal, show
		eoweð	appear, present, reveal, show
eorþbuend	earth-dweller, human	eower	you (plural)
		eowere	you (plural)
eorþbuende	earth-dweller, human	eowerne	you (plural)
		eoweþ	appear, present, reveal, show
eorþbuendra	earth-dweller, human	eowic	you (plural)
eorþbuendum	earth-dweller, human	eowra	you (plural)
		eowre	you (plural), your
eorþcund	earthly	eowrum	you (plural)
eorþcunde	earthly	erat	was (Latin)
eorþcyning	earthly-king	ered	plough
eorþcyninges	earthly-king	erede	plough
eorþdraca	earth--dwelling-dragon	erian	plough
		ermig	in-pain
eorþe	earth, earth-building	esa	but-which, evil-spirit, fairy, Germanic-pagan-god, the-Aesir-or-Ases, the-mouth, which
eorþreced	earth-building, subterranean-building		
eorþrice	earth-kingdom		
eorþscræf	cave, grave	esne	labourer, man, retainer
eorþscrafa	cave, grave		
eorþscrafu	cave, grave	esol	ass, donkey
eorþsele	earth-dwelling, earth-hall	esolas	ass, donkey
		est	consent, favour, grace
eorþweall	dyke, earthwork		
eorthweard	a-surrounding-earth-work, earth-dwellers, perhaps	este	favourable, gracious
		estig	gracious
		estum	consent, favour, grace
eorþweg	earthly-road-or-path	et	and, and (Latin)
eorþwege	earthly-road-or-path	etan	eat
eorþwela	earthly-possession	etc	because
eorþwelan	earthly-possession	eteð	eat
eoten	giant, monster	eternam	eternal (Latin)
eotena	giant, monster	eteþ	eat
eotenas	giant, monster	eþbegete	easily-gotten
eotenisc	giant-made, gigantic, troll-made	eþe	easy, pleasant

Word List (*Ænglisc* to English)

Ænglisc	English
eþel	country, home, homeland, homeland, native-land, noble
eþeldream	homeland-joy
eþeldreamas	homeland-joy
eþeleard	native-land
eþeleardum	native-land
eþeles	homeland
eþelland	native-land
eþel-land	native-land
eþelleas	exiled, homeless
eþelleasum	exiled, homeless
eþelmearc	country, nation
eþelmearce	country, nation
eþelriht	right-to-a-native-land
eþelrihtes	right-to-a-native-land
eþelseld	noble-settlement
eþelsetl	noble-settlement
eþelstæf	child, heir
eþelstaþol	secure-homeland
eþelstaþolas	secure-homeland
eþelstol	capital-city, high-place, home, national-fortress, national-homeland, native-habitation, noble-place
eþelstolas	home, national-homeland, native-habitation
eþelstow	homeland, native-place
eþelstowe	homeland, native-place
eþelþrym	native-power, noble-power
eþelturf	homeland, native-soil
eþelweard	king, noble-guardian
eþelweardas	king, noble-guardian
eþelwearde	king, noble-guardian
eþelwyn	noble-delight, noble-land
eþgesyne	easily-seen, plentiful
eþle	country, homeland, native-land, punishment
eþulstæfe	child, heir
eþyl	country, native-land
eþylstæf	child, heir
eþyltyrf	homeland, native-soil
etiam	also, also (Latin)
etonisc	giant-made, gigantic, troll-made
ettan	graze, pasture
etted	graze, pasture
ettede	graze, pasture
eunuch	eunuch
eunuchi	eunuch
euthenia	prosperity
Evan	Eve (name)
exle	shoulder

F, f

Ænglisc	English
facen	crime, deceit, evil, fault, sin, treachery
facenful	deceitful
facenfyllan	deceitful
facenlice	deceitful
facenstæf	deceitful-action, evil-act
facenstafas	deceitful-action, evil-act
facna	deceit, evil, sin, treachery
facne	deceit, evil, faults, sin, treachery
facnes	deceit, evil, sin, treachery
factor	maker, maker (Latin)
fæc	moment, time
fæcna	deceitful, malicious
fæcne	deceitful, malicious
fæd	decorated
fædan	decorated
fædde	decorated
fæder	father, father's, paternal-uncle
fædera	paternal-uncle

Word List (Ænglisc to English)

Ænglisc	English	Ænglisc	English
fæderæþelu	hereditary-endowment, paternal	fæghðe	enmity, feud, hostility
fæderæþelum	hereditary-endowment, paternal	fæghþe	enmity, feud, hostility
fæderenmæg	paternal-male-relative	fægir	fair, lovely, pleasant
fæderenmæge	paternal-male-relative	fægne	accursed, dead, doomed, glad, joyous
fædergeard	father's-land, paternal-dwelling	faegnian	be-delighted, be-happy
fædergeardum	father's-land, paternal-dwelling	fægnode	be-delighted, be-happy
fæðergearwe	feather-arrow, feathering	fægran	fair, lovely, pleasant
fæðergearwum	feather-arrow, feathering	fægre	beautifully, fair, justly, lovely, pleasant, pleasantly, well
fæðm	body, breast, embrace, grasp	fægriað	become-beautiful
fæðme	body, breast, embrace, grasp	fægrian	become-beautiful
fæðmian	embrace, swim-on	fægriaþ	become-beautiful
fæðmie	embrace, swim-on	fægrost	beautifully, justly, pleasantly, well
fæðmum	body, breast, embrace, grasp	fægroste	fair, lovely, pleasant
fægan	accursed, dead, doomed, doomed-one	fægum	accursed, dead, doomed
fæge	accursed, dead, doomed, fated	fæhð	enmity, feud, hostility
fægean	accursed, dead, doomed	fæhða	enmity, feud, hostility
fægen	glad, joyous, pleased	fæhðe	enmity, feud, hostility
fæger	beautiful, beautifully, fair, fairly, lovely, pleasant	fæhðo	enmity, feud, hostility
fægere	beautifully, fair, fairly, gloriously, good, justly, lovely, pleasant, pleasantly, well	fæhðu	enmity, feud, hostility
		fæhþ	enmity, feud, hostility
		fæhþa	enmity, feud, hostility
		fæhþe	enmity, feud, hostility
		fæhþo	enmity, feud, hostility
fægerra	fair, fairer, lovely, pleasant	fæhþu	enmity, feud, hostility
fægerum	fair	fæla	many, much
fæges	accursed, dead, doomed	fæle	faithful, reliable
		fælsian	cleanse, purify
		fælsode	cleanse, purify

Word List (Ænglisc to English)

Ænglisc	English
fæmnan	female, maid, virgin, woman, woman's
fæmne	female, maid, virgin, woman
fæmnum	female, maid, virgin, woman
fæng	achieve, grasp, seize, take
fær	calamity, conveyance, journey, peril, vessel
færcyle	calamitous-cold
færde	accomplish, bring, fare, go, obtain, travel
færdon	accomplish, bring, fare, go, obtain, travel
fære	calamity, conveyance, journey, peril, vessel
færeð	go, proceed, travel
færen	accomplish, bring, fare, go, obtain, travel
færes	calamity, peril
færeþ	go, proceed, travel
færgripe	sudden-grasping
færgripum	sudden-grasping
færgryre	sudden-horror
færgryrum	sudden-horror
færinga	suddenly
færlice	suddenly, violently
færnið	sudden-violence
færniða	sudden-violence
færniþ	sudden-violence
færniþa	sudden-violence
færsceaða	violent-attacker
færsceaðan	violent-attacker
færsceaþa	violent-attacker
færsceaþan	violent-attacker
færspel	announcement, bad-news, news
færstice	a-stabbing-pain, stabbing-pain, stitch
færwundra	sudden-marvel, terrifying-wonder
fæsl	offspring, progeny
fæsle	offspring, progeny
fæst	fast, firm, firmly-attached, solid
fæste	enclosure, fast, fasten, fastened, firm, firmly, firmly-attached, securely, solid, solidly
fæsten	enclosure, stronghold
fæstengeat	fortress-gate
fæstengeates	fortress-gate
fæstenne	enclosure, stronghold
fæsthydig	faithful, resolute, steadfast
fæsthydigne	faithful, resolute, steadfast
fæstlice	decisively, firmly, permanently
fæstne	fast, firm, firmly-attached, solid
fæstnian	contract-for, fasten, provide-assurances-that, secure, settle-upon
fæstnung	covenant, protection, stability
fæstor	fast, firmly, securely, solidly
fæstræd	steadfast
fæstrædne	steadfast
fæstum	fast, fastened, firm, firmly-attached, solid
fæt	cup, gold-ornament, gold-plate, vessel
fæted	adorned-with-gold, ornamented
fætedhleor	cheek-decorated
fætedhleore	cheek-decorated
fætels	bag, sack
fætelse	bag, sack
fætgold	ornamented-gold
fæþergearwe	feather-arrow, feathering
fæþergearwum	feather-arrow, feathering
fæþm	body, breast, embrace, grasp

Word List (*Ænglisc* to English)

Ænglisc	English
fæþme	body, breast, embrace, grasp
fæþmian	embrace, swim-on
fæþmie	embrace, swim-on
fæþmum	body, breast, embrace, grasp
fætt	adorned-with-gold, gold-ornament, gold-plate, ornamented
fættan	adorned-with-gold, ornamented
fætte	adorned-with-gold, ornamented
fættum	gold-ornament, gold-plate
fætum	gold-ornament, gold-plate
fæwundor	sudden-marvel, terrifying-wonder
fæx	hair
fag	blood-stained, criminal, guilty, hostile, ornamented, outlawed, shining, stained
fage	blood-stained, ornamented, shining, stained
fagne	blood-stained, ornamented, shining, stained
fagum	blood-stained, criminal, guilty, hostile, ornamented, outlawed, shining, stained
fah	blood-stained, coloured, criminal, guilty, hostile, ornamented, outcast, outlawed, shining, stained
fahne	blood-stained, ornamented, shining, stained
fam	foam
famig	foam-covered, foamy
famige	foam-covered, foamy
famigheals	foamy-prowed
famiheals	foamy-prowed
fana	banner, standard
fand	devise, find
fandian	examine, rummage-through, test
fandigan	examine, rummage-through, test
fandode	examine, rummage-through, test
fandung	discovery, investigation
fandunga	discovery, investigation
fane	blood-stained, criminal, guilty, hostile, ornamented, outlawed, shining, stained
fant	baptismal-font
fante	baptismal-font
far	go, proceed, travel
fara	criminal, guilty, hostile, outlawed
farað	go, proceed, travel, travelling
faraðlacende	sailor, sailors, swimmer
faran	go, proceed, ride, travel
faraþ	go, proceed, travel
faraþlacende	sailor, swimmer
fare	course, go, going, proceed, travel, travels, way
fareð	fares, go, proceed, sailor, travel
fareðlacende	sailor
fareðlacendum	sailor, travelling-sailors
faren	go, ride, travel
fareþ	fares, go, proceed, sailor, travel
fareþlacende	sailor
fareþlacendum	sailor
faroð	bank, shore
faroðe	bank, shore

Word List (*Ænglisc* to English)

Ænglisc	English	Ænglisc	English
faroðlacend	sailor, swimmer	feaum	few
faroðlacende	sailor, swimmer, travelling-sailors	feax	hair
		feaxe	hair
farones	pharaoh's	feccende	bring, carry-away, fetch
faroþ	bank, shore		
faroþe	bank, shore	fed	bear, feed, give-birth-to
faroþlacend	sailor, swimmer		
faroþlacende	sailor, swimmer	feða	foot-soldier, troop
faru	course, going, way	fedað	bear, feed, give-birth-to
Fastitocalon	a-large-whale		
fatu	cup, vessel	fedan	bear, feed, give-birth-to
faum	criminal, guilty, hostile, outlawed		
		feðan	foot-soldier, troop
fea	a-little, at-all, few, hardly, little, livestock, wealth	fedaþ	bear, feed, give-birth-to
		feddan	bear, feed, give-birth-to
feaht	fight, fighting		
feala	many, much	fedde	bear, feed, give-birth-to
fealdan	fold		
fealene	fallow	feðe	going, movement-power, pace
fealh	depart, escape, penetrate, reach		
		feðecempa	walking-warrior
feall	depart, escape, penetrate	feded	bear, feed, give-birth-to
feallan	die, fall, fall-dead, fall-onto, fall-to, flow	feðegang	journey-on-foot, walking
feallen	fall, flow	feðegange	journey-on-foot, walking
feallende	die, fall, fall-dead, fall-onto, fall-to	feðegest	guest-travelling-on-foot
fealleþ	die, fall, fall-dead, fall-onto, fall-to	feðegestum	guest-travelling-on-foot
fealo	many, much	feðelast	footpath, footstep
fealohilte	golden-hilt, yellow-hilt	feðelaste	footpath, footstep
fealone	dusky, grey, yellow	feðeleas	footless, without-feet
fealu	dusky, grey, yellow	feder	father
fealwe	dusky, grey, yellow	feðer	feather, wing
feara	few	feðera	feather, wing
fearm	cargo	feðerhama	feather-covering, feather-home, wings
fearme	cargo		
feasceaft	bereft, destitute, indigent, miserable, poor	feðerhaman	feather-covering, feather-home, wings
		feðerhoma	feather-covering, feather-home, wings
feasceafte	bereft, indigent, miserable, poor		
		feðerhoman	feather-covering, feather-home, wings
feasceaftig	destitute, indigent, poor		
		fedeþ	bear, feed, give-birth-to
feasceaftum	bereft, indigent, miserable, poor		
		feðewig	foot-battle

Word List (Ænglisc to English)

Ænglisc	English	Ænglisc	English
feðewiges	foot-battle	fengon	achieve, grasp, seize, take
feferfuige	feverfew (tanacetum parthenium)	fenhleoðu	fen-cliff, fen-slope
fegan	attach, confine, join	fenhleoþu	fen-cliff, fen-slope
fegeð	attach, confine, join	fenhlið	fen-cliff, fen-slope
fegere	fair	fenhliþ	fen-cliff, fen-slope
fegeþ	attach, confine, join	fenhop	dry-land-in-a-marsh
fehð	achieve, grasp, seize, take	fenhopu	dry-land-in-a-marsh
		fenn	fen, marsh, moor
fehþ	achieve, grasp, seize, take	fenne	fen, marsh, moor
		feo	livestock, wealth
fel	file	feoð	hate
fela	file, many, much	feofor	fever
felafricgende	knowledgeable, well-informed, wise	feofore	fever
		feogan	cattle, hate, hating
felageomor	very-sad	feoh	cattle, goods, livestock, money, wealth
felahror	very-strong		
felaleof	very-dear		
felaleofan	dearly-loved, very-dear	feohgifre	greedy-for-property
		feohgift	cattle-gift, property-gift, wealth-gift
felamodig	very-brave		
felamodigra	very-brave	feoh-gift	cattle-gift, money-
felan	feel, perceive	feohgiftum	cattle-gift, property-gift, wealth-gift
felasinnig	very-sinful		
felasinnigne	very-sinful	feohgyft	cattle-gift, property-gift, wealth-gift
felawlonc	very-proud		
feld	field, plain	feohgyfte	cattle-gift, property-gift, wealth-gift
felda	field, plain		
feldas	field, plain	feohgyftum	cattle-gift, property-gift, wealth-gift
feldhus	tent		
feldhusum	tent	feohleas	ineligible-for-wergild, without-compensation
feleleas	insensible, without-sensation		
feleþ	feel, perceive	feoh-leas	moneyless, without-cattle
fell	hide, skin		
fellum	hide, skin	feoht	battle, fight
felon	savagely	feohtan	fight, fighting, struggle
femnan	female, maid, virgin, woman		
		feohte	battle, fight, struggle
femnena	virgins'	feol	die, fall, fall-dead, fall-onto, fall-to, felled
fen	fen, marsh, moor		
fenfreoðo	refuge-in-the-fens		
fenfreoþo	refuge-in-the-fens	feolan	escape, penetrate, reach, to--depart-from
feng	achieve, grasp, seize, take, took		
		feoldan	fold
fenge	grasp	feolheard	file-hard
fengel	king, prince	feolhearde	file-hard
fengelad	fen-passage, fen-path		

Word List (*Ænglisc* to English)

Ænglisc	English
feoll	die, fall, fall-dead, fall-onto, fall-to, flow
feollan	fell
feollon	die, fall, fall-dead, fall-onto, fall-to, flow
feon	exult, hate, rejoice
feond	adversary, and, devil, enemy, fiend
feonda	adversary, devil, enemy, fiend
feondas	adversary, devil, enemy, fiend
feonde	adversary, devil, enemy, fiend
feondes	adversary, devil, enemy, fiend
feondgrap	fiend-grip, hostile-grasp
feondgrapum	fiend-grip, hostile-grasp
feondræs	hostile-attack
feondscaða	hostile-enemy
feondscaþa	hostile-enemy
feondsceaða	hostile-enemy
feondsceaðan	hostile-enemy
feondsceaþa	hostile-enemy
feondsceaþan	hostile-enemy
feondscipe	adversary, enmity, hostility
feondum	adversary, devil, enemy, fiend, fiends
feor	distant, far, from-afar
feora	life, living-being, person, spirit
feorbuend	foreigner, outsider
feorcyþðe	distant-acquaintance
feorcyþðu	distant-acquaintance
feorcyþþe	distant-acquaintance
feorcyþþu	distant-acquaintance
feorð	mind, soul, spirit
feorða	fourth
feorðan	fourth
feorðe	fourth
feore	life, living-being, person, spirit
feores	life, living-being, person, spirit
feorg	life, living-being, person, spirit
feorgbold	body, spirit-house
feorgbona	killer, murderer
feorh	life, living-being, person, spirit
feorhbana	killer, murderer
feorhbanan	killer, murderer
feorhbealo	murderous-evil
feorhbealu	murderous-evil
feorhbenn	deadly-wound
feorhbennum	deadly-wound
feorhberend	living-being
feorhberendra	living-being
feorhbona	killer, murderer
feorhbonan	killer, murderer
feorhcwale	death
feorhcwalu	death
feorhcwealm	death, murder
feorhcynn	living-family, race
feorhcynna	living-family, race
feorhdæg	life-days
feorhdaga	life-days
feorheacen	animate, living
feorheaceno	animate, living
feorhgeniðla	mortal-enemy
feorhgeniðlan	mortal-enemy
feorhgeniþla	mortal-enemy
feorhgeniþlan	mortal-enemy
feorhhus	body, life-house, spirit-house
feorh-hus	body, life-house
feorhhyrde	life's-guardian
feorhlast	bloody-track
feorhlastas	bloody-track
feorhlean	compensation-for-life
feorhlege	death, life-laying
feorhlegu	death, life-laying
feorhnere	salvation
feorhseoc	mortally-wounded
feorhsweng	deadly-stroke, mortal-blow
feorhwund	deadly-wound
feorhwunde	deadly-wound

Word List (Ænglisc to English)

Ænglisc	English
feorlondum	far-lands
feorm	care, food, goods, handling, management, possessions, provisions, upkeep
feorme	care, food, goods, handling, management, possessions, provisions, upkeep
feormend	caretaker, host, patron, provider, up-keeper
feormendleas	without-a-caretaker, without-a-polisher
feormendlease	without-a-caretaker, without-a-polisher
feormendra	caretaker, host, patron, provider, up-keeper
feormian	entertain, look-after, polish-off
feormynd	caretaker, host, patron, provider, up-keeper
feorr	far, from-afar
feorran	distant-past, far, far-off, from-afar, remove, take-away, withdraw
feorrancund	from-a-distant-country
feorrancundum	from-a-distant-country
feorren	distant-past, far-off, from-afar
feorres	distant, far, far-from
feorþ	mind, soul, spirit
feorþa	fourth
feorþan	fourth
feorþe	fourth
feorum	life, living-being, person, spirit
feorweg	distant-journey, distant-way
feorwegas	distant-journey, distant-way
feorwegum	distant-journey, distant-way
feos	livestock, wealth
feoþ	hate
feower	4, four
feoþer	4, four
feower and feowertig	44, forty four
feoþer and feoþertig	44, forty four
feower and feowertigoþa	forty fourth
feower and fiftig	54, fifty four
feoþer and fiftig	54, fifty four
feower and fiftigoþa	fifty fourth
feower and hundeahtatig	84, eighty four
feoþer and hundeahtatig	84, eighty four
feower and hundeahtatigoþa	eighty fourth
feower and hundendleftig	114, a hundred and fourteen
feoþer and hundendleftig	114, a hundred and fourteen
feower and hundnigontig	94, ninety four
feoþer and hundnigontig	94, ninety four
feower and hundnigontigoþa	ninety fourth
feower and hundseofontig	74, seventy four
feoþer and hundseofontig	74, seventy four
feower and hundseofontigoþa	seventy fourth
feower and hundteontig	104, a hundred and four
feoþer and hundteontig	104, a hundred and four
feower and sixtig	64, sixty four
feoþer and sixtig	64, sixty four
feower and sixtigoþa	sixty fourth
feower and þritig	34, thirty four
feoþer and þritig	34, thirty four
feower and þritigoþa	thirty fourth
feower and twentig	24, twenty four
feoþer and tpentig	24, twenty four

Word List (Ænglisc to English)

Ænglisc	English	Ænglisc	English
feower and twentigoþa	twenty fourth	*ferhð*	mind, soul, spirit
feowera	four	*ferhðcearig*	sorrowful-in-spirit
feowerteoþa	fourteenth	*ferhðcofa*	breast, spirit-chamber
feowertig	40, forty	*ferhðcofan*	breast, spirit-chamber
feopertig	40, forty		
feowertigoþa	fortieth	*ferhðe*	mind, soul, spirit
feowertine	14, fourteen	*ferhðes*	mind, soul, spirit
feopertine	14, fourteen	*ferhðfreca*	bold-in-spirit
feowertyne	fourteen	*ferhðfrecan*	bold-in-spirit
feran	accomplish, bring, fare, flow, go, obtain, travel, travelled	*ferhðgeniðla*	deadly-enemy
		ferhðgeniðlan	deadly-enemy
		ferhðgleaw	clever, intelligent
		ferhðgleawe	clever, intelligent
ferð	mind, soul, spirit	*ferhðloca*	body, spirit-enclosure
ferde	accomplish, bring, fare, go, obtain, transported, travel	*ferhðlocan*	body, spirit-enclosure
ferðe	fierce-minded, mind, soul, spirit	*ferhðum*	mind, soul, spirit
		ferhtgereaht	life-right, what-is-just-and-right
ferðgrim	fierce-minded, travelling-horrible	*ferhþ*	mind, soul, spirit
ferðloca	body, spirit-enclosure	*ferhþcearig*	sorrowful-in-spirit
		ferhþcofa	breast, spirit-chamber
ferð-loca	breast, heart, spirit-enclosure	*ferhþcofan*	breast, spirit-chamber
ferðlocan	body, spirit-enclosure	*ferhþe*	mind, soul, spirit
ferdon	accomplish, bring, fare, go, obtain, travel	*ferhþes*	mind, soul, spirit
		ferhþfreca	bold-in-spirit
		ferhþfrecan	bold-in-spirit
fere	accomplish, bring, calamity, fare, go, obtain, peril, travel	*ferhþgeniþla*	deadly-enemy
		ferhþgeniþlan	deadly-enemy
		ferhþgleaw	clever, intelligent
fered	go, travel	*ferhþgleawe*	clever, intelligent
ferede	bring, carry, depart, go, transport	*ferhþloca*	body, spirit-enclosure
feredon	bring, carry, depart, go, transport	*ferhþlocan*	body, spirit-enclosure
ferend	traveller, travellers	*ferhþum*	mind, soul, spirit
ferende	accomplish, bring, fare, go, obtain, travel	*ferhweard*	protection
		ferhwearde	protection
		ferian	bring, carry, depart, go, transport
fergað	bring, carry, depart, go, transport	*ferigeað*	bring, carry, depart, go, transport
fergaþ	bring, carry, depart, go, transport	*ferigeaþ*	bring, carry, depart, go, transport
ferh	life, living-being, person, spirit	*ferion*	carry

Word List (Ænglisc to English)

Ænglisc	English	Ænglisc	English
ferlorene	abandon, destroy, lose	feþera	feather, wing
ferode	bring, carry, depart, go, transport	feþerhama	feather-covering, feather-home, wings
fers	sentence, verse	feþerhaman	feather-covering, feather-home, wings
fersc	fresh	feþerhoma	feather-covering, feather-home, wings
ferþ	mind, soul, spirit	feþerhoman	feather-covering, feather-home, wings
ferþe	fierce-minded, mind, soul, spirit	feþewig	foot-battle
ferþgrim	fierce-minded	feþewiges	foot-battle
ferþloca	body, spirit-enclosure	feþra	feather, wing
ferþ-loca	breast, heart, spirit-enclosure	fetigan	bring, carry-away, fetch
ferþlocan	body, spirit-enclosure	fetigean	bring, carry-away, fetch
fet	foot, link-hilted-sword?	fetod	bring, carry-away, fetch
fetelhilt	link-hilted-sword?	fetor	fetter, shackle
feter	fetter	fexe	hair
feterian	fasten, fetter	fiat	let-it-be-done
feterum	fetter	fiersn	heel
feþa	foot-soldier, troop	fiersna	heel
feþað	make-walk, put-back-on-feet	fif	5, five
feþan	foot-soldier, make-walk, put-back-on-feet, troop	fif and feowertig	45, forty five
		fif and feoþertig	45, forty five
		fif and feowertigoþa	forty fifth
		fif and fiftig	55, fifty five
feþaþ	make-walk, put-back-on-feet	fif and fiftigoþa	fifty fifth
		fif and hundeahtatig	85, eighty five
feþe	going, movement-power, pace	fif and hundeahtatigoþa	eighty fifth
feþecempa	walking-warrior	fif and hundendleftig	115, a hundred and fifteen
feþecempan	walking-warrior		
feþegang	journey-on-foot, walking	fif and hundnigontig	95, ninety five
		fif and hundnigontigoþa	ninety fifth
feþegange	journey-on-foot, walking	fif and hundseofontig	75, seventy five
feþegeorn	eager-to-travel-by-foot	fif and hundseofontigoþa	seventy fifth
feþegest	guest-travelling-on-foot	fif and hundteontig	105, a hundred and five
feþegestum	guest-travelling-on-foot	fif and sixtig	65, sixty five
feþelast	footpath, footstep	fif and sixtigoþa	sixty fifth
feþelaste	footpath, footstep	fif and þritig	35, thirty five
feþelastum	footpath, footstep	fif and þritigoþa	thirty fifth
feþeleas	footless, without-feet	fif and twentig	25, twenty five
feþer	feather, wing	fif and tþentig	25, twenty five

Word List (*Ænglisc* to English)

Ænglisc	English	*Ænglisc*	English
fif and twentigoþa	twenty fifth	firum	fish, for-men, human-beings, men, to-men
fife	five, giant-kin		
fifelcynn	giant-kin		
fifelcynnes	giant-kin	fisc	fish
fifta	fifth	fisca	fish
fiftena	fifteen	fiscas	fish, the-fishes
fifteoþa	fifteenth	fiþerleas	featherless, flightless
fiftig	50, fifty		
fiftiges	fifty	fiþrum	feather, wing
fiftigoþa	fiftieth	fitt	fighting, poem, song
fiftine	15, fifteen	fitte	fighting, poem, song
fiftyno	fifteen	flæsc	body, flesh
filio	son (Latin)	flæsce	body, flesh
filium	son (Latin)	flæsces	flesh
findað	devise, find	flæschoma	body, flesh
findan	devise, find	flæsc-homa	body
findaþ	devise, find	flæschoman	body, flesh
findeð	devise, find	flah	deceitful, treacherous, wicked
findest	devise, find		
findeþ	devise, find	flan	arrow, spear
finger	finger	flana	arrow, spear
fingra	finger	flanboga	arrow-bow
fingras	finger	flanbogan	arrow-bow
fingrum	finger	flane	arrow, spear
finit	the-end	flanes	arrow, spear
Finnsburuh	Finnsburgh (place)	fleag	flee, fly
finol	fennel	fleah	flee, fly
fiond	fiend	fleam	flight, rout
fionda	adversary, devil, enemy, fiend	fleame	flight, rout
		fleat	float, swim
fira	human-beings, men	flema	exile
firas	human-beings, men, people	fleogan	flee, fly
		fleogeð	flee, fly, flying
firen	crime, guilt, sin, torment	fleogende	flee, fly, flying
		fleogeþ	flee, fly
firena	crime, guilt, sin, torment	fleoh	flee, flown, fly
		fleohnet	fly-net, thin-curtain
firendæd	crime, sin, sinful-deed	fleon	avoid, flee, fleeing, fly-from
firendæda	crime, sin, sinful-deed	fleonde	avoid, flee, fly-from
		fleotan	float, swim
firene	sin	fleotend	floater, sailor
firenum	extremely, violently	fleotende	float, swim
firgenstream	mountain-current, mountain-stream	fleotendra	floater, sailor
		flet	hall
firgenstreamas	forest-streams	fletgesteald	hall-goods
firgenstreamum	mountain-current, mountain-stream	fletgestealdum	hall-goods
		fletræst	bed-in-the-hall
firnum	extremely, violently	fletræste	bed-in-the-hall

Word List (Ænglisc to English)

Ænglisc	English
fletsittende	courtiers, hall-sitters, warriors
fletsittendum	courtiers, hall-sitters, warriors
flett	hall
flette	hall
flettgesteald	hall-goods
flettwað	hall-wandering
flettwaðas	hall-wandering
flettwaþ	hall-wandering
flettwaþas	hall-wandering
fletwerod	hall-troop
fliht	flight
flihte	flight
flitan	contend, fight
flite	contend, fight
flitende	contend, fight
flod	current, deluge, flood, stream, water, water-body, wave
floda	current, flood, stream, water, water-body, wave
flodas	current, flood, stream, water, water-body, wave
flode	current, flood, stream, water, water-body, wave
flodes	current, flood, stream, water, water-body, wave
flodgræg	flood-grey
flodweg	sea-path, sea-way
flodwegas	sea-path, sea-way
flodyþ	sea-wave
flogen	flee, fly
flor	floor
flore	floor
flot	sea, the-sea
flota	fish, floater, sailor, ship
flotan	fish, floater, sailor, sailors, ship
flothere	fleet
flotherge	fleet
flotmonn	sailor, shipman
flotmonna	sailor, shipman
flotweg	ship-route
flowan	flow, flowing
flowende	flow
flugon	flee, fly
flyht	flight
flying	flight
flyman	cast-out, drive-out
flymde	cast-out, drive-out
fo	take
fodder	fodder, food
foddor	food
fodre	fodder, food
fodres	fodder, food
fohten	fight
folc	folk, nation, people, tribe
folca	folk, folk-ruler, nation, people, tribe, tribes
folcagend	folk-ruler
folcagende	folk-ruler
folcbearn	descendant, folk-child
folcbearnum	descendant, folk-child
folccwen	folk-queen, folk-woman
folccyning	folk-king
folccyningas	folk-king
folccyninge	folk-king
folcdriht	folk-multitude
folce	folk, nation, people, tribe
folces	folk, nation, people, people-lord, the-people, tribe
folcfrea	people-lord
folcfrean	people-lord
folcgesið	national-companion
folcgesiðas	national-companion
folcgesiþ	national-companion
folcgesiþas	national-companion
folcgestælla	companion, supporter
folcgestælna	companion, supporter
folcgestealla	companion, supporter
folcgesteallan	companion, supporter

Word List (Ænglisc to English)

Ænglisc	English
folcgestreon	national-wealth
folcgestreonum	national-wealth
folcgetæl	people-number
folcgetrum	host, national-army
folcgetrume	host, national-army
folclond	national-land
folclondes	national-land, nation-land
folcmægð	nation, people
folcmægþ	nation, people
folcmægþa	nation, people
folcmære	famous, renowned-to-peoples
folcmæro	famous, renowned-to-peoples
folcred	national-leadership
folcriht	family-entitlement
folcrihta	family-entitlement
folcscare	common-people's-land, nation
folcscaru	common-people's-land, nation
folcsceare	common-people's-land, nation
folcstede	battlefield, folk-stead, national-capital, palace
folcstyde	battlefield, national-capital, palace
folctoga	chieftain, commander
folctogan	chieftain, commander
folcum	nation, people, tribe
folcwer	human-being, man
folcweras	human-being, man
foldan	earth, earth-dwellers, earthly-building, ground, lands, the-earth
foldbold	earthly-building
foldbuend	earth-dwellers, human-beings, men, people
foldbuende	earth-dwellers, human-beings, men, people
foldbuendum	earth-dwellers, human-beings, men, people
folde	earth, ground
foldhrerendra	earth-stalking
foldu	lands, path
foldweg	path, track-on-the-earth, way
foldwegas	path, track-on-the-earth, way
foldwege	path, track-on-the-earth, way
foldwegum	earth-ways
folen	penetrate, reach
folgað	following, people-following
folgaþ	people-following
folgedon	follow
folgeras	followers
folgian	follow, obey, serve
folgod	follow, obey, serve
folgode	follow, obey, serve
folkes	folk
follc	folk
folm	hand, palm
folma	hand, palm
folman	hand, palm
folme	hand, palm
folmum	hand, palm
fon	achieve, catch, grasp, seize, take
fond	devise, find
for	because, because-of, before, before-spatial, during, for, go, going, in-front-of, in-presence-of, journey, on-account-of, proceed, ride, therefore, travel, way-of-life
for þon	because, therefore
foran	before, go, in-front, proceed, travel
forane	ahead-of-time, back, before-me, first, in-the-other-direction
forbærnan	burn-up
forbærnedne	burn-up

Word List (*Ænglisc* to English)

Ænglisc	English
forbærst	break, fail
forbarn	burn-up
forbead	forbid
forbeah	avoid, flee-from
forbeodan	forbid
forbeornan	burn-up
forberan	endure, put-up-with
forbernde	burn-up
forberstan	break, fail
forbigan	debase, humiliate
forbigde	debase, humiliate
forbiged	debase, humiliate
forbodene	forbid
forbogen	flee-from
forborsten	break, fail
forbræcon	break, transgress
forbrecan	break, transgress
forbrocen	break, transgress
forbugan	avoid, flee-from, for-surrendering
forbugon	flee-from
forburnon	burn-up
forbyrnan	burn-up
forcearf	cut-off
forceorfan	cut-off
forcurfon	cut-off
ford	ford, place-to-cross-water
forð	away, ford, forth, forward, forwards, from-now-on, from-then-on, hence, thence
forda	ford, place-to-cross-water
fordæmed	condemn, sentence-to-death
forðam	because, for-that-reason, since, therefore
forðan	because, for, for-that-reason, since, therefore
fordeman	condemn, sentence-to-death
forð-feran	depart, die, go-forth
forð-ferde	depart, die, go-forth
forð-fered	depart, die, go-forth
forðgeorn	eager-to-press-forward-in-battle, valiant
forðgerimed	all-told, counted-out
forðgesceaft	creation, destiny, destiny-creation
forðgewiten	dead, departed
forðgewitenum	dead, departed
forðhere	vanguard
forðherge	vanguard
forðian	carry-out
fordon	corrupt, ruin, undo
forðon	because, for-that-reason, since, therefore
fordraf	compel, drive-away, impel
fordrifan	compel, drive-away, impel
forðryne	onward-course
forðsiþ	journey-forth
forðsiþes	journey-forth
forðweard	eternal, future, ongoing, pilot, steersman
forðwearde	from-then-on
forðweardum	eternal, future, ongoing
forðweg	death, way-forth
forðwegas	death, way-forth
forðwege	death, way-forth
forðylman	cover, enclose, shut-up
forðylmed	cover, enclose, shut-up
fore	before, for, going, grows-old, instead-of, in-the-presence-of, journey, on-account-of, way-of-life
forealdað	grows-old
forealdaþ	grows-old
foregenga	escort, servant
foreldit	delays, very-famous
foremære	very-famous
foremærost	very-famous
foremeahtig	pre-eminently-powerful

Word List (*Ænglisc* to English)

Ænglisc	English
foremeahtige	pre-eminently-powerful
foremihtig	pre-eminently-powerful
foresædan	say-before, say-previously
foresædon	say-before, say-previously
foresecgan	say-before, say-previously
foresnotor	eminently-wise, very-wise
fore-snotor	clever, prudent
foresnotre	eminently-wise, very-wise
foreþanc	forethought, judiciousness, prudence
foreweall	protecting-wall
foreweallas	protecting-wall
foreweard	bargain, covenant, promise
forewyrcend	servant, subordinate
forewyrcendum	servant, subordinate
for-faran	get-in-front-of, obstruct
for-faren	get-in-front-of, obstruct
for-for	get-in-front-of, obstruct
for-foron	get-in-front-of, obstruct
forgeaf	bestow-upon, give, grant
forgeafe	bestow-upon, give, grant
forgeafon	give, grant
forgeald	pay-back, requite, reward
forgeate	forget
forgefe	bestow-upon, give, grant
forgeton	forget
forgiefan	bestow-upon, give, grant
forgiefen	give, grant
forgiefene	bestow-upon, give, grant
forgieldan	pay-back, requite, reward
forgietan	forget
forgif	bestow-upon, give, grant
forgifan	give, grant
forgifð	bestow-upon, give, grant
forgifen	bestow-upon, give, grant
forgifþ	bestow-upon, give, grant
forgolden	pay-back, requite, reward
forgrand	destroy
forgrap	attack, seize
forgrindan	destroy
forgripan	attack, seize
forgrunden	destroy, destroyed
forgyldan	pay-back, repaid, requite, reward
forgylde	pay-back, requite, reward
forgyldon	pay-back, requite, reward
forgyman	neglect, not-observe
forgymdon	neglect, not-observe
forgymeð	neglect, not-observe
forgymeþ	neglect, not-observe
forgyteð	forget
forgyteþ	forget
forhabban	restrain, restrain-oneself
forhatena	accursed-one, devil
forhealdan	forsake, rebel-against
forhealden	forsake, rebel-against
forhealdene	forsake, rebel-against
forheard	very-hard
forheardne	very-hard
forheawan	cut-down, cut-to-pieces, cut-up, hew
forheawen	cut-down, cut-to-pieces, cut-up, hew
forhelan	conceal, cover-up
forhele	conceal, cover-up
forheow	cut-down, hew

Word List (*Ænglisc* to English)

Ænglisc	English	*Ænglisc*	English
forheowon	cut-down, hew	*forlætaþ*	allow, allow-to-escape, avoid, leave-behind, let, release, relinquish
forhicgan	disdain, reject		
forhicge	disdain, reject		
forhogian	disdain, scorn		
forhogode	disdain, scorn	*forlæte*	allow, allow-to-escape, avoid, leave-behind, let, release, relinquish
forholen	hidden		
forht	feared, frightened, timid		
forhtan	dreadful	*forlæteð*	allow, allow-to-escape, avoid, leave-behind, let, release, relinquish
forhtedon	be-frightened		
forhtiað	be-frightened		
forhtian	be-frightened, fear		
forhtiaþ	be-frightened	*forlæten*	abandon, allow, allow-to-escape, avoid, leave, leave-behind, let, release, relinquish
forhtlice	timidly		
forlacan	betray, deceive, mislead		
forlacen	betray, deceive, mislead	*forlæteþ*	allow, allow-to-escape, avoid, leave-behind, let, release, relinquish
forlæd	lead-astray, lead-to-destruction, mislead		
forlædan	lead-astray, lead-to-destruction, mislead	*forleas*	abandon, destroy, lose
forlædd	lead-astray, lead-to-destruction, mislead	*forlec*	betray, deceive, mislead
forlæddan	lead-astray, lead-to-destruction, mislead	*forleogan*	commit-perjury-regarding, lie-about
forlædde	lead-astray, lead-to-destruction, mislead	*forleos*	for-lose
forlæran	misdirect, misinform	*forleosan*	abandon, destroy, for-lose, lose
forlærde	misdirect, misinform	*forlet*	abandon, abandoned, abandoning, allow, allow-to-escape, avoid, leave, leave-behind, let, release, relinquish
forlæred	misdirect, misinform		
forlæt	allow, allow-to-escape, avoid, leave-behind, let, release, relinquish		
forlætað	allow, allow-to-escape, avoid, leave-behind, let, release, relinquish	*forleton*	abandon, allow, allow-to-escape, avoid, leave, leave-behind, let, release, relinquish
forlætan	abandon, allow, allow-to-escape, avoid, leave, leave-behind, let, let-go, neglect, release, relinquish, to-forsake	*forlicgan*	have-sex-with
		forliger	fornication, seduction
		forligre	fornication, seduction
		forlor	destruction, loss
		forlore	destruction, loss

Word List (Ænglisc to English)

Ænglisc	English	Ænglisc	English
forloren	abandon, destroy, lose	forscyldigian	condemn, declare-to-be-guilty
forlugan	commit-perjury-regarding, lie-about	forseah	despise, reject
		forsendan	send-away
forlycgan	have-sex-with	forsended	send-away
forlygre	fornication, seduction	forseon	despise, reject
		forsewen	neglected
forlyres	fornication, seduction	forsiðian	die, pass-away
		forsiðod	die, pass-away
forma	first	forsiteð	go-blind, hinder, obstruct, resist
formærne	very-famous		
forman	first	forsiteþ	go-blind, hinder, obstruct, resist
formoni	too-many-a		
fornam	do-away-with, swept-away, take-away	forsiþian	die, pass-away
		forsiþod	die, pass-away
		forsittan	go-blind, hinder, obstruct, resist
fornamon	do-away-with, take-away		
		forslean	beat-up, destroy, kill
forniman	do-away-with, take-away	forslegen	beat-up, destroy, kill
		forsoc	refuse, refused
fornom	do-away-with, swept-away, take-away	forsocon	refuse
		forspanan	entice, urge
		forspeon	entice, urge
fornoman	do-away-with, take-away	forspildan	ruin, spoil, waste
		forst	frost
fornumen	do-away-with, take-away	forstandan	hinder, prevent, protect, understand
forod	useless, vain	forste	frost
foron	go, proceed, ride, travel	forstelan	deprive, steal-away
		forstes	frost
forsacan	refuse	forstod	hinder, prevent, protect, understand
forsæcgan	defame, falsely-accuse, slander	forstode	hinder, prevent, protect, understand
forsæt	go-blind, hinder, obstruct, resist	forstodon	hinder, prevent, protect, understand
forsæton	go-blind, hinder, obstruct, resist	forstolene	deprive, steal-away
forsceaf	drive-back	forswapan	drive-off, sweep-away
forsceap	monstrous-thing		
forsceape	monstrous-thing	forswapen	drive-off, sweep-away
forsceop	change, transform-negatively		
		forswealg	devour, swallow
forscieppan	change, transform-negatively	forswelgan	devour, swallow
		forswelge	devour, swallow
forscrifan	condemn, judge	forsweop	drive-off, sweep-away
forscrifen	condemn, judge		
forscufan	drive-back	forsweorcan	go-blind, of-the-eyes-become-dark
forscyldeguda	condemn, declare-to-be-guilty		
		forsweran	renounce

Word List (*Ænglisc* to English)

Ænglisc	English	*Ænglisc*	English
forswiðe	excessively, utterly	*forþwegas*	death, way-forth
forswiþe	excessively, utterly	*forþwege*	death, way-forth
forsworceð	go-blind, of-the-eyes-become-dark	*forþylman*	cover, enclose, shut-up
forsworceþ	go-blind, of-the-eyes-become-dark	*forþylmed*	cover, enclose, shut-up
forsworen	renounce	*fortis*	strength (Latin)
forswulge	devour, swallow	*forwearð*	be-destroyed, perish
forþ	away, ford, forth, forwards, from-now-on, from-then-on, hence, thence	*forwearþ*	be-destroyed, perish
		forwegan	kill
		forwegen	kill
		forweorðan	be-destroyed, perish
forþam	because, for-that-reason, since, therefore	*forweorðe*	be-destroyed, perish
		forweorn	refuse
		forweorone	decayed
forþan	because, for-that-reason, since, therefore	*forweorp*	throw
		forweorpan	cast-out, throw-away
forþbære	creative, productive	*forweorþan*	be-destroyed, perish
forþbæro	creative, productive	*forweorþe*	be-destroyed, perish
forþ-feran	depart, die, go-forth	*forworht*	barricade, close-up, destroy, lose, ruin
forþ-ferde	depart, die, go-forth		
forþ-fered	depart, die, go-forth	*forworhte*	barricade, close-up, destroy, lose, ruin
forþgeorn	eager-to-press-forward-in-battle, valiant	*forwræc*	banish, drive-away
		forwrat	slice-to-death
forþgerimed	all-told, counted-out	*forwrecan*	banish, drive-away
forþgesceaft	creation, destiny	*forwritan*	slice-to-death
forþgewiten	dead, departed	*forwunded*	wound-badly
forþgewitenum	dead, departed	*forwundian*	wound-badly
forþhere	vanguard	*forwundod*	wound-badly, wounded
forþherge	vanguard		
forþian	carry-out	*forwurpe*	cast-out, throw-away
forþolian	do-without, endure-the-absence-of	*forwyrcan*	barricade, close-up, destroy, lose, ruin
forþon	because, for, for-that, for-that-reason, since, therefore	*forwyrd*	destruction, ruin
		forwyrnan	oppose, refuse, withhold
forþringan	drive-away	*forwyrnde*	oppose, refuse, withhold
forþryne	onward-course		
forþsiþ	journey-forth	*forwyrne*	oppose, refuse, withhold
forþsiþes	journey-forth		
forþweard	eternal, future, ongoing, pilot, steersman	*fostercyld*	foster-child
		fot	foot
		fote	foot
forþwearde	from-then-on	*fotes*	foot
forþweardum	eternal, future, ongoing	*fotgemearc*	foot-measure
forþweg	death, way-forth	*fotgemearces*	foot-measure

Word List (*Ænglisc* to English)

Ænglisc	English	*Ænglisc*	English
fotlast	track, trail-of-footsteps	frec	bold, daring, greedy
fotmæl	foot-measure	freca	man, warrior
fotum	foot	frecan	man, warrior
fracod	criminal, shameful, vile	frece	bold, daring, greedy
		frecen	danger, dangerous, peril, perilous
fracodes	criminal, shameful, vile	frecenra	dangerous, perilous
		frecna	danger, peril
fracodlice	criminally, shamefully, vilely	frecnan	dangerous, evil, perilous
fracoðlice	criminally, shamefully, vilely	frecne	danger, dangerous, dangerously, evil, harshly, peril, perilous, severely
fracoþlice	criminally, shamefully, vilely		
fræcne	dangerously, harshly, severely	frecnen	dangerous, evil, perilous
frægn	ask, asked, find-out, learned	frecnes	danger, peril
		frefran	cheer, comfort, console
fræt	break-faith, consume, eat	frefred	cheer, comfort
frætewum	armour, break-faith, ornaments, trappings, treasure	frefrede	cheer, comfort
		fremaþ	acts
		fremde	alien, foreign, strange
fræton	break-faith, consume, eat	fremdes	alien, foreign, strange
frætwa	armour, trappings, treasure	fremdu	alien, foreign, strange
frætwan	adorn, decorate		
frætwe	armour, ornaments, trappings, treasure	fremdum	alien, foreign, strange
frætwed	adorn, decorate	freme	advantage, benefit
frætwian	adorn, decorate	fremed	do, perform
frætwum	armour, possessions, trappings, treasure, treasures	fremeð	advance, carry-out, do, further, make, perpetuate, support
		fremede	advance, carry-out, do, further, make, perform, perpetuate, support
fram	away, bold, forth, from, strong		
franca	lance, spear	fremedon	advance, carry-out, do, further, make, perpetuate, support
francan	lance, spear		
frea	king, lord, lord-of, master	fremena	advantage, benefit
		fremest	advance, carry-out, do, further, make, perpetuate, support
freadrihten	king, lord		
freadrihtnes	king, lord		
freamærne	renowned		
frean	king, lord		
freawine	friendly-lord	fremeþ	advance, carry-out, do, further, make, perpetuate, support
freawrasn	lordly-chain		
freawrasnum	lordly-chain		

Word List (*Ænglisc* to English)

Ænglisc	English	*Ænglisc*	English
fremmað	advance, carried-out, carry-out, do, further, make, perpetuate, support	*freogan*	cherish, love
		freoge	cherish, love
		freolecu	beautiful, glorious
		freolic	beautiful, free, glorious
fremman	advance, bring, carry-out, do, further, make, perform, perpetrate, perpetuate, support	*freolice*	beautiful, glorious
		freolico	beautiful, glorious
		freolicu	beautiful, glorious
		freolucu	beautiful, glorious
fremmaþ	advance, carry-out, do, further, make, perpetuate, support	*freom*	free, happy, noble
		freomæg	free, noble-kinsman
		freomægum	free, noble-kinsman
		freomagum	free, noble-kinsman
fremme	advance, carry-out, do, further, make, perpetuate, support	*freomann*	free, noble-man
		freomanna	free, noble-man
		freomen	free, noble-man
		freond	friend, lover, relative
fremmen	advance, carry-out, do, further, make, perpetuate, support	*freonda*	friend, friends, relative
fremu	advantage, benefit		
fremum	advantage, benefit	*freondas*	friend, relative
freo	free, happy, noble, woman	*freondlar*	friendly-advice
		freondlarum	friendly-advice
freobearn	noble-child, noble-son	*freondlaþu*	friendship
		freondleas	friendless, lord-less
freobearnum	noble-child	*freond-leas*	friend-less
freoburh	noble-city	*freondleasne*	friendless, lord-less
freod	affection, good-will, peace	*freondlice*	amicably, in-a-friendly-manner
freoð	cherish, love	*freondlicor*	amicably, in-a-friendly-manner
freode	affection, good-will, peace		
		freondlufu	friendship, love
freoðiaþ	refuge	*freondmynd*	amorous-intention
freoðo	peace, protection, safety	*freondmynde*	amorous-intention
		freondscipe	friendship, love-relationship
freoðobeacen	protection-beacon, protection-sign	*freondscype*	friendship, love-relationship
freoðoburh	protecting-city	*freondsped*	success-in-making-friends
freodom	freedom		
freoðoscealc	peace-minister	*freondum*	friend, relative
freoðoscealcas	peace-minister	*freora*	free, happy, noble
freoðosped	success-in-maintaining-peace	*freorig*	chill, chilly, cold, freezing
freoðowær	peace-treaty	*freoþ*	cherish, love
freoðowære	peace-treaty	*freoþian*	cherish, defend, protect
freoðowong	peaceful-field		
freodrihten	noble-lord	*freoþo*	peace, protection, safety
freodryhtne	noble-lord		
freoðuwebbe	peace-weaver		
freog	love		

89

Word List (*Ænglisc* to English)

Ænglisc	English
freoþobeacen	protection-beacon, protection-sign
freoþoburh	protecting-city
freoþode	cherish, defend, protect
freoþoscealc	peace-minister
freoþoscealcas	peace-minister
freoþosped	success-in-maintaining-peace
freoþoþeaw	peaceful-disposition, peaceful-virtue
freoþoþeawas	peaceful-disposition, peaceful-virtue
freoþowær	peace-treaty
freoþowære	peace-treaty
freoþowong	peaceful-field
freoþuwebbe	peace-weaver
freowine	noble-lord
fretan	break-faith, consume, eat
fricgan	ask, find-out, inquire, try-to-find-out
fricgcean	ask, find-out, inquire, try-to-find-out
fricgean	ask, find-out, inquire, try-to-find-out
fricgen	ask, find-out, inquire, try-to-find-out
friclan	desire, seek
frið	peace, security, tranquillity
friðcandel	peace-candle, the-sun
friðe	peace, security, tranquillity
friðgedal	death
friðian	cherish, defend, protect
friðo	peace, protection, safety
friðotacen	peace-sign, protection-sign
friðusibb	peace-marriage, peace-pledge
frige	affections, ask, embraces, find-out, inquire, lady, love, try-to-find-out
frigesscit	grows-cold (Latin)
frignan	ask, find-out
frigu	affections, embraces, love
frin	ask, find-out
frinan	ask, find-out
frind	friends
frineð	ask, find-out
frineþ	ask, find-out
frioðowære	peace-agreement
frioðuwær	peace-agreement
frioðuwære	peace-agreement
frioþowære	peace-agreement
frioþuwær	peace-agreement
frioþuwære	peace-agreement
friþ	beautiful, peace, security, stately, tranquillity
friþcandel	peace-candle, the-sun
friþe	beautiful, peace, security, stately, tranquillity
friþes	peace, security, tranquillity
friþgedal	death
friþian	cherish, defend, protect
friþion	protect
friþo	peace, protection, safety
friþotacen	peace-sign, protection-sign
friþu	peace, protection, safety
friþusibb	peace-marriage, peace-pledge
frod	ancient, astute, experienced, old, wise
froda	old, wise
frodan	old, wise
frode	old, wise
frodran	old, wise
frofer	consolation

Word List (*Ænglisc* to English)

Ænglisc	English	*Ænglisc*	English
frofor	comfort, consolation, relief, solace	frumsceaft	creation, first-creation, home, origin
frofra	consolation	frumsceafta	first-creation, home, origin
frofre	away, comfort, consolation, satisfaction	frumsceafte	first-creation, home, origin
from	away, bold, brave, descendants, forth, from, splendid, strong	frumstol	original-habitation
		fryðo	peace, protection, safety
		frymð	beginning, origin
fromcyme	descendants, posterity	frymða	beginning, origin
		frymðe	beginning, origin
fromcynn	descendants, progeny	frymdi	entreating
		frymþ	beginning, origin
fromcynne	descendants, progeny	frymþa	beginning, origin
		frymþe	beginning, origin
frome	bold, strong	frynd	friend, friends, relative
fromlad	departure		
fromlice	boldly, quickly, vigorously	fryþo	peace, protection, safety
fromne	bold, strong	fugel	bird
fromsiþ	departure	fugelas	birds
fromum	bold, strong	fugele	bird
fromweard	departing, doomed-to-die	fugla	fowl
		fuglas	bird
fromweardum	departing, doomed-to-die	fugle	bird
		fugles	bird
fruma	beginning, cause, creation, creator, founder, leader, origin, progenitor	fuglum	bird
		fugol	bird
		fuhton	fight, fighting, fought
		fuit	he-was (Latin)
fruman	beginning, cause, creation, creator, founder, leader, origin, progenitor	ful	beaker, completely, cup, entirely, foul, full, fully, impure, impure-person, rotten, unclean, very
frumbearn	first-born-child		
frumbearne	first-born-child	fula	foul, impure, impure-person, rotten, unclean
frumcyn	from-kin		
frumgar	chief, leader		
frumgara	chief, leader	fulan	foul, impure, impure-person, rotten, unclean
frumgaran	chief, leader		
frumgaras	chief, leader		
frumgare	chief, leader	fulboren	live-born
frumgarum	chief, leader	fulborenum	fully-born-one, live-born
frumhrægl	original-garment		
frumhrægle	original-garment	fule	foul, impure, impure-person, rotten, unclean

Word List (Ænglisc to English)

Ænglisc	English	Ænglisc	English
fulgangan	complete, fulfil	furður	any-more, farther, further
fulgon	penetrate, reach	furh	furrow
full	beaker, cup, entirely, full, very	furþor	any-more, farther, further
fullæstan	help	furþum	already, before, even, first
fullæstu	help	furþur	any-more, farther, further
fulle	beaker, cup, full, fullness	fus	brave, eager, noble, quick, striving, zealous
fulleode	strengthen, support		
fulleodon	strengthen, support	fuse	brave, eager, noble, quick, striving, zealous
fullgan	strengthen, support		
fullian	fulfil		
fullum	foul, full, impure, impure-person, rotten, unclean	fuslic	ready
		fuslicu	ready
fullwen	baptism?-one-occurrence, in-poetry	fusne	brave, eager, noble, quick, striving, zealous
fullwona	baptism?-one-occurrence, in-poetry	fyftyne	fifteen
		fyl	death, destruction, fall
fulne	full		
fulneah	almost, very-nearly	fylde	cause-to-fall, complete, fell, fill, filled, fulfil
fultum	help, support		
fultumes	help, support		
fulwian	baptize	fylgan	follow, obey, observe, pursued
fulwiht	baptism		
fundað	go, hasten, strive-after, wish-for	fylgde	follow, obey, observe
fundast	go, hasten, strive-after, wish-for	fylgean	follow, obey, observe
fundaþ	go, hasten, strive-after, wish-for	fylian	follow
funde	devise, find, found, go	fyligan	follow, obey, observe
fundedon	go, hasten, strive-after, wish-for	fyll	death, destruction, fall, feasting, fullness, repletion
funden	devise, find		
fundian	go, hasten, strive-after, wish-for	fyllað	complete, fill, fulfil
		fyllan	cause-to-fall, complete, fell, fill, fulfil
fundiaþ	go, hasten, strive-after, wish-for		
fundode	go, hasten, strive-after, wish-for	fyllaþ	complete, fill, fulfil
		fylle	death, destruction, fall, feasting, fullness, fully, repletion
fundon	devise, find		
furðor	any-more, farther, further		
furðum	already, before, even, first	fylstan	help, support
		fylste	help, support

Word List (*Ænglisc* to English)

Ænglisc	English	*Ænglisc*	English
fylston	help, support	*fyren*	crime, fiery, fire-made, flaming, guilt, sin, torment, wickedness
fylwerig	wounded, wounded-to-death, wound-weary		
fylwerigne	wounded, wounded-to-death, wound-weary	*fyrena*	crime, guilt, sin, torment
		fyrendæd	evil-or-criminal-deed
fynd	adversary, devil, enemy, fiend	*fyrendæda*	evil-or-criminal-deed
		fyrendædum	evil-or-criminal-deed
fyore	life, living-being, person, spirit	*fyrenðearf*	dire-need
		fyren-ðearf	dire-distress
fyr	far, fire, from-afar	*fyrenðearfe*	dire-need
fyra	human-beings, men	*fyrene*	crime, fiery, fire-made, flaming, guilt, sin, torment
fyrbend	fire-forged-band		
fyrbendum	fire-forged-band		
fyrd	army, military-campaign	*fyrenearfeða*	dire-suffering
		fyrenearfeðe	dire-suffering
fyrde	army, companion-in-arms, military-campaign	*fyrenearfeþa*	dire-suffering
		fyrenearfeþe	dire-suffering
		fyrenlice	savagely
fyrdgestealla	companion-in-arms, retainer	*fyrenþearf*	dire-need
		fyren-þearf	dire-distress
fyrdgesteallum	companion-in-arms, retainer	*fyrenþearfe*	dire-need
		fyrenu	aflame
fyrdgetrum	warrior-band	*fyrenum*	extremely, violently
fyrdhom	army-suit	*fyres*	fire
fyrdhrægl	armour, mail-coat	*fyrgebræc*	fire-sound
fyrdhwæt	army-vigorous	*fyrgenbeam*	mountain-tree
fyrdhwate	army-vigorous	*fyrgenbeamas*	mountain-tree
fyrdleoð	martial-song	*fyrgenheafde*	mountain-top
fyrdleoþ	martial-song	*fyrgenheafod*	mountain-top
fyrdraca	fire-dragon	*fyrgenholt*	mountain-wood
fyrðran	further, hasten	*fyrgenstream*	mountain-stream
fyrdrinc	soldier, warrior	*fyrhðe*	soul
fyrdrinces	soldier, warrior	*fyrheard*	fire-hardened, tempered
fyrdsearo	armour, war-trappings		
		fyrleoht	fire-light
fyrdsearu	armour, war-trappings	*fyrmest*	first, foremost
		fyrn	earlier, formerly, long-ago
fyrdwic	encampment, military-camp		
		fyrndaeg	long-ago-day
fyrdwicum	encampment, military-camp	*fyrndagum*	long-ago-day
		fyrngearum	ancient-years
fyrdwyrðe	worthy-in-battle	*fyrngeflit*	former-strife
fyrdwyrþe	worthy-in-battle	*fyrngeflitan*	enemy
fyre	fire	*fyrngeflitu*	former-strife
fyredon	bring, carry, depart, go, transport	*fyrngeweorc*	ancient-work, long-ago-craftsmanship

Word List (*Ænglisc* to English)

Ænglisc	English	*Ænglisc*	English
fyrngewinn	ancient-fight, long-ago-struggle	*gæleð*	chant, sing
		gæleþ	chant, sing
fyrngewinnes	ancient-fight, long-ago-struggle	*gæst*	demon, ghost, goes, guest, soul, spirit, stranger
fyrnmann	long-ago-person		
fyrnmanna	long-ago-person	*gæsta*	demon, ghost, goes, soul, spirit
fyrnstream	distant-current		
fyrnstreama	distant-current, distant-streams	*gæstas*	guest, stranger
		gæste	demon, ghost, soul, spirit
fyrnum	extremely, fiery, violently		
		gæstes	demon, ghost, soul, spirit
fyrnwita	ancient-sage, old-wise-man		
		gæsthalge	holy-spirit
fyrnwitan	ancient-sage, old-wise-man	*gæstlic*	ghastly, ghostly, holy, spiritual
fyrr	far, from-afar	*gæþ*	acquire, carry-out, go, goes, observe, overrun, take-place
fyrst	period, time		
fyrste	period, time		
fyrþran	further, hasten		
fyrwet	curiosity	*gæworht*	carry-out, create, do, make, work
fyrwylm	fire-flame		
fyrwylmum	fire-flame	*gafol*	tax, tribute
fyrwyt	curiosity	*gafole*	tax, tribute
fysan	force, hurry, impel, urge	*gahuuem*	undertaking
		gahwem	folly, undertaking
		gal	folly, lust, luxury
fysde	force, hurry, impel, urge	*galan*	chant, sing, song
		galdor	chant, chanting, incantation, instrument, magic, sing, song, spell

G, g

Ænglisc	English	*Ænglisc*	English
ga	acquire, carry-out, go, goes, observe, overrun, take-place	*galdre*	chant, chanting, incantation, instrument, magic, sing, song, spell
Gabriel	Gabriel (name)		
gad	goes, lack, need, want	*galferhð*	lustful
		galferhþ	lustful
gað	acquire, carry-out, go, observe, overrun, take-place	*galga*	gallows
		galgan	gallows
		galgmod	fierce, gallows-like, gloomy, stern
gaderian	gather	*galgtreow*	gallows-tree
gæd	lack, need, want	*galgtreowum*	gallows-tree
gæð	acquire, carry-out, go, goes, observe, overrun, take-place	*galmod*	lecherous
		galmoda	lecherous
gædeling	companion	*galnys*	lechery, lust
gædelinges	companion, companions	*galnysse*	lechery, lust
		galscipe	folly, lasciviousness, luxury
gædelingum	companion, companions		
		gamela	old

Word List (Ænglisc to English)

Ænglisc	English	Ænglisc	English
gamele	old	garcwealm	death-in-battle, spear-death
gamelum	old	GAR-DENA	spear-Danes
gamen	amusement, joy, mirth, play, sport	gar-Dene	spear-Danes
gamene	amusement, amusing, joy, joyful, mirth, mirthful, play, playful, sport, sporty	gar-Denum	spear-Danes
		gare	spear
		gares	spear
		gargewinn	spear-battle
gamol	ancient, old	gargewinnes	spear-battle
gamolfeax	grey-haired, old-hair, old-haired	garholt	spear-forest, spear-wood
gamolferhð	old	garmittinge	spear-meeting
gamolferhþ	old	garmundes	spear-hand, spear-mound
gan	acquire, carry-out, go, move, observe, overrun, take-place, to-go, walk	garræs	spear-attack
		garsecg	ocean, sea, to-the-deep
ganet	gannet, sea-bird	garsecges	ocean, sea, the-sea
ganetes	gannet, sea-bird	Garulf	Garulf (name)
gang	departure, flow, go, going, stream, take-place, track, walk	garum	spears
		garwiga	spear-warrior
		garwigan	spear-warrior
gangænde	go, walk	garwigend	spear-warrior
gangan	go, going, take-place, walk	gast	angel, demon, ghost, soul, spirit
gange	departure, flow, go, go, going, stream, take-place, track, walk	gasta	demon, ghost, soul, spirit
		gastae	demon, ghost, spIrIt
		gastas	demon, ghost, soul, spirit, spirits
gangende	go, walk	gastbona	soul-murderer, spirit-murderer, the-devil
ganges	departure, flow, go, going, stream, take-place, track		
		gastcofan	spirit-box
gangon	go, walk	gastcyning	Soul-king, Spirit-king
ganot	gannet, goose, sea-bird	gastcyninge	Soul-king, Spirit-king
		gaste	demon, ghost, soul, spirit
ganotes	gannet, sea-bird		
gar	spear	gastes	demon, ghost, soul, spirit, spirit
gara	spear		
garas	spear, spears	gastgedal	death
garbeam	spear-shaft	gastlic	ghastly, ghostly, holy, spiritual
garbeames	spear-shaft		
garberend	spear-bearer, warrior	gastlice	spirit-of
		gastum	guest, spirit, stranger
garberendra	spear-bearer, warrior	gaþ	acquire, carry-out, go, observe, overrun, take-place
garcene	battle-brave, spear, spear-brave		

Word List (Ænglisc to English)

Ænglisc	English	Ænglisc	English
ge	and, both, both...and, cuckoo, either...or, you, you (plural)	geapes	high, spacious, wide
		geapne	bent, crooked, curved, high, spacious, wide
geac	cuckoo	geapum	high, spacious, wide
geacsian	discover, find-out, learn	gear	year
		geara	finished, formerly, long-since, once, prepared, ready, spare, year, years-ago, yore
geador	together		
geæfnan	affect, make		
geæfndon	carry-out, construct		
geæfned	carry-out, construct		
geæhted	consider, deliberate-on, discuss, esteemed, mention, praise, prized	gearcian	prepare
		geard	dwelling, enclosure, ground, land, yard
		geardæg	days-of-old, days-of-yore, former-day
geæhtlan	consideration, esteem, esteemed, prized	gear-dæg	year-day
		geardagum	days-of-old, days-of-yore, former-day, olden-days, year-days
geæhtle	consideration, esteem		
geændade	end, reach-an-agreement, stop	geardas	dwelling, enclosure, ground, land
geæþele	renowned	geardum	dwelling, enclosure, ground, land
geaf	gave, give		
geafon	give, given	geare	clearly, entirely, finished, gear, prepared, readily, ready
geagnod	acquire, dedicate, obtain, own		
geahsod	discover, find-out, learn		
		geareofolm	ready-handed
geald	gold, pay, pay-back, repay, yield	gearo	finished, prepared, ready
gealdor	chant, chanting, incantation, instrument, magic, sing, song, spell	gearolice	certainly, clearly
		gearone	finished, prepared, ready
		gearoþoncol	quick-witted
gealga	gallows	gearoþoncolre	quick-witted
gealgan	gallows	gearowe	finished, prepared, ready
gealgean	avenge, defend, protect		
gealgtreow	gallows-tree	gearrim	year-number
gealgtreowe	gallows-tree	gearrimum	year-number
gealp	boast, brag, exult, yelp	geartorht	annually-bright
		geartorhte	annually-bright
gean	again, still, yet	gearu	finished, prepared, ready
geanoðe	meeting		
geanoþe	meeting	gearum	year
geap	bent, crooked, curved, high, spacious, wide	gearwad	adorn, equip, prepare

96

Word List (*Ænglisc* to English)

Ænglisc	English	*Ænglisc*	English
gearwan	clothing, equipment, trappings	gebæran	bearing, behave, comport-oneself
gearwe	clearly, clothing, entirely, equipment, finished, prepared, readily, ready, trappings	gebærdon	behave, comport-oneself
		gebære	behaviour, cry
		gebæro	behaviour, comportment, demeanour
gearwian	adorn, equip, prepare	gebæted	to-bridle, to-halter
gearwor	clearly, clothing, entirely, equipment, readily, trappings	geband	bind
		gebannan	command, order
		gebarn	be-burned, burn
gearwost	accomplished, clearly, entirely, readily, skilled	gebeacnod	point-out, show
		gebead	announce, give, grant, make-known, offer, proclaim
gearwum	clothing, equipment, trappings	gebeag	bow, coil, lie-down, of-a-dragon-coil, rest-inactive, sit-down, stoop, submit, turn-away
geascodan	found-out		
geascodon	ask, discover, find-out		
geasne	deprived-of, lacking, without	gebeah	bow, coil, lie-down, of-a-dragon-coil, rest-inactive, sit-down, stoop, submit, turn-away
geat	gate		
Geates	Geats		
Geatmæcgum	Geatish-man		
Geatmecga	Geatish-man		
geatolic	decorated, magnificent	gebearg	preserve, save
		gebearh	preserve, save
geatwa	equipment, treasures	gebeaten	beat, pound, strike-against
geaxode	discover, find-out, learn	gebed	prayer
		gebedda	sexual-partner, spouse
gebad	announce, attain, await, continue, endure, endured, expect, experience, give, grant, live, live-to-enjoy, make-known, offer, proclaim, remain, stay, wait, waited	gebeddan	partner, sexual-partner, spouse
		gebeddum	sexual-partner, spouse
		gebede	prayer
		gebeded	driven
		gebedscipe	sexual-intercourse, sleeping-together
gebæd	ask, pray	gebegde	bowed
gebædda	sexual-partner, spouse	gebeodan	announce, give, grant, make-known, offer, proclaim
gebæded	dispatch, impel, impelled, urge	gebeor	beer-drinker, beer-drinking-buddy
gebær	bear, carry, give-birth-to	gebeoras	beer-drinker, beer-drinking-buddy

Word List (Ænglisc to English)

Ænglisc	English
gebeorg	protection
gebeorge	protection
gebeorh	protector
gebeorscipe	beer-party, feast
gebeorum	beer-drinker, beer-drinking-buddy
gebeot	vow
gebeotedon	boast, vow
gebetan	amend, compensate, improve, increase, remedy, restore
gebette	amend, amended, compensate, increase, restore
gebettest	amend, compensate, increase, restore
gebicge	buy
gebidan	attain, await, continue, experience, live, live-to-enjoy, remain, stay, wait
gebidanne	continue, experience, live, live-to-enjoy, stay, wait
gebiddað	ask, pray
gebiddan	pray
gebiddaþ	ask, pray
gebidde	ask
gebide	await, continue, endure, expect, experience, live, live-to-enjoy, look, stay, wait
gebideð	experience, experienced, live-to-enjoy
gebiden	attain, await, continue, endure, expect, experience, live, live-to-enjoy, remain, stay, wait
gebidenne	experience, live-to-enjoy
gebidenra	experience, live-to-enjoy
gebideþ	experience, live-to-enjoy
gebidon	attain, await, experience, remain
gebiesgad	occupied
gebind	band, binding, fastening
gebindað	bind
gebindaþ	bind
gebland	mixed
geblanden	blend-with
gebletsad	bless
gebletsade	bless
gebletsod	bless, blessing
gebletsode	bless
geblissad	become-happy, delight, get-drunk, have-fun, make-happy
geblodegod	bloody, make-bloody
geblonden	corrupted, infected, mixed-in, mixed-with
gebod	command, precept
geboden	offer
gebodode	announced
gebogen	bow, coil, lie-down, of-a-dragon-coil, rest-inactive, sit-down, stoop, submit, turn-away
gebogenan	bow, lie-down, of-a-dragon-coil, rest-inactive, sit-down, stoop, submit, turn-away
gebohte	buy, get, get-in-exchange
gebohtest	bought
gebolgen	angry, enraged, enraged-from
gebolgne	angry, enraged, enraged-from
gebond	bound
geboren	bear, born, carry, give-birth-to
geborenum	born
geborgen	preserve, save

Word List (*Ænglisc* to English)

Ænglisc	English	*Ænglisc*	English
gebræc	break, breaking, burst, clashing, destroy, of-curiosity, subdue, torment, transgress, transgress-a-commandment	gebrohte	bring
		gebrohten	bring
		gebrohton	bring
		gebroþer	brethren
		gebroþor	brethren, brother, fellow-Christian, fellow-monk
gebræcon	break, broken, destroy, subdue	gebroþra	brother, fellow-Christian, fellow-monk
gebræd	draw-a-sword, feign, mail-coat-rings, move, pretend, swing, weave	gebroþru	brethren, brother
		gebroþrum	brother, fellow-Christian, fellow-monk
gebrægd	break, breaking, burst, clashing, destroy, drawn, transgress	gebudon	offer
		gebulge	cause-anger-in, enrage
gebrecan	break, destroy, subdue	gebun	dwell, live, settle
		gebunden	bind, bound
gebregd	manipulation, movement	gebundene	bind
		gebundenne	bound
gebringan	bring	gebylde	encourage, to-embolden
gebringe	bring		
gebroced	afflict, crush, hurt	gebyrd	birth, origin, race
gebrocede	afflict, crush, hurt	gebyrdo	birth, origin, race
gebrocen	break, breaking, broken, burst, clashing, destroy, of-curiosity, subdue, torment, transgress, transgress-a-commandment	gebyrdum	birth, origin, race
		gebyrede	birth
		gebyrgde	eat, taste
		gebyrge	bury, eat, taste
		gebyrgenne	grave
		gebysgad	occupy, trouble
		gebysmrian	degrade, dishonour, mock, revile
gebrocian	afflict, crush, hurt	gebysnode	instruct-by-example, set-an-example
gebrocod	afflict		
gebroden	draw-a-sword, feign, mail-coat-rings, move, pretend, swing, weave	gecamp	battle
		gecampe	battle
		geceapian	buy
		geceapod	bought, buy
gebroðor	brother, fellow-Christian, fellow-monk	geceas	accept, choose, chosen, seek-out, select
gebroðra	brother, fellow-Christian, fellow-monk	gecenne	declare
		geceos	accept, choose, chosen, seek-out, select
gebroðru	brother		
gebroðrum	brother, fellow-Christian, fellow-monk	geceosað	accept, choose, seek, seek-out, select
gebroht	bring, brought		

Word List (*Ænglisc* to English)

Ænglisc	English	*Ænglisc*	English
geceosaþ	accept, choose, seek-out, select	gecwæþ	quote, said, say
		gecweden	spoken-of
geceoseð	chooses	gecwedene	say
geceosenne	accept, choose, chosen, seek-out, select	gecwemað	be-pleased
		gecyd	make-known, reveal, say, tell
gecnawan	find-out, know, perceive, recognise, recognize, understand	gecyðan	make-known, reveal, say, tell
		gecyðanne	make-known, reveal, say, tell
gecnaweð	find-out, know, perceive, perceives, recognize	gecyðde	make-known, reveal, say, tell
		gecyddest	proclaim, testament
gecnaweþ	find-out, know, perceive, recognize	gecyðed	make-known, reveal, say, tell
gecned	kneed	gecyged	call, name, speak, summon
gecoren	accept, choose, seek-out, select	gecynd	nature
gecorenan	accept, choice, choose, seek-out, select	gecynde	inheritance, natural
		gecyndne	natural
		gecypan	buy
gecorene	accept, choose, seek-out, select	gecyre	choose
		gecyrre	turn
gecorone	accept, choose, chosen, seek-out, select	gecyrred	change, convert, turn, turn-back
		gecyste	kiss
gecoste	excellent, proven	gecyþan	make-known, reveal, say, tell
gecranc	cringe, fall, fall-in-battle, perish	gecyþanne	make-known, reveal, say, tell
gecrang	fall-in-battle, fell-in-battle	gecyþde	make-known, reveal, say, tell
gecringan	cringe, fall, perish	gecyþed	make-known, reveal, say, tell
gecrong	fall-in-battle, fell		
gecrungen	cringe, fall, perish	gecyþed!	made-known
gecrungon	cringe, fall, perish	gedæde	act, cause, do, make, perform, put, take
gecunnad	explore, find-out, know, make-trial-of, test, try, try-out		
		gedælan	allot, deal-in, divide, engage-in, participate-in, share
gecunnade	know, make-trial-of, test, try		
gecunnian	know, make-trial-of, test, try	gedælde	allot, deal-in, divide, engage-in, participate-in, separated, share
gecwæð	quote, said, say		
gecwæde	quote, say		
gecwædon	quote, say		
gecwæman	gratify, please, serve	gedæled	allot, deal-in, divide, engage-in, participate-in, share
gecwæmde	gratify, please, serve		
		geðafode	agree-to, consent

Word List (Ænglisc to English)

Ænglisc	English	Ænglisc	English
geðah	endure, prosper, thrive	gedreas	fail, fall, fell, perish
gedal	division, lot, part, piece, portion, separation, share	gedrefed	afflict, beset, stir-up, trouble
		gedreht	afflict, oppress, torment
gedale	division, lot, part, piece, portion, separation, share	gedrehte	afflict, oppress, torment
		gedreogeð	endures
gedaled	allot, deal-in, divide, engage-in, participate-in, share	gedreosan	fail, fall, perish
		gedreoseð	fail, fall, perish
		gedreoseþ	fail, fall, perish
gedeaf	sink-in	gedriht	company, multitude, nation, people, troop
gedeð	act, cause, do, make, perform, put, sink-in, take	geðring	throng
		gedrogen	do, endure, experience, fulfil, perform, suffer
gedefe	fitting, good, improper, proper, seemly, suitable, wrong, wrongly	gedrohtnunge	monastic-life, monastic-rule, way-of-life
gedemed	judge, praise		
gedeþ	act, cause, do, make, perform, put, sink-in, take	gedroren	fail, fall, perish
		gedrorene	fallen
		geðrungen	advance, press, press-forward, throng
gedidon	did		
gedigan	overcome, survive		
gedigde	overcome, survive	gedruron	fail, fall
gedigeð	overcome, survive	gedryht	company, troop
gedigest	overcome, survive	geðuht	appear, seem, think
gedigeþ	overcome, survive	geðungen	distinguished, excellent, grown
gedo	act, cause, do, make, perform, put, take	gedwild	error, folly, heresy, sin
gedoð	act, cause, do, make, perform, put, take	gedwilde	error, folly, heresy, sin
		gedwolen	perverted, sinful, wrong
geðoht	thought		
gedon	act, bring-to-pass, cause, do, done, make, perform, put, take	gedwolene	perverted, sinful, wrong
		gedwyld	error, folly, heresy, sin
geðonce	thanks, thought	gedwylde	error, folly, heresy, sin
gedoþ	act, cause, do, make, perform, put, take	gedyde	act, cause, do, make, perform, put, take
gedræg	assembly, multitude		
geðread	afflict, oppress	gedydon	act, cause, do, make, perform, put, take
geðreadne	afflict		
gedreag	assembly, multitude, tumult	gedygan	overcome, survive

Word List (Ænglisc to English)

Ænglisc	English	Ænglisc	English
gedyrsod	glorify, honour	gefaran	go, proceed, travel
geearnaþ	deserving, earn, merit	gefare	fare
		gefaren	go, proceed, travel
geearnod	deserving, earn, merit	gefea	happiness, joy
		gefeah	exult, rejoice
geearnung	desert, merit, virtue	gefealleð	die, fall, fall-dead, fall-onto, fall-to
geearnunga	desert, merit, virtue		
geearnunge	desert, merit, virtue	gefealleþ	die, fall, fall-dead, fall-onto, fall-to
geeawed	appear, present, reveal, show		
		gefean	happiness, joy
geefsod	shave, shear	gefecgan	bring, carry-away, fetch
geendod	end, reach-an-agreement, stop		
		gefeg	attach, confine, join
geendode	ended	gefeged	attach, confine, confined, join
geendung	ending		
geendunge	ending	gefegon	exult, rejoice
geeode	acquire, carry-out, conquered, go, observe, overrun, take-place	gefeh	exult, rejoice
		gefele	feel, feels, perceive
		gefeleð	feel, feels, perceive
		gefeleþ	feel, perceive
geeodon	acquire, carry-out, go, observe, overrun, take-place	gefelled	fulfil
		gefeng	achieve, grasp, seize, take
		gefengon	seize, take
geeuenlæhton	be-like, emulate, equal, match	gefeoh	rejoice
		gefeoht	battle, fight, struggle
gefæccan	bring, carry-away, fetch	gefeohtan	battle, fight, struggle
		gefeohte	battle, fight, struggle
gefæg	pleasing	gefeol	die, fall, fall-dead, fall-onto, fall-to
gefægnod	be-delighted, be-happy		
gefægon	exult, rejoice	gefeoll	die, fall, fall-dead, fall-onto, fall-to
gefægra	fair, pleasing		
gefælsod	cleanse, purify	gefeormedon	entertain, look-after, polish-off
gefæra	companion		
gefæran	companion	gefeormod	entertain, look-after, polish-off
gefæstnod	contract-for, fasten, provide-assurances-that, secure, settle-upon		
		gefera	companion, comrade
		geferan	companion, companions
gefæstnodon	contract-for, fasten, provide-assurances-that, secure, settle-upon	geferde	accomplish, bring, fare, go, obtain, travel
gefætte	bring, carry-away, fetch	geferdon	accomplish, bring, carry, depart, fare, go, obtain, transport, travel
gefandod	examine, rummage-through, test		
gefangen	seize, take		
gefara	companion, follower		

Word List (*Ænglisc* to English)

Ænglisc	English	*Ænglisc*	English
gefere	accomplish, bring, carry, depart, fare, go, obtain, transport, travel	gefrægen	ask, famous, find-out, knowledge, report, respected, well-known
gefered	accomplish, bring, carry, depart, fare, go, obtain, transport, travel	gefrægn	ask, famous, find-out, heard-of, knowledge, report, respected, well-known
geferede	accomplish, bring, carry, depart, fare, go, obtain, transport, travel	gefrægnod	ask, find-out
		gefrætewod	adorn, decorate
		gefrætwad	adorn, decorate
geferedon	accomplish, bring, carry, depart, fare, go, obtain, transport, travel	gefrætwade	adorn, decorate
		gefrætwed	adorned
		gefrætwod	adorn, decorate
		gefran	hear-of, learn, learned
geferian	accomplish, bring, carry, depart, fare, go, obtain, transport, travel	gefrege	known
		gefremed	advance, carry-out, do, further, make, perpetuate, support
geferum	companion		
gefeterode	fasten, fetter	gefremede	advance, carry-out, do, further, make, perpetuate, support
gefetian	bring, carry-away, fetch		
gefetige	bring, carry-away, fetch	gefremeden	advance, carry-out, do, further, make, perpetuate, support
gefetrade	better		
gefette	fetched	gefremedon	advance, carry-out, do, further, make, perpetuate, support
geflæmdest	put-to-flight		
geflemed	put-to-flight		
geflit	contest, dispute	gefremian	accomplish
geflota	fish, floater	gefremman	advance, carry-out, do, further, make, perpetuate, support
geflotan	fish, floater		
geflymed	cast-out, drive-out		
gefohten	fight, fighting	gefremmanne	advance, carry-out, do, further, make, perpetuate, support
gefon	seize, take		
gefondad	examine, rummage-through, test		
		gefremmed	committed
gefor	go, proceed, travel	gefretewodon	adorn, decorate
geforan	go, proceed, travel	gefricge	ask, find-out, inquire, try-to-find-out
geforðad	forth		
geforon	go, proceed		
geforþod	carry-out	gefricgeað	ask, find-out, inquire, try-to-find-out
gefræge	famous, knowledge, report, respected, well-known		
		gefricgean	ask, find-out, inquire, try-to-find-out

Word List (*Ænglisc* to English)

Ænglisc	English	*Ænglisc*	English
gefricgeaþ	ask, find-out, inquire, try-to-find-out	*gegæþ*	acquire, carry-out, go, observe, overrun, take-place
gefriðode	cherish, defend, protect	*gegan*	acquire, carry-out, go, observe, overrun, take-place
gefrinan	hear-of, learn		
gefriþod	cherish, defend, protect	*gegangan*	acquire, attain, go, going, happen, ongoing, reach, take-place, walk
gefriþode	cherish, defend, protect		
gefrugnon	ask, find-out, learned-of	*gegangeð*	acquire, attain, go, going, happen, ongoing, reach, take-place, walk
gefrunen	ask, find-out, hear-of, inquire, learn, try-to-find-out		
		gegangenne	acquire, attain, go, happen, reach, take-place, walk
gefrungon	ask, find-out, inquire, try-to-find-out	*gegangeþ*	acquire, attain, go, going, happen, ongoing, reach, take-place, walk
gefrunon	ask, find-out, hear-of, inquire, learn, try-to-find-out		
gefullod	baptize	*gegarwod*	adorn, equip, prepare
gefullode	baptize		
gefyldan	cause-to-fall, complete, fell, fill, fulfil	*gegaþ*	acquire, carry-out, go, observe, overrun, take-place
gefylde	complete, fill, fulfil	*gegearcod*	prepare
gefyllan	cause-to-fall, complete, fell, fill, fulfil	*gegearewod*	adorn, equip, prepare
		gegearwigean	adorn, equip, prepare
gefylle	complete, fill, fulfil		
gefylled	complete, felled, fill, filled, fulfil	*gegearwod*	adorn, equip, prepare
gefylste	assist	*gegenge*	agreeable, appropriate
gefyrðred	further, hasten		
gefyrn	earlier, formerly, long-ago	*gegeorcode*	prepare
		gegired	adorn, dress, equip, prepare
gefyrþred	further, hasten		
gefysde	readying	*gegiredan*	adorn, dress, equip, prepare
gefysed	force, hurry, impel, urge		
		gegncwida	conversation, reply
gegaderie	gather	*gegncwide*	conversation, reply
gegæð	acquire, carry-out, go, observe, overrun, take-place	*gegnum*	away, directly, forwards
		gegnunga	certainly, indeed, plainly
gegærwan	adorn, dress, equip, prepare	*gegododon*	give-property-to

Word List (Ænglisc to English)

Ænglisc	English	Ænglisc	English
gegongeð	acquire, attain, going, happen, ongoing, reach, take-place	gehalgode	bless, consecrate, dedicate
gegongen	acquire, attain, go, going, happen, ongoing, reach, take-place, walk	gehalgodum	bless, consecrate, dedicate
		gehat	promise
		gehata	promise
		gehatað	promise
		gehatan	call
gegongeþ	acquire, attain, going, happen, ongoing, reach, take-place	gehataþ	call
		gehate	be-named, call, command, name, promise
gegrap	grasp, seize, take	gehaten	be-named, call, command, name, promise
gegremed	anger, enrage		
gegremede	anger, enrage		
gegremian	enrage	gehatheort	headstrong, hot-hearted, rash
gegremod	anger, enrage		
gegremode	anger, enrage	gehatum	promise
gegrettan	address, attack, greet, injure, play-a-harp, speak-to, touch	gehðo	care, sorrow
		geheaðerian	confine
		geheaðerod	confine
		geheald	hold, keep, rule
gegrette	address, attack, greet, injure, play-a-harp, speak-to, touch	gehealdan	hold, keep, rule
		gehealde	hold, keep, rule
		gehealdeþ	hold, keep, rule
		gehealdon	hold
gegrind	clash, impact	geheapen	heaped
gegripon	grasp, seize, take	geheaþerian	confine
gegrunden	ground-up	geheaþerod	confine
gegrundene	grind, sharpen	geheawe	cut, hew
gegyred	adorn, dress, equip, prepare	geheawen	cut, hew
		gehedde	achieve, perform
gegyrede	adorn, dress, equip, prepare	gehegan	achieve, perform
		gehende	close-by, within-reach-of
gegyrwan	adorn, dress, equip, prepare	geheold	hold, keep, rule
gegyrwed	adorn, dress, equip, prepare	gehergod	harry, raid, ravage
		gehet	be-named, call, command, had, name, promise
gehæfte	bind, fetter		
gehæfted	bind, fetter		
gehæl	heal	geheton	be-named, call, command, name, promise
gehæle	save		
gehæled	comfort, heal, make-whole		
		gehicgenne	sword-hilt, think
gehælede	comfort, heal, make-whole, saving	gehiltum	sword-hilt
		gehiwodon	disguise
gehalgod	bless, consecrate, dedicate	gehladene	burden, laden, load, take-in

105

Word List (*Ænglisc* to English)

Ænglisc	English	*Ænglisc*	English
gehlædene	burden, laden, load, take-in	gehwæþer	both, either-of-two
gehlæste	adorn, load, weigh-down	gehwæþere	both, either-of-two
		gehwæþres	both, either-of-two
		gehwæþrum	both, either-of-two
gehleat	get, obtain, receive-by-lot, to-cast-lots	gehwam	each, every
		gehwane	each, every
gehleod	burden, laden, load, take-in	gehwearf	go, move, turn
		gehwelcne	each, every
gehleop	gallop, leap, mount-a-horse	gehweorfe	turn
		gehwer	always, everywhere, somewhere, wherever
gehliðo	cliff, hill, slope		
gehlidu	roof, vault		
gehliþo	cliff, hill, slope	gehwilc	each
gehlyn	heard	gehwilce	each, every
gehlyston	listen	gehwilces	each, every
gehnægde	humble, humiliate	gehwilcne	each
gehnægdon	address, attack	gehwilcre	each
gehnæged	humble, humiliate	gehwilcum	each, every
gehnæst	conflict	gehwone	each, every
gehnæste	conflict	gehwylc	each, every, every-one
gehogod	intend, resolve, wish-for		
gehogodest	intend, resolve, wish-for	gehwylce	each, every
		gehwylces	each, every
		gehwylcne	each, every
gehola	confidant, friend, protector, supporter	gehwylcre	each, every, works
		gehwylcum	each, every
geholena	confidant, supporter	gehwyrfed	change, go, move
gehroden	adorned, covered, decorated	gehydað	hidden
		gehydde	hidden, hide
gehrodene	adorned, covered, decorated	gehyded	concealed
		gehygd	mind, thought
gehrorene	fallen	gehyge	consider, think
gehþo	care, sorrow	gehyld	holding, protection
gehugod	minded	gehyrað	belong, belong-to, hear, obey
gehuuæs	each		
gehwa	each, every, everyone	gehyraþ	belong, belong-to, hear, obey
gehwæðer	both, either-of-two	gehyrde	belong, belong-to, harden, hear, heard, make-hard, obey, temper
gehwæðere	both, either-of-two		
gehwæðrum	both, either-of-two		
gehwæm	each, every, everyone		
		gehyrdeð	harden, make-hard, temper
gehwæne	each, every		
gehwær	always, each, every, everywhere, on-every-side, somewhere	gehyrdeþ	harden, make-hard, temper
		gehyrdon	belong, belong-to, hear, obey
gehwære	each, every	gehyre	belong, belong-to, hear, obey
gehwæs	both, each, every		

Word List (Ænglisc to English)

Ænglisc	English	Ænglisc	English
gehyrest	belong, hear, obey	gelæstan	carry-out, endure, follow, help, last, perform, serve, show, stand-by
gehyrst	belong, hear, obey		
gehyrsteð	decorate, ornament		
gehyrsteþ	decorate, ornament		
geican	augment, grow, increase	gelæste	carry-out, endure, follow, help, last, perform, serve, stand-by
geiceað	augment, grow, increase		
geicean	augment, grow, increase	gelæston	carry-out, endure, follow, help, last, perform, serve
geiceaþ	augment, grow, increase		
		gelafede	wash
geicte	augment, grow, increase	gelagu	expanse, surface
		gelamp	exist, happen, occur
geinnod	inward, within	gelang	belonging, present
geiode	acquire, carry-out, go, observe, overrun, take-place	gelaþ	enemy, hostile
		gelaþe	enemy, hostile
		geldenne	gilded, gilt, golden
gelac	commotion, play, rolling, sport, tumult	geleafa	faith
		geleafan	belief, faith
gelacna	cure	geleafful	believing
gelacum	commotion, play, sport, tumult	geleaffulne	believing
		geleah	betray, deceive, lie
gelad	journey, path, route, way	geled	lay
		gelenge	belonging, close-of-time, imminent, related
gelað	enemy, hostile		
gelaðe	enemy, hostile		
gelædað	bring, conduct, do, lead, take	geleorene	departed
		geleornian	learn, study
gelædaþ	bring, conduct, do, lead, take	geleornod	learn, study
		geleornode	learn, study
gelædde	bring, conduct, do, lead, take	gelettan	let
		gelette	hinder, hindered, prevent
gelæde	bring, conduct, do, lead, take	gelic	alike, like, similar-to
gelæded	bring, conduct, do, lead, take	gelica	companion, equal, like
gelæg	be-situated, die-down, laying, lie, lie-dead, lying, situated	gelicade	likened
		gelican	companion, equal, like
		gelice	alike, also, as, like, similarly, similar-to
gelæran	instruct, teach		
gelærdon	instruct, teach		
gelæred	instruct, teach	gelicode	be-liking-to, please
gelærede	instruct, teach	gelicost	alike, also, as, like, most-like, most-similarly, similarly, similar-to
gelæset	serve, stand-by		
gelæst	carry-out, endure, follow, help, last, perform, serve		
		geliefan	believe, believe-in, grant, trust

Word List (*Ænglisc* to English)

Ænglisc	English	Ænglisc	English
geliefde	believe, grant, trust	gemæne	common, controlled, general, subdued, to-become-multiplied, universal
geliefed	believe, grant, trust		
gelignian	show-to-be-a-liar		
gelignod	show-to-be-a-liar		
gelimpan	happen	gemænigfealda	to-become-multiplied
gelimpe	exist, happen, occur		
gelimpeð	exist, happen, occur	gemænra	common, controlled, general, subdued, universal
gelimpeþ	exist, happen, occur		
gelimplic	suitable		
geliste	cause-longing, longing, please	gemænscipe	communion
		gemænum	common, controlled, general, subdued, universal
gelocen	fasten, intertwine, lock, weave		
geloden	burden, laden, load, take-in	gemærsod	made-famous
		gemærsodest	made-great
gelogodon	lodge, place	gemætte	dream
gelome	frequently, often	gemagas	family, kindred, kinsman, male-relative
gelomp	exist, happen, occur		
gelong	belonging, present		
Gelpan	boast	gemah	bad, shameless
geludon	grow, spring	geman	be-mindful-of, pay-attention-to, remember
gelumpe	exist, happen, occur		
gelumpen	exist, happen, occur		
gelyfað	believe	gemanan	partaking
gelyfan	believe, believe-in, trust	gemang	assembly, mixture, multitude
gelyfde	believe, believe-in, trust	gemanode	admonish, remind, warn
gelyfe	believe, believe-in, trust	gemealt	burn-up, dissolve, melt
gelyfed	advanced	gemearca	create, design, designate, mark, note, remark, stain
gelyfeð	believe, believe-in, trust		
gelyfenne	believe	gemearces	border, end-of-life, limit, mark, term
gelyfeþ	believe, believe-in, trust	gemearcian	to-mark
gelyste	cause-longing, please	gemearcod	create, design, designate, mark, note, remark, stain
gemacod	do, make		
gemæc	companion, equal, spouse	gemearcode	create, design, designate, mark, note, remark, stain
gemæcca	mate, partner, spouse		
		gemedu	consent
gemæccum	mate, partner, spouse	gemenged	combined, confused, mingle, mix, mixed
gemæcne	companion, equal, spouse	gemet	ability, appropriate, capacity, fitting, law, measure, right, rule
gemælde	speak		
gemænden	mention, tell-of		

Word List (*Ænglisc* to English)

Ænglisc	English	*Ænglisc*	English
gemete	ability, capacity, law, means, measure, meet, met, rule	*gemunde*	be-mindful-of, pay-attention-to, remember
gemeted	encounter, meet, met	*gemundon*	be-mindful-of, pay-attention-to, remember
gemetfæst	slow-to-anger		
gemeting	encounter, meeting	*gemunon*	be-mindful-of, remember
gemette	encounter, measure, measure-out, meet, traverse	*gemyltan*	be-melted, burn-up, dissolve, melt
gemetton	encounter, measure, measure-out, meet, traverse	*gemynd*	intellect, memory, mind, remembrance, thought
gemilsa	mitigate	*gemynda*	intellect, memory, thought
gemilsige	have-mercy-on		
gemiltsa	have-mercy, show-mercy	*gemynde*	bring-to-mind, intellect, memory, mindful, thought
gemind	thoughts	*gemyndgad*	bring-to-mind, remind
gemindige	mindful		
gemittan	encounter, meet	*gemyndi*	mindful
gemitte	encounter, meet	*gemyndig*	keeping-in-mind, mindful, mindful-of, remembering
gemitton	encounter, meet		
gemon	be-mindful-of, pay-attention-to, remember, remembers	*gemyndum*	his-mind, intellect, memory, thought
gemong	assembly, mixture, multitude	*gemyne*	be-mindful-of, pay-attention-to, remember
gemonge	assembly, mixture, multitude	*gemynt*	intend, mean, think
gemoniað	admonish, remind, warn	*gemynted*	intend, mean, think
		gemyrre	obstruct
gemoniaþ	admonish, remind, warn	*gen*	again, further, still, yet
gemonige	admonish, remind, warn	*gena*	again, still, until-now, yet
gemot	assembly, council, fight, meeting	*genægdan*	address, attack
		genæged	address, attack
gemotes	fight, meeting	*genæs*	escape-from, survive
gemunað	be-mindful-of, pay-attention-to, remember	*genæson*	wielded
		genam	seize, take, taken, took
gemunan	be-mindful-of, remember	*genaman*	take
gemunaþ	be-mindful-of, pay-attention-to, remember	*gename*	take
		genamon	seize, take
		genap	darken, grow-dark
		gende	go

Word List (*Ænglisc* to English)

Ænglisc	English	*Ænglisc*	English
geneahe	abundance, enough, often, sufficiently, very	geniht	abundance, enough, sufficiency
geneahhe	constantly, enough, often, sufficiently, very	genihtsum	abundant, sufficient
		genim	take
		geniman	seize, take
		genime	take
genealæhton	approach, come-near	genimeð	take
		genimeþ	take
genealecan	approach, come-near	genipu	darkness
		geniwad	afresh, make-anew, renew, repeat
genearwad	afflict, become-confined, become-narrow, confine, oppress	geniwod	afresh, make-anew, renew, repeat
		genog	enough, many, much, numerous
genearwod	afflict, become-confined, become-narrow, confine, oppress	genoge	enough, many, much, numerous, sufficiently
geneat	companion, retainer	genoh	enough, many, much, numerous
geneatas	companion, retainer, vassal	genohra	enough, many, much, numerous
geneðde	dare, risk, to-venture	genom	take
geneðdon	dare, risk, to-venture	genumen	seize, take
genehe	enough, often, sufficiently, very	genunga	completely, entirely
genehhe	abundantly	genydde	force, impel-by-necessity
genehost	enough, often, sufficiently, very	genyded	force, impel-by-necessity
genemned	call, name, named	genyðerad	condemn, oppress, put-down
geneosode	find-out, inspect, seek-out, visit	genyþerad	condemn, oppress, put-down
genered	protect, save	genyttod	enjoy, make-use-of
generede	protect, save, saved	geo	formerly, help, of-old, once
generedes	deliverance		
generian	protect, save	geoc	help
generigan	protect, save	geoce	help, help-, support
genesan	escape	geocor	bitter, harsh, sad
genesen	escape-from, survive	geofen	ocean, sea
		geofena	gift, grace
geneþan	dare, risk, to-venture	geofenes	ocean, sea
geneþde	dare, risk, to-venture	geofian	gift, provide-with-benefits
geneþdon	dare, risk, to-venture		
gengan	go		
gengde	go	geofon	ocean, sea
gengdon	go	geofonhus	ocean-house, ship
genge	go, walk	geofum	gift, grace
gengword	complaint, lament, mournful-word	geogoð	youngster, youth
		geogoðe	youth

Word List (Ænglisc to English)

Ænglisc	English
geogoðfeore	youth
geogoðfeorh	youth
geogoðhad	youth-hood
geogoðhade	youth-hood
geogoþ	youngster, youth
geogoþe	youth
geogoþfeore	youth
geogoþfeorh	youth
geogoþhad	youth-hood
geogoþhade	youth-hood
geoguðe	youth
geoguðfeore	youth
geoguþ	youth
geoguþe	youth
geoguþfeore	youth
geolorand	yellow-shield
geolow	yellow
geolwe	yellow
geomor	miserable, sad, sadness
geomore	miserably, sadly
geomorfrod	miserable-with-age
geomorlic	miserable, sad
geomormod	miserable, miserable--minded, sad, sorrowful-in-mind
geomormode	miserable--minded, miserably, sad, sad-minded
geomormodum	miserable--minded, sad
geomorne	miserable, sad
geomorre	miserable, sad, sorrow
geomra	be-miserable, be-sad, mourn
geomran	miserable, sad
geomre	miserable, sad
geomres	mournful
geomrian	be-miserable, be-sad, mourn
geomrode	be-miserable, be-sad, mourn
geomuru	miserable, sad
geond	around, over, through, throughout
geondbrædan	spread-throughout
geondbræded	spread-throughout
geondfolen	completely-filled
geondhwearf	pass-through
geondhweorfan	pass-through
geondhweorfeð	pass-through
geondhweorfeþ	pass-through
geondsceawað	look-around
geondsceawaþ	look-around
geondsceawian	look-around
geondseh	look-over, survey
geondsendan	send-throughout
geondsended	send-throughout
geondseon	look-over, survey
geondsprengan	sprinkle-about
geondsprengde	sprinkle-about
geondþencan	consider, think-through
geondþence	consider, think-through
geondþenceð	consider, think-through
geondþenceþ	consider, think-through
geong	go, going, the-young, walk, young
geonga	young, young-man
geongan	young
geonge	young
geonges	youth's
geongne	young
geongon	go, walk
geongordom	allegiance, service
geongordome	allegiance, service
geongordomes	allegiance, service
geongra	a-servant follower, more-junior, subservient
geongum	young
geopenod	opened
georn	diligent, eager, serious
georne	diligent, eager, eagerly, earnestly, exactly, gladly, serious, very-eager, well
geornful	very-eager
geornlice	eagerly, exactly, gladly

Word List (Ænglisc to English)

Ænglisc	English	Ænglisc	English
geornor	destiny, eagerly, earnestly, exactly, gladly, well	gerena	adorned
		gereno	ornament
geosceaft	destiny, foreordination	gerenod	adorn, decorate, prepare-a-trick, set-a-trap
geosceaftgast	ancient-spirit, fated-spirit	gereord	speech, voice
		gereorda	hospitality
geosceaftgasta	ancient-spirit, fated-spirit	gereorded	speak, spoke
		gereordu	hospitality
geotan	flow, kill, pour, shed-blood	gereordum	feast, of-peoples
		geres	the-year's
geotena	flow, pour	gerestan	rest
geotende	flow, kill, pour, shed-blood	gerestest	rested
		geriht	assign, direct, set-up
gerad	able, control, float, ready, ride, sail	gerihte	a-right, duty, justice, law, obligation, rule, truth, what-is-right
gerade	able, ready		
geræcan	attain, get, obtain, reach	gerihtlæcan	make-straight
geræd	advise, instruct, make-decisions, rule	gerihtlæced	make-straight
		gerim	number
gerædde	advisement	gerisne	appropriate, fitting
gerædest	advise, instruct, make-decisions, rule	gerisno	what-is-appropriate
		gerume	broad, empty, expansive, roomy, spacious, un-oppressed, wide
gerædu	harness, trappings		
geræfa	prefect, reeve, steward		
geræhte	extend, get, give, obtain, offer, reach, reach-with-a-weapon, wound	gerumlicor	farther-away, liberally, widely
		gerymde	clear, enlarge, make-space-for, manifest, open-up
geræhton	extend, get, give, obtain, offer, reach, reach-with-a-weapon, wound	gerymdon	clear, enlarge, make-space-for, manifest, open-up
		gerymed	clear, enlarge, make-space-for, manifest, open-up
geræsde	attack		
gere	clearly, entirely, readily		
gerefa	prefect, reeve, steward	gerynum	mysteries
		gerysne	appropriate, fitting, what-is-appropriate
gerefan	prefect, reeve, steward	gerysnu	what-is-appropriate
geregnad	adorn, decorate, prepare-a-trick, set-a-trap	gesaca	enemy, opponent
		gesacan	enemy, opponent
		gesacu	battle, strife
geregnode	adorn, decorate, prepare-a-trick, set-a-trap	gesacum	enemy, opponent
		gesæd	say, spoken, tell
		gesæde	say, tell
geren	ornament	gesægd	say, tell

Word List (*Ænglisc* to English)

Ænglisc	English	*Ænglisc*	English
gesægde	say, tell	*gesceafta*	creation
gesæged	cause-to-fall, destroy, fell	*gesceafte*	creation
		gesceaftum	creatures
gesægon	observe, see	*gesceap*	action, arrange, creation, form, genitalia, shape
gesælde	cause-to-fall, destroy, fell, happen, sealed, take-place	*gesceapen*	arrange, create, design, make, shape
gesæled	bind, fetter, moor		
gesælige	blessed, blessedly, happily, happy	*gesceapene*	arrange, create, design, make
gesæliglic	blessed, happy	*gesceapo*	action, creation, form, genitalia, shape
gesæt	inhabit, live, one-sitting-beside, settle, sit	*gesceapu*	action, creation, form, genitalia, shape
gesætla	fellow-judge, one-sitting-beside	*gesceat*	dart-to, shoot, shoot-arrows, shot, throw-a-spear
gesætlan	fellow-judge, one-sitting-beside		
gesæton	inhabit, live, settle, sit	*gesceawað*	consider, look-upon, respect, show, show-consideration-for, showing
gesætte	appoint, create, establish, ordain, place, set, settle	*gesceawaþ*	consider, look-upon, respect, show, show-consideration-for
gesættnys	law		
gesættnysse	law		
gesætton	appoint, create, establish, ordain, place, set, settle	*gesceawod*	consider, consider-to-be, look-upon, respect, show, show-consideration-for
gesaga	say, tell		
gesawe	look, perceive, saw, see		
gesawon	look, perceive, see	*gesced*	decide, determine, divide, separate
gescad	discernment, separation, understanding	*gesceft*	creation
gescæphwil	appointed-time, appointed-while, death	*gesceod*	harm, injure
		gesceop	allot, arrange, assign, create, created, design, made, make
gescæphwile	appointed-time, appointed-while, death	*gescer*	allot, assign, cleave, cut, hew
gescær	cleave, cut, hew, shear	*gescerede*	allot, assign
gescaft	creation	*gesceþðan*	harm, injure
gesceaft	creation, creator, decree, the-created-world, world, worldly-creation	*gesceþþan*	harm, injure
		gescieppan	create, shape
		gescipe	fate
		gescod	harm, injure

113

Word List (Ænglisc to English)

Ænglisc	English
gescop	create, shape
gescopon	create, shape
gescot	launching, shooting, shot, throwing
gescotes	launching, shooting, shot, throwing
gescraf	impose, ordain, prescribe
gescyld	defend, protect, shield
gescylt	defend, protect, shield
gescype	arrange, create, design, make
gescyred	allot, allotted, assign, look, ordain
geseah	look, observe, perceive, see
geseald	consign, give, give-up, sell
gesealde	consign, gave, give, give-up, sell
gesealdon	consign, give, give-up, sell
gesec	attack, desire, go-to, seek, seek-out, visit, wish-for
gesecan	attack, desire, go-to, seek, seek-out, visit, wish-for
gesecanne	attack, desire, go-to, seek, seek-out, visit, wish-for
gesece	attack, desire, go-to, seek, seek-out, visit, wish-for
gesecean	attack, desire, go-to, seek, seek-out, visit, wish-for
geseceð	attack, desire, go-to, seek, seek-out, seeks, visit, wish-for
geseceþ	attack, desire, go-to, seek, seek-out, visit, wish-for
gesegan	look, perceive, see
gesegen	observe, see
geseglian	sail
geseglod	sail
geseglode	sail
gesegon	look, perceive, see
geselda	hall-companion
geseldan	hall-companion
gesellan	consign, give, give-up, sell
gesene	clear, evident, manifest
geseo	look, perceive, see
geseoð	look, perceive, see
geseon	look, observe, perceive, see
geseoþ	look, perceive, see
geset	seat
geseted	appoint, create, establish, ordain, place, set, settle
geseten	inhabit, live, settle, sit
gesetena	established
gesett	appoint, create, establish, ordain, place, set, settle
gesettan	appoint, establish
gesette	appoint, composed, create, establish, ordain, place, set, settle
gesettest	foundation
gesetton	appoint, create, establish, ordain, place, set, settle
gesetu	seat, settles
gesib	related
gesibb	kinsman, kinswoman, related, relative
gesibbra	kinsman, kinswoman, related, relative
gesibbum	kinsman, kinswoman, related, relative
gesicclod	become-sick
gesið	companion, company, follower
gesiða	companion, company, follower

Word List (*Ænglisc* to English)

Ænglisc	English	*Ænglisc*	English
gesiðas	companion, company, follower	*gesloh*	beat, erect-a-tent, forge, get-by-fighting, kill, obtain-by-killing, slay, strike
gesiððas	companion, company, follower		
gesiðða	companion, company, follower	*geslyht*	battle
		geslyhta	battle
gesiðes	companion, company, follower	*gesmyrode*	anoint, apply-a-lotion, embrocate
gesiðum	companion, company, follower	*gesne*	destitute, forlorn, lacking, without
gesiene	clear, evident, manifest	*gesoht*	desire, seek
gesigan	descend, fall, go, move, sink	*gesohtan*	attack, desire, go-to, seek, seek-out, visit, wish-for
gesihð	look, perceive, see, sight, sight-power, view, vision	*gesohte*	attack, desire, go-to, seek, seek-out, sought, visit, wish-for
gesihðe	sight, sight-power, view, vision		
gesihþ	look, perceive, see, sight, sight-power, view, vision	*gesohtest*	attack, desire, go-to, seek, seek-out, visit, wish-for
		gesohton	attack, desire, go-to, seek, seek-out, visit, wish-for
gesihþe	sight, sight-power, view, vision		
gesiþ	companion, company, follower	*gesohtun*	sought
		gesome	friendly, peaceable, united
gesiþa	companion, company, follower	*gesomnad*	assemble, congregate
gesiþas	companion, company, follower	*gesomnie*	assemble
gesiþes	companion, company, follower	*gesomnod*	assemble, congregate
gesiþþas	companion, company, follower	*gespæc*	say, speak
		gespan	fastening
gesiþþe	companion, companions, company, follower	*gespearn*	perch-upon
		gespedeð	be-speedy, be-successful, be-wealthy
gesiþum	companion, company, follower, together	*gespedeþ*	be-speedy, be-successful, be-wealthy
geslægene	beat, erect-a-tent, forge, kill, strike		
		gespeon	attach, fasten
geslean	get-by-fighting, obtain-by-killing	*gespeow*	succeed
		gespon	enticement, persuasion
geslegene	beat, erect-a-tent, forge, kill, strike	*gespong*	clasp, fastening
		gesponne	fastening
geslogon	get-by-fighting, obtain-by-killing, obtained-by-fighting	*gespræc*	say, speak, speak-to
		gespræce	say, speak, speak-to

Word List (*Ænglisc* to English)

Ænglisc	English	*Ænglisc*	English
gespræcon	say, speak, speaking, speak-to	*gesundne*	healthy, sound, whole
gespræconn	say, speak, speak-to, spoken-about	*gesundran*	healthy, sound, whole
gesprang	grow, leap, spread, spring, spurt	*gesundrod*	separate, sunder
		gesundrode	separate, sunder
gesprece	say, speak, speak-to	*gesupe*	sip
gesprong	grow, leap, spread, spring, spurt	*geswac*	abandon, betray, deceive, depart
gestæled	admit, confess	*geswæse*	beloved, dear, own, sweet
gestah	arise, ascend, climb, get-onto, mount	*geswearc*	become-gloomy, darken, grow-dark
gestaþelað	establish, found		
gestaþelade	establish, found	*geswence*	weary
gestaþelaþ	establish, found	*geswenced*	afflict, injure, torment
gestaþelod	establish		
gestaþelode	establish, found	*geswencte*	afflict, injure, torment
gesteal	foundation		
gestefnde	appoint, arrange, ordain	*gesweorc*	darkness, mist
		gesweorce	become-gloomy, darken, grow-dark
gestepte	advance, elevate, erect, raise, support	*gesweostor*	sister
gestigan	ascend, mount	*geswicað*	abandon, betray, deceive, depart, diminish
gestigen	ascend, mount		
gestigest	arise, climb, get-onto, mount	*geswicaþ*	abandon, betray, deceive, depart, diminish
gestigon	ascend, mount		
gestilled	to-still-cause-to-be-still	*geswiceð*	fail
gestod	be, exist, extend, remain, stand	*geswiðrod*	diminish, disappear, vanish
gestodon	be, exist, extend, remain, stand	*geswinc*	effort, hardship, labour
gestop	step	*geswincdæg*	hardship-day
gestreon	property, treasure, wealth	*geswinc-dæg*	day-of-toil
		geswincdagum	hardship-day
gestreona	property, treasure	*geswing*	clash, surge
gestrynan	acquire, beget, get	*geswiþrod*	diminish, disappear, vanish
gestrynde	acquire, beget, get		
gestsele	guest-hall	*geswutelod*	make-clear, make-manifest, reveal
gestylled	to-still-cause-to-be-still	*geswutelode*	make-clear, make-manifest, reveal
gestyran	direct, guide, rule		
gestyrde	guide, restrain	*geswyce*	turn-from
gesund	healthy, safe, sound, uncorrupted, unharmed, whole	*gesyhð*	look, perceive, see
		gesyhðe	sight, sight-power, view, vision
gesunde	healthy, sound, whole	*gesyhst*	look, perceive, see
		gesyhþ	look, perceive, see

Word List (*Ænglisc* to English)

Ænglisc	English	*Ænglisc*	English
gesyhþe	sight, sight-power, view, vision	geteohhian	appoint, arrange, assign, intend
gesylle	consign, give, give-up, sell	geteohhod	appoint, arrange, assign, intend
gesyne	clear, evident, manifest, seen	geteoþ	adorn, arrange, create, ordain, prepare
gesyngad	do-evil, sin		
gesynta	health, salvation, welfare	geþægon	accept, eat, partake-of, receive, take
gesynto	health, salvation, welfare	geþafa	a-consenter, ally, helper, supporter
gesyntum	health, salvation, welfare	geþafode	agree-to, consent, permitted
gesyrwed	equip-with-armour, plan, plot	geþah	accept, eat, endure, partake-of, prosper, receive, thrive, took thought
getacnod	betoken, show-by-signs	geþanc	
getæce	allot, assign, instruct, show, teach	geþancie	consider, thank
		geþancmeta	consider, think-about
getæhte	allot, assign, instruct, show, teach	geþancmetian	consider, think-about
getæhton	allot, assign, instruct, show, teach	geþancum	thanks, thought
getæl	number	geþeah	accept, eat, partake-of, receive, take
getæse	advantageous, agreeable	geþeaht	advice, scheme, thought
getalum	number	geþeahtne	be-stretched-out-upon, cover, cover-over
getan	flow, kill-by-shedding-the-blood-of, pour		
		geþearfod	have-occasion-to, need
geteah	bring, bring-up, draw-a-sword, educate, grant, take	geþegen	accept, receive, take
		geþenc	consider, imagine, intend, plan, think
getealdon	consider, count, reckon, tell, think		
geteld	tent	geþencan	think
geteled	consider, count, reckon, tell, think	geþencean	consider, imagine, intend, plan, think
getenge	near, on	geþenod	be-humiliated, serve
geteoð	adorn, arrange, create, ordain, prepare	geþeodde	enter-a-monastic-order, join
		geþeode	language
geteode	appoint, arrange, assign, intend	geþeoh	endure, prosper, thrive
geteoh	appoint, arrange, assign, bring, bring-up, draw-a-sword, educate, grant, intend, take	geþeon	endure, prosper, thrive
		geþicgan	accept, receive, take
		geþigen	prosper, thrive
		geþigon	prosper, thrive

Word List (*Ænglisc* to English)

Ænglisc	English	*Ænglisc*	English
geþinge	agreement, conclusion, settlement-term	geþring	crowding, thronging, tumult
geþingea	agreement, conclusion, settlement-term, term-of-settlement	geþruen	forged
		geþrungen	advance, press, press-forward, throng
geþinged	arrange, ask, determine, intend, intercede-for, settle, speak	geþuht	appear, seem, think
		geþuhton	appear, seem
		geþungen	distinguished, endure, excellent, grown, prosper, successful, thrive, virtuous
geþingeð	intend-to-go		
geþinges	agreement, conclusion, settlement-term, term-of-settlement		
		geþungon	excellent, successful, virtuous
		geþwære	obedient
geþingeþ	intend-to-go	geþyld	longsuffering, patience, patient
geþingo	agreement, conclusion, settlement-term, term-of-settlement		
		geþyldig	longsuffering, patient
		geþyldum	patience
geþingod	arrange, ask, determine, intend, intercede-for, settle, speak	geþywe	accustomed, usual
		getiðad	give, grant, tithe
		getigðode	give, grant
		getigþode	give, grant
geþingþo	office, rank	getimbro	building, material, timbering
geþoht	mind, thought, thoughts		
		getimode	happen
geþohtas	mind, thought, thoughts	getingnys	rhetoric
		getingnysse	rhetoric
geþohte	mind, thought	Getiþa	bestow
geþolian	allow, endure, forgo, lose, suffer	getiþad	give, grant, tithe
		getogen	bring, bring-up, draw-a-sword, educate, grant, take
geþolianne	allow, endure, forgo, lose, suffer		
geþolode	allow, endure, forgo, lose, suffer	getogene	educated
		getoht	battle
geþonce	thanks, thought	getohte	battle
geþoncum	thanks, thought	getreowe	believe
geþræc	force, host, pressure, violence	getreowra	faithful, true, trustworthy
geþrang	advance, battle-throng, crowd, press, press-forward, press-of-battle, throng, tumult	getrimede	address, arrange, comfort, exhort, ordain, prepare, strengthen
		getrum	company, troop
geþread	afflict, oppress	getrume	company, troop
geþreadne	afflict	getruwedon	make-an-agreement, trust

Word List (*Ænglisc* to English)

Ænglisc	English	*Ænglisc*	English
getruwode	make-an-agreement, trust	geweald	command, control, might, power
getruwodest	make-an-agreement, trust	gewealdan	control, govern, rule, wield
getrymmed	address, arrange, comfort, exhort, ordain, prepare, strengthen	gewealde	command, control, might, power
		gewealdene	control, govern, rule, wield
getrywð	believe, trust	gewealdenne	control, govern, rule, wield
getrywe	faithful, true, trustworthy	gewealdon	strengthen
getryweð	trusting	gewealdum	command, control, might, power, wielding
getrywþ	believe, trust		
getugon	drawing		
getwæfan	deprive-of, end, prevent, stop	gewearð	agreement, be, became, become, suit
getwæfde	deprive-of, end, prevent, stop	gewearþ	agreement, be, become, suit
getwæfed	deprive-of, end, prevent, stop	gewef	destiny
		gewegan	fight
getwæfeð	deprive-of, end, prevent, stop	gewelgad	enriched
		gewemde	defile, destroy, profane
getwæfeþ	deprive-of, end, prevent, stop	gewemmed	defile, destroy, profane
getwæman	hinder, separate		
getyþa	bestow		
geuðe	allow, grant, like, offer, wish	gewendan	alter, change, go, take-oneself, turn
geunnan	allow, grant, like, offer, wish	gewende	alter, change, flex-take-oneself, go, gore, take-oneself, turn
geunne	allow, grant, like, offer, wish		
geuþe	allow, grant, like, offer, wish	geweold	control, govern, rule, wield
gewac	be-useless, break, fail	geweoldum	control, govern, rule, wield
gewaden	go, move, wade	geweorc	construction, creation, work, working, workmanship
gewæde	armour, clothing		
gewædu	armour, clothing		
gewand	end, fly, go, result, twist, wave-in-a-circular-motion, wind	geweorces	construction, creation, work, workmanship
gewanod	diminish, wane, waste-away	geweorðad	cherish, give-worthiness-to, honour, worship
gewat	depart, departed, die, go, went-out		
gewealc	rolling, sea-swell, tossing	geweorðan	cherish, give-worthiness-to, honour, worship
gewealcen	toss-around		

Word List (*Ænglisc* to English)

Ænglisc	English	*Ænglisc*	English
geweorðod	cherish, give-worthiness-to, honour, worship	gewissode	advise, guide, point-out, show
geweorðode	cherish, honour, worship	gewit	depart, die, go
geweorkes	work	gewita	king's-councillor, wise-man, witness
geweornie	wither-away	gewitað	depart, die, go
geweorþad	cherish, give-worthiness-to, honour, worship	gewitan	depart, departed, die, go, king's-councillor, wise-man, witness
geweorþade	cherish, honour, worship	gewitaþ	depart, die, go
geweorþan	cherish, give-worthiness-to, honour, worship	gewite	depart, die, go
geweorþod	cherish, give-worthiness-to, honour, worship	gewiteð	depart, die, go, going
		gewiten	depart, go
geweorþode	cherish, honour, worship	gewitene	depart, die, go
		gewitenes	depart, departed, die, go
geweox	grow, increase	gewiteþ	depart, die, go, goes
gewered	clothe, cover, defend, protect	gewitloca	mind, understanding
		gewitlocan	mind, understanding, wit's-enclosure
gewergad	make-weary		
gewexen	grow, increase	gewitnad	punish, torment
gewiciað	camp	gewitnian	punish, torment
gewiciaþ	camp	gewiton	depart, die, go
gewidost	far-apart, most-widely-separated	gewitt	wit
		gewitte	consciousness, head, knowledge, understanding, wit
gewidre	storm		
gewidru	storm	gewittig	wise
gewin	contention, strife, struggle, war	gewlitegad	become-beautiful, become-bright, make-beautiful
gewindan	escape		
gewinn	battle, conflict, strife, struggle, war	gewlitegod	garnished, well-adorned
gewinnan	conquer, win	gewlo	ornamented
gewinne	contention, strife, struggle, war	gewod	go, move, wade
		geworden	agreement, be, become, suit
gewinnes	contention, strife, struggle, war	geworht	accomplish, achieve, carry-out, construct, create, do, make, perform, work
gewiofu	destiny		
gewis	certain, trustworthy		
gewisade	advise, guide, point-out, show		
gewislice	certainly, truly		
gewislicost	certainly, truly		
gewiss	certain, trustworthy		
gewissan	certain, trustworthy		

Word List (*Ænglisc* to English)

Ænglisc	English	*Ænglisc*	English
geworhte	accomplish, achieve, carry-out, construct, create, do, make, perform, work	gewundode	wound
		gewunedon	dwell, inhabit, live, remain
		gewunian	remain, remain-with, stand-by
geworhtest	created, worked	gewunigen	dwell, inhabit, live, remain
geworhtne	carry-out, create, do, make, work	gewunne	fight, gain, obtain, struggle, work
geworhton	carry-out, construct, create, do, make, work	gewunnen	fight, gain, obtain, struggle, work
		gewunod	remain-with, stand-by
gewræc	avenge, be-exiled, drive-out, exile, expel, punish, speak-about, utter	gewunode	remain-with, stand-by
		gewurde	been
gewrec	avenge, be-exiled, drive-out, exile, expel, punish, speak-about, utter	gewurðien	cherish, honour, worship
		gewurðnys	honour
		gewurðnysse	honour
gewrecen	avenge, be-exiled, drive-out, exile, expel, punish, speak-about, utter	gewurðod	cherish, honour, honoured, worship
		gewurþad	cherish, give-worthiness-to, honour, worship
gewrecene	avenge, be-exiled, drive-out, exile, expel, punish, speak-about, utter	gewurþe	become
		gewurþien	cherish, honour, worship
gewreged	accuse, stir-up	gewurþnys	honour
gewrit	book, document, letter-Scripture, writing	gewurþnysse	honour
		gewurþod	cherish, honour, worship
gewritu	book, document, letter-Scripture, writing	gewylnung	desire
		gewylnunga	desire
gewritum	writing	gewyrc	action, carry-out, create, do, make, struggle, work
gewrixle	bargain, exchange, receive-in-exchange, substitute, varying-words	gewyrcan	accomplish, achieve, carry-out, create, do, make, perform, work
gewrixled	exchange, exchange-of-words, substitute	gewyrce	carry-out, create, do, make, work
gewrohtest	created	gewyrcean	carry-out, create, do, make, work
gewrytum	book, document, letter-Scripture, writing	gewyrht	accomplished-deed, merit
gewundian	wound	gewyrhtum	accomplished-deed, merit
gewundod	wound		

Word List (Ænglisc to English)

Ænglisc	English	Ænglisc	English
gewyrpte	recover	giestum	guest, stranger
geywan	appear, present, reveal, show	giet	previously, still, yet
		gieta	previously, still, yet
gid	poem, song, speech	gif	if
gidd	poem, song, speech	gifa	gift, giver, grace
gidda	poem, song, speech	gifan	give
giddum	poem, song, speech	Gifðum	Gifthas (a-Germanic-people)
gied	poem, song, speech		
giedd	poem, riddle, song, speech, word	gife	gift, give, give-up, grace, grant, relinquish
giedde	poem, song, speech		
gief	give	gifeðe	give, given, give-up, grant, granted, lot, predetermined-situation, relinquish
giefað	give		
giefaþ	give		
giefe	given		
giefl	morsel, piece-of-food	gifen	give, give-up, grant, ocean, relinquish, sea
gieflum	morsel, piece-of-food	gifena	gift, grace
giefstol	gift-seat	gifest	give
giefstolas	gift-seat	gifeþe	give, give-up, grant, granted, lot, predetermined-situation, relinquish
giefu	favour, gift, grace		
gield	compensation, offering, substitute		
gieldan	pay, pay-back, repay, yield	gifheall	gift-hall
		gifhealle	gift-hall
gielde	compensation, offering, substitute	gifre	greedy, useful
		gifrost	greedy, most-greedy
giellan	yell	gifsceatt	gift
gielleð	yell	gifsceattas	gift
gielleþ	yell	gifstol	gift-dispensing-hall, gift-seat
gielp	boasting, pride		
gielpan	boast, exult	Gifþum	Gifthas (a-Germanic-people)
gielpes	boasting, pride		
gielpsceaþan	boasting, pride	giftum	gift
gieman	care-about, keep, keep-to, look-after	gifu	gift, give, given, giving, grace
gien	again, now, still, yet	gifum	gift, grace
giena	still, until-now, yet	gigant	giant
gieng	go, walk	giganta	giant
gierede	adorn, dress, equip, prepare	gigantas	giant, giants
		gigantmæcg	giant
gierwaþ	adorn, dress, equip, prepare	gigantmæcgas	giant
		gihuaes	compensation, each
giestas	guest, visitor	gild	compensation, offering, substitute
giestliðnyss	hospitality		
giestliðnysse	hospitality	gilp	boasting, pride
giestliþnyss	hospitality	gilpcwide	boasting-speech
giestliþnysse	hospitality		

Word List (*Ænglisc* to English)

Ænglisc	English	*Ænglisc*	English
gilphlæden	expert-in-giving-praise, loaded-with-boasting, praise-giving	gistmægen	guests, visiting-troop, visitors
		gistum	guest, stranger
		git	previously, still, yet, you-two
gim	gem, precious-jewel		
gimfæst	generous, huge, spacious	gitsian	be-greedy, covet
		gitsiende	be-greedy, covet
gimfæste	generous, huge, spacious	giunge	young
		giungne	ground-down
gimm	gem, precious-jewel	glad	bright, glide, glided, pleasant, shining, slide
gimmas	gem, precious-jewel		
gimmerice	jewel-kingdom		
ginfæst	generous, huge, spacious	gladiað	bright, pleasant, shine, shining
ginfæstan	generous, huge, spacious	gladian	shine
		gladiaþ	bright, pleasant, shine, shining
ginfæstum	generous, huge, spacious		
		gladu	bright, pleasant, shining
gingæste	youngest		
ginn	spacious, wide	gladum	bright, pleasant, shining
ginnan	spacious, wide		
ginne	spacious, wide	glæd	bright, pleasant, shining
gio	before, care, formerly, of-old, once, sad, sorrow	glæde	bright, pleasant, shining
giofan	give	glædlic	bright, pleasant, shining
giogoð	youth		
giogoðe	youth	glædlice	brightly, happily
giogoþ	youth	glædman	gracious, kind
giogoþe	youth	glædmod	happy, joyful, of-glad-mood
gioguðe	youth		
giogup	young-people, youth	glædmode	happy, joyful
gioguþe	youth	glædne	bright, pleasant, shining
giohðe	care, sorrow		
giohðo	care, sad, sorrow	glædstede	altar, glowing-coals
giohþe	care, sorrow	glæm	beauty, brightness, splendour
giohþo	care, sad, sorrow		
giomorgyd	lament, sad-song	glæmes	beauty, brightness, splendour
giomormod	miserable--minded, sad		
		glappan	buck-bean
giondwlitan	examine, look-over	glappe	buck-bean
giong	go, walk, young	gleam	beauty, splendour
giongorscipe	allegiance, service	gleaw	learned, prudent, skilful, wise
girwan	adorn, dress, equip, prepare		
		gleawan	skilful, wise
gisel	hostage	gleawe	skilful, wise
gist	guest, stranger	gleawferhð	discerning, prudent, wise
gistas	guest, stranger		

Word List (*Ænglisc* to English)

Ænglisc	English	*Ænglisc*	English
gleawferhþ	discerning, prudent, wise	gnyrn	complaint, outcry
gleawhydig	clever, intelligent, wise	god	advantage, benefit, excellent, god, God (name), God-heathen, good, goods, good-thing, pagan-god, property
gleawne	skilful, wise		
gleawra	skilful, wisdom, wise		
gleawum	skilful, wise		
gled	ember, glowing-coal	goda	advantage, benefit, gods, good, good-one, goods, good-thing, of-good, property
gledegesa	glowing-embers, horror-of-glowing-embers		
gledstyde	altar, glowing-coals		
gledum	ember, glowing-coal	godaes	advantage, good
gleo	entertainment, music	godan	advantage, benefit, good, good-one, goods, good-thing, property
gleobeam	entertainment-wood, harp, music-wood		
gleobeames	entertainment-wood, harp, music-wood	godas	God-heathen, Gods
		godcund	divine, sacred
gleodream	delight-in-entertainment, fun, joy	godcunde	divine, sacred
		godcundlic	divine, sacred
		godcundlicum	divine, sacred
gleoma	splendour	goddre	good-one
gleomann	minstrel, scop	gode	advantage, benefit, god, God (name), God-heathen, good, good-one, goods, good-thing, property, to-god
gleomannes	minstrel, scop		
glidan	glide, slide		
glidon	glide, slide		
glitinian	glint, shine		
gliwedon	make-delightful		
gliwian	make-delightful	godes	advantage, benefit, divine, give-property-to, God-heathen, God-heathen's, God's (name), good, good-doer, goods, good-thing, property, wellbeing
gliwstafum	joyously		
glof	glove		
glofe	the-glove		
Gloria	glory (Latin)		
gneað	frugal, miserly		
gneaþ	frugal, miserly		
gnorn	lamentation, mourning, sorrow		
gnornað	lament, mourn	godfæder	good-father
gnornaþ	lament, mourn	godfremmend	good-doer
gnorngende	lament, mourn	godfremmendra	good-doer
gnornian	lament, mourn	godian	give-property-to
gnornod	lament, mourn	godlecran	excellent, fair, goodly
gnornode	lament, lamentation, mourn, mourning, sorrow		
		godlic	divine, excellent, fair, godlike, goodly
gnornung	mourned	godlice	excellent, fair, goodly
gnornword	complaint, lament, mournful-word		

Word List (*Ænglisc* to English)

Ænglisc	English	*Ænglisc*	English
godne	advantage, benefit, good, good-one, goods, good-thing, property	*goldmaþmas*	golden-treasure
		goldsele	gold-hall
		goldsmiþe	goldsmith
		goldsmiþu	goldsmith
godnys	goodness, virtue	*goldweard*	gold-guardian, gold-lord, guardian-of-gold
godnysse	goodness, virtue		
godra	advantage, benefit, good, good-one, goods, good-thing, property	*goldwine*	gold-friend, gold-giving, i.e.-generous-lord
godspedig	rich, successful	*gold-wine*	gold-friend
godspellic	occurring-in-the-Gospels	*goldwlanc*	gold-proud, resplendent-with-gold
godspellicum	occurring-in-the-Gospels	*goma*	jaws, mouth
godsunu	godson	*goman*	jaws, mouth
godum	advantage, benefit, God-heathen, good, good-one, goods, good-thing, property	*gomban*	tribute, tribute-tribute
		gombe	
		gombon	tribute
		gomel	old
Godwine	Godwin (name)	*gomela*	old
gofol	tax, tribute	*gomelan*	old
gold	gold	*GomelaScilding*	Old-descendants-of-Scyld (name)
goldæht	golden-belongings		
goldbeorht	gold-adorned	*gomele*	old
goldburg	gilded-city	*gomelfeax*	grey-haired, old-haired
goldburgum	gilded-city		
golde	gold	*gomelra*	old
golden	pay, pay-back, repay, yield	*gomelswyrd*	old-worthy
		gomelum	old
goldes	gold	*gomen*	amusement, entertainment, joy, mirth, pastime, play, pleasure, sport
goldfag	decorated-with-gold, gilded		
goldfah	decorated-with-gold, gilded		
goldfahne	decorated-with-gold, gilded	*gomene*	amusement, joy, mirth, play, sport
goldgiefa	gold-giver, king	*gomenwaþ*	happy-journey, pleasure-trip
goldgiefan	gold-giver, king	*gomenwaþe*	happy-journey, pleasure-trip
goldgifa	gold-giver, king		
goldgifan	gold-giver, king	*gomenwudu*	harp, joy-wood
goldgyfa	gold-giver, king	*gomol*	old
goldgyfan	gold-giver, king	*gongan*	go, walk
goldhladen	gold-laden	*gonge*	go, walk
goldhroden	decorated-with-gold	*gongen*	go, walk
goldhwæte	eager-for-gold	*good*	good
goldmaðm	golden-treasure	*goodes*	good
goldmaðmas	golden-treasure	*Gotena*	the-Goths
goldmaþm	golden-treasure	*Got-land*	Goth-land

Word List (Ænglisc to English)

Ænglisc	English	Ænglisc	English
govern	national-territory	grenne	green
grædig	fierce, greedy, ravenous	grenre	green
		greot	cry, dust, earth, gravel, grit, sand
grædige	fierce, greedy, ravenous	greotan	cry
grædigne	greedily	greote	gravel, sand
græf	grave	greotende	cry
græg	grey	greoteþ	cry
grægan	grey	greow	flourish, grow
græge	grey	gretan	address, approach, attack, greet, injure, play-a-harp, speak-to, touch
græghama	grey-coat		
grægmæl	grey-in-colour, grey-marked		
græs	grass	greted	address, approach, attack, greet, injure, play-a-harp, speak-to, touch
græsmoldan	grass-covered, grass-covered-earth		
græsmolde	grass-covered-earth		
gram	angry, angry-one, hostile, the-devil, the-evil-one, warrior	greteð	address, attack, greet, injure, play-a-harp, speak-to, touch
grama	anger, rage		
graman	anger, angry, angry-one, hostile, rage, the-devil, the-evil-one, warrior	greteþ	address, attack, greet, injure, play-a-harp, speak-to, touch
grame	angry, angry-one, hostile, the-devil, the-evil-one, warrior	grette	address, approach, attack, greet, injure, play-a-harp, speak-to, touch
gramena	angry, angry-one, hostile, the-devil, the-evil-one, warrior	gretton	address, attack, greet, injure, play-a-harp, speak-to, touch
grames	angry, angry-one, hostile, the-devil, the-evil-one, warrior		
		grið	peace, truce
gramum	angry, angry-one, hostile, the-devil, the-evil-one, warrior	grim	bitter, dire, fierce, grim, savage, severe
grap	grasp, handgrip, seize, take	grima	face-protector, metal-mask
grape	grasp, handgrip	grimhelm	face-protector, helmet
grapian	grasp, seize, touch		
grapode	grasp, seize, touch	grimhelmas	face-protector, helmet, helmet-with-a-metal-face-protector
grapum	grasp, handgrip		
great	great, huge, large		
greate	great, huge, large		
gremian	anger, enrage	grimlic	fierce, grim, savage
grenan	green	grimma	bitter, dire, fierce, savage, severe
grene	green		
grenes	green		

Word List (Ænglisc to English)

Ænglisc	English
grimman	be-fierce, bitter, dire, fierce, rage, savage, savagely, severe
grimme	bitter, dire, fierce, fiercely, grim, grimly, savage, severe, severely
grimmeð	be-fierce, rage
grimmeþ	be-fierce, rage
grimmon	face-protector, metal-mask
grimne	bitter, dire, fierce, savage, severe
grimre	bitter, dire, fierce, savage, severe
grindan	grind, sharpen
grindel	bar, bolt
grindlas	bar, bolt
gripan	grasp, seize, take
gripe	attack, grasp, onslaught, seize, take
gripeð	grasp, seize, take
gripen	grasp, seize
gripeþ	grasp, seize, take
gripon	grasp, seize, take
gristbitian	gnash-one's-teeth
griþ	peace, truce
grome	angry, angry-one, hostile, the-devil, the-evil-one, warrior
gromheort	angry-hearted, hostile
gromhydig	angry-hearted, angry--minded, hostile
gromra	angry, angry-one, hostile, the-devil, the-evil-one, warrior
growan	flourish, grow
groweð	grows
growende	flourish, grow
growendra	flourish, grow
grummon	clamour
grund	bottom, earth, ground, sea-bottom
grundas	earth, ground, sea-bottom, the-floor, the-ground
grundbuend	earth-dweller
grundbuendra	earth-dweller
grunde	earth, ground, sea-bottom, the-ground
grundes	earth, ground, sea-bottom
grundhyrde	bottom-ruler
grundleas	bottomless
grundlease	bottomless, without-end
grundleasne	bottomless
grundsele	sea-bottom-hall
grundwela	earth-joy, earth-wealth
grundwelan	earth-joy, earth-wealth
grundwong	area-of-ground, bottom-surface, ground-bottom, sea-bottom
grundwyrgen	bottom-dwelling-criminal, outlaw
grundwyrgenne	bottom-dwelling, bottom-dwelling-criminal, outlaw
grymetende	roaring
grymma	grim
grymme	fiercely, severely
grynn	affliction, grief, injury
grynna	affliction, grief, injury
gryra	horror, terror, violence
gryre	horror, terror, violence
gryrebroga	terror
gryrefah	horribly-coloured
gryrefahne	horribly-coloured, terribly-coloured
gryregeatwe	terrifying-armour
gryregeatwum	terrifying-armour
gryregiest	terrifying-visitor
gryregieste	terrifying-visitor
gryregist	terrifying-visitor
gryreleoð	song-of-terror, terror-song
gryreleoða	terror-song
gryreleoþ	song-of-terror, terror-song
gryreleoþa	terror-song

Word List (*Ænglisc* to English)

Ænglisc	English	*Ænglisc*	English
gryrelic	terrible	*guðhere*	army, Guthere's (name)
gryrelicne	terrible		
gryresið	terrible-expedition	*guðhergum*	army
gryresiðas	terrible-expedition	*guðhorn*	war-horn
gryresiþ	terrible-expedition	*guðhreð*	victory-in-battle
gryresiþas	terrible-expedition	*guðkyning*	war-king
gryrum	horror, terror, violence	*guðlaf*	battle-remaining
		Guðlafes	Guthulf's (name)
guð	battle, combat, war	*guðleoð*	martial-anthem, war-song
guða	combat, war		
guðbeorn	warrior	*guðplega*	martial-sport, war-play
guðbill	battle-bill, sword		
guðbilla	battle-bill, sword	*guðræs*	attack
guðbord	shield, war-board	*guðræsa*	attack
guðbordes	shield, war-board	*guðreouw*	fierce-in-battle
guðbyrne	battle-mail-coat, battle-shield, mail-coat	*guðrinc*	warrior
		guðrinca	warrior
		guðrof	brave-in-battle, renowned-in-battle
guðceare	battle-churl, battle-misery		
		guðsceaða	martial-injurer, warlike-enemy
guðcearu	battle-misery		
guðcræft	battle-strength, skill-in-war	*guðscear*	carnage, slaughter
		guðsceare	carnage, slaughter
guðcyning	war-king	*guðsceorp*	armour-and-weapons, martial-equipment
guðdeað	death-in-battle		
guðe	combat, fight, war		
Guðere	Guthere (name)	*guðsearo*	armour, war-trappings, weapons
guðfana	war-banner		
guðfanum	war-banner	*guðsele*	battle-hall
guðflan	spear, war-arrow	*guðspell*	battle-account
guðflana	spear, war-arrow	*guðsweord*	battle-sword
guðfloga	battle-flyer, dragon	*guðþracu*	violence, warlike-attack
guðflogan	battle-flyer, dragon		
guðfreca	warrior	*guðþræce*	violence, warlike-attack
guðfrecan	warrior		
guðfremmend	warrior	*guðþreat*	war-troop
guðfremmendra	warrior	*guðum*	combat, war
guð-Geata	battle-Geat	*guðweard*	warlord
guðgeatawum	armour, battle-gear	*guðwerig*	combat-weary, dead
guðgemot	battle, combat	*guðwerigne*	combat-weary, dead, weary-from-combat
guðgetawa	armour, battle-gear		
guðgetawe	armour, battle-gear		
guðgewæda	armour	*guðwiga*	warrior
guðgewæde	armour	*guðwine*	ally, friend-in-battle
guðgewædo	armour	*guðwinum*	ally, friend-in-battle
guðgewædu	armour	*guðwudu*	spear-wood
guðgeweorca	action-in-battle	*guldan*	paid
guðhafoc	excessive-appetite	*guldon*	pay, pay-back, repay, yield
guðhelm	battle-helmet		

Word List (*Ænglisc* to English)

Ænglisc	English	*Ænglisc*	English
gulpon	boast, exult	*guþfloga*	battle-flyer, dragon
guma	hero, man, men, person	*guþflogan*	battle-flyer, dragon
		guþfreca	warrior
guman	man, men, person	*guþfrecan*	warrior
gumcynn	the-human-race	*guþfremmend*	warrior
gumcynne	the-human-race	*guþfremmendra*	warrior
gumcynnes	the-human-race	*guþ-Geata*	battle-Geat
gumcynnum	the-human-race	*guþgeatawum*	armour, battle-gear
gumcyst	excellence, virtue	*guþgemot*	battle, combat
gumcyste	excellence, virtue	*guþgetawa*	armour, battle-gear
gumcystum	excellence, virtue	*guþgetawe*	armour, battle-gear
gumdream	human-joy, joy, pleasure	*guþgewæda*	armour
		guþgewæde	armour
gumdryhten	troop-lord	*guþgewædo*	armour
gumena	man, men, person	*guþgewædu*	armour
gumfeþa	troop-men	*guþgeweorc*	action-in-battle
gummann	man	*guþgeweorca*	action-in-battle
gummanna	man	*guþhelm*	battle-helmet
gumrinc	man	*guþhere*	army
gumrincum	man	*guþhergum*	army
gumstol	hall, men-seat, troop-seat	*guþhorn*	war-horn
		guþhreþ	victory-in-battle
gumstole	hall, men-seat, seat-of-men, troop-seat	*guþkyning*	war-king
		guþlaf	battle-remaining, Guthlaf (name)
gumþeod	nation, people		
gumþeoda	nation, people	*guþleoþ*	martial-anthem, war-song
gumum	man, person		
guþ	battle, combat, war	*guþmod*	warlike
guþa	combat, war	*guþplega*	martial-sport, war-play
guþbeorn	warrior		
guþbill	battle-bill, sword	*guþræs*	attack
guþbilla	battle-bill, sword	*guþræsa*	attack
guþbord	shield, war-board	*guþreouw*	fierce-in-battle
guþbordes	shield, war-board	*guþrinc*	warrior
guþbyrne	battle-mail-coat, battle-shield, mail-coat	*guþrinca*	warrior
		guþrof	brave-in-battle, renowned-in-battle
guþceare	battle-churl, battle-misery	*guþscear*	carnage, slaughter
		guþsceare	carnage, slaughter
guþcearu	battle-misery	*guþsceaþa*	martial-injurer, warlike-enemy
guþcræft	battle-strength, skill-in-war		
		guþsceorp	armour-and-weapons, martial-equipment
guþcyning	war-king		
guþdeaþ	death-in-battle		
guþe	combat, war	*guþsearo*	armour, war-trappings, weapons
guþfana	war-banner		
guþfanum	war-banner	*guþsele*	battle-hall
guþflan	spear, war-arrow	*guþspell*	battle-account
guþflana	spear, war-arrow	*guþsweord*	battle-sword

Word List (Ænglisc to English)

Ænglisc	English	Ænglisc	English
guþbracu	violence, warlike-attack	gylp	boast, boasting, pride
guþbræce	violence, warlike-attack	gylpan	boast
guþþreat	war-troop	gylpe	boast, boasting, exult, pride
guþum	combat, war	gylpeð	boast
guþweard	warlord	gylpeþ	boast
guþwerig	combat-weary, dead	gylpplega	boasting-sport
guþwerigne	combat-weary, dead, weary-from-combat	gylpplegan	boasting-sport
		gylpspræc	boasting-speech
		gylpspræce	boastful-speech, boasting-speech
guþwiga	warrior		
guþwine	ally, friend-in-battle	gylpword	boastful-speech
guþwinum	ally, friend-in-battle	gylpworda	boastful-speech
gy	yet	gylpwordum	boastful-speech
gyd	poem, song, speech	gylt	crime, guilt, sin
gydd	poem, song, speech	gyltum	crime, faults, guilt, sin
gyddian	make-a-speech, speak		
gyddode	make-a-speech, speak	gym	care-about, keep, keep-to, look-after
gyddum	poem, song, speech	gyman	care-about, keep, keep-to, look-after
gydenan	goddess	gymden	care-about, keep, keep-to, look-after
gydene	goddess		
gyf	give, give-up, grant, if, relinquish	gymdon	care-about, keep, keep-to, look-after
gyfan	give	gymeð	care-about, keep, keep-to, look-after
gyfe	gave		
gyfeðe	granted	gymeþ	care-about, keep, keep-to, look-after
gyfen	give, give-up, grant, ocean, relinquish, sea	gynn	spacious, wide
		gynne	spacious, wide
gyfenes	ocean, sea	gyrdan	girded, weapon-fastened
gyfeþe	give, give-up, grant, granted, relinquish	gyrde	adorn, dress, dressing, equip, prepare, staff
gyld	compensation, offering, pay-back, repay, substitute		
		gyrded	girded, weapon-fastened
gyldan	all-golden, completely-gilded, pay-back, repay	gyrede	adorn, dress, equip, prepare
gylden	gilded, gilt, golden	gyredon	adorn, dress, equip, prepare
gyldenhilt	golden-hilt		
gyldenne	gilded, gilt, golden	gyrla	apparel, dress
gyldnum	gilded, gilt, golden	gyrlan	apparel, dress
gylede	shout, yell	gyrn	affliction, desire, grief, injury, yearn-for
gylian	shout, yell		
gylleð	yells		
gyllende	yell, yelling	gyrnan	desire, yearn-for

Word List (*Ænglisc* to English)

Ænglisc	English
gyrnde	desire, yearn-for
gyrne	complaint, outcry
gyrnwracu	revenge-for-injury
gyrnwræce	injury-wreak, revenge, revenge-for-injury
gyrwað	adorn, dress, equip, prepare
gyrwan	adorn, dress, equip, prepare
gyrwaþ	adorn, dress, equip, prepare
gyse	yes
gysel	hostage
gyst	guest, stranger
gystað	be-greedy, covet
gystas	guest, stranger
gystaþ	be-greedy, covet
gyste	guest, guest-house, guest-room, stranger
gystern	guest-house, guest-room
gysterne	guest-house, guest-room
gystran	yesterday
gystum	guest, stranger
gyt	be-greedy, covet, previously, still, yet, you-two
gyta	previously, still, yet
gytesæl	drinking-happiness
gytesalum	drinking-happiness
gytsað	be-greedy, covet
gytsaþ	be-greedy, covet
gytsian	be-greedy, covet

H, h

Ænglisc	English
habbað	have
habban	have, having, possess, to-have
habbaþ	have
habben	have
had	family, gender, nature, office, position
hade	family, gender, nature, office, position
hades	family, gender, nature, office, position, the-order
hador	bright, brightly, brightness, clear
hadre	brightly, brightness
hæahsetle	high-seat
hæbbað	have
hæbbaþ	have
hæbbe	have
hæðe	the-heath
hæðen	heathen, pagan
hæðenan	heathen, pagan
hæðencynn	heathen-nation, pagan-people
hæðene	heathen, pagan
hæðenes	heathen, pagan
hæðenra	heathen, pagan
hæðenscype	paganism
hæðne	heathen, pagan
hæðnum	heathen, pagan
hæðstapa	heath-walker
hæf	ocean, sea
hæfd	have, possess
hæfð	have
hæfde	had, have, possess
hæfdon	have
hæfen	lift, raise-up
hæfst	have
hæft	bind, captive, captivity, fetter, haft, hilt, slave
hæftan	bind, fetter
hæfte	haft, hilt
hæfteclommum	binding-chains
hæfþ	have
hæftmece	hafted-sword
hæftnyd	captivity, slavery
hæfton	bind, captive, hilt, slave
hægel	hail
hægl	hail
hægles	hail
hæglfare	hail-storm
hæglfaru	hail-storm

Word List (*Ænglisc* to English)

Ænglisc	English
hægsteald	young-man, young-warrior
hægstealdas	young-warriors
hægstealdmann	young-warrior
hægstealdmen	young-warrior
hægstealdra	young-man, young-warrior
hægtessan	witch, witchery
hægtesse	witch
hæl	healthy, hero, man, safe, sound, warrior, whole
hælæð	hero, man, warrior
hælæþ	hero, man, warrior
hælan	comfort, heal, make-whole
hældon	comfort, heal, make-whole
hæle	cure, healing, health, hero, man, salvation
hæleð	hero, heroes, man, men, warrior
hæleða	hero, man, of-men, warrior
hæleðhelm	helmet-of-invisibility, heroic-helmet
hæleðum	hero, man, to-men, warrior
hælend	saviour, the-Saviour
hælende	the-Saviour
hælendes	the-Saviour
hælendne	saviour
hæleþ	hero, heroes, man, warrior
hæleþa	hero, heroes, hero's, man, warrior
hæleþas	hero, man, warrior
hæleþhelm	helmet-of-invisibility, heroic-helmet
hæleþum	hero, man, warrior
hælo	cure, good, healing, health, healthy, salvation, sound
hælon	hit
hælu	cure, healing, health, salvation
hæman	have-sex-with
hæmed	fornication, sexual-intercourse
hæmede	fornication, sexual-intercourse
hæncgest	horse, steed
hær	hair
hærfest	harvest
hærgtraf	heathen-temple
hærgtrafum	heathen-temple
hæs	behest, bidding, command
hæse	bidding, command
hæst	violence, violent
hæste	violence, violently
hæstne	violent
hæþen	heathen, pagan
hæþena	heathen, pagan
hæþenan	heathen, pagan
hæþencynn	heathen-nation, pagan-people
hæþene	heathen, pagan
hæþenes	heathen, pagan
hæþenra	heat, heathen, heathenry, pagan, paganism
hæþenscype	paganism
hæþne	heathen, pagan
hæþnum	heathen, pagan
hæþstapa	heath-walker
hæto	heat
hættode	scalped
hafa	have
hafað	has, have, having, head, holds, they-have
hafala	head
hafalan	head
hafast	have
hafaþ	has, have, head
hafelan	head
hafen	lift, raise-up
hafenade	brandish, raise
hafenian	brandish, lift-up, raise
hafenod	lift-up, raise
hafenode	brandish, lift-up, raise
hafest	you-have
hafo	have

Word List (*Ænglisc* to English)

Ænglisc	English
hafoc	hawk
hafu	have, ocean, sea
Hafuc	hawk
haga	enclosure
hagan	enclosure
hagle	hail
hagol	hail
hagosteald	young-man, young-warrior
hagostealdes	young-man, young-warrior
hal	healthy, safe, sound, unhurt, whole
halan	healthy, safe, sound, whole
hale	healthy, safe, sound, whole
haleg	consecrated, holy
halegu	consecrated, holy, saint, the-holy-one
haleted	hail, salute
halettan	hail, salute
halette	hail, salute
halga	consecrated, holy, saint, the-holy-one
halgad	hallowed
halgan	consecrated, holy, saint, the-holy-one
halgena	consecrated, holy, saint, the-holy-one
halgian	bless, consecrate, dedicate
halgodest	hallowed
halgum	consecrated, hallowed, holy, saint, the-holy-one
halgungboc	holy-book
halig	consecrated, holy, saint, the-holy-one
haligan	consecrated, holy, saint, the-holy-one
haligdomes	holy-judgement
halige	consecrated, holy, saint, the-holy-one
haliges	consecrated, holy, saint, the-holy-one
haligne	holy
haligra	holy, saints
haligre	consecrated, holy, saint, the-holy-one
haligum	holy
haligwæter	holy-water
haligwætere	holy-water
halre	virtuous
hals	neck
halse	neck
halsfæst	intimately?-earnestly?
halsige	beseech
ham	dwelling, estate, home, homewards
hama	covering, garment, home
haman	covering, garment
hamas	dwelling, estate, home, homes
hame	dwelling, estate, home
hamelode	mutilated
hamer	hammer
hamere	hammer
hames	dwelling, estate, home
hamora	hammers
hamsittende	living-at-home
hamsittendra	living-at-home
hamsittendum	living-at-home
hamweorðung	honour-done-to-a-home
hamweorðunge	honour-done-to-a-home
hamweorþung	honour-done-to-a-home
hamweorþunge	honour-done-to-a-home
hand	hand, hand-to-hand-combat, side
handa	hand, hand-to-hand-combat, side
handæ	hand, hand-to-hand-combat, side
handbana	hand, hand-killer, hand-to-hand-killer
handbanan	hand, hand-killer, hand-to-hand-killer
handbona	hand, hand-killer, hand-to-hand-killer

Word List (*Ænglisc* to English)

Ænglisc	English
handbonan	hand, hand-killer, hand-to-hand-killer
handgesceaft	creation, handiwork
handgestealla	close-companion, comrade
handgesteallan	close-companion, comrade
handgeweorc	creation, handiwork
handgewriþen	hand-twisted
handgewriþene	hand-twisted
handgyft	wedding-gift
handlean	hand-revenge, repayment, reward
handmægen	bodily-might
handon	hand, hand-to-hand-combat, side
handplega	fighting, hand-play, martial-sports
handplegan	fighting, hand-play, martial-sports
handrof	brave-in-action, renowned-for-action
handrofra	brave-in-action, renowned-for-action
handscale	hand-picked-troop
handscalu	hand-picked-troop
handspor	claw
handsporu	claw
handum	hand, hand-to-hand-combat, side
handweorc	creation, handiwork
handwurmes	hand-worm's
hangað	hang
hangaþ	hang
hangella	hanging-thing
hangian	hang
hangode	hang
har	grey, grey-haired, hoary, old-man
hara	grey, hoary, old-man
Haraldes	Harald (name)
hare	grey, hoary, old-man
hares	grey, hoary, old-man
harne	grey, hoary, old, old-man
harum	grey, hoary, old-man
harungdæg	old-age-day
harungdagas	old-age-day
hasewanpadan	hazel-feathered-ones
hasu	grey
haswe	grey
hat	be-named, call, command, enticing, exiting, fervent, fervid, heat, hot, hotly, intense, name, promise
hatað	be-named, call, command, name, named, promise
hatan	be-named, call, command, enticing, exiting, fervent, hot, intense, name, order, promise
hataþ	be-named, call, command, name, promise
hate	be-named, call, command, enticing, exiting, fervent, hot, hotly, intense, name, named, promise
haten	be-named, call, called, command, name, order, promise
hatene	be-named, call, command, name, promise
hates	enticing, exiting, fervent, hot, intense
hatheort	headstrong, hot-hearted, rash
hatian	attack, hate, persecute, treat-with-hatred
hatne	enticing, exiting, fervent, hot, intense
hatode	attack, hate, persecute, treat-with-hatred
haton	enticing, exiting, fervent, hot, intense

Word List (*Ænglisc* to English)

Ænglisc	English
hatost	enticing, exiting, fervent, hot, hottest, intense
hatran	enticing, exiting, fervent, hot, intense
hattæ	is-named
hatte	be-named, call, command, name, promise
hauest	have
he	exalted, he, high, it, she
hea	exalted, high
heaburh	high-principal-city
heaðobyrne	battle-mail-coat
heaðodeor	brave-in-battle
heaðofyr	battle-flame, violent-flame
heaðofyrum	battle-flame, violent-flame
heaðogrim	battle-grim
heaðolac	battle--play
heaðolace	battle--play
heaðolaces	battle--play
heaðoliðendum	expedition, travelling-soldiers
heaðomære	battle-famous
heaðoræs	battle-onslaught
heaðoræsa	battle-onslaught
heaðoreaf	war-equipment, weapons
heaðorinc	warrior
heaðorincas	warrior
heaðorinces	warrior
heaðorincum	warrior
heaðorof	battle-brave
heaðoscearp	battle-sharp
heaðoscearpe	battle-sharp
heaðosioc	sick-from-battle, wounded
heaðosiocum	sick-from-battle, wounded
heaðosteapne	battle-tall
heaðotorht	battle-bright, challenging, clear
heaðowæd	armour-suit
heaðowædum	armour-suit
heaðowelm	violent-flame
heaðoweorc	battle-work

Ænglisc	English
heaðowylm	violent-flame
heaðowylma	violent-flame
heaðowylmas	violent-flame
heaðufyr	battle-flame, violent-flame
heaðufyres	battle-flame, violent-flame
heaðusweng	battle-blow, stroke
heaðuswenge	battle-blow, stroke
heaf	lamentation, wailing
heafde	chief, face, head, leader, top
heafdon	chief, head, leader, top
heafdum	chief, head, leader, top
heafena	heaven
heafo	ocean, sea
heafoc	hawk
heafod	chief, head, leader, top
heafodbeorg	head-protection
heafodbeorge	head-protection
heafodgerim	head-count
heafodgerimes	head-count
heafodmæg	chief, head
heafodmægum	chief, head
heafodmaga	chief, head
heafodsien	eye, eyesight, vision
heafodsiene	eye, eyesight, vision
heafodswima	intoxication, swimming-head
heafodsyne	eye, eyesight, vision
heafodweard	chief-leader, death-watch, head-watch
heafodweardas	chief-leader
heafodwearde	death-watch, head-watch
heafodwisa	chief-master, originator
heafola	head
heafolan	head
heafu	ocean, sea
heagum	exalted, high
heah	exalted, high
heahan	high
heahcining	high-king
heahcininges	high-king
heahcyninc	high-king

Word List (*Ænglisc* to English)

Ænglisc	English
heahcyning	high-king
heahcyninges	high-king
heahfæder	God-the-Father, high-father
heahfædere	God-the-Father, high-father
heahflod	deep-water, flood
heahfyr	big-fire, high
heahgeræfan	chief-overseer
heahgerefa	chief-overseer
heahgerefan	chief-overseer
heahgesceaft	noble-creation
heahgesceafta	noble-creation
heahgesceap	high-destiny
heahgestreon	exalted-treasure
heahgestreona	exalted-treasure
heahgetimbro	high-buildings
heahkyning	high-king
heahlufan	high-love, noble-love
heahlufu	high-love, noble-love
heahne	exalted, high
heahnisse	high-ness
heahran	superior
heahreced	citadel, high-building, temple
heahrodor	the-high-heaven
heahrodore	the-high-heaven
heahsele	high-hall
heahsetl	high-seat, throne
heahsteap	tall, towering
heahstede	high-place
heahstefn	high-stemmed
heahþrea	tremendous-calamity
heahþrymnesse	great-glory
heal	hall
healærn	hall--building
healærna	hall--building
heald	hold, keep, rule
healdað	hold, keep, rule
healdan	hold, keep, preserve, retain, rule
healdaþ	hold, keep, rule
healde	hold, keep, rule
healdeð	hold, keep, rule
healðegn	hall-warrior, retainer
healðegnas	hall-warrior, retainer
healðegnes	hall-warrior, retainer
healdend	owner, ruler
healdest	hold, keep, rule
healdeþ	hold, keep, rule
healf	half, part, side
healfa	half, side
healfe	half, side
healfne	half
healfre	half, side
healgamen	enjoyment, hall-entertainment, hall-games
healic	haughty, noble, proud
heall	hall
healle	a-hall, hall
healp	help
healreced	hall--building
heals	neck
healsbeag	necklace, neck-ring
healsbeaga	necklace, neck-ring
healsbeah	necklace, neck-ring
healsbege	necklace, neck-ring
healse	neck
healsgebedda	intimate-bed-fellow
healsian	beseech, entreat
healsittend	hall-inhabitant, hall-sitter
healsittendra	hall-inhabitant, hall-sitter
healsittendum	hall-inhabitant, hall-sitter
healsmægeð	beloved-woman
healsmægeþ	beloved-woman
healsode	beseech, entreat
healþegn	hall-warrior, retainer
healþegnas	hall-warrior, retainer
healþegnes	hall-warrior, retainer
healwudu	hall-wood
hean	abject, depressed, exalted, high, humiliated, lowly, miserable
heane	humiliated, lowly, miserable
heanlic	humiliating, shameful

Word List (*Ænglisc* to English)

Ænglisc	English
heanne	exalted, high, humiliated, lowly, miserable
heanum	exalted, high
heap	heap, host, multitude
heape	heap, host, multitude
heapum	heap, host, hosts, multitude
hearan	superior
heard	hard, miserable, stern, strong, tough, warrior
hearda	hard, miserable, tough, warrior
heardan	hard, miserable, tough, warrior
hearde	firmly, greatly, hard, miserable, severely, tough, warrior
heardecg	hardened-edge, sword
heardes	hard, miserable, tough, warrior
heardgripe	firm-gripped
heardhicgende	resolute, stern, tough-minded
heardlice	hard, vigorously
heardmod	resolute, tough-minded
heardmode	resolute, tough-minded
heardne	hard, hard-warrior, miserable, tough, warrior
heardost	hard, miserable, tough, warrior
heardra	hard, miserable, tough, warrior
heardræd	constant, firm
heardrædne	constant, firm
heardran	hard, miserable, tough, warrior
heardsælig	unhappy, unlucky
heardsæligne	unfortunate, unhappy, unlucky
heardum	hard, miserable, tough, warrior
heare	exalted, high
hearh	heathen-shrine
hearm	damage, harm, insult, misery, pain
hearma	damage, harm, insult, misery, pain
hearmas	damage, harm, insult, misery, pain
hearmcwyde	condemnation, curse
hearme	damage, harm, insult, misery, pain
hearmes	damage, harm, insult, misery, pain
hearmloca	harmful-enclosure
hearmlocan	harmful-enclosure
hearmplega	fight, harmful-struggle
hearmscaþa	destructive-enemy, harmful-attacker
hearmsceare	evil-allotment, evil-share, punishment
hearmscearu	evil-allotment, evil-share, punishment
hearmstæf	harm
hearmstafas	harm
hearmtan	harmful-or-evil-twig
hearmtanas	harmful-or-evil-twig
hearpan	harp
hearpe	harp
hearra	as-a-superior, leader, lord
hearran	superior
heaþobyrne	battle-mail-coat
heaþodeor	brave-in-battle
heaþodeorum	brave-in-battle
heaþofyr	battle-flame, violent-flame
heaþofyrum	battle-flame, violent-flame
heaþogeong	warlike
heaþogrim	battle-grim
heaþolac	battle--play
heaþolace	battle--play
heaþolaces	battle--play
heaþoliðend	expedition, travelling-soldiers
heaþoliðende	expedition, travelling-soldiers

Word List (Ænglisc to English)

Ænglisc	English
heaþolinde	battle-wood
heaþoliþend	expedition, travelling-soldiers
heaþoliþende	expedition, travelling-soldiers
heaþoliþendum	expedition, travelling-soldiers
heaþomære	battle-famous
heaþoræs	battle-onslaught, battle-rush
heaþoræsa	battle-onslaught
heaþoreaf	war-equipment, weapons
heaþorinc	warrior
heaþorincas	warrior
heaþorinces	warrior
heaþorincum	warrior
heaþorof	battle-brave
heaþorofe	battle-brave
heaþoscearp	battle-sharp
heaþoscearpe	battle-sharp
heaþosioc	sick-from-battle, wounded
heaþosiocum	sick-from-battle, wounded
heaþosteap	battle-tall
heaþosteapa	battle-tall
heaþosteapne	battle-tall
heaþoswat	battle-blood
heaþoswata	battle-blood
heaþoswate	battle-blood
heaþotorht	battle-bright, challenging, clear
heaþowæd	armour-suit
heaþowædum	armour-suit
heaþowelm	violent-flame
heaþoweorc	battle-work
heaþowylm	violent-flame
heaþowylma	violent-flame
heaþowylmas	violent-flame
heaþufyr	battle-flame, violent-flame
heaþufyres	battle-flame, violent-flame
heaþusweng	battle-blow, stroke
heaþuswenge	battle-blow, stroke
heaum	exalted, high
heawan	cut, cut-down, hew, kill
heawen	cut-down, hew, kill
hebban	lift, raise-up
heben	care-about, heaven
hedan	care-about
hedde	care-about
hefaenricaes	heaven-kingdom's, lift
hefeð	lift, raise-up
hefene	heaven
hefeþ	lift, raise-up
hefian	heavy, oppressive, painful
hefig	heavy, oppressive, painful
hefige	heavy, oppressive, painful
hefigran	heavy, oppressive, painful
hefoncyninges	heaven-king
hefone	heaven
hefonrices	heaven-kingdom
hegan	achieve, perform
hehðe	glory, height, highest-point
hehðu	glory, height, highest-point
hehra	superior
hehsta	highest, most-high
hehstan	highest, most-high
hehste	highest, most-high
hehstne	highest, most-high
heht	be-named, call, command, commanded, commands, name, order, promise
hehþe	glory, height, highest-point
hehþu	glory, height, highest-point
hel	conceal, hide
helan	conceal, hide
helde	allegiance
heldor	hell-gate
heldora	hell-gate
heleða	healing
helend	healer
hellbend	hell-bond
hellbendum	hell-bond

Word List (*Ænglisc* to English)

Ænglisc	English
helldor	hell-door, hell-gate
helldora	hell-door, hell-gate
helle	fell, hell
hellebryne	hell-burning
helleheaf	hell-lamentation, hell-wailing
helleheafas	hell-lamentation, hell-wailing
hellesceaða	devil, hellish-enemy
hellesceaþa	devil, hellish-enemy
hellewite	hell-pain, hell-torment
hellewites	hell-pain, hell-torment
hellfirena	hell-fire-like
hellgeþwing	hell-torture
hellme	handle
hellsceaða	devil, enemy-from-hell, fiendish-enemy
hellsceaþa	devil, enemy-from-hell, fiendish-enemy
helltrega	hell-misery, hell-torment
helltregum	hell-misery, hell-torment
helm	cover, defence, helmet, lord, protection
helmas	defence, helmet, lord, protection
helmberend	helmet-wearer, warrior
helme	defence, helmet, lord, protection, shield
helmes	defence, helmet, lord, protection
helmum	defence, helmet, lord, protection
help	help
helpan	help, to-help
helpe	aid, help
helpend	help
helruna	demon, hell-inhabitant
helrunan	demon, hell-inhabitant
helsceaðan	devil, hellish-enemy
helsceaþan	devil, hellish-enemy
Hengest	Hengest (name)
heo	he, it, once, she, they
heodæg	today
Heodeninga	Hedening's (name)
heofena	heaven, of-heaven, of-heavens
heofenas	heaven
heofenes	heaven
heofenlic	heavenly
heofenstolas	the-heavens
heofenum	heaven, the-heavens
heofna	heaven, heaven's
heofne	heaven
heofnes	heaven
heofnum	heaven
heofon	heaven, sky
heofona	heaven
heofonas	heaven, heaven's
heofoncyning	heaven-king
heofoncyninge	heaven-king
heofoncyninges	heaven-king
heofones	heaven, heaven's
heofonfugel	heaven-bird
heofonfugla	heaven-bird
heofonfuglas	heaven-bird
heofonlic	heavenly
heofonlican	heavenly
heofonlicne	heavenly
heofonrice	heaven-kingdom
heofon-rice	kingdom-of-heaven
heofonrices	heaven-kingdom, heaven-kingdom's, heavenly-structure
heofontimber	heavenly-structure
heofonum	heaven, heaven-guardian
heofonweard	heaven-guardian, heaven-lord
heofonweardes	heaven-guardian, heaven-lord
heold	hold, keep, preserve, retain, rule
heoldan	hold, keep, rule
heolde	held, hold, keep, rule
heoldon	held, hold, keep, preserve, retain, rule

Word List (*Ænglisc* to English)

Ænglisc	English
heolfor	blood, gore
heolfre	blood, gore
heolfrig	bloody, gory
heoloþhelm	cloak-of-invisibility, helmet-of-invisibility
heoloþhelme	cloak-of-invisibility, helmet-of-invisibility
heolster	concealment, darkness, hiding-place
heolstor	concealment, confining, cover, dark, darkness, hiding-place
heolstorsceado	concealing-darkness
heolstran	confining, dark
heolstre	concealment, dark, darkness, from-here, hiding-place
heonan	from, from-here, hence
heonane	from-here, hence
heonengange	from-here, from-here-goes
heonon	from-here, hence
heonone	from-here, hence
heononweard	disappearing, going-away
heora	it, their
heorawulfas	battle-wolf, warrior
heord	care, custody
heorð	area-surrounding-a-fireplace, hearth
heorðe	area-surrounding-a-fireplace, hearth
heorðgeneat	hearth-companion
heorð-geneat	hearth-companion
heorðgeneatas	hearth-companion
heorðgeneatum	hearth-companion
heorðwerod	hearth-troop
heore	pleasant, secure
heorodreore	blood, sword-gore
heorodreorig	bloody, combat-blood-drenched
heorodreorigne	bloody, combat-blood-drenched
heorogifre	battle-greedy
heorogrim	battle-grim
heorohocyht	sword-hooked
heorohocyhtum	sword-hooked
heoroswealwe	battle-swallow, hawk
heorosweng	sword-stroke
heorot	deer, hart, stag
heorowearh	sword, violent-outlaw
heorowulf	battle-wolf, sword, violent-outlaw, warrior
heorr	hinge
heorra	as-a-superior, leader, lord
heorras	hinge
Heorrenda	Heorrenda (name)
heort	hart, stag
heortan	heart
heorte	heart
heorþ	area-surrounding-a-fireplace, hearth
heorþe	area-surrounding-a-fireplace, hearth
heorþgeneat	hearth-companion
heorþ-geneat	hearth-companion
heorþgeneatas	hearth-companion
heorþgeneatum	hearth-companion
heorþwerod	hearth-troop
heortlufan	heart-of-love
heortum	heart
heoru	pleasant, secure, sword
heorudreor	blood, sword-gore
heorudreore	blood, sword-gore
heorugrimm	battle-grim
heorugrimme	battle-grim
heoruwæpen	sword, sword-weapon
heoruwæpnum	sword, sword-weapon
heow	cut, cut-down, hew, kill
heowan	hewed
heowon	cut, cut-down, hew, kill
heowun	hew
her	here, here-living
herbuende	here-living
herbuendra	here-living
here	army, enemy-army, host, multitude

Word List (*Ænglisc* to English)

Ænglisc	English	*Ænglisc*	English
herebroga	war-terror	*herewædum*	army-garment, mail-coat
herebrogan	war-terror	*herewæsm*	martial-vigour, warlike-stature
herebyrne	battle-mail-shirt	*herewæsmun*	martial-vigour, warlike-stature
herecist	selected-war-troop	*herewæpa*	warrior
hereciste	selected-war-troop	*herewæpan*	warrior
herecyste	selected-war-troop	*herewic*	military-encampment
hered	extol, praise	*herewicum*	military-encampment
herede	extol, praise	*herewisa*	war-leader
heredon	praise	*herewosa*	savage-warrior
herefleman	from-behind	*herewosan*	savage-warrior
herefolc	army	*herewulf*	battle-wolf, warrior
herefolces	army	*herg*	altar, hell, idol, pagan-temple, residence, sacred-grove
herefugol	army-bird, war-bird	*herga*	army, host, multitude
herefugolas	army-bird, war-bird	*hergan*	army, honour
heregeatu	war-equipment, weapons-and-armour	*hergas*	armies, army, host, multitude
heregrima	war-mask	*herge*	army, host, multitude, praise
heregriman	war-mask	*hergen*	praise
herehuþ	booty, loot, war-spoils	*herges*	army, host, multitude
herehuþe	booty, loot, plunder, war-spoils	*hergian*	attack, harry, plunder, raid, ravage
herelafum	battle-leavings	*hergode*	attack, harry, plunder, raid, ravage
heremæcgas	warrior	*hergum*	altar, army, hell, host, idol, multitude, pagan-temple, residence, sacred-grove
heremecg	warrior		
herenes	praise		
herenet	army-net, mail-coat		
herenið	armed-conflict		
hereniþ	armed-conflict		
herepad	army-coat, mail-coat		
herereaf	plunder, war-spoils		
hererinc	warrior		
heresceaft	spear, war-shaft		
heresceafta	spear, war-shaft		
heresceorp	war-dress		
heresped	success-in-war		
herestræl	army-arrow		
herestræt	war-road	*herheard*	altar, idol, pagan-temple, residence, sacred-grove
herestræta	war-road		
heresweg	martial-sound		
heresyrcan	army-mail-coat		
heresyrce	army-mail-coat	*heriað*	praise
hereteam	booty	*herian*	extol, praise
hereteame	booty	*herige*	army, host, multitude, praise
herewæd	army-garment, mail-coat	*herigean*	honour, praise
herewæða	warrior	*herigen*	praise
herewæðan	warrior		

Word List (*Ænglisc* to English)

Ænglisc	English	*Ænglisc*	English
heriges	army, host, multitude	*hi*	a, consider, it, the, they, think, this
heroden	praise	*hicgan*	consider, think
herodon	praise	*hicgeaþ*	think
herpað	path-for-an-army, swath-cut-through-opponents	*hider*	here, hither, to-here, to-this-world
		hie	he, it
herpaþ	path-for-an-army, swath-cut-through-opponents	*hiera*	it
		hieran	belong, hear, obey
herra	as-a-superior, leader, lord	*hierde*	belong, hear, obey
		hiered	belong, hear, obey
herran	elevate, make-higher, superior	*hierran*	superior
		hig	it, they
herteames	booty	*hige*	intention, it, mind, thought
herum	hair	*higeðoncol*	clever, intelligent, thoughtful
het	be-named, bid, call, command, commanded, name, ordered, promise	*higeðoncolre*	clever, intelligent, thoughtful
		higefrod	wise
hete	be-named, call, command, enmity, hate, name, promise	*higefrofer*	consolation
		higegleawe	wise-soul
		higemæðum	mind-wearying, weary-minded
hetelic	hateful	*higemæþum*	mind-wearying, weary-minded
hetend	enemy, hater		
hetende	enemy, hater	*higerof*	brave-minded
hetenið	enmity-act, hate-act, hateful-attack	*higerofe*	brave-minded
		higerofne	brave-minded
heteniðas	enmity-act, hate-act, hateful-attack	*higes*	intention, mind, thought
heteniþ	enmity-act, hate-act, hateful-attack	*higesorg*	mental-sorrow
		higesorga	mental-sorrow
heteniþas	enmity-act, hate-act, hateful-attack	*higeteonan*	hostility, insult
hetespræc	hateful-speech	*higeþihtig*	strong-minded
hetespræce	hateful-speech	*higeþihtigne*	strong-minded
hetesweng	hostile-blow	*higeþoncol*	clever, intelligent, thoughtful
heteswengeas	hostile-blow		
heteþanc	hateful-thought	*higeþoncolre*	clever, intelligent, thoughtful
heteþancum	hateful-thought		
heteþoncol	hostile, malevolent	*higeþryð*	pride
heteþoncolne	hostile, malevolent	*higeþryðe*	pride
heton	be-named, call, command, name, order, promise	*higeþrymm*	bravery, courage
		higeþrymmum	bravery, courage
		higeþryþ	pride
Hettend	enemies, enemy, persecutor	*higeþryþe*	pride
		higetreow	faithfulness
hettendra	enemy, persecutor	*higetreowa*	faithfulness
hettendum	enemy, persecutor		

Word List (Ænglisc to English)

Ænglisc	English	Ænglisc	English
higum	intention, mind, thought	hildeleoma	light-of-battle, light-of-dragon-flame, sword
hiht	hope, joy, trust		
hihte	trust	hildeleoman	light-of-battle, light-of-dragon-flame, sword
hihtful	hope-full, joy-full		
hihtfulne	hope-full, joy-full		
hihtleasne	despairing, without-hope	hildeleoþ	battle-song
		hildemeceas	warrior
hihtlic	hopeful, joyous	hildemecg	warrior
hild	battle, combat, war	hildemecgas	warrior
hilda	battles	hildenædran	arrow, battle-snake
hilde	battle, combat, of-battle, war	hildenædre	arrow, battle-snake
		hilderæs	attack-in-battle
hildebil	battle-bill, sword	hilderand	battle-shield
hildebill	battle-bill, sword	hilderandas	battle-shield
hildebille	battle-bill, sword	hilderinc	warrior
hildeblac	sword-pale	hilderinca	warrior
hildebord	battle-board, shield	hilderincas	warrior
hildebordum	battle-board, shield	hilderince	warrior
hildecalla	herald	hilderinces	warrior
hildecumbor	war-banner	hildesceorp	armour, battle-equipment, weapons
hildecyst	band-of-picked-men, battle-troop		
hildecystum	band-of-picked-men, battle-troop	hildesetl	battle-seat, saddle
		hildestrengo	battle-strength
hildedeor	brave-in-battle	hildeswat	battle-sweat, blood, perhaps-its-fiery-breath, perhaps-poison
hilde-deor	battle-bold		
hildedior	brave-in-battle		
hildediore	brave-in-battle		
hildefreca	warrior	hildesweg	war-noise
hildefrecan	warrior	hildetux	battle-tooth
hildegeatwa	armour-and-weapons, war-equipment	hildetuxum	battle-tooth
		hildewæpen	battle-weapon
		hildewæpnum	battle-weapon
hildegeatwe	armour-and-weapons, war-equipment	hildewisa	military-leader
		hildewisan	military-leader
		hildewulf	battle-wolf, warrior
hildegicel	battle-icicle	hildewulfas	battle-wolf, warrior
hildegicelum	battle-icicle	hildfreca	warrior
hildegrædig	battle-greedy	hildfrecan	warrior
hildegrædige	battle-greedy	hildfruma	battle-leader
hildegrap	battle-grip	hildfruman	battle-leader
hildehlæmm	battle-crash	hildlata	cowardly
hildehlæmmum	battle-crash	hildlatan	cowardly
hildehlemm	battle-crash	hildþracu	battle-violence
hildehlemma	battle-crash	hildþræce	battle-violence
hildeleoð	battle-song	hilt	sword-hilt
		hilte	sword-hilt
		hilted	hilted

Word List (*Ænglisc* to English)

Ænglisc	English	*Ænglisc*	English
hiltum	sword-hilt	*hit*	appearance, he, it, she, this, your
him	family-members, for-his, he, him, himself, his, it, last, she, them, they, to-him	*hiw*	appearance, colour, form, hue
		hiwa	hues
hina	family-members	*hiwan*	family-members
hindan	behind, the-rear	*hiwe*	appearance, colour, form
hindema	last		
hindeman	last	*hiwian*	disguise
hine	eager-to-get-away, he, him, himself, it, she, they	*hiwum*	family-members
		hladan	burden, laden, load, take-in
hinfus	eager-to-get-away	*hlade*	burden, laden, ladle, load, take-in
hiniongae	from-here-goes		
hinionge	death, from-here-goes	*hladen*	burden, laden, load, take-in
hinnsið	death, departure	*hlæder*	ladder, stairs
hinnsiþ	death, departure	*hlædræ*	ladder, stairs
hinsiðe	death, departure	*hlæfdian*	lady, mistress
hinsiþ	death, departure	*hlæfdigan*	lady, mistress
hinsiþe	death, departure	*hlæfdige*	lady, mistress
hio	it	*hlæst*	burden, load
hiofan	lament	*hlæstan*	adorn, load, weigh-down
hiofen	heaven		
hiofena	heavenly	*hlæste*	burden, load
hiofende	lament	*hlæw*	barrow, graveyard, hill, mound, mounds
hiofenrices	heaven's-kingdom		
hiold	hold, keep, rule	*hlæwe*	barrow, den, graveyard, hill, mound
hiora	it		
hiorodrync	sword-drink, wound		
hiorodryncum	sword-drink, wound	*hlaf*	bread, lady, loaf
hioroserce	battle-mail-coat, sword-mail-coat	*hlafdian*	lady, mistress
		hlafdige	lady, mistress
hiorosercean	battle-mail-coat, sword-mail-coat	*hlaford*	husband, lord, master
hioroweallan	violently-boil-or-surge	*hlaforde*	husband, lord
		hlafordes	husband, lord
hioroweallende	violently-boil-or-surge	*hlafordleas*	without-a-lord
		hlafordlease	without-a-lord
hiowbeorht	hue-bright	*hlafordum*	husband, lord
hira	it, their	*hlafurd*	lord
hire	a, her, it	*hlamm*	resound, roar
hired	family, household, monastic-community, retinue	*hlanc*	lank, lean
		hlanca	lank, lean
		hlaw	barrow, graveyard, hill, mound
hiredmann	house-man		
hiredmen	house-man	*hlawe*	barrow, graveyard, hill, mound
his	he, his, it, she, this		

Word List (*Ænglisc* to English)

Ænglisc	English	*Ænglisc*	English
hleahtor	jubilation, laughter, mirth	*hleorberg*	face-protection, face-protector
hleapan	gallop, leap, mount-a-horse	*hleorbergan*	face-protection, face-protector
hleapeð	gallop, leap, mount-a-horse	*hleorbolster*	pillow
hleapeþ	gallop, leap, mount-a-horse	*hleosceorp*	protective-clothing, protective-ornament
hleat	get, obtain, receive-by-lot, to-cast-lots	*hleosceorpe*	protective-clothing, protective-ornament
hlehhan	laughing	*hleotan*	get, obtain, receive-by-lot, to-cast-lots
hlemmeð	crash, crashes, resound, roar	*hleoþa*	cliff, hill, slope
		hleoþo	cliff, hill, slope
hlemmeþ	crash, resound, roar	*hleoþor*	language, song, sound, speech, voice
hlencan	mail-coat		
hlence	mail-coat		
hleo	covering, lord, protecting, protection, protective-board, protector, refuge, shelter	*hleoþorcwydas*	word
		hleoþorcwyde	word
		hleoþorstede	conversation-place
		hleoþrade	speak
		hleoþre	language, speech, voice
hleobord	protective-board	*hleoþrian*	speak
hleobordum	protective-board	*hleoþrode*	speak, spoke
hleoburh	protective-city, stronghold	*hleoþrum*	language, speech, voice
hleoðo	cliff, hill, slope	*hleoþu*	cliff, hill, slope
hleoðor	language, song, sound, speech, voice	*hleow*	covering, lord, protection, protector, refuge
hleoðorcwydas	word	*hleowfeðer*	protecting-wing
hleoðorcwyde	word	*hleowfeðrum*	protecting-wing
hleoðorstede	conversation-place	*hleowfeþer*	protecting-wing
hleoðrade	speak	*hleowfeþrum*	protecting-wing
hleoðre	language, speech, voice	*hleowlora*	one-lacking-protection
hleoðrian	speak	*hleowstol*	protecting-city
hleoðrode	speak, spoke	*hleowstole*	protecting-city
hleoðrum	language, speech, voice	*hlid*	roof, vault
hleoðu	cliff, hill, slope	*hlið*	cliff, hill, slope
hleomæg	protecting-kinsman	*hliðe*	cliff, hill, slope
hleo-mæg	protector-kinsman	*hliðes*	cliff, hill, slope
hleomæges	protecting-kinsman	*hlifade*	loom, stand-tall, tower
hleomaga	protecting-kinsman	*hlifian*	loom, stand-tall, tower
hleomagum	protecting-kinsman		
hleonian	cover, shelter	*hlifigan*	loom, stand-tall, tower
hleor	face		

Word List (*Ænglisc* to English)

Ænglisc	English	*Ænglisc*	English
hlifige	loom, stand-tall, tower	hlynsode	make-music, resound
hlifigean	loom, stand-tall, tower	hlystan	listen
		hlytm	lot
hlihende	laugh	hlytme	lot
hlihhan	laugh	Hnæf	Hnaef (name)
hlimbed	rest-bed	Hnæfe	Hnaef (name)
hlimman	crash, resound, roar	hnægan	humble, humiliate
hlimmeð	crash, resound, roar	hnægde	address, attack
hlimmeþ	crash, resound, roar	hnag	bend-down, bent-down, bow, humble, ignoble, illiberal, lowly, mean, sink-down
hlinduru	confining-door, door		
hlioðo	cliff, hill, slope		
hlioðorcwidum	voice		
hlioþo	cliff, hill, slope		
hlisfullice	excellently, honourably, reputably	hnagran	bent-down, humble, ignoble, illiberal, lowly, mean
hliþ	cliff, hill, slope	hnah	bend-down, bent-down, bow, humble, ignoble, illiberal, lowly, mean, sink-down
hliþe	cliff, hill, slope		
hliþes	cliff, hill, slope, the-cliffs		
hliuade	loom, stand-tall, tower		
		hnahran	bent-down, humble, ignoble, illiberal, lowly, mean
hlodon	burden, laden, load, take-in		
hloh	laugh	hneaw	miserly, stingy
hlud	loud, noisy	hneawlice	in-a-miserly-way, stingily
hludast	loudest		
hlude	loud, loudly, noisy	hnigan	bend-down, bow, sink-down
hludne	loud, noisy		
hlummen	resound, roar	hnigon	bend-down, bow, sink-down
hlummon	crash, resound, roar		
hlumon	resound, roar	hnitan	clash-together
hlutor	clear, pure	hniton	clash-together
hluttrum	clear, pure	ho	hang, suspend
hlydan	be-noisy, make-noise	hoðma	concealment, darkness
hlydde	be-noisy, make-noise	hoðman	concealment, darkness
hlyn	din, music, roar, sound	hoe	headland, heel
		hof	building, court, dwelling, house, lift, raise-up
hlynede	roar, shout		
hlynian	roar, shout		
hlynnan	roar, shout	hofe	building, dwelling, house
hlynneð	clashes		
hlynode	roar, shout	hofu	building, dwelling, dwellings, house
hlynsian	make-music, resound	hofum	building, dwelling, house

Word List (Ænglisc to English)

Ænglisc	English
hogedon	intend, resolve, wish-for
hogian	intend, resolve, wish-for
hogod	resolve, think
hogode	intend, resolve, think, wish-for
hogodon	intend, resolve, wish-for
hoh	headland, heel, promontory
hohful	anxious, thoughtful, troubled
hol	hole
hold	faithful, favourable, generous, gracious, loyal, of-a-lord, of-a-retainer
holde	faithful, generous, gracious, loyal, of-a-lord, of-a-retainer
holdlice	holding
holdne	faithful, generous, gracious, loyal, of-a-lord, of-a-retainer
holdost	faithful, generous, gracious, loyal, of-a-lord, of-a-retainer
holdra	faithful, generous, gracious, loyal, of-a-lord, of-a-retainer
holinga	without-cause
holm	ocean, water
holma	ocean, water
holmærn	sea-building, ship
holmærna	sea-building, ship
holmas	ocean, water
holmclif	sea-cliff
holmclife	sea-cliff
holmclifu	sea-cliff
holme	island, ocean, water
holmes	ocean, water
holmmægen	sea-might
holmmægne	sea-might
holmwylm	sea-current, sea-surge, sea-wave
holmwylme	sea-current, sea-surge, sea-wave
holt	forest, wood
holte	forest, the-woods, wood
holtes	forest, wood
holtwudu	forest, grove, timber, wood
holunge	in-vain, without-reason
homer	hammer
homera	hammer
hon	hang, suspend
hond	hand, hand-to-hand-combat, side
honda	hand, hand-to-hand-combat, side
hondgemot	battle, hand-meeting
hondgemota	battle, hand-meeting
hondgesella	close-companion
hondgesellum	close-companion
hondgestealla	close-companion, comrade
hondgesteallan	close-companion, comrade
hondgeweorc	creation, handiwork
hondgeweorce	creation, handiwork
hondlocen	hand-linked
hondplegan	hand-play
hondræs	hand-onslaught, hand-to-hand-combat
hondscole	hand-picked-troop
hondslyht	battle, counterattack
hondsweng	hand-thrust, sword-stroke
hondum	hand, hand-to-hand-combat, side
hondwundor	hand--made-wonder, marvel
hondwundra	hand--made-wonder, marvel
hongað	hang
hongaþ	hang
hongiað	hang
hongiaþ	hang
hopian	expect, hope
hord	a-hoard, hoard, treasure, treasures
hordærn	hoard-building, treasury

Word List (*Ænglisc* to English)

Ænglisc	English	*Ænglisc*	English
hordærna	hoard-building, treasury	horwyrðe	hoard-worthy, treasure-worthy
hordærne	hoard-building, treasury	horwyrþe	hoard-worthy, treasure-worthy
hordburh	treasure-city	hos	band, company
hordcofa	treasure-chamber, treasury	hose	band, company
		hosp	insult, reproach
hord-cofa	hoard-cove, treasure-chamber	hoþma	concealment, darkness
hordcofan	treasure-chamber, treasury	hoþman	concealment, darkness
horde	hoard, treasure	hra	carrion, corpse, corpses
hordes	hoard, treasure		
hordfate	vessel	hraðe	hasty, immediately, quick, quickly
hordgestreon	hoard-treasure		
hordgestreona	hoard-treasure	hræd	hasty, quick
hordgestreonum	hoard-treasure	hrædding	deliverance, rescuers
hordlocan	hoard-lock		
hordmadum	hoard-treasure	hræddinge	deliverance, rescuers
hordweard	dragon, hoard-guardian, treasurer, usually	hrædlice	quickly, speedily
		hræðre	heart, mind, spirit
hordwela	hoarded-treasure, hoard-wealth	hrædwyrde	hasty-speech, hasty-words, quick-worded
hordwelan	hoarded-treasure, hoard-wealth		
		Hræfen	raven
hordweorþung	hoard-worthiness, treasure	hræfn	ravens
		hrægl	clothing, garment
hordweorþunge	hoard-worthiness, treasure	hrægla	clothing, garment
		hrægle	clothing, garment
hordwynn	hoard-delight, hoard-treasure	hrægles	clothing, garment
		hræs	carrion, corpse, corpses
hordwynne	hoard-delight, hoard-treasure		
		hræþe	immediately, quickly
hordwyrðne	hoard-worthy, treasure-worthy	hræþre	heart, mind, spirit
		hræw	carrion, corpse, corpses
hordwyrþne	hoard-worthy, treasure-worthy		
		hrafyl	slaughter
horn	horn	hran	affect, injure, touch
hornas	horns	hraþe	hasty, immediately, quick, quickly
hornboga	horn-bow		
hornbogan	horn-bow	hraþor	immediately, quickly
horngestreon	pinnacles	hream	noise, outcry
hornreced	gabled-building	hreame	noise, outcry
hornsele	gabled-hall	hreas	be-ruined, fall, sink
hornum	horn	hreaw	carrion, corpse, corpses, distress, grieve
hors	horse		
hors-þegn	horse-thane		

Word List (Ænglisc to English)

Ænglisc	English
hreawic	battlefield, corpse-place
hreð	glory, victory
hreðe	cruel, harsh, immediately, quickly, terrible
hreðeadegost	the-most-awesome
hreðer	heart, mind, spirit
hreðerloca	spirit-chamber, the-body
hreðerlocan	spirit-chamber, the-body
hreðra	heart, mind, spirit
hreðre	heart, mind, spirit
hreðsigor	victory
hreðsigora	victory
hrefn	raven
hrefne	raven
hreman	cry-out
hremge	boastful, exultant
hremig	boastful, exultant
hremige	exultant
hremm	raven
hremmas	raven
hreo	fierce, rough, savage, violent, wild
hreof	rough-in-texture
hreofum	rough, rough-in-texture
hreoh	fierce, rough, storm, tempest, violent
hreohmod	sad, troubled
hreon	fierce, rough, violent
hreopon	cry, scream, shout
hreorge	ruined
hreosan	be-ruined, fall, sink
hreosende	be-ruined, fall, sink
hreoum	fierce, rough, violent
hreow	grieving, sorrow
hreowa	grieving, sorrow
hreowan	distress, grieve
hreowcearig	miserable, sad-minded
hreoweð	distress, grieve
hreoweþ	distress, grieve
hreowig	miserable, sad
hreowige	miserable, sad
hreowigmod	grieving-minded, sad-or-grieving-mind
hreowigmode	grieving-minded
hreowlice	cruelly
hrepian	touch
hrepode	touch
hreran	move, stir, stir-up
hrerde	move, stir
hrered	move, stir
hreþ	glory, victory
hreþe	cruel, harsh, immediately, quickly, terrible
hreþer	heart, mind, spirit
hreþerbealo	mental-distress
hreþerloca	spirit-chamber, the-body
hreþerlocan	spirit-chamber, the-body
hreþra	heart, mind, spirit
hreþre	heart, mind, spirit
hreþsigor	victory
hreþsigora	victory
hricg	back, ridge, spine, surface
hrið	snow-storm
hrim	frost, hoar-frost, rime
hrimceald	frosty-cold
hrim-ceald	frosty, ice-cold
hrimcealde	frosty-cold
hrime	hoar-frost, rime
hrimgicel	icicle
hrim-gicel	icicle
hrimgicelum	icicle
hrimigost	frostiest
hrinan	affect, injure, touch
hrincg	back, ridge, spine, surface
hrinde	frost-covered
hrine	affect, injure, touch
hring	link-in-a-chain-or-in-chainmail, ring
hringa	link-in-a-chain-or-in-chainmail, ring
hringan	clang, clank, ring
hringas	link-in-a-chain-or-in-chainmail, ring, rings
hringboga	coiled-creature, dragon, ring-loop

Word List (Ænglisc to English)

Ænglisc	English
hringbogan	coiled-creature, dragon, ring-loop
hringde	ring-made
hringdon	clang, clank, ring
hringe	back, chain, ridge, ring, spine, surface
hringed	ring-made
hringedstefna	ring-stemmed-ship
hringedstefnan	ring-stemmed-ship
hringiren	chainmail, ring-iron
hringloca	chainmail, ring-iron
hringlocan	chainmail, ring-iron
hringmæl	ring-ornamented
hringmæled	ring-ornamented
hringmere	ringed-pool
hringnaca	ring-prowed-ship
hringnet	mail-coat, ring-net
hringsele	ring-hall, treasure-hall
hringþege	ring-receiving
hringþegu	ring-receiving
hringum	link-in-a-chain-or-in-chainmail, ring
hringweorðung	neck-ring-wearing
hringweorðunge	neck-ring-wearing
hringweorþung	neck-ring-wearing
hringweorþunge	neck-ring-wearing
hrinon	affect, injure, touch
hriþ	snow-storm
hroden	adorned, covered, decorated, redden
hroðor	benefit, pleasure
hroðra	benefit, pleasure
hroðre	benefit, pleasure
hrof	helmet-crown, roof, sky-roof
hrofas	roofs
hrofe	a-roof, helmet-crown, sky-roof
hrofes	helmet-crown, sky-roof
hrofsele	roofed-hall
hronfisc	whale
hronfixas	whale
hronrad	the-sea, the-whale-road
hron-rad	sea, whale-road
hronrade	the-sea, the-whale-road

Ænglisc	English
hropan	cry, scream, shout
hror	brave, vigorous
hroran	brave, vigorous
hrostbeages	woodwork
hroþor	benefit, pleasure
hroþra	benefit, pleasure
hroþre	benefit, pleasure
hrungeat	beams
hruron	be-ruined, fall, sink
hrusan	ground, soil, the-earth
hruse	earth, ground, soil, the-earth
hrycg	back, ridge, spine, surface
hryðge	snowy
hryðig	snowy
hryman	scream, yell
hrymde	scream, yell
hryre	death, decay, fall, ruin
hrysedon	shake
hrysian	shake
hryþge	snowy
hryþig	snowy
hu	how, how-now!, oh!
huaet	derision, what-of
hucs	derision
hucse	derision
huðe	plunder, prey, treasure
huilpan	sea-bird
Humbra	Humber (place)
hun	dog, hundred
hund	dog, hound, hundred
hundeahtatig	80, eighty
hundeahtatigoþa	eightieth
hundendleftig	110, a hundred and ten
hundnigontig	90, ninety
hundnigontigoþa	ninetieth
hundred	one-hundred
hundseofontig	70, seventy
hundseofontigoþa	seventieth
hundteontig	100, a hundred, one-hundred
hundteontigoþa	hundredth

Word List (Ænglisc to English)

Ænglisc	English	Ænglisc	English
hundteontigoþa and forma	hundred and first	hwæne	anyone, each, which, who
hundtwelftig	120, a hundred and twenty, one-hundred-and-twenty	hwænne	as-long-as, until, when
hundtþelftig	120, a hundred and twenty	hwær	anywhere, everywhere, where
hundum	dog, hound	hwærf	go, move, turn
hunger	hunger	hwæs	something, that-which, what
hungor	famine, hunger	hwæt	active, bold, brave, hear, indeed, listen, quick, so, something, that-which, what, what-of, wheat-crop, whether, who
hungri	hungry		
hunig	honey		
hunigsmæccas	honey-savouring		
hunteontig	one-hundred		
hupeban	hipbone		
hupseax	hip-carried-sax, short-sword	hwætewæstm	wheat-crop
huru	indeed, truly	hwætewæstma	wheat-crop
hus	building, family, house, household	hwæþer	whether, whether, which-of-two
husa	building, family, house, household	hwæþere	but, however, in-any-case, nevertheless, yet
husc	derision		
husce	derision	hwæþre	however, in-any-case, nevertheless
huse	building, family, house, household	hwæt-hwegu	something
huses	building, family, house, household	hwætran	active, bold, brave, quick
huþe	plunder, prey, treasure	hwætred	counsel
		hwætt	bold, valiant
huuæt	what, what-of	hwale	whale
huuet	what-of	hwam	anyone, each, which, who
huuit	white		
hwa	anyone, each, what, which, who	hwan	anyone, each, which, who
hwæder	to-where, whither	hwanan	from-where, whence
hwæðer	whether, which-of-two	hwanon	from-where, whence
		hwar	anywhere, everywhere, where
hwæðere	but, however, in-any-case, nevertheless, yet	hwata	active, bold, brave, quick
hwæðre	however, in-any-case, nevertheless	hwate	active, bold, brave, quick
hwæl	whale	hwaþere	however, in-any-case, nevertheless
hwæles	whale, whale's		
hwælmere	the-sea, whale-lake	hwatum	active, bold, brave, quick
hwælweg	the-sea, whale-path, whale-way	hwealf	arch, arched, vault, vaulted

Word List (Ænglisc to English)

Ænglisc	English	Ænglisc	English
hwealfum	arched, vaulted	hwitan	bright, shining, white
hwearf	crowd, go, move, throng, turn, went	Hwitanwyllesgeat	Whitwell-Gap (place)
hwearfian	approach	hwite	bright, shining, white
hwearflicra	transitory	hwitlocced	blond-haired, shining-haired, white-haired
hwearfode	approach		
hwearfum	crowd, throng		
hwelc	any, some-kind-of, someone, what, what-kind-of, which	hwitloccedu	blond-haired, shining-haired, white-haired
hwelp	cub, puppy, whelp	hwitne	bright, shining, white
hwene	somewhat, to-some-extent	hwitost	bright, shining, white
		hwitre	bright, shining, white
hweop	threaten	hwon	a-little, anyone, each, little, somewhat, trifle, which, who
hweorfað	turn		
hweorfan	go, move, turn, turn-to		
hweorfaþ	turn	hwone	anyone, each, which, who
hweorfeð	go, move, turn		
hweorfeþ	go, move, turn	hwonne	as-long-as, until, when
hwergen	somewhere, where		
hwet	encourage, what-of	hwopan	threaten
hweteð	encourage	hworfan	go, move, turn
hweteþ	encourage	hwurfe	go, move, turn
hwettan	encourage	hwurfon	go, move, turn
hwette	encourage	hwy	for-what-reason, why
hwetton	encourage		
hwi	for-what-reason, why	hwyder	to-where, where, whither
hwider	to-where, whither	hwylc	any, some, some-kind-of, someone, what, what-kind-of, which
hwil	time, while		
hwilc	any, some-kind-of, someone, what, what-kind-of		
		hwylce	any, some-kind-of, someone, such, what, what-kind-of
hwilce	any, some-kind-of, someone, what, what-kind-of		
		hwylcere	any, some-kind-of, someone, what, what-kind-of
hwilcne	which		
hwile	awhile, for-a-time, sometimes, time, while		
		hwylcne	any, some-kind-of, someone, what, what-kind-of
hwilen	transitory		
hwilnan	transitory, while	hwylcum	any, some-kind-of, someone, what, what-kind-of
hwilon	often, sometimes		
hwilpe	sea-bird		
hwilum	bright, often, sometimes	hwyrfað	change, go, move
		hwyrfan	change, go, move
hwit	bright, shining, white	hwyrfaþ	change, go, move
hwita	bright, shining, white	hwyrfde	change, go, move

Word List (*Ænglisc* to English)

Ænglisc	English	*Ænglisc*	English
hwyrfeð	go, move, turn	hygegalan	lascivious, wanton
hwyrfeþ	go, move, turn	hygegeomor	miserable, sad
hwyrft	escape, going, movement, possible-movement, turning	hygegeomorne	miserable, sad, sad-of-heart
		hygegiomor	miserable, sad
		hygeleas	foolish, thoughtless
hwyrftum	escape, going, movement, possible-movement, turning	hygelease	foolish, thoughtless
		hygeleast	folly, thoughtlessness
		hygeleaste	folly, thoughtlessness
hy	consider, it, them, they, those, who, your	hygemeðe	mind-wearying, weary-minded
		hygemeþe	mind-wearying, weary-minded
hycgað	consider, think	hygerof	brave-minded, brave--minded
hycgan	consider, plan, resolve, think, to-plan		
		hygerofe	brave--minded
hycgaþ	consider, think	hygesceaft	mind, thought
hycge	consider, think	hygesceaftum	mind, thought
hycgean	consider	hygesorg	mental-sorrow
hycgendne	consider, considering, think	hygesorga	mental-sorrow
		hygesorge	mental-sorrow
hyð	harbour	hygeteona	hostility, injury, insult
hydað	harbour, moor, mooring	hygeteonan	hostility, insult
		hygewælm	spiritual-agitation
hydan	harbour, hide, moor, mooring	hygewlonc	haughty, proud-minded
hydaþ	harbour, moor, mooring	hyhsta	highest, most-high
		hyht	bliss, hope, joy, trust
hyddon	hide	hyhtan	rejoice
hyde	hide	hyhte	hope, joy, trust
hyðe	harbour	hyhtlease	despairing, without-hope
hydeð	hide		
hyðelic	favourable	hyhtlic	hopeful, joyful, pleasant
hydeþ	hide		
hydig	careful, thoughtful	hyhtwynn	joy, pleasure
hyðweard	harbour-master	hyhtwynna	joy, pleasure
hyge	courage, heart, intention, mental-bond, mind, mind's, soul, spiritual-attachment, thought	hyldan	bend-down, lean
		hylde	bend-down, lean
		hyldemæg	close-kinsman
		hyldemaga	close-kinsman
		hyldo	allegiance, favour, grace, loyalty, protection
hygebend	mental-bond, spiritual-attachment		
hygebendum	mental-bond, spiritual-attachment	hylt	hilt, sword-hilt
hygebliþe	joyful-hearted	hym	he, him, it, she
hygebliþran	joyful-hearted		
hygegal	lascivious, wanton		

Word List (*Ænglisc* to English)

Ænglisc	English	*Ænglisc*	English
hynan	despise, humiliate, injure, insult, kill, lay-low	*hyredmann*	man, servant, serving
hynð	humiliation, shame	*hyredmen*	man, servant, serving
hynða	humiliation, shame	*hyrnan*	corner
hynde	despise, humiliate, injure, insult, kill, lay-low	*hyrne*	corner
		hyrnednebba	horny-beaked
		hyrnednebban	hard-beaked
hynðo	humiliation, shame	*hyrst*	armour, jewel, ornament
hynðu	humiliation, shame		
hyne	he, him, it, she	*hyrsta*	jewel, ornament, ornaments
hyned	despise, injure, insult		
		hyrstan	decorate, ornament
hynþ	humiliation, shame	*hyrste*	jewel, ornament
hynþa	humiliation, shame	*hyrsted*	decorate, ornament
hynþo	humiliation, shame	*hyrstedne*	decorate, ornament
hynþu	humiliation, shame	*hyrstum*	jewel, ornament
hyra	belong, it, their, they	*hyrtan*	be-bold, take-heart
hyrað	belong, hear, obey	*hyrte*	be-bold, take-heart
hyræð	obeys	*hys*	he, his, it, she, warrior
hyran	belong, hear, obey		
hyraþ	belong, hear, obey	*hysas*	warrior, youth
hyrdan	harden, make-hard, temper	*hyse*	warrior, youth
		hyssa	warrior, youth, youthful-warriors
hyrdas	guardian, pastor, shepherd		
		hyssas	warrior, youth
hyrde	belong, encouraged, family, guardian, hear, heard, household, keeper, monastic-community, obey, pastor, retinue, shepherd	*hysses*	warrior, youth
		hyt	heat, it, that
		hyþ	harbour, plunder, prey, treasure
		hyþe	harbour, plunder, prey, treasure
		hyþweard	harbour-master
hyrdon	belong, hear, heard, obey, obeyed	**I, i**	
hyre	belong, hear, her, it, obey	*Iacob*	Jacob (name)
		iamiamque	right-now (Latin)
hyred	family, household, monastic-community, retinue	*ic*	augment, I, me
		icte	augment, grow, increase
hyredcniht	servant, serving-boy, serving-man	*icton*	augment, grow, increase
hyredcnihtas	servant, serving-boy, serving-man	*idel*	desolate, idle, useless, void
hyredes	family, household, monastic-community, retinue	*idelhende*	empty-handed, idle-handed
		Ides	a-woman, lady, woman

Word List (Ænglisc to English)

Ænglisc	English	Ænglisc	English
idesa	lady, woman	ingehyde	intent, meaning, purport
idese	lady, woman	ingelde	warrior
idesum	lady, woman	ingemann	native
idlu	desolate, idle, useless, void	ingemen	native
iecan	augment, grow, increase	ingenga	in-goer, ingoing, intruder, visitor
iecte	augment, grow, increase	ingesteald	household-contents, in-placed
ieg	island	ingeþanc	private-thought
iege	island	ingeþancum	private-thought
Iesum	Jesus (name) (Latin)	inlende	local, native
iewan	appear, present, reveal, show	inn	chamber, dwelling, house, in, inside, into, on, onto
iewde	appear, present, reveal, show	inna	in
iewe	appear, present, reveal, show	innan	in, inside, into, inwardly, within
ige	island	innanweard	inwardly, within, within-deep
iglond	island		
III	same, three-times	inne	chamber, dwelling, house, inside, within
ilca	same	inneweard	inward, within, within-deep
ilcan	same		
ilce	same	innewerdne	inward, within
ilfetu	swan	innianfill	inward, within
in	chamber, dwelling, house, in, into, on, onto, within, you-two	innoþ	guts, innards, stomach
inc	us-two, you-two	innoþe	guts, innards, insides, stomach
incer	you, you-two	insittend	person-sitting-within
incgelaf	sword	insittendra	person-sitting-within
incgelafe	sword	intinga	cause, reason
incit	you-two	into	into
incre	you-two	inuenta	found (Latin)
incrum	you-two	inweaxan	grow
indrihten	noble	inwidda	devious, evil-one
indryhten	noble	inwidhlemm	evil-wound
indryhto	nobility	inwidhlemmas	evil-wound
inflede	flooded, in-flooded, water-filled, water-full	inwidsorg	evil-sorrow, malicious
infrod	very-wise	inwidsorge	evil-sorrow
infrodum	very-wise	inwit	deceit, evil
ingang	entrance, in-going	inwitfeng	evil-grasp
ingefolc	native-people	inwitfull	crafty, cunning, malicious
ingefolca	native-people		
ingehyd	intent, meaning, purport	inwitfulle	crafty, cunning, malicious

Word List (*Ænglisc* to English)

Ænglisc	English	*Ænglisc*	English
inwitgæst	evil-guest, evil-visitor, malicious-alien	irenna	iron, iron-sword, sword
inwithrof	evil-roof	irenþreat	iron-armed-troop, iron-threat, troop
inwitnet	evil-net, evil-web, malice-net, malice-web	irnan	hasten, move-quickly, run
inwitnið	evil, hostility	is	be, become, exist, ice, ice-cold, is, this, to-be
inwitniðas	offences		
inwitniþ	evil, hostility	Isace	Isaac (name)
inwitniþa	evil, hostility	iscald	ice-cold
inwitniþas	evil, hostility	iscaldne	ice-cold
inwitscear	evil-slaughter, malicious-slaughter	isceald	ice-cold
		is-ceald	ice-cold
inwitsearo	evil-malice, malice	iscealdne	ice-cold
inwitsorge	evil-sorrow, malicious	ise	ice
		isen	iron, steel
inwitsorh	evil-malice, evil-sorrow, malicious	isenes	iron, steel
		isern	iron, made-iron, steel
inwitspell	malice-story, woe-story	iserna	iron, made-iron
inwitþanc	crafty-thought	isernbyrnan	iron-coat, iron-mail-coat
inwitþancum	crafty-thought, evil-thought	isernbyrne	iron-mail-coat
inwyxð	grows	isernes	iron, steel
inwyxeð	grow	isernscur	arrows, battle, iron-shower
inwyxeþ	grow		
iofore	ever-before	isernscure	arrows, battle, iron-shower
iogoþe	formerly, youth		
Iohannes	John (name)	isgebind	binding-ice, fettering-ice
iomeowlan	old-woman		
iomeowle	old-woman	isgebinde	binding-ice, fettering-ice, ice-binding
Iosep	Joseph (name)		
Iosephes	Joseph's (name)		
ipselos	high (Latin)	isig	icy
Iraland	Ireland	isig-feðera	icy-feathered
iren	iron, iron-sword, sword	isigfeþera	icy-feathered
		isig-feþera	icy-feathered
irena	iron, iron-sword, sword	Israela	Israel
		iu	formerly, of-old, once
irenbend	iron-bond, iron-fetter		
irenbenda	iron-bond, iron-fetter	Iudeas	Judas (name)
irenbendum	iron-bond, iron-fetter	Iulius	July (name)
irenbyrnan	iron-coat, iron-mail-coat	iumonn	ancient-man
		iumonna	ancient-man
irenbyrne	iron-mail-coat	iustus	just (Latin)
irenes	iron, iron-sword	iuwine	former-lord, old-friend
irenheard	iron-hard		

Word List (*Ænglisc* to English)

Ænglisc	English
K, k	
kyning	king
kyninga	of-kings
kyninges	king
kyningwuldor	glorious-king, king-glory
L, l	
la	indeed, oh!-ah!-indeed!
labor	work (Latin)
lac	offering, play, present, sacrifice
laca	offering, present, sacrifice
lacan	fly, leap, play
lace	offer
laceð	fly, leap, play
lacende	fly, leap, play
laceþ	fly, leap, play
lacnað	healed
lacnaþ	healed
lacum	offering, present, sacrifice
lad	journey, path, route, way
lað	evil, harm, hateful, inimical, injury, loathed, loathsome, unwelcome
laðan	hateful, the-hateful-one
laðbite	hateful-wound
lade	journey, path, route, way
laðe	the-hateful-one
laðere	the-hateful-one
laðes	harm, injury, the-hateful-one
laðestan	the-hateful-one
laðgeteona	hateful-enemy
laðgeteonan	hateful-enemy
ladigan	excuse
laðlic	hateful, unpleasant
laðlice	despicably, hatefully, nastily
laðlicost	despicably, hatefully, nastily, wretchedly
laðlicu	unpleasant
laðne	the-hateful-one
laðost	the-hateful-one
laðra	foes, the-hateful-one
laðran	the-hateful-one
laðscipe	harm, injury, misfortune
laðtreow	hateful-tree
laðum	the-hateful-one
laðwende	hostile
laðwendne	hostile
laðwendo	hostile
læca	physicians
læce	doctor, physician
læces	doctor, physician
læd	bring, conduct, do, lead, take
lædað	bring, conduct, do, lead, take
lædan	bring, conduct, do, lead, take
lædaþ	bring, conduct, do, lead, take
læðð	injury, wrong
læðða	injury, wrong
lædde	bring, conduct, do, lead, led, take
læddest	bring, conduct, do, lead, take
læddon	bring, conduct, do, lead, take
læððum	injury, wrong
læde	bring, conduct, do, lead, take
læded	bring, conduct, do, lead, take
læf	bequeath, leave
læfan	bequeath, leave
læfde	bequeath, leave
læfed	bequeath, leave
læg	be-situated, die-down, extend, lay, lay-dead, lie, lie-dead, lying, situated

Word List (*Ænglisc* to English)

Ænglisc	English	*Ænglisc*	English
læge	die-down, lay-dead, lie, lie-dead, lying, situated	*læstan*	carry-out, endure, follow, help, last, lasting, perform, serve
lægon	be-situated, die-down, extend, lay-dead, lie, lie-dead, lying, situated	*læste*	carry-out, endure, follow, footprint, help, last, perform, serve, trace, track
lægun	lay		
læn	benefit, gift, loan	*læsten*	carry-out, endure, follow, help, last, perform, serve
lænan	free-for-the-taking, give, grant, lend, loaned, perishable, temporary, transitory	*læstes*	carry-out, endure, follow, help, last, perform, serve
lændæg	transitory-days, transitory-life	*læt*	allow, ignore, lazy, let, lethargic, neglect, slow
lændaga	transitory-days, transitory-life		
lændagas	transitory-days, transitory-life	*lætað*	allow, ignore, let, neglect
læne	free-for-the-taking, granted, lean, lent, loaned, perishable, temporary, transitory	*lætan*	allow, ignore, let, neglect
		lætaþ	allow, ignore, let, neglect
lænes	free-for-the-taking, perishable, temporary, transitory	*lætbyrd*	delayed-labour
		lætbyrde	delayed-labour, late-birth
lænum	free-for-the-taking, perishable, temporary, transitory	*læte*	allow, ignore, let, neglect
		læteð	allow, allowing, ignore, let, neglect
lær	instruct, teach		
læran	advise, exhort, instruct, instructed, teach	*læten*	allow, let
		læteþ	allow, ignore, let, neglect
lærde	advise, exhort, instruct, teach	*læþþ*	injury, wrong
		læþþa	injury, wrong
lære	instruct, teach	*læþþum*	injury, wrong
læred	advise, exhort, teach	*laf*	leaving, legacy, remainder, remnant, what-is-left
læren	instruct, teach		
lærig	border, edge	*lafan*	left
læs	insignificant, less, lest, small	*lafe*	legacy, remainder, remnant, what-is-left
læsest	insignificant, less, lest, small	*lafian*	wash
		lago	ocean, sea, waters
læssa	fewer, less, smaller	*lagon*	die-down, lay-dead, lie, lie-dead, lying, situated
læssan	fewer, less, smaller		
læst	carry-out, endure, follow, help, last, perform, serve	*lagosið*	sea-journey
		lagosiða	sea-journey

158

Word List (Ænglisc to English)

Ænglisc	English	Ænglisc	English
lagosiþ	sea-journey	landsocne	search-for-land
lagosiþa	sea-journey	landwara	land-people
lagostreamum	sea-current	landweard	land-guardian
lagu	law, ocean, sea, waters	lang	long, tall
		langa	long, tall
lagucræftig	sea-wise, skilled-at-sailing	langað	long, longing, summon, yearn-for
laguflod	ocean, sea, the-sea, waters	langaþ	long, longing, summon, yearn-for
laguflode	ocean, sea, waters	lange	for-a-long-time, long, tall
lagulad	sea-route		
lagu-lad	ocean-journey, water-way	langian	long, summon, yearn-for
lagulade	sea-route	langne	long, tall
lagustræt	sea-road	langode	long, summon, yearn-for
lagustræte	sea-road		
lagustream	sea-current	langoþe	longing, unhappiness
lagustreamas	sea-current		
lah	lend	langre	long, tall
lamb	lamb	langsum	enduring, long
lambyrd	ineffective-labour, lame	langsumu	enduring, long
		langtwidig	granted-for-a-long-time, lasting
lambyrde	ineffective-labour, lame, lame-birth	langunghwil	longing-while
		langunghwila	longing-while
lamp	befall, happen	lansumum	enduring, long
lamrindum	earth-rind	lar	learning, precept, teaching
land	country, dry-land, land, the-land		
		lara	learning, precept, teaching
landa	country, dry-land, land		
		larcwide	instruction, teaching
landbuende	earth-dwellers, humans	larcwidum	instruction, teaching
		lare	learning, precept, teaching
landbuendum	earth-dwellers, humans		
		larena	learning, precept, teaching
lande	country, dry-land, land, the-land		
		lareow	teacher
landes	country, dry-land, land	lareowes	teacher
		larum	learning, precept, teaching, teachings
landfruma	land-holding-king, prince		
		last	footprint, the-track, trace, track
landgemyrce	land-edge, shoreline		
landgemyrcu	land-edge, shoreline	lastas	footprint, trace, track
landgeweorc	national-edifice	laste	footprint, trace, track, tracks
landmann	inhabitant, native		
landmanna	inhabitant, native		
landriht	land-right, property-right	lastum	footprint, trace, track
		lastweard	follower, pursuer
landscipe	land, region		
landsocn	search-for-land		

Word List (*Ænglisc* to English)

Ænglisc	English	*Ænglisc*	English
lastword	subsequent-reputation, track-word	leag	betray, deceive, lie
		leahtor	crime, sin, vice
		leahtra	sins
lastworda	subsequent-reputation, track-word	leahtrum	crime, sin, vice
		lealden	hold, preserve, retain
lata	late, slack	lean	blame, compensation, loan, reproach, retribution, reward
late	late		
laþ	evil, harm, hateful, hostile, inimical, injury, unwelcome		
		leana	compensation, loan, retribution, reward
laþan	hateful, the-hateful-one	leanast	repay, reward, take-vengeance-for
laþbite	hateful-wound		
laþe	the-hateful-one, the-loathed	leane	compensation, loan, retribution, reward
laþere	the-hateful-one	leanes	compensation, loan, retribution, reward
laþes	harm, injury, the-hateful-one		
		leanian	repay, reward, take-vengeance-for
laþestan	the-hateful-one		
laþgeteona	hateful-enemy	leanige	repay, reward, take-vengeance-for
laþgeteonan	hateful-enemy		
laþlic	hateful, unpleasant	leanode	repay, reward, take-vengeance-for
laþlice	despicably, hatefully, nastily		
		leanum	compensation, loan, retribution, reward
laþlicost	despicably, hatefully, nastily	leap	corpse
laþlicu	unpleasant	leas	bereft-of, devoid-of, false, lacking, less, lying, without
laþne	the-hateful-one		
laþost	the-hateful-one		
laþra	enemy, the-hateful-one	leasan	false, lacking, lying, without
laþran	the-hateful-one	lease	false, lacking, lying, without
laþre	the-hateful-one		
laþscipe	harm, injury, misfortune	leaslice	deceitfully, falsely
		leasne	false, lacking, lying, without
laþtreow	hateful-tree		
laþum	of-enemies, the-hateful-one	leassceaweras	spy
		leassceawere	spy
laþwende	hostile	leasum	false, lacking, lying, without
laþwendemod	hostile, malicious		
laþwendne	hostile	leasung	falsehood, lie
laþwendo	hostile	leasunga	falsehood, lie
latteow	guide, leader	leax	salmon
leaf	a-leaf, belief, leaf	leccan	irrigate, water
leafa	belief, faith	lecgað	lay
leafnesword	allowing-word, permission-word	lecgan	lay
		lecgaþ	lay
leafum	leaf	lecge	lay

Word List (Ænglisc to English)

Ænglisc	English
lef	feeble, infirm, sickly
leg	die-down, fire, flame, lay, lay-dead, lays, lie, lie-dead, lying, situated
legde	laid, lay
legdon	lay
legdraca	breathing-dragon, fire
legdun	laid
lege	fire, flame, lay
legeð	lay
legen	be-situated, extend, lie
leger	grave, lying-place-bed, lying-with
legerbedd	deathbed, grave
legerbedde	deathbed, grave
legere	grave, lying-place-bed
legeþ	lay
legge	lay
lemedon	disable, lame
lemian	disable, lame
lencten	spring
lende	landed
leng	belonging, for-a-long-time, long, longer
lenge	belonging, imminent, of-time-close, related
lengest	for-a-long-time, long, the-longest
lengo	distance, length
lengra	long, tall
lengran	long, tall
lengre	quickly, soon
leod	king, lord, man, member-of-tribe, nation, people, person, prince
leoð	poem, song
leoda	king, man, nation, people, person, prince
leodan	grow, spring
leodbealewa	harm-to-the-whole-people, national-evil
leodbealo	harm-to-the-whole-people, national-evil
leodburg	national-city
leodbyrig	national-city
leoðcræftig	skilled-in-poetry, skilled-in-song
leodcyning	people-king
leode	king, man, nation, people, person, prince
leodfruma	patriarch, people, people-founder, people-leader, prince
leodfruman	patriarch, people-founder, people-leader, prince
leodgeard	national-territory
leodgebyrgea	people-protector
leodgebyrgean	people-protector
leodhata	people-enemy, tyrant
leodhatan	people-enemy, tyrant
leodhryre	people-fall
leodhryres	people-fall
leodmæg	co-national, relative, tribal-member
leodmægen	national-army
leodmægenes	national-army
leodmægnes	national-army
leodmagum	co-national, relative, tribal-member
leoðocræft	limb-skill
leoðocræftum	limb-skill
leodon	king, man, person, prince
leoðosyrcan	limb-mail-coat
leoðosyrce	limb-mail-coat
leodsceaða	enemy, threat-to-a-people
leodsceaðan	enemy, threat-to-a-people
leodsceaþa	enemy, threat-to-a-people
leodsceaþan	enemy, threat-to-a-people
leodscipe	nation, people
leodþeaw	people-custom

Word List (Ænglisc to English)

Ænglisc	English
leodþeawum	people-custom
leodum	king, man, nation, people, person, prince
leodweard	leadership, people-ruling
leodwer	people-man, people-person
leodweras	people-man, people-person
leof	beloved, dear, love
leofa	beloved, dear, love, loved
leofað	as-the-living, exist, live
leofan	beloved, dear, love, loved
leofast	exist, live
leofaþ	as-the-living, exist, live, living
leofe	beloved, beloveds, dear, love, loved
leofes	beloved, dear, life, love, loved
leofestan	beloved, dear, love, loved
leofian	live
leoflic	dear, delightful, precious
leofne	beloved, dear, love, loved
leofost	beloved, dear, love, loved
leofra	beloved, dear, love, loved
leofran	beloved, dear, love, loved
leofre	beloved, dear, love, loved
leoftæl	kind
leofum	beloved, dear, love, loved
leogan	betray, deceive, lie
leoge	betray, deceive, lie
leoht	bright, easy, irrigate, life, light, lightweight, water
leohtan	bright, light
leohte	brightly, clearly, irrigate, life, light, lightly, water
leohtes	bright-creator, creator, life, light, of-lights
leohtfruma	bright-creator, light-creator
leohtfruman	bright-creator, light-creator
leohtne	bright, light
leohtra	bright, light
leohtum	bright, light
leolc	fly, leap, play
leoma	heavenly-body, light-beam, luminary
leoman	heavenly-body, light-beam, luminary
leomena	heavenly-body, light-beam, luminary
leomu	branch, limb
leomum	branch, limb
leon	lend
leorna	consider, learn
leornian	consider, learn
leornode	consider, learn
leoþ	poem, poetry, song
leoþcræftig	skilled-in-poetry, skilled-in-song
leoþocræft	limb-skill
leoþocræftum	limb-skill
leoþosyrcan	limb-mail-coat
leoþosyrce	limb-mail-coat
leoþu	limb, member
lepeþ	feed-a-hawk
leppan	feed-a-hawk
lesse	smaller
let	allow, ignore, let, neglect
Letan	left
letanias	litany
letanie	litany
lete	allow, ignore, let, neglect
leton	allow, ignore, let, neglect
lettan	hinder, prevent
letton	hinder, prevent
libban	exist, live

Word List (*Ænglisc* to English)

Ænglisc	English	*Ænglisc*	English
lic	body, likeness	liden	sail, travel
lica	body, likeness	liðend	sailor, traveller
licað	be-liking-to, please	liðende	sailor, traveller
licaþ	be-liking-to, please	liðendum	sail, travel
lice	body, likeness	lides	ship, ship's
lices	bodily, body, likeness	lidmann	sailor
		lidmanna	sailor
licgað	die-down, lay-dead, lie, lie-dead, lying, situated	lidmen	sailor
		liðost	gracious, pleasant
		liðsa	grace, joy, love, peace
licgan	be-situated, die-down, extend, lay-dead, lie, lie-dead, lying, situated	liðsum	grace, joy, love, peace
		liðum	limb, member
		lif	life
licgaþ	die-down, lay-dead, lie, lie-dead, lying, situated	lifað	as-the-living
		lifan	allow, grant
		lifaþ	as-the-living
licgean	die-down, lay-dead, lie, lie-dead, lying, situated	lifbysig	struggling-for-life
		lifceare	anxiety-about-life
		lifcearu	anxiety-about-life
licgende	die-down, lay-dead, lie, lie-dead, lying, situated	lifd	live
		lifdagas	life-days
licgendre	die-down, lay-dead, lie, lie-dead, lying, situated	lifdagum	life-days
		lifde	exist, live
		lifdon	exist, live
lichama	body	life	allow, grant, life
lichaman	body	lifes	life, life's
lichoma	body	liffæst	hearty, lively, vigorous
lic-homa	body, flesh		
lichoman	body	liffæstan	hearty, lively, vigorous
lichryre	death		
lician	be-liking-to, please	liffrea	life-lord, living-lord
licode	be-liking-to, please	Lif-frea	Life-lord
licodon	be-liking-to, please	liffrean	life-lord, living-lord
licrest	cemetery	lifge	live
licreste	cemetery	lifgedal	death
licsar	bodily-wound	lifgend	living-person
licsyrce	mail-coat	lifgende	live, living
licwund	bodily-wound	lifgendne	live, living
licwunde	bodily-wound	lifgendra	as-the-living
lid	ship	lifgendum	live, living
lið	die-down, lay-dead, lie, lie-dead, limb, lying, member, situated, the-body	lifgenra	living-person
		lifgesceaft	life-circumstance
		lifgesceafta	life-circumstance
		lifiað	live
lide	ship	lifian	live
liðe	gracious, kind, pleasant	lifiaþ	live
		lifiende	living

Word List (*Ænglisc* to English)

Ænglisc	English	*Ænglisc*	English
lifigan	live	*limnacod*	having-naked-limbs
lifige	live	*limpan*	befall, exist, happen, occur
lifigende	live	*limpeð*	exist, happen, occur
lifigendra	as-the-living	*limpeþ*	exist, happen, occur
lifigendum	live	*limum*	branch, limb
lifwraðe	life-protection	*limwerig*	weary-limbed
lifwraðu	life-protection	*limwerigne*	weary-limbed
lifwraþe	life-protection	*Lincylene*	Lincoln (place)
lifwraþu	life-protection	*lind*	linden-wood-shield, shield
lifwynn	life-joy	*linda*	shields
lifwynna	life-joy	*lindcroda*	battle, shield-crashing
lig	fire, flame	*lindcrodan*	battle, shield-crashing
ligas	fire, flame	*linde*	lindens, linden-wood-shield
ligdraca	breathing-dragon, fire	*lindgestealla*	linden-wood, shield-wood
lige	fire, flame	*lindhæbbend*	linden-wood, shield-possessor, warrior
ligeð	die-down, lay-dead, lie, lie-dead, lying, situated	*lindhæbbende*	linden-wood, shield-possessor, warrior
ligegesa	fire-terror	*lindhæbbendra*	linden-wood, shield-possessor, warrior
ligegesan	fire-terror	*lindplega*	linden-wood, shield-play, warrior
ligen	falsehood, lie, untruth	*lindplegan*	linden-wood, shield-play, warrior
ligenum	falsehood, lie, untruth	*lindum*	linden-wood-shield
ligenword	lying-word	*lindwig*	linden-wood-shield-bearing-army
ligenwordum	lying-word	*lindwiga*	linden-wood, shield-bearing
liges	fire, flame	*lindwiggend*	linden-wood, shield-bearing
ligeþ	die-down, lay-dead, lie, lie-dead, lying, situated	*lindwiggende*	linden-wood, shield-bearing
ligetorn	feigned-injury	*linnan*	cease-from, lose
ligetorne	feigned-injury	*linsetcorn*	linseed
ligewyrhtum	deception	*liodan*	grow, spring-up
ligge	fire, flame	*liodende*	grow, spring-up
Ligoraceaster	Leicester (place)	*liodgeard*	country
ligst	die-down, lay-dead, lie, lie-dead, lying, situated	*lioðobend*	bond, fetter
		lioðobendum	bond, fetter
ligyð	fire-wave	*liofan*	love
ligyðum	fire-wave	*liofwendum*	gracious
ligyþ	fire-wave	*lioht*	light
ligyþum	fire-wave		
lihtan	alight, dismount		
lihte	alight, dismount, light		
lim	branch, cement, limb, lime, mortar		
lime	cement, lime, mortar		

Word List (Ænglisc to English)

Ænglisc	English	Ænglisc	English
liþobend	bond, fetter	lociað	gaze-on, look, see
liþobendum	bond, fetter	locian	gaze-on, look, see
liss	grace, joy, love, peace	lociaþ	gaze-on, look, see
		locod	look
lissa	grace, joy, love, peace	locode	look
		loða	cloak
lisse	grace, joy, love, peace	loðum	cloak
		lof	glory, love, praise, praised, reputation
lissum	grace, joy, love, peace	lofdæd	famous-deed, praiseworthy-action
list	craft, skill	lof-dæd	praiseworthy-deed
lista	craft, skill	lofdædum	famous-deed, praiseworthy-action
listas	craft, skill		
listum	artfully, craft, cunningly, skill	lofe	bent-on-glory, glory, life, love, praise, reputation
litel	little		
liþ	die-down, lay-dead, lie, lie-dead, limb, lying, member, situated	lofgeorn	bent-on-glory, eager-for-fame, eager-for-praise
liþan	sail, travel	lof-georn	eager-for-praise
liþe	gracious, kind, pleasant	lofgeornost	bent-on-glory, eager-for-fame
liþend	sailor, traveller	lofian	praise
liþende	sailor, traveller	lofsum	glorious, praiseworthy
liþendum	sail, travel		
liþnes	gentleness	log	blame, reproach
liþnesse	gentleness	logian	lodge, place
liþost	gracious, pleasant	logon	blame, reproach
liþsa	grace, joy, love, peace	lomp	exist, happen, occur
		lond	country, dry-land, land, realm
liþsum	grace, joy, love, peace	londbuend	earth-dwellers, humans
liþu	limb, member		
liþum	limb, member	londbuendum	earth-dwellers, humans
lithwæge	beer-cup, wine-cup		
litla	little	londe	country, dry-land, land
litle	little		
lixan	shine	londes	country, dry-land, land, lands
lixeð	splendidly		
lixte	shine, shone	londriht	land-right, property-right
lixton	shine		
locast	gaze-on, look, see	londrihtes	land-right, property-right
locen	locked, securely-linked		
		londryht	land-right, property-right
locene	locked, securely-linked		
		londstede	country, location-on-land
locenra	fasten, intertwine, lock, weave		
		long	long, tall

Word List (*Ænglisc* to English)

Ænglisc	English	*Ænglisc*	English
longade	long, longing, summon, yearn-for	*lufien*	cherish, love
longaþ	longing, unhappiness	*lufode*	cherish, love
		lufsum	loving
longaþes	longing, unhappiness	*luftacen*	friendship-token, love-token
longe	ancient-treasure, for-a-long-time, long, tall	*lufu*	kind-action, love, settlement
longgestreon	ancient-treasure, long-accumulated-treasure	*lufum*	kind-action, love, settlement
		lumpen	befall, happen
longgestreona	ancient-treasure, long-accumulated-treasure	*lumpon*	befall, happen
		lungre	quickly, soon
		lust	desire, lust, pleasure
longsum	enduring, long, long-lasting, overlong, wearisome	*lustas*	lust, pleasure
		luste	lust, pleasurable, pleasure
longsumne	long-lasting, overlong, wearisome	*lustum*	gladly, joyfully, lust, pleasure, with-pleasure
longung	longing, sadness	*lux*	light (Latin)
longunge	longing, sadness	LXXX	eighty
losað	escape, perish, to-be-lost	*lybban*	exist, live
		lyblac	sorcery, witchcraft
losade	escape, perish, to-be-lost	*lyblaca*	sorcery, witchcraft
		lyblace	sorcery, witchcraft
losaþ	escape, perish, to-be-lost	*lyðra*	wicked
		lyfað	allow, as-the-living, grant
losian	escape, perish, to-be-lost	*lyfan*	believe
		lyfaþ	allow, as-the-living, grant
loþa	cloak		
loþum	cloak	*lyfde*	as-the-living
loue	love	*lyfdon*	exist, live
lucan	fasten, intertwine, lock, weave	*lyfe*	life
		lyfes	life, life's
lucon	fasten, intertwine, lock, weave	*lyfiendne*	the-living
		lyfode	lived
Lucos	Luke (name)	*lyft*	air, breeze, clouds, sky, the-air
ludon	grow, spring		
lufan	kind-action, love, settlement	*lyfte*	clouds, sky, the-air, the-sky
lufe	kind-action, love, settlement	*lyftedoras*	sky-enclosure
		lyftfloga	air-flier, flying-thing
lufen	kind-action, love, settlement	*lyftgeswenced*	travailed-by-the-wind, weather-beaten
lufiað	cherish, love		
lufian	cherish, love	*lyfthelm*	the-air
lufiaþ	cherish, love		

Word List (*Ænglisc* to English)

Ænglisc	English	*Ænglisc*	English
lyftsceaþa	airborne-pest, flying-molester	*maððumwelan*	precious-possession, treasure
lyftsceaþan	airborne-pest, flying-molester	*maðelian*	address, harangue, speak
lyftswift	air-swift, swift-flying	*maðelod*	address, harangue, speak
lyftswiftne	air-swift, swift-flying	*maðelode*	address, harangue, speak
lyftwynn	delight-in-the-air, flying-joy	*madm*	precious-thing, treasure
lyftwynne	delight-in-the-air, flying-joy	*madma*	precious-thing, treasure, treasures
lygenum	falsehood, lie, untruth	*maðma*	precious-thing, treasure, treasures
lyhð	blame, reproach	*maðmæhta*	treasure, valuable-possession
lyhþ	blame, reproach	*madmas*	precious-thing, treasure
lysan	ransom, release	*maðmas*	precious-thing, treasure
lystan	cause-longing, please	*madme*	precious-thing, treasure
lyste	cause-longing, please	*madmum*	precious-thing, treasure
lysteþ	cause-longing, longs-for, please	*maðmum*	precious-thing, treasure
lyt	few, little, small-number	*maðþum*	precious-thing, treasure
lytegian	act-cunningly	*maðþumfæt*	treasure
lytel	little, short, small	*maðþumsweord*	precious-sword
lythwon	few, little	*mæca*	men
lytlað	become-smaller, diminish	*mæcg*	man, son
lytlaþ	become-smaller, diminish	*mæcga*	man, son
lytle	little, short, small	*mæcgea*	kinsmen
lytlian	diminish, lessen	*mæcgum*	man, son
lytligan	become-smaller, diminish	*maecti*	decency, might
lytlod	diminish, lessen	*mæð*	decency, propriety
lytlode	diminish, lessen	*mædæg*	age, day, era
lytlum	little, short, small	*mæden*	girl, maiden, virgin

M, m

Ænglisc	English	*Ænglisc*	English
		mædene	girl, maiden, virgin
ma	great, more, stout	*mædenman*	maiden, young-girl
macian	do, make	*mæder*	mother
maððum	precious-thing, treasure	*Mæðhilde*	Matilda (name)
maððumsigla	precious-jewel	*mæðlan*	speak
maððumsigle	precious-jewel	*mæðmæht*	treasure, valuable-possession
maððumwela	precious-possession, treasure		

Word List (*Ænglisc* to English)

Ænglisc	English	*Ænglisc*	English
mæg	avail, be-able-to, be-strong, family, kindred, kinsman, maiden, male-relative, may, may-be, nation, to-be-able-to, wife, woman	mægeneacen	empowered, might-endowed
		mægenellen	bravery, power
		mægenes	army, host, might, power, strength, troop
		mægenfultum	mighty-support, weapon
mæga	kinsman	mægenfultuma	mighty-support, weapon
mægburg	family, nation, race, tribe		
mægburge	family, nation, race, tribe	mægenheap	military-troop
		mægenheapum	military-troop
mægburh	family, nation, race, tribe	maegenraes	mighty-swing
		maegenrof	mighty, powerful
mægð	clan, girl, people	mægenstrang	main-strong
mægða	clan, girl, kindred, maiden, people, woman	mægenstranga	main-strong
		mægenstrengo	mighty-strength
		mægenstrengu	mighty-strength
mægðe	clan, kindred, people	mægenwudu	power-wood, spear
		mæges	kindred, kinsman, male-relative
mægðhad	virginity		
mægðhade	virginity	mægeþ	army, girl, maiden, woman
mægðum	girl, maiden, woman		
mæge	avail, be-strong, female-relative, feminine-relative, may	mægna	army, host, might, power, strength, troop
		mægne	army, host, might, power, strength, troop
mægeð	army, girl, maiden, woman		
mægen	army, be-strong, host, may, might, power, strength, to-be-able-to, troop	mægnes	army, host, might, power, strength, troop
		mægnu	army, host, might, power, strength, troop
mægena	virtue		
mægenagend	hero, might-owner	mægþ	clan, girl, maiden, nation, people, tribe
mægenagendra	hero, might-owner		
mægenbyrþen	immense-load, mighty-burden	mægþa	clan, girl, kindred, maiden, people, woman
mægenbyrþenne	immense-load, mighty-burden		
mægencorðor	mighty-company	mægþe	clan, kindred, people
mægencorðrum	mighty-company		
mægencorþor	mighty-company	mægþhad	virginity
mægencorþrum	mighty-company	mægþhade	virginity
mægencræft	might, strength	mægþum	clan, girl, kindred, maiden, people, woman
mægene	army, host, might, power, strength, troop		
		mægum	family

Word List (*Ænglisc* to English)

Ænglisc	English
mægwine	friendly-male-relative
mægwinum	friendly-male-relative
mægyn	army, host, might, power, strength, troop
mæhtum	mighty
mæl	cross, mark, measure, occasion, sign, time
mæla	cross, mark, sign, time
mælan	speak
mælceare	contemporary-trouble-or-sorrow, time-trouble
mælcearu	contemporary-trouble-or-sorrow, time-trouble
mældæges	age, day, era
mældagum	age, day, era
mælde	speak
mæles	cross, mark, sign, time
mælgesceaft	time-events
mælgesceafta	time-events
mælo	cross, mark, sign, time
mælum	cross, mark, sign, time
mænað	mention, tell-of
mænan	mention, moan, relate, speak-of, tell-of
mænaþ	mention, tell-of
mænde	mention, moan, relate, speak-of, tell-of
mændon	mention, tell-of
mæne	sinful, wicked
mæned	mention, moan, relate, speak-of, tell-of
mænegeo	multitude
mænego	host, multitude, multitudes
mænegum	many
mænig	many
mænige	host, multitude
mænigeo	multitude
mænigfeald	many, numerous
mænigfealde	many, numerous
mænigfealdian	to-become-multiplied
mænigne	many
mænigo	host, many, multitude
mæniu	multitude
mæra	excellent, famous, splendid
mærað	glorify, honour, praise
mæran	excellent, famous, glorify, honour, noble, praise, splendid
mæraþ	glorify, honour, praise
mærð	fame, famous-exploit
mærða	fame, famous-exploit, praised
mærðe	fame, famous-exploit
mærðo	fame, famous-exploit
mærðu	fame, famous-exploit
maere	confine, excellent, famous, glorious, majestic, notorious, splendid
mæres	excellent, famous, splendid
Mæringa	Maering (place)
mærlice	gloriously, splendidly
mærne	excellent, famous, splendid, splendidly
mæro	excellent, famous, splendid
mæron	excellent, famous, splendid
mærost	excellent, famous, splendid
mærra	excellent, famous, formed, splendid

Word List (*Ænglisc* to English)

Ænglisc	English
mærsian	glorify, praise
mærsigende	glorify, praise
mærþ	fame, famous-exploit
mærþa	fame, famous-exploit
mærþe	fame, famous-exploit
mærþo	fame, famous-exploit
mærþu	fame, famous-exploit
mæru	excellent, famous, splendid
mærum	excellent, famous, splendid
mæssan	mass, service
mæsse	mass, service
mæssepreost	mass, priest
mæst	greatly, mast, most, very, very-much
mæsta	greatly, most, very, very-much
mæste	greatly, mast, most, very, very-much
mæstne	greatly, most, very, very-much
mæt	measure, measure-out, traverse
mætan	dream
mæte	poor, small
mæþ	decency, propriety
mæþlan	speak
mæþmæht	treasure, valuable-possession
mæton	measure, measure-out, traverse
mætost	poor, small
mæw	gull, mew, sea-gull, sea-mew
mæwes	gull, gulls, sea-mew
maga	family, kindred, kinsman, male-kinsman, male-relative, may, son, stomach, young-man
magan	avail, be-able, be-able-to, be-competent, be-strong, can, female-relative, male-relative, may, son, to-be-able-to, young-man
magas	family, kindred, kinsman, male-relative, relatives
magaþiht	powerful-bellied
magaþihtan	powerful-bellied
mage	female-relative, may
magnificat	let-Him-be-exalted
mago	male-kinsman, son, young-man
magoðegn	man, retainer, servant
magodriht	men-band
magon	avail, be-able-to, be-strong, may, to-be-able-to
magoræswa	leader, warrior-chief
magorinc	male-relative, man
magorinca	male-relative, man
magorincas	male-relative, man
magorince	male-relative, man
magoþegn	man, retainer, servant
magoþegna	man, retainer, servant
magoþegnum	man, retainer, servant
magotimber	child, progeny
magotimbre	child, progeny
magotudor	male-offspring
magotudre	male-offspring
magum	family, kindred, kinsman, male-relative
maguþegn	man, retainer, servant
maguþegnas	man, retainer, servant
maguþegne	man, retainer, servant
magwlite	family-resemblance

Word List (Ænglisc to English)

Ænglisc	English	Ænglisc	English
man	admonish, a-man, anyone, anyone-used-to-form-passive-sense, bad, crime, criminal, evil, false, man, man, men, one, remind, sin, someone	mannan	man
		manncynnes	humanity, mankind
		mannes	man, man's, person
		mannon	man
		mannum	man, person
		manod	admonish, exhort, warn
manað	admonish, remind, warn	manode	admonish, exhort, remind, warn
manaþ	admonish, remind, warn	manscaða	criminal-destroyer
		manscaþa	criminal-destroyer
mancyn	humanity, mankind	mansceaða	criminal, sinner
mancynn	humanity, mankind	mansceaðan	criminal, sinner
mancynne	humanity, mankind	mansceaþa	criminal, sinner
mancynnes	humanity, mankind	mansceaþan	criminal, sinner
mandæd	crime, sin	manscilde	sin
mandædum	crime, sin	manscyldig	criminal, sinful
mandrihten	liege-lord	manscyligne	criminal, sinful
mandrihtne	liege-lord	manum	bad, criminal, evil, false
mandryhten	liege-lord		
mandryhtne	liege-lord	mara	bigger, greater, more
mandryhtnes	liege-lord		
mane	crime, evil, sin, wickedness	maran	bigger, great, greater, more, much
		Marcus	Mark's (name)
manega	many	mare	bigger, greater, more
manegum	many		
manes	crime, sin	Marian	Mary (name)
manfæhð	criminally-hostile	Marie	Mary (name)
manfæhðu	criminally-hostile, wickedness	martyrdom	martyrdom
		maþðum	precious-thing, treasure
manfæhþ	criminally-hostile		
manfæhþu	criminally-hostile, wickedness	maþðumgife	treasure-gift, treasure-giving
manfordædla	evil-doer	maþðumgifu	treasure-gift, treasure-giving
manfordædlan	evil-doer	maþelade	speak
manian	admonish, exhort, remind, warn	maþelian	address, harangue, speak
manig	many	maþelod	address, harangue, speak
manige	many		
manigeo	host, multitude	maþelode	address, harangue, speak
manigne	many		
manigra	many		
manigre	many	Matheus	Matthew's (name)
manigum	many	maþm	treasure
manlice	manly, noble	maþma	precious-thing, treasure
mann	man, man's, person		
manna	man, men, of-man's, person	maþmæhta	treasure, valuable-possession

Word List (*Ænglisc* to English)

Ænglisc	English	*Ænglisc*	English
maþmas	precious-thing, treasure	meara	horse, horses
maþme	precious-thing, treasure	mearas	horse
		mearc	border, boundary, end-of-life, limit, mark, region, term
maþmgestreon	treasure		
maþmgestreona	treasure	mearcað	create, design, designate, mark, note, remark, stain
maþmum	precious-thing, treasure		
maþþum	precious-thing, treasure	mearcaþ	create, design, designate, mark, note, remark, stain
maþþumfæt	treasure		
maþþumgife	treasure-gift, treasure-giving	mearce	border, end-of-life, limit, mark, term
maþþumgifu	treasure-gift, treasure-giving	mearcian	create, design, designate, mark, note, remark, stain
maþþumgyfa	king, treasure-giver		
maþþumsigla	precious-jewel	mearcode	create, design, designate, mark, note, remark, stain
maþþumsigle	precious-jewel		
maþþumsweord	precious-sword		
maþþumwela	precious-possession, treasure	mearcstapa	walker-in-border-regions
		mearcstapan	walker-in-border-regions
maþþumwelan	precious-possession, treasure	mearcþreat	vanguard
		mearcþreate	vanguard
me	firm, I, me, mine, my, myself, strong, to-me	mearcweard	border-guardian
		mearcweardas	border-guardian
		meare	horse
meaglum	firm, strong	mearg	horse
meagol	firm, strong	mearh	horse
meaht	avail, be-strong, might, power, strength, to-be-able-to	mearn	be-sorrowful, mourn, regret
		mearum	horse
		mec	I, me, my
meahtan	avail, be-strong, to-be-able-to	meca	sword
		mece	sword
meahte	avail, be-able-to, be-strong, may, might, mighty, power, strength, to-be-able-to	meces	sword
		mecum	sword, swords
		med	compensation, reward
		meda	compensation, reward
meahtig	mighty, powerful		
meahtigra	mighty, powerful	mede	compensation, reward
meahton	avail, be-strong, to-be-able-to		
		meðe	sad, tired, worn-out
meahtum	power, strength	meðel	council, discourse, speech, utterance
mealt	burn-up, dissolve, melt		
		meðelstede	assembly-place, meeting-place
mear	horse		

Word List (*Ænglisc* to English)

Ænglisc	English
meðelword	formal-utterance, speech
meðelwordum	formal-utterance, speech
meder	mother
medo	compensation, mead, reward
medoærn	mead-hall
medobenc	mead-bench
medobence	mead-bench
medoburg	mead-city
medobyrig	mead-city
medodrinc	mead, mead-drinking
medodrince	mead, mead-drinking
medoful	mead-cup
medoheal	mead-hall
medoheall	mead-hall
medohealle	mead-hall
medostig	path-to-the-mead-hall
medostigge	path-to-the-mead-hall
medowerig	drunk, hung-over
medowerige	drunk, hung-over
medowerigum	drunk, hung-over
medu	mead
medubenc	mead-bench
medubence	mead-bench
medudream	mead-joy
medu-drinc	mead-drink
medugal	drunk-with-mead
medu-heall	mead-hall
medum	compensation, reward
meduseld	mead-hall
medu-setl	mead-seat
mege	female-relative
mehte	avail, be-strong, to-be-able-to
melda	accuser, informant
meldan	accuser, informant
melo	flour, meal
meltan	burn-up, dissolve, melt
men	men
mencgan	mingle
mene	necklace
menegu	many
mengan	blend, mingle, mix
mengeo	multitude
menigeo	host, multitude
meniu	multitude
menn	man, person
mennen	handmaid, slave
mennisc	human, human-being, people, race
mennisces	human, human-being, people, race
menniscra	human, human-being, people, race
menniscum	human, human-being, people, race
meodo	mead
meododream	mead-joy
meododreama	mead-joy, mead-joys
meodoheall	mead-halls
meodosetl	mead-seat, place-at-mead-drinking
meodosetla	mead-seat, place-at-mead-drinking
meodowong	mead-hall-ground, mead-plain
meodowongas	mead-hall-ground, mead-plain
meodubenc	mead-bench
meodubence	mead-bench
meoduburgum	mead-city, mead-towns
meoduful	mead-cup
meodugal	drunk-with-mead
meodugales	drunk-with-mead
meoduhealle	mead-hall
meoduscenc	mead-cup
meoduscencum	mead-cup
meolc	milk
meolce	milk
meoluc	milk
meoto	thought
meotod	creator, the-Creator, the-measurer
meotodes	creator's, death, the-Creator, the-measurer's
meotodsceaft	death, doom, fate
meotud	the-Creator

Word List (*Ænglisc* to English)

Ænglisc	English	*Ænglisc*	English
meotudes	the-Creator	meridie	the-south
meotudgesceaft	death, doom, fate	messepreost	mass, mass-priest, priest
meowlan	maiden, woman		
meowle	maiden, woman	messepreoste	mass, priest
meox	dung, filth	metan	encounter, find, measure, measure-out, meet, traverse
mercels	mark, target		
mercelses	mark, target		
mere	lake, mere, ocean, pond, pool, sea, the-sea	mete	food, meat
		meted	find, meet
		metelist	food-lack
mereciest	sea-chest	meteliste	food-lack
merecieste	sea-chest	metend	the-Measurer
meredeor	sea-animal	metes	eating-strong, food, meat, the-food
merefara	sailor, seafarer		
merefaran	sailor, seafarer	meteþiht	eating-strong, food-strong
merefisc	sea-fish		
merefixa	sea-fish	meteþihtan	eating-strong, food-strong
mereflod	ocean, sea		
mereflode	ocean, sea, sea-flow	meþe	sad, tired, worn-out
meregrund	lake-bottom, sea-bottom	meþel	council, discourse, speech, utterance
meregrundas	lake-bottom, sea-bottom	meþelstede	assembly-place, meeting-place
merehrægl	sail, sea-garment	meþelword	formal-utterance, speech
merehrægla	sail, sea-garment		
merehus	sae-house, ship	meþelwordum	formal-utterance, speech
mere-hus	sea-house		
merehuses	sae-house, ship	meþle	council, discourse, speech, utterance
merelad	sea-route		
merelade	sea-route	metod	creator, the-Creator
mereliðend	sailor	metode	the-Creator
mereliðende	sailor	metodes	creations, the-Creator
mereliþend	sailor		
mereliþende	sailor	metodsceaft	death, doom, fate
merestræt	sea-path	metodsceafte	death, doom, fate
merestræta	sea-path	mette	encounter, find, meet
merestream	sea-stream, sea-water		
merestreamas	sea-stream, sea-streams, sea-water	metton	encounter, meet
		mettrum	infirm, weak
		mettrume	infirm, weak
merestrengo	sea-strength, swimming-strength	metudæs	the-Creator, the-measurer's
mereweard	sea-lord	metudes	the-Creator
merewerges	sea-weary	miccla	great
merewerig	sea-weary	miccle	greatly, much
mere-werig	sea-weary	miccles	greatly, much, very, very-much
merewif	sea-woman		
mergen	morning	miccli	much
mergenne	morning		

Word List (*Ænglisc* to English)

Ænglisc	English	*Ænglisc*	English
micclum	greatly, much, very, very-much	*middelniht*	midnight, night-middle
micel	great, large, much, very	*middelnihtum*	midnight, night-middle
micela	great	*midde-weard*	middling, mid-ward
micelan	great	*middum*	mid, middle
miceles	greatly, much, very, very-much	*middungeard*	conceal, middle-earth
micelne	greatly, much, very, very-much	*miðendne*	conceal, hide
micla	great, much	*midne*	mid, middle
miclade	increase, make-greater	*midre*	mid, middle
miclan	great, much	*miht*	avail, be-strong, might, power, strength, to-be-able-to
micle	greatly, much, very, very-much	*mihta*	avail, might, mighty, power, strength
micles	greatly, much, very, very-much	*mihte*	avail, be-strong, power, strength, to-be-able-to
miclian	increase, make-greater		
miclum	greatly, much, very, very-much	*mihten*	avail, be-strong, to-be-able-to
micro	little (Latin)	*mihtig*	mighty, powerful, the-mighty-one
mid	also, amid, among, and, by-means-of, conceal, hide, in-addition, through, together-with, with, with-before, within	*mihtiga*	mighty, powerful, the-mighty-one
		mihtigan	mighty, powerful, the-mighty-one
		mihtiges	mighty, powerful, the-mighty-one
miðan	conceal, hide	*mihtigne*	mighty, powerful, the-mighty-one
midd	mid, middle		
middaneard	earth, middle-earth, middle-world, the-earth, the-world	*mihtmod*	might-mood, power-emotion, strong-inclination
middan-eard	middle-earth, world	*mihton*	avail, be-strong, might, power, to-be-able-to
middaneardlic	earthly, worldly		
middaneardlice	earthly, worldly		
middangeard	earth, middle-earth, middle-world, the-earth, the-world, world	*mihtum*	power, strength
		mil	mile
		milde	gentle, merciful, mild
middangearde	earth, middle-earth, middle-world, the-earth, the-world	*mildsa*	pity
		mildse	mercy
		mildum	gentle, merciful, mild
middangeardes	earth, middle-earth, middle-world, the-earth, the-world	*mildust*	gentle, merciful, mild
		milgemearc	measurement-in-miles
midde	middle	*milgemearces*	measurement-in-miles

Word List (*Ænglisc* to English)

Ænglisc	English	*Ænglisc*	English
milpaðas	mile-track	*misthleoþum*	misty-slope
milpæð	mile-track	*misthliþ*	misty-slope
milpæþ	mile-track	*mistig*	misty
milpaþas	mile-track	*mistige*	misty
milts	favour, kindness, mercy	*miþan*	conceal, hide
miltse	favour, kindness, mercy, mild	*miþendne*	conceal, concealed, hide
miltsian	have-mercy, show-mercy	*mnodhete*	hate, hatred
miltsum	favour, kindness, mercy	*mod*	anxiety, arrogance, courage, heart, mind, mood, mood-mind, pride, spirit, thoughts
Mimming	Mimming (name)		
min	mine, my		
mina	mine		
mine	affection, desire, intention, love, memory, mind, mine, my, to-me	*modceare*	anxiety, grief, mind-sadness, sadness
		modcearig	anxious-minded, sad-hearted
		mod-cearig	anxious, mood-caring, sorrowful
mines	mine, my	*modcearu*	anxiety, mind-sadness
minne	mine		
minra	mine	*moðhe*	moth
minre	mine, my	*mode*	arrogance, courage, heart, mind, mood, pride, spirit
minum	mine		
mirigðe	mirth		
mislic	various	*modega*	proud, valiant
mislice	various-ways	*modelice*	bravely
mislicum	various	*moder*	mother
missan	miss-a-target	*modes*	arrogance, courage, heart, mind, mind's, pride, proud, spirit
missarum	half-year, season, year		
missenlic	different, diverse, various	*modgan*	proud, valiant
		modge	proud, valiant
missenlice	diversely, in-different-ways-or-places, variously	*modgeðance*	mind, plan, understanding
		modgehygd	thought
missenlicum	different, diverse, various	*modgehygdum*	thought
		modgemynd	intelligence, memory, mood-mind, thought
missera	half-year, season, year		
missere	half-year, season, year	*modges*	proud, valiant
		modgeþanc	mind, mind-plans
misserum	half-year, season, year	*modgeþance*	plan, understanding
		modgeþoht	intelligence, thought, understanding
mist	mist, smoke		
mistas	mist, smoke	*modgeþohte*	intelligence, thought, understanding
miste	miss-a-target		
mistglom	misty-gloom		
mistglome	misty-gloom		

Word List (Ænglisc to English)

Ænglisc	English	Ænglisc	English
modgeþonc	conception, mind, plan, purpose, understanding	molde	earth, world
		moldern	earth-building, grave
modgeþonce	mind, plan, understanding	mon	anyone-used-to-form-passive-sense, man, one, someone
modgewinna	mental-trouble	mona	moon
modgewinnan	mental-trouble	monað	admonish, month, remind, warn
modgidanc	mind-plans, mind-sad		
		monan	moon
modgiomor	mind-sad	monaþ	admonish, month, remind, warn
modgum	proud, valiant		
modheap	proud-troop	moncynn	humanity, mankind
modheapum	proud-troop	moncynnæs	humanity, mankind's
modhwatu	strong-soul	moncynne	humanity, mankind
modi	proud, valiant	moncynnes	humanity, mankind, mankind's, month
modig	arrogant, bold, brave, proud, valiant		
		monðes	month
modiga	proud, valiant	mondream	joy, revelry
modigan	proud, valiant	mondreama	joy, revelry
modige	proud, valiant	mondreamum	joy, revelry
modiges	proud, valiant	mondrihten	liege-lord
modiglic	brave, proud	mondryhten	liege-lord, man-lord
modiglicran	brave, proud	mondryhtnes	liege-lord
modigra	proud, valiant	monðwære	gentle, kind
modigre	proud, valiant	monðwærust	gentle, kind
modlufan	heart-love, mood-love, ponder	monegum	many
		monge	many, moans
modlufu	heart-love, mood-love	monig	many
		monige	many
modor	mother	moniges	many
modsefa	mind, spirit	monigfealde	manifold
mod-sefa	mind, spirit	monlica	human-effigy, statue
modsefan	distress, mind, spirit	monn	man, person
modsorg	distress, grief	monna	man, person
modþracu	courage	monnan	man
modþræce	courage	monn-cynn	mankind
modþryðo	arrogance	monnes	man, man's, men, person
modþryþo	arrogance		
modum	arrogance, courage, heart, mind, pride, spirit	monnum	man, mankind, people-number, person
modur	mother	monoð	month
modwlonc	proud-minded	monrim	people-number, population
mod-wlonc	haughty, mood-proud		
		monþes	month
molda	head-crown	monþwære	gentle, kind
moldan	earth, head-crown, the-dust, the-mould, the-world, world	monþwærust	gentle, kind
		monwisa	sinful-way
		monwisan	sinful-way

Word List (*Ænglisc* to English)

Ænglisc	English	*Ænglisc*	English
mor	hilly-region, moor, mountain, mountainous-region	*morþorbealo*	murder, slaughter
		morþorbed	death-bed
		morþorhete	hatred-resulting-from-murder
moras	hilly-region, moor, mountain	*morþorhetes*	hatred-resulting-from-murder
morð	death, destruction, murder	*morþra*	crime, murder, sin, torment
morðbeala	murderous-evil		
morðbealu	murderous-evil	*morþre*	crime, murder, sin, torment
morðer	crime, murder, sin, torment	*morþres*	crime, murder, sin, torment
morðes	death, destruction, murder	*mortuis*	death (Latin)
morðor	crime, murder, sin, torment	*most*	to-be-able-to, to-be-allowed-to
morðorbealo	murder, slaughter	*moste*	to-be-able-to, to-be-allowed-to
morðra	crime, murder, sin, torment	*mosten*	to-be-able-to, to-be-allowed-to
morðre	crime, murder, sin, torment	*moston*	to-be-able-to, to-be-allowed-to, were-able-to
morðres	crime, murder, sin, torment		
more	hilly-region, moor, mountain	*mot*	may, to-be-able-to, to-be-allowed-to
morgen	morning	*motan*	be-allowed-to, may, meet, might, to-be-able-to, to-be-allowed-to
morgena	morning		
morgenceald	morning-cold		
morgencolla	morning-slaughter		
morgencollan	morning-slaughter	*mote*	may, might, to-be-able-to, to-be-allowed-to
morgenleoht	dawn, morning-light		
morgenlong	morning-long		
morgenlongne	morning-long	*moten*	to-be-able-to, to-be-allowed-to
morgensweg	morning-noise		
morgentid	morning-time, morning--time	*moþþe*	moth
		moton	be-able, may, to-be-able-to, to-be-allowed-to
morgne	morning		
morhop	moor-retreat		
morhopu	moor-retreat	*Moyses*	Moses (name)
morna	morning	*muð*	door, mouth, opening
morþ	death, destruction, murder	*muða*	door, estuary, mouth-of-a-river, opening
morþbeala	murderous-evil		
morþbealu	murderous-evil		
morþer	crime, murder, sin, torment	*muðan*	door, opening
		muðbona	biter-to-death, deadly-words, mouth-bane
morþes	death, destruction, murder		
morþor	crime, murder, sin, torment, violence		

Word List (Ænglisc to English)

Ænglisc	English	Ænglisc	English
muðbonan	biter-to-death, deadly-words, mouth-bane	muþ-fulne	mouthful
		myccle	the-greatest
		mycclum	greatly, much, very, very-much
muðe	door, mouth, mouths, opening	mycel	great, much
muð-ful	mouthful	mycele	much
muð-fulne	mouthful	mycelre	greatly, much, very, very-much
multon	burn-up, dissolve, melt	mycle	greatly, much, very, very-much
munan	be-mindful-of, pay-attention-to, remember	myclum	greatly, much, very, very-much
mund	hand, protection	mylenscearpan	ground-sharp
mundbora	guardian, help, protector	myltestre	floozy, prostitute, slut
mundbyrd	help, patronage, protection	myndgað	bring-to-mind, remind
mundbyrdan	intercede, protect	myndgaþ	bring-to-mind, remind
mundbyrde	help, patronage, protection	myndgian	bring-to-mind, remind
mundgripe	hand-grasp	myndgiend	bring-to-mind, remind
mundum	hand		
munecon	monks		
murcnung	grief	myne	desire, intention, love, memory
murcnunge	grief		
murn	fear	mynster	church, monastery
murnan	be-sorrowful, mourn, regret	mynsterlic	monastic
		mynsterlicre	monastic
murne	be-sorrowful, mourn, regret	mynstermann	minster-inhabitant, minster-man, monk
murnende	be-sorrowful, mourn, regret	mynstermen	minster-inhabitant, minster-man, monk
murnon	be-sorrowful, mourn, regret	mynstermenn	minster-inhabitant, minster-man, monk
muþ	door, mouth, opening	mynstre	monastery
		myntan	intend, mean, think
muþa	door, estuary, mouth-of-a-river, opening	mynte	intend, mean, think
		mynteð	intend, mean, think
		mynteþ	intend, mean, think
muþan	door, opening	mynton	intend, mean, think
muþbona	biter-to-death, deadly-words, mouth-bane	myrcan	dark
		myrce	dark, Mercia (place), Mercians, sign
muþbonan	biter-to-death, deadly-words, mouth-bane	myrcels	sign, token, warning
		myrcelse	sign, token, warning
		Myrceon	Mercia
muþe	door, mouth, opening	myrðe	affliction, trouble
		myrðu	affliction, trouble
muþ-ful	mouthful	myrþe	affliction, trouble

Word List (Ænglisc to English)

Ænglisc	English
myrþu	affliction, trouble

N, n

Ænglisc	English
na	never, no, nor, not, not-at-all
naca	boat, ship
nacan	ship
nacod	naked
næbbe	have
næbben	have
nædran	serpent, snake
nædre	serpent, snake
næfð	have
næfdon	have
næfne	except-for, except-that, unless
næfre	address, ever, never
næfþ	have
nægan	address, attack
nægl	claw, finger-or-toe-nail, nail
nægla	claw, finger-or-toe-nail, nail
nægled	decorated-with-nails, nailed
næglede	decorated-with-nails, nailed
næglum	claw, finger-or-toe-nail, nail
næledbord	nailed-board, ship
nænegum	none, not-any
nængum	none, not-any
næni	none
nænig	none, not-any
nænigne	none, not-any
nænigra	none, not-any
nænigum	none, not-any
nænne	none, not-one
nære	to-be
næron	to-be
næs	cliff, earth, ground, headland, never, none, not-at-all, not-emphatic, to-be
næshleoðum	headland-slope
næshleoþum	headland-slope
næshlið	headland-slope
næshliþ	headland-slope
næss	bluff, earth, ground
nagon	control, have, own, possess, rule, some
nah	control, have, own, possess, rule
nahte	control, have, own, possess, rule
nahton	control, have, own, possess, rule
na-hwæðer	neither...nor
na-hwæþer	neither...nor
nalæs	in-no-way, never, not-at-all, not-emphatic
nalas	never, not-at-all, not-emphatic
nales	never, not-at-all, not-emphatic
nallas	never, not-at-all, not-emphatic
nalles	never, not-at-all, not-emphatic, take
nam	take
nama	name, named
naman	name, names, take
namcuþ	whose-name-is-known
namcuþre	whose-name-is-known
name	take
namon	name, take, took
nan	none, not-one
nanðing	nothing
nanne	none, not-one
nanþing	nothing
nanum	any
nap	darken, grow-dark, obscure
nat	be-aware-of, know, not, not-at-all
nateshwon	not-at-all, not-by-any-means
nathwær	somewhere-or-other
nathwæt	something-or-other
nathwylc	a-certain, some-kind, some-kind-of
nathwylces	a-certain, some-kind, some-kind-of

Word List (*Ænglisc* to English)

Ænglisc	English	*Ænglisc*	English
nathwylcum	a-certain, some-kind, some-kind-of	nearwaþ	afflict, become-confined, become-narrow, confine, oppress
nawiht	nothing		
ne	be, do-not, have, near, neither, no, nor, not, to, to-be, was-not, will-not	nearwe	confinement, difficulty, narrow, narrow-place, near, oppressive, tightly
neah	near		
neahbuend	neighbour	nearwian	afflict, become-confined, become-narrow, confine, oppress
neahbuendum	neighbour		
nealæcan	approach, come-near, draw-near		
nealæced	approach, draw-near	nearwode	afflict, become-confined, become-narrow, confine, oppress
nealæcte	approach, draw-near		
nealæhte	approach, come-near	neat	companion, cow, employ, ox, retainer, use, vassal
nealles	never, not-at-all, not-emphatic		
		neawest	nearness, proximity, touch
nean	from-nearby, near		
near	nearer	neb	beak, bill, nose
nearo	difficulty, narrow, oppressive, tight-place	neðde	dare, risk, to-venture
		neðdon	dare, risk, to-venture
		nede	business, by-force, duty, errand, force, necessarily, necessity
nearocræft	confining-strength, keeping-secure, near-strength		
nearocræftum	confining-strength, keeping-secure, near-strength	neðende	dare, risk, to-venture
		nedfere	needed-journey, nephew
nearofag	closely-confined, confined-hostility	nefa	nephew
		nefan	nephew
nearofages	closely-confined, confined-hostility	nefne	except-for, except-that, unless
nearon	to-be	nefre	never
nearore	narrow, oppressive	nefuglas	carrion-bird, death-bird
nearoþearf	oppressive-misery		
nearoþearfe	oppressive-misery	nefugol	carrion-bird, death-bird
nearu	confinement, difficulty, full-of-hardship, narrow, narrow-place		
		negledcnearrum	nailed-knorrs
		neh	near
		nehst	most-recently
nearwað	afflict, become-confined, become-narrow, confine, oppress	nehstan	most-recently, next, recent
		neidfaerae	desire, needed-journey
nearwan	narrow, oppressive	nele	desire, intend, will, wish

Word List (*Ænglisc* to English)

Ænglisc	English	*Ænglisc*	English
nellað	desire, intend, will, wish	*neowel*	deep, precipitous, steep
nellaþ	desire, intend, will, wish	*neowelne*	deep, precipitous, steep
nelle	desire, desires, intend, will, wish	*neowle*	deep, precipitous, steep
nemde	call, name	*nere*	protect, save
nemdon	call, name	*nereð*	protect, save
nemed	call, name	*nerede*	protect, save
nemnað	call, name	*nereþ*	protect, save
nemnan	call, name	*nergan*	protect, save
nemnaþ	call, name	*nergean*	protect, save
nemne	except-for, except-that, unless	*nergend*	preserver, saviour
nemþe	except, unless	*nergende*	saviour
nenig	business, none	*nergendes*	saviour
nenne	any	*nerian*	protect, save
neod	business, delight, desire, duty, errand, lack, longing, necessity, pleasure	*nerion*	save
		nesan	escape-from, survive
		nest	food, provisions
		netele	nettle
neoðan	below, beneath	*neþan*	dare, risk, to-venture
neode	business, duty, errand, necessity	*neþde*	dare, risk, to-venture
		neþdon	dare, risk, to-venture
neodlaðu	desire	*neþeð*	dare, risk, to-venture
neodlaðum	desire	*neþende*	dare, risk, to-venture
neodlaþu	desire	*neþeþ*	dare, risk, to-venture
neodlaþum	desire	*next*	most-recently
neodlice	eagerly, earnestly	*nicer*	water-monster
neoðone	below, beneath	*nicera*	water-monster
neomegende	sound-harmoniously	*niceras*	water-monster
neomian	sound-harmoniously	*nicorhus*	water-monster-house
neon	from-nearby, near		
neorxnawange	paradise	*nicorhusa*	water-monster-house
neorxnawanges	paradise		
neorxnawong	paradise	*nicras*	water-monster
neorxnawonge	paradise	*nið*	affliction, attack, enmity, evil, hatred, hostility, malice, oppression, strife
neorxnawonges	paradise		
neosan	find-out, inspect, seek-out, visit		
		niða	affliction, attack, compel, enmity, evil, force, hatred, men, oppression, strife
neosian	find-out, inspect, seek-out, visit		
neot	enjoy, use		
neotan	employ, enjoy, held, use	*niðas*	affliction, attack, enmity, evil, hatred, men, oppression, strife
neoþan	below, beneath		
neoþeweard	down, downwards		
neoþeweardne	down, downwards		
neoþone	below, beneath	*niðða*	men

182

Word List (*Ænglisc* to English)

Ænglisc	English	*Ænglisc*	English
niððas	men	*nigon and hundeahtatig*	89, eighty nine
niðdraca	evil-dragon		
niððum	men	*nigon and hundeahtatigoþa*	eighty ninth
niðe	affliction, attack, enmity, evil, hatred, oppression, strife	*nigon and hundendleftig*	119, a hundred and nineteen
niðer	down, downwards	*nigon and hundnigontig*	99, ninety nine
niðerian	condemn, oppress, put-down	*nigon and hundnigontigoþa*	ninety ninth
niðerweard	downward		
niðes	affliction, attack, enmity, evil, hatred, oppression, strife	*nigon and hundseofontig*	79, seventy nine
		nigon and hundseofontigoþa	seventy ninth
niðgæst	evil-visitor, malicious-stranger	*nigon and hundteontig*	109, a hundred and nine
niðgeteon	violent-attack	*nigon and sixtig*	69, sixty nine
niðgeteone	violent-attack	*nigon and sixtigoþa*	sixty ninth
nidgripe	hostile-grasp	*nigon and þritig*	39, thirty nine
Niðhad	Nithad (name)	*nigon and þritigoþa*	thirty ninth
niðheard	brave-in-battle, tough	*nigon and twentig*	29, twenty nine
niðhedig	malice-mindful	*nigon and tpentig*	29, twenty nine
nið-hedig	battle-resolved	*nigon and twentigoþa*	twenty ninth
niðhedige	malice-mindful		
niðhycgende	intending-evil	*nigonhund*	nine-hundred
niðsele	evil-hall, hostile-hall	*nigonteoþa*	nineteenth
niðþa	men	*nigontine*	19, nineteen
niðum	affliction, attack, enmity, evil, hatred, oppression, strife	*nigoþa*	ninth
		nigoþan	ninth
		nihgan	next
niðwundor	terrifying-spectacle	*niht*	night, nights
niede	by-force, necessarily, needs, of-necessity	*nihta*	night
		nihtbealu	night-evil
		nihtbealwa	night-evil
niedwædla	beggar, poor-man	*nihte*	night
niehstan	most-recently	*nihtes*	night
nigen	nine	*nihtfeormung*	hospitality-for-the-night, lodging
nigene	nine		
nigenhund	nine-hundred	*nihtfeormunge*	hospitality-for-the-night, lodging
nigoða	ninth		
nigoðan	ninth	*nihtgerim*	night-number
nigon	9, nine	*nihthelm*	night-covering
nigon and feowertig	49, forty nine	*nihtlang*	night-long
nigon and feopertig	49, forty nine	*nihtlangne*	night-long
nigon and feowertigoþa	forty ninth	*nihtlong*	night-long
		nihtlongne	night-long
nigon and fiftig	59, fifty nine	*nihtrest*	bed
nigon and fiftigoþa	fifty ninth	*nihtreste*	bed
		nihtscua	night-darkness

Word List (Ænglisc to English)

Ænglisc	English	Ænglisc	English
nihts-cua	night's-cover	niþ	affliction, attack, enmity, evil, hatred, hostility, malice, oppression, strife, trouble
nihtscuwan	night-darkness		
nihtum	night, nights		
nihtwaco	night-wakefulness, night-watch		
niht-waco	night-watch	niþa	affliction, attack, enmity, evil, hatred, men, oppression, strife, warrior
nihtweorc	night-work		
nihtweorce	night-work		
nim	take		
nimað	take	niþas	affliction, attack, enmity, evil, hatred, men, oppression, strife
niman	take		
nimaþ	take		
nime	take		
nimeð	take	niþða	men
nimest	take	niþdraca	evil-dragon
nimeþ	take	niþe	affliction, attack, enmity, evil, hatred, oppression, strife
nimþe	except		
niobedd	death-bed		
niod	delight, desire, lack, longing, pleasure	niþer	down, downwards
		niþerian	condemn, oppress, put-down
niode	delight, desire, lack, longing, pleasure	niþerweard	downward
nioðor	down, downwards	niþes	affliction, attack, enmity, evil, hatred, oppression, strife
nior	nearer		
niosað	find-out, inspect, seek-out, visit		
niosan	find-out, inspect, seek-out, visit	niþgæst	evil-visitor, malicious-stranger
niosaþ	find-out, inspect, seek-out, visit	niþgeteon	violent-attack
		niþgeteone	violent-attack
niosian	find-out, inspect, seek-out, visit	niþgeweorc	deed-in-battle, evil-deed
		niþgeweorca	deed-in-battle, evil-deed
niotað	enjoy, use		
niotan	enjoy, use	niþgrim	grievous, horrific, terrible
niotaþ	enjoy, use		
nioþor	down, downwards	nithgripe	hostile-grasp
niowan	fresh, new, unheard-of	niþheard	brave-in-battle, tough
nip	darkness	niþhedig	malice-mindful
nipan	darken, grow-dark, obscure	niþ-hedig	battle-resolved
		niþhedige	malice-mindful
nipeð	darken, grow-dark	niþhycgende	intending-evil
nipen	grow-dark, obscure	niþre	below
nipende	darken, grow-dark	niþsele	evil-hall, hostile-hall
nipeþ	darken, grow-dark	niþþa	humanity's, men
nipon	grow-dark, obscure	niþþas	men
nis	be, to-be	niþþum	men

Word List (Ænglisc to English)

Ænglisc	English	Ænglisc	English
niþum	affliction, attack, enmity, evil, hatred, men, oppression, strife	norðdæle	the-north, the-northern-part
		norðmann	northern-man
		Norð-mann	north-man
niþwundor	terrifying-spectacle	norðmanna	northern-man, Northmen
nitor	fresh, shining		
niwan	fresh, new, unheard-of	Norðmannum	Northmen (name)
		norðmen	northern-man
niwe	fresh, new, unheard-of	norðmonna	northern-man
		norðmonnum	northern-man
niwes	fresh, new, recently, unheard-of	norð-weard	northward
		norþ	from-the-north, north
niwiað	afresh, make-anew, renew, repeat	norþan	from-the-north
		norþanwind	north-wind
niwian	afresh, make-anew, renew, repeat	norþdæl	the-north, the-northern-part
niwiaþ	afresh, make-anew, renew, repeat	norþdæle	the-north, the-northern-part
niwra	fresh, new, unheard-of	norþerna	of-the-north
		norþmann	northern-man
niwre	fresh, new, unheard-of	Norþ-mann	north-man
		norþmanna	northern-man
niwtyrwyd	recently-tarred	Norþmannum	Northmen (name)
niwtyrwydne	recently-tarred	norþmen	northern-man, Northmen
no	never, nor, not, not-at-all		
		norþmonna	northern-man
noden	employ, use	norþmonnum	northern-man
noðer	and-not, neither	norþ-weard	northward
nohwæðere	however-not, yet-not-at-all	nosan	headland, promontory
nohwæðre	however-not, yet-not-at-all	nose	headland, promontory
nohwæþere	however-not, yet-not-at-all	nostrum	ours (Latin)
		noþ	loot, plunder
nohwæþre	however-not, yet-not-at-all	noþe	loot, plunder
		noþer	and-not, neither
noldan	desire, intend, will, wish	nu	employ, now
		nudon	employ, use
nolde	desire, intend, will, wish, wished	numen	take
		nunc	now (Latin)
noldon	desire, intend, will, wish	nusquam	never, never (Latin)
		nyd	business, compulsion, duty, errand, necessity
nom	take		
noma	name, the-name		
noman	name	nydan	force, impel-by-necessity
non	3pm, ninth-hour		
norð	from-the-north, north	nydbad	enforced-payment, tariff, toll
norðan	from-the-north		

Word List (*Ænglisc* to English)

Ænglisc	English
nydbade	enforced-payment, tariff, toll
nyde	by-force, compulsion, down, necessarily, necessity, need, subjected
nyðer	down, downwards
nydfara	exile
nydgestealla	companion-in-necessity, comrade
nydgesteallan	companion-in-necessity, comrade
nydwracu	enforced-distress, misery
nyhstan	most-recently
nyhtes	night
nymðe	except, unless
nymeð	take
nymeþ	take
nymþe	except, unless
nys	to-be
nyste	be-aware-of, know
nyston	be-aware-of, know
nyt	beneficial, useful
nyþer	down, downwards
nytt	beneficial, benefit, use, useful, utility
nyttade	enjoy, make-use-of
nytte	beneficial, benefit, use, useful
nyttian	enjoy, make-use-of
nyt-wyrðe	useful
nyt-wyrþe	useful

O, o

Ænglisc	English
o	always, eternally, ever
oboren	carry, wear
obtenebrescit	grows-dark (Latin)
occidente	the-west (Latin)
oð	as-far-as, until, up-to
oð þæt	until
oððæt	until
oðða	or, went-away
oðeodon	went-away
oðer	another, a-second, next, of, one-of-two, other, second
oðerne	another, each-other
oðferede	carry-away
oðferian	carry-away
oðgan	went-away
oðiewan	show
oðiewde	show
oðiewdest	show
oðle	country, native-land
oðre	another, a-second, one-of-two, other
oðres	another, a-second, one-of-two, other
oðrum	another, a-second, one-of-two, other, the-others
oðþæt	until
oðþringan	deprive, drive-out
oðþringeð	deprive, drive-out
oðþrong	deprive, drive-out
oðwand	escape
oðwendan	divert, withdraw
oðwindan	escape
oðwitan	blame, reproach
oðwunden	escape
oðwundon	escape
of	away, away-from, from, of, off, out, out-of
ofæt	fruit
ofætes	fruit
ofaslean	cut-off, strike-off
ofclipian	call, get-by-calling
ofclypode	call, get-by-calling
ofdune	down
ofeode	exit, go-out-of
ofer	above, across, after, against, despite, during, edge, over, overcome, shore, throughout, without
ofercoman	overcoming
ofercomon	overcome
ofercuman	overcome
ofercumen	overcome
ofercwom	overcome
oferdrencan	make-too-drunk

Word List (*Ænglisc* to English)

Ænglisc	English	*Ænglisc*	English
oferdrencte	make-too-drunk	*ofermaðmum*	extravagant-treasure
oferdrifan	defeat, overcome	*ofermægen*	overpowering-might, superior-strength
ofereode	end, overcome, pass-over, traverse	*ofermægene*	overpowering-might, superior-strength
ofereodon	end, pass-over, traverse	*ofermægnes*	overpowering-might, superior-strength
oferfæðmed	covered		
oferfæþmed	covered	*ofermaþm*	extravagant-treasure
oferfaran	cross, go-over, traverse	*ofermaþmum*	extravagant-treasure
oferferan	traverse		
oferferde	traverse	*ofermede*	pride
oferfered	traverse	*ofermetto*	arrogance, pride
oferflat	beat, best, overcome	*ofermod*	arrogance, arrogant, overconfidence, pride, proud
oferfleon	flee-from		
oferflitan	beat, best, overcome	*ofermoda*	arrogant, proud
oferforan	cross, go-over, traverse	*ofermode*	pride
		ofermodes	pride
ofergan	end, pass-over, traverse	*ofersawon*	look-upon, observe, oversee, see, supervise
ofergeaton	forget		
ofergietan	forget	*ofersecan*	overstress, overwhelm
oferhelmað	cover-over, overhang	*oferseon*	look-upon, observe, oversee, see, supervise
oferhelmaþ	cover-over, overhang		
oferhelmian	cover-over, overhang	*ofersittan*	refrain-from, renounce
oferhidig	arrogant, proud	*ofersitte*	refrain-from, renounce
oferhigian	outlast, overtake, pass	*ofersohte*	overstress, overwhelm
oferhogode	be-too-proud-for, despise	*oferswað*	overcome, vanquish
oferhycgan	be-too-proud-for, despise	*oferswam*	swim-across
		oferswaþ	overcome, vanquish
oferhyda	arrogance, conceit, pride	*oferswimman*	swim-across
oferhydig	arrogant, proud	*oferswyðan*	overcome, vanquish
oferhygd	arrogance, conceit, pride	*oferswyðeð*	overcome, vanquish
		oferswyðeþ	overcome, vanquish
oferhygda	arrogance, conceit, pride	*oferswyþan*	overcome, vanquish
oferhygde	arrogance, conceit, pride	*oferswyþeþ*	overcome, vanquish
		oferwearp	cast-down, in-wrestling-throw
ofermaðm	extravagant-treasure	*oferweorp*	throw-down
		oferweorpan	cast-down, in-wrestling-throw

Word List (Ænglisc to English)

Ænglisc	English	Ænglisc	English
oferwinnan	outfight, overcome, vanquish	ofor	above, across, after, against, despite, during, over, throughout, without
oferwunnen	outfight, overcome, vanquish		
ofest	haste, speed	ofost	haste, speed
ofeste	haste, speed	ofoste	haste, speed
ofestlice	hurriedly, quickly	ofostlice	hurriedly, quickly
ofestum	hastily, speedily	ofostum	hastily, speedily
ofet	fruit	ofrað	make-an-offering-or-oblation
ofetes	fruit		
offerede	carry-off	ofraþ	make-an-offering-or-oblation
offerian	carry-off		
offrian	make-an-offering-or-oblation, offer	ofre	edge, shore
		ofsæt	sit-upon
ofgæfon	give-up, leave, relinquish	ofsættum	oppress, possess
		ofsceamian	humiliate, shame
ofgan	exit, go-out-of	ofsceamod	humiliate, shame
ofgeaf	give-up, leave, relinquish	ofsceat	shooting, spear-shooting
ofgeafon	give-up, leave, relinquish	ofsceotan	shooting, spear-shooting
ofgeafun	give-up, leave, relinquish	ofscet	shooting, spear-shooting
ofgefan	give-up, leave, relinquish	ofsettan	oppress, possess
		ofsittan	sit-upon
ofgiefan	give-up, leave, relinquish	ofslægen	destroy, slay
		ofslagen	kill, strike-down
ofgif	give-up, leave, relinquish	ofslean	destroy, kill, slay, strike-down
ofgifan	give-up, leave, relinquish	ofslegene	kill, strike-down
		ofslogon	destroy, slay
ofgifen	give-up, leave, relinquish	ofsloh	destroy, kill, slay, slayed, strike-down
ofgyfan	give-up, leave, relinquish	ofste	haste, speed
		ofstlice	hurriedly, quickly
oflætan	leave-behind, let-go, relinquish, sacramental-wafer	ofstonden	withstood
		ofstum	hastily, speedily
		oft	deny, frequently, often
oflæte	sacramental-wafer		
oflætest	leave-behind, let-go, relinquish	ofteah	deny, deprive, remove, take-away, withdraw, withhold
oflangian	be-overcome-with-longing	ofteon	deny, deprive, remove, take-away, withdraw, withhold
oflet	leave-behind, let-go, relinquish		
oflongad	be-overcome-with-longing, of-longing	ofþecgan	destroy
		ofþegde	destroy
		ofþyncan	displease

Word List (*Ænglisc* to English)

Ænglisc	English	*Ænglisc*	English
ofþyrstan	thirst-for, to-be-thirsty	onbitan	eat, partake-of
		onbleot	sacrifice
ofþyrsted	thirst-for, to-be-thirsty	onblotan	sacrifice
		onbræd	burst, move
oftihð	remove, take-away, withdraw, withhold	onbrægd	burst, move
		onbregdan	burst, move
oftihþ	remove, take-away, withdraw, withhold	onbryrd	encourage, inspire
		onbryrdan	encourage, inspire
oftogen	deny, deprive	onbryrde	encourage, inspire
oftor	frequently, often	onbyrigan	experience, taste
oftost	frequently, often	oncearbendum	anchor-cable
oftugon	deny, deprive	oncerbend	anchor-cable
oht	calamity, enmity	oncierran	return
ohwær	anywhere	oncirde	alter, change, return, turn
oleccan	charm, flatter		
olecung	charm, flattery, seduction	oncirran	return
		oncnawan	know, recognize, understand
olecunge	charm, flattery, seduction	oncneow	know, recognize, understand
oliccan	praise		
ombeht	officer, servant	oncniow	know, recognize, understand
ombiht	command, officer, servant, service	oncwæð	answer, reply-to, say, speak
ombihtscealc	retainer, servant	oncwædon	answer, reply-to
ombihtscealcum	retainer, servant	oncwæþ	answer, reply-to, say, speak
ombihtþegn	serving-man		
ombihtþegne	serving-man	oncweðan	answer, reply-to, say, speak
ombihtum	officer, servant		
omig	corroded, rusty	oncweden	answer, reply-to
omige	corroded, rusty	oncweþan	answer, reply-to, say, speak
omnia	everything (Latin)		
omnipotentem	all-powerful (Latin)		
on	about, allow, alone, among, grant, in, into, kindle, like, of, offer, on, one, onto, swing-open, upon, wish	oncwyð	answers
		oncyð	distress, grief
		oncyrrap	anchor-rope, cable
		oncyrrapum	anchor-rope, cable, tether
		oncyrreð	alter, change, return, turn
onælan	kindle	oncyrreþ	alter, change, return, turn
onæled	kindle		
onarn	swing-open		
onbad	await	oncyþ	distress, grief
onband	loose, release, unbind	oncyþðe	distress, grief
		oncyþþe	distress, grief
onbat	eat, partake-of	ond	and, be-useful-to
onberan	carry, wear	onðah	be-useful-to, prosper
onbidan	await		
onbindan	loose, release, unbind	onðeon	be-useful-to, prosper

Word List (Ænglisc to English)

Ænglisc	English	Ænglisc	English
ondhwearf	turn-against	onfoð	accept, receive, take, take-up
ondhweorfan	turn-against	onfoh	accept, receive, take, take-up
ondlang	accompanying, entire, extended	onfon	accept, receive, take, take-up
ondlangne	accompanying, entire, extended	onfond	discover, experience, find, find-out, found, realize
ondlean	retaliation, revenge		
ondlong	accompanying, entire, extended		
ondlonge	accompanying, entire, extended	onfoþ	accept, receive, take, take-up
ondlongne	the-length	onfunde	discover, experience, find
ondrædað	dread, fear, frighten		
ondrædan	dread, fear, frighten	onfunden	discover, experience, find, find-out, realize
ondrædaþ	dread, fear, frighten		
ondrædeþ	dread, fear, frighten		
ondred	dread, dreaded, fear, frighten	onfundon	find-out, realize
ondrede	dread, fear, frighten	ongæt	perceive, understand
ondredon	dread, fear, frighten		
ondrysne	awe-inspiring, fearful, terrible, venerable	ongalan	recite-a-charm
		ongan	attempt, begin, try, undertake, undertook
ondsaca	adversary, enemy		
ondsacan	adversary	ongangan	approach, attack
ondslyht	battle, counterattack	ongann	attempt, begin, try, undertake
ondsware	answer, reply		
ondswarode	answer, reply	ongeador	together
ondswaru	answer, reply	ongeald	atone-for, be-punished-for, pay-for
ondwrað	wrathful		
onegan	dread, fear		
onemn	beside, by	ongean	again, against, attempt, back, begin, begins, opposite, towards, try, undertake
onettan	hurry, move-rapidly		
onette	hurry, move-rapidly		
onetteð	hurry, move-rapidly		
onetteþ	hurry, move-rapidly		
onetton	hurry, move-rapidly	ongeat	grasp, perceive, understand
onfand	discover, experience, find	ongeaton	grasp, perceive, understand
onfangen	accept, receive	ongietan	grasp, perceive, understand
onfeng	accept, receive, received, take, take-up	ongieten	grasp, perceive, understand, understood
onfengon	accept, receive, take, take-up	ongildan	repaid
onfindan	discover, experience, find, find-out, realize	ongin	attempt, begin, try, undertake

Word List (Ænglisc to English)

Ænglisc	English
onginnað	attempt, begin, try, undertake
onginnan	attempt, begin, try, undertake
onginnaþ	attempt, begin, try, undertake
onginneð	attempt, begin, try, undertake
onginnen	attempt, begin, try, undertake
onginneþ	attempt, begin, try, undertake
ongit	perceive, understand
ongitan	perceive, understand
ongite	perceive, understand
ongon	attempt, begin, try, undertake
ongonn	attempt, begin
ongunn	attempt, undertake
ongunnan	attempt, begin, try, undertake
ongunne	attempt, begin, try, undertake
ongunnen	attempt, begin, try, undertake
ongunnon	attempt, begin, tried, try, undertake
ongyldan	atone-for, be-punished-for, pay-for
ongyn	attempt, begin, try, undertake
ongynneð	attempt, begin, try, undertake
ongynneþ	attempt, begin, try, undertake
ongyrede	strip, unclothe
ongyrwan	strip, unclothe
ongytan	perceive, understand
ongyton	perceive, understand
onhætan	inflame, kindle
onhæted	inflame, kindle
onhawian	gaze-at, observe
onhawoden	gaze-at, observe
onhebban	exalt, increase, raise-up
onhlytme	disappointed, disheartened, dispirited
onhof	exalt, increase, raise-up
onhohsnian	put-a-stop-to
onhohsnode	put-a-stop-to
onhread	adorn
onhreodan	adorn
onhreran	move, stir-up
onhrered	move, stir-up
onhweorfan	change, reverse, turn
onhworfen	change, changed, reverse, turn
onirnan	swing-open
onlædan	bring-in, introduce
onlædde	bring-in, introduce
onlætan	release
onlæteð	release
onlæteþ	release
onlag	give, grant, granted, land, lent, loaned
onlah	give, grant, granted, land, lent, loaned
onleac	open, unlock
onleah	give, grant, granted, land, lent, loaned
onleon	give, grant, granted, land, lent, loaned
onlicnæs	likeness
onlicnes	likeness
onlicnesse	likeness
onlucan	open, unlock
onlut	bow
onlutan	bow
onlysan	loose, release
onlysde	loose, release
onman	esteem, remember, think-worthy
onmedla	arrogance, pomp, pride
onmedlan	arrogance, pomp, pride
onmode	one-minded

Word List (*Ænglisc* to English)

Ænglisc	English	*Ænglisc*	English
onmunan	consider-worthy-of, esteem, remember, think-worthy	onsite	fear, occupy, seated, sit-on-or-in
onmunde	consider-worthy-of, esteem, remember, think-worthy	onsittan	dread, fear, occupy, sit-on-or-in
		onslæpan	fall-asleep
		onslæpen	fall-asleep
onmunon	esteem, remember, think-worthy	onslep	fall-asleep
		onslepon	fall-asleep
onnied	oppression	onspeon	unfasten
onriht	fitting, proper, right	onsponnan	unfasten
onrihtne	fitting, proper, right	onspringan	burst-apart
onsacan	attack	onsprungon	burst-apart
onsæce	deprive	onstealde	begin, establish, established, exemplify, initiate, institute
onsægde	dedicate, offer-a-sacrifice		
onsæge	attacking, fatal		
onsæl	loosen, reveal, untie	onstealdest	begin, exemplify, initiate, institute
onsælan	loosen, reveal, untie		
onsæton	dread, fear	onsteled	establish, institute
onsage	accusation, assertion	onstellan	begin, establish, exemplify, initiate, institute
onsagu	accusation, assertion		
		onsund	healthy, sound, uninjured, whole
onsceacan	shake		
onsceoc	shake	onsundne	healthy, sound, uninjured, whole
onsceotan	open		
onsceote	open	onsundran	apart, privately, secretly, separately
onsecan	deprive		
onsecgan	dedicate, offer-a-sacrifice	onsundron	apart, privately, separately
onsegon	look-upon, observe, watch	onswaf	swing, turn
		onswifan	swing, turn
onsend	deliver-up, dispatch, send	onsyn	beauty, face, figure, sight
onsendan	deliver-up, dispatch, send	ontendnyss	incitement, kindling, spark
onsende	deliver-up, dispatch, send	onþah	be-useful-to, prosper
onsended	deliver-up, dispatch, send	onþeon	be-useful-to, prosper
onsendeð	deliver-up, dispatch, send	ontyhtan	impel, incite
		ontyhte	impel, incite
onsendeþ	deliver-up, dispatch, send	ontynan	open, reveal
		ontyndnys	incitement, kindling, spark
onsendon	deliver-up, dispatch, send		
		ontyneð	open, opened, reveal
onseon	look-upon, observe, watch		
		ontyneþ	open, reveal

Word List (*Ænglisc* to English)

Ænglisc	English	*Ænglisc*	English
onwacan	arise, awake, be-born, begin	*orc*	cask, pitcher
onwacnigeað	awaken	*orcas*	cask, pitcher
onwadan	seize, take	*orcneas*	monsters
onwæcan	weaken	*ord*	beginning, front, front-of-troop-fighter, point, prince, source, spear, troop, vanguard
onwæcen	weaken		
onwæcnan	awake		
onwæcneð	awake		
onwæcneþ	awake	*orðanc*	ingenious
onweald	control, ownership	*ordbana*	murderer
onwendan	change, transgress-a-commandment	*ordbanan*	murderer
		orde	front, front-of-troop-fighter, point, prince, source, spear, troop, vanguard
onwende	movement		
onwended	change, transgress-a-commandment		
onwendeð	change, transgress-a-commandment	*ordfruma*	author, chief, chief-of, creator, leader
onwendeþ	change, transgress-a-commandment	*ordfruman*	author, author-of, chief, creator, leader
onwendon	change, transgress-a-commandment	*Ordlaf*	Ordlaf (name)
		orðonc	art, contrivance, skill
onwindan	untie, unwind	*orðoncum*	art, contrivance, skill
onwindeð	untie, unwind	*ordwyga*	warrior
onwindeþ	untie, unwind	*ore*	army-front, beginning, origin
onwoc	arise, awake, be-born, begin		
		oreð	breath
onwocan	arise, awake, be-born, begin	*oreðe*	breath
		oreðes	breath
onwoce	arise, awake, be-born, begin	*oret*	battle
		oreþ	breath
onwocon	arise, awake, be-born, begin	*oreþe*	breath
		oreþes	breath
onwod	seize, take	*oretmæcgas*	warrior
onwreoh	display, reveal	*oretmecg*	warrior
onwreon	display, reveal	*oretmecgas*	warrior
onwriðan	unwrap	*oretta*	warrior
onwriþan	unwrap	*orette*	battle
op	out-of	*orfeorme*	empty, lacking, useless, without
open	open, visible		
opene	open, visible	*oriente*	the-east (Latin)
openian	open	*orlæggifre*	belligerent, war-mongering
openlice	openly, publicly		
or	army-front, beginning, border, origin	*orleahtre*	blameless
		orlegceap	war-spoils
		orlege	battle
ora	border, edge, shoreline	*orleges*	battle
		orleghwil	battle-time, battle-while
oran	border, edge, shoreline		

Word List (Ænglisc to English)

Ænglisc	English
orleghwila	battle-time, battle-while
orleghwile	battle-time, battle-while
orlegnið	war
orlegniþ	war
orlegweorc	affliction-of?-war
ormæte	boundless, unlimited
orsawle	inanimate, lifeless, without-a-soul
orsorg	unconcerned-by, untroubled-with
orsorge	unconcerned-by, untroubled-with
orþanc	art, contrivance, skill
orþancum	art, contrivance, skill
orþonc	art, contrivance, skilful, skill
orþoncum	art, contrivance, skill
ortrywe	despairing, faithless, hopeless, traitorous
oruð	breath
oruþ	breath
orwearde	unguarded
orwena	despairing-of, without-hope-of
os	but-which, evil-spirit, fairy, Germanic-pagan-god, the-Aesir-or-Ases
Oslac	Oslac (name)
oþ	as-far-as, since, until, up-to
oþ þæt	until
oþbær	carry-along, carry-away
oþberan	carry-along, carry-away
oþðæt	until
oþðe	or
oþeodon	went-away
oþer	another, a-second, next, one-of-two, other, second
oþerne	another, a-second, one-of-two, other
oþerre	another, a-second, one-of-two, other
oþferede	carry-away
oþferian	carry-away
oþgan	went-away
oþiewan	show
oþiewde	show
oþiewdest	show
oþle	country, native-land
oþre	another, a-second, one-of-two, other, the-other
oþres	another, a-second, one-of-two, other
oþrum	another, a-second, one-of-two, other, others
oþþæt	until
oþþe	deprive, or, went-away
oþþringan	deprive, drive-out
oþþringeð	deprive, drive-out
oþþringeþ	deprive, drive-out
oþþrong	deprive, drive-out
oþwand	escape
oþwendan	divert, withdraw
oþwindan	escape
oþwitan	blame, reproach
oþwunden	escape
oþwundon	escape
owðer	both, each, either
ower	anywhere
owiht	anything, at-all, nothing, something
owihte	anything, at-all, nothing, something
owþer	both, each, either

P, p

Ænglisc	English
pæþ	path
pandher	the-panther
paralisyn	paralysis
paralysis	paralysis
Passus	spread-out
patrem	the-father (Latin)
Patri	father (Latin)
Paulus	Paul (name)
peccatorum	of-sins (Latin)
penig	penny
per	by (Latin)
Petrus	Peter (name)

Word List (*Ænglisc* to English)

Ænglisc	English
Pilato	Pilate (name)
Pilatus	Pilate (name)
plega	festivity, fighting, sport
plegan	amuse-oneself, mock, play, sport
plegian	amuse-oneself, mock, play, sport
plegodan	played
plegode	amuse-oneself, mock, play, sport
pleno	full (Latin)
pondus	weight (Latin)
Pontio	Pontius (name)
pontisca	Pontius (name)
ponus	work (Latin)
port	harbour, port
post	post
poste	post
prass	military-force
prasse	military-force
pregnant	child, offspring
preost	priest
principio	the-first (Latin)
pyt	hole, pit

Q, q

Ænglisc	English
que	which (Latin)
quem	who (Latin)

R, r

Ænglisc	English
racentægum	chain
racentan	chain
racente	chain
racentum	chain
racu	cloud, smoke
rad	control, expedition, float, journey, ride, road, sail
rade	expedition, journey, ride, road
raðe	immediately, quickly
raecan	extend, get, give, obtain, offer, reach, reach-with-a-weapon, wound
ræcede	building, palace
ræd	advice, counsel, decree, gain, ordinance, plan, profit
ræda	counsel, decree, gain, ordinance, plan, profit
rædað	advise, instruct, make-decisions, rule
rædan	advise, give-counsel, instruct, make-decisions, read, rule
rædas	counsel, decree, gain, ordinance, plan, profit
rædaþ	advise, instruct, make-decisions, rule
rædbora	counsellor
rædde	advise, instruct, make-decisions, rule
ræde	counsel, decree, gain, ordinance, plan, profit
rædend	ruler
rædes	counsel
rædfæst	disordered, righteous, wise
rædleas	disordered, foolish, miserable
rædlease	disordered, foolish, miserable
ræfndon	carry-out, do
ræfnian	carry-out, do
ræghar	lichen-grey
ræhte	extend, get, give, obtain, offer, reach, reach-with-a-weapon, wound
ræhton	extend, get, give, obtain, offer, reach, reach-with-a-weapon, wound
ræran	build, create, elevate, raise
rærde	build, create, elevate, raise
rærdon	build, create, elevate, raise

Word List (*Ænglisc* to English)

Ænglisc	English	*Ænglisc*	English
ræs	attack, onslaught, rush	reccan	care-about, consider, narrate, tell
ræsan	attack, hasten, rush	recce	care-about, cares-for, consider
ræsbora	guide, leader		
ræsde	attack, hasten, rush	recceð	care-about, consider
ræsed	hasten, rush		
ræseð	attack	reccendne	smoke, steam
ræseþ	attack	recceþ	care-about, consider
ræst	bed, resting-place	rece	smoke
ræste	bed, rest, resting-place, sleep	reced	building, palace
		receda	building, palace
ræsum	attack, onslaught, rush	recede	building, palace
		recedes	building, palace
ræswa	king, leader, lord	recene	immediately, quickly
ræswan	king, leader, lord	reðan	cruel, harsh, terrible
rancstræt	a-large-magnificent?-road	reðe	cruel, fierce, harsh, terrible
rancstræte	a-large-magnificent?-road	reðemode	fierce, savage
		reðran	prepare
rand	shield, shield-boss	reðre	cruel, harsh, terrible
randas	shield	reducant	led
rande	shield	reducat	led (Latin)
randgebeorh	shield-defence	regn	rain
randwiga	shield-warrior	regnas	rain
randwigan	shield-warrior	regnheard	very-tough
randwiggend	shield-warrior	regnhearde	very-tough
randwiggendra	shield-warrior	regnian	adorn, decorate, prepare-a-trick, set-a-trap
randwigum	shield-warrior		
rasian	explore, ransack		
rasod	explore, ransack	rehte	narrate, tell
raþe	immediately, quickly	Remissionem	remission (Latin)
read	red	renian	adorn, decorate, prepare-a-trick, set-a-trap
reada	red		
reade	red		
readfah	red-stained	renig	rainy
readum	red	renodest	adorn, decorate, prepare-a-trick, set-a-trap
reaf	clothing		
reafað	despoil, rob		
reafaþ	despoil, rob	renweard	building-guardian
reafeden	despoil, rob	renweardas	building-guardian
reafian	despoil, rob	reoc	furious, savage
reafige	despoil, rob	reocan	smoke, steam
reafode	despoil, rob	reocende	smoke, steam
reafum	clothing	reodan	redden
rec	smoke	reodne	red
recan	be-interested-in, care-about	reon	row, swim
		reonigmod	weary
recas	smoke	reonigmode	weary
		reord	language, voice

196

Word List (*Ænglisc* to English)

Ænglisc	English	*Ænglisc*	English
reordade	speak	ricne	a-powerful, immediately, mighty, powerful
reordberend	human-being, speech-bearer		
reordberendum	human-being, speech-bearer	ricone	immediately, quickly
		ricost	mighty, powerful
reorde	language, speech, voice	ricra	mighty, powerful
		ricsast	have-power
reordian	speak	ricsian	dominate, oppress, rule
reordigean	speak		
reordode	speak	ricum	mighty, powerful
reotað	cry, lament	ridan	control, float, ride, rode, sail
reotan	cry, lament		
reotaþ	cry, lament	ridda	horseman, rider
reoteð	cry, lament	ride	control, float, ride, sail
reoteþ	cry, lament		
reotig	mournful, weeping	rideð	control, float, ride, sail
reotugu	mournful, weeping		
replete	fill	riden	ride
rest	bed, rest, resting-place, sleep	ridend	horseman, rider
		rideþ	control, float, ride, sail
restað	be-quiet, rest		
restan	be-quiet, rest	ridon	ride
restaþ	be-quiet, rest	rightly	a-right, duty, justice, law, obligation, rule, truth, what-is-right
reste	bed, be-quiet, rest, resting-place, sleep		
		riht	a-right, duty, fitting, just, justice, law, laws, obligation, right, rule, true, truth, what-is-right
restestow	rest-place		
restestowe	rest-place		
reston	be-quiet, rest		
resurrectionem	resurrection (Latin)		
resurrexit	arose (Latin)		
reþan	cruel, harsh, terrible	rihtan	assign, direct, fitting, just, right, set-up, true
reþe	cruel, fierce, harsh, terrible		
reþehygdig	right-thinking	rihte	a-right, assign, correctly, direct, duty, fitting, just, justice, law, obligation, right, rightly, rule, set-up, true, truly, truth, what-is-right
reþemod	fierce, savage		
reþemode	fierce, savage		
reþran	prepare		
reþre	cruel, harsh, terrible		
rib	rib		
rica	mighty, powerful		
rican	mighty, powerful		
rice	great, immediately, kingdom, mighty, powerful, reign, rule	rihtne	fitting, just, right, true
		rihtum	fitting, just, right, true
ricene	immediately, quickly	rihtwis	righteous
rices	kingdom, kingdom's, rule	rihtwisra	righteous
		rim	count, number, total
		rimcræfte	number-reckoning

Word List (*Ænglisc* to English)

Ænglisc	English
rimde	the-host
rime	count, counted, number, total
rimes	count, number, total
rimgetæl	number
rimgetel	number
rinc	man, warrior
rinca	man, warrior
rincas	man, warrior
rince	man, warrior
rinces	man, warrior
rincgetæl	warrior-number
rincum	man, warrior
riodan	control, float, ride, sail
rixað	rule
rixian	dominate, oppress, rule
rixode	dominate, oppress, rule
rod	cross, rood
rode	cross, firmament
rodera	firmament, heaven, heavens, sky
roderas	firmament, heavens, sky
roderum	firmament, heavens, sky, the-firmament, the-skies
rodetacen	cross-sign
rodetacne	cross-sign
rodor	firmament, heaven, heavens, sky
rodora	firmament, heavens, sky
rodore	heaven
rodores	firmament, heavenly-dwelling, heavens, sky, the-heavens
rodorstol	heavenly-dwelling
rodorstolas	heavenly-dwelling
rodortunglum	heavenly-body, star
rodortungol	heavenly-body, star
rof	bold, helmet, noble, sky-crown, sky-roof, strong
rofan	noble, strong
rofe	noble, strong
rofes	helmet, sky-crown, sky-roof
rofne	noble, strong
rofra	noble, strong
rofum	noble, strong
rohte	be-interested-in, care-about
rohton	be-interested-in, care-about
rom	ram-male-sheep
romigan	extend, make-more-spacious?
rommes	ram-male-sheep
Romwarum	the-Romans
rond	round-shield, shield
rondas	round-shield
ronde	shield
rondhæbbend	shield-owner, warrior
rondhæbbendra	shield-owner, warrior
rondwiggend	shield-warrior
rondwiggende	shield-warrior
rowan	row, swim
ruh	coarse, hairy, rough, shaggy
rum	broad, empty, expansive, room, roomy, space, spacious, time, un-oppressed, wide
rume	broad, delighting-in-spaciousness, empty, expansive, for-a-long-distance, for-a-long-time, frequently, roomy, spacious, spaciously, un-oppressed, wide, widely
rumgal	delighting-in-spaciousness
rumheort	large-hearted
rumlice	liberally, widely
rumne	broad, empty, expansive, roomy, spacious, un-oppressed, wide

Word List (*Ænglisc* to English)

Ænglisc	English	*Ænglisc*	English
rumor	for-a-long-distance, for-a-long-time, frequently, spaciously, widely	sæcce	battle
		sæce	battle, strife
		sæcgan	say, tell
		sæcir	tide-turning
rumre	broad, empty, expansive, roomy, spacious, un-oppressed, wide	sæcyning	sea-king
		sæcyninga	sea-king
		sæd	sated, satiated, seed
rumum	broad, empty, expansive, roomy, spacious, un-oppressed, wide	sæda	seed
		sædan	say, tell
		sædberende	seed-bearing
		sædberendes	seed-bearing
run	counsel, discussion, secret-meditation	sæde	said, say, tell
		sædeor	sea-creature
rune	counsel, discussion	sædne	satiated
runstæf	rune, runic-letter	sædon	say, tell
runstafas	rune, runic-letter	sædraca	sea-dragon
runum	counsels	sædracan	sea-dragon
runung	private-conversation, whispering	sæfisc	sea-fish
		sæfisca	sea-fish
		sæflod	flood, sea-current, tide
rununga	private-conversation, whispering	sæfor	sea-voyage
		sæ-for	sea-voyage
runwita	close-advisor	sæfore	sea-voyage
rycene	immediately, quickly	sægan	cause-to-fall, destroy, fell
ryht	a-right, duty, justice, law, obligation, rule, truth, what-is-right	sægd	say
		sægde	said, say, tell
ryhte	properly, rightly	sægdest	say, tell
ryman	clear, enlarge, make-space-for, manifest, open-up	sægdon	say, tell
		sæge	say, tell
		sægeap	sea-roomy
rymde	clear, enlarge, make-space-for, manifest, open-up	sægeð	say, tell
		sægenga	sea-goer
		sægeþ	say, tell
ryne	course, flow, running	sægon	look, perceive, see
		sægrund	sea-bottom
		sægrundas	sea-bottom

S, s

		sægrunde	sea-bottom
		sægst	say, tell
sacan	contest, fight, struggle	sæl	castle, hall, happiness, joy, occasion, time
sacu	battle, strife		
sadol	saddle	sæla	happiness, joy, occasion, time
sadolbeorht	saddle-bright		
sæ	lake, sea	sælac	sea-booty, sea-offering
sæbat	sea-boat, ship		
sæcc	battle, strife		

Word List (*Ænglisc* to English)

Ænglisc	English	*Ænglisc*	English
sælace	sea-booty, sea-offering	sæne	lazy
sælad	sea-voyage	sænra	lazy
sælade	sea-voyage	sæ-rima	seacoast, seashore
sælan	bind, fetter, happen, moor, take-place	særinc	sailor, seaman
		særinca	sailor, seaman
sæld	hall, palace, residence	særyric	sea
		særyrica	sea-reeds
sælða	hall, palace, residence	sæs	sea
		sæsið	sea-journey
sælde	bind, fetter, moor	sæsiðe	sea-journey
sældon	bind, fetter, moor	sæsiþ	sea-journey
sæled	bind	sæsiþe	sea-journey
sæles	happiness, joy, occasion, time	sæstream	sea-current
		sæstreamas	sea-current
sælida	sailor, seafarer	sæstreamum	sea-current
sælidan	sailor, seafarer	sæt	inhabit, live, sat, settle, settled, sit
sæliðend	sailor, seaman		
sælig	blessed, happy	sætan	ambush, inhabit, lie-in-wait-for, live, sat, settle, sit
sæliglice	blessedly, happily		
sæliþend	sailor, seaman		
sæliþende	sailor, sailors, seaman	sæte	inhabit, live, settle, sit
sælþa	hall, palace, residence	sæton	inhabit, live, settle, sit
		sæweall	sea-wall, water-wall
sælum	happiness, joy, occasion, time	sæwealle	sea-wall, water-wall
		sæwong	beach, sea-beach, sea-surface
sælwongas	prosperous-earth, prosperous-ground		
		sæwongas	beach, sea-beach, sea-surface
sæm	sea		
sæmann	sailor, seaman	sæwudu	sea-horse, ship
sæmanna	sailor, seaman	sæwylm	sea-surge, wave
sæmannum	sailor, seaman	sæwylmas	sea-surge, wave
sæmearas	sea-horse, sea-steed, ship	saga	say, tell
		sagast	say, tell
sæmearh	sea-horse, ship	sagona	report, story
sæmeðe	sea-weary, tired-out-from-sailing	sagu	report, story
		sah	sank
sæmen	sailor, seaman	Saharie	Sarah (name)
sæmeþe	sea-weary, tired-out-from-sailing	sal	bond, collar, rope
		sale	bond, collar, rope
sæmra	weaker	salo	castle, dark, dusky, hall
sæmran	weaker		
sænaca	sea-ship	salowigpada	having-a-dark-coat
sænacan	sea-ship, seaward	salum	happiness, joy, occasion, time
sænæss	seaside-headland		
sænæssas	seaside-headland	saluwigpadan	dark-coated-ones
sændan	send, send-away, throw, to-send	salwed	blackened, darkened

Word List (*Ænglisc* to English)

Ænglisc	English	*Ænglisc*	English
salwigfeðera	the-dark-feathered-one	*sarigmod*	sad-minded
salwigfeþera	the-dark-feathered-one	*sarigmodum*	sad-minded
		sarigne	painful, sad
salwigpad	having-a-dark-coat	*sarlic*	pained, painful, sad
samnian	assemble, congregate	*sarlicre*	pained, painful, sad
		sarnissum	distress, pain
samod	also, at-the-same-time, together, together-with, too	*sarnys*	distress, pain
		sarnysse	distress, pain
		sarost	painful, unhappy
		sarra	painful, unhappy
samworht	partly-constructed, unfinished	*sarum*	painful, unhappy
		saul	soul
sanct	saint	*saula*	being, soul, spirit
sancta	holy, saint	*saule*	being, soul
sanctan	saint	*saulum*	being, soul, spirit
sancte	saint	*sawan*	plant-seeds, sow
sancto	holy (Latin)	*saweð*	sewing
Sanctorum	of-the-saints (Latin)	*sawele*	being, soul, spirit
sanctum	holy (Latin)	*sawelleas*	dead, without-a-soul
sanctus	holy, saint	*sawelleasne*	dead, without-a-soul
sand	beach, sand, shore	*sawen*	plant-seeds, sow
sande	beach, sand, shore	*sawl*	being, soul, spirit
sang	compose, sing, singing, song	*sawla*	being, human-being, so, soul, souls, spirit
sanges	singing, song	*sawlberend*	human-being, man, person, soul-bearer
sapan	ointment, salve, soap	*sawlberendra*	human-being, man, person, soul-bearer
sape	ointment, salve, soap	*sawldreor*	life-blood
		sawldreore	life-blood
sar	affliction, pain, painful, sore, sorrow, sorrowful, unhappy	*sawle*	being, soul, spirit
		sawlhord	body, soul-hoard
		sawlum	being, soul, spirit
sara	soreness	*sawol*	being, soul, spirit
sare	affliction, grievously, pain, painful, painfully, sorely, soreness, sorrow, sorrowfully, unhappy	*sawolleas*	dead, without-a-soul
		sawolleasne	dead, without-a-soul
		sawon	look, perceive, see
		sawul	being, soul, spirit
		sawuldrior	life-blood
sarferhð	sad-minded, unhappy	*sawuldriore*	life-blood
		sawulleas	dead, without-a-soul
sarferhþ	sad-minded, unhappy	*sawulleasne*	dead, without-a-soul
		scacan	brandish, depart, flee, hasten, shake
sarig	painful, sad, sorrowful	*scacen*	brandish, depart, flee, hasten, shake
sarigferð	sad-minded, unhappy	*scadeþ*	borders
		scaduhelm	shadow-covering
sarigferþ	sad-minded, unhappy	*scaduhelma*	shadow-covering

Word List (Ænglisc to English)

Ænglisc	English	Ænglisc	English
scæcen	brandish, depart, flee, hasten, shake	sceaðum	destroyer, enemy, scabbard, sheath, warrior
scæð	scabbard, sheath		
scæðum	scabbard, sheath	sceaf	advance, cause-to-move-forward, expel, push-out, thrust
scæron	cleave, cut, hew		
scæþ	scabbard, sheath		
scæþum	scabbard, sheath		
scal	be-obliged, have-the-habit-of, must, shall, should, would	sceaft	arrow-shaft, creation, shaft-of-wheat, spear-shaft
scamian	be-ashamed	sceafta	arrow-shaft, shaft-of-wheat, spear-shaft
scamiende	be-ashamed		
scamigan	be-ashamed		
scan	destroyer, shine, shining, shone	sceal	be-obliged, have-the-habit-of, man, must, ought-to, shall, shall-be, should, warrior, would
scaþan	destroyer, enemy, warrior		
sceacan	brandish, depart, flee, hasten, shake		
sceaceð	brandish, depart, flee, hasten, shake	scealc	man, warrior
		scealcas	man, warrior
sceacen	brandish, depart, flee, hasten, shake	scealcum	man, men, warrior
		sceall	be-obliged, have-the-habit-of, must, shall, should, would
sceaceþ	brandish, depart, flee, hasten, shake		
sceacol	plectrum	scealt	be-obliged, have-the-habit-of, must, shall, shall-you, should, slut, would
sceað	scabbard, sheath		
sceaða	destroyer, enemy, warrior		
sceadan	decide, determine, divide, separate	sceand	slut, whore
		sceande	slut, whore
sceade	darkness, shadow	sceap	sheep
sceaðe	scabbard, sheath	sceape	sheep
sceadeð	decide, determine, divide, separate, separated	sceard	sheared
		scearde	shattered
		scearp	discerning, keen, sharp, shrewd
sceaðen	harm, hurt		
sceaðena	destroyer, enemy, warrior	scearpe	discerning, keen, sharp, shrewd
sceadenmæl	pattern-welder-sword	scearpne	discerning, keen, sharp, shrewd
sceadeþ	decide, determine, divide, separate	sceat	amount, earth-covering, earth-surface, garment, money, property, region, shoot, shoot-arrows, surface, throw-a-spear, wealth
sceado	darkness, shadow		
sceaðona	destroyer, enemy, warrior		
sceadu	darkness, shadow		
sceadugenga	shadowy-walker, walker-in-shadow		

Word List (Ænglisc to English)

Ænglisc	English
sceata	covering, earth-covering, earth-surface, garment
sceatas	earth-covering, earth-surface, garment
sceate	earth-covering, earth-surface, garment
sceates	amount, money, property, wealth
sceaþ	scabbard, sheath
sceaþa	destroyer, enemy, warrior
sceaþe	scabbard, sheath
sceaþen	harm, hurt
sceaþena	destroyer, enemy, warrior
sceaþona	destroyer, enemy, warrior
sceaþum	destroyer, enemy, scabbard, sheath, warrior
sceatt	amount, earth-covering, earth-surface, garment, money, payment, property, wealth
sceatta	earth-covering, earth-surface, garment
sceattas	amount, money, property, wealth
sceattes	amount, money, property, wealth
sceattum	amount, earth-covering, earth-surface, garment, money, property, wealth
sceatum	earth-covering, earth-surface, garment
sceawa	consider, look-upon, respect, show, show-consideration-for
sceawað	consider, look-upon, respect, sees, show, show-consideration-for
sceawaþ	consider, look-upon, respect, show, show-consideration-for
sceawedon	consider, look-upon, respect, show, show-consideration-for
sceawiað	consider, look-upon, respect, show, show-consideration-for
sceawian	consider, look-at, look-upon, respect, see, show, show-consideration-for
sceawiaþ	consider, look-upon, respect, show, show-consideration-for
sceawigan	consider, look-upon, respect, show, show-consideration-for
sceawige	consider, look-upon, respect, show, show-consideration-for
sceawode	consider, look-upon, respect, show, show-consideration-for
sceawodon	consider, look-upon, respect, show, show-consideration-for
sceððan	allot, assign, harm, scabbard
sceðe	scabbard, sheath
sceðþan	allot, assign
sceft	arrow-shaft, shaft-of-wheat, spear-shaft
scefte	shaft

Word List (Ænglisc to English)

Ænglisc	English
scel	be-obliged, have-the-habit-of, must, shall, should, would
scencan	serve-liquid-to
scencte	serve-liquid-to
scene	bright, brilliant, shining
scennum	bright, brilliant, shining
scenost	bright, brilliant, shining
scenran	bright, brilliant, shining
sceoc	brandish, depart, flee, hasten, shake
sceod	harm, injure
sceof	advance, cause-to-move-forward, expel, push-out, thrust
sceolan	shall
sceolde	be-obliged, have-the-habit-of, must, shall, should, should-be, would
sceolden	be-obliged, have-the-habit-of, must, shall, should, would
sceoldest	be-obliged, have-the-habit-of, must, shall, should, would
sceoldon	be-obliged, have-the-habit-of, must, shall, should, would
sceole	be-obliged, have-the-habit-of, must, shall, should, would
sceolon	be-obliged, have-the-habit-of, must, shall, should, would
sceolu	company
sceome	genitals, shame
sceomian	be-ashamed
sceomiende	be-ashamed
sceond	disgrace, insult, shame
sceonde	disgrace, insult, shame
sceone	bright, brilliant, shining
sceonost	bright, brilliant, shining
sceop	arrange, create, created, design, make, poet, shoot, shoot-arrows
sceope	shaped
sceotan	shoot, shoot-arrows, throw-a-spear
sceote	rush
sceoteð	shoot, shoot-arrows, throw-a-spear
sceotend	archer, spearman
sceotendra	archer, spearman
sceotendum	archer, spearman
sceoteþ	shoot, shoot-arrows, throw-a-spear
Sceotta	Scots, The-Scots
scepen	arrange, create, cut, design, make, shaper
sceppend	creator
sceran	cut
scerian	allot, assign
scerne	dung
scepðan	harm, injure
scepe	scabbard, sheath
scepede	harm, injure
sceppan	allot, assign, harm, injure, scabbard
sceppe	harm, injure
sciene	bright, brilliant, shining
scienost	bright, brilliant, shining
scieppan	arrange, create, design, make
scieppend	creator, shaper
scieran	cleave, cut, hew
scild	shield
scildas	shield
scildburh	shield-wall
scildig	guilty, sinful
scildweall	shield-wall
scile	be-obliged, have-the-habit-of, must, shall, should, would

Word List (Ænglisc to English)

Ænglisc	English	Ænglisc	English
scilling	shilling, silver-coin	scoc	brandish, depart, flee, hasten, shake
scima	brightness, radiance	scod	harm, injure
sciman	brightness, radiance	scodon	harm, injure
scinað	shine	scofen	advance, cause-to-move-forward, expel, push-out, thrust
scinan	shine, shining		
scinaþ	shine		
scine	shines		
scineð	shine		
scineþ	shine	scolde	be-obliged, have-the-habit-of, must, ought-to, shall, should, would
scinn	evil-spirit, ghost		
scinna	evil-spirit, ghost, shine		
scinnum	evil-spirit, ghost	scoldon	be-obliged, have-the-habit-of, must, shall, should, would
scinon	shine		
scio	die, fly, go-quickly		
scion	die, fly, go-quickly	scole	host, multitude
scionon	shine	scolu	host, multitude
scip	ship	scomu	genitals, shame
scipe	ship	scop	arrange, create, created, design, make, poet, scop, singer, story-teller
scipes	ship		
scipflotan	sailors		
sciphere	fleet, naval-force		
scipherge	fleet, naval-force	scopes	poet, singer, story-teller
scippend	shaper		
scipu	ship	scorene	sheared
scir	bright, district, division, radiant, shining, shire	scoten	shoot, shoot-arrows, shot, throw-a-spear
		scotendum	archer, spearman
scira	bright, radiant, shining	scralletan	resound, sound-loudly
sciran	bright, radiant, shining	screoda	creep, numbered
		scriðað	move-fast
scire	bright, district, radiant, shining, shire	scriðan	creep, glide
		scrifan	impose, ordain, prescribe
scirecg	keen-edged	scrifeð	impose, ordain, prescribe
scireð	cleave, cut, hew		
scireþ	cleave, cut, hew	scrifeþ	impose, ordain, prescribe
scirham	having-bright-garments		
		scrin	shrine
scirhame	having-bright-garments	scrine	shrine
		scring	shrivel
scirian	allot, assign, ordain	scripað	creep, glide
scirmæled	brightly-decorated	scripan	creep, glide
scirne	bright, radiant, shining	scripaþ	creep, glide
		scucca	demon
scirum	bright, radiant, shining	scuccum	demon
Scittisc	Scottish		

Word List (Ænglisc to English)

Ænglisc	English	Ænglisc	English
scufan	advance, cause-to-move-forward, expel, push-out, thrust	scylda	shield
		scyldan	defend, protect, shield
		scyldas	shield
scufeð	advance, cause-to-move-forward, expel, push-out, thrust	scyldburh	shield-wall
		scylde	defend, fault, protect, shield, shielded
scufeþ	advance, cause-to-move-forward, expel, push-out, thrust	scyldfreca	shield-man, warrior
		scyldfrece	sinful-greed
		scyldfrecu	sinful-greed
		scyldfull	guilty, sinful
scufon	advance, cause-to-move-forward, expel, push-out, thrust	scyldfullum	guilty, sinful
		scyldfulra	guilty, sinful
		scyldi	guilty
		scyldig	guilty, sinful
scufun	advance, cause-to-move-forward, expel, push-out, thrust	scyldige	guilty, sinful
		scyldwiga	shield-warrior
		scyle	be-obliged, have-the-habit-of, must, shall, should, would
sculan	be-obliged, have-the-habit-of, have-to, must, ought-to, shall, should, would		
		scylfa	platform, shelf
		scylfan	platform, shelf
		scylun	hasten, shall-we
sculon	battle-storm, be-obliged, have-the-habit-of, must, ought-to, shall, shall-we, should, would	scyndan	hasten
		scynded	hasten
		scyndeð	surged
		scyndeþ	surged
		scyne	bright, brilliant, shining
scur	battle-storm, shower, storm	scyneð	shines
		scynost	bright, brilliant, shining
scuras	battle-storm, shower, storm	scynra	shining
		scynscaþa	ghostly-or-magical-enemy
scurbeorge	storm-shields		
scurboga	rainbow	scype	ship
scurbogan	rainbow	scypen	shed
scurheard	battle-hard, shower	scypon	ship
scursceade	protection-from-storm	scyppend	creator, district, shaper
scursceadu	protection-from-storm	scyppende	shaper
scurum	battle-storm, incite, shower, storm, storms	scyr	district, region, shire
		scyran	clear-up, cleave, cut, declare, hew, make-known
scyhtan	incite		
scyhte	incite	scyre	district, region, shire
scyld	defend, protect, shield	scyred	allot, assign, ordain
		scyreð	allot, assign, ordain

Word List (Ænglisc to English)

Ænglisc	English
scyrede	allot, assign, ordain
scyreþ	allot, assign, ordain
scyte	shooting, spear-shooting, spear-throwing
se	afflicted, be, be-afflicted, he, it, it-shall, let, she, so, that, that-in, the, this, those, to-be, when, where, which, who, you
seað	be-afflicted, be-troubled, boil, seeing
seah	look, perceive, saw, see
sealde	consign, give, give-up, sealed, sell, sold
sealdest	consign, gave, give, give-up, sell
sealdon	consign, give, give-up, sell
sealma	bed
sealman	bed
sealobrun	deep-brown
sealt	salt, salty
sealte	salt, salty
sealtne	salt, salty
sealtstan	salt-stone
sealtstanes	salt-stone
sealt-yð	salt-wave
sealtyþ	salt-wave
sealt-yþ	salt-wave
sealtyþa	salt-wave, salty-waves
searað	barren, become-dried-out
searaþ	barren, become-dried-out
searian	barren, become-dried-out
searo	armour, art, cunning, skill, trap, trick, weaponry
searobend	cunning-bond
searobende	cunning-bond
searobendum	cunning-bond
searocræftig	craftily-witted
searoðoncol	clever, cunning, skilful
searofah	cunningly-decorated
searogimm	skilfully-made-jewel
searogimma	skilfully-made-jewel
searogimmas	skilfully-made-jewel, skilfully-made-jewels
searogrim	grim-in-battle
searohæbbend	armour-possessor, human-being, man, warrior
searohæbbendra	armour, armoured, armour-possessor, human-being, man, warrior
searonet	armour, mail-coat
searonið	armed-strife, battle, treachery
searoniða	armed-strife, battle, treachery
searoniðas	armed-strife, battle, treachery
searoniþ	armed-strife, battle, treachery
searoniþa	armed-strife, battle, treachery
searoniþas	armed-strife, battle, treachery
searoþonc	cunning, skill-in-contrivance
searoþoncelra	clever, cunning, skilful
searoþoncol	clever, cunning, skilful
searoþoncum	cunning, skill-in-contrivance
searowundor	marvel, strange-wonder
searwum	armour, art, cunning, skill, trap, trick, weaponry
seaþ	be-afflicted, be-troubled, boil, hole, pit, seeing
seaþe	hole, pit
seax	a-blade, blade, knife, sax, seax
seaxe	knife, sax, Saxons, seax

Word List (*Ænglisc* to English)

Ænglisc	English	*Ænglisc*	English
seaxses	knife, sax, seax	sefa	heart, mind, spirit
sec	attack, desire, go-to, man, seek, seek-out, visit, wish-for	sefan	mind, spirit
		seft	gently, softly
		sefte	comfortable, soft
secan	attack, desire, go-to, seek, seek-out, to-seek, visit, wish-for	sefteadig	comfortably-happy, rich-in-luxuries
		sege	say, tell
		segeð	say, tell
secce	battle, strife	segelgyrd	sail-yard
sece	attack, desire, go-to, seek, seek-out, visit, wish-for	segen	account, banner, look, see, sign, story
		segene	account, story
seceað	attack, desire, go-to, seek, seek-out, visit, wish-for	segeþ	say, tell
		segl	sail
secean	attack, desire, go-to, seek, seek-out, visit, wish-for	seglian	sail
		seglod	sail
		seglode	sail
seceaþ	attack, desire, go-to, seek, seek-out, visit, wish-for	seglrad	sail-road, the-sea
		seglrade	sail-road, the-sea
		segn	banner, sign, standard
seceð	attack, desire, go-to, seek, seek-out, seeks, visit, wish-for	segnad	bless, consecrate
		segnade	bless, consecrate, sign-of-the-cross
secen	attack, desire, go-to, seek, seek-out, visit, wish-for	segnas	banner, sign
		segncyning	banner-king
secest	attack, desire, go-to, seek, seek-out, visit, wish-for	segne	banner, sign
		segnian	bless, consecrate, sign-of-the-cross
seceþ	attack, desire, go-to, seek, seek-out, visit, wish-for	sel	better, castle, good, hall
		selast	excellence
secg	man, sword, warrior, warriors	seld	hall, palace, residence
secga	man, men's	seldan	seldom
secgað	say, tell, told	seldcymas	infrequent-visit
secgan	man, say, tell, told	seldcyme	infrequent-visit
secgas	man	seldguma	retainer, servant
secgaþ	say, tell	sele	hall, happiness, house, joy, occasion, time
secge	man, say, sword, tell		
secgeað	say, tell		
secgean	say, tell	seleð	consign, give, give-up, sell
secgeaþ	say, tell		
Secgena	Secgen (name)	seledream	hall-joy
secggende	say, tell	seledreamas	hall-joy
secgrofra	sword-brave	seledreorig	miserable-because-lacking-a-hall
secgum	man, might		
secula	time (Latin)	seleful	ceremonial-cup, hall-cup
seculorum	of-times (Latin)		

Word List (Ænglisc to English)

Ænglisc	English
selegyst	hall-guest
selerædend	hall-councillor
selerædende	hall-councillor
selerest	hall-bed
selereste	hall-bed
selesecg	hall-man, retainer, warrior
sele-secg	hall-hero, retainer
selesecgas	hall-man, retainer, warrior
selest	good
selesta	good
selestan	good
seleste	good
seleþ	consign, give, give-up, sell
seleþegn	hall-thane, warrior
seleweard	hall-guard
self	her, him, own, same, self
selfa	her, him, own, self
selfcyning	absolute-king, personal-ruler
selfe	her, him, own, self
selfes	her, him, own, self
selfne	her, him, own, self, yourself
selfra	her, him, own, self
selfre	her, him, own, self
selfsceafte	directly-created
selfum	her, him, own, self
sella	better, good
sellan	give, good, sell
selle	consign, give, give-up, sell
sellend	giver
sellic	marvellous, rare
sellice	marvellous, rare
sellicra	rarer
selost	good
selra	good
selran	good
selre	good
seman	reconcile, settle
semian	continue, lie, lie-at-rest, lie-in-wait, stay
semninga	all-at-once, immediately, suddenly
semper	always (Latin)
sencan	cause-to-sink, death, sink, submerge, thrust-down
sendan	cause-to-go, hurl, send, throw
sende	send, throw
sended	send, throw
sendeð	send, sends, throw
sendeþ	send, throw
sendon	send, throw
sened	send
senescunt	grows-old (Latin)
senna	sin
sensu	sense (Latin)
sent	send, throw
seo	he, her, his, it, she, sick, so, that, that-in, the, this, those, to-be, which, who, wounded
seoc	sick, wounded
seoce	sick, wounded
seoðan	be-afflicted, be-troubled, boil, seeing
seoððan	after, afterwards, since, when
seofad	lament, sigh
seofade	lament, sigh
seofan	seven
seofedun	lament, sigh
seofene	seven
seofian	lament, sigh
seofoðan	seventh
seofon	7, seven
seofon and feowertig	47, forty seven
seofon and feopertig	47, forty seven
seofon and feowertigoþa	forty seventh
seofon and fiftig	57, fifty seven
seofon and fiftigoþa	fifty seventh
seofon and hundeahtatig	87, eighty seven
seofon and hundeahtatigoþa	eighty seventh

Word List (Ænglisc to English)

Ænglisc	English
seofon and hundendleftig	117, a hundred and seventeen
seofon and hundnigontig	97, ninety seven
seofon and hundnigontigoþa	ninety seventh
seofon and hundseofontig	77, seventy seven
seofon and hundseofontigoþa	seventy seventh
seofon and hundteontig	107, a hundred and seven
seofon and sixtig	67, sixty seven
seofon and sixtigoþa	sixty seventh
seofon and þritig	37, thirty seven
seofon and þritigoþa	thirty seventh
seofon and twentig	27, twenty seven
seofon and tpentig	27, twenty seven
seofon and twentigoþa	twenty seventh
seofone	seven
seofonfeald	seven-fold, seven-times-as-large
seofonteoþa	seventeenth
seofontine	17, seventeen
seofoþa	seventh
seolf	her, him, own, self
seolfa	her, him, own, self
seolfor	silver
seolfre	silver
seolhbaþo	ocean, seal-baths
seomade	continue, lie, lie-at-rest, lie-in-wait, stay
seomedon	continue, lie, lie-at-rest, lie-in-wait, stay
seomian	continue, lie, lie-at-rest, lie-in-wait, stay, swinging-in
seomode	continue, lie, lie-at-rest, lie-in-wait, stay
seomodon	continue, lie, lie-at-rest, lie-in-wait, stay
seon	look, perceive, see
seono	muscle-fibre, sinew
seonobend	sinew-bond
seonobende	sinew-bond
seonobenn	injury-to-a-sinew-or-muscle
seonobennum	injury-to-a-sinew-or-muscle
seonowe	muscle-fibre, sinew
seoþan	be-afflicted, be-troubled, boil, seeing
seoþðan	after, afterwards, since, when
seoþþan	after, afterwards, since, when
seow	plant-seeds, sow
seowed	knit, link, sew
seowian	knit, link, sew
Serafhin	Seraphim (name)
sess	seat
sesse	seat
setan	inhabit, live, settle, sit
sete	appoint, create, establish, ordain, place, set, settle
seþeah	nevertheless
setl	place, residence, seat, throne
setla	place, residence, seat, throne
setlað	bring-to-a-halt, settle
setlan	bring-to-a-halt, settle
setlaþ	bring-to-a-halt, settle, settling
setle	place, residence, seat, setting, throne
setles	place, residence, seat, throne
setlgang	setting
setlgange	setting
setlum	place, residence, seat, throne
settan	appoint, create, establish, ordain, place, set, set-down, settle
sette	appoint, create, establish, ordain, place, set, settle
settest	set
setton	appoint, create, establish, ordain, place, set, settle

Word List (Ænglisc to English)

Ænglisc	English
sexbenn	knife-wound, wound-from-a-sax
sexbennum	knife-wound, wound-from-a-sax
si	be, let, to-be
siae	friendship, to-be
sib	friendship, happiness, peace
sibæðeling	noble-relative
sibæðelingas	noble-relative
sibæþeling	noble-relative
sibæþelingas	noble-relative
sibb	friendship, happiness, peace
sibbe	friendship, happiness, peace
sibbegedriht	peaceful-company, troop-of-relatives
sibblufan	friendship, love
sibblufu	friendship, love
sibgebyrd	blood-relation
sibgebyrdum	blood-relation
sibgedriht	peaceful-company, troop-of-relatives
siblufan	friendship, love
siblufu	friendship, love
siclian	become-sick
sicut	thus-as (Latin)
sid	broad, extensive, extensively, generally, wide
sið	custom, destiny, expedition, fate, habit, journey, late, occasion, time, voyage
sida	custom, destiny, expedition, fate, habit, journey, occasion, time
sidan	broad, extensive, side, wide
siðast	late
siðboda	expedition-messenger
siððan	after, afterwards, since, when
side	broad, extensive, extensively, far, side, wide, widely
siðe	custom, destiny, expedition, fate, habit, journey, occasion, time
siðedon	go, journey, travel
siðes	custom, destiny, expedition, fate, habit, journey, occasion, time
siðestan	late, later, since
siðfæt	expedition, journey, path, road
sidfæþm	capacious, of-a-ship-broad-beamed
sidfæþme	capacious, of-a-ship-broad-beamed
sidfæþmed	capacious, of-a-ship-broad-beamed
siðfate	expedition, journey, path, road
siðfrom	ready-for-a-journey
siðfrome	ready-for-a-journey
siðian	go, journey, travel
siðie	go, journey, travel
siðien	go, journey, travel
sidland	wide-or-extensive-land
sidne	broad, extensive, wide
siðode	go, journey, travel
sidra	broad, extensive, wide
sidrand	broad-shield
sidre	broad, extensive, wide
siðþan	after
siðwerod	expeditionary-force, invading-army
sie	be, sight-power, to-be
sien	sight-power, to-be, vision
siene	sight-power, vision
siex	6, six, six-hundred
siex and feowertig	46, forty six
siex and feopertig	46, forty six

Word List (*Ænglisc* to English)

Ænglisc	English	*Ænglisc*	English
siex and fiftig	56, fifty six	sigegyrd	wand
siex and hundeahtatig	86, eighty six	sigehræmig	victorious-exultant
		sigehreð	triumph, victory
siex and hundendleftig	116, a hundred and sixteen	sigehreðig	triumphant
		sigehreþ	triumph, victory
siex and hundnigontig	96, ninety six	sigehreþig	triumphant
		sigehwil	victory-time
siex and hundseofontig	76, seventy six	sigehwila	victory-time
		sigel	gem, victory
siex and hundteontig	106, a hundred and six	sigeleas	defeated, vanquished
siex and sixtig	66, sixty six	sigelease	defeated, vanquished
siex and þritig	36, thirty six		
siex and twentig	26, twenty six	sigeleasne	defeated, vanquished
siex and þpentig	26, twenty six		
siex-hund	six-hundred	sigeres	victory
siextig	sixty	sigerof	famous-for-victories, victorious
siextine	16, sixteen		
sig	to-be	sigerofe	famous-for-victories, victorious
sigað	sink		
sigan	descend, fall, go, move, sink	sigerofra	victorious-strong
		sigeþ	descend, fall, go, move, sink
sigaþ	sink		
sige	victory	sigeþeod	victorious-people
sigebeam	cross-of-victory, tree-of-victory, victorious-cross, victorious-tree, victory-cross, victory-tree	sigeþeode	victorious-people
		sigeþuf	victory-banner
		sigeþufas	victory-banner
		sigewæpen	victory-weapon
		sigewæpnum	victory-weapon
		sigewif	victorious-women
sigebeorna	victory-warriors	sigewong	victory-field
sigeð	descend, fall, go, move, sink	sigisiþa	broach, successful
		sigla	broach, jewel, necklace
sigedrihten	the-victorious-Lord, victory-king, victory-lord	sigle	broach, brooch, jewel, necklace
sigeeadig	blessed-with-victories, victorious	siglu	gem
		sigon	descend, fall, go, move, sink
sigefæst	triumphant, victorious	sigor	victory
sigefæstran	triumphant, victorious	sigora	victory
		sigore	victory
Sigeferð	Sigeferth (name)	sigoreadig	blessed-with-victory, victorious
Sigeferþ	Sigeferth (name)		
sigefest	victorious	sigores	victory
sigefolc	victorious-people	sigorfæst	victorious
sigefolca	victorious-people, victory-folk	sigorlean	reward-for-victory
		sigorleanum	reward-for-victory
sigefolce	victorious-people	sigoro	victory

Word List (Ænglisc to English)

Ænglisc	English	Ænglisc	English
sile	give	sing	sing
sima?	chain, fetter	singað	singing
simble	always	singal	continual, perpetual
simle	always, continually, ever	singala	always, continually, perpetually
simon	chain, fetter	singalan	continuously
sin	her, his, its	singale	continual, perpetual
sinc	jewels, riches, treasure, treasures	singales	always, continually, perpetually
sinca	riches, treasures	singan	compose, sing
sincan	sink, subside	singeð	sing
since	because, for-that-reason, riches, treasures	singende	sing
		singeþ	sing
		sinhere	massive-army
sincende	sink, subside	sinherge	massive-army
sinces	riches, treasures	sinhiwan	married-couple
sincfæt	precious-object, treasure-cup	sinhiwum	married-couple
		sinnan	care-about, notice, pay-attention-to
sincfag	decorated-with-treasure	sinne	her, his, its
sincfage	decorated-with-treasure	sinnihte	in-perpetual-night
		sinre	her, his, its
sincfato	precious-object, treasure-cup	sinsorg	great-sorrow
		sinsorgna	great-sorrow
sincgestreon	treasure	sint	to-be
sincgestreona	treasure	sinum	her, his, its
sincgestreonum	treasure	sio	that-in, the, those
sincgifa	king, lord, treasure-giver	siodo	custom, good-conduct, manner, morality
sincgifan	king, lord, treasure-giver	siofa	minds
sincgyfa	king, lord, treasure-giver	siofan	minds
		sioleð	sea
sincgyfan	king, lord, treasure-giver	sioleða	sea
		sioleþ	sea
sinchroden	adorned-with-treasure	sioleþa	sea
		siomian	continue, lie, lie-at-rest, lie-in-wait, stay
sincmaðþum	treasure		
sincmaþþum	treasure	site	established
sincþege	treasure-receiving	siteð	established, he-sits, sits
sincþego	treasure-receiving		
sincþegu	treasure-receiving	sitest	sit
sinc-þegu	treasure-receipt	siteþ	established
sind	they-are, to-be	siþ	custom, destiny, expedition, fate, habit, journey, late, lot, occasion, time, venture, voyage
sinder	cinder, slag		
sindon	they-are, to-be		
sindrum	cinder, slag		
sine	her, his, its		
sines	her, his, its		

Word List (Ænglisc to English)

Ænglisc	English	Ænglisc	English
siþa	custom, destiny, expedition, fate, habit, journey, occasion, time	six and hundnigontigoþa	ninety sixth
		six and hundseofontigoþa	seventy sixth
siþade	go, travel	six and sixtigoþa	sixty sixth
siþast	late	six and þritigoþa	thirty sixth
siþboda	expedition-messenger	six and twentigoþa	twenty sixth
		sixta	sixth
siþðan	after, afterwards, since, when	sixteoþa	sixteenth
		sixtig	60, sixty
siþe	custom, destiny, expedition, fate, habit, journey, occasion, time	sixtigoþa	sixtieth
		slægen	beat, erect-a-tent, forge, kill, strike
		slæp	sleep
siþedon	go, journey, travel	slæpe	sleep
siþes	custom, destiny, expedition, fate, habit, journey, occasion, time	slaga	killer, slayer
		slagan	killer, slayer
		slat	cut, slit, tear, torture
		slea	beat, erect-a-tent, forge, kill, strike
siþestan	late, later, since		
siþfæt	expedition, journey, path, road	sleac	slow, sluggish
		sleah	beat, erect-a-tent, forge, kill, strike
siþfate	expedition, journey, path, road		
		slean	beat, erect-a-tent, forge, kill, strike
siþfrom	ready-for-a-journey		
siþfrome	ready-for-a-journey	slege	blow, killing
siþian	go, journey, travel	slegefæge	doomed-to-die-by-blows
siþie	go, journey, travel		
siþien	go, journey, travel	sliðe	cruel, savage
siþode	go, journey, travel	sliðen	dire, evil, hard
siþon	custom, destiny, expedition, fate, habit, journey, occasion, time	sliðheard	cruel
		sliðhearda	cruel
		sliðne	cruel, savage
		sliðra	cruel, savage
siþþan	after, afterwards, established, inhabit, later, since, thenceforth, when	slit	cut, tear, torture
		slitan	cut, slit, tear, torture
		slite	cut, tear, torture
		sliteð	cut, tear, torture
siþwerod	expeditionary-force, invading-army	sliten	slit, tear
		sliteþ	cut, tear, torture
sittað	established	sliþe	cruel, savage
sittan	inhabit, live, settle, sit, sitting	sliþen	cruel, dire, evil, hard, savage
sittaþ	established	sliþheard	cruel
sitte	sit	sliþhearda	cruel
six and feowertigoþa	forty sixth	sliþne	cruel, savage
six and fiftigoþa	fifty sixth	sliþra	cruel, savage
six and hundeahtatigoþa	eighty sixth	sliton	slit, tear

Word List (*Ænglisc* to English)

Ænglisc	English	*Ænglisc*	English
slog	beat, erect-a-tent, forge, kill, strike	snotera	clever, intelligent, skilful, wise, wiser
sloge	beat, erect-a-tent, forge, kill, strike	snoteran	clever, intelligent, skilful, wise
slogon	beat, erect-a-tent, forge, kill, strike	snotere	clever, intelligent, skilful, wise
sloh	beat, erect-a-tent, forge, kill, strike, striking	snoterost	wisest
		Snotingaham	Nottingham (place)
		snotor	clever, intelligent, skilful, wise, wise-man
smæl	narrow, small		
smæte	pure		
smætum	pure	snotorlice	wisely
smeagan	examine, think	snotorlicor	wisely
smeðe	smooth	snotra	clever, intelligent, skilful, wise
smeðne	smooth		
smið	a-smith, metal-worker, smith	snottor	clever, intelligent, skilful, wise
smiðas	metal-worker, smith, smiths	snottra	clever, intelligent, skilful, wisdom, wise
smiðcræftega	skilled-in-metal-craft	snottre	clever, intelligent, skilful, wise
smiþ	metal-worker, smith		
smiþa	metal-worker, smith	snude	immediately, quickly
smiþas	metal-worker, smith	snyredon	hurry, move-quickly
smiþcræftega	skilled-in-metal-craft	snyrian	hurry, move-quickly
smiþes	metal-worker, smith	snytra	cleverness, intelligence, skill, wisdom
smylte	tranquil		
smyrian	anoint, apply-a-lotion, embrocate	snytro	cleverness, intelligence, skill, wisdom
snað	cut		
snædan	cut, devour, slice	snytru	cleverness, intelligence, skill, wisdom
snaþ	cut		
snaw	snow		
snedeþ	cut, devour, slice		
snel	bold, quick	snytrum	wisdom, wise
snella	bold, quick	snyttru	cleverness, intelligence, skill, wisdom
snelle	bold, quick, quickly		
snellic	bold, quick		
snellice	quickly	snyttrum	cleverness, intelligence, skill, wisdom
snelra	bold, quick		
sneome	swiftly		
sner	harp, string	socn	visit
snere	harp, string	socne	visit
sniðan	cut	soð	justice, rectitude, righteousness, true, truly, truth, truthful
sniome	quickly		
sniomor	quickly		
sniþan	cut	soðan	true
sniwan	snow	soðcyning	the-true-king
sniwde	snow	soðcyninges	the-true-king
sniwed	snow		

Word List (*Ænglisc* to English)

Ænglisc	English	*Ænglisc*	English
soðe	justice, rectitude, righteousness, true, truth	*somod*	also, together, together-with
soðfæst	honest, just, righteous, trustworthy, truth-firm	*somwist*	cohabitation, living-together
		sona	at-once, dune, immediately, soon
soðfæste	honest, just, righteous, trustworthy, truth-fastened	*sondbeorg*	dune, sand-bank
		sondbeorgum	dune, sand-bank
		sonde	beach, sand, shore
		song	sing, singing, song
soðfæstra	honest, just, righteous, trust, trustworthy, truthful	*sorg*	distress, grief, pain, sorrow, trouble
		sorga	distress, grieve, pain, sorrow, take-pains-over, to-be-sorrowful, worry-about
soðgeleafa	true-belief		
soðgeleafan	true-belief		
soðgied	or-poem, song, true-story		
		sorgcearig	sorrowful
soð-gied	true-tale	*sorge*	distress, pain, sorrow
soðlice	truly		
soðne	true, truly	*sorgedon*	grieve, take-pains-over, to-be-sorrowful, worry-about
soðra	true		
soðum	gently, true		
softe	gently, softly		
soht	desire, seek	*sorgful*	miserable, sorrowful
sohtan	attack, desire, go-to, seek, seeking, seek-out, visit, wish-for	*sorgfulre*	miserable, sorrowful
		sorgian	grieve, take-pains-over, to-be-sorrowful, worry-about
sohte	attack, desire, go-to, seek, seek-out, visit, wish-for		
		sorgiende	grieve, take-pains-over, to-be-sorrowful, worry-about
sohten	attack, desire, go-to, seek, seek-out, visit, wish-for		
		sorglufu	sorrowful-love, unhappy-love
sohtest	attack, desire, go-to, seek, seek-out, sought, visit, wish-for	*sorgum*	distress, pain, sorrow
		sorh	distress, pain, sorrow
		sorhcearig	sorrowful
sohton	attack, desire, go-to, seek, seek-out, sought, visit, wish-for	*sorhful*	miserable, sorrowful
		sorhfull	miserable, sorrowful
		sorhfullne	miserable, sorrowful
som	friendly, peaceable, united	*sorhfulne*	miserable, sorrowful
some	the-same	*sorhg*	distress, pain, sorrow
somed	also, together, together-with		
somnigean	assemble, congregate	*sorhleas*	unmolested, without-sorrow

Word List (*Ænglisc* to English)

Ænglisc	English	*Ænglisc*	English
sorhleoð	burial-hymn, lament	*sparian*	abstain-from, save, use-sparingly
sorhleoþ	burial-hymn, lament		
sorhword	sorrowing-word	*sparode*	abstain-from, save, use-sparingly
sorhworda	sorrowing-word		
sorhwylm	sorrow, sorrow-wave	*spearca*	spark
		spearcan	spark
sorhwylmas	sorrow, sorrow-wave	*specan*	say, speak
		sped	means, power, prosperity, quickness, riches, speed, success
sorhwylmum	sorrow, sorrow-wave		
soþ	justice, rectitude, righteousness, true, truly, truth	*spedan*	be-quick, be-successful, be-wealthy
soþan	true		
soþcyning	the-true-king	*spedaþ*	be-quick, be-successful, be-wealthy
soþcyninges	the-true-king		
soþe	justice, rectitude, righteousness, true, truth	*speddropa*	effective-drop, successful-drop
soþfæst	honest, just, righteous, trustworthy, truth-firm	*speddropum*	effective-drop, successful-drop
		spede	power, prosperity, speed, success
soþfæste	honest, just, righteous, trustworthy	*spedge*	successful
		spedig	successful
		spedum	successful
soþfæstra	honest, just, righteous, trustworthy	*spel*	speech, story
		spell	message, speech, story
soþgeleafa	true-belief	*spella*	speech, story
soþgeleafan	true-belief	*spellboda*	messenger
soþgied	or-poem, song, true-story	*spellbodan*	messenger
		spellum	message, speech, story
soþ-gied	true-tale		
soþlice	truly	*spenn*	attach, fasten
soþne	true	*speon*	entice, urge
soþra	true	*speone*	entice, urge
soþum	gently, true	*speow*	succeed
spæc	language, speech	*spere*	spear
spæce	language, speech	*sperenið*	battle, spear-strife
span	entice, spin, twist, urge, wring	*spereniþ*	battle, spear-strife
		speru	spear
spanan	entice, urge	*spilde*	destroy, kill, spoil
spang	buckle, clasp	*spildsið*	journey-of-destruction
spangum	buckle, clasp		
spannan	attach, fasten	*spildsiðe*	journey-of-destruction
sparedon	abstain-from, save, use-sparingly		
		spildsiþ	journey-of-destruction

Word List (Ænglisc to English)

Ænglisc	English	Ænglisc	English
spildsiþe	journey-of-destruction	spyrian	ask, go, investigate, make-a-track, travel
spillan	destroy, kill, spoil	squalescit	grows-dirty (Latin)
spinnan	spin, twist, wring	staca	pin, spike, stake
spiritui	spirit (Latin)	stacan	pin, spike, stake
spiritum	the-spirit (Latin)	staðelian	establish, found
spiwan	spit, spit-out	staðol	foundation, location, position, security, stance, state, support
spiwe	spit, spit-out		
spor	spoor, trace, track		
spornan	perch-upon		
spowan	succeed	staðolas	foundation, location, position, security, stance, state, support
spræc	conversation, say, speak, speak-to, speech		
spræca	conversation, speech	staðole	foundation, location, position, security, stance, state, station, support
spræce	conversation, say, speak, speaking, speak-to, speech		
		staðolwang	location-for-settlement, piece-of-land
spræcon	say, speak, speak-to		
sprang	burst-forth, grow, leap, spread, spring, spurt	staðolwangas	location-for-settlement, piece-of-land
spreca	councillor		
sprecað	say, speak, speak-to	stæð	beach, river-bank, shore
sprecan	say, speak, speak-to		
sprecaþ	say, speak, speak-to	stæðe	beach, river-bank, shore
sprece	say, speak, speak-to		
spreceð	speaking	stædefæste	steadfastly, unyieldingly
sprecen	say, speak, speak-to		
sprengan	break, split	stæðweall	retaining-bank, shoreline-as-barrier8
sprengde	break, split		
spriceð	say, speak, speak-to		
spriceþ	say, speak, speak-to	stæð-weall	shore-wall
springan	burst-forth, grow, leap, spread, spring, spurt	stæðweallas	retaining-bank, shoreline-as-barrier8
sprong	grow, leap, spread, spring, spurt	stæl	admit, place, place-of, position
sprungen	burst-forth, spread, spring	stælan	admit, confess, place, position
sprungon	burst-forth, grow, leap, spread, spring, spurt	stæle	place, position
		stælgiest	burglar, thieving-intruder
sprycst	say, speak, speak-to	stæl-here	marauding-army
sprytan	sprout	stæmne	voice
spyrede	ask, go, investigate, make-a-track, travel	stænen	stone, stone-made
		stænenne	stone, stone-made
		stænnene	stone, stone-made

Word List (*Ænglisc* to English)

Ænglisc	English	*Ænglisc*	English
stæppan	step	*stanhliþ*	stone-slope-or-cliff
stæppe	step	*stanhliþe*	stone-slope, stone-slope-or-cliff
stæþ	beach, river-bank, shore	*stanhliþo*	stone-slope-or-cliff
stæþe	beach, river-bank, shore	*stanhofu*	stone-halls
		stantorr	stone-tower
stæþweall	retaining-bank, shoreline-as-barrier8	*stapol*	base, front-step, pediment, support
stæþ-weall	shore-wall	*stapole*	base, front-step, pediment, support
stæþweallas	retaining-bank, shoreline-as-barrier8	*stapulum*	base, front-step, pediment, support
stah	arise, arisen, ascend, climb, get-onto, mount, rise	*starað*	gaze, stare
		staraþ	gaze, stare
		starede	gaze, stare
		staredon	gaze, stare
stan	stone	*starian*	gaze, stare
stanbeorh	hill, stone-burial-mound, stone-cliff	*starie*	gaze, stare
		starige	gaze, stare
stanboga	stone-arch	*staþe*	beach, river-bank, shore
stanbogan	stone-arch		
stanburg	stone-city, stone-fort	*staþel*	foundation, location, position, security, stance, state, support
stanbyrig	stone-city, stone-fort		
stancleofu	stone-cliff		
stanclif	stone-cliff		
stan-clif	stony-cliff	*staþelian*	establish, found
stanclifu	stone-cliff	*staþelum*	foundation, location, position, security, stance, state, support
standað	be, exist, extend, remain, stand		
standan	be, exist, extend, remain, stand		
standaþ	be, exist, extend, remain, stand	*staþol*	foundation, location, position, security, stance, state, support
stande	be, exist, extend, remain, stand		
standeð	be, exist, extend, remain, stand	*staþolas*	foundation, location, position, security, stance, state, support
standen	stand		
standeþ	be, exist, extend, remain, stand, standing	*staþole*	foundation, location, position, security, stance, state, support
stane	stone		
stanfah	decorated-paved-with-stones	*staþolwang*	location-for-settlement, piece-of-land
Stanford	Stamford (place)		
stang	stab	*staþolwangas*	location-for-settlement, piece-of-land
stanhleoþu	stone-slope-or-cliff		
stanhlið	stone-slope-or-cliff		
stanhliðo	stone-slope-or-cliff		

Word List (*Ænglisc* to English)

Ænglisc	English	*Ænglisc*	English
staþu	beach, river-bank, shore	steppan	step
stealc	steep	stepte	advance, elevate, erect, raise, support
steallian	happen	stepton	advance, elevate, erect, raise, support
steam	moisture, steam	stercedferhð	harsh-spirited
steame	moisture, steam	stercedferhðe	harsh-spirited
steap	deep, high, steep	stercedferhþ	harsh-spirited
steape	above, deep, high, steep	stercedferhþe	harsh-spirited
steapes	deep, high, steep	sticaþ	prick, stab, stick
steapheah	erect, towering	stice	sticking
steapne	deep, high, steep	stician	prick, stab, stick
stearcheort	strong-hearted	stið	brave, hard, stern, stiff, strong
stearn	sea-swallow, tern		
stede	place, position	stiðe	hard, strong, very-much, well
stedefæst	steadfast, unyielding		
stedefæste	steadfast, unyielding	stiðferhð	resolute, stern
stedeheard	very-hard	stiðferhþe	strong-mind
stedehearde	very-hard	stiðhicgende	brave, resolute
stefn	prow, root, stave, stem, stern, stump, time, turn, voice	stiðhydig	resolute, stern
		stiðlic	strong
		stiðlice	boldly, firmly
stefna	prow, root, stave, stern, stump	stiðmod	brave, resolute, strong
stefnan	appoint, arrange, ordain, prow, root, stave, stern, stump	stiðmoda	brave, resolute, strong
		stiðra	hard, strong
stefne	prow, root, stave, stern, stump, voice	stiðum	hard, strong
		stiep	deprivation?
stefnum	stern	stiepe	deprivation?
stemn	voice	stieran	guide, restrain
stemne	voice	stig	road, track
stemnettan	stand-firm	stigan	arise, ascend, climb, get-onto, mount, rise
stemnetton	stand-firm		
stenc	fragrance, odour, smell, stench	stige	arise, climb, get-onto, mount, road, track
steor	correction, guidance, punishment		
		stigen	ascend, rise
		stigon	arise, ascend, climb, get-onto, mount, rise
steor-bord	starboard		
steore	correction, guidance, punishment	stigwita	household-counsellor, leader
		stigwitum	household-counsellor, leader
steorra	star		
steorrum	star	stihtan	command, order
stepan	advance, elevate, erect, raise, support	stihte	command, order
		stillan	to-still-cause-to-be-still
stepe	advance, elevate, erect, raise, support		

Word List (Ænglisc to English)

Ænglisc	English	Ænglisc	English
stille	motionless, quiet, still	stondeþ	be, exist, extend, remain, stand
stincan	follow-a-scent, smell	stop	step
stingan	stab	stopon	step
stinge	sting	stor	incense
stirende	steering	storm	attack, storm, tempest
stiþ	brave, hard, stern, stiff, strong	stormas	storm
stiþe	hard, strong, very-much, well	storme	storm
		stormum	storms
stiþferhþ	resolute, stern	stow	place
stiþfrihþ	resolute, stern	stowe	place
stiþhicgende	brave, resolute	stræl	arrow
stiþhydig	resolute, stern	stræla	arrow
stiþlic	strong	strælas	arrow
stiþlice	boldly, firmly	stræle	arrow
stiþmod	brave, resolute, strong	strælum	arrow
		stræt	road, street
stiþmoda	brave, resolute, strong	stræte	road, street
		strand	seashore, strand
stiþra	hard, strong	strande	seashore, strand
stiþum	hard, strong	strang	powerful, strong
stod	be, exist, extend, remain, stand, stood	stranga	powerful, strong
		strangan	powerful, strong
stodan	be, exist, extend, remain, stand, stood	strange	powerful, strong
		strangne	powerful, strong
stode	stood	strangre	powerful, strong
stodon	be, exist, extend, remain, stand	strangum	powerful, strong
		stream	current, river, stream
stol	castle, establishment, seat, throne	streamas	current, river, rivers, streams
stole	castle, establishment, seat, throne	streame	current, river, stream
		streames	current, river
stolenne	stolen	streamstað	river-bank, shore
stonc	follow-a-scent, smell	streamstaðe	river-bank, shore
stondað	be, exist, extend, remain, stand, standing	streamstaþ	river-bank, shore
		streamstaþe	river-bank, shore
		streamum	current, river
stondan	be, exist, extend, remain, stand	streamweall	current-wall, gunwale
stondaþ	be, exist, extend, remain, stand	stred	scatter, strew
		stregan	scatter, strew
stonde	be, exist, extend, remain, stand	streng	bowstring, cord, rope
stondeð	be, exist, extend, remain, stand	strengðo	force, strength, vigour
		strenge	strength

Word List (Ænglisc to English)

Ænglisc	English	Ænglisc	English
strengel	lord, ruler	styrian	disturb, mention, stir-up, tell-about
strengeo	strength	styrman	rage, storm
strengest	powerful, strong	styrmde	rage, storm
strenglic	strong	styrmdon	rage, storm
strenglicran	strong	styrne	grave, hard, stern
strengo	strength	styrnmode	sternly, with-determination
strengþo	force, strength, vigour	sub	under
strengum	bowstring, cord, powerful, rope, strong	suð	from-the-south, south
strið	battle, contest, fight, struggle	suðan	from-the-south
		suðe-weard	southward
striðe	battle, contest, fight, struggle	suðfolc	southern-nation, southern-people
striþ	battle, contest, fight, struggle	suðfolcum	southern-nation, southern-people
striþe	battle, contest, fight, struggle	suðmonn	southern-man
		suðmonna	southern-man
strong	powerful, strong	suðon	from-the-south
stronglic	strong	suðportice	south-porch
stronglican	strong	suð-stæð	south-shore
strongum	powerful, strong	suðweg	southern-direction, way-from-the-south
strudan	carry-off, plunder		
strude	carry-off, plunder	suðwegum	southern-direction, way-from-the-south
strudende	carry-off, plunder		
strudon	carry-off, plunder	suðwind	south-wind
strynan	acquire, beget, get	sue	as, illness-only-instance-is-at
strynde	acquire, beget, get		
stryndon	acquire, beget, get	suht	illness-only-instance-is-at
stund	awhile, time		
stundum	from-time-to-time	suhterga	nephew
styde	location, place, situation	suhtergefæderan	man-and-paternal-uncle
style	steel	suhtria	nephew
stylecg	having-steel-edges	suhtrian	nephew
stynt	be, exist, extend, remain, stand	suhtriga	nephew
		suhtrigan	nephew
styple	steeple	sules	plough
styran	guide, restrain	sulh	plough
styrde	guide, restrain, stirred	sulhgeteogo	ploughing-implements
styrede	disturb, mention, stir-up, tell-about	sulhgeweorc	plough-making
		sulhgeweorces	plough-making
styreþ	disturb, mention, stir-up, tell-about	sum	a, a-certain, a-certain-amount, a-certain-one, one, some
styrge	disturb, mention, stir-up, tell-about		

Word List (Ænglisc to English)

Ænglisc	English
sume	a-certain, a-certain-one, some, some-of
sumeres	summer
sumes	a-certain, a-certain-one, some
sumne	a-certain, a-certain-one, some
sumor	summer
sumorlang	summer-long
sumorlangne	summer-long
sumum	a-certain, a-certain-one, some, son
suna	son
sund	sailing, sea, swimming, the-sea, water
sunde	sailing, sea, swimming, the-sea, water
sundes	sailing, sea, swimming, the-sea, water
sundgebland	stirred-up-water, water-mixing
sundhelm	water-protection
sundhelme	water-protection
sundhwat	quick-swimming
sundhwate	quick-swimming
sundnytt	swimming
sundnytte	swimming
sundor	apart, separately
sundorgecynd	strange-nature
sundornytt	special-assignment, special-duty
sundornytte	special-assignment, special-duty
sundorspræc	private-conversation
sundorspræce	private-conversation
sundoryrfe	inherited-private-property
sundoryrfes	inherited-private-property
sundreced	sea-building
sundrian	separate, sunder
sundwudu	sea-wood, ship
sunganges	clockwise, sun-going, sunwise
sungen	compose, sing
sungon	compose, sing
sunnan	sun
sunnandæg	Sunday
sunnbeam	sunbeam, sunshine
sunne	sun, the-sun
sunnon	care-about, notice, pay-attention-to
suno	son
sunt	they (Latin), they-are (Latin)
sunu	son
sunum	son
sunwlitegost	sunniest
supan	sip
susl	misery, torment
susla	torment
susle	misery, torment
suslhofe	torment-of-hell
suþ	from-the-south, south
suþan	from-the-south
suþern	southern
suþerne	southern
suþe-weard	southward
suþfolc	southern-nation, southern-people
suþfolcum	southern-nation, southern-people
suþmonn	southern-man
suþmonna	southern-man
suþon	from-the-south
suþ-stæp	south-shore
suþweg	southern-direction, way-from-the-south
suþwegum	southern-direction, way-from-the-south
suþwind	south-wind
suua	as
suuyltit	dies
swa	abandon, also, as, as-if, in-such-a-way-that, likewise, so, so-as, such, such-as, thus, when, whosoever
swa hwilc swa	whosoever
swac	abandon, betray, deceive, depart
swaðe	footstep, path, track

Word List (Ænglisc to English)

Ænglisc	English	Ænglisc	English
swaðrian	become-calm, subside	swatigne	bloody, sweaty
swaðu	footstep, path, track	swatswaðu	blood--stained, track
swæcca	scents	swatswaþu	blood--stained, track
swæf	lie-dead, sleep	swealg	swallow
swæfne	dream, sleep	swealh	swallow
swæfon	lie-dead, sleep	swealt	die
swæfun	lie-dead, sleep	sweart	black, dark, swarthy
swægende	crash, make-noise, roar, rush	sweartan	black, dark
swær	sluggish, weak	swearte	black, dark
swæran	sluggish, weak	sweartlast	leaving-black-tracks
swærbyrde	weak-birth	sweartne	black, dark
swærtbyrd	black-labour, cyanotic-birth	sweartnys	blackness
		sweartnysse	blackness
swærtbyrde	black-labour, cyanotic-birth	sweartost	black, dark
		sweartra	darkness
swærtum	black, dark	sweartum	black, dark
swæs	beloved, dear, own, sweet	swebban	kill, put-to-sleep
		sweðrian	cease
swæsendu	dinner, feasting, meal	sweðrode	cease
		swefað	lie-dead, sleep
swæsendum	dinner, feasting, meal	swefan	death-sleep, lie-dead, sleep
swæslice	easily, pleasantly	swefaþ	lie-dead, sleep
swætan	bleed, sweat	swefeð	kill, lie-dead, put-to-sleep, sleep
swæþer	whichever	swefeþ	kill, lie-dead, put-to-sleep, sleep
swancor	lithe, thin, trim, weak	swefl	sulphur
swang	fly, strike, whip	swefn	dream, sleep
swanrad	sea, swan-road	swefna	dream, sleep
swanrade	sea, swan-road	swefne	dream, sleep
swar	heavy, oppressive	swefote	slumber
sware	heavy, oppressive	swefyl	sulphur
swase	beloved, dear, own, sweet	sweg	music, noise, sound
		swegan	crash, make-noise, roar, rush
swat	blood, sweat		
swate	blood, sweat	swege	music, sound
swates	blood, sweat	swegel	sky
swatfag	blood-stained	Sweghleoþor	sound
swatfah	blood-stained	swegl	bright, shining, the-heavens, the-sky
swaþe	footstep, path, track		
swaþredon	become-calm, subside	sweglbosmas	the-heavens
		sweglcyning	heaven-king
swaþrian	become-calm, subside	swegle	bright, shining, the-heavens, the-sky
swaþu	footstep, path, track	swegles	heaven, the-heavens, the-sky
swaþul	heat?-flame?		
swaþule	heat?-flame?	swegltorht	heaven-bright
swatig	bloody, sweaty	swegltorhtan	heaven-bright

Word List (Ænglisc to English)

Ænglisc	English	Ænglisc	English
sweglwered	covered-in-brightness	sweorde	sword
		sweordes	sword, swords
swelan	burn	sweordfreca	sword-warrior
swelc	such, such-as, such-a-thing	sweordfrecan	sword-warrior
		sweordplegan	sword-play
swelce	such, such-as, such-a-thing	sweordum	sword, swords
		sweordwigend	sword-warrior
swelgað	swallow	sweordwigendra	sword-warrior
swelgan	swallow	sweordwund	sword-wounded
swelgaþ	swallow	sweostar	sister
swellan	swell	sweostor	sister
sweltan	die	sweot	host, troop
swencan	afflict, injure, torment	sweotol	clear, manifest
		sweotolan	clear, manifest
swencte	afflict, injure, torment	sweotole	clearly, openly, plainly
sweng	stroke	sweotolian	make-clear, make-manifest, reveal
swenge	stroke		
swenges	stroke	sweotollice	clearly
swengum	stroke	sweotule	clearly, openly
sweofot	sleep	sweotum	host, troop
sweofote	sleep	swerian	swear
sweog	resound, roar	sweta	sweet
sweogon	resound, roar	swete	sweet
sweoloð	flames, heat	sweþrian	cease
sweoloðe	flames, heat	sweþrode	cease
sweoloþ	flames, heat	swetne	sweet
sweoloþe	flames, heat	swettra	sweeter
sweolt	die	swican	abandon, betray, deceive, depart
sweora	neck		
sweoran	neck	swicce	scent
sweorcan	become-gloomy, darken, grow-dark	swice	abandon, betray, deceitful, deceive, depart, escape, such
sweorceð	become-gloomy, darken, darkening, grow-dark		
		swician	betray, deceive
sweorcendferhð	gloomy	swicode	betray, deceive
sweorcendferhðe	gloomy	swicol	deceitful, untrustworthy
sweorcendferhþ	gloomy		
sweorcendferhþe	gloomy	swicole	deceitful, untrustworthy
sweorceþ	become-gloomy, darken, grow-dark	swicon	abandon, betray, deceive, depart
sweord	sword		
sweorda	sword	swið	mighty, strong
sweordbealo	sword-evil, violence	swiðan	strengthen, support
sweordberend	man, sword-wearer, warrior	swiðe	exceedingly, much, very, very-much, very-sustaining
sweordberende	man, sword-wearer, warrior		
		swiðfeorm	very-sustaining

Word List (Ænglisc to English)

Ænglisc	English
swiðferhð	bold, brave
swiðferhðum	bold, brave
swiðferhþe	bold, brave
swiðferhþes	bold, brave
swiðhicgende	brave, resolute, strong-minded
swiðlic	extremely, greatly
swiðlice	extremely, greatly
swiðmod	bold-hearted, proud-minded
swiðne	right-hand
swiðor	exceedingly, very, very-much
swiðost	exceedingly, strongest, very, very-much
swiðra etc	right-hand
swiðrade	diminish, disappear, vanish
swiðran	right, right-hand
swiðre	right
swiðrian	diminish, disappear, vanish
swiðrode	diminish, disappear, vanish
swifan	stroke, sweep, swipe
swifeð	sleeps, stroke, sweep, swipe
swifeþ	stroke, sweep, swipe
swift	swift
swifta	swift
swiftne	swift
swiftust	swiftest
swige	quiet, silent
swigedon	become-silent, be-silent
swigian	become-silent, be-silent
swigode	become-silent, be-silent
swigra	quiet, silent
swilc	such, such-as, such-a-thing
swilce	also, as, as-if, likewise, so, so-as, such, such-as, thus
swilces	such, such-as, such-a-thing
swilcum	such, such-as, such-a-thing
swima	fainting, head-spinning, head-swimming
swiman	fainting, head-spinning, head-swimming
swimmað	fly, sail, swim, swimmers
swimman	fly, sail, swim
swimmaþ	fly, sail, swim
swin	wild-boar
swincan	labour, struggle, toil
swingan	fly, strike, whip
swingeð	fly, strike, whip
swingeþ	fly, strike, whip
swinlic	swine-likeness, wild-boar-banner, wild-boar-image, wild-boar-sign
swinlicum	swine-likeness, wild-boar-banner, wild-boar-image, wild-boar-sign
swinsian	be-musical, make-music, sing
swinsigende	be-musical, make-music, sing
swioðol	fire
swioðole	fire
swioþol	fire
swioþole	fire
swirman	swarming
swiþ	mighty, strong
swiþan	strengthen, support
swiþe	exceedingly, great, greatly, very, very-much, very-sustaining
swiþfeorm	very-sustaining
swiþferhþ	bold, brave
swiþferhþe	bold, brave
swiþferhþes	bold, brave
swiþferhþum	bold, brave
swiþhicgende	brave, resolute, strong-minded

Word List (Ænglisc to English)

Ænglisc	English	Ænglisc	English
swiþlic	extremely, greatly	swyðe	exceedingly, very, very-much
swiþlice	extremely, greatly		
swiþmod	bold-hearted, proud-minded	swyðferhð	bold, brave
		swyðor	exceedingly, very, very-much
swiþne	right-hand		
swiþor	exceedingly, very, very-much	swylc	such, such-as, such-a-thing
swiþost	exceedingly, very, very-much	swylce	also, as, as-if, just-as, likewise, so, so-as, such, such-as, such-a-thing
swiþra	stronger		
swiþra etc	right-hand		
swiþrade	diminish, disappear, vanish	swylcne	such, such-as, such-a-thing
swiþran	right, right-hand	swylcra	such, such-as, such-a-thing
swiþre	right, right-hand		
swiþrian	diminish, disappear, vanish	swylcum	such, such-as, such-a-thing
swiþrode	diminish, disappear, vanish	swylt	death
		swyltdæg	death-day
switolost	the-clearest	swyltdæge	death-day
swogan	resound, roar	swylte	death
swogen	resound, roar	swyltit	dies, fly
swogende	roar	swymman	fly, sail, swim
swoncre	lithe, supple, thin, trim, weak	swyn	wild-boar
		swynsode	be-musical, make-music, sing
swor	swear		
sworcenferð	insensible, unconscious, with-darkened-mind	swyrd	sword
		swyrdgeswing	sword-cutting, sword-swinging
sworcenferþ	insensible, unconscious, with-darkened-mind	swyrdgifu	sword-giving
		swyrdum	sword
		swyster	sister
sword	swords	swytelað	made-known
swulces	such, such-as, such-a-thing	swyþ	mighty, strong
		swyþe	exceedingly, very, very-much
swulge	swallow		
swuncon	labour, struggle	swyþferhþ	bold, brave
swurd	sword	swyþor	exceedingly, very, very-much
swurde	sword		
swurdleoma	sword-gleam	sy	after, afterwards, be, it-is, the, to-be, whether
swustersunu	nephew, sister's-son		
swutele	law-maker		
swutelung	explanation, revelation	sybbe	friendship
		sybcwide	friendliness
swutelunge	explanation, revelation	syððan	after, afterwards, since, when
swutol	clear, manifest	syððon	since
swyð	mighty, strong	syddra	wide

Word List (Ænglisc to English)

Ænglisc	English	Ænglisc	English
syðþan	after, afterwards, since, when	symble	always, continually, feast
syfanwintre	seven-years-old	symle	always, continually, crime, ever, feast, forever, sin
syfone	seven		
Sygegealdor	tribute		
syle	give, grant	syn	crime, sin, they
syleð	consign, give, give-up, sell	synbysig	guilty, sinful
		syncfatum	precious-treasures
syleþ	consign, give, give-up, sell	synd	they, to-be
		syndan	they-are
sylf	her, herself, him, himself, own, self, yourself	synderlic	singular, special
		synderlicre	singular, special
		syndolh	large-wound
sylfa	her, him, himself, own, self, yourself	syndon	they-are, to-be
		syndrig	distinct, separate, special
sylfan	her, him, his-self, own, self, suicide		
		synfullum	sinful
sylfcwale	suicide	syngales	always, continually, perpetually
sylfcwalu	suicide		
sylfe	her, him, own, self	syngian	do-evil, sin
sylfes	her, him, own, self	syngige	sin
sylfne	her, him, himself, own, self	synn	crime, guilt, sin
		synna	crime, guilt, sin
sylfor	silver	synne	crime, guilt, sin
sylfra	her, him, own, self	synnig	sinful, sinner
sylfre	her, him, own, self, to-her	synnigra	sinful, sinner
		synnihte	perpetual-night
sylfum	her, him, own, self, to-himself	synnum	crime, guilt, sin
		synscaðan	sinful-devil, sinful-enemy
syll	floor		
syllað	consign, give, give-up, sell	synscaþan	sinful-devil, sinful-enemy
syllan	consign, give, give-up, good, sell, the-better	synsceaþa	sinful-devil, sinful-enemy
		synsceaþan	sinful-devil, sinful-enemy
syllaþ	consign, give, give-up, sell	synsnæd	large-piece-of-food
sylle	consign, floor, give, give-up, sell	synsnædum	large-piece-of-food
		synt	to-be
syllic	marvellous, rare	syrcan	mail-coat
syllicran	marvellous, rare	syrce	mail-coat
syllicre	marvellous, rare	syrede	equip-with-armour, plan, plot
syllon	consign, give, give-up, sell		
		syrwan	equip-with-armour, plan, plot
symbel	feast		
symbelwerig	drunk, feast-wary	syþðan	after, afterwards, since, when
symbelwynn	feast-joy		
symbelwynne	feast-joy	syþþan	after, afterwards, since, when
symbla	feast		

Word List (*Ænglisc* to English)

Ænglisc	English
syx	six
syxhund	six-hundred
syxtig	sixty

T, t

Ænglisc	English
tacen	sign, token
tacn	sign, token
tacne	sign, token
tacnian	betoken, show-by-signs
tæcan	allot, assign, instruct, show, teach
tæcaþ	allot, assign, instruct, show, teach
tæfl	perhaps-referring-to-chess, tables—a-board-game
tæfle	perhaps-referring-to-chess, tables—a-board-game
tægel	tail
tæhte	allot, assign, instruct, show, teach
tæleð	blaming
tæsan	tear, tease-wool, wound
tæsde	tear, tease-wool, wound
talað	claim, consider
talade	numbered
talast	claim, consider
talaþ	claim, consider
talian	claim, consider
talige	claim, consider
tan	branch, twig
tanum	branch, twig
teaforgeapa	red-coloured
teag	band, cord, fetter
teage	band, cord, fetter
teagum	chains
teah	bring, bring-up, draw-a-sword, educate, grant, take
teala	well
tealde	consider, count, reckon, tell, think
tealdon	consider, count, reckon, tell, think
team	descendant, progeny
teames	descendant, progeny
teamum	descendant, progeny
tear	tear
tearas	tear
tearighleor	having-a-tear-stained-face
tela	well
telg	dye, ink
telga	branch, twig
telgan	branch, twig
telge	consider, count, reckon, tell, think
telgum	branch, twig
tellan	consider, count, reckon, tell, think
temað	bring-forth, engender, propagate
teman	bring-forth, engender, propagate
temaþ	bring-forth, engender, propagate
temian	tame
temiaþ	tame
tene	ten
tenet	holds (Latin)
teng	go, hurry
tengan	go, hurry
teoche	race, species, troop
teoða	tenth
teodan	adorn, arrange, create, ordain, prepare
teoðan	tenth
teode	adorn, arrange, create, ordain, prepare, settle, titled
teodod	adorn, settle
teoh	race, species, troop
teohh	race, species, troop
teohha	race, species, troop
teohhe	race, species, troop

Word List (Ænglisc to English)

Ænglisc	English
teohhian	appoint, arrange, assign, intend
teohhode	appoint, arrange, assign, intend
teon	accuse, adorn, arrange, bring, bring-up, create, drag, draw, draw-a-sword, educate, grant, ordain, prepare, settle, take
teona	injury, malice, wrong
teonan	injury, malice, wrong
teonhete	malicious-hatred
teonum	injury, malice, wrong
teonwit	contention, strife
teonwordum	rebuke
teorað	fail
teoraþ	fail
teosu	harm, injury
teoþa	tenth
teoþan	tenth
teran	tear
terre	earth
Tertia	third (Latin)
tiadæ	offering, titled
tiber	offering, sacrifice
tibre	offering, sacrifice
tid	hour, time, times
tið	boon, favour, gift, grant
tida	hour, time
tiða	recipient, sharer
tiddæg	allotted-time, lifespan
tiddæge	allotted-time, lifespan
tide	hour, time
tiðe	boon, favour, gift, grant
tidege	allotted-time, lifespan
tiðiað	give, grant
tiðian	give, grant
tiedrað	bring-forth, produce, propagate
tiedran	bring-forth, produce, propagate
tiedraþ	bring-forth, produce, propagate
tien	10, ten
tigelum	bricks
tihte	draw, persuade, pull, teach
tihting	exhortation, instruction
tihtinge	exhortation, instruction
tiid	time
tiir	fame, glory, honour
til	for, good, to
tile	good
tilian	till, to, towards, until, work-for
tilien	till, to, towards, until, work-for
till	good
tilmodig	good, righteous
tilmodigne	good, righteous
tilne	good
tilode	till, to, towards, until, work-for
tilra	good
tilu	good
timber	building, building-material, timber
timbran	build, construct, erect
timbred	build, construct, erect
timbrede	build, construct, erect
timbrien	build
timian	happen
tiode	adorn, arrange, create, ordain, prepare
tir	fame, glory, honour
tire	fame, glory, honour
tireadge	glorious
tireadig	famous, glorious, victorious
tireadigra	famous, glorious, victorious
tireadigum	famous, glorious, victorious
tires	fame, glory, honour

Word List (Ænglisc to English)

Ænglisc	English	Ænglisc	English
tirfæst	famed, famous, glorious, victorious	to-faran	disperse, separate
tirfæste	glorious, glory-fastened, victorious	to-faren	disperse, separate
		to-for	disperse, separate
tirfæstra	triumph-tough	toforan	be-dispersed, before, in-front-of, scatter
tirleas	honour, humiliated, or-fame, vanquished, without-glory	to-foron	disperse, separate
		togædere	together
		togædre	together
tirleases	honour, humiliated, or-fame, vanquished, without-glory	togeanes	against, before, opposite, towards
		togen	bring, bring-up, draw-a-sword, educate, grant, take
tiþ	boon, favour, gift, grant		
		togenes	against, before, opposite, towards
tiþa	recipient, sharer		
tiþe	boon, favour, gift, grant	togengan	go-away
		togengdon	go-away
tiþian	give, grant	toglad	shatter, split
tiþiaþ	give, grant	toglidan	shatter, split
to	also, as, burst-apart, excessively, for, forth, from, in, into, onwards, shatter, so, to, too, very, why	tohladan	build-separate-piles, separate-into-piles
		tohlidan	burst, spring-apart
		tohlidene	burst, spring-apart
		tohlodon	build-separate-piles, separate-into-piles
to hwon	why		
to þæs	so	tohtan	battle, fight
tobærst	burst-apart, shatter	tohte	battle, fight
toberstan	burst-apart, shatter	tolucan	destroy, disassemble, pull-apart
tobræc	to-break		
tobræd	divide, tear-apart		
tobrægd	divide, tear-apart	tomiddes	amid, in-the-middle, in-the-middle-of
tobrecan	break-apart, destroy		
tobredon	divide, tear-apart	torht	bright
tobregdan	divide, tear-apart	torhtan	bright
tobrocen	break-apart, destroy	torhte	bright
toð	tooth	torhtlic	bright
todælan	divide, separate	torhtlicne	bright
todælden	divide, separate	torhtmod	glorious, noble
toðmægenes	tooth-power	torhtum	bright
toðon	tooth	torn	anger, grievous, miserable, misery, trouble, troubled
todræfed	driven-away		
todraf	destroyed, drive-apart	torna	anger, misery, trouble
todrifan	drive-apart		
toðum	tooth	torne	anger, grievous, miserable, misery, trouble, troubled
toemnes	alongside		
tofaran	be-dispersed, scatter	torngemot	bitter-meeting

Word List (Ænglisc to English)

Ænglisc	English
tornost	grievous, miserable, troubled
torr	tower, watchtower
torras	towers
torre	tower, watchtower
toscufeð	do-away
toscufeþ	do-away
toslitan	cut-apart, rip-apart
tosliteð	cut-apart, rip-apart
tosliteþ	cut-apart, rip-apart
tosomne	together
tosyndrodost	separate
totær	tear-apart
toteran	tear-apart
toþ	tooth
toþon	tooth
toþum	tooth
totwæman	break-up, divide, separate
totwæmed	break-up, divide, separate
totweman	break-up, divide, separate
toward	toward
toweard	approaching, for, future, towards, with-respect-to
toweardan	approaching, future
toweccan	arouse, begin
towehton	arouse, begin
towurpe	cast-down
træd	step-on, tread
træde	step-on, tread
træf	building, pavilion, tent
træfe	building, pavilion, tent
travel	lay
tredað	step-on, tread
tredan	step-on, tread
tredaþ	step-on, tread
treddan	step, tread
treddode	step, tread
tredeð	step-on, tread
tredeþ	step-on, tread
trega	affliction, grief, pain
tregan	affliction, grief, pain
tregena	affliction, grief, pain
trem	distance, length
treocyn	a-kind-of-tree, kind-of-tree
treow	agreement, faith, honour, loyalty, pledge, promise, tree, trust
treowa	agreement, faith, fidelity, pledge, promise, trust, truth
treowan	believe, trust
treowcynn	kind-of-tree
treowcynnes	kind-of-tree
treowde	believe, trust
treowe	agreement, faith, kind-of-tree, pledge, promise, tree, trust
treowes	tree
treowgeþofta	trusted-friends
treowian	be-faithful
treowige	be-faithful
treowloga	oath-breaker, traitor
treowlogan	oath-breaker, traitor
treowræden	agreement, covenant
treowrædenne	agreement, covenant
treowum	agreement, faith, pledge, promise, step-on, trees, trust
triedeð	step-on, tread
triedeþ	step-on, tread
trimian	address, arrange, comfort, exhort, ordain, prepare, strengthen
triow	trinity
trode	footprint, track
trodu	footprint, track
truly	a-right, duty, justice, law, obligation, rule, truth, what-is-right
trum	firm, steadfast, tough
trumne	firm, steadfast
truwian	make-an-agreement, trust
truwode	make-an-agreement, trust
tryddode	step, tread

Word List (Ænglisc to English)

Ænglisc	English
trym	distance, length
trymed	encourage, exhort
trymeð	address, arrange, comfort, exhort, ordain, prepare, strengthen
trymede	address, arrange, comfort, encourage, exhort, ordain, prepare, strengthen
trymedon	address, arrange, comfort, exhort, ordain, prepare, strengthen
trymeþ	address, arrange, comfort, exhort, ordain, prepare, strengthen
trymian	address, arrange, comfort, encourage, exhort, ordain, prepare, strengthen
trymman	address, arrange, comfort, exhort, ordain, prepare, strengthen
trywe	faithful, true, trustworthy
tu	both, twain, two
tū	2 (accusative neuter), 2 (nominative neuter), two (accusative neuter), two (nominative neuter)
tuddor	offspring
tuddorsped	fertility, success-in-offspring
tuddorteonde	bringing-forth-offspring
tuddorteondra	bringing-forth-offspring
tudor	offspring
tudra	offspring
tudre	awake, offspring
tudres	offspring
tun	dwelling, tongue, town, village
tunece	tunic
tungan	tongue
tunge	tongue
tungel	heavenly-body-such-as-the-sun, moon, planets, stars
tungla	the-heavens
tunglum	heavenly-body-such-as-the-sun, moon, planets, stars
tungol	heavenly-body, heavenly-body-such-as-the-sun, moon, planets, star, stars
turf	soil, turf
turfa	soil, turf
turfon	soil, turf
twa	200, 2 (accusative feminine), 2 (accusative neuter), 2 (nominative feminine), 2 (nominative neuter), twain, twice, two, two (accusative feminine), two (accusative neuter), two (nominative feminine), two (nominative neuter), two hundred
tpa	200, 2 (accusative feminine), 2 (accusative neuter), 2 (nominative feminine), 2 (nominative neuter), two (accusative feminine), two (accusative neuter), two (nominative feminine), two (nominative neuter), two hundred
twa and feowertigoþa	forty second
twa and fiftigoþa	fifty second
twa and hundeahtatigoþa	eighty second

Word List (*Ænglisc* to English)

Ænglisc	English
twa and hundnigontigoþa	ninety second
twa and hundseofontigoþa	seventy second
twa and sixtigoþa	sixty second
twa and þritigoþa	thirty second
twa and twentigoþa	twenty second
twa þūsend	2000, two thousand
tpa þūsend	2000, two thousand
twægen	two
twæm	two
twam	2 (dative feminine), 2 (dative masculine), 2 (dative neuter), 2 (instrumental feminine), 2 (instrumental masculine), 2 (instrumental neuter), two, two (dative feminine), two (dative masculine), two (dative neuter), two (instrumental feminine), two (instrumental masculine), two (instrumental neuter)
tpam	2 (dative feminine), 2 (dative masculine), 2 (dative neuter), 2 (instrumental feminine), 2 (instrumental masculine), 2 (instrumental neuter), two (dative feminine), two (dative masculine), two (dative neuter), two (instrumental feminine), two (instrumental masculine), two (instrumental neuter)
twega	2 (genitive feminine), 2 (genitive masculine), 2 (genitive neuter), two, two (genitive feminine), two (genitive masculine), two (genitive neuter), two-things
tpega	2 (genitive feminine), 2 (genitive masculine), 2 (genitive neuter), two (genitive feminine), two (genitive masculine), two (genitive neuter)
twegen	2, 2 (accusative masculine), 2 (nominative masculine), twain, two, two (accusative masculine), two (nominative masculine)

Word List (*Ænglisc* to English)

Ænglisc	English	Ænglisc	English
tƿegen	2, 2 (accusative masculine), 2 (nominative masculine), two, two (accusative masculine), two (nominative masculine)	*tweo*	doubt, dubiousness, uncertainty
		tweode	be-fearful, doubt, hesitate
		tweon	be-fearful, doubt, dubiousness, hesitate
		tweonum	between, twixt
twegen and feowertig	42, forty two	*twig*	branch, twig
		twige	branch, twig
tƿegen and feoƿertig	42, forty two	*tydran*	propagate
		tydre	cowardly, weak
twegen and fiftig	52, fifty two	*tyhð*	accuse
tƿegen and fiftig	52, fifty two	*tyhtað*	draw, persuade, pull, teach
twegen and hundeahtatig	82, eighty two	*tyhtan*	draw, persuade, pull, teach
tƿegen and hundeahtatig	82, eighty two	*tyhtaþ*	draw, persuade, pull, teach
twegen and hundendleftig	112, a hundred and twelve	*tyhþ*	accuse
tƿegen and hundendleftig	112, a hundred and twelve	*tymað*	beget, bring-forth, engender
twegen and hundnigontig	92, ninety two	*tyman*	beget, bring-forth, engender, procreate
tƿegen and hundnigontig	92, ninety two	*tymaþ*	beget, bring-forth, engender
twegen and hundseofontig	72, seventy two	*tymdon*	beget, bring-forth, engender
tƿegen and hundseofontig	72, seventy two	*tyn*	ten
		tynan	insult, revile
twegen and hundteontig	102, a hundred and two	*tyndon*	insult, revile
		tyne	ten
tƿegen and hundteontig	102, a hundred and two	*tyr*	fame, glory, honour
		tyreadig	glorious
twegen and sixtig	62, sixty two	*tyrf*	soil, turf
tƿegen and sixtig	62, sixty two		
twegen and þritig	32, thirty two		
tƿegen and þritig	32, thirty two		

Þ, þ

Ænglisc	English
twegen and twentig	22, twenty two
tƿegen and tƿentig	22, twenty two
twegin	two
twelf	12, twelve
tƿelf	12, twelve
twelfe	twelve
twelfta	twelfth
twentig	20, twenty
tƿentig	20, twenty
twentigoþa	twentieth

Ænglisc	English
þa	being, being-the-case, it-being-the-case-that, man, minister, nobleman, officer, that, that-in, the, them, then, there, this, those, was, when, who, yet
þæ	their

Word List (*Ænglisc* to English)

Ænglisc	English
þægn	man, minister, nobleman, officer, retainer, servant, thane
þægne	man, minister, nobleman, officer, retainer, servant, thane
þæm	that-in, the, there, those
þæne	that-in, the, this, those
þænne	than, than-that, then, when
þær	that-in, there, therein, where, wherein-such-a-case-where
þær inne	therein
þær to	thereto
þæra	that-in, the, there, those
þære	of-the, that, that-in, the, there, those
þærfe	need
þæron	in-it, therein, thereon
þæs	because, for-that-reason, so, that, that-in, that-was, the, these, this, this-was, those
þæsas	because, for-that-reason
þæt	be, he, in-order-that, it, she, so-that, that, that-in, the, those, which, who
þætte	so-that, that, which, which
þafian	agree-to, consent
þafodest	agree-to, consent
þag	endure, prosper, thrive
þah	endure, prosper, thrive
þam	than, that, that, that-in, the, the, them, then, this, those, those
þan	from-there, than, that-in, the, then, thence, those
þanan	from-there, thence
þanc	agree-to, consent, grace, mercy, thanks, thought
þancast	thank
þance	thank, thanks, thought
þancedon	thank
þances	pensive, thanks, thought
þanchycgende	pensive, prudent
þanciað	thank
þancian	thank
þanciende	thank
þancode	thank
þancodon	thank
þancolmod	thoughtful, wise
þancung	thanksgiving
þane	the, those
þanon	from-there, thence
þanonne	from-there, thence
þar	there, wherein-such-a-case-where
þara	that-in, the, those
þarf	needs, these
þas	that-in, these, this
þat	that-in, the, those
þe	although, as, dead, death, endure, have, however, it, nevertheless, than, that, that-in, the, thee, then, this, those, thou, though, to-thee, to-you, where, which, who, you
þeah	although, be-stretched-out-upon, endure, holds, however, nevertheless, prosper, though, thrive, yet
þeah þe	although, even-if

Word List (*Ænglisc* to English)

Ænglisc	English	*Ænglisc*	English
þeaht	be-stretched-out-upon, conceal, cover, cover-over	þecce	be-stretched-out-upon, cover, cover-over
þeahte	be-stretched-out-upon, conceal, cover, cover-over	þeccean	be-stretched-out-upon, cover, cover-over
þeahtian	consider, deliberate, ponder	þecen	covering, roof, thatch
þeahtode	consider, deliberate, ponder	þecene	covering, roof, thatch
þeahton	be-stretched-out-upon, cover, cover-over	þecest	be-stretched-out-upon, cover, cover-over
þearf	have-occasion-to, lacking, need, needs, requirement	þegen	man, minister, nobleman, officer, retainer, servant, thane
þearfa	lacking, needing, needy, poor	þegenas	man, minister, nobleman, officer, retainer, servant, thane
þearfan	have-occasion-to, need		
þearfe	need		
þearfendre	have-occasion-to, need	þegenlice	nobly
þearft	have-occasion-to, need	þegn	man, minister, nobleman, officer, retainer, servant, thane, warrior
þearfum	lacking, needing, needy, poor	þegna	man, minister, nobleman, officer, retainer, servant, thane
þearl	excessive, severe, strong, violent		
þearle	extremely, greatly, horribly, severely, violently	þegnas	man, minister, nobleman, officer, retainer, servant, thane
þearlmod	mighty, severe, violent		
þeaw	custom, habit, manner, practice, virtue	þegne	man, minister, nobleman, officer, retainer, servant, thane
þeawas	custom, habit, manner, manners, virtue	þegnes	man, minister, nobleman, officer, retainer, servant, thane
þeawfæst	virtuous		
þeawum	custom, habit, manner, virtue	þegnian	serve
þec	thou, you	þegnode	serve
þeccan	be-stretched-out-upon, conceal, cover, cover-over	þegnscipe	service, servitude
		þegnscipes	service, servitude
		þegnsorg	sorrow-for-followers

Word List (*Ænglisc* to English)

Ænglisc	English	*Ænglisc*	English
þegnum	man, minister, nobleman, officer, retainer, servant, thane	þeoda	enter-a-monastic-order, nation, nations, people, peoples
þegnung	meal, service	þeodan	enter-a-monastic-order, join
þegnunge	meal, service	þeodcyning	people-king
þegon	accept, eat, partake-of, receive	þeod-cyning	people-king
þegun	accept, eat, partake-of, receive	þeodcyninga	people-king
		þeodcyningas	people-king
þeh	although, nevertheless, though	þeodcyninges	people-king
		þeode	nation, people
þehton	be-stretched-out-upon, cover, cover-over	þeoden	faithful-to-a-lord, king, lord, prince
		þeodenhold	faithful-to-a-lord
þellfæsten	board-stronghold, plank-fastening	þeodenholde	faithful-to-a-lord
		þeodenholdra	faithful-to-a-lord
þellfæstenne	board-stronghold, plank-fastening	þeodenleas	lord-less
		þeodenlease	lord-less
þencað	consider, imagine, intend, plan, think	þeodenmadm	royal-treasure
		þeodenmadmas	royal-treasure
þencan	board-stronghold, intend, plank-fastening, resolve, think	þeodgestreon	national-treasure
		þeodgestreona	national-treasure
		þeodgestreonum	national-treasure
		þeodguma	national-warrior
		þeodhere	national-army
þencaþ	consider, imagine, intend, plan, think, thinking	þeodherga	national-army
		þeodkyning	people-king
		þeodlanda	country, empire, nation, national-homeland
þence	consider, imagine, intend, plan, think		
þencean	consider, imagine, intend, plan, think	þeodlond	country, empire, nation, national-homeland
þenceð	consider, imagine, intend, plan, think	þeodnas	king, lord
þencest	consider, imagine, intend, plan, think	þeodne	king, lord
		þeodnes	king, lord, prince's
þenceþ	consider, imagine, intend, plan, think	þeodsceaða	national-enemy, people-destroyer
þenden	as-long-as, during-that-time, king, meanwhile, so-long-as, while	þeodsceaþa	national-enemy, people-destroyer
		þeodscipe	nation, people
		þeodþrea	national-disaster, national-distress, people-disaster, people-distress
þengel	king, lord, ruler		
þenian	be-humiliated, serve		
þenode	be-humiliated, serve		
þeo	hip, servant, slave, thigh		
þeod	nation, people		

Word List (Ænglisc to English)

Ænglisc	English	Ænglisc	English
þeodþreaum	national-disaster, national-distress, people-disaster, people-distress	þider	there, thither, to-there
		þigeð	accept, consumes, eat, partake-of, receive
þeodum	nation, people		
þeodwiga	mighty-warrior	þigen	prosper, thrive
þeof	thief	þigeþ	accept, eat, partake-of, receive
þeofes	thief		
þeon	endure, prosper, thrive	þigon	prosper, thrive
		þihtan	powerful
þeos	darkness, death-day, these, this	þin	thou, you, your, yours
þeostra	darkness, shadow	þina	thou, you
þeostre	dark, gloomy	þincan	appear, seem
þeostru	darkness, shadow	þince	appear, seem
þeostrum	dark, darkness, gloomy, shadow	þinceað	appear, seem
		þincean	appear, seem
þeow	servant, slave	þinceaþ	appear, seem
þeowa	servant, slave	þinceð	appear, seem, thinks
þeowan	servant, slave		
þeowdom	service, servitude, slavery	þinceþ	appear, seem
		þincg	assembly, circumstance, contest, meeting, thing
þeowdome	service, servitude, slavery		
þeowdon	serve		
þeowe	female-slave	þindan	swell
þeowen	female-servant, female-slave	þine	thou, you, your
		þinen	female-servant, handmaid
þeowian	serve		
þeowige	serve	þinene	female-servant, handmaid
þeowmennen	female-slave, maidservant		
		þinenne	female-servant, handmaid
þeownyd	slavery		
þeowra	female-slave	þines	thou, you
þer	there	þing	assembly, circumstance, circumstances, contest, meeting, thing, things
þes	these, this		
þet	that		
þewhile	often, sometimes		
þi	closely, therefore		
þicce	closely, thickly	þinga	assembly, by, circumstance, contest, meeting, thing
þicgan	accept, eat, partake-of, receive		
þicgeað	accept, eat, partake-of, receive	þingade	arrange, ask, determine, intend, intercede-for, settle, speak
þicgean	accept, eat, partake-of, receive		
þicgeaþ	accept, eat, partake-of, receive	þingan	intend-to-go
þiclice	pressingly, thickly		

Word List (*Ænglisc* to English)

Ænglisc	English	*Ænglisc*	English
þinge	assembly, circumstance, contest, meeting, thing	*þoliað*	allow, endure, forgo, lose, suffer
þinges	assembly, circumstance, contest, meeting, thing	*þolian*	allow, endure, forgo, hold-out, lose, suffer
		þoliaþ	allow, endure, forgo, lose, suffer
þingian	arrange, ask, determine, intend, intercede-for, settle, speak	*þolien*	allow, endure, forgo, lose, suffer
		þoligende	allow, endure, forgo, lose, suffer
þingode	arrange, ask, determine, intend, intercede-for, settle, speak	*þolodan*	allow, endure, forgo, lose, suffer
		þolode	allow, endure, forgo, lose, suffer
		þon	from, from-there, than, that-in, the, then, those
þinne	thou, you, your, yours		
þinra	thou, you, your	*þonan*	from-there, thence
þinre	thou, you, your	*þonc*	thanks, thought
þinum	king, lord, thou, you, your, yours	*þoncol*	thoughtful, wise
		þoncsnotturra	thanks-worthy, thought-wiser
þioda	nation's		
þiodcyning	people-king	*þoncwyrðe*	thanks-worthy, thank-worthy
þioden	king, lord	*þoncwyrþe*	thanks-worthy, thank-worthy
þis	dish, these, this		
þisne	these, this	*þone*	than, than-that, that, that-in, the, then, those, who, whom
þison	these, this		
þissa	these, this		
þisse	these, this	*þonne*	from-there, than, than-that, that, that-in, the, then, thence, they, this, those, when, while
þissere	these, this		
þisses	these, this		
þissum	these, this		
þisum	these, this		
þoht	intend, resolve, think	*þonon*	from-there, thence
þohte	consider, imagine, intend, plan, resolve, think	*þonosnotturra*	have-occasion-to, thought-wiser
		þorfte	have-occasion-to, need, needing
þohton	consider, imagine, intend, plan, think	*þorfton*	have-occasion-to, need
þolad	endure, hold-out		
þolað	allow, endure, forgo, lose, suffer	*þorftun*	need
		þræcrof	brave-in-battle
þolade	endure, endured, hold-out	*þræcrofe*	brave-in-battle
		þræcwig	violent-battle
þolaþ	allow, endure, forgo, lose, suffer	*þræcwiges*	violent-battle
		þrag	period, season, time
þoledon	allow, endure, forgo, lose, suffer	*þrage*	advance, for-a-time, period, season, time

Word List (*Ænglisc* to English)

Ænglisc	English	*Ænglisc*	English
þragum	sometimes	þreo þūsend	3000, three thousand
þrang	advance, press, press-forward, throng	þreohund	three-hundred
		þreonihta	three-nights
þrea	oppression	þreora	3 (genitive feminine), 3 (genitive masculine), 3 (genitive neuter), three, three (genitive feminine), three (genitive masculine), three (genitive neuter)
þreagan	afflict, oppress		
þrealic	dire, oppressive		
þrean	afflict		
þreanedla	dire-distress		
þreanedlan	dire-distress		
þreanyd	dire-distress		
þreanydum	dire-distress, in-distress		
þreat	band, company, troop	þreotine	13, thirteen
		þreotteoð	thirteenth
þreatas	company, troop	þreotteoða	thirteenth
þreate	company, troop	þreotteoþ	thirteenth
þreatedon	menace, press	þreotteoþa	thirteenth
þreatian	menace, press	þri	3, 3 (accusative masculine), 3 (nominative masculine), three, three (accusative masculine), three (nominative masculine)
þreatum	company, troop		
þreaweorc	oppressive-affliction		
þrecwudu	power-wood, spear		
þreo	300, 3 (accusative feminine), 3 (accusative neuter), 3 (nominative feminine), 3 (nominative neuter), three, three (accusative feminine), three (accusative neuter), three (nominative feminine), three (nominative neuter), three hundred		
		þri and feowertig	43, forty three
		þri and feopertig	43, forty three
		þri and fiftig	53, fifty three
		þri and hundeahtatig	83, eighty three
		þri and hundendleftig	113, a hundred and thirteen
		þri and hundnigontig	93, ninety three
		þri and hundseofontig	73, seventy three
		þri and hundteontig	103, a hundred and three
þreo and feowertigoþa	forty third	þri and sixtig	63, sixty three
þreo and fiftigoþa	fifty third	þri and þritig	33, thirty three
þreo and hundeahtatigoþa	eighty third	þri and twentig	23, twenty three
		þri and tpentig	23, twenty three
þreo and hundnigontigoþa	ninety third	þridda	third
		þriddan	the-third, third
þreo and hundseofontigoþa	seventy third	þrie	three
þreo and sixtigoþa	sixty third		
þreo and þritigoþa	thirty third		
þreo and twentigoþa	twenty third		

Word List (*Ænglisc* to English)

Ænglisc	English	*Ænglisc*	English
þrim	3 (dative feminine), 3 (dative masculine), 3 (dative neuter), 3 (instrumental feminine), 3 (instrumental masculine), 3 (instrumental neuter), three, three (dative feminine), three (dative masculine), three (dative neuter), three (instrumental feminine), three (instrumental masculine), three (instrumental neuter)	þrowode	endure, suffer
		þrungen	crowd, press, throng
		þrungon	advance, crowd, hastened, press, press-forward, throng
		þry	three
		þryð	company, host, strength
		þryðge	mighty, powerful
		þryðig	mighty, powerful
		þryðlic	mighty, powerful
		þrydlicost	mighty, powerful
		þryðswyð	strong-and-powerful, very-mighty
		þryðum	company, host, strength
		þryðword	brave-speech, powerful-word
		þrym	force, glory, host, majesty, power, three, troop
þrindan	swell		
þrindende	swell		
þringan	advance, crowd, press, press-forward, throng	þrymfæst	glorious, mighty, powerful
		þrymfæste	glorious, mighty, powerful
þrio	three		
þrist	audacious, bold, shameless	þrymfæstne	glorious, mighty, powerful
þriste	audacious, bold, boldly, resolutely, shameless, shamelessly	þrymful	mighty, powerful
		þrymlic	glorious, magnificent
		þrymm	force, glory, host, majesty, power, renown, troop
þristhydig	bold--minded		
þritig	30, thirty	þrymmas	force, glories, glory, host, majesty, power, troop
þritigoþa	thirtieth		
þrittig	thirty		
þrittiges	thirty	þrymme	mightily, strength
þriwa	advance, three-times, thrice	þrymmes	mightily
		þrymmum	mightily
þrong	advance, crowd, press, press-forward, throng	þrynes	trinity
		þrynesse	trinity
		þrysman	become-dark, become-smoky
þrosm	smoke		
þrowad	endure, suffer	þrysmaþ	become-dark, become-smoky
þrowade	endure, suffer, suffered		
		þryþ	company, host, strength
þrowedon	endure, suffer		
þrowian	endure, suffer	þryþærn	hall, majestic-building
þrowigean	endure, suffer		

Word List (Ænglisc to English)

Ænglisc	English	Ænglisc	English
þryþe	company, host, strength	þurhwadan	go-through, penetrate, pierce
þryþge	mighty, powerful	þurhwaden	penetrate, pierce
þryþig	mighty, powerful	þurhwod	go-through, penetrate, pierce
þryþlic	mighty, powerful		
þryþswyþ	strong-and-powerful, very-mighty	þurhwodon	penetrate, pierce
		þurhwunade	remain
þryþum	company, host, strength	þurhwunian	remain
		þurst	thirst
þryþword	brave-speech, powerful-word	þurstig	eager, needing, thirsty
þu	banner, thou, you	þuruh	by-means-of, for-the-sake-of, through
þuf	banner		
þufas	banner	þus	in-this-way, thousand, thus
þuhte	appear, seem, think		
þuhton	appear, seem	þusend	thousand, thousands
þunar	thunder		
þunede	groan, make-a-booming-noise, resound	þūsend	1000, a thousand
		þusenda	thousand
		þusendmælum	in-thousands
þunian	be-lifted-up, be-prominent, groan, make-a-booming-noise, resound	þusendo	thousand
		þwean	cleanse, wash
		þweorh	crooked, depraved, perverse
þureð	Thureth (name)	þwoh	cleanse, wash
þureþ	Thureth (name)	þy	any, because, by, by-this, crush, for-that-reason, that-in, the, those
þurfan	have-occasion-to, need		
þurh	break-through, by, by-means-of, for, for-the-sake-of, from, penetrate, sake-of, through		
		þyð	crush, oppress, press
		þyder	there, thither, to-there
þurhbræc	break-through, penetrate	þyhtig	strong
		þyle	orator, spokesman
þurhbrecan	break-through, penetrate	þyn	your
		þyncan	appear, seem, think
þurhdeaf	dive-or-swim-through	þynceð	appear, seem
		þynceþ	appear, seem
þurhdrifan	drive-a-nail-through, pierce	þyne	your
		þynum	your
þurhdufan	dive-or-swim-through	þyrel	hole, opening
		þyrs	demon, giant, ogre
þurhetan	eat-through	þys	these, this
þurhetone	eat-through	þyslic	like-this, similar
þurhfon	get-through, penetrate	þyslicu	like-this, similar
		þysne	these, this
þurhteon	accomplish, carry-out	þyssa	these, this
		þysse	these, this

Word List (*Ænglisc* to English)

Ænglisc	English
þyssere	these, this
þysses	these, this
þysson	these, this
þyssum	these, this
þystre	dark, darkness, gloomy, shadow, shadowy
þystro	darkness, shadow
þystru	darkness, shadow
þystrum	darkness, shadow, shadowy
þysum	these, this
þyþ	crush, oppress, press
þywað	crush, oppress, press
þywan	crush, oppress, press
þywaþ	crush, oppress, press

U, u

Ænglisc	English
uard	allow, ward
uðe	allow, bestow, grant, like, offer, wish
uðgenge	depart, departing
uðwitan	wide-men
uðwytegung	philosophy
uðwytegunge	philosophy
uerc	above, work-of
ueþer	wing
ufan	above, down-from-above
ufara	later
ufaran	later
ufera	later
uferan	later
ufe-weard	upward
ufon	above, down-from-above
ufor	higher-up
uhta	dawn, period-just-before-dawn, twilight
uhtan	before-dawn, dawn, early-morning, morning-twilight
uhtceare	dawn-sadness, early-morning-misery, sadness
uhtcearu	dawn-sadness, early-morning-misery
uhte	dawn, early-morning, morning-twilight
uhtfloga	dawn-flier
uhtflogan	dawn-flier
uhthlem	ruckus-at-dawn
uhtna	dawn, early-morning, morning-twilight
uhtsceaða	dawn-enemy, nocturnal-attacker
uhtsceaþa	dawn-enemy, nocturnal-attacker
uhttid	dawn, early-morning, morning-twilight
uitam	life (Latin)
umborwesende	being-a-child
umborwesendum	being-a-child
unarlic	contemptible, dishonourable
unarlice	dishonourably, sinfully
unbefohten	uncontested, un-fought
unbefohtene	uncontested, un-fought
unbliðe	sad, sorrowful, unhappy
unbliþe	sad, sorrowful, unhappy
unbyrnende	un-burning
unc	us, we-two
uncer	we-two
uncerne	we-two
unclæne	unclean
uncran	we-two
uncre	we-two
uncres	we-two
uncuð	strange
uncuðe	strange
uncuðes	strange
uncuðne	strange

Word List (*Ænglisc* to English)

Ænglisc	English	*Ænglisc*	English
uncuðra	strange	unforcuðlice	bravely, honourably, nobly
uncuþ	strange, unknowing, unknown	unforcuþ	brave, highly-regarded, noble, reputable
uncuþe	strange		
uncuþes	strange	unforcuþlice	bravely, honourably, nobly
uncuþne	strange		
uncuþra	strange	unforht	brave, not-timid-or-afraid, resolute
undearninga	un-secretly		
under	by-means-of, in-the-shelter-of, subject, under	unforhte	brave, bravely, not-timidly-or-fearfully, not-timid-or-afraid, resolute
underðeodde	subject, submit		
undereotone	under-eaten		
underfænge	accept, receive	unfreme	unprofitable-thing
underfeng	accept, receive	unfremu	unprofitable-thing
underflowan	flow-under	unfreondlice	in-an-unfriendly-way
underflowen	flow-under	unfricgende	un-asking
underfon	accept, receive	unfricgendum	un-asking
underne	clear, manifest, obvious	unfrod	not-old, young
		unfrodum	not-old, young
undernmæl	morning--time	unfrom	not-brave, not-vigorous
underþeodan	subject, submit		
underþeodde	subject, submit	ungeara	just-now, momentarily, recently, shortly, soon
undor	by-means-of, in-the-shelter-of, under		
undyrne	clear, clearly, manifest, manifestly, obvious, openly	ungedefe	improper, wrong
		ungedefelice	wrongly
unearg	brave, not-fearful, not-timid, resolute	ungefullod	un-baptised
		ungelic	unlike
unearge	brave, not-fearful, not-timid, resolute	ungelice	differently, unlike
		ungemete	extremely, immeasurably, very
unfæcne	non-fraudulent, sincere	ungesibb	un-peaceful, unrelated
unfæge	not-doomed-to-die		
unfæger	ugly, unlovely	ungesibbum	un-peaceful, unrelated
unfægere	in-an-ugly-or-unpleasant-way		
		ungeþeod	divided, separate
unfægne	not-doomed-to-die	ungeþeode	divided, separate
unfæle	ugly, wicked	ungifre	rapacious, voracious
unfære	in-an-ugly-or-unpleasant-way	ungleaw	ineffective?, not-smart, unwise
unfeor	not-far	ungnyðe	abundant
unfliten	unassailed	ungrene	not-green
unflitne	unassailed	ungyfeðe	not-given
unforcuð	brave, highly-regarded, noble, reputable	ungyfeþe	not-given
		unhæl	evil, sick, unsound
		unhælo	evil, sick, unsound

Word List (*Ænglisc* to English)

Ænglisc	English
unheanlice	not-disgracefully, not-ignobly
unheore	monstrous, wild
unheoru	monstrous, wild
unhiore	monstrous, wild
unhlisa	dishonour
unhlisan	dishonour
unhlitme	disappointed, disheartened, dispirited
unhror	un-stirring
unhyldo	disfavour, displeasure
unhyre	monstrous, wild
unicum	only (Latin)
unigmetes	immeasurably
unlæd	evil, wicked
unlædan	evil, wicked
unland	false-land, non-land
unleof	hateful, unloved
unleofe	hateful, unloved
unliðe	harsh, severe, unpleasant
unlifigende	dead, unliving
unliþe	harsh, severe, unpleasant
unlonde	false-land, non-land
unlyfigende	dead, unliving
unlyfigendes	dead, unliving
unlyfigendne	dead, unliving
unlyfigendum	dead, unliving
unlytel	great, not-little
unlytle	great, not-little
unmæðlice	immoderately, without-restraint
unmæne	free-from-evil
unmæte	huge, vast
unmæþlice	immoderately, without-restraint
unmurnlice	remorselessly, willingly, without-compunction, without-grouching
unnan	allow, bestow, grant, like, offer, wish
unnon	bestow, grant
unnyt	useless
unorne	simple
unræd	evil, folly, mischief, treachery, unruly
unræde	evil, folly, mischief, treachery
unræden	folly, unadvised-act
unrædes	evil, folly, mischief, treachery
unriht	crime, sin, un-right, un-rightful-act
unrihte	crime, guiltily, sin, un-rightful-act, unrightfully, wrongly
unrihtwisnys	sinfulness, unrighteousness
unrihtwisnysse	sinfulness, unrighteousness
unrim	countless-number
unrime	countless
unrimu	innumerable
unrot	dejected
unrote	dejected
unryhte	un-right
unsælga	miserable, unfortunate, wicked
unsælig	miserable, unfortunate, wicked
unsceððiga	innocent
unscildigan	innocent
unscomlice	indecently, shamelessly
unscyldig	innocent
unscyldigan	innocent
unsnyttru	foolishness, un-wise
unsnyttrum	foolishness, un-wise
unsofte	roughly, with-difficulty
unspedig	unpromising, unsuccessful
unspedigran	unpromising, unsuccessful
unstilnes	disturbance, tumult
unswæslic	unpleasant
unswæslicne	unpleasant
unswiðe	not-strongly, not-very-much
unswiðor	not-strongly, not-very-much
unswiþe	not-strongly, not-very-much

Word List (*Ænglisc* to English)

Ænglisc	English	*Ænglisc*	English
unswiþor	not-strongly, not-very-much	unwillum	involuntarily, unintentionally, unwillingly
unsyfra	filthy, impure, lecherous, unclean	unwrecen	un-avenged
unsyfre	filthy, impure, lecherous, unclean	unwundod	unwounded
unsynnig	guiltless	unwurðlice	dishonourably, unworthily
unsynnigne	guiltless	unwurþlice	dishonourably, unworthily
unsynnum	guiltlessly		
untæle	blameless	up	up, upon, upwards
unþanc	displeasure, ingratitude	upganga	disembarking, landing
unþances	displeasure, ingratitude	upgangan	disembarking, landing
unþinged	un-atoned, without-intercession	uphea	elevated, high, tall, up-high
untreowa	deceptive, faithless, false, untrue	upheofon	heaven-above
		uplang	upright
untreowe	deceptive, faithless, false, untrue	uplican	lofty, supreme
		uplicne	lofty
untrum	infirm, sick	uplyft	the-heavens
untrume	infirm, sick	uplyfte	upper-air
untryoð	treachery, untruthfulness	upp	up, upon
		uppe	above, up
untryoða	treachery, untruthfulness	upplican	on-high
		uppriht	upright
untryoþ	treachery, untruthfulness	uproder	heaven, heaven-above, the-heavens
untryoþa	treachery, untruthfulness	uprodor	heaven, heaven-above, the-heavens
untydras	evil-offspring, misshapen-birth	ure	we
		ures	we
untydre	evil-offspring, misshapen-birth	urigfeðera	dewy-feathered
		urig-feðera	dewy-feathered
unwaclic	not-small, not-weak	urigfeþera	dewy-feathered
unwaclice	bravely, forcefully, not-weakly, toughly, unwaveringly	urig-feþera	dewy-feathered
		urigfeþra	dewy-feathered
		uriglast	damp-track, dewy-path
unwaclicne	not-small, not-weak		
unwærlice	carelessly, unwarily	urne	we
unwar	gullible, unwary	urnen	run
unware	gullible, unwary	urnon	hasten, move-quickly, run
unwealt	steady		
unwearnum	irresistibly	urum	we
unweaxen	immature, not-adult, un-grown, young	us	upon-us, us, we, we-two
unwemme	unspoiled, virgin	user	we-two
unwered	unprotected-from	userne	ours, we
		usic	us, we

Word List (Ænglisc to English)

Ænglisc	English
usser	we, we-two
usses	we
ussum	out, us, we
ut	out, outwards
utan	outside
utanweard	outside
utanweardne	outside
ute	out, outside
uter-mere	open-sea, outer-sea
ute-weard	outward
utfus	ready-for-departure
uþe	allow, bestow, grant, like, offer, wish
uþgenge	depart, departing
uþwytegung	philosophy
uþwytegunge	philosophy
uton	exit, let-us, outside
utsiþ	exit, way-out
utweard	out-guarding, outward-turned, turned-outwards
uuære	were
uueard	ward
uuene	think
uueorc	work-of
uueorðae	of-worth
uueorþae	of-worth
uueorþe	of-worth
uueorudes	troops
uuereda	army
uuihte	anything
uuiorðe	of-worth
uuiorðeð	will-be
uuiorþe	of-worth
uuiorþeþ	will-be
uuiurðit	will-be
uuiurþit	will-be
uuldurfadur	glory-father, wonder
uundra	wonder, world-kingdom
uuoruldrice	world-kingdom
uuraþe	wrathfully
uuuldor	glory
uuuldorfæder	glory-father
uuundra	wonder
uuurðmynt	honour
uuurþmynt	honour
uuyrde	destroyed
uuyrican	made
uuyrþeþ	will-be

V, v

Ænglisc	English
vi	six
VII	seven

W, w

Ænglisc	English
wa	miserable, woe, woeful
wac	slender, weak
waca	arise, be-born, be-wakeful, keep-watch, wake
wacað	weaken
wacan	arise, be-born, be-wakeful, keep-watch, wake
wace	frailty, slender, weak
wacian	become-or-be-weak
waciaþ	awaken
wacne	slender, weak
wacran	slender, weak
wada	sea, water
wadan	go, move, stride-over, wade
waden	stride-over, wade
wado	sea, water
waðol	wanders
wadu	sea, water
waðum	sea, wave
wæccan	be-awake, be-watchful, wake
wæccende	be-awake, be-watchful, wake
wæccendne	be-awake, be-watchful, wake
wæcnan	arise, come-to-exist
wæcned	arise, come-to-exist
wæd	clothing, garment, sea, water
wæda	clothing, garment
wædes	sea, water, water's
wædla	destitute, poor
wædlum	destitute, poor
wædo	clothing, garment
wædum	clothing, garment

Word List (*Ænglisc* to English)

Ænglisc	English	*Ænglisc*	English
wæfersyn	display, show, spectacle	wælceasega	corpse-chooser, raven
wæfersyne	display, show, spectacle	wælclomm	deadly-bond, fetter
		wælclommum	deadly-bond, fetter
wæfre	restless, wandering	wældeað	slaughter, violent-death
wæg	bear, billow, carry, carry-out, move, path, perform, road, sea, water, wave, way, wear	wældeaþ	slaughter, violent-death
		wældreor	slaughter-blood
		wældreore	slaughter-blood
		wæle	battlefield, corpses, the-pool
wægbora	underwater-creature, wave-bearer	wælfæhð	deadly-feud
		wælfæhða	deadly-feud
wægbord	deck	wælfæhþ	deadly-feud
wæge	cup, sea, water, wave	wælfæhþa	deadly-feud
wægfaru	wave-passage	wælfag	marked-by-death, slaughter-stained
wægholm	ocean, wave-sea		
wæglidend	sailor, sea-traveller	wælfagne	marked-by-death, slaughter-stained
wæg-lidend	wave-traveller		
wæglidende	sailor, sea-traveller	wælfeall	slaughter-perhaps-a-spelling-of
wæglidendum	sailor, sea-traveller		
wægliþend	sailor, sea-traveller	wælfelda	slain-field
wæg-liþend	wave-traveller	wælfus	eager-for-slaughter
wægliþende	sailor, sailors, sea-traveller	wælfyll	slaughter-full
		wælfylla	slaughter-full
		wælfylle	slaughter-full
wægliþendum	sailor, sea-traveller	wælfylles	slaughter-full
wægon	bear, carry, carry-out, move, perform, wear	wælfyllu	slaughter-full
		wælfyr	corpse-fire, deadly-fire, pyre
wægstream	stream, wave-current	wælfyra	corpse-fire, deadly-fire, pyre
wægsweord	wavy[ornamented]-sword	wælfyre	corpse-fire, deadly-fire, pyre
wægþæl	ship, wave-plane		
wægþel	ship, wave-plane	wælgæst	murderous-spirit
wæg-þel	ship, wave-planking	wælgar	deadly-spear
wægþele	ship, wave-plane	wælgara	deadly-spear
wægþreat	wave-host	wælgifre	greedy-for-carrion
wægþreate	wave-host	wælgifru	greedy-for-carrion
wæl	battlefield, carnage, corpses, slaughter	wælgifrum	greedy-for-carrion
		wælgrim	deadly, dire
wælbedd	grave, slaughter-bed	wælgryre	deadly-terror
wælbedde	grave, slaughter-bed	wælherigas	death-dealing-army
wælbend	death-bond	wælherige	death-dealing-army
wælbende	death-bond	wælhlem	battle-crash, battle-deadly, battle-deadly-crash, deadly-attack
wælbleat	deadly		
wælbleate	deadly		

Word List (Ænglisc to English)

Ænglisc	English	Ænglisc	English
wælhlencan	battle, mail-coat-slaughter	wælsleaht	carnage, deadly-battle, slaughter
wælhlence	battle, mail-coat-slaughter	wælsleahta	deadly-battle, slaughter
wælhreow	bloody, fierce, savage	wælslihta	battle-slaughter
		wælspera	deadly-spear, killing-spear
wælig	prosperous, rich		
wælisc	enslaved, foreign	wælspere	deadly-spear
wælisca	enslaved, foreign	wæl-spere	deadly-spear
wællgrim	cruel, deadly, dire, fierce	wælsteng	corpse-pole, spear
		wælstenge	corpse-pole, spear
wællregn	murderous-rain	wælstow	battlefield
wællseax	slaughter-knife	wælstowe	battlefield
wællseaxe	slaughter-knife	wælstream	deadly-current
wælm	current, flame, surge	wælstreamas	deadly-current
wælmes	current, flame, surge	wælsweng	deadly-blow
wælmist	blindness, death, slaughter-mist	wælswenge	deadly-blow
		wælwulf	carnage-wolf, warrior
wælmiste	blindness, death, slaughter-mist		
		wælwulfas	carnage-wolf, warrior
wælnet	mail-coat, slaughter-net		
		wæn	wagon
wælnið	deadly-hostility	wæpen	weapon
wælniðas	deadly-hostility	wæpenes	weapon
wælniðe	deadly-hostility	wæpengewrixles	passage-of-arms
wælniþ	deadly-hostility	wæpenþracu	armed-conflict, weapon-storm
wælniþas	deadly-hostility		
wælniþe	deadly-hostility	wæpenþræce	armed-conflict, weapon-storm
wælræs	murderous-attack		
wælræse	murderous-attack	wæpmonn	male-person, man
wælrap	death-ropes, immobility	wæpna	weapon
		wæpne	weapon
wælrapas	death-ropes, immobility	wæpned	male, weaponed
		wæpnedcynn	male-gender
wælreaf	battle, booty, slaughter-spoils	wæpnedcynnes	male-gender
		wæpnedmann	male-person, man
wælrec	deadly-smoke, fumes	wæpnedmen	male-person, man
		wæpnes	weapon
wælreow	bloodthirsty, bloody, fierce, savage	wæpnum	weapon
		wær	covenant, honest, keeping, promise, protection, true, trustworthy
wælreowe	bloodthirsty, bloody, fierce, savage		
wælrest	grave, slaughter-bed		
wælreste	grave, slaughter-bed	wæran	man, they-were, to-be, were
wælsceaft	slaughter-shaft, spear		
		wæras	man
wælsceaftas	slaughter-shaft, spear	wærð	agreement, be, become, suit
wælscel	carnage		

Word List (*Ænglisc* to English)

Ænglisc	English	*Ænglisc*	English
wære	faithful, pledges, protection, to-be, was, were	wætere	river, water
		wæteregesa	terrifying-water, water-terror
wærfæst	faithful, honourable, trustworthy	wæteregesan	terrifying-water, water-terror
wærfæstne	faithful, honourable	wæteres	river, water
wærfæstra	faithful, honourable	wæterþisa	ship, water-rusher, watery, whale
wærleas	faithless, traitorous, treacherous	wæteryð	water-wave
wærlecum	masculine	wæteryðum	water-wave
wærlice	guilefully, truthfully, warily	wæteryþ	water-wave
		wæteryþum	water-wave
wærlices	masculine	wæteþ	moisten, to-wet
wærlicum	masculine	wæþrea	sea-menace
wærloga	deceitful-one, devil, liar	wætre	river, water
		wætres	river, water
wærlogan	deceitful-one, deceitful-ones, devil, liar	wætrum	river, water
		wætte	moisten, to-wet
		wag	wall
wærlogona	deceitful-one, devil, liar	wage	wall
		wagon	bear, carry, carry-out, move, perform, wear
wæron	to-be, was, were		
wærþ	agreement, be, become, suit		
		wagum	wall
wærum	honest, true, trustworthy	wald	forest, wood
		walde	forest, wood
wæs	to-be, was	walden	ruler
wæstm	fruit, fruits, increase, stature	waldend	king, lord-of, master, ruler, the-Lord
wæstma	fruit, increase, planted, stature	waldende	king, ruler, the-Lord
wæstmas	fruit, increase, produce, stature	waldendes	king, ruler, the-Lord, the-lord's
wæstme	fruit, increase, stature	waldest	rule
		waldswæþ	forest-track
		waldswaþum	forest-track
wæstmes	fruit, increase, stature	wale	female-slave, maidservant
wæstmum	fruit, increase, stature	walo	bodies
		walu	a-protective-ridge, battlefield, battle-helmet, corpses
wæstum	fruit, increase, stature		
wæt	moist, wet	wan	dark, dusky, fight, gain, obtain, struggle, work
wæta	liquid, moisture		
wætan	liquid, moisten, moisture, the-water, to-wet	wana	lacking, wanting, without
wæteð	moisten, to-wet	wanað	waning
wæter	river, water	wancgturf	ground-turf, land, soil, turf
wætera	river, water		

Word List (*Ænglisc* to English)

Ænglisc	English	*Ænglisc*	English
wand	fly, go, twist, wave-in-a-circular-motion, wind	warigeaþ	beware, defend, hold, possess, protect
wandian	draw-back, flinch	warnað	take-heed, take-warning, warn
wandode	draw-back, flinch		
wandrode	wondered	warnaþ	take-heed, take-warning, warn
wang	earth-root, earth-route, field, land-layout, plain-surface, root	warnian	take-heed, take-warning, warn
		warod	guard, occupy, protect
wange	earth-root, earth-route, field, land-layout, plain-surface	waroð	seaside, shore
		waroðas	seaside, shore
wanhal	sickly, unhealthy, weak	warode	beware, defend, guard, hold, occupy, possess, protect
wanhalum	sickly, unhealthy, weak		
		waroðe	seaside, shore
wanhydig	careless, reckless	waron	to-be
wanian	diminish, wane, waste-away	waroþ	seaside, shore
		waroþas	seaside, shore
wanigean	bewail, lament	waroþe	seaside, shore
wann	dark, dusky, fight, gain, obtain, struggle, work	waroþum	shore
		wast	be-aware-of, know
		wat	be-aware-of, know, know, knows, observe
wanna	dark, dusky		
wanre	dark, dusky		
war	seaweed	waþema	wave
warað	beware, defend, hold, possess, protect	waþum	sea, wave
		wawa	evil, woe
		wawan	evil, woe
waraþ	beware, defend, hold, possess, protect	we	distress, we
		wea	distress, grief, harm, woe
ware	covenant, keeping, promise, protection, seaweed	weadæda	woe-deeds
		weagesið	evil-companion
		weagesiðas	evil-companion
wariað	beware, defend, hold, possess, protect	weagesiþ	evil-companion
		weagesiþas	evil-companion
		weaht	arouse, awake, kindle-a-fire, produce, set-in-motion
warian	beware, defend, guard, hold, occupy, possess, protect		
		weal	cliff, the-wall, wall
wariaþ	beware, defend, hold, possess, protect	wealaf	woeful-remnant
		wealafe	woeful-remnant
		wealand	foreign-country
warigeað	beware, defend, hold, possess, protect	wealandum	foreign-country
		wealas	slave, Welsh
		wealcan	toss-around

Word List (Ænglisc to English)

Ænglisc	English
weald	command, control, forest, might, power, wood
wealdan	control, direct, govern, rule, wield, wielded
wealdas	forest, wood
wealde	control, forest, govern, rule, the-weald, wield, wood
wealden	direct, wield
wealdend	governor, king, lord, ruler, ruler-of, ruling, the-Lord, wielder
wealdende	king, ruler, the-Lord
wealdendes	king, ruler, the-Lord
Wealdest	you-wield
wealfæsten	walled-stronghold
wealgat	gate-in-a-wall
wealgate	gate-in-a-wall
wealh	slave
wealic	miserable, woeful
weall	cliff, rampart, wall
weallað	boil, seethe
weallan	boil, seethe, surge
weallas	cliff, wall
weallaþ	boil, seethe
weallclif	wall-cliff
wealle	cliff, wall
weallendan	welling
weallende	boil, seethe
weallendu	boil, seethe
wealles	cliff, wall
weallfæsten	fortified-dwelling, walled-town
weallfæstenna	fortified-dwelling, walled-town
weallinde	boil, seethe
weallstana	wall-stones
weallsteap	of-a-cliff-steep-as-a-wall, wall-steep
weallsteapan	of-a-cliff-steep-as-a-wall, wall-steep
weallsteape	of-a-cliff-steep-as-a-wall, wall-steep
weallum	cliff, wall
weallwalan	house-walls
wealstan	wall-stone
wealsteal	foundation, location-for-walls
wealweode	roll-around, thrash-about, wallow
wealwian	roll-around, thrash-about, wallow
wealwigende	roll-around, thrash-about, wallow
wean	distress, grief, harm, misery, woe, woes
weana	distress, grief, harm, miseries, trouble, woe
weard	agreement, guard, guardian, guardianship, keeper, king, lord, oversight, protector, responsibility, to, towards, ward
wearð	agreement, be, became, become, happen, suit, was, worthy
weardade	guard, inhabit, rule
weardas	guardian, king, lord, protector
wearde	guardian, guardianship, king, lord, oversight, protector, responsibility
weardes	guardian, king, lord, protector
weardiað	guard, guarding, inhabit, inhabiting, rule
weardian	dwell-in, guard, inhabit, keep, protect, rule
weardiaþ	guard, inhabit, rule
weardigan	guard, inhabit, keep, rule
weardode	dwell-in, guard, inhabit, keep, protect, rule
weardodon	guard, inhabit, rule
weardum	guardian, king, lord, protector

Word List (Ænglisc to English)

Ænglisc	English	Ænglisc	English
wearh	criminal	wecceþ	arouse, awake, kindle-a-fire, produce, set-in-motion
wearn	refusal		
wearne	refusal		
wearp	reflex-change, throw, throw-down, transform, warped	wedd	agreement, pledge
		wedde	agreement, pledge
wearþ	agreement, be, become, happen, suit	weder	storm, weather, wind
		wedera	storm, weather, wind
weaspell	bad-news-telling, disaster-news, disaster-story	wederum	weather
		wedres	storm, weather, wind
weaspelle	bad-news-telling, disaster-news, disaster-story	wedum	clothing, garment
		wefan	contrive, devise, weave
weaþearf	dire-need		
weaþearfe	dire-need	weg	altar, idol, path, road, sea, water, wave, way
Weax	wax		
weaxað	grow, increase		
weaxan	grow, increase, wax	wegan	bear, carry, carry-out, move, perform, wear
weaxaþ	grow, increase		
weaxeð	grow, increase, waxing	wegas	sea, water, waves
		wegbrade	plantain
weaxen	grow, wax	wege	bear, carry, carry-out, move, perform, wear
weaxende	grow, increase		
weaxendum	grow, increase		
weaxeþ	grow, increase	wegeð	bear, carry, carry-out, move, perform, wear
web	hanging, tapestry, woven-fabric		
weccað	arouse, awake, awaking, kindle-a-fire, produce, set-in-motion	wegeþ	bear, carry, carry-out, move, perform, wear
weccan	arouse, awake, kindle-a-fire, produce, set-in-motion	wegfarende	travelling, wayfaring
		wegflota	ship, wave-floater
		wegon	bear, carry, carry-out, move, perform, wear
weccaþ	arouse, awake, kindle-a-fire, produce, set-in-motion		
		wehte	arouse, awake, kindle-a-fire, produce, set-in-motion
weccean	arouse, awake, kindle-a-fire, produce, set-in-motion		
		wel	almost-everywhere, well
		wel hwær	almost-everywhere
wecceð	arouse, awake, kindle-a-fire, produce, set-in-motion	wela	happiness, prosperity, riches
		welan	happiness, prosperity, riches

Word List (Ænglisc to English)

Ænglisc	English	Ænglisc	English
Welande	Weland's (name)	wende	alter, anticipate, believe, change, consider, expect, go, reflex-take-oneself, turn, wend
weler	lip		
weleras	lip, lips		
welerum	lips		
welhold	very-faithful		
welhreowan	bloody, fierce, savage	wended	go, turn, wend
		wendeð	alter, change, go, reflex-take-oneself, turn
welhwær	everywhere		
welhwylc	each, every		
welhwylcra	each, every	wenden	alter, change, go, reflex-take-oneself, turn
welig	prosperous, rich		
weligne	prosperous, rich		
well	well	wendeþ	alter, change, go, goes-to, reflex-take-oneself, turn
welþungen	accomplished, cultivated, excellent		
Welund	Welund (name)	wendon	alter, anticipate, believe, change, consider, expect, go, reflex-take-oneself, turn
wemað	convince, lead-astray, persuade		
weman	attract, convince, entice, lead-astray, persuade, treat		
		wene	accustom, anticipate, believe, consider, expect, think
wemaþ	convince, lead-astray, persuade		
wemde	attract, entice, treat		
wemed	attract, entice, treat	wened	accustom
wemman	defile, destroy, profane	weneð	anticipate, believe, consider, expect
wen	anticipate, belief, believe, consider, expect, expectation, hope	wenede	accustom, entice, habituate, retainer-gifts, train
		weneþ	anticipate, believe, consider, expect
wena	belief, expectation		
wenað	anticipate, believe, consider, considering, expect	wenian	accustom, entice, habituate, retainer-gifts, train
wenan	anticipate, belief, believe, consider, expect, expectation, mind	wennan	accustom
		wenne	wen
		wenum	belief, expectation, hopes
wenaþ	anticipate, believe, consider, expect	weobedd	altar
		weofod	altar
wenchichenne	little-wen	weofode	altar
wend	alter, change, go, reflex-take-oneself, turn	weol	boil, seethe
		weold	control, controlled, direct, govern, rule, wield
wendan	alter, change, go, reflex-take-oneself, translate, turn, wend	weoldon	control, direct, govern, rule, wield
		weoll	boil, seethe

Word List (Ænglisc to English)

Ænglisc	English	Ænglisc	English
weop	cry, weep	weorðen	agreement, be, become, suit, worded
weora	man		
weorada	hosts		
weorc	deed, labour, pain, suffering, work, work-of, works	weorðfull	honoured, valued
		weorðiað	cherish, honour, worship
weorca	deed, labour, pain, suffering, work	weorðian	cherish, honour, worship
weorcan	construct, do, make	weorðinga	honour
weorce	deed, difficult, grievous, labour, pain, painful, suffering, work	weorðlic	honourably, worthily
		weorðlican	worthiness
		weorðlice	honourably, nobly
		weorðlicost	honourably, nobly
weorces	deed, labour, pain, suffering, work	weorðmynd	distinction, glory, honour, reverence
weorcsum	painful, trouble-causing	weorðmynda	distinction, honour, worth-minded
weorcsumne	painful, trouble-causing	weorðmynde	distinction, honour
		weorðmyndum	honourably, nobly
weorctheos	servant, slave	weorðode	cherish, honour, worship
weorcþeow	servant, slave		
weorcum	agreement, deed, labour, pain, suffering, work, works	weorðung	honour
		weorne	evaporate
		weorod	army, band, company, host, throng
weorð	agreement, be, become, dear-to, price, prized, suit, treasure, worded, worthy	weoroda	army, band, company, host, throng
		weorode	army, band, company, host, throng, troop
weorða	worthiness		
weorðað	agreement, be, become, suit, worded	weorold had	secular-life
		weorpan	reflex-change, throw, throw-down, transform
weorðade	cherish, honour, worship		
weorðae	become, of-worth	weorpaþ	reflex-change, throw, throw-down, transform
weorðan	become, happen, price, treasure		
weorðaþ	agreement, be, become, suit, worded	weorþ	agreement, be, become, dear-to, price, prized, suit, treasure, worded, worthy
weorðe	agreement, be, become, price, suit, treasure, worded		
		weorþad	cherish, honour, worship
weorðeð	agreement, be, become, suit, worded	weorþade	cherish, honour, worship
		weorþae	become, of-worth

Word List (*Ænglisc* to English)

Ænglisc	English	*Ænglisc*	English
weorþan	become, happen, price, treasure	*weotena*	king's-councillor, wise-man, witness
weorþaþ	agreement, be, become, suit, worded	*weotode*	allot, assign
		weox	grew, grow, increase, wax, waxed
weorþe	agreement, be, become, deserving-of, esteemed, honoured, of-worth, price, suit, treasure, worded, worthy	*weoxon*	grow, increase, wax
		wepan	cry, weep
		wer	man
		wera	man, men, of-man
		weras	man, men
weorþeð	agreement, be, become, becomes, suit, worded	*werðeode*	nation's-men
		were	man
		wered	army, band, company, defend, host, protect, throng, wear
weorþen	agreement, be, become, suit, worded		
weorþeþ	agreement, be, become, suit, worded	*wereð*	clothe, cover, defend, protect
		wereda	army, band, company, host, hosts, throng
weorþfull	honoured, valued		
weorþian	cherish, honour, worship	*werede*	army, band, clothe, company, cover, defend, host, protect, throng, wear
weorþiaþ	cherish, honour, worship		
weorþinga	honour		
weorþlic	honourably, worthily	*weredes*	army, band, company, host, throng
weorþlice	honourably, nobly		
weorþlicost	honourably, nobly		
weorþmynd	distinction, glory, honour, reverence	*weredon*	clothe, cover, defend, protect
weorþmynda	distinction, honour, worth-minded	*weredum*	army, band, company, host, throng
weorþmynde	distinction, honour		
weorþmyndum	honourably, nobly	*weres*	man
weorþode	cherish, honour, worship	*wereþ*	clothe, cover, defend, protect
weorþra	deserving-of, esteemed, honoured, worthy	*werg*	accursed, accursed-one, criminal, outlaw, wicked
weorþscipe	worthiness	*wergan*	accursed, accursed-one, criminal, outlaw, wicked
weorþung	honour		
weoruda	hosts		
weorude	army, band, company, host, throng	*wergas*	accursed, accursed-one, criminal, outlaw, wicked
weorudes	situation, troops	*wergðo*	curse, punishment
weoruld	situation, the-world, way-of-life		

Word List (*Ænglisc* to English)

Ænglisc	English	*Ænglisc*	English
werge	miserable, sad, weak, weary, wound-incapacitated	wermægð	human-kindred, nation, nation-of-men, tribe
wergend	defender	wermægða	human-kindred, nation, nation-of-men, tribe
wergendra	defender		
wergian	make-weary		
wergþo	curse, punishment	wermægþ	human-kindred, nation, nation-of-men, tribe
wergum	accursed, accursed-one, criminal, miserable, outlaw, sad, weak, weary, wicked, wound-incapacitated		
		wermægþa	human-kindred, nation, nation-of-men, tribe
werhðo	curse, punishment	werod	army, band, company, host, throng, troop
werhþo	curse, punishment		
werian	clothe, cover, defend, protect, unprotected-from, wear	weroda	army, band, company, host, throng
		werode	army, band, company, host, throng
werig	accursed, accursed-one, criminal, exhausted, miserable, outlaw, sad, weak, weary, wicked, wound-incapacitated	werodes	army, band, company, host, throng
		werodum	army, band, company, host, throng
werige	miserable, miserably, sad, sadly, weak, wearily, weary, wound-incapacitated	werþeod	nation, people
		werþeoda	nation, people
		werþeode	nation, people
		werud	army, band, company, host, throng
werigean	clothe, cover, defend, protect		
werigferðe	weary	weruda	army, band, company, host, throng
werigferhð	weary		
werigferhðe	weary		
werigferhþ	weary	werudes	army, band, company, host, throng
werigferhþe	weary		
werigferþe	weary		
werigmod	evil-minded, miserable, suffers, weary	werum	man
		wes	be, to-be, was
		wesað	be
werigne	miserably, sadly, wearily	wesan	be, happen, to-be
		Wesseaxe	West-Saxons
werlic	masculine	Wesseaxena	West-Saxon
werloga	devil, liar, traitor	west	from-the-west, west
werlogan	devil, liar, traitor	westan	from-the-west
		weste	barren, desolate, uninhabited, waste

Word List (Ænglisc to English)

Ænglisc	English	Ænglisc	English
westem	fruit, increase, stature	wida	spacious, wide
westen	desert, wasteland, wilderness	widan	extensive, spacious, wide, widely
westende	west-end	widbrad	extensive
westenne	desert, wasteland, wilderness	widbradne	extensive
westne	barren, desolate, uninhabited, waste	widcuðne	famous, widely-known
		widcuþ	famous, widely-known
westu	be, to-be	widcuþes	famous, widely-known
weter	water		
wexað	grow, increase	widcuþne	famous, widely-known
wexan	grow, increase		
wexaþ	grow, increase	wiððon	afterwards
wexe	grow, increase	widdor	far, widely
wexendra	grow, increase	wide	always, extensively, far, far-and-wide, spacious, wide, widely
wibed	altar		
wic	abode, castle, dwelling, habitation, mansion		
		wideferhð	always, ever, forever
wica	castle, dwelling, habitation, mansion	wideferhþ	always, ever, forever
wican	be-useless, break, fail	wiðeræhtes	on-the-other-side, opposite
wicg	horse		
wicga	horse	wiðerbreca	adversary, enemy
wicge	horse	wiðerbrecan	adversary, enemy
wic-gerefa	wick-reeve	wiðermedo	enmity, opposition
wician	camp, lodge	wiðertrod	retreat, return
wicing	pirate	wiðfeng	grapple-with, seize
wicinga	viking	widfloga	far-flying-one
wicingas	viking	widflogan	far-flying-one
wicingum	viking	widfolc	extensive-kindred
wicod	camp, lodge	wiðfon	grapple-with, seize
wicode	camp, lodge	widgil	ample, broad, extensive
wicstede	dwelling-place		
wicum	castle, dwelling, habitation, mansion	widgillan	ample, broad, extensive
wicun	castle, dwelling, habitation, mansion	wiðgripan	grapple-with
		wiðhabban	withstand
wid	spacious, wide	wiðhæfde	withstand
wið	against, along, beside, exchange, forwards, near, onto, to, to-the-east, towards, with	wiðhogian	reject
		wiðhogode	reject
		widl	filth
		widland	extensive-land
		widlast	distant-journey, far-and-wide, far-wandering
wið eastan	to-the-east		
wið suðan	to-the-south		
wið uppan	above, upwards		

Word List (*Ænglisc* to English)

Ænglisc	English	*Ænglisc*	English
widlastum	distant-journey, far-and-wide, far-wandering	wigblac	shining-armour, war-bright
widle	filth	wigbord	battle-shield
widlond	broad, extensive-land	wigcræft	strength-in-battle
		wigcræftig	strong-in-war
widlum	filth	wigcræftigne	strong-in-war
widmære	widely-famous	wigcyrm	battle-din
widne	spacious, wide	wige	battle, war
widost	far, widely	wigeð	bear, carry, carry-out, move, perform, wear
widre	far, more-remotely, spacious, wide, widely	wigena	warrior
		wigend	warrior, warriors
wiðre	resistance	wigendra	warrior
wiðres	resistance	wiges	battle, war
wiðsacan	forsake, oppose, resist	wigeþ	bear, carry, carry-out, move, perform, wear
wiðsace	forsake, oppose, resist	wigfreca	warrior
widsceope	widely-distributed	wigfrecan	warrior
widscofen	extensive, widespread	wigfruma	war-leader
		wigfruman	war-leader
wiðstandan	resist, withstand	wigge	battle, war
wiðstanden	resist, withstand	wiggend	warrior
wiðstod	resist, withstand	wiggendra	warriors
wiðstodon	resist, withstand	wiggendum	warrior
wiðstondan	resist, withstand	wiggetawe	armour, war-accoutrements
widweg	distant-path		
widwegas	distant-path	wiggetawum	armour, war-accoutrements
wif	the-wife, wife, woman, women	wiggryre	war-terror
wifa	wife, woman	wigheafola	helmet, war-head
wife	wife, woman	wigheafolan	helmet, war-head
wifes	wife, woman	wigheap	war-band
wiflufan	love-for-a-woman	wigheard	battle-hard
wiflufu	love-for-a-woman	wigheardne	battle-hard
wifman	the-wife, woman	wighete	enmity, war--hate
wifmann	woman	wighryre	fall-in-battle
wifmon	the-wife, woman	wighyrstum	war-trappings
wifmyne	love-of-a-wife, love-of-a-woman, wife-love, woman-love	wigleoð	battle-cry, trumpet-call, war-song
		wigleoþ	battle-cry, trumpet-call, war-song
wifum	wife, woman	wiglic	warlike
wig	battle, strife, war	wigplega	battle, martial-sport
wiga	warrior	wig-plega	battle, war-play
wigan	fight, warrior	wigplegan	battle, martial-sport
wigbealu	horror-of, war-violence	wigrædenne	warfare
wigbil	war-sword	wigrod	battle-road

Word List (*Ænglisc* to English)

Ænglisc	English	*Ænglisc*	English
wigsð	military-expedition	*wilgesið*	dear-companion, willing-companion, willing-follower
wigsigor	victory-in-war		
wigsmið	warrior, war-smith		
wigsmiðum	warrior, war-smith	*wilgesiþ*	dear-companion, willing-companion, willing-follower
wigsmiþ	warrior, war-smith		
wigsmiþas	war-smiths		
wigsmiþum	warrior, war-smith	*willa*	delight, desire, pleasure, purpose, will, wish
wigsped	success-in-battle		
wigspeda	success-in-battle		
wigsteal	battle-place	*willað*	desire, intend, will, wish
wigsþ	military-expedition		
wigtig	wise	*willan*	be-willing, delight, desire, intend, pleasure, purpose, want, will, wish
wigum	battle, war		
wigweorðung	idol-worship, offering-to-an-idol		
wigweorðunga	idol-worship, offering-to-an-idol	*willaþ*	desire, intend, will, wish
wigweorþung	idol-worship, offering-to-an-idol	*wille*	desire, intend, will, wish, wish-to
wigweorþunga	idol-worship, offering-to-an-idol	*willeburnan*	stream, well-water
		willeburne	well-spring
wihaga	battle-hedge, shield-wall	*willende*	desire, intend, will, wish
wihagan	battle-hedge, shield-wall	*willflod*	good-or-desired-flood
wiht	anything, at-all, being, by-any-means, creature, thing, whit	*willgebroðor*	good-brothers
		willgebroþor	good-brothers
		willgeðofta	good-companion
		willgeðoftan	good-companion
wihta	beings	*willgesiðða*	good-companion
wihtæ	anything	*willgesiððas*	good-companion
wihte	anything, at-all, by-any-means, welcome-guest	*willgesiþþa*	good-companion
		willgesiþþas	good-companion
		willgestealla	good-companion
wilcuma	welcome-guest	*willgesteallum*	good-companion
wilcuman	welcome-guest	*willgesweostor*	good-sisters
wilda	wild	*willgeþofta*	good-companion
wilde	untamed, wild, wild-animal	*willgeþoftan*	good-companion
		willum	delight, desire, pleasure, purpose, will, wish
wildeor	wild-animal		
wildne	wild		
wildra	wild	*wilna*	delight, desire, pleasure, purpose, will, wish
wildres	beast's		
wildu	wild		
wile	desire, intend, will, wish	*wilnian*	desire, petition-for, wish-for
wilgeofa	delight-giver	*wilsið*	desired-expedition
		wilsiþ	desired-expedition

Word List (*Ænglisc* to English)

Ænglisc	English	*Ænglisc*	English
wilt	desire, intend, will, wish	*winetreow*	friendship-promise
		winetreowe	friendship-promise
wimman	woman	*wingal*	drunk-with-wine, wine-drunk
wimmanna	woman		
win	wine	*win-gal*	intoxicated, wine-gay
wina	friend, lord		
winærn	hall, wine-building	*wingeard*	vineyard
winærnes	hall, wine-building	*wingedrinc*	wine-drinking
winas	friend, lord	*wingedrince*	wine-drinking
wincel	corner	*wingedrync*	wine-drinking
Wincestre	Winchester (place)	*winhatan*	invitation-to-drink-wine
wincle	corner		
wind	wind	*winhate*	invitation-to-drink-wine
windæg	struggle-day, toil-day		
		winia	friend, lord
windagum	struggle-day, toil-day	*winigea*	friend, lord
		winn	contention, strife, struggle, war
windan	fly, go, turn, twist, wave-in-a-circular-motion, wind		
		winnað	fight, gain, obtain, struggle, work
windas	winds	*winnan*	fight, gain, obtain, struggle, work
windblond	wind-mixing, wind-swirling		
		winnaþ	fight, gain, obtain, struggle, work
winde	wind		
windge	windswept, windy	*winnende*	fight, gain, obtain, struggle, work
windgeard	home-of-the-winds, wind-home		
		winreced	hall, wine-building
windig	windswept, windy	*winsad*	drunken
windige	windswept, windy	*winsade*	drunken
wine	friend, friends, lord, wine	*winsadum*	drunken
		winsæl	wine-hall
winedrihten	friend-and-lord	*winsalo*	wine-hall
winedrihtne	friend-and-lord	*winsele*	wine-hall
winedryhten	friend-and-lord	*winter*	winter, year
wine-dryhten	friend-lord	*wintercald*	winter-cold
winedryhtnes	friend-and-lord	*wintercealde*	winter-cold
wineleas	friendless, friend-less, lord-less	*wintercearig*	winter-churlishness, winter-despondency, wintry-minded
wineleasum	friendless, lord-less		
winemæg	dear-kinsman		
wine-mæg	dear-, friend-kinsman	*winter-cearig*	sorrowful, winter-caring
winemæga	dear-kinsman	*winterstund*	short-time, winter-hour
winemægum	dear-kinsman		
winemaga	dear-kinsman	*winterstunde*	short-time, winter-hour
winemagas	dear-kinsman		
winemagum	dear-kinsman	*wintra*	winter, winters, year
wines	friend, lord	*wintres*	winter, year
wineþearfende	friend-needing	*wintrum*	winter, year

Word List (*Ænglisc* to English)

Ænglisc	English	*Ænglisc*	English
wintrys	winter, year	*wissian*	advise, declare, guide, make-known, point-out, reveal, show
winum	friend, lord		
wiorðe	of-worth, will-be		
wiorðeð	of-worth, will-be		
wiorþe	of-worth, will-be	*wisson*	be-aware-of, know
wiorþeþ	of-worth, will-be	*wist*	abundance, feast, food, plenty, provision, provisions
wir	armlet, precious-metal, ring, wire, wire-ornament		
		wistan	be-aware-of, know
wira	armlet, precious-metal, ring, wire, wire-ornament	*wiste*	abundance, be-aware-of, food, know, observe, plenty, provisions
wire	armlet, precious-metal, ring, wire, wire-ornament		
		wistfylle	food-fill, food-full
		wistfyllo	food-fill, food-full
wirum	armlet, precious-metal, ring, wire, wire-ornament	*wiston*	be-aware-of, know, wish
		wisum	conduct, manner, way, wise
wis	wise		
wisa	guide, leader, wise	*wit*	we, we-two
wisade	advise, guide, point-out, show	*wita*	counsellor, king's-councillor, misery, punishment, torments, torture, wise-man, witness
wisan	conduct, guide, leader, manner, way		
wisdom	wisdom		
wisdome	wisdom	*witan*	be-aware-of, blame, depart, die, go, king's-councillor, know, observe, reproach, wise-man, witness
wise	conduct, manner, way, wise		
wisfæst	wise		
wisfæste	wise, wise-fast		
wishidig	wise		
wishycgende	wise--thinking	*wite*	be-aware-of, blame, consciousness, head, know, knowledge, misery, punishment, reproach, suffer, torture, understanding, wit
wishydig	wise		
wisian	advise, guide, point-out, show		
wisie	advise, guide, point-out, show		
wisige	advise, guide, point-out, show		
wislic	certain, true	*witebroga*	dreadful-torment
wislice	carefully, wisely	*witebrogan*	dreadful-torment
wislicne	certain, true	*witega*	wise
wisna	conduct, manner, way	*witehus*	torment-house
		witelac	punishment
wisode	advise, guide, point-out, show	*witelocc*	flame, hair, tormenting-lock
wisra	wise	*witeloccas*	flame, hair, tormenting-lock
wisse	be-aware-of, know		

263

Word List (Ænglisc to English)

Ænglisc	English	Ænglisc	English
witena	king's-councillor, wise-man, witness	witt	consciousness, head, knowledge, understanding, wit
witeswinge	punishment, torment	witum	misery, punishment, torture
witeswingum	punishment, torment		
wiþ	against, along, being, beside, creature, exchange, forwards, from, near, onto, to, to-the-east, towards, with	wiurðit	will-be
		wiurþit	will-be
		wlanc	proud, rich, splendid
		wlancan	proud, rich, splendid
		wlance	proud, rich, splendid
		wlances	proud, rich, splendid
		wlancne	proud, rich, splendid
wiþ eastan	to-the-east	wlat	gaze, look
wiþ suþan	to-the-south	wlatian	look-for
wiþ uppan	above, upwards	wlatode	look-for
wiþeræhtes	on-the-other-side, opposite	wlence	arrogance, pride, splendour
wiþerbreca	adversary, enemy		
wiþerbrecan	adversary, enemy	wlenco	arrogance, pride, splendour
wiþerlean	pay-back, retaliation		
wiþermedo	enmity, opposition	wlencu	arrogance, pride, splendour
wiþertrod	retreat, return		
wiþfeng	grapple-with, seize	wlitað	gaze, look
wiþfon	grapple-with, seize	wlitan	gaze, look
wiþgripan	grapple-with	wlitaþ	gaze, look
wiþhabban	withstand	wlite	beauty, brightly-shining, brightness, splendour
wiþhæfde	withstand		
wiþhogian	reject		
wiþhogode	reject	wlitebeorht	brightly-shining, brilliant
wiþre	resistance		
wiþres	resistance	wlitebeorhte	brightly-shining, brilliant
wiþsacan	forsake, oppose, resist		
		wlitebeorhtne	brightly-shining, brilliant
wiþsace	forsake, oppose, resist		
		wlitebeorhtum	brightly-shining, brilliant
wiþstandan	resist, withstand		
wiþstanden	resist, withstand	wlitegan	beautiful, bright
wiþstod	resist, withstand	wlitegost	beautiful, bright
wiþstodon	resist, withstand	wlitegra	beautiful, bright
wiþstondan	resist, withstand	wliten	gaze, look
wiþþon	afterwards	wlitesciene	beautiful, bright, brilliant
witian	allot, assign		
witig	wise	wliteseon	beautiful-sight, spectacle
witiga	knowing-man		
witod	allot, assign, known	wlitest	gaze, look
witode	allot, assign	wlitig	beautiful, bright
witodes	allot, assign	wlitigað	become-beautiful, become-bright, make-beautiful
witon	know, observe		

Word List (Ænglisc to English)

Ænglisc	English	Ænglisc	English
wlitigaþ	become-beautiful, become-bright, make-beautiful	wodon	go, move, stride-over, wade
wlitige	beautiful, bright	wodum	crazy, insane
wlitigian	become-beautiful, become-bright, make-beautiful	woerðfullost	honoured, valued
		woerþfullost	honoured, valued
		woh	evil, perverse, twisted
wlitigigan	become-beautiful, become-bright, make-beautiful	wohbogen	perversely-twisted
		wolcen	cloud, heaven, sky, the-sky
wlitigre	beautiful, bright	wolcna	cloud, the-skies, the-sky
wliton	gaze, look		
wlonc	proud, rich, splendid	wolcne	cloud, the-sky
wlonce	proud, rich, splendid	wolcnu	cloud, clouds, the-sky
wlonces	proud, rich, splendid		
wloncne	proud, rich, splendid	wolcnum	cloud, clouds, the-sky
wloncum	proud, rich, splendid		
wlytegan	beautiful, bright	woldagas	days-of-pestilence
wndra	wonder	woldan	desire, intend, will, wish
woc	arise, be-born, be-wakeful, keep-watch, wake	wolde	desire, intend, will, wish, wished, would
wocan	arise, be-born, be-wakeful, keep-watch, wake	wolden	desire, intend, will, wish
		woldest	desire, intend, will, wish
woce	arise, be-born, be-wakeful, keep-watch, wake	woldon	desire, intend, will, wish
wocon	arise, be-born, be-wakeful, keep-watch, wake	wollenteare	with-welling-tears
		wolues	the-wolf's
		wom	evil, perverse, twisted
wocor	offspring, progeny	woma	tumult
wocre	offspring, progeny	womcwidas	evil-speech
wocun	arise, be-born, be-wakeful, keep-watch, wake	womcwide	evil-speech
		womfull	defiled, guilty, sinful
wod	crazy, go, insane, move, stride-over, wade	womm	evil, sin, spot, stain
		womma	evil, sin, spot, stain
		womme	evil, sin, spot, stain
woðbora	counsellor, prophet, speaker	wommes	blot
woðboran	counsel, counsellor, prophet, speaker	wommum	evil, sin, spot, stain
		womscyldig	guilty, sinful
woðcræft	poetry-art	won	dark, dusky, fight, gain, obtain, struggle, work
woðcræfte	poetry, poetry-art		
woðgiefu	song, speech, word-gift	wonað	a-field
		wond	turn, twist, wind
wodnys	insanity, madness	wonfeax	dark-haired
wodnysse	insanity, madness		

Word List (*Ænglisc* to English)

Ænglisc	English	Ænglisc	English
wong	earth-root, earth-route, field, land-layout, plain, plain-surface	*wordcwida*	command, utterance, word
		wordcwydas	command, utterance, word
wongas	earth-root, earth-route, field, land-layout, plain-surface	*wordcwyde*	command, utterance, word
		wordcwydum	command, utterance, word
wonge	earth-root, earth-route, field, land-layout, plain-surface	*worde*	speech, utterance, word, words
wongstede	place	*worden*	agreed, agreement, be, become, happen, suit, worded
wonhyd	carelessness, daring		
wonhydum	carelessness, daring		
wonhygdum	carelessness, daring		
wonn	dark, dusky, fight, gain, misery, obtain, struggle, work	*wordes*	speech, utterance, word
		wordgemearc	declaration
wonna	dark, dusky	*wordgemearcum*	declaration
wonnan	dark, dusky	*wordgyd*	elegy, lay, poem, song
wonne	dark, dusky		
wonsæli	unhappy	*wordhord*	word-hoard, word-treasury
wonsceaft	misery, unhappiness		
wonsceaftum	misery, unhappiness	*worðig*	enclosure-surrounding-a-dwelling
wop	lamentation, weeping		
wope	lamentation, weeping	*wordlean*	reward-for-words
		wordleana	reward-for-words
wora	evil, perverse, twisted	*worðmyndum*	honourably, nobly
		wordon	speech, utterance, word
worc	deed, labour, pain, suffering, work	*wordriht*	word-right
worca	deed, labour, pain, suffering, work	*wordrihta*	word-right
		wordsige	word-successful
worces	work	*wordsnotor*	word-wise
worcsige	work-successful	*wordum*	speech, utterance, word, words
worcþeow	servant, slave, working-slave		
		worhtan	working
worcþeowe	working-slave	*worhte*	carry-out, create, do, make, work
worcum	deed, labour, pain, suffering, work	*worhtest*	created, worked
word	speech, utterance, word, words	*worhton*	carry-out, create, do, make, work
worda	speech, utterance, word	*woriað*	become-worn, crumble, wander
wordbeot	verbal-promise, word-vows	*worian*	become-worn, crumble, wander
wordbeotung	verbal-promise	*woriaþ*	become-worn, crumble, wander
wordbeotunga	verbal-promise, words-promised		

Word List (Ænglisc to English)

Ænglisc	English
worie	become-worn, crumble, wander, worn
world	the-world
worn	large-number, many-things, multitude
worna	large-number, many-things, multitude
wornas	flocking
worngehat	promise
wornum	large-number, many-things, multitude
worold	situation, the-world, way-of-life
worold-ar	worldly-honour
woroldare	worldly-honour
woroldcyning	earthly-king
worold-cyning	earthly-king
woroldcyninga	earthly-king
worolde	situation, the-world, way-of-life
woroldræden	worldly-leadership
woroldrædenne	worldly-leadership
worþig	enclosure-surrounding-a-dwelling
worþmyndum	honourably, nobly
worude	army, band, company, host, throng
woruld	situation, the-world, way-of-life, world, worldly-honour
worulda	worlds
woruldar	worldly-honour
woruldbuend	earth-dweller, human-being
woruldbuendra	earth-dweller, human-being
woruldcandel	the-sun, world-candle
woruldcyingas	earthly-king
woruldcyning	earthly-king
worulddream	earthly-joy
worulddreama	earthly-joy
worulddugeða	worldly-excellence, worldly-honour
worulddugeðum	worldly-excellence, worldly-honour
worulddugeþa	worldly-excellence, worldly-honour
worulddugeþum	worldly-excellence, worldly-honour
woruldduguð	worldly-excellence, worldly-honour
woruldduguþ	worldly-excellence, worldly-honour
worulde	situation, the-world, way-of-life, world, world-edge, worldly
woruldende	world-edge, world-end
woruldfeoh	earthly-goods
woruldgesælig	happy, prosperous, rich-in-earthly-possessions
woruldgesceaft	the-created-world, worldly-creation
woruldgesceafta	the-created-world, worldly-creation
woruldgesceafte	the-created-world, worldly-creation
woruldgestreon	earthly-wealth
woruldgestreona	earthly-wealth
woruldgestreonum	earthly-wealth
woruldlic	worldly
woruldlicra	worldly
woruldmæg	earthly-male-relative
woruldmagas	earthly-male-relative
woruldnytt	worldly-benefit
woruldnytte	worldly-benefit
woruldrice	the-world-kingdom, world-kingdom, worldly-strength
woruldstrenga	worldly-strength
woruldstrengu	worldly-strength
woruldwisdom	secular-learning, worldly-wisdom
woruldwysdome	secular-learning, worldly-wisdom
woruldyrmðo	earthly-misery
woruldyrmþo	earthly-misery
woþa	songs

Word List (Ænglisc to English)

Ænglisc	English	Ænglisc	English
woþbora	counsellor, prophet, speaker	wræce	avenge, be-exiled, distress, drive-out, exile, expel, misery, punish, retribution, revenge, speak-about, utter, vengeance, wrack
woþboran	counsellor, prophet, speaker		
woþcræft	poetry-art		
woþcræfte	poetry-art		
woþgiefu	song, speech, word-gift		
wrace	distress, exile, misery, retribution, revenge, vengeance	wræces	agony, exile, misery, vengeance
		wræclast	exile-track, miserable-track
wracu	distress, misery, retribution, revenge, vengeance	wræc-last	misery-track, path-of-exile
		wræclastas	exile-track, miserable-track
wrað	angry, cruel, evil, wrathful, wroth	wræclic	exiled, wretched
wraða	angry, cruel, evil, wrathful	wræclicne	exiled, wretched
		wræcmæcgas	banished-man, exile
wraðan	angry, cruel, evil, wrathful	wræcmecg	banished-man, exile
		wræcmon	exile
wraðe	angrily, angry, cruel, cruelly, cruelty, evil, with-evil-consequence, wrathful	wræcna	exiled-person, wretch
		wræcon	avenge, be-exiled, drive-out, exile, expel, force, punish, speak-about, tell, utter, wreak
wraðlic	cruel, evil		
wraðlice	cruelly, evilly, with-evil-consequence		
		wræcsið	exile-journey
wraðmod	angrily, angry	wræcsiðum	exile-journey
wraðra	angry, cruel, evil, wrathful	wræcsiþ	exile-journey
		wræcsiþa	exile, exile-journey
wraðum	angrily, angry, cruel, cruelly, evil, with-evil-consequence, wrathful	wræcsiþas	exile-journey
		wræcsiþum	exile-journey
		wræcstow	exile-place
wræc	avenge, be-exiled, drive-out, exile, expel, force, misery, punish, speak-about, tell, utter, vengeance, wreak	wræcstowe	exile-place
		wrægistre	female-accuser
		wræstan	pluck-with-a-plectrum
		wræte	decoration, jewel, ornament
wræca	exiled-person, wretch	wrætlic	curious, marvellous, splendid, wondrous
wræcca	exile, exiled-person, wanderer, wretch	wrætlice	splendidly, wondrous, wondrously
		wrætlicne	curious, splendid, wondrous
		wrætlicra	ornament

Word List (Ænglisc to English)

Ænglisc	English
wrætlicran	curious, splendid, wondrous
wrætlicu	curious, splendid, wondrous
wrætt	decoration, jewel, ornament
wrætta	decoration, jewel, ornament
wrættum	decoration, jewel, ornament
wrah	conceal, cover, hide, protect
wraþ	angry, cruel, cruelty, evil, hostile, wrathful, wroth
wraþa	angry, cruel, evil, wrathful
wraþan	angry, cruel, evil, wrathful
wraþe	angrily, angry, cruel, cruelly, cruelty, evil, with-evil-consequence, wrath, wrathful, wrathfully
wrathfully	cruelty
wraþlic	cruel, evil
wraþlice	cruelly, evilly, with-evil-consequence
wraþmod	angrily, angry
wraþra	angry, cruel, evil, wrathful
wraþum	angrily, angry, cruel, cruelly, evil, with-evil-consequence, wrathful
wreah	conceal, hide, protect
wrec	avenge, be-exiled, drive-out, exile, expel, punish, speak-about, utter
wrecan	avenge, be-exiled, drive-out, exile, expel, force, punish, speak-about, tell, utter, wreak
wrecca	adventurer, avenger, exile, outcast, stranger, wretch
wreccan	wake-up
wreccea	traveller
wreccena	adventurer, avenger, exile, outcast
wrece	avenge, be-exiled, drive-out, exile, expel, punish, speak, speak-about, utter
wrecen	avenge, be-exiled, drive-out, exile, expel, force, punish, speak-about, tell, utter, wreak
wrecend	avenger
wregan	accuse, stir-up
wrehton	wake-up
wreo	conceal, hide, protect
wreon	conceal, cover, hide, protect
wreoþenhilt	having-a-wound-or-wrapped-hilt
wridað	flourish, grow
wriðade	flourish, grow
wridan	flourish, grow
wriðan	flourish, grow
wridaþ	flourish, grow
wriðende	flourish, grow
wridendra	flourish, grow
wridian	flourish, grow
wriðian	flourish, grow
wriðon	bandage, bind, fetter
wrigen	cover, hide
wrigon	cover, hide
wrihst	conceal, hide, protect
writan	carve, engrave, write
writen	carve, engrave, write
wriþade	flourish, grow
wriþan	bandage, bind, fetter, flourish, grow

Word List (Ænglisc to English)

Ænglisc	English	Ænglisc	English
wriþende	flourish, grow	wuhte	anything, at-all, by-any-means
wriþian	flourish, grow		
wriþon	bandage, bind, fetter	wuldor	glorious-fame, glory, honour, praise, splendour
wrixl	exchange		
wrixlan	exchange, exchange-of-words, substitute	wuldorblæd	glorious-fame, wondrous-success
wrixle	exchange	wuldorcining	glorious-king, glory-king
wroht	blame, condemnation, crime, enmity, sin, strife	wuldorcyning	glorious-king, glory-king
		wuldorcyninge	glorious-king, glory-king
wrohte	blame, condemnation, crime, enmity, sin, strife	wuldorcyninges	glorious-king, glory-king
		wuldordreames	praise-rejoicing
wrohtes	blame, condemnation, crime, enmity, sin, strife	wuldorfæder	glorious, glory-father
		wuldorfæst	glorious, heavenly
		wuldorfæstan	glorious, heavenly
		wuldorfæstne	glorious, heavenly
wrohtgeteme	sinful-host?	wuldorgast	glorious-spirit
wrohtscipe	crime, sin	wuldorgesteald	glorious-dwelling
wrugon	conceal, hide, protect	wuldorgestealdum	glorious-dwelling
		wuldorgyfa	glorious-gift
wry	conceal, hide, protect, wrap	wuldorgyfe	glorious-gift
		wuldorsped	glorious-prosperity, glorious-success
wrymeð	to-warm		
wrymeþ	to-warm	wuldorspedum	glorious-prosperity, glorious-success
wryon	conceal, hide, protect	wuldortorht	gloriously-bright
wucan	week	wuldortorhtan	gloriously-bright
wucu	week	wuldre	glory, honour, splendour
wuda	forest, ship, the-woods, widow, wood	wuldres	glory, honour, of-glory, splendour, wondrous, world
wudewan	widow		
wudu	cross, forest, shield, tree, wood, woods	wuldrian	praise
wudubeam	forest-tree	wuldris	glory, honour, splendour
wudubeame	forest-tree		
wudubeames	forest-tree	wuldurcyninge	glorious-king, glory-king
wudubledum	forest-fruit		
wudufæsten	forest-stronghold, wooden-stronghold	wuldurfadur	glory-father
		wulf	the-wolf, wolf
wudurec	wood-smoke	wulfas	wolf
wuduwan	widow	wulfe	wolf
wuduwe	widow	wulfhleoþu	wolf--inhabited-hillside
wuht	anything		
wuhta	being, creature	wulfhlið	wolf--inhabited-hillside

Word List (*Ænglisc* to English)

Ænglisc	English	*Ænglisc*	English
wulfhliþ	wolf--inhabited-hillside	*wundordeað*	marvellous-death, strange-death
wulfum	wolf	*wundordeaðe*	marvellous-death, strange-death
wull	wool	*wundordeaþ*	marvellous-death, strange-death
wulle	wool		
wuna	dwell, inhabit, live, remain	*wundordeaþe*	marvellous-death, strange-death
wunað	dwell, dwells, inhabit, live, remain	*wundorgiefe*	wondrous-gift
wunade	dwell, inhabit, live, remain	*wundorgiefu*	wondrous-gift
		wundorlic	marvellous, strange, wondrous
wunast	living	*wundorlicne*	wondrous
wunaþ	dwell, inhabit, live, remain	*wundorlicran*	marvellous, strange, wondrous
wund	wound, wounded	*wundorsion*	marvellous-sight
wunda	wounds	*wundorsiona*	marvellous-sight
wunde	fly, wound, wounded, wounds	*wundorsmiþ*	marvellous-smith
wunden	fly, go, turn, twist, wave-in-a-circular-motion, wind	*wundorsmiþa*	marvellous-smith
		wundra	marvel, wonder
		wundre	marvel, wonder
wundenfeax	having-curly-hair	*wundrian*	be-amazed, marvel, wonder
wundenhals	twisted-prow, wounded-neck	*wundrigende*	be-amazed, marvel, wonder
wundenlocc	braided-hair		
wundenmæl	twisted-sword, wound-sword	*wundrodon*	be-amazed, marvel, wonder
wundenstefna	ship, twisted-staves, wound-staves	*wundrum*	marvellously, wondrous, wondrously
wunder	marvel, wonder		
wunderfæt	vessel, wondrous-cup	*wundrung*	amazement, wonder
		wundrunge	amazement, wonder
wunderfatum	vessel, wondrous-cup	*wundum*	wound, wounded
		wundun	wounded
wunderlicu	marvellous, strange, wondrous	*wundur*	marvel, wonder
		wundurmaððum	marvellous-treasure
wundian	wound	*wundurmaþþum*	marvellous-treasure
wundiaþ	wound	*wunedon*	dwell, inhabit, live, remain
wundnum	fly, go, twist, wave-in-a-circular-motion, wind	*wuniað*	dwell, inhabit, live, remain
wundon	fly, go, turn, twist, wave-in-a-circular-motion, wind	*wunian*	dwell, dwelling, inhabit, live, remain
		wuniaþ	dwell, dwelling, inhabit, live, remain
wundor	marvel, miracle, wonder	*wuniende*	dwell, inhabit, live, remain
wundorbebod	strange-command		
wundorbebodum	strange-command	*wunne*	fight, gain, obtain, struggle, work

Word List (*Ænglisc* to English)

Ænglisc	English	*Ænglisc*	English
wunnon	fight, gain, obtain, struggle, work	wurman	dragon, serpents, snake, worm
wunod	dwell, live, remain	wurþon	reflex-change, throw, throw-down, transform
wunode	dwell, dwelled, inhabit, live, remain	wurþan	agreement, be, become, suit, wording
wunodon	dwell, inhabit, live, remain	wurþaþ	agreement, be, become, suit, wording
wunung	dwelling, house		
wununge	dwelling, house	wurþe	agreement, be, become, deserving-of, esteemed, honoured, suit, wording, worth, worthy
wurðað	agreement, be, become, suit, wording		
wurðan	agreement, be, become, suit, wording		
wurðaþ	agreement, be, become, suit, wording	wurþeþ	agreement, be, become, suit, wording
wurde	agreement, be, become, suit, wording	wurþian	cherish, esteem, honour, worship
wurðe	agreement, be, become, deserving-of, esteemed, honoured, suit, wording, worth, worthy	wurþiaþ	cherish, honour, worship
		wurþlice	honourably, nobly
		wurþlicor	honourably, nobly, worthier
wurðeþ	agreement, be, become, suit, wording	wurþmyndum	honourably, nobly
		wurþmynt	cherish, honour
		wurþode	cherish, esteem, honour, worship
wurðiað	cherish, honour, worship		
wurðian	cherish, honour, worship	wurþran	deserving-of, esteemed, honoured, worthy
wurðlice	honourably, nobly, worthiness	wuton	let-us
		wutun	let-us
wurðlicor	honourably, nobly	wycce	witch
wurðmyndum	honourably, nobly	wyccum	witch
wurðmynt	cherish, honour	wyde	wide
wurðode	cherish, esteem, honour, worship	wydewan	widow
		wydewe	widow
wurdon	agreement, be, became, become, happen, suit, wording	wyle	cruel, desire, intend, will, wish, wishes
		wylfen	cruel, rapacious, wolfish
wurðran	deserving-of, esteemed, honoured, worthy	wylfenne	cruel, rapacious, wolfish
		wyll	boil
wurdun	had-been	wylla	well-spring

272

Word List (Ænglisc to English)

Ænglisc	English
wyllað	desire, intend, will, wish
wyllan	boil, delight, desire, pleasure, purpose, will, wish
wyllaþ	desire, intend, will, wish
wylle	desire, intend, will, wish
wylleburne	stream, well-water
wylm	current, flame, surge, welling
wylmas	current, flame, surge
wylme	current, flame, surge
wylmhat	flaming-hot
wylmhatne	flaming-hot
wyln	female-servant, slave
wylt	desire, intend, will, wish
wyn	delight, happiness, joy
wyndæg	joyful-day
wyndagum	joyful-day
wynleas	joyless
wynleasne	joyless
wynleasran	joyless
wynlic	beautiful, joyful
wynlicran	beautiful, joyful
wynlicu	beautiful, joyful
wynn	delight, happiness, joy
wynna	delight, happiness, joy
wynne	delight, happiness, joy
wynnum	delight, delightfully, happiness, joy, joyously
wynstre	left
wynsum	beautiful, delightful, pleasant, pleasing
wynsuman	beautiful, delightful, pleasant
wynsumast	beautiful, delightful, pleasant, sweetest
wynsume	beautiful, delightful, pleasant
wynsumne	beautiful, delightful, pleasant
wynsumra	pleasant
wyrcan	action, form, make, produce, struggle
wyrcð	works
wyrce	carry-out, create, do, make, work
wyrcean	carry-out, create, created, do, make, work
wyrceð	carry-out, create, do, make, work
wyrceþ	carry-out, create, do, make, work
wyrd	destiny, event, fate
wyrð	agreement, be, become, suit, wording
wyrda	destiny, fate
wyrdan	destroy, injure
wyrde	deserving-of, destiny, destroy, destroyed, fate, fates, injure
wyrðe	become, deserving-of, esteemed, honoured, worthy
wyrðig	worthy
wyrðne	worthy
wyrðra	deserving-of, esteemed, honoured, worthy
wyrgean	curse
wyrhta	artisan, craftsman, workman
wyrhtan	builders
wyrican	dragon, made
wyrm	dragon, serpent, snake, worm
wyrman	to-warm
wyrmas	dragon, snake, worm
wyrmcynn	dragon-kind, serpent-kind, snake-kind, worm-kind
wyrmcynnes	dragon-kind, serpent-kind, snake-kind, worm-kind

Word List (Ænglisc to English)

Ænglisc	English	Ænglisc	English
wyrme	dragon, snake, worm	wyrþe	become, deserving-of, esteemed, honoured, worthy
wyrmes	dragon, snake, worm	wyrþeþ	bottom, will-be
wyrmfah	decorated-with-worms, serpent-like, snakes	wyrþne	worthy
		wyrþra	deserving-of, esteemed, honoured, worthy
wyrmhord	dragon-hoard		
wyrmhorda	dragon-hoard	wyrtruma	bottom, lower-end, root
wyrmlic	dragon-body, serpent-body, snake-body, worm-body	wyrtruman	bottom, lower-end, root
		wyrtum	herb, plant, root, vegetable
wyrmlicum	dragon-body, serpent-body, snake-body, worm-body	wyruldcyning	earthly-king
		wyruldcyninga	earthly-king
		wysan	conduct, manner, way
wyrmsele	dragon-hall, serpent-hall, snake-hall, worm-hall	wyscan	wish
		wyscte	wish, wished
		wyste	be-aware-of, know
wyrmum	dragon, snake, worm	wyt	we-two
		wyta	misery, punishment, torture
wyrnan	deny, refuse		
wyrnde	deny, refuse	wytan	know
wyrndon	refused	wytum	misery, punishment, torture
wyrnest	deny, refuse		
wyrp	alteration, change, throwing		

X, x

wyrpan	recover		
wyrpe	alteration, change	XII	twelve
wyrpel	jess-strap-for-a-falcon's-leg	XIIa	twelve
		XIII	thirteen
wyrplas	jess-strap-for-a-falcon's-leg	XL	forty
		XVIII	eighteen
wyrs	worse	XVna	fifteen
wyrsa	worse	XXX	thirty
wyrsan	worse	XXXtiges	thirty
wyrse	worse		
wyrstan	worst		
wyrt	herb, plant, root, vegetable		

Y, y

wyrta	herbs		
wyrte	herb, plant, root, vegetable	ycað	augment, grow, increase
		ycan	augment, grow, increase
wyrþ	agreement, be, become, suit, wording	ycaþ	augment, grow, increase
		yð	wave

Word List (*Ænglisc* to English)

Ænglisc	English	*Ænglisc*	English
yða	current, wave, waves	ylfa	elf, elves, fairy, goblin
yðan	destroy, lay-waste	ylfe	elf, fairy, goblin
yðde	destroy, lay-waste	ylfete	swan
yðe	current, easy, pleasant, wave	ylfetu	swan
		ymb	about, after, around, concerning
yðelice	easily		
yðgebland	surging-water	ymbbearh	surround-with-protection
yðgeblond	surging-water		
yðgewinn	wave-struggle, wave-tumult	ymbbeorgan	surround-with-protection
yðgewinne	wave-struggle, wave-tumult	ymbclyppan	embrace, hug
		ymbclypte	embrace, hug
yðgewinnes	wave-struggle, wave-tumult	ymbe	about, after, around, a-swarm-of-bees, at, encircle
yðlad	sea-voyage		
yðlade	sea-voyage	ymbefeng	encircle, surround
yðlaf	beach	ymbefon	encircle, surround
yðlafe	beach	ymbehwearf	circle-about
yðlida	ship, wave-sailor	ymbehweorfan	circle-about
yðlidan	ship, wave-sailor	ymbeode	process, walk-around
yðmearas	ship, wave-sailor, wave-sailors	ymbesittend	neighbour, one-living-nearby
yðmearh	ship, wave-sailor	ymbesittendra	neighbour, one-living-nearby
yðum	current, the-waves, wave	ymbgan	process, walk-around
yfel	bad, badly, evil, mischief, wickedness	ymbhwyrft	about-turns
		ymbhycgenne	about-think
		ymbhycggannae	about-think, besiege
yfele	bad, badly, evil, evilly, wickedness	ymbsæt	besiege, sit-round
yfeles	evil, wickedness	ymbsæton	besiege, sit-around, sit-round, surround
yfla	evil, wickedness		
yflaes	evil	ymbseald	clothe, surround, surrounded
yfles	evil, same, wickedness	ymbsellan	clothe, surround
ylcan	same	ymbseten	besiege, sit-round
ylda	men, of-time	ymbsittan	besiege, sit-around, sit-round, surround
yldan	delay, prolong		
ylde	age, men, old-age	ymbsittend	neighbour, one-living-nearby
yldesta	elder, leader		
yldestan	elder, leader	ymbsittendra	neighbour, one-living-nearby
yldo	age, men, old-age		
yldra	elder, parent	ymbstandend	bystander, one-standing-around
yldre	elder, parent		
yldrum	elder, parent	ymbstandendra	bystander, one-standing-around
yldu	old-age		
yldum	men	ymbutan	about

Word List (*Ænglisc* to English)

Ænglisc	English
yppan	dais, raised-platform-for-high-seat
yppe	dais, raised-platform-for-high-seat
yrfe	inheritance, livestock, property
yrfelaf	heirloom, inherited-sword
yrfelafe	heirloom, inherited-sword
yrfes	inheritance, livestock, property
yrfestol	ancestral-city, inherited-seat-or-homeland
yrfestole	ancestral-city, inherited-seat-or-homeland
yrfeweard	heir, son
yrfewearda	heir, son
yrfeweardas	heir, son
yrhðo	cowardice
yrhþo	cowardice
yrmða	misery, wretchedness
yrmðe	misery, wretchedness
yrmðu	misery, wretchedness
yrmðum	misery, wretchedness
yrmþa	about, misery, wretchedness
yrmþe	misery, wretchedness
yrmþu	hardship, misery, wretchedness
yrmþum	misery, wretchedness
yrnan	run
yrnende	hasten, move-quickly, run
yrnendum	hasten, move-quickly, run, running
yrre	anger, angry, ire
yrremod	angry, enraged
yrringa	angrily
yrrum	angry
yrþ	crop, ploughing
ys	is, to-be
yslan	ember, glowing-coal
ysle	ember, glowing-coal
yþ	current, wave
yþa	current, the-waves, wave, waves
yþan	destroy, lay-waste
yþde	destroy, lay-waste
yþe	current, easy, pleasant, wave
yþelice	easily
yþgebland	surging-water
yþgeblond	surging-water
yþgesene	easily-seen, plentiful
yþgewinn	wave-struggle, wave-tumult
yþgewinne	wave-struggle, wave-tumult
yþgewinnes	wave-struggle, wave-tumult
yþlad	sea-voyage
yþlade	sea-voyage
yþlaf	beach
yþlafe	beach
yþlida	ship, wave-sailor
yþlidan	ship, wave-sailor
yþmearas	ship, wave-sailor
yþmearh	ship, wave-sailor
yþum	current, wave
ywan	appear, present, reveal, show
ywde	appear, present, reveal, show

Word List (English to Ænglisc)

English	Ænglisc	English	Ænglisc
0-9		34	feower and þritig, feoþer and þritig
1	an	35	fif and þritig
2	twegen, tþegen	36	siex and þritig
3	þri	37	seofon and þritig
4	feower, feoþer	38	eahta and þritig
5	fif	39	nigon and þritig
6	siex	40	feowertig, feoþertig
7	seofon	41	an and feowertig, an and feoþertig
8	eahta	42	twegen and feowertig, tþegen and feoþertig
9	nigon		
10	tien	43	þri and feowertig, þri and feoþertig
11	endleofan		
12	twelf, tþelf	44	feower and feowertig, feoþer and feoþertig
13	þreotine		
14	feowertine, feoþertine	45	fif and feowertig, fif and feoþertig
15	fiftine		
16	siextine	46	siex and feowertig, siex and feoþertig
17	seofontine		
18	eahtatine	47	seofon and feowertig, seofon and feoþertig
19	nigontine		
20	twentig, tþentig	48	eahta and feowertig, eahta and feoþertig
21	an and twentig, an and tþentig		
22	twegen and twentig, tþegen and tþentig	49	nigon and feowertig, nigon and feoþertig
23	þri and twentig, þri and tþentig	50	fiftig
		51	an and fiftig
24	feower and twentig, feoþer and tþentig	52	twegen and fiftig, tþegen and fiftig
25	fif and twentig, fif and tþentig	53	þri and fiftig
		54	feower and fiftig, feoþer and fiftig
26	siex and twentig, siex and tþentig	55	fif and fiftig
		56	siex and fiftig
27	seofon and twentig, seofon and tþentig	57	seofon and fiftig
		58	eahta and fiftig
28	eahta and twentig, eahta and tþentig	59	nigon and fiftig
		60	sixtig
29	nigon and twentig, nigon and tþentig	61	an and sixtig
30	þritig	62	twegen and sixtig, tþegen and sixtig
31	an and þritig		
32	twegen and þritig, tþegen and þritig	63	þri and sixtig
33	þri and þritig		

Word List (English to Ænglisc)

English	*Ænglisc*	English	*Ænglisc*
64	*feower and sixtig, feoper and sixtig*	90	*hundnigontig*
		91	*an and hundnigontig*
65	*fif and sixtig*	92	*twegen and hundnigontig, þpegen and hundnigontig*
66	*siex and sixtig*		
67	*seofon and sixtig*		
68	*eahta and sixtig*		
69	*nigon and sixtig*	93	*þri and hundnigontig*
70	*hundseofontig*	94	*feower and hundnigontig, feoper and hundnigontig*
71	*an and hundseofontig*		
72	*twegen and hundseofontig, þpegen and hundseofontig*	95	*fif and hundnigontig*
		96	*siex and hundnigontig*
		97	*seofon and hundnigontig*
73	*þri and hundseofontig*	98	*eahta and hundnigontig*
74	*feower and hundseofontig, feoper and hundseofontig*	99	*nigon and hundnigontig*
		100	*hundteontig*
75	*fif and hundseofontig*	101	*an and hundteontig*
		102	*twegen and hundteontig, þpegen and hundteontig*
76	*siex and hundseofontig*		
77	*seofon and hundseofontig*	103	*þri and hundteontig*
		104	*feower and hundteontig, feoper and hundteontig*
78	*eahta and hundseofontig*		
79	*nigon and hundseofontig*	105	*fif and hundteontig*
		106	*siex and hundteontig*
80	*hundeahtatig*		
81	*an and hundeahtatig*	107	*seofon and hundteontig*
82	*twegen and hundeahtatig, þpegen and hundeahtatig*	108	*eahta and hundteontig*
		109	*nigon and hundteontig*
83	*þri and hundeahtatig*	110	*hundendleftig*
84	*feower and hundeahtatig, feoper and hundeahtatig*	111	*an and hundendleftig*
		112	*twegen and hundendleftig, þpegen and hundendleftig*
85	*fif and hundeahtatig*		
86	*siex and hundeahtatig*		
87	*seofon and hundeahtatig*	113	*þri and hundendleftig*
88	*eahta and hundeahtatig*		
89	*nigon and hundeahtatig*		

Word List (English to *Ænglisc*)

English	*Ænglisc*	English	*Ænglisc*
114	feower and hundendleftig, feoper and hundendleftig	2 (accusative masculine)	twegen, tpegen
		2 (accusative neuter)	tū, twa, tpa
115	fif and hundendleftig	2 (dative feminine)	twam, tpam
116	siex and hundendleftig	2 (dative masculine)	twam, tpam
		2 (dative neuter)	twam, tpam
117	seofon and hundendleftig	2 (genitive feminine)	twega, tpega
		2 (genitive masculine)	twega, tpega
118	eahta and hundendleftig	2 (genitive neuter)	twega, tpega
119	nigon and hundendleftig	2 (instrumental feminine)	twam, tpam
120	hundtwelftig, hundtpelftig	2 (instrumental masculine)	twam, tpam
200	twa, tpa	2 (instrumental neuter)	twam, tpam
300	þreo		
1000	þūsend	2 (nominative feminine)	twa, tpa
2000	twa þūsend, tpa þūsend	2 (nominative masculine)	twegen, tpegen
3000	þreo þūsend	2 (nominative neuter)	tū, twa, tpa
1 (accusative feminine)	an-e	3 (accusative feminine)	þreo
1 (accusative masculine)	an-ne	3 (accusative masculine)	þri
1 (accusative neuter)	an	3 (accusative neuter)	þreo
1 (dative feminine)	anre	3 (dative feminine)	þrim
1 (dative masculine)	an-um	3 (dative masculine)	þrim
1 (dative neuter)	an-um	3 (dative neuter)	þrim
1 (genitive feminine)	an-re	3 (genitive feminine)	þreora
1 (genitive masculine)	an-es	3 (genitive masculine)	þreora
1 (genitive neuter)	an-es	3 (genitive neuter)	þreora
1 (instrumental feminine)	an-re	3 (instrumental feminine)	þrim
1 (instrumental masculine)	an-e	3 (instrumental masculine)	þrim
1 (instrumental neuter)	an-e	3 (instrumental neuter)	þrim
1 (nominative feminine)	an	3 (nominative feminine)	þreo
1 (nominative masculine)	an	3 (nominative masculine)	þri
1 (nominative neuter)	an	3 (nominative neuter)	þreo
2 (accusative feminine)	twa, tpa	3pm	non

Word List (English to Ænglisc)

English	Ænglisc

A, a

English	Ænglisc
a	a, an, anes, enne, hi, hire, sum
a hundred	hundteontig
a hundred and eight	eahta and hundteontig
a hundred and eighteen	eahta and hundendleftig
a hundred and eleven	an and hundendleftig
a hundred and fifteen	fif and hundendleftig
a hundred and five	fif and hundteontig
a hundred and four	feower and hundteontig, feoper and hundteontig
a hundred and fourteen	feower and hundendleftig, feoper and hundendleftig
a hundred and nine	nigon and hundteontig
a hundred and nineteen	nigon and hundendleftig
a hundred and one	an and hundteontig
a hundred and seven	seofon and hundteontig
a hundred and seventeen	seofon and hundendleftig
a hundred and six	siex and hundteontig
a hundred and sixteen	siex and hundendleftig
a hundred and ten	hundendleftig
a hundred and thirteen	þri and hundendleftig
a hundred and three	þri and hundteontig
a hundred and twelve	twegen and hundendleftig, tpegen and hundendleftig
a hundred and twenty	hundtwelftig, hundtpelftig
a hundred and two	twegen and hundteontig, tpegen and hundteontig
a thousand	þūsend
abandon	alecgan, alecgean, alede, aledon, alegde, alegdon, anforlætan, anforleten, ferlorene, forlætan, forlæten, forleas, forleosan, forlet, forleton, forloren, geswac, geswicað, geswicaþ, swa, swac, swican, swice, swicon
abandoned	forlet
abandoning	forlet
abbot	abbod, abbude
a-better	betera, beteran, betere, betest, betost, betst, betsta, betstan, betste
abide	abidan
ability	gemet, gemete
a-bishop	byscop
abject	hean
a-blade	seax
able	gerad, gerade
a-boat	bates
abode	wic
about	abutan, an, be, bi, big, embe, on, ymb, ymbe, ymbutan, yrmþa
about-think	ymbhycgenne, ymbhycggannae
about-turns	ymbhwyrft
above	bufan, ofer, ofor, steape, uerc, ufan, ufon, uppe, wið uppan, wiþ uppan
Abraham (name)	Abrame
a-breakthrough	dagaz
a-brood	cynren
absolute-king	selfcyning
abstain-from	sparedon, sparian, sparode
abundance	geneahe, geniht, wist, wiste
abundant	genihtsum, ungnyðe
abundantly	genehhe

Word List (English to Ænglisc)

English	Ænglisc	English	Ænglisc
abyss	dæl, dala, dalo, deop	accursed-one	forhatena, werg, wergan, wergas, wergum, werig
a-cave	eorðscræfe		
accept	anfenge, ceosan, ciosan, cure, curon, ðicgean, geceas, geceos, geceosað, geceosaþ, geceosenne, gecoren, gecorenan, gecorene, gecorone, geþægon, geþah, geþeah, geþegen, geþicgan, onfangen, onfeng, onfengon, onfoð, onfoh, onfon, onfoþ, þegon, þegun, þicgan, þicgeað, þicgean, þicgeaþ, þigeð, þigeþ, underfænge, underfeng, underfon	accusation	onsage, onsagu
		accuse	cwiðan, cwiðe, cwiðed, cwiþan, cwiþe, cwiþed, gewreged, teon, tyhð, tyhþ, wregan
		accuser	melda, meldan
		accustom	wene, wened, wenede, wenian, wennan
		accustomed	geþywe
		a-certain	nathwylc, nathwylces, nathwylcum, sum, sume, sumes, sumne, sumum
		a-certain-amount	sum
		a-certain-one	sum, sume, sumes, sumne, sumum
accompanying	andlang, andlong, andlongne, ondlang, ondlangne, ondlong, ondlonge	achieve	agan, ahæfen, ahafen, ahebban, ahof, ahofon, fæng, fehð, fehþ, feng, fengon, fon, gefeng, gehedde, gehegan, geworht, geworhte, gewyrcan, hegan
accomplish	færde, færdon, færen, feran, ferde, ferdon, fere, ferende, geferde, geferdon, gefere, gefered, geferede, geferedon, geferian, gefremian, geworht, geworhte, gewyrcan, þurhteon		
		a-consenter	geþafa
accomplished	gearwost, welþungen		
accomplished-deed	gewyrht, gewyrhtum		
according-to	æfter		
account	segen, segene		
accursed	fægan, fæge, fægean, fæges, fægne, fægum, werg, wergan, wergas, wergum, werig		

Word List (English to Ænglisc)

English	Ænglisc	English	Ænglisc
acquire	ægnian, agnian, begeat, begeate, begeaton, beget, begietan, begieten, begytan, bigeat, eode, eodon, eow, eowde, ga, gað, gæð, gæþ, gan, gaþ, geagnod, geeode, geeodon, gegæð, gegæþ, gegan, gegangan, gegangeð, gegangenne, gegangeþ, gegaþ, gegongeð, gegongen, gegongeþ, geiode, gestrynan, gestrynde, strynan, strynde, stryndon	address	gegrettan, gegrette, gehnægdon, genægdan, genæged, getrimede, getrymmed, gretan, greted, greteð, greteþ, grette, gretton, hnægde, maðelian, maðelod, maðelode, maþelian, maþelod, maþelode, næfre, nægan, trimian, trymeð, trymede, trymedon, trymeþ, trymian, trymman
acquisition	ceap, ceapas, ceape	adhere	cleofiað, cleofian, cleofiaþ
acre	æcer, æcera, æceras	admit	gestæled, stæl, stælan
across	ofer, ofor	admonish	abead, abeod, abeodan, abude, gemanode, gemoniað, gemoniaþ, gemonige, man, manað, manaþ, manian, manod, manode, monað, monaþ
act	dædon, deð, deþ, do, doð, don, doþ, drohtende, drohtian, dyde, dydest, dydon, gedæde, gedeð, gedeþ, gedo, gedoð, gedon, gedoþ, gedyde, gedydon		
act-cunningly	lytegian		
action	angin, dæd, dæda, dæde, dædum, gesceap, gesceapo, gesceapu, gewyrc, wyrcan		
action-in-battle	guðgeweorca, guþgeweorc, guþgeweorca		
active	hwæt, hwætran, hwata, hwate, hwatum		
acts	fremaþ		

Word List (English to *Ænglisc*)

English	*Ænglisc*	English	*Ænglisc*
adorn	frætwan, frætwed, frætwian, gearwad, gearwian, gefrætewod, gefrætwad, gefrætwade, gefrætwod, gefretewodon, gegærwan, gegarwod, gegearewod, gegearwigean, gegearwod, gegired, gegiredan, gegyred, gegyrede, gegyrwan, gegyrwed, gehlæste, geregnad, geregnode, gerenod, geteoð, geteoþ, gierede, gierwaþ, girwan, gyrde, gyrede, gyredon, gyrwað, gyrwan, gyrwaþ, hlæstan, onhread, onhreodan, regnian, renian, renodest, teodan, teode, teodod, teon, tiode	advance	fremeð, fremede, fremedon, fremest, fremeþ, fremmað, fremman, fremmaþ, fremme, fremmen, geðrungen, gefremed, gefremede, gefremeden, gefremedon, gefremman, gefremmanne, gestepte, geþrang, geþrungen, sceaf, sceof, scofen, scufan, scufeð, scufeþ, scufon, scufun, stepan, stepe, stepte, stepton, þrage, þrang, þringan, þriwa, þrong, þrungon
		advanced	gelyfed
		advantage	freme, fremena, fremu, fremum, god, goda, godaes, godan, gode, godes, godne, godra, godum
adorned	gefrætwed, gehroden, gehrodene, gerena, hroden	advantageous	getæse
		adventurer	wrecca, wreccena
adorned-with-gold	fæted, fætt, fættan, fætte	adversary	andsaca, feond, feonda, feondas, feonde, feondes, feondscipe, feondum, fionda, fynd, ondsaca, ondsacan, wiðerbreca, wiðerbrecan, wiþerbreca, wiþerbrecan
adorned-with-treasure	sinchroden		
		advice	geþeaht, ræd

Word List (English to Ænglisc)

English	Ænglisc	English	Ænglisc
advise	geræd, grædest, gewisade, gewissode, læran, lærde, læred, rædað, rædan, rædaþ, rædde, wisade, wisian, wisie, wisige, wisode, wissian	affliction	bisgo, bisgum, bisigu, broc, broce, bysigu, bysigum, grynn, grynna, gyrn, myrðe, myrðu, myrþe, myrþu, nið, niða, niðas, niðe, niðes, niðum, niþ, niþa, niþas, niþe, niþes, niþum, sar, sare, trega, tregan, tregena
advisement	gerædde		
Aelfhere's (name)	ælfheres		
Aethelred's (name)	Æþelrædes		
affect	geæfnan, hran, hrinan, hrine, hrinon	affliction-of?-war	orlegweorc
		a-field	wonað
affection	freod, freode, mine	aflame	fyrenu
affections	breost-cofa, frige, frigu	afresh	geniwad, geniwod, niwiað, niwian, niwiaþ
afflict	brocian, ðrean, dreccan, dreceð, dreceþ, drefan, drefde, dreht, drehte, drep, drepan, drepen, dropen, eglan, gebroced, gebrocede, gebrocian, gebrocod, geðread, geðreadne, gedrefed, gedreht, gedrehte, genearwad, genearwod, geswenced, geswencte, geþread, geþreadne, nearwað, nearwaþ, nearwian, nearwode, swencan, swencte, þreagan, þrean	after	æfter, eft, efter, embe, ofer, ofor, seoððan, seoþðan, seoþþan, siððan, siðþan, siþðan, siþþan, sy, syððan, syðþan, syþðan, syþþan, ymb, ymbe
		after-speaking	æftercweþend, æftercweþendra
		afterward	eft
		afterwards	æfter, eft, seoððan, seoþðan, seoþþan, siððan, siþðan, siþþan, sy, syððan, syðþan, syþðan, syþþan, widðon, wiþþon
		again	eft, gean, gen, gena, gien, ongean
		against	æt, ofer, ofor, ongean, togeanes, togenes, wið, wiþ
		age	ældo, ealdað, ealdaþ, ealdian, ealdor, eldo, mædæg, mældæges, mældagum, ylde, yldo
afflicted	se	ages	a

284

Word List (English to Ænglisc)

English	Ænglisc	English	Ænglisc
agony	wræces	a-large-whale	Fastitocalon
a-good	bonus	alarmed	acol
agreeable	gegenge, getæse	alas!	eal, eala
agreed	worden	Aldhelm (name)	ealdelm
agreement	endian, geþinge, geþingea, geþinges, geþingo, geweard, gewearþ, geworden, treow, treowa, treowe, treowræden, treowrædenne, treowum, wærð, wærþ, weard, weard, wearþ, wedd, wedde, weorcum, weorð, weorðað, weorðaþ, weorðe, weorðeð, weorðen, weorþ, weorþaþ, weorþe, weorþeð, weorþen, weorþeþ, worden, wurðað, wurðan, wurðaþ, wurde, wurðe, wurðeþ, wurdon, wurþan, wurþaþ, wurþe, wurþeþ, wyrð, wyrþ	a-leaf	leaf
		ale-beaker	ealowæg, ealowæge, ealuwæg, ealuwæge
		ale-bench	ealne, ealobenc, ealobence, ealubence
		ale-depriving	ealuscerwen
		ale-dispensing	ealuscerwen
		ale-drinker	ealodrincend, ealodrincende
		Alfred (name)	Ælfred
		alien	elðeodig, elþeodig, fremde, fremdes, fremdu, fremdum
		alien-being	ælwiht, ælwihta
		alien-spirit	ellorgæst, ellorgast
		alight	lihtan, lihte
		alike	gelic, gelice, gelicost
		a-little	fea, hwon
		alive	cucra, cwic, cwican, cwice, cwicera, cwices, cwicne, cwico, cwicra
agree-to	ðafian, ðanc, geðafode, geþafode, þafian, þafodest, þanc	all	a, æghwilc, ælc, ales, eal, eall, ealle, ealles, eallra, eallum, ealne, ealra, ealre
a-hall	healle		
ahead-of-time	forane		
a-hoard	hord	all-at-once	semninga
aid	helpe	all-creatures	allwihta, alwihta, eallwihta
ailment	cnyssan, coðu, coþu, coþum	allegiance	geongordom, geongordome, geongordomes, giongorscipe, helde, hyldo
air	lyft		
airborne-pest	lyftsceaþa, lyftsceaþan		
air-flier	lyftfloga		
air-swift	lyftswift, lyftswiftne	all-golden	ealgylden, eallgylden, gyldan
a-killing-one	cwellendum		
a-kind-of	cynn	all-good	ealteawne
a-kind-of-tree	treocyn	all-green	ælgrene
a-king	Cyning	all-iron	ealliren, eallirenne
a-large-magnificent?-road	rancstræt, rancstræte	all-mankind	eormencynn, eormencynnes

Word List (English to Ænglisc)

English	Ænglisc	English	Ænglisc
allot	dælað, dælan, dælaþ, dælde, dældon, dæle, dæleð, dæleþ, dælon, gedælan, gedælde, gedæled, gedaled, gesceop, gescer, gescerede, gescyred, getæce, getæhte, getæhton, sceððan, sceðþan, scerian, sceþþan, scirian, scyred, scyreð, scyrede, scyreþ, tæcan, tæcaþ, tæhte, weotode, witian, witod, witode, witodes	allow-to-escape	forlæt, forlætað, forlætan, forlætaþ, forlæte, forlæteð, forlæten, forlæteþ, forlet, forleton
		all-powerful (Latin)	omnipotentem
		all-ready	ealgearo, ealles, eallgearo
		all-ruler	allmectig, allwalda, alwalda, alwaldan, alwaldend, alwealdan, eallwealda
		all-timbered	æltimbred
		all-told	forðgerimed, forþgerimed
		ally	geþafa, guðwine, guðwinum, guþwine, guþwinum
allotted	gescyred	almighty	ællmihtig, ælmehtig, ælmihtegan, ælmihtgian, ælmihtig, ælmihtiga, ælmihtigan, ælmihtiges, ælmihtigne, allmectig
allotted-time	tiddæg, tiddæge, tidege		
allow	alyfan, alyfde, alyfed, an, ðoliaþ, ðolode, forlæt, forlætað, forlætan, forlætaþ, forlæte, forlæteð, forlæten, forlæteþ, forlet, forleton, geþolian, geþolianne, geþolode, geuðe, geunnan, geunne, geuþe, læt, lætað, lætan, lætaþ, læte, læteð, læten, læteþ, let, lete, leton, lifan, life, lyfað, lyfaþ, on, þolað, þolaþ, þoledon, þoliað, þolian, þoliaþ, þolien, þoligende, þolodan, þolode, uard, uðe, unnan, uþe		
		almost	fulneah
		almost-everywhere	wel, wel hwær
		alms	ælmessan, ælmyssan, ælmysse
		almsman	ælmesmann, ælmesmannum
		alone	ænne, an, ana, ane, anes, anne, annesse, anon, anra, anre, anum, on
		alone-walker	angenga, angengea
		along	æfter, emnlange, wið, wiþ
		alongside	toemnes
		already	furðum, furþum
		also	ea, eac, ec, etiam, gelice, gelicost, mid, samod, somed, somod, swa, swilce, swylce, to
allowing	læteð		
allowing-word	leafnesword		
		also (Latin)	etiam

Word List (English to Ænglisc)

English	Ænglisc	English	Ænglisc
altar	*glædstede, gledstyde, herg, hergum, herheard, weg, weobedd, weofod, weofode, wibed*	amusement	*gamen, gamene, gomen, gomene*
		amuse-oneself	*plegan, plegian, plegode*
		amusing	*gamene*
		an	*an*
alter	*gewendan, gewende, oncirde, oncyrreð, oncyrreþ, wend, wendan, wende, wendeð, wenden, wendeþ, wendon*	ancestor	*ærfæder, cneowmæg, cneowmægas, cneowmagas, ealdfæder*
		ancestors	*cneomægum*
		ancestral-city	*yrfestol, yrfestole*
alteration	*wyrp, wyrpe*	anchor	*ancor, ancre*
although	*ðeah, ðeah ðe, ðeh, þe, þeah, þeah þe, þeh*	anchor-cable	*oncearbendum, oncerbend*
		anchor-rope	*oncyrrap, oncyrrapum*
altogether	*æghwam, eallunga, ealra, ealre*	ancient	*frod, gamol*
always	*a, æfre, ealneg, gehwær, gehwer, o, simble, simle, singala, singales, symble, symle, syngales, wide, wideferhð, wideferhþ*	ancient-fight	*fyrngewinn, fyrngewinnes*
		ancient-hostility	*ærgewinn*
		ancient-man	*iumonn, iumonna*
		ancient-riches	*ærwelan, æwela*
		ancient-sage	*fyrnwita, fyrnwitan*
		ancient-spirit	*geosceaftgast, geosceaftgasta*
always (Latin)	*semper*	ancient-treasure	*ærgestreon, ærgeweorc, longe, longgestreon, longgestreona*
am	*eom*		
a-man	*man*		
amazement	*wundrung, wundrunge*		
		ancient-work	*fyrngeweorc*
ambush	*sætan*	ancient-years	*fyrngearum*
amen	*amen*	and	*7, ac, and, end, et, feond, ge, mid, ond*
amend	*betan, bete, gebetan, gebette, gebettest*	and (Latin)	*et*
		and-not	*noðer, noþer*
amended	*gebette*	an-earl's-treasures	*eorlgestreona*
amicably	*freondlice, freondlicor*	an-end	*ende*
		angel	*ærendgast, engel, engla, englas, engle, engles, englum, engyl, gast*
amid	*æfter, mid, tomiddes*		
among	*æfter, mid, on*		
amorous-intention	*freondmynd, freondmynde*		
		angelic	*engla*
amount	*sceat, sceates, sceatt, sceattas, sceattes, sceattum*	angel-kin	*engelcynn, engelcynna*
		angels	*angla, engla, englas, englum*
ample	*widgil, widgillan*		

Word List (English to Ænglisc)

English	Ænglisc	English	Ænglisc
anger	abealch, abelgan, abolgen, and, anda, andan, gegremed, gegremede, gegremod, gegremode, grama, graman, gremian, torn, torna, torne, yrre	announce	abead, abeodan, aboden, abudon, bead, beoð, beodan, beodeð, beodeþ, beoþ, biodan, boden, bude, budon, gebad, gebead, gebeodan
		announced	gebodode
Angle-kin	Angel-cynn, engelcynn, engelcynna	announcement	færspel
		annually-bright	geartorht, geartorhte
		a-noble	æþele
Angles	Engle	anoint	gesmyrode, smyrian
angrily	wraðe, wraðmod, wraðum, wraþe, wraþmod, wraþum, yrringa	another	eac, ellor, elra, elran, oðer, oðerne, oðre, oðres, oðrum, oþer, oþerne, oþerre, oþre, oþres, oþrum
angry	abelgan, abolgen, belgan, bolgenmod, eorres, gebolgen, gebolgne, gram, graman, grame, gramena, grames, gramum, grome, gromra, wrað, wraða, wraðan, wraðe, wraðmod, wraðra, wraðum, wraþ, wraþa, wraþan, wraþe, wraþmod, wraþra, wraþum, yrre, yrremod, yrrum	answer	7sware, andsware, andswarede, andswaredon, andswarian, andswarod, andswarode, andswarodon, andswaru, andwyrdan, andwyrde, oncwæð, oncwædon, oncwæþ, oncweðan, oncweden, oncweþan, ondsware, ondswarode, ondswaru
angry-hearted	gromheort, gromhydig	answers	oncwyð
angry--minded	gromhydig	anticipate	wen, wenað, wenan, wenaþ, wende, wendon, wene, weneð, weneþ
angry-one	gram, graman, grame, gramena, grames, gramum, grome, gromra		
animal	deor		
animals	deor	anxiety	breost-cearu, mod, modceare, modcearu
animate	feorheacen, feorheaceno		
Anlaf (name)	Anlaf, Anlafe	anxiety-about-life	lifceare, lifcearu
Anlaf's (name)	Anlafes	anxious	ceara, cearað, cearaþ, cearian, hohful, mod-cearig
Anna (name)	Annan		
		anxious-minded	modcearig

Word List (English to Ænglisc)

English	Ænglisc	English	Ænglisc
any	ælc, æne, ænegum, ænges, ængum, ænig, ænige, æniges, ænigne, ænigra, ænigre, ænigum, ænyg, anegum, hwelc, hwilc, hwilce, hwylc, hwylce, hwylcere, hwylcne, hwylcum, nanum, nenne, þy	appearance	anlicnes, anlicnesse, anlycnysse, hit, hiw, hiwe
		apple	æple, æppel
		apple-dark	æppelfealo, æppelfealowe, æppelfealuwe
		apply-a-lotion	gesmyrode, smyrian
		appoint	aseted, asettan, asette, asetton, gesætte, gesætton, geseted, gesett, gesettan, gesette, gesetton, gestefnde, geteode, geteoh, geteohhian, geteohhod, sete, settan, sette, setton, stefnan, teohhian, teohhode
any-more	furðor, furður, furþor, furþur		
anyone	hwa, hwæne, hwam, hwan, hwon, hwone, man		
anyone-used-to-form-passive-sense	man, mon		
anything	aht, aweox, awiht, awuht, edwihtan, edwihte, owiht, owihte, uuihte, wiht, wihtæ, wihte, wuht, wuhte		
		appointed-time	gescæphwil, gescæphwile
		appointed-while	gescæphwil, gescæphwile
anything-else	elles		
anywhere	ahwær, hwær, hwar, ohwær, ower	approach	genealæhton, genealecan, gretan, greted, grette, hwearfian, hwearfode, nealæcan, nealæced, nealæcte, nealæhte, ongangan
apart	onsundran, onsundron, sundor		
apostle	apostol, apostoles		
a-powerful	ricne		
apparel	gyrla, gyrlan		
appear	ætæwde, æteowan, æteowde, ætywan, ðuhte, ðyncan, eaweð, eaweþ, eowdon, eoweð, eoweþ, geðuht, geeawed, geþuht, geþuhton, geywan, iewan, iewde, iewe, þincan, þince, þinceað, þincean, þinceaþ, þinceð, þinceþ, þuhte, þuhton, þyncan, þynceð, þynceþ, ywan, ywde	approaching	toweard, toweardan
		appropriate	gegenge, gemet, gerisne, gerysne
		appropriate-for-a-queen	cwenlic
		a-prince	ealdor
		a-protective-ridge	walu
		arch	hwealf
		arched	hwealf, hwealfum
		archer	sceotend, sceotendra, sceotendum, scotendum
		are	eart
		area-of-ground	grundwong

Word List (English to Ænglisc)

English	Ænglisc	English	Ænglisc
area-surrounding-a-fireplace	heorð, heorðe, heorþ, heorþe	armour	breostweorðung, breostweorðunge, breostweorþung, breostweorþunge, byrnhomon, frætewum, frætwa, frætwe, frætwum, fyrdhrægl, fyrdsearo, fyrdsearu, gewæde, gewædu, guðgeatawum, guðgetawa, guðgetawe, guðgewæda, guðgewæde, guðgewædo, guðgewædu, guðsearo, guþgeatawum, guþgetawa, guþgetawe, guþgewæda, guþgewæde, guþgewædo, guþgewædu, guþsearo, hildesceorp, hyrst, searo, searohæbbendra, searonet, searwum, wiggetawe, wiggetawum
a-right	gerihte, rightly, riht, rihte, ryht, truly		
arise	aras, aris, arisað, arisan, arisaþ, arisen, arison, aspringan, asprungen, astag, astah, asteah, astelidæ, astigan, astigeð, astigeþ, awacan, awæcniað, awæcnian, awæcniaþ, awoc, awocon, gestah, gestigest, onwacan, onwoc, onwocan, onwoce, onwocon, stah, stigan, stige, stigon, waca, wacan, wæcnan, wæcned, woc, wocan, woce, wocon, wocun		
arisen	stah		
arises	arisað		
ark	earc		
arm	bog, bogum, earm, earme, earmon, earmum		
armed-conflict	herenið, hereniþ, wæpenþracu, wæpenþræce	armour-and-weapons	guðsceorp, guþsceorp, hildegeatwa, hildegeatwe
armed-strife	searonið, searoniða, searoniðas, searoniþ, searoniþa, searoniþas	armoured	searohæbbendra
		armour-possessor	searohæbbend, searohæbbendra
armies	hergas		
armlet	beag, beaga, beagas, beage, beages, beagum, beah, begas, wir, wira, wire, wirum	armour-suit	heaðowæd, heaðowædum, heaþowæd, heaþowædum
		arm-ring	earmbeag, earmbeaga
arm-ornament	earmread, earmreade		

Word List (English to *Ænglisc*)

English	*Ænglisc*	English	*Ænglisc*
army	fyrd, fyrde, guðhere, guðhergum, guþhere, guþhergum, here, herefolc, herefolces, herga, hergan, hergas, herge, herges, hergum, herige, heriges, mægeð, mægen, mægene, mægenes, mægeþ, mægna, mægne, mægnes, mægnu, mægyn, uuereda, weorod, weoroda, weorode, weorude, wered, wereda, werede, weredes, weredum, werod, weroda, werode, werodes, werodum, werud, weruda, werudes, worude	arrange	gesceap, gesceapen, gesceapene, gesceop, gescype, gestefnde, geteoð, geteode, geteoh, geteohhian, geteohhod, geteoþ, geþinged, geþingod, getrimede, getrymmed, sceop, scepen, scieppan, scop, stefnan, teodan, teode, teohhian, teohhode, teon, þingade, þingian, þingode, tiode, trimian, trymeð, trymede, trymedon, trymeþ, trymian, trymman
		arranged	aræd
		arrival	cime, cyme
		arrive	becom, becoman, becomon, becuman, becwom, com, coman, come, comon, cumað, cuman, cumaþ, cume, cumen, cumene, cumenra, cwom, cwoman, cwome, cwomon, cymð, cyme, cymeð, cymen, cymest, cymeþ, cymþ
army-arrow	herestræl		
army-bird	herefugol, herefugolas		
army-coat	herepad		
army-front	or, ore		
army-garment	herewæd, herewædum		
army-mail-coat	heresyrcan, heresyrce		
army-net	herenet		
army-suit	fyrdhom		
army-vigorous	fyrdhwæt, fyrdhwate		
a-roof	hrofe	arrogance	bælc, mod, mode, modes, modþryðo, modþryþo, modum, oferhyda, oferhygd, oferhygda, oferhygde, ofermetto, ofermod, onmedla, onmedlan, wlence, wlenco, wlencu
arose	aras		
arose (Latin)	resurrexit		
around	abutan, embe, geond, ymb, ymbe		
arouse	aweahte, aweccan, awehte, toweccan, towehton, weaht, weccað, weccan, weccaþ, weccean, wecceð, wecceþ, wehte	arrogant	modig, oferhidig, oferhydig, ofermod, ofermoda

Word List (English to *Ænglisc*)

English	*Ænglisc*	English	*Ænglisc*
arrow	flan, flana, flane, flanes, hildenædran, hildenædre, stræl, stræla, strælas, stræle, strælum	ask	abiddan, acsian, ahsian, ahsode, ahsodon, ascian, axian, axoden, axude, bæd, bædon, bena, benan, biddan, bidde, bydde, frægn, fricgan, fricgcean, fricgean, fricgen, frige, frignan, frin, frinan, frineð, frineþ, geascodon, gebæd, gebiddað, gebiddaþ, gebidde, gefrægen, gefrægn, gefrægnod, gefricge, gefricgeað, gefricgean, gefricgeaþ, gefrugnon, gefrunen, gefrungon, gefrunon, geþinged, geþingod, spyrede, spyrian, þingade, þingian, þingode
arrow-bow	flanboga, flanbogan		
arrows	isernscur, isernscure		
arrow-shaft	sceaft, sceafta, sceft		
art	orðonc, orðoncum, orþanc, orþancum, orþonc, orþoncum, searo, searwum		
artery	ædra, ædre, ædrum, edrum		
artfully	listum		
artisan	wyrhta		
as	also, alswa, ða, ðe, gelice, gelicost, sue, suua, swa, swilce, swylce, þe, to		
as-a-superior	hearra, heorra, herra		
ascend	gestah, gestigan, gestigen, gestigon, stah, stigan, stigen, stigon		
a-second	oðer, oðre, oðres, oðrum, oþer, oþerne, oþerre, oþre, oþres, oþrum	asked	frægn
		as-long-as	ðenden, hwænne, hwonne, þenden
		a-smith	smið
a-servant follower	geongra	ass	esol, esolas
as-far-as	oð, oþ	assemble	gesomnad, gesomnie, gesomnod, samnian, somnigean
ash	axan, axe		
ashamed	æwiscmod		
ash-army	æschere		
ash-bearer	æscberend, æscberendra	assembly	ðing, ðinga, ðinges, gedræg, gedreag, gemang, gemong, gemonge, gemot, þincg, þing, þinga, þinge, þinges
ash-tree	æsc, æsca, æscum, asca		
ash-warrior	æscwiga		
ash-wood	æscholt, æscplega, æscplegan, æscrof, æscrofe, æsctir	assembly-place	meðelstede, meþelstede
ash-woods	aelicce, æscþræcu, æscþraelicce	assertion	onsage, onsagu
ashy	blac, blacne		
as-if	swa, swilce, swylce		

Word List (English to *Ænglisc*)

English	*Ænglisc*	English	*Ænglisc*
assign	geriht, gesceop, gescer, gescerede, gescyred, getæce, getæhte, getæhton, geteode, geteoh, geteohhian, geteohhod, rihtan, rihte, sceððan, sceðþan, scerian, sceþþan, scirian, scyred, scyreð, scyrede, scyreþ, tæcan, tæcaþ, tæhte, teohhian, teohhode, weotode, witian, witod, witode, witodes	attack	attack, beaduræs, ecgþracu, ecgþræce, ehtan, ehtende, ehtnys, ehtnysse, ehton, forgrap, forgripan, gegrettan, gegrette, gehnægdon, genægdan, genæged, geræsde, gesec, gesecan, gesecanne, gesece, gesecean, geseceð, geseceþ, gesohtan, gesohte, gesohtest, gesohton, gretan, greted, greteð, greteþ, grette, gretton, gripe, guðræs, guðræsa, guþræs, guþræsa, hatian, hatode, hergian, hergode, hnægde, nægan, nið, niða, niðas, niðe, niðes, niðum, niþ, niþa, niþas, niþe, niþes, niþum, ongangan, onsacan, ræs
assist	gefylste		
associates	drihtgesiða		
assume	benam, beniman, benumen, binom		
a-stabbing-pain	færstice		
as-the-living	leofað, leofaþ, lifað, lifaþ, lifgendra, lifigendra, lyfað, lyfaþ, lyfde		
astute	frod		
asunder	asyndrod		
a-superior	betera, beteran, betere, betest, betost, betst, betsta, betstan, betste		
		attack-in-battle	hilderæs
		attacking	onsæge
a-surrounding-earth-work	eorþan, eorthweard	attacking-woman	aglæcwif
		attain	gebad, gebidan, gebiden, gebidon, gegangan, gegangeð, gegangenne, gegangeþ, gegongeð, gegongen, gegongeþ, geræcan
a-swarm-of-bees	ymbe		
at	æt, be, ymbe		
at-all	aht, awiht, awuht, fea, owiht, owihte, wiht, wihte, wuhte		
atheling	æþele, æþeling		
Athelstan (name)	æþelstan		
at-once	æne, ætsomne, sona		
atone-for	angeald, ongeald, ongyldan		
attach	fegan, fegeð, fegeþ, gefeg, gefeged, gespeon, spannan, spenn		

293

Word List (English to Ænglisc)

English	Ænglisc	English	Ænglisc
attempt	angan, ongan, ongann, ongean, ongin, onginnað, onginnan, onginnaþ, onginneð, onginnen, onginneþ, ongon, ongonn, ongunn, ongunnan, ongunne, ongunnen, ongunnon, ongyn, ongynneð, ongynneþ	avenger	wrecca, wreccena, wrecend
		avoid	fleon, fleonde, forbeah, forbugan, forlæt, forlætað, forlætan, forlætaþ, forlæte, forlæteð, forlæten, forlæteþ, forlet, forleton
		avoiding	bibugeð
		await	abidan, bad, basnedon, basnian, beodan, bidan, bideð, bideþ, bidon, gebad, gebidan, gebide, gebiden, gebidon, onbad, onbidan
attend-to	beweotede, beweotode, bewitiað, bewitian, bewitiaþ, bewitigað, bewitigaþ		
at-the-same-time	samod		
attract	weman, wemde, wemed	awaiting	bidað
audacious	ðrist, ðriste, þrist, þriste	awake	awacan, aweahte, aweccan, awehte, awoc, awocon, onwacan, onwæcnan, onwæcneð, onwæcneþ, onwoc, onwocan, onwoce, onwocon, tudre, weaht, weccað, weccan, weccaþ, weccean, wecceð, wecceþ, wehte
augment	ecan, geican, geiceað, geicean, geiceaþ, geicte, ic, icte, icton, iecan, iecte, ycað, ycan, ycaþ		
augmented	eacen, eacne, eacnum, eci, ecne		
author	ordfruma, ordfruman		
author (Latin)	auctor		
author-of	ordfruman	awaken	onwacnigeað, waciaþ
avail	dege, mæg, mæge, magan, magon, meaht, meahtan, meahte, meahton, mehte, miht, mihta, mihte, mihten, mihton	awaking	weccað
		away	anyman, awage, aweg, forð, forþ, fram, frofre, from, gegnum, of
		away-from	of
avenge	awræce, awrecan, ealgian, ealgode, gealgean, gewræc, gewrec, gewrecen, gewrecene, wræc, wræce, wræcon, wrec, wrecan, wrece, wrecen	away-go	a-gan
		awe	egesa, egesan, egesum, egsa, egsan
		awe-inspiring	andrysne, andrysnum, egesful, egesfull, ondrysne
		awhile	hwile, stund
		a-woman	Ides

Word List (English to Ænglisc)

English	Ænglisc
Æ, æ	
Ælfric (name)	Ælfrices
Ælfric's (name)	Ælfrices
Æthelmaer (name)	Æþlmær
Æthelwold (name)	Aðeluuold, Aðelwold, Aþeluuold, Aþelwold
B, b	
back	bæc, eft, forane, hricg, hrincg, hringe, hrycg, ongean
bad	gemah, man, manum, yfel, yfele
badly	earme, yfel, yfele
bad-news	færspel
bad-news-telling	weaspell, weaspelle
bag	fætels, fætelse
bake	a, abacæ, abacan
baker	bæcere
band	bend, bendum, ðreat, gebind, hos, hose, teag, teage, þreat, weorod, weoroda, weorode, weorude, wered, wereda, werede, weredes, weredum, werod, weroda, werode, werodes, werodum, werud, weruda, werudes, worude
bandage	wriðon, wriþan, wriþon
band-of-men	beornþreat
band-of-picked-men	hildecyst, hildecystum
bane	bana
banish	acwæð, acwæþ, acweðan, acweþan, acwið, acwiþ, acwyð, acwyþ, forwræc, forwrecan
banished-man	wræcmæcgas, wræcmecg
bank	faroð, faroðe, faroþ, faroþe
banner	cumbles, cumblum, cumbol, eaforheafodsegn, fana, segen, segn, segnas, segne, þu, þuf, þufas
banner-conflict	cumbolgehnastes
banner-king	segncyning
banner-warrior	cumbolwiga, cumbolwigan
baptism	fulwiht
baptism?-one-occurrence	fullwen, fullwona
baptismal-font	fant, fante
baptize	fulwian, gefullod, gefullode
bar	grindel, grindlas
bare	bær, bare, barnum, baro, baru
bargain	ceap, ceapas, ceape, foreweard, gewrixle
barley-crop	berewæstm, berewæstma
barm	beorma, beorman
barren	searað, searaþ, searian, weste, westne
barricade	forworht, forworhte, forwyrcan
barrier	clustor, clustro
barrow	beorg, beorgas, beorge, beorges, beorgum, beorh, biorgas, biorges, biorh, hlæw, hlæwe, hlaw, hlawe
base	arleas, stapol, stapole, stapulum
bath	bæð, bæþ, baþu
bathe	baþian
bathhouses	burnsele
bath-road	bæðweg, bæþweg

Word List (English to Ænglisc)

English	Ænglisc	English	Ænglisc
battle	aelicce, æscplega, æscplegan, æscþræcu, æscþraelicce, beadowe, beadu, beaduwe, beadwa, beadwe, camp, campe, comp, compe, compwig, compwige, feoht, feohte, gecamp, gecampe, gefeoht, gefeohtan, gefeohte, gesacu, geslyht, geslyhta, getoht, getohte, gewinn, guð, guðgemot, guþ, guþgemot, hild, hilde, hondgemot, hondgemota, hondslyht, isernscur, isernscure, lindcroda, lindcrodan, ondslyht, oret, orette, orlege, orleges, sacu, sæcc, sæcce, sæce, searonið, searoniða, searoniðas, saroniþ, searoniþa, searoniþas, secce, sperenið, spereniþ	battle-brave	æscrof, æscrofe, garcene, heaðorof, heaþorof, heaþorofe
		battle-bright	heaðotorht, heaþotorht
		battle-churl	guðceare, guþceare
		battle-clothing	beaduscrud, beaduscruda
		battle-coat	beaduserce, beadusercean
		battle-crash	hildehlæmm, hildehlæmmum, hildehlemm, hildehlemma, wælhlem
		battle-cry	wigleoð, wigleoþ
		battle-deadly	wælhlem
		battle-deadly-crash	wælhlem
		battle-din	wigcyrm
		battle-equipment	hildesceorp
		battle-famous	heaðomære, heaþomære
		battlefield	campstede, folcstede, folcstyde, hreawic, wæl, wæle, wælstow, wælstowe, walu
		battle-flame	heaðofyr, heaðofyrum, heaðufyr, heaðufyres, heaþofyr, heaþofyrum, heaþufyr, heaþufyres
battle-account	guðspell, guþspell		
battle-bill	guðbill, guðbilla, guþbill, guþbilla, hildebil, hildebill, hildebille	battle-flyer	guðfloga, guðflogan, guþfloga, guþflogan
battle-blood	heaþoswat, heaþoswata, heaþoswate	battle-garment	beadohrægl
		battle-gear	guðgeatawum, guðgetawa, guðgetawe, guþgeatawum, guþgetawa, guþgetawe
battle-blow	heaðusweng, heaðuswenge, heaþusweng, heaþuswenge		
battle-board	hildebord, hildebordum	battle-Geat	guð-Geata, guþ-Geata
battle-bold	hilde-deor	battle-gleam	beadoleoma
		battle-glory	æsctir

Word List (English to Ænglisc)

English	Ænglisc	English	Ænglisc
battle-greedy	heorogifre, hildegrædig, hildegrædige	battle-road	wigrod
		battle-row	bordhreoða, bordhreoþa
battle-grim	heaðogrim, heaþogrim, heorogrim, heorugrimm, heorugrimme	battle-rush	heaþoræs
		battles	hilda
		battle-seat	hildesetl
		battle-sharp	beaduscearp, heaðoscearp, heaðoscearpe, heaþoscearp, heaþoscearpe
battle-grip	hildegrap		
battle-hall	guðsele, guþsele		
battle-hard	scurheard, wigheard, wigheardne		
		battle-shield	guðbyrne, guþbyrne, hilderand, hilderandas, wigbord
battle-hedge	wihaga, wihagan		
battle-helmet	guðhelm, guþhelm, walu	battle-slaughter	wælslihta
battle-icicle	hildegicel, hildegicelum	battle-snake	hildenædran, hildenædre
battle-leader	hildfruma, hildfruman	battle-song	hildeleoð, hildeleoþ
		battle-storm	sculon, scur, scuras, scurum
battle-leavings	herelafum		
battle-light	beadoleoma	battle-strength	guðcræft, guþcræft, hildestrengo
battle-mail-coat	guðbyrne, guþbyrne, heaðobyrne, heaþobyrne, hioroserce, hiorosercean		
		battle-swallow	heoroswealwe
		battle-sweat	hildeswat
		battle-sword	beadomecas, beadomece, guðsweord, guþsweord
battle-mail-shirt	herebyrne		
battle-mask	beadogrima, beadogriman		
		battle-tall	heaðosteapne, heaþosteap, heaþosteapa, heaþosteapne
battle-misery	guðceare, guðcearu, guþceare, guþcearu		
battle-onslaught	beaduræs, heaðoræs, heaðoræsa, heaþoræs, heaþoræsa	battle-throng	geþrang
		battle-time	orleghwil, orleghwila, orleghwile
battle-place	wigsteal	battle-tooth	hildetux, hildetuxum
battle-play	beadulac, beadulace	battle-troop	hildecyst, hildecystum
battle--play	heaðolac, heaðolace, heaðolaces, heaþolac, heaþolace, heaþolaces	battle-violence	hildþracu, hildþræce
		battle-weapon	hildewæpen, hildewæpnum
		battle-while	orleghwil, orleghwila, orleghwile
battle-proclaimer	beadohata		
battle-remaining	guðlaf, guþlaf		
battle-resolved	nið-hedig, niþ-hedig		

Word List (English to Ænglisc)

English	Ænglisc	English	Ænglisc
battle-wolf	heorawulfas, heorowulf, herewulf, hildewulf, hildewulfas	be-afflicted	se, seað, seaþ, seoðan, seoþan
		beak	neb
		beaker	bunan, bune, ful, full, fulle
battle-wood	heaþolinde		
battle-work	beaduweorc, beaduweorces, heaðoweorc, heaþoweorc	be-allowed-to	motan
		beam	beam, beama, beaman, beamas, beame, beames
be	be, beo, beoð, beon, beoþ, bið, bioð, bist, biþ, byð, byþ, eart, gestod, gestodon, gewearð, gewearþ, geworden, is, ne, nis, se, si, sie, standað, standan, standaþ, stande, standeð, standeþ, stod, stodan, stodon, stondað, stondan, stondaþ, stonde, stondeð, stondeþ, stynt, sy, þæt, wærð, wærþ, wearð, wearþ, weorð, weorðað, weorðaþ, weorðe, weorðeð, weorðen, weorþ, weorþaþ, weorþe, weorþeð, weorþen, weorþeþ, wes, wesað, wesan	be-amazed	wundrian, wundrigende, wundrodon
		beam-of-light	beam, beama, beaman, beamas, beame, beames
		beams	hrungeat
		bear	ac, acende, acennan, acenned, bær, bæran, bære, bæron, Beo-wulf, Bera, berað, beran, beraþ, bere, bereð, beren, bereþ, beron, bireð, bireþ, boren, byreð, byreþ, cende, cennað, cennan, cennaþ, cenned, fed, fedað, fedan, fedaþ, feddan, fedde, feded, fedeþ, gebær, geboren, wæg, wægon, wagon, wegan, wege, wegeð, wegeþ, wegon, wigeð, wigeþ
be-able	magan, moton		
be-able-to	can, cann, canst, con, const, cuðe, cuðon, cunnan, cunne, cunnon, cuþe, cuþon, mæg, magan, magon, meahte	bearing	gebæran
		be-ashamed	scamian, scamiende, scamigan, sceomian, sceomiende
beach	sæwong, sæwongas, sand, sande, sonde, stæð, stæðe, stæþ, stæþe, staþe, staþu, yðlaf, yðlafe, yþlaf, yþlafe	beast	deor, deores
		beasts	deora
		beast's	wildres
beacon	beacen, becn		
Beadohild (name)	Beadohilde		

298

Word List (English to Ænglisc)

English	Ænglisc	English	Ænglisc
beat	beatað, beatan, beataþ, beateð, beaten, beateþ, beot, beotan, beoton, cnysed, cnysede, cnyssan, gebeaten, geslægene, geslegene, gesloh, oferflat, oferflitan, slægen, slea, sleah, slean, slog, sloge, slogon, sloh	be-bold	bealdian, bealdode, hyrtan, hyrte
		be-born	awacan, awoc, awocon, onwacan, onwoc, onwocan, onwoce, onwocon, waca, wacan, woc, wocan, woce, wocon, wocun
		be-brave	bealdian, bealdode
		be-burned	gebarn
		became	becoman, geweard, weard, wurdon
be-attached	cleofiað, cleofian, cleofiaþ	because	because, etc, for, for þon, forðam, forðan, forðon, forþam, forþan, forþon, since, þæs, þæsas, þy
beat-up	forslean, forslegen		
beautiful	ænlic, ænlicu, cyrten, cyrtenu, fæger, freolecu, freolic, freolice, freolico, freolicu, freolucu, friþ, friþe, wlitegan, wlitegost, wlitegra, wlitesciene, wlitig, wlitige, wlitigre, wlytegan, wynlic, wynlicran, wynlicu, wynsum, wynsuman, wynsumast, wynsume, wynsumne		
		because-of	be, bi, big, for
		become	beon, geweard, gewearþ, geworden, gewurþe, is, wærð, wærþ, weard, wearþ, weorð, weorðað, weorðae, weorðan, weorðaþ, weorðe, weorðeð, weorðen, weorþ, weorþae, weorþan, weorþaþ, weorþe, weorþeð, weorþen, weorþeþ, worden, wurðað, wurðan, wurðaþ, wurde, wurðe, wurðeþ, wurdon, wurþan, wurþaþ, wurþe, wurþeþ, wyrð, wyrðe, wyrþ, wyrþe
beautiful-as-a-fairy	ælfscyne		
beautifully	cymlice, cymlicor, fæger, fægere, fægre, fægrost		
beautiful-sight	wliteseon		
beauty	ansien, ansyn, ansyne, glæm, glæmes, gleam, onsyn, wlite		
		become-beautiful	fægriað, fægrian, fægriaþ, gewlitegad, wlitigað, wlitigaþ, wlitigian, wlitigigan
be-awake	wæccan, wæccende, wæccendne		
be-aware-of	nat, nyste, nyston, wast, wat, wisse, wisson, wistan, wiste, wiston, witan, wite, wyste	become-bright	beorhte, beorhtian, beorhtode, gewlitegad, wlitigað, wlitigaþ, wlitigian, wlitigigan

Word List (English to Ænglisc)

English	Ænglisc	English	Ænglisc
become-calm	drusade, drusian, swaðrian, swaþredon, swaþrian	bed	bed, bedd, bedde, beddes, beddrest, beddreste, beddum, bedrest, bedreste, nihtrest, nihtreste, ræst, ræste, rest, reste, sealma, sealman
become-cold	col, colian, colode		
become-confined	genearwad, genearwod, nearwað, nearwaþ, nearwian, nearwode	be-delighted	faegnian, fægnode, gefægnod
become-dark	ðrysman, ðrysmaþ, þrysman, þrysmaþ	be-deprived-of	beleas, belegde, beleosan, beloren, belorene
become-day	dagian, dagige		
become-dried-out	searað, searaþ, searian	be-destroyed	forwearð, forwearþ, forweorðan, forweorðe, forweorþan, forweorþe
become-gloomy	geswearc, gesweorce, sweorcan, sweorceð, sweorceþ		
become-happy	blissian, blissigende, geblissad	bed-in-the-hall	fletræst, fletræste
		be-dispersed	tofaran, toforan
become-narrow	genearwad, genearwod, nearwað, nearwaþ, nearwian, nearwode	bedroom	bur, bure, burum
		been	gewurde
		beer	beor, beore
		beer-cup	lithwæge
become-or-be-weak	wacian	beer-drinker	gebeor, gebeoras, gebeorum
become-pale	blacað, blacaþ, blacian	beer-drinking	beorþege, beorþegu
become-pregnant	eacnian, eacniendra	beer-drinking-buddy	gebeor, gebeoras, gebeorum
become-proud	astag, astah, asteah, astigan, astigeð, astigeþ	beer-hall	beorsele, biorsele
		beer-man	beorscealc, beorscealca
becomes	weorþeð		
become-sick	gesicclod, siclian	beer-party	gebeorscipe
become-silent	swigedon, swigian, swigode	bees	beon
		bee-wolf	Beo-wulf
becomes-loathed	alaðað, alaðaþ, alaþaþ	be-exiled	gewræc, gewrec, gewrecen, gewrecene, wræc, wræce, wræcon, wrec, wrecan, wrece, wrecen
become-smaller	lytlað, lytlaþ, lytligan		
become-smoky	ðrysman, ðrysmaþ, þrysman, þrysmaþ		
become-worn	woriað, worian, woriaþ, worie	be-faithful	treowian, treowige
be-competent	magan		

Word List (English to Ænglisc)

English	Ænglisc	English	Ænglisc
befall	alimpan, becom, becoman, becomon, becuman, becwom, befælled, befyllan, befylled, begeat, begeate, begeaton, beget, begietan, begytan, belamp, belimpan, bigeat, lamp, limpan, lumpen, lumpon	begin	angan, awacan, awoc, awocon, began, begann, beginnan, ongan, ongann, ongean, ongin, onginnað, onginnan, onginnaþ, onginneð, onginnen, onginneþ, ongon, ongonn, ongunnan, ongunne, ongunnen, ongunnon, ongyn, ongynneð, ongynneþ, onstealde, onstealdest, onstellan, onwacan, onwoc, onwocan, onwoce, onwocon, toweccan, towehton
be-fearful	tweode, tweon		
be-fierce	grimman, grimmeð, grimmeþ		
before	ær, ærðon, æror, ærþan, ærþon, ærur, ætforan, beforan, biforan, for, foran, fore, furðum, furþum, gio, toforan, togeanes, togenes		
		beginning	angin, anginn, fruma, fruman, frymð, frymða, frymðe, frymþ, frymþa, frymþe, or, ord, ore
before-dawn	uhtan		
before-me	forane		
before-spatial	for		
be-frightened	forhtedon, forhtiað, forhtian, forhtiaþ		
		begins	ongean
began	began	be-good	deah, dohte, dohtest, dugan, duge
beget	afedan, afeded, astrienan, astrynde, aweahte, aweccan, awehte, cennan, cenned, cennede, gestrynan, gestrynde, strynan, strynde, stryndon, tymað, tyman, tymaþ, tymdon	begot	acende
		be-greedy	gitsian, gitsiende, gystað, gystaþ, gyt, gytsað, gytsaþ, gytsian
		be-happy	faegnian, fægnode, gefægnod
		behave	bæran, drohtende, drohtian, gebæran, gebærdon
beggar	ælmesmann, ælmesmannum, niedwædla	behaves	drohtende
		behaviour	gebære, gebæro
		behead	beheafdian, beheafdod
		beheld	befeng
		behest	hæs
		behind	æftan, beæftan, behindan, hindan

Word List (English to Ænglisc)

English	Ænglisc	English	Ænglisc
behold	behealdan, beheold, beheoldon	belong	gehyrað, gehyraþ, gehyrde, gehyrdon, gehyre, gehyrest, gehyrst, hieran, hierde, hiered, hyra, hyrað, hyran, hyraþ, hyrde, hyrdon, hyre
be-humiliated	geþenod, þenian, þenode		
being	beoð, beon, bið, biþ, saula, saule, saulum, sawele, sawl, sawla, sawle, sawlum, sawol, sawul, þa, wiht, with, wuhta	belonging	gelang, gelenge, gelong, leng, lenge
		belong-to	gehyrað, gehyraþ, gehyrde, gehyrdon, gehyre
being-a-boy	cnihtwesende		
being-a-child	umborwesende, umborwesendum	beloved	deoran, deore, deorestan, deorre, diore, dyre, dyrne, dyrnne, dyrum, geswæse, leof, leofa, leofan, leofe, leofes, leofestan, leofne, leofost, leofra, leofran, leofre, leofum, swæs, swase
beings	wihta		
being-the-case	ða, þa		
be-interested-in	recan, rohte, rohton		
bejewelled	beaghroden, beahhroden, beahhrodene		
belief	geleafan, leaf, leafa, wen, wena, wenan, wenum		
believe	geliefan, geliefde, geliefed, gelyfað, gelyfan, gelyfde, gelyfe, gelyfeð, gelyfenne, gelyfeþ, getreowe, getrywð, getrywþ, lyfan, treowan, treowde, wen, wenað, wenan, wenaþ, wende, wendon, wene, weneð, weneþ	beloved-land	eardlufan, eardlufe
		beloveds	leofe
		beloved-woman	healsmægeð, healsmægeþ
		below	neoðan, neoðone, neoþan, neoþone, niþre
		be-melted	gemyltan
		be-mindful-of	geman, gemon, gemunað, gemunan, gemunaþ, gemunde, gemundon, gemunon, gemyne, munan
believe-in	geliefan, gelyfan, gelyfde, gelyfe, gelyfeð, gelyfeþ	be-miserable	geomra, geomrian, geomrode
believing	geleafful, geleaffulne	bemoan	cwanian
be-lifted-up	þunian	be-musical	swinsian, swinsigende, swynsode
be-like	efenlæcan, geeuenlæhton		
be-liking-to	gelicode, licað, licaþ, lician, licode, licodon	be-named	gehate, gehaten, gehet, geheton, hat, hatað, hatan, hataþ, hate, haten, hatene, hatte, heht, het, hete, heton
belligerent	orlæggifre		

Word List (English to Ænglisc)

English	Ænglisc	English	Ænglisc
bench	benc, bence, bencum	bequeath	læf, læfan, læfde, læfed
bench-floor	bencþelu	be-quick	spedan, spedaþ
bench-sitters	bencsittende, bencsittendum	be-quiet	restað, restan, restaþ, reste, reston
bench-sound	bencsweg	bereave	bedreas, bedreosan, bedroren, bedruron, befeallan, befeallen, befeallene, bereafian
bend	abeag, abugan		
bend-down	hnag, hnah, hnigan, hnigon, hyldan, hylde		
beneath	neoðan, neoðone, neoþan, neoþone	bereft	bereafod, berofen, bidæled, feasceaft, feasceafte, feasceaftum
beneficial	nyt, nytt, nytte		
benefit	arstaf, arstafum, freme, fremena, fremu, fremum, god, goda, godan, gode, godes, godne, godra, godum, hroðor, hroðra, hroðre, hroþor, hroþra, hroþre, læn, nytt, nytte	bereft-of	leas
		be-ruined	hreas, hreosan, hreosende, hruron
		be-sad	geomra, geomrian, geomrode
		beseech	bæd, bædon, beden, biddan, halsige, healsian, healsode
benefit-from	bræc, breac, bruc, brucað, brucan, brucaþ, bruce, bruceð, bruceþ	beset	drefan, drefde, gedrefed
		beside	be, bi, big, onemn, wið, wiþ
be-noisy	hlydan, hlydde	besides	eac, elles
bent	beag, geap, geapne	besiege	ymbhycgannae, ymbsæt, ymbsæton, ymbseten, ymbsittan
bent-down	hnag, hnagran, hnah, hnahran		
bent-on-glory	lofe, lofgeorn, lofgeornost	be-silent	swigedon, swigian, swigode
be-obliged	scal, sceal, sceall, scealt, scel, sceolde, sceolden, sceoldest, sceoldon, sceole, sceolon, scile, scolde, scoldon, sculan, sculon, scyle	be-sinking	bisenceð
		be-situated	gelæg, læg, lægon, legen, licgan
		be-sorrowful	ceara, cearað, cearaþ, cearian, mearn, murnan, murne, murnende, murnon
be-of-use	dugan	be-speedy	gespedeð, gespedeþ
be-overcome-with-longing	oflangian, oflongad	best	oferflat, oferflitan
be-pleased	gecwemað	bestow	ann, Getiþa, getyþa, uðe, unnan, unnon, uþe
be-prominent	þunian		
be-punished-for	angeald, ongeald, ongyldan		

Word List (English to Ænglisc)

English	Ænglisc	English	Ænglisc
bestow-upon	*forgeaf, forgeafe, forgefe, forgiefan, forgiefene, forgif, forgifð, forgifen, forgifþ*	bewail	*cwiðan, cwiðdon, cwiðe, cwiðed, cwiþan, cwiþdon, cwiþe, cwiþed, wanigean*
be-stretched-out-upon	*geþeahtne, þeah, þeaht, þeahte, þeahton, þeccan, þecce, þeccean, þecest, þehton*	be-wakeful	*waca, wacan, woc, wocan, woce, wocon, wocun*
		beware	*warað, waraþ, wariað, warian, wariaþ, warigeað, warigeaþ, warode*
be-strong	*mæg, mæge, mægen, magan, magon, meaht, meahtan, meahte, meahton, mehte, miht, mihte, mihten, mihton*	be-watchful	*wæccan, wæccende, wæccendne*
		be-wealthy	*gespedeð, gespedeþ, spedan, spedaþ*
be-successful	*gespedeð, gespedeþ, spedan, spedaþ*	be-willing	*willan*
		beyond	*begeondan*
Bethlehem (place)	*Bethleem, Bethlem*	bid	*abead, abeodan, aboden, abudon, bæd, bædon, bead, bebead, beden, beodan, biddan, biddu, boden, budon, het*
betoken	*getacnod, tacnian*		
be-too-proud-for	*oferhogode, oferhycgan*		
betray	*ameldian, ameldod, beswac, beswicað, beswican, beswicaþ, beswicen, beswicene, forlacan, forlacen, forlec, geleah, geswac, geswicað, geswicaþ, leag, leogan, leoge, swac, swican, swice, swician, swicode, swicon*		
		bidding	*hæs, hæse*
		bide	*bad, bidan, biden, bidon*
		big-fire	*heahfyr*
		bigger	*mara, maran, mare*
		bill	*neb*
		billow	*wæg*
betrays	*beswicaþ*		
be-troubled	*seað, seaþ, seoðan, seoþan*		
better	*bet, beteran, bot, gefetrade, sel, sella*		
between	*betuh, betux, betweonan, betweox, tweonum*		
betwixt	*betuh*		
be-useful-to	*ond, onðah, onðeon, onþah, onþeon*		
be-useless	*gewac, wican*		
beverage	*drinc*		

Word List (English to *Ænglisc*)

English	*Ænglisc*	English	*Ænglisc*
bind	bind, bindað, bindan, bindaþ, binde, bindeð, bindeþ, bond, bunden, bundenne, bundon, geband, gebindað, gebindaþ, gebunden, gebundene, gehæfte, gehæfted, gesæled, hæft, hæftan, hæfton, sælan, sælde, sældon, sæled, wriðon, wriþan, wriþon	black	blac, blaca, blace, blacum, blæc, brun, swærtum, sweart, sweartan, swearte, sweartne, sweartost, sweartum
		blackberry-bush	brember, brembrum
		blackened	salwed
		black-labour	swærtbyrd, swærtbyrde
		blackness	sweartnys, sweartnysse
		blade	blæd, ecg, ecga, ecge, ecgum, seax
		blame	ætwitan, ætwiton, lean, log, logon, lyhð, lyhþ, oðwitan, oþwitan, witan, wite, wroht, wrohte, wrohtes
binding	gebind		
binding-chains	hæfteclommum		
binding-ice	isgebind, isgebinde		
bind-with-fetters	asælan		
bird	fugel, fugele, fuglas, fugle, fugles, fuglum, fugol	blameless	orleahtre, untæle
		blaming	tæleð
		bleed	swætan
birds	fugelas	blend	mengan
birth	gebyrd, gebyrdo, gebyrdum, gebyrede	blending	bland
		blend-with	geblanden
bishop	bisceop, bisceope	bless	benedicite, bletsian, gebletsad, gebletsade, gebletsod, gebletsode, gehalgod, gehalgode, gehalgodum, halgian, segnad, segnade, segnian
bite	bat, bit, bitan, bite		
biter-to-death	muðbona, muðbonan, muþbona, muþbonan		
bitter	afor, biter, biteran, bitere, biteres, biþeaht, bitre, bitres, bitresta, bitter, geocor, grim, grimma, grimman, grimme, grimne, grimre	blessed	eadega, eadga, eadge, eadhreðig, eadhreðige, eadhreþig, eadhreþige, eadig, eadigan, gesælige, gesæliglic, sælig
bitter-experience	bealusiþ		
bitterly	bitre		
bitter-meeting	torngemot		
bitterness	biter, bitre, bitres	blessedly	gesælige, sæliglice
		blessedness	eadignes, eadignesse
		blessed-with-victories	sigeeadig
		blessed-with-victory	sigoreadig

Word List (English to Ænglisc)

English	Ænglisc	English	Ænglisc
blessing	blætsiað, bletsung, bletsunga, bletsunge, gebletsod	bloody-and-fierce	blodreow
		bloody-toothed	blodigtoð, blodigtoþ
		bloody-track	feorhlast, feorhlastas
blind	blind, blindum	bloom	blowan
blinded	blende, blindne	blossom	blostm, blostmum
blindness	wælmist, wælmiste	blossom-brightly	beorhtblowan, beorhtblowende
bliss	blis, bliss, blisse, blission, blysse, hyht	blossoming	blæd, blostmum
blithe	bliðu	blossoms	blædum
blond-hair	blandenfeax	blot	wommes
blond-haired	hwitlocced, hwitloccedu	blow	blawan, drepe, slege
blood	blod, blode, dreor, dreore, heolfor, heolfre, heorodreore, heorudreor, heorudreore, hildeswat, swat, swate, swates	blowing	blæst
		bluff	næss
		boar	bar, eofor
		board	bord, borda, bordes, bordum
		boar-decorated-spear	eoferholt
bloodied	blode	board-stronghold	þellfæsten, þellfæstenne, þencan
bloodier	dreorlicre		
blood-relation	sibgebyrd, sibgebyrdum	boar-image	eoforlic
		boar's-head-banner	eaforheafodsegn
bloodshed	blodgyte	boar's-head-sign	eaforheafodsegn
blood-stained	blode, blodfag, dreorfah, fag, fage, fagne, fagum, fah, fahne, fane, swatfag, swatfah	boar's-head-symbol	eaforheafodsegn
		boar-spear	eoferspreot, eoferspreotum
		boast	beot, beotedan, beotian, beotode, gealp, gebeotedon, Gelpan, gielpan, gulpon, gylp, gylpan, gylpe, gylpeð, gylpeþ
blood--stained	swatswaðu, swatswaþu		
bloodthirsty	wælreow, wælreowe		
bloody	blodfag, blodge, blodig, blodigan, blodige, blodigian, blodigne, dreorig, dreorigne, driorig, driorigne, geblodegod, heolfrig, heorodreorig, heorodreorigne, swatig, swatigne, wælhreow, wælreow, wælreowe, welhreowan	boast-about	begylpan
		boastful	hremge, hremig
		boastful-speech	gylpspræce, gylpword, gylpworda, gylpwordum
		boasting	gielp, gielpes, gielpsceaþan, gilp, gylp, gylpe
		boasting-speech	gilpcwide, gylpspræc, gylpspræce

Word List (English to *Ænglisc*)

English	*Ænglisc*	English	*Ænglisc*
boasting-sport	*gylpplega, gylpplegan*	bold	*arod, bald, beadurof, beald, bealde, caf, cafne, cene, deorlic, deorlice, ðrist, ðriste, ellenþrist, ellenþriste, fram, frec, frece, from, frome, fromne, fromum, hwæt, hwætran, hwætt, hwata, hwate, hwatum, modig, rof, snel, snella, snelle, snellic, snelra, swiðferhð, swiðferhðum, swiðferhþe, swiðferhþes, swiþferhþ, swiþferhþe, swiþferhþes, swiþferhþum, swyðferhð, swyþferhþ, þrist, þriste*
boasting-word	*beotword, beotwordum*		
boat	*æsc, bat, bates, naca*		
boat-guardian	*batweard, batwearde*		
bodies	*walo*		
bodily	*lices*		
bodily-might	*handmægen*		
bodily-wound	*licsar, licwund, licwunde*		
body	*bancofa, bancofan, banfæt, banfatu, banhus, banloca, bodig, fæðm, fæðme, fæðmum, fæþm, fæþme, fæþmum, feorgbold, feorhhus, feorh-hus, ferðloca, ferðlocan, ferhðloca, ferhðlocan, ferhþloca, ferhþlocan, ferþloca, ferþlocan, flæsc, flæsce, flæschoma, flæsc-homa, flæschoman, lic, lica, lice, lices, lichama, lichaman, lichoma, lic-homa, lichoman, sawlhord*		
		bold-hearted	*swiðmod, swiþmod*
		bold-in-battle	*beadurof*
		bold-in-spirit	*ferhðfreca, ferhðfrecan, ferhþfreca, ferhþfrecan*
		boldly	*baldlice, bald-lice, baldlicost, caflice, fromlice, stiðlice, stiþlice, þriste*
body-of-retainers	*duguð, duguþ*		
Boethius (name)	*boethia*		
		bold--minded	*þristhydig*
boil	*seað, seaþ, seoðan, seoþan, weallað, weallan, weallaþ, weallende, weallendu, weallinde, weol, weoll, wyll, wyllan*	bolt	*grindel, grindlas*
		bond	*bend, bendum, clammum, clom, clomm, clommas, clomme, clommum, lioðobend, lioðobendum, lioþobend, lioþobendum, sal, sale*
		bone	*ban, bane, banum*
		bone-chamber	*bancofa, bancofan*

Word List (English to *Ænglisc*)

English	*Ænglisc*	English	*Ænglisc*
bone-enclosure	banloca	both	æghwæðer, æghwæðre, æghwæðres, æghwæðrum, æghwæt, æghwæþer, æghwæþre, æghwæþres, æghwæþrum, ægþer, ba, bam, bega, begea, begen, begra, bu, butu, ge, gehwæðer, gehwæðere, gehwæðrum, gehwæs, gehwæþer, gehwæþere, gehwæþres, gehwæþrum, owðer, owþer, tu
bone-helm	banhelm		
bone-house	banhus		
boneless	banleas, banlease		
bone-ring	banhring, banhringas		
book	bec, boc, gewrit, gewritu, gewrytum		
books	bec		
boon	tið, tiðe, tiþ, tiþe		
booty	herehuþ, herehuþe, hereteam, hereteame, herteames, wælreaf		
border	brerd, gemearces, lærig, mearc, mearce, or, ora, oran		
border-guardian	mearcweard, mearcweardas		
borders	scadeþ		
bore	bær, borian, borige, cende	both...and	æg-hwæðer, æg-hwæþer, ge
born	acenned, boren, byreð, byreþ, geboren, geborenum	bottom	botm, botme, grund, wyrþeþ, wyrtruma, wyrtruman
		bottom-dwelling	grundwyrgenne
boroughs	burga	bottom-dwelling-criminal	grundwyrgen, grundwyrgenne
bosom	bearm, bearme, bearmum, bosm, bosme, breostum	bottomless	grundleas, grundlease, grundleasne
		bottom-ruler	grundhyrde
		bottom-surface	grundwong
		bough	bog, bogum
		bought	gebohtest, geceapod
		bound	bende, gebond, gebunden, gebundenne
		boundary	mearc
		boundary-watcher	endesæta
		boundless	ormæte
		bound-prow	bundenstefna
		bound-stave	bundenstefna

Word List (English to Ænglisc)

English	Ænglisc	English	Ænglisc
bow	abeag, abugan, beah, boga, bogan, bugan, bugeð, bugeþ, bugon, gebeag, gebeah, gebogen, gebogenan, hnag, hnah, hnigan, hnigon, onlut, onlutan	brave	anhydig, bald, beald, bealde, cene, cenoste, cenra, cenre, cenum, collenferð, collenferhð, collenferhðe, collenferhþ, collenferhþe, collenferþ, collenferþe, deor, deore, deorlic, deorlice, deormod, deorum, dior, dyrstig, from, fus, fuse, fusne, hror, hroran, hwæt, hwætran, hwata, hwate, hwatum, modig, modiglic, modiglicran, stið, stiðhicgende, stiðmod, stiðmoda, stiþ, stiþhicgende, stiþmod, stiþmoda, swiðferhð, swiðferhðum, swiðferhþe, swiðferhþes, swiðhicgende, swiþferhþ, swiþferhþe, swiþferhþes, swiþferhþum, swiþhicgende, swyðferhð, swyþferhþ, unearg, unearge
bowed	gebegde		
bowl	bolla, bollan		
bowstring	streng, strengum		
boy	cniht, cnihtas, cnihtum, cnyhtum		
bracelet	earmbeag, earmbeaga, earmread, earmreade		
brag	gealp		
braided-hair	wundenlocc		
braided-sword	brodenmæl, brogdenmæl		
bramble	brember, brembrum, brer, brerum		
branch	blado, blæd, blæda, blædæ, blædu, leomu, leomum, lim, limum, tan, tanum, telga, telgan, telgum, twig, twige		
brandish	acweccan, acweht, acwehte, asceacan, asceoc, hafenade, hafenian, hafenode, scacan, scacen, scæcen, sceacan, sceaceð, sceacen, sceaceþ, sceoc, scoc	brave-in-action	handrof, handrofra
brass	ær		

Word List (English to Ænglisc)

English	Ænglisc	English	Ænglisc
brave-in-battle	æscrof, beaducafa, beadurof, beadurofes, beoducaf, guðrof, guþrof, heaðodeor, heaþodeor, heaþodeorum, hildedeor, hildedior, hildediore, niðheard, niþheard, þræcrof, þræcrofe	break-faith	fræt, frætewum, fræton, fretan
		breaking	gebræc, gebrægd, gebrocen
		break-through	þurh, þurhbræc, þurhbrecan
		break-up	totwæman, totwæmed, totweman
		breast	bosm, bosme, breost, breosta, breostcofa, breostcofan, breostum, fæðm, fæðme, fæðmum, fæþm, fæþme, fæþmum, ferð-loca, ferðcofa, ferðcofan, ferþcofa, ferþcofan, ferþ-loca
brave-in-deeds	dæda, dædcene		
brave-in-killing	cwyldrof		
bravely	baldlice, baldlicost, cene, ellenlice, modelice, unforcuðlice, unforcuþlice, unforhte, unwaclice		
brave-minded	deormod, higerof, higerofe, higerofne, hygerof		
		breast-adornment	breostweorðung, breostweorðunge, breostweorþung, breostweorþunge
brave--minded	hygerof, hygerofe		
bravery	cenðu, cenþu, eorlscipe, eorlscype, higeþrymm, higeþrymmum, mægenellen		
		breast-care	breostceare, breostcearu
		breast-chamber	breostcofan
brave-speech	þryðword, þryþword	breast-hoard	breosthord
bread	hlaf	breast-net	breostnet
break	abrecan, abrocen, abrocene, bærst, beroþor, berstan, bræc, bræce, bræcon, breat, brecað, brecan, brecaþ, breotan, brocen, burston, forbærst, forberstan, forborsten, forbræcon, forbrecan, forbrocen, gebræc, gebræcon, gebrægd, gebrecan, gebrocen, gewac, sprengan, sprengde, wican	breast-surge	breostwylm
		breath	æðm, æðme, æþm, æþme, blæd, oreð, oreðe, oreðes, oreþ, oreþe, oreþes, oruð, oruþ
		breathing-dragon	legdraca, ligdraca
		breeding	cennan
		breeze	blæst, lyft
		brethren	gebroþer, gebroþor, gebroþru
		briar	brember, brembrum
		briars	brerum
		bricks	tigelum
		bride	bryd, bryda, bryde
		bridge	bricg, bricge
		bridge-guard	bricgweard, bricgweardas
break-apart	tobrecan, tobrocen		

Word List (English to *Ænglisc*)

English	*Ænglisc*	English	*Ænglisc*
bridge-keeper	bricgweard, bricgweardas	brilliant	scene, scennum, scenost, scenran, sceone, sceonost, sciene, scienost, scyne, scynost, wlitebeorht, wlitebeorhte, wlitebeorhtne, wlitebeorhtum, wlitesciene
brier	brer, brerum		
bright	beorht, beorhta, beorhtan, beorhte, beorhtne, beorhtost, beorhtra, beorhtre, beorhtum, blac, brun, brune, brunne, byrhtan, glad, gladiað, gladiaþ, gladu, gladum, glæd, glæde, glædlic, glædne, hador, hwilum, hwit, hwita, hwitan, hwite, hwitne, hwitost, hwitre, leoht, leohtan, leohtne, leohtra, leohtum, scene, scennum, scenost, scenran, sceone, sceonost, sciene, scienost, scir, scira, sciran, scire, scirne, scirum, scyne, scynost, swegl, swegle, torht, torhtan, torhte, torhtlic, torhtlicne	bring	ætbær, ætbæron, ætberan, bringað, bringan, bringaþ, bringe, bringeð, bringeþ, broht, brohtan, brohte, brohton, brungen, færde, færdon, færen, feccende, feran, ferde, ferdon, fere, ferede, feredon, ferende, fergað, fergaþ, ferian, ferigeað, ferigeaþ, ferode, fetigan, fetigean, fetod, fremman, fyredon, gebringan, gebringe, gebroht, gebrohte, gebrohten, gebrohton, gefæccan, gefætte, gefecgan, geferde, geferdon, gefere, gefered, geferede, geferedon, geferian, gefetian, gefetige, gelædað, gelædaþ, gelædde, gelæde, gelæded, geteah
bright-creator	leohtes, leohtfruma, leohtfruman		
bright-edged	brunecg		
brighter	beorhtra, brigda		
brightly	beorhte, glædlice, hador, hadre, leohte		
brightly-decorated	brunfag, brunfagne, scirmæled		
brightly-shining	wlite, wlitebeorht, wlitebeorhte, wlitebeorhtne, wlitebeorhtum		
brightness	bearhtm, bearhtme, glæm, glæmes, hador, hadre, scima, sciman, wlite		

Word List (English to Ænglisc)

English	Ænglisc	English	Ænglisc
bring-forth	acennan, afedan, afeded, cennan, cenned, cennede, eacnian, eacniendra, temað, teman, temaþ, tiedrað, tiedran, tiedraþ, tymað, tyman, tymaþ, tymdon	brother	beroþor, breþer, broðer, broðor, broðru, broðrum, broþer, broþor, broþra, broþru, broþrum, gebroðor, gebroðra, gebroðru, gebroðrum, gebroþor, gebroþra, gebroþru, gebroþrum
bring-in	onlædan, onlædde		
bringing-forth-offspring	tuddorteonde, tuddorteondra	brother-gold	broðorgyld, broþorgyld
brings	bringeð	brother-payment	broðorgyld, broþorgyld
bring-to	ætbær, ætbæron, ætberan	brother's	broþra
bring-to-a-halt	setlað, setlan, setlaþ	brought	brohte, gebroht
bring-to-mind	gemynde, gemyndgad, myndgað, myndgaþ, myndgian, myndgiend	brought-forth	akende
		brown	brun, brune, brunne
		Brunanburh (place)	Brunanburh
		buck-bean	glappan, glappe
		bucket	anbre
bring-to-pass	gedon	buckle	spang, spangum
bring-up	geteah, geteoh, getogen, teah, teon, togen	build	betimbran, betimbred, betimbrede, betimbredon, betimbrian, bytlian, ræran, rærde, rærdon, timbran, timbred, timbrede, timbrien
briny-deep	Brim		
Britain	Brytene		
Britain (place)	bretene, Brytene		
broach	sigisiþa, sigla, sigle		
broad	brad, brada, bradan, brade, bradnæ, bradre, gerume, rum, rume, rumne, rumre, rumum, sid, sidan, side, sidne, sidra, sidre, widgil, widgillan, widlond	build-around	beworhton, bewyrcan
		builders	wyrhtan
		building	aerist, ærn, ærnes, bold, bolda, botl, botle, ederas, edor, edoras, eoderas, eodor, eodur, getimbro, hof, hofe, hofu, hofum, hus, husa, huse, huses, ræcede, reced, receda, recede, recedes, timber, træf, træfe
broadly	brade		
broad-shield	sidrand		
broadsword	bradswurd, bradswyrd		
broken	abrocen, burston, gebræcon, gebrocen		
bronze	ær, ærnum		
brooch	sigle		
brook	broc, broce	building-guardian	renweard, renweardas

312

Word List (English to Ænglisc)

English	Ænglisc	English	Ænglisc
building-material	timber	burst	bærst, berstan, bræc, bræce, bræcon, brecað, brecan, brecaþ, brocen, burston, gebræc, gebrægd, gebrocen, onbræd, onbrægd, onbregdan, tohlidan, tohlidene
building-owner	boldagend, boldagendra		
build-separate-piles	tohladan, tohlodon		
burden	gehladene, gehlædene, gehleod, geloden, hladan, hlade, hladen, hlæst, hlæste, hlodon		
burgh-floor	buruhðelu	burst-apart	onspringan, onsprungon, to, tobærst, toberstan
burglar	stælgiest		
burial-hymn	sorhleoð, sorhleoþ		
burial-mound	byrgenne	burst-forth	sprang, springan, sprungen, sprungon
burial-site	birgenne		
buried	byrigde	bury	bedealf, bedelfan, byrgan, gebyrge
burn	bærnan, beorn, beswælan, beswæled, born, burnon, byrnan, byrnende, gebarn, swelan	business	nede, nenig, neod, neode, nyd
		busy	bisgo, bisgum, bisigu, bysig, bysige, bysigu, bysigum
burned	beorn, born, burnon, byrnan, byrnende	but	ac, butan, buton, hwæðere, hwæþere
burning	brand, bryne, byrnað, byrnende	butter	butan, buteran, butere
burning-flame	brynewylm, brynewylmum	but-which	esa, os
burning-gleam	bryneleoma	buy	bi, bicgan, bycgan, ceapian, gebicge, gebohte, geceapian, geceapod, gecypan
burning-wood	brond, bronda, brondas, bronde		
burnt-offering	brynegield, brynegielde	by	æt, be, bi, big, onemn, þinga, þurh, þy
burn-up	forbærnan, forbærnedne, forbarn, forbeornan, forbernde, forburnon, forbyrnan, gemealt, gemyltan, mealt, meltan, multon	by (Latin)	per
		by-any-means	wiht, wihte, wuhte
		by-days	dæiges
		by-fastened	bifæsteð
		by-force	nede, niede, nyde
		by-means-of	be, bi, big, ðurh, mid, þurh, þuruh, under, undor
		bystander	ymbstandend, ymbstandendra
		by-this	þy

C, c

Word List (English to Ænglisc)

English	Ænglisc	English	Ænglisc
cable	oncyrrap, oncyrrapum	care	bisgo, bisgum, bisigu, bysigu, bysigum, carfulnys, carfulnysse, cear, ceare, cearo, cearu, cearum, feorm, feorme, gehðo, gehþo, gio, giohðe, giohðo, giohþe, giohþo, heord
calamitous-cold	færcyle		
calamity	bealu-sið, bealu-siþ, fær, fære, færes, fere, oht		
call	acigan, acigde, aclænsian cleanse, ceallian, cigan, cigde, cigean, cigeð, cigeþ, cirman, cleopað, cleopaþ, cleopian, clipian, clypian, clypode, cygan, cygde, gecyged, gehatan, gehataþ, gehate, gehaten, gehet, geheton, genemned, hat, hatað, hatan, hataþ, hate, haten, hatene, hatte, heht, het, hete, heton, nemde, nemdon, nemed, nemnað, nemnan, nemnaþ, ofclipian, ofclypode	care-about	besceawian, bisceawað, bisceawaþ, gieman, gym, gyman, gymden, gymdon, gymeð, gymeþ, heben, hedan, hedde, recan, reccan, recce, recceð, recceþ, rohte, rohton, sinnan, sunnon
		careful	hydig
		carefully	wislice
		carefulness	carfulnys, carfulnysse
		care-house	cearseld, cearselda
called	haten	careless	carleas, carleasan, wanhydig
came	com, comon, cwoman	carelessly	unwærlice
camp	gewiciað, gewiciaþ, wician, wicod, wicode	carelessness	wonhyd, wonhydum, wonhygdum
		care-place	cear-seld
can	can, cann, canst, con, const, cuðe, cuðon, cunnan, cunne, cunnon, cuþe, cuþon, magan	cares-for	recce
		caretaker	feormend, feormendra, feormynd
		cargo	fearm, fearme
cancel-out	awægan	carnage	guðscear, guðsceare, guþscear, guþsceare, wæl, wælscel, wælsleaht
candle	candel, condel		
capacious	sidfæþm, sidfæþme, sidfæþmed		
capacity	gemet, gemete		
capital-city	eðelstol, eþelstol	carnage-wolf	wælwulf, wælwulfas
capital-crime	cwealmbealu	carried-out	fremmað
captive	hæft, hæfton	carrion	hra, hræs, hræw, hreaw
captivity	hæft, hæftnyd		
		carrion-bird	nefuglas, nefugol

Word List (English to Ænglisc)

English	Ænglisc	English	Ænglisc
carry	ætbær, ætbæron, ætberan, bær, bæran, bæron, berað, beran, beraþ, bere, bereð, beren, bereþ, beron, bireð, bireþ, boren, byreð, byreþ, ferede, feredon, fergað, fergaþ, ferian, ferigeað, ferigeaþ, ferion, ferode, fyredon, gebær, geboren, geferdon, gefere, gefered, geferede, geferedon, geferian, oboren, onberan, wæg, wægon, wagon, wegan, wege, wegeð, wegeþ, wegon, wigeð, wigeþ	carry-out	æfnan, æfnde, berenedon, berenian, efnan, efnde, efne, eode, eodon, eowde, forðian, forþian, fremeð, fremede, fremedon, fremest, fremeþ, fremmað, fremman, fremmaþ, fremme, fremmen, ga, gað, gæð, gæþ, gæworht, gan, gaþ, geæfndon, geæfned, geeode, geeodon, geforþod, gefremed, gefremede, gefremeden, gefremedon, gefremman, gefremmanne, gegæð, gegæþ, gegan, gegaþ, geiode, gelæst, gelæstan, gelæste, gelæston, geworht, geworhte, geworhtne, geworhton, gewyrc, gewyrcan, gewyrce, gewyrcean, læst, læstan, læste
carry-along	oþbær, oþberan		
carry-away	ætbær, ætbæron, ætberan, ætwæg, ætwegan, feccende, fetigan, fetigean, fetod, gefæccan, gefætte, gefecgan, gefetian, gefetige, oðferede, oðferian, oþbær, oþberan, oþferede, oþferian		
carry-off	ætferede, ætferian, areafian, areafod, offerede, offerian, strudan, strude, strudende, strudon	carry-up-to	ætbær, ætbæron, ætberan
		carve	agrafan, agrof, ceorfan, curfon, writan, writen
carry-off-from	ætferede	carved	agrof
		cask	orc, orcas
		cast	beweorpan, beworpen, biworpen
		cast-down	afylled, aweorpan, aworpene, oferwearp, oferweorpan, towurpe

Word List (English to Ænglisc)

English	Ænglisc	English	Ænglisc
castle	burg, burga, burgum, burh, burhfæsten, burhstede, byrig, ceaster, ceastra, ceastre, ceastrum, sæl, salo, sel, stol, stole, wic, wica, wicum, wicun	cause-to-sink	sencan
		causeway	bricg, bricge
		cave	cofa, cofan, eorðscræf, eorðscrafa, eorðscrafu, eorþscræf, eorþscrafa, eorþscrafu
castle-dweller	ceasterbuend, ceasterbuendum	cease	alæg, alicgan, alicgean, aswamað, aswamaþ, aswamian, sweðrian, sweðrode, sweþrian, sweþrode
castle-halls	burgsalum		
cast-out	aweorpan, aworpene, flyman, flymde, forweorpan, forwurpe, geflymed	cease-from	linnan
castrated-man	belisnod, belisnode	cement	lim, lime
catch	fon	cemetery	licrest, licreste
catholic (Latin)	catholicam	ceremonial-cup	seleful
cattle	ceap, ceapa, ceapas, ceape, feogan, feoh	certain	cuð, cuðe, cuðes, cuðra, cuþ, cuþe, cuþes, cuþra, gewis, gewiss, gewissan, wislic, wislicne
cattle-gift	feohgift, feoh-gift, feohgiftum, feohgyft, feohgyfte, feohgyftum	certainly	aninga, anunga, gearolice, gegnunga, gewislice, gewislicost
cause	dædon, deð, deþ, do, doð, don, doþ, dyde, dydest, dydon, fruma, fruman, gedæde, gedeð, gedeþ, gedo, gedoð, gedon, gedoþ, gedyde, gedydon, intinga	chain	hringe, racentægum, racentan, racente, racentum, sima?, simon
		chainmail	hringiren, hringloca, hringlocan
cause-anger-in	belgan, gebulge	chains	teagum
cause-longing	geliste, gelyste, lystan, lyste, lysteþ	challenging	heaðotorht, heaþotorht
cause-to-be-burned	bærnan		
cause-to-drink	drencan, drencte	chamber	cofa, cofan, in, inn, inne
cause-to-fall	fylde, fyllan, gefyldan, gefyllan, gesæged, gesælde, sægan	chamberlain	burþen, burþene
		champion	cempa, cempan
cause-to-go	sendan		
cause-to-move-forward	sceaf, sceof, scofen, scufan, scufeð, scufeþ, scufon, scufun		

Word List (English to Ænglisc)

English	Ænglisc	English	Ænglisc
change	awend, awendan, awende, cirdon, cyrran, cyrreð, cyrreþ, edwendan, edwenden, forsceop, forscieppan, gecyrred, gehwyrfed, gewendan, gewende, hwyrfað, hwyrfan, hwyrfaþ, hwyrfde, oncirde, oncyrreð, oncyrreþ, onhweorfan, onhworfen, onwendan, onwended, onwendeð, onwendeþ, onwendon, wend, wendan, wende, wendeð, wenden, wendeþ, wendon, wyrp, wyrpe	cherish	freoð, freogan, freoge, freoþ, freoþian, freoþode, friðian, friþian, gefriðode, gefriþod, gefriþode, geweorðad, geweorðan, geweorðod, geweorðode, geworþad, geweorþade, geweorþan, geweorþod, geweorþode, gewurðien, gewurðod, gewurþad, gewurþien, gewurþod, lufiað, lufian, lufiaþ, lufien, lufode, weorðade, weorðiað, weorðian, weorðode, weorþad, weorþade, weorþian, weorþiaþ, weorþode, wurðiað, wurðian, wurðmynt, wurðode, wurþian, wurþiaþ, wurþmynt, wurþode
changed	onhworfen		
channel	ædre		
chant	asingan, asinge, asungen, gæleð, gæleþ, galan, galdor, galdre, gealdor		
chanting	galdor, galdre, gealdor	chessboard	bleobord, bleobordes
charity	ælmyssan, ælmysse	chest	breost, breosta, breostcofa, breostcofan, breostum, earc, earce
charm	oleccan, olecung, olecunge		
cheek-decorated	fætedhleor, fætedhleore	chicken	cicen
cheer	byldan, bylde, bylded, frefran, frefred, frefrede	chide	cide
cheered	arette		
cheese	cyse		

Word List (English to Ænglisc)

English	Ænglisc	English	Ænglisc
chief	aldorwisa, frumgar, frumgara, frumgaran, frumgaras, frumgare, frumgarum, heafde, heafdon, heafdum, heafod, heafodmæg, heafodmægum, heafodmaga, ordfruma, ordfruman	choose	ceosan, ciosan, cure, curon, geceas, geceos, geceosað, geceosaþ, geceosenne, gecoren, gecorenan, gecorene, gecorone, gecyre
chief-leader	heafodweard, heafodweardas	chooses	geceoseð
		chose	ceas
chief-master	heafodwisa	chosen	geceas, geceos, geceosenne, gecorone
chief-of	ordfruma	Christ (name)	Crist, Criste
chief-overseer	heahgeræfan, heahgerefa, heahgerefan	Christ (name) (Latin)	Christum
		Christian	cristene
		Christ's (name)	Cristes
chieftain	aldorþegn, folctoga, folctogan	church	circean, cirice, cyrcan, cyrican, mynster
child	bearn, bearna, bearne, bearnes, bearnum, byras, byre, cild, cilde, cildes, eðelstæf, eðulstæfe, eðylstæf, eþelstæf, eþulstæfe, eþylstæf, magotimber, magotimbre, pregnant	church (Latin)	ecclesiam
		cinder	axan, axe, sinder, sindrum
		circle	beag, beaga, beagas, beage, beages, beagum, beah, begas
		circle-about	ymbehwearf, ymbehweorfan
		circlet	beahwriða, beahwriðan, beahwriþa, beahwriþan
child-bearing	bearngebyrdo		
child-like	cildisc	circular-ornament	beag
children	barnum, bearn, bearnum	circumstance	ðing, ðinga, ðinges, þincg, þing, þinga, þinge, þinges
children's	bearna		
child's	cildes	circumstances	þing
chill	freorig	citadel	heahreced
chilly	freorig	cities	burgum, Ceastra, ceastrum
chin-protector	cinberg, cinberge	citizen	burgleoda, burhleod, burhleodum
choice	cista, cyst, cystum, gecorenan	citizens	burgum, burgwara, burhwara, burhwaras, burhwarena
		city	burg, burhstede, byrig

Word List (English to Ænglisc)

English	Ænglisc	English	Ænglisc
city-dweller	burgleoda, burhleod, burhleodum, ceasterbuend, ceasterbuendum	clear	beorht, beorhta, beorhtan, beorhte, beorhtne, beorhtost, beorhtra, beorhtre, beorhtum, beredon, berian, byrhtan, cuð, cuðe, cuðes, cuðra, cuþ, cuþe, cuþes, cuþra, gerymde, gerymdon, gerymed, gesene, gesiene, gesyne, hador, heaðotorht, heaþotorht, hlutor, hluttrum, ryman, rymde, sweotol, sweotolan, swutol, underne, undyrne
city-dwellers	burgsittendra, burgwara, burhsittende, burhsittendum, burhwara, burhwaras, burhwarena		
city-gate	burhgeat, burhgeate		
city-place	burgsteall, burgstede		
city-riches	burhwela, burhwelan		
city-walls	burgtunas		
claim	talað, talast, talaþ, talian, talige	clearly	cuðlice, eaðe, geare, gearolice, gearwe, gearwor, gearwost, gere, leohte, sweotole, sweotollice, sweotule, undyrne
clamour	grummon		
clan	mægð, mægða, mægðe, mægþ, mægþa, mægþe, mægþum		
clang	hringan, hringdon		
clank	hringan, hringdon	clear-up	scyran
clash	gegrind, geswing	cleave	cleofan, clufon, gescær, gescer, scæron, scieran, scireð, scireþ, scyran
clashes	hlynneð		
clashing	gebræc, gebrægd, gebrocen		
clash-together	hnitan, hniton		
clasp	befangen, befealdan, befealdest, befon, befongen, bifongen, clyppað, clyppan, clyppaþ, clyppe, clypte, gespong, spang, spangum	cleaved	cleofiað, clufan
		clever	ferhðgleaw, ferhðgleawe, ferhþgleaw, ferhþgleawe, fore-snotor, gleawhydig, higeðoncol, higeðoncolre, higeþoncol, higeþoncolre, searoðoncol, searoþoncelra, searoþoncol, snotera, snoteran, snotere, snotor, snotra, snottor, snottra, snottre
claw	clea, handspor, handsporu, nægl, nægla, næglum		
clean	clæne		
cleanse	aþwean, aþwoh, ðwoh, fælsian, fælsode, gefælsod, þwean, þwoh		
cleansed	clænre		

319

Word List (English to Ænglisc)

English	Ænglisc	English	Ænglisc
cleverness	snytra, snytro, snytru, snyttru, snyttrum	clothe	gewered, wereð, werede, weredon, wereþ, werian, werigean, ymbseald, ymbsellan
cliff	clif, clifu, clifum, gehliðo, gehliþo, hleoðo, hleoðu, hleoþa, hleoþo, hleoþu, hlið, hliðe, hliðes, hlioðo, hlioþo, hliþ, hliþe, hliþes, næs, weal, weall, weallas, wealle, wealles, weallum	clothing	gearwan, gearwe, gearwor, gearwum, gewæde, gewædu, hrægl, hrægla, hrægle, hrægles, reaf, reafum, wæd, wæda, wædo, wædum, wedum
climb	gestah, gestigest, stah, stigan, stige, stigon	cloud	racu, wolcen, wolcna, wolcne, wolcnu, wolcnum
clinging	clibbor	clouds	lyft, lyfte, Wolcnu, wolcnum
cloak	loða, loðum, loþa, loþum	coal	col
		coarse	ruh
cloak-of-invisibility	heoloþhelm, heoloþhelme	coast-guard	endesæta
		coffer	earc, earce
clockwise	sunganges	cohabitation	somwist
close	beleac, belocen, belucan, belucon	coil	gebeag, gebeah, gebogen
close-advisor	runwita	coiled-creature	hringboga, hringbogan
close-by	gehende		
close-companion	eaxlgestealla, eaxlgesteallan, handgestealla, handgesteallan, hondgesella, hondgesellum, hondgestealla, hondgesteallan	cold	cald, caldast, calde, caldum, ceald, cealde, cealdost, cealdum, col, colran, freorig
		coldest	cealdost
		collar	sal, sale
		colour	bleo, bleom, bleos, hiw, hiwe
close-kinsman	hyldemæg, hyldemaga	coloured	fah
closely	ðicce, þi, þicce	coloured-board	bleobord, bleobordes
closely-confined	nearofag, nearofages	combat	guð, guða, guðe, guðgemot, guðum, guþ, guþa, guþe, guþgemot, guþum, hild, hilde
close-of-time	gelenge		
closet	cofa, cofan		
close-up	forworht, forworhte, forwyrcan		
cloth	clað, claþ, claþe	combatant	aglæca
		combat-blood-drenched	heorodreorig, heorodreorigne

Word List (English to Ænglisc)

English	Ænglisc	English	Ænglisc
combat-weary	*guðwerig, guðwerigne, guþwerig, guþwerigne*	command	*abead, abeod, abeodan, abude, ambyht, ambyhto, bannan, bead, bebead, bebeod, bebeodan, bebeode, bebod, beboden, bebodu, bebudon, beodan, bisen, bisne, boden, budon, bysen, bysene, bysna, gebannan, gebod, gehate, gehaten, gehet, geheton, geweald, gewealde, gewealdum, hæs, hæse, hat, hatað, hatan, hataþ, hate, haten, hatene, hatte, heht, het, hete, heton, ombiht, stihtan, stihte, weald, wordcwida, wordcwydas, wordcwyde, wordcwydum*
combined	*gemenged*		
come	*acuman, acumen, becom, becoman, becomon, becuman, becwom, com, coman, come, comon, cumað, cuman, cumaþ, cume, cumen, cumene, cumenra, cwom, cwoman, cwome, cwomon, cymð, cyme, cymeð, cymen, cymest, cymeþ, cymþ*		
come-near	*genealæhton, genealecan, nealæcan, nealæhte*		
comes	*cymeð*		
Cometa (name)	*cometa*		
come-to-be	*alamp, alimpan, alumpen*		
come-to-exist	*wæcnan, wæcned*		
come-to-pass	*alimpan*	commanded	*bebead, Heht, het*
comfort	*frefran, frefred, frefrede, frofor, frofre, gehæled, gehælede, getrimede, getrymmed, hælan, hældon, trimian, trymeð, trymede, trymedon, trymeþ, trymian, trymman*	commander	*folctoga, folctogan*
		commandment	*bebod, bebodu, bodscipe*
		commands	*heht*
		commend	*betæcan, betæhte*
		commiseration	*earminge*
		commit	*bebead, bebeod, bebeodan, befæstan, befæste, berenedon, berenian, bifæstan, bifæste&th*
comfortable	*sefte*		
comfortably-happy	*sefteadig*		
coming	*cime, cumað, cumen, cyme*	commit-perjury-regarding	*forleogan, forlugan*
		committed	*gefremmed*
		common	*gemæne, gemænra, gemænum*
		common-people's-land	*folcscare, folcscaru, folcsceare*
		commotion	*gelac, gelacum*
		communion	*gemænscipe*

321

Word List (English to Ænglisc)

English	Ænglisc	English	Ænglisc
communion (Latin)	*communionem*	company	*cempan, ðreatum, driht, drihta, dugeða, dugeðe, dugeðum, dugeþa, dugeþe, dugeþum, dugoða, dugoðe, dugoþa, dugoþe, duguð, duguða, duguðe, duguðum, duguþ, duguþa, duguþe, duguþum, eored, gedriht, gedryht, gesið, gesiða, gesiðas, gesiððas, gesiððe, gesiðes, gesiðum, gesiþ, gesiþa, gesiþas, gesiþes, gesiþþas, gesiþþe, gesiþum, getrum, getrume, hos, hose, sceolu, þreat, þreatas, þreate, þreatum, þryð, þryðum, þryþ, þryþe, þryþum, weorod, weoroda, weorode, weorude, wered, wereda, werede*
companion	*folcgestælla, folcgestælna, folcgestealla, folcgesteallan, gædeling, gædelinges, gædelingum, gefæra, gefæran, gefara, gefera, geferan, geferum, gelica, gelican, gemæc, gemæcne, geneat, geneatas, gesið, gesiða, gesiðas, gesiððas, gesiððe, gesiðes, gesiðum, gesiþ, gesiþa, gesiþas, gesiþes, gesiþþas, gesiþþe, gesiþum, neat*		
companion-in-arms	*fyrde, fyrdgestealla, fyrdgesteallum*		
companion-in-necessity	*nydgestealla, nydgesteallan*	compel	*fordraf, fordrifan, niða*
companions	*gædelinges, gædelingum, geferan, gesiþþe*	compensate	*betan, bete, gebetan, gebette, gebettest*
		compensation	*bot, bote, broðorgyld, broþorgyld, gield, gielde, gihuaes, gild, gyld, lean, leana, leane, leanes, leanum, med, meda, mede, medo, medum*
		compensation-for-life	*feorhlean*
		complain-about	*cwanian*
		complaint	*gengword, gnornword, gnyrn, gyrne*

Word List (English to Ænglisc)

English	Ænglisc	English	Ænglisc
complete	ealgearo, ealles, eallgearo, fulgangan, fylde, fyllað, fyllan, fyllaþ, gefyldan, gefylde, gefyllan, gefylle, gefylled	concealing-darkness	heolstorsceado
		concealment	heolster, heolstor, heolstre, hoðma, hoðman, hoþma, hoþman
		conceit	oferhyda, oferhygd, oferhygda, oferhygde
completely	deope, diope, ealle, eallenga, eallinga, ful, genunga	conceive	cennan, cenned, cennede, eacnian, eacniendra
completely-filled	geondfolen		
completely-gilded	ealgylden, gyldan	conception	modgeþonc
comportment	gebæro	concerning	be, ymb
comport-oneself	gebæran, gebærdon	conclusion	geþinge, geþingea, geþinges, geþingo
compose	sang, singan, sungen, sungon	condemn	fordæmed, fordeman, forscrifan, forscrifen, forscyldeguda, forscyldigian, genyðerad, genyþerad, niðerian, niþerian
composed	gesette		
compulsion	nyd, nyde		
comrade	gefera, handgestealla, handgesteallan, hondgestealla, hondgesteallan, nydgestealla, nydgesteallan		
		condemnation	hearmcwyde, wroht, wrohte, wrohtes
co-national	leodmæg, leodmagum	conduct	gelædað, gelædaþ, gelædde, gelæde, gelæded, læd, lædað, lædan, lædaþ, lædde, læddest, læddon, læde, læded, wisan, wise, wisna, wisum, wysan
conceal	bediglan, bedyrnan, bedyrnded, bedyrndon, bedyrned, beþeahte, beþeahton, beþeccan, bewreon, biþ, biþeaht, biwrah, biwrigen, biwrigon, ðeaht, ðeahte, ðeccan, dyre, dyrnan, dyrnde, forhelan, forhele, hel, helan, mid, miðan, middungeard, miðendne, miþan, miþendne, þeaht, þeahte, þeccan, wrah, wreah, wreo, wreon, wrihst, wrugon, wry, wryon		
		confess	andette, gestæled, stælan
		confidant	gehola, geholena
		confine	fegan, fegeð, fegeþ, gefeg, gefeged, geheaðerian, geheaðerod, geheaþerian, geheaþerod, genearwad, genearwod, maere, nearwað, nearwaþ, nearwian, nearwode
concealed	gehyded, miþendne	confined	ænga, ænge, enge, gefeged

Word List (English to Ænglisc)

English	Ænglisc	English	Ænglisc
confined-hostility	nearofag, nearofages	consider	aðohte, ahicgan, ahycgan, aþencan, aþohte, besceawian, bewand, bewindað, bewindan, bewindaþ, bewunden, bisceawað, bisceawaþ, biwunden, eahtedon, eahtian, eahtodan, eahtode, ehtigað, ehtigaþ, geæhted, gehyge, geondþencan, geondþence, geondþenceð, geondþenceþ, gesceawað, gesceawaþ, gesceawod, getealdon, geteled, geþancie, geþancmeta, geþancmetian, geþenc, geþencean, hi, hicgan, hy, hycgað, hycgan, hycgaþ, hycge, hycgean, hycgendne, leorna, leornian, leornode, reccan, recce, recceð, recceþ, sceawa, sceawað, sceawaþ, sceawedon, sceawiað, sceawian, sceawiaþ, sceawigan
confinement	nearu, nearwe		
confining	heolstor, heolstran		
confining-door	hlinduru		
confining-strength	nearocræft, nearocræftum		
conflict	gehnæst, gehnæste, gewinn		
confused	gemenged		
confusion	bland		
congregate	gesomnad, gesomnod, samnian, somnigean		
conquer	alecgan, alecgean, alede, aledon, alegde, alegdon, gewinnan		
conquered	geeode		
consciousness	gewitte, wite, witt		
consecrate	gehalgod, gehalgode, gehalgodum, halgian, segnad, segnade, segnian		
consecrated	haleg, halegu, halga, halgan, halgena, halgum, halig, haligan, halige, haliges, haligre		
consent	ðafian, ðanc, est, estum, geðafode, gemedu, geþafode, þafian, þafodest, þanc		
		consideration	geæhtlan, geæhtle
		considering	hycgendne, wenað
		consider-to-be	gesceawod
		consider-worthy-of	onmunan, onmunde

Word List (English to *Ænglisc*)

English	*Ænglisc*	English	*Ænglisc*
consign	*geseald, gesealde, gesealdon, gesellan, gesylle, sealde, sealdest, sealdon, seleð, seleþ, selle, syleð, syleþ, syllað, syllan, syllaþ, sylle, syllon*	continual	*edneowe, singal, singale*
		continually	*simle, singala, singales, symble, symle, syngales*
		continue	*bad, beodan, bidan, bideð, bideþ, bidon, gebad, gebidan, gebidanne, gebide, gebiden, semian, seomade, seomedon, seomian, seomode, seomodon, siomian*
consolation	*frofer, frofor, frofra, frofre, higefrofer*		
console	*frefran*		
consort	*cwen*		
constant	*heardræd, heardrædne*		
constantly	*geneahhe*	continuously	*singalan*
constrain	*æsæled, asælan*	contract-for	*fæstnian, gefæstnod, gefæstnodon*
construct	*æfnan, æfnde, asmiðigen, asmiþigen, asmiþod, besmiþian, besmiþod, betimbran, betimbred, betimbrede, beworht, beworhte, bewyrcan, efnan, efnde, efne, geæfndon, geæfned, geworht, geworhte, geworhton, timbran, timbred, timbrede, weorcan*	contrivance	*orðonc, orðoncum, orþanc, orþancum, orþonc, orþoncum*
		contrive	*aðohte, aþencan, aþohte, wefan*
		control	*agan, gerad, geweald, gewealdan, gewealde, gewealdene, gewealdenne, gewealdum, geweold, geweoldum, nagon, nah, nahte, nahton, onweald, rad, ridan, ride, rideð, rideþ, riodan, weald, wealdan, wealde, weold, weoldon*
construction	*geweorc, geweorces*		
consume	*fræt, fræton, fretan*		
consumes	*þigeð*		
contemporary-trouble-or-sorrow	*mælceare, mælcearu*		
contemptible	*unarlic*	controlled	*gemæne, gemænra, gemænum, weold*
contemptuously	*bysmerlice*		
contend	*flitan, flite, flitende*	conversation	*gegncwida, gegncwide, spræc, spræca, spræce*
contention	*gewin, gewinne, gewinnes, teonwit, winn*		
		conversation-place	*hleoðorstede, hleoþorstede*
contest	*ðing, ðinga, ðinges, geflit, sacan, strið, striðe, strib, striþe, þincg, þing, þinga, þinge, þinges*	convert	*awend, awendan, awende, cirdon, cyrran, cyrreð, cyrreþ, gecyrred*

Word List (English to Ænglisc)

English	Ænglisc	English	Ænglisc
conveyance	fær, fære	count	getealdon, geteled, rim, rime, rimes, tealde, tealdon, telge, tellan
convince	wemað, weman, wemaþ		
convulsive-fever	dweores, dweorh		
cool	col, colian, colode, colran	counted	rime
		counted-out	forðgerimed, forþgerimed
copper	ar		
cord	streng, strengum, teag, teage	countenance	andwlita, andwlitan
		counterattack	hondslyht, ondslyht
corn	corn, corna	countless	unrime
corner	hyrnan, hyrne, wincel, wincle	countless-number	unrim
		country	eard, earda, eardas, earde, eardes, eðel, eðelmearc, eðelmearce, eðle, eðyl, eþel, eþelmearc, eþelmearce, eþle, eþyl, land, landa, lande, landes, liodgeard, lond, londe, londes, londstede, oðle, oþle, þeodlanda, þeodlond
corpse	drihtne, drihtneum, hra, hræs, hræw, hreaw, leap		
corpse-chooser	wælceasega		
corpse-fire	wælfyr, wælfyra, wælfyre		
corpse-pile	ecgwal, ecgwale		
corpse-place	hreawic		
corpse-pole	wælsteng, wælstenge		
corpses	hra, hræs, hræw, hreaw, wæl, wæle, walu		
correction	steor, steore	courage	ellen, elne, elnes, higeþrymm, higeþrymmum, hyge, mod, mode, modes, modþracu, modþræce, modum
correctly	rihte		
corroded	omig, omige		
corrupt	fordon		
corrupted	geblonden		
corruption	brosnung		
corselet	byrnan, byrne, byrnende, byrnhom, byrnhomas, byrnum	courageous	ellenrof, ellenrofe, ellenrofum
		courageously	eornoste
Costontinus (name)	Costontinus	courage-work	ellenweorc, ellenweorca
cottage	bur, bure, burum		
cough?-clear-one's-throat?	cohhetan	course	fare, faru, ryne
		court	hof
council	gemot, meðel, meþel, meþle	courtiers	bencsittende, bencsittendum, fletsittende, fletsittendum
councillor	spreca		
counsel	hwætred, ræd, ræda, rædas,ræde, rædes, run, rune, woðboran	covenant	fæstnung, foreweard, treowræden, treowrædenne, wær, ware
counsellor	rædbora, wita, woðbora, woðboran, woþbora, woþboran		
counsels	runum		

Word List (English to *Ænglisc*)

English	*Ænglisc*	English	*Ænglisc*
cover	bedraf, bedrifan, bedrifenne, begeotan, begoten, behelan, beholen, behreosan, belecgan, belegde, beseald, besellan, beþeahte, beþeahton, beþeccan, beþenede, beþenian, bewegan, bewegen, beworht, beworhte, bewreon, bewrigen, bewrigene, bewrigenum, bewyrcan, bihrorene, bilecgað, bilecgaþ, bilegde, biþeaht, biwrah, biwrigen, biwrigon, ðeaht, ðeahte, ðeccan, forðylman, forðylmed, forþylman, forþylmed, geþeahtne, gewered, helm, heolstor, hleonian, þeaht, þeahte, þeahton, þeccan, þecce, þeccean, þecest, þehton, wereð, werede, weredon, wereþ, werian, werigean	cover-over	geþeahtne, oferhelmað, oferhelmaþ, oferhelmian, þeaht, þeahte, þeahton, þeccan, þecce, þeccean, þecest, þehton
		cover-up	forhelan, forhele
		covet	gitsian, gitsiende, gystað, gystaþ, gyt, gytsað, gytsaþ, gytsian
		cow	cu, neat
		cowardice	yrhðo, yrhþo
		cowardly	earg, earges, eargra, earh, hildlata, hildlatan, tydre
		craft	list, lista, listas, listum
		craftily	cræftig
		craftily-witted	searocræftig
		craftsman	wyrhta
		crafty	cræftig, inwitfull, inwitfulle
		crafty-thought	inwitþanc, inwitþancum
		cramped	ænga, ænge, enge
		crash	cnossað, cnossaþ, cnossian, hlemmeð, hlemmeþ, hlimman, hlimmeð, hlimmeþ, hlummon, swægende, swegan
		crash-against	cnysedan, cnyssað, cnyssan, cnyssaþ
covered	belegde, biþeaht, biþeahte, gehroden, gehrodene, hroden, oferfæðmed, oferfæþmed	crashes	hlemmeð
		crash-together	bihlemman, bihlemmeð, bihlemmeþ
covered-in-brightness	sweglwered	crazy	wod, wodum
covering	hama, haman, hleo, hleow, sceata, þecen, þecene		

Word List (English to *Ænglisc*)

English	*Ænglisc*	English	*Ænglisc*
create	*gæworht, gemearca, gemearcod, gemearcode, gesætte, gesætton, gesceapen, gesceapene, gesceop, gescieppan, gescop, gescopon, gescype, geseted, gesett, gesette, gesetton, geteoð, geteoþ, geworht, geworhte, geworhtne, geworhton, gewyrc, gewyrcan, gewyrce, gewyrcean, mearcað, mearcaþ, mearcian, mearcode, ræran, rærde, rærdon, sceop, scepen, scieppan, scop, sete, settan, sette, setton, teodan, teode, teon, tiode, worhte, worhton, wyrce, wyrcean, wyrceð, wyrceþ*	creation	*ærsceaft, forðgesceaft, forþgesceaft, fruma, fruman, frumsceaft, gescaft, gesceaft, gesceafta, gesceafte, gesceap, gesceapo, gesceapu, gesceft, geweorc, geweorces, handgesceaft, handgeweorc, handweorc, hondgeweorc, hondgeweorce, sceaft*
		creations	*metodes*
		creative	*forþbære, forþbæro*
		creator	*fruma, fruman, gesceaft, leohtes, meotod, metod, ordfruma, ordfruman, sceppend, scieppend, scyppend*
		creator's	*meotodes*
		creature	*wiht, with, wuhta*
created	*gesceop, geworhtest, gewrohtest, sceop, scop, worhtest, wyrcean*	creatures	*gesceaftum*
		creep	*screoda, scriðan, scripað, scripan, scripaþ*

Word List (English to Ænglisc)

English	Ænglisc	English	Ænglisc
crime	facen, firen, firena, firendæd, firendæda, fyren, fyrena, fyrene, gylt, gyltum, leahtor, leahtrum, man, mandæd, mandædum, mane, manes, morðer, morðor, morðra, morðre, morðres, morþer, morþor, morþra, morþre, morþres, symle, syn, synn, synna, synne, synnum, unriht, unrihte, wroht, wrohte, wrohtes, wrohtscipe	cross	beam, beama, beaman, beamas, beame, beames, crux, mæl, mæla, mæles, mælo, mælum, oferfaran, oferforan, rod, rode, wudu
		cross (Latin)	crux
		cross-beam	eaxlgespann, eaxlgespanne
		cross-of-victory	sigebeam
		cross-sign	rodetacen, rodetacne
		crowd	geþrang, hwearf, hwearfum, þringan, þrong, þrungen, þrungon
		crowding	geþring
criminal	fag, fagum, fah, fane, fara, faum, fracod, fracodes, man, mansceaða, mansceaðan, mansceaþa, mansceaþan, manscyldig, manscyligne, manum, wearh, werg, wergan, wergas, wergum, werig	crown	beag
		cruel	blodreow, hreðe, hreþe, reðan, reðe, reðre, reþan, reþe, reþre, sliðe, sliðheard, sliðhearda, sliðne, sliðra, sliþe, sliþen, sliþheard, sliþhearda, sliþne, sliþra, wællgrim, wrað, wraða, wraðan, wraðe, wraðlic, wraðra, wraðum, wraþ, wraþa, wraþan, wraþe, wraþlic, wraþra, wraþum, wyle, wylfen, wylfenne
criminal-destroyer	manscaða, manscaþa		
criminally	fracodlice, fracoðlice, fracoþlice		
criminally-hostile	manfæhð, manfæhðu, manfæhþ, manfæhþu		
		cruelly	hreowlice, wraðe, wraðlice, wraðum, wraþe, wraþlice, wraþum
cringe	cringan, Criste, crong, crungen, crungon, gecranc, gecringan, gecrungen, gecrungon		
		cruelty	wraðe, wraþ, wraþe, wrathfully
		crumble	woriað, worian, woriaþ, worie
crooked	depravedly, geap, geapne, þweorh		
crop	yrþ		

Word List (English to Ænglisc)

English	Ænglisc	English	Ænglisc
crush	gebroced, gebrocede, gebrocian, þy, þyð, þyþ, þywað, þywan, þywaþ	current	eagor-stream, egstream, egstreamum, flod, floda, flodas, flode, flodes, stream, streamas, streame, streames, streamum, wælm, wælmes, wylm, wylmas, wylme, yða, yðe, yðum, yþ, yþa, yþe, yþum
cry	cirm, cyrm, gebære, greot, greotan, greotende, greoteþ, hreopon, hropan, reotað, reotan, reotaþ, reoteð, reoteþ, weop, wepan		
		current-flame	cearwælm, cearwælmum, cearwylm, cearwylmas
cry-out	cirman, cleopað, cleopaþ, cleopian, clypian, clypode, hreman	current-wall	streamweall
cub	hwelp	curse	awyrgan, awyrged, hearmcwyde, wergðo, wergþo, werhðo, werhþo, wyrgean
cuckoo	ge, geac		
cultivated	welþungen		
cultivated-field	æcer		
cunning	cræfte, inwitfull, inwitfulle, searo, searoðoncol, searoþonc, searoþoncelra, searoþoncol, searoþoncum, searwum	cursed-one	awyrgda
		curved	biwunden, geap, geapne
		custody	heord
		custom	ðeaw, ðeawum, sið, siða, siðe, siðes, siodo, siþ, siþa, siþe, siþes, siþon, þeaw, þeawas, þeawum
cunning-bond	searobend, searobende, searobendum		
cunningly	listum	cut	bite, geheawe, geheawen, gescær, gescer, heawan, heow, heowon, scæron, scepen, sceran, scieran, scireð, scireþ, scyran, slat, slit, slitan, slite, sliteð, sliteþ, snað, snædan, snaþ, snedeþ, sniðan, sniþan
cunningly-decorated	searofah		
cup	bunan, bune, dryncfæt, fæt, fatu, ful, full, fulle, wæge		
cure	gelacna, hæle, hælo, hælu		
curiosity	fyrwet, fyrwyt		
curious	wrætlic, wrætlicne, wrætlicran, wrætlicu		
		cut-apart	toslitan, tosliteð, tosliteþ

Word List (English to Ænglisc)

English	Ænglisc	English	Ænglisc
cut-down	aheawan, aheawen, forheawan, forheawen, forheow, forheowon, heawan, heawen, heow, heowon	dare	dear, dearr, dearst, dorste, dorston, durran, durre, durron, dyrre, geneðde, geneðdon, geneþan, geneþde, geneþdon, neðde, neðdon, neðende, neþan, neþde, neþdon, neþeð, neþende, neþeþ
cut-off	becearf, beceorfan, beheowan, beheowe, beslægene, beslean, besloh, forcearf, forceorfan, forcurfon, ofaslean	daring	deor, deore, deorlic, deorlice, deorum, dior, dollic, dollicra, ellenþrist, ellenþriste, frec, frece, wonhyd, wonhydum, wonhygdum
cut-off-from	beheowan, beheowe		
cut-out	ceorfan, curfon		
cut-to-pieces	forheawan, forheawen		
cut-up	forheawan, forheawen	dark	blac, blaca, blace, blacum, blæc, brun, brune, brunne, deorc, deorcan, deorce, deorcum, digol, dim, dimman, dimme, eorp, heolstor, heolstran, heolstre, myrcan, myrce, salo, swærtum, sweart, sweartan, swearte, sweartne, sweartost, sweartum, þeostre, þeostrum, þystre, wan, wann, wanna, wanre, won, wonn, wonna, wonnan, wonne
cyanotic-birth	swærtbyrd, swærtbyrde		
Cyneweard (name)	Cyneweard		

D, d

English	Ænglisc	English	Ænglisc
dais	yppan, yppe		
damage	hearm, hearma, hearmas, hearme, hearmes		
damp-track	uriglast		
Danes (name)	Dæne		
danger	broga, frecen, frecna, frecne, frecnes		
dangerous	frecen, frecenra, frecnan, frecne, frecnen		
dangerously	fræcne, frecne	dark-coated-ones	saluwigpadan
		darken	blatan, blatende, genap, geswearc, gesweorce, nap, nipan, nipeð, nipende, nipeþ, sweorcan, sweorceð, sweorceþ
		darkened	dænnede, salwed
		darkening	sweorceð
		dark-haired	wonfeax

Word List (English to *Ænglisc*)

English	*Ænglisc*	English	*Ænglisc*
darkness	genipu, gesweorc, heolster, heolstor, heolstre, hoðma, hoðman, hoþma, hoþman, nip, sceade, sceado, sceadu, sweartra, þeos, þeostra, þeostru, þeostrum, þystre, þystro, þystru, þystrum	days	dæg, daga, dagas, dagum
		days-of-old	ærdagum, geardæg, geardagum
		days-of-pestilence	woldagas
		days-of-yore	geardæg, GEARDAGUM
		day's-work	dægweorc, dægweorce, dægweorces
		day-time	dægtid
dart-to	gesceat	day-while	dæghwil, dæhwila
dash	cnossað, cnossaþ, cnossian	dead	aldorleas, aldorleasne, ðe, dead, deaðdege, deade, deadne, deadum, deaþdege, ealdorleas, ealdorleasne, fægan, fæge, fægean, fæges, fægne, fægum, forðgewiten, forðgewitenum, forþgewiten, forþgewitenum, guðwerig, guðwerigne, guþwerig, guþwerigne, sawelleas, sawelleasne, sawolleas, sawolleasne, sawulleas, sawulleasne, þe, unlifigende, unlyfigende, unlyfigendes, unlyfigendne, unlyfigendum
dash-against	cnysedan, cnyssað, cnyssan, cnyssaþ		
daughter	dæhter, dehter, dohter, dohtor, dohtra, dohtrum		
David (name)	Dauit		
dawn	ær, ærdæg, ærdæge, ærdagum, dægred, dagað, dagian, dagige, morgenleoht, uhta, uhtan, uhte, uhtna, uhttid		
dawn-enemy	uhtsceaða, uhtsceaþa		
dawn-flier	uhtfloga, uhtflogan		
dawn-sadness	uhtceare, uhtcearu		
day	dæg, dæge, dæges, dæiges, daga, dagas, dagum, doemid, dogera, dogor, dogora, dogore, dogores, dogra, dogrum, mædæg, mældæges, mældagum		
day (Latin)	die	dead-incapacitated-by-death	deaðwerig, deaðwerigne, deaþwerig, deaþwerigne
daybreak	ærdæg, ærdæge, ærdagum		
day-count	dogorgerim, dogorgerimes		
day-number	dægrim, dægrime, dægrimes		
day-of-toil	geswinc-dæg		

Word List (English to Ænglisc)

English	Ænglisc	English	Ænglisc
deadly	ætterne, ættren, ættrynne, dædhata, wælbleat, wælbleate, wælgrim, wællgrim	deal-in	dælað, dælan, dælaþ, dælde, dældon, dæle, dæleð, dæleþ, dælon, gedælan, gedælde, gedæled, gedaled
deadly-attack	wælhlem		
deadly-battle	wælsleaht, wælsleahta	dealing	dælan
deadly-blow	wælsweng, wælswenge	deal-with	ateah, ateon
		dear	deora, deoran, deore, deorestan, deorre, diore, dyre, dyrne, dyrnne, dyrum, geswæse, leof, leofa, leofan, leofe, leofes, leofestan, leoflic, leofne, leofost, leofra, leofran, leofre, leofum, swæs, swase
deadly-bond	wælclomm, wælclommum		
deadly-calamity	cwealmþrea		
deadly-current	wælstream, wælstreamas		
deadly-enemy	ealdorgewinna, ferhðgeniðla, ferhðgeniðlan, ferhþgeniþla, ferhþgeniþlan		
deadly-feud	wælfæhð, wælfæhða, wælfæhþ, wælfæhþa	dear-	wine-mæg
		dear-companion	wilgesið, wilgesiþ
		dearest	deorost
deadly-fire	wælfyr, wælfyra, wælfyre	dear-kinsman	winemæg, winemæga, winemægum, winemaga, winemagas, winemagum
deadly-hostility	wælnið, wælniðas, wælniðe, wælniþ, wælniþas, wælniþe		
deadly-smoke	wælrec		
deadly-spear	wælgar, wælgara, wælspera, wælspere, wæl-spere	dearly-loved	felaleofan
		dear-to	dyre, weorð, weorþ
deadly-stroke	feorhsweng		
deadly-terror	wælgryre		
deadly-words	muðbona, muðbonan, muþbona, muþbonan		
deadly-wound	feorhbenn, feorhbennum, feorhwund, feorhwunde		

Word List (English to Ænglisc)

English	Ænglisc	English	Ænglisc
death	aldorgedal, cwalm, cwealm, cwealme, cwealmes, ðe, deað, deaðcwalu, deaðcwalum, deaðe, deaðes, deaþ, deaþcwalu, deaþcwalum, deaþe, deaþes, deoð, deoþ, ealdorgedal, ellorsið, ellorsiþ, feorhcwale, feorhcwalu, feorhcwealm, feorhlege, feorhlegu, forðweg, forðwegas, forðwege, forþweg, forþwegas, forþwege, friðgedal, friþgedal, fyl, fyll, fylle, gastgedal, gescæphwil, gescæphwile, hinionge, hinnsið, hinnsiþ, hinsiðe, hinsiþ, hinsiþe, hryre, lichryre, lifgedal, meotodes, meotodsceaft, meotudgesceaft, metodsceaft, metodsceafte, morð, morðes, morþ, morþes, sencan, swylt	death-blood	cwealmdreor
		death-bond	wælbend, wælbende
		death-danger	aldorbealu
		death-day	deaðdæg, deaðdæge, deaðdege, deaþdæg, deaþdæge, deaþdege, deoðdaege, ðeos, deoþdaege, endedæg, endedogor, endedogores, swyltdæg, swyltdæge, þeos
		death-dealing-army	wælherigas, wælherige
		death-hall	deaðsele, deaþsele
		death-in-battle	garcwealm, guðdeað, guþdeaþ
		deathly-home	deaþe, deaþwic
		death-place	deaþwic
		death-ropes	wælrap, wælrapas
		death-shadow	deaðscua, deaþscua
		death-sleep	swefan
		death-tree	deaðbeam, deaðbeames, deaþbeam, deaþbeames
		death-watch	heafodweard, heafodwearde
		debase	byfigynde, bygan, forbigan, forbigde, forbiged
death (Latin)	mortuis		
death-beam	deaðbeam, deaðbeames, deaþbeam, deaþbeames	decapitate	beheafdian
		decay	brosnað, brosnaþ, brosnian, brosnung, hryre
deathbed	legerbedd, legerbedde	decayed	brosnade, forweorone
death-bed	deaðbedd, deaðbedde, deaþbedd, deaþbedde, morþorbed, niobedd	decays	brosnað
		deceit	facen, facna, facne, facnes, inwit
death-bird	nefuglas, nefugol		

Word List (English to Ænglisc)

English	Ænglisc	English	Ænglisc
deceitful	dyrnan, dyrne, dyrnra, dyrnum, facenful, facenfyllan, facenlice, fæcna, fæcne, flah, swice, swicol, swicole	decorate	frætwan, frætwed, frætwian, gefrætewod, gefrætwad, gefrætwade, gefrætwod, gefretewodon, gehyrsteð, gehyrsteþ, geregnad, geregnode, gerenod, hyrstan, hyrsted, hyrstedne, regnian, renian, renodest
deceitful-action	facenstæf, facenstafas		
deceitfully	leaslice		
deceitful-one	wærloga, wærlogan, wærlogona		
deceitful-ones	wærlogan		
deceive	bepæcan, bepæceð, bepæceþ, beswac, beswicað, beswican, beswicaþ, beswicen, beswicene, forlacan, forlacen, forlec, geleah, geswac, geswicað, geswicaþ, leag, leogan, leoge, swac, swican, swice, swician, swicode, swicon	decorated	fæd, fædan, fædde, geatolic, gehroden, gehrodene, hroden stanfah
		decorated-paved-with-stones	
		decorated-with-bone	banfag
		decorated-with-gold	goldfag, goldfah, goldfahne, goldhroden
deceived	beswican, beswicen	decorated-with-nails	nægled, næglede
decency	maecti, mæð, mæþ	decorated-with-treasure	beaghroden, beahhroden, beahhrodene, sincfag, sincfage wyrmfah
deception	ligewyrhtum		
deceptive	untreowa, untreowe		
decide	gesced, sceadan, sceadeð, sceadeþ	decorated-with-worms	
decided	aræd		
decision	dom	decoration	wræte, wrætt, wrætta, wrættum
decisively	fæstlice		
deck	wægbord	decree	gesceaft, ræd, ræda, rædas, ræde
declaration	wordgemearc, wordgemearcum	dedicate	ægnian, agnian, bebead, bebeod, bebeodan, geagnod, gehalgod, gehalgode, gehalgodum, halgian, onsægde, onsecgan
declare	areccean, asæde, asecgan, benemde, benemdon, benemnan, cen, cennan, gecenne, scyran, wissian		
declared	bodedan		
declare-to-be-guilty	forscyldeguda, forscyldigian	deed	dæd, dæda, dæde, dædum, dydest, weorc, weorca, weorce, weorces, weorcum, worc, worca, worcum

Word List (English to Ænglisc)

English	Ænglisc	English	Ænglisc
deed-doer	dædfruma, dædfruman	defile	besmitan, besmiten, gewemde, gewemmed, wemman
deed-hater	dædhata		
deed-in-battle	niþgeweorc, niþgeweorca	defiled	womfull
deeds	dæda, dædrof, dædum	degrade	bysmeredon, bysmerian, gebysmrian
deem	deman, demde, demed	degrading	bismorlic, bismorlicum
deemed	demed, doemed, doemid	dejected	unrot, unrote
deeming	doma	delay	yldan
deep	deop, deopan, dyrne, neowel, neowelne, neowle, steap, steape, steapes, steapne	delayed-labour	lætbyrd, lætbyrde
		delays	foreldit
		deliberate	þeahtian, þeahtode
		deliberate-on	geæhted
		deliberate-upon	eahtedon, eahtian, eahtodan, eahtode, ehtigað, ehtigaþ
deep-brown	sealobrun		
deeply	deope, diope		
deepness	deopnesse	delight	blissian, blissigende, dream, geblissad, neod, niod, niode, willa, willan, willum, wilna, wyllan, wyn, wynn, wynna, wynne, wynnum
deep-water	heahflod		
deer	heorot		
defame	forsæcgan		
defeat	oferdrifan		
defeated	sigeleas, sigelease, sigeleasne		
defence	helm, helmas, helme, helmes, helmum	delightful	leoflic, wynsum, wynsuman, wynsumast, wynsume, wynsumne
defend	beorgan, ealgian, ealgode, ealgodon, freoþian, freoþode, friðian, friþian, gealgean, gefriðode, gefriþod, gefriþode, gescyld, gescylt, gewered, scyld, scyldan, scylde, warað, waraþ, wariað, warian, wariaþ, warigeað, warigeaþ, warode, wered, wereð, werede, weredon, wereþ, werian, werigean	delightfully	wynnum
		delight-giver	wilgeofa
		delight-in-entertainment	gleodream
		delighting-in-spaciousness	rume, rumgal
		delight-in-the-air	lyftwynn, lyftwynne
		deliver	alynnan
		deliverance	generedes, hrædding, hræddinge
		deliver-up	onsend, onsendan, onsende, onsended, onsendeð, onsendeþ, onsendon
defender	wergend, wergendra	deluge	flod
		demeanour	gebæro

Word List (English to Ænglisc)

English	Ænglisc	English	Ænglisc
demon	*gæst, gæsta, gæste, gæstes, gast, gasta, gastae, gastas, gaste, gastes, helruna, helrunan, scucca, scuccum, þyrs*	departed	*forðgewiten, forðgewitenum, forþgewiten, forþgewitenum, geleorene, gewat, gewitan, gewitenes*
den	*denn, dennes, hlæwe*	departing	*fromweard, fromweardum, uðgenge, uþgenge*
denounce	*ameldian, ameldod*	departure	*fromlad, fromsiþ, gang, gange, ganges, hinnsið, hinnsiþ, hinsiðe, hinsiþ, hinsiþe*
deny	*oft, ofteah, ofteon, oftogen, oftugon, wyrnan, wyrnde, wyrnest*		
Deor (name)	*Deor*	depraved	*depravedly, þweorh*
depart	*afera, aferian, aferige, fealh, feall, ferede, feredon, fergað, fergaþ, ferian, ferigeað, ferigeaþ, ferode, forð-feran, forð-ferde, forð-fered, forþ-feran, forþ-ferde, forþ-fered, fyredon, geferdon, gefere, gefered, geferede, geferedon, geferian, geswac, geswicað, geswicaþ, gewat, gewit, gewitað, gewitan, gewitaþ, gewite, gewiteð, gewiten, gewitene, gewitenes, gewiteþ, gewiton, scacan, scacen, scæcen, sceacan, sceaceð, sceacen, sceaceþ, sceoc, scoc, swac, swican, swice, swicon, uðgenge, uþgenge, witan*	depressed	*hean*
		deprivation?	*astypan, astypednes, stiep, stiepe*
		deprive	*ageat, ageotan, agotene, bedælan, bedæled, bedreosan, bedroren, bedrorene, befeallan, befeallen, befeallene, begrindan, begrindeð, begrindeþ, begrunden, benam, beniman, benumen, bereafan, bereafian, bereofan, berofan, berofen, berofene, bið, bidælde, bidæled, bidroren, bidrorene, binom, biþ, forstelan, forstolene, oðþringan, oðþringeð, oðþrong, ofteah, ofteon, oftogen, oftugon, onsæce, onsecan, oþþe, oþþringan, oþþringeð, oþþringeþ, oþþrong*

337

Word List (English to Ænglisc)

English	Ænglisc	English	Ænglisc
deprive-by-striking	beslægene, beslean, besloh	desert	geearnung, geearnunga, geearnunge, westen, westenne
deprived	binom		
deprived-of	bireafod, geasne		
deprive-of	bedreas, bedreosan, bedroren, bedruron, beheowan, beheowe, beliðan, belidenne, belipan, benæman, beneotan, beneote, beneoteð, beneoteþ, bescierian, bescyrede, besnyðede, besnyðian, besnyþede, besnyþian, bineat, biscyred, getwæfan, getwæfde, getwæfed, getwæfeð, getwæfeþ	deserve	acsian, ahsian, ahsode, ahsodon
		deserving	earna, earnian, geearnaþ, geearnod
		deserving-of	weorþe, weorþra, wurðe, wurðran, wurþe, wurþran, wyrde, wyrðe, wyrðra, wyrþe, wyrþra
		design	gemearca, gemearcod, gemearcode, gesceapen, gesceapene, gesceop, gescype, mearcað, mearcaþ, mearcian, mearcode, sceop, scepen, scieppan, scop
deprive-of-by-falling-off	bihrorene		
depth	deop	designate	gemearca, gemearcod, gemearcode, mearcað, mearcaþ, mearcian, mearcode
Derby (place)	Deoraby		
derision	huaet, hucs, hucse, husc, husce		
descend	awæcniað, awæcnian, awæcniaþ, gesigan, sigan, sigeð, sigeþ, sigon		
descendant	afera, aforan, eafera, eaferan, eaferum, eafora, eaforan, eaforum, eafrum, folcbearn, folcbearnum, team, teames, teamum		
descendants	cneorim, cneowrim, from, fromcyme, fromcynn, fromcynne		
descendent	cneomæg, cneomagum		
descent	æðelu, æþelo, æþelu		

Word List (English to Ænglisc)

English	Ænglisc	English	Ænglisc
desire	friclan, gesec, gesecan, gesecanne, gesece, gesecean, geseceð, geseceþ, gesoht, gesohtan, gesohte, gesohtest, gesohton, gewylnung, gewylnunga, gyrn, gyrnan, gyrnde, lust, mine, myne, neidfaerae, nele, nellað, nellaþ, nelle, neod, neodlaðu, neodlaðum, neodlaþu, neodlaþum, niod, niode, noldan, nolde, noldon, sec, secan, sece, seceað, secean, seceaþ, seceð, secen, secest, seceþ, soht, sohtan, sohte, sohten, sohtest, sohton, wile, willa, willað, willan, willaþ, wille, willende, willum	destiny	forðgesceaft, forþgesceaft, geornor, geosceaft, gewef, gewiofu, sið, siða, siðe, siðes, siþ, siþa, siþe, siþes, siþon, wyrd, wyrda, wyrde
desired-day	dægwilla, dægwillan	destiny-creation	forðgesceaft
desired-expedition	wilsið, wilsiþ	destitute	feasceaft, feasceaftig, gesne, wædla, wædlum
desires	nelle	destroy	a, aæðan, aæþan, abreat, abrecan, abredwade, abreot, abreotan, abreoten, abrocen, abrocene, abroten, acwealde, acwellan, agetan, ahiþan, awægan, bræc, bræce, bræcon, brecað, brecan, brecaþ, brocen, ferlorene, forgrand, forgrindan, forgrunden, forleas, forleosan, forloren, forslean, forslegen, forworht, forworhte, forwyrcan, gebræc, gebræcon, gebrægd, gebrecan, gebrocen, gesæged, gesælde, gewemde, gewemmed, ofslægen, ofslean, ofslogon, ofsloh, ofþecgan, ofþegde, sægan, spilde, spillan, tobrecan, tobrocen, tolucan, wemman, wyrdan, wyrde
desolate	idel, idlu, weste, westne		
despairing	hihtleasne, hyhtlease, ortrywe		
despairing-of	orwena		
despicably	laðlice, laðlicost, laþlice, laþlicost		
despise	forseah, forseon, hynan, hynde, hyned, oferhogode, oferhycgan		
despite	ofer, ofor	destroyed	abreoðan, abreoðe, abreoþan, abreoþe, ageted, awyrdan, awyrded, forgrunden, todraf, uuyrde, wyrde
despoil	reafað, reafaþ, reafeden, reafian, reafige, reafode		

Word List (English to Ænglisc)

English	Ænglisc	English	Ænglisc
destroyer	scan, scaþan, sceaða, sceaðena, sceaðona, sceaðum, sceaþa, sceaþena, sceaþona, sceaþum	devour	ahiþan, forswealg, forswelgan, forswelge, forswulge, snædan, snedeþ
destruction	bealewa, bealu, bealuwa, bealwa, forlor, forlore, forwyrd, fyl, fyll, fylle, morð, morðes, morþ, morþes	dewy-feathered	urigfeðera, urig-feðera, urigfeþera, urig-feþera, urigfeþra
destructive-enemy	hearmscaþa	dewy-path	uriglast
detain	behabban, behæfdon	did	dyde, gedidon
determine	gesced, geþinged, geþingod, sceadan, sceadeð, sceadeþ, þingade, þingian, þingode	die	cringan, crong, crungen, crungon, feallan, feallende, fealleþ, feol, feoll, feollon, forð-feran, forð-ferde, forð-fered, forsiðian, forsiðod, forsiþian, forsiþod, forþ-feran, forþ-ferde, forþ-fered, gefealleð, gefealleþ, gefeol, gefeoll, gewat, gewit, gewitað, gewitan, gewitaþ, gewite, gewiteð, gewitene, gewitenes, gewiteþ, gewiton, scio, scion, swealt, sweltan, sweolt, witan
determined	anræd, aræd		
devil	deofla, deofle, deofles, deoflum, deofol, feond, feonda, feondas, feonde, feondes, feondum, fionda, forhatena, fynd, hellesceaða, hellesceaþa, hellsceaða, hellsceaþa, helsceaðan, helsceaþan, wærloga, wærlogan, wærlogona, werloga, werlogan		
		die?-conceal-oneself?	deagan, deog
		died	dead
		die-down	gelæg, læg, læge, lægon, lagon, leg, licgað, licgan, licgaþ, licgean, licgende, licgendre, lið, ligeð, ligeþ, ligst, liþ
devilish	deofolcund, deofolcunda		
devil's	deofles		
devious	inwidda		
devise	ahicgan, ahycgan, fand, findað, findan, findaþ, findeð, findest, findeþ, fond, funde, funden, fundon, wefan	dies	suuyltit, swyltit
		different	missenlic, missenlicum
		differently	ungelice
		difficult	earfoðlic, earfoþlic, weorce
devoid-of	leas		

Word List (English to Ænglisc)

English	Ænglisc	English	Ænglisc
difficulty	earfeðu, earfeþa, earfeþo, earfeþu, earfoða, earfoþa, earfoþe, nearo, nearu, nearwe	dire-need	fyrenðearf, fyrenðearfe, fyrenþearf, fyrenþearfe, weaþearf, weaþearfe
dignity	ar, ara, aræred, aran, are, arena, arna, arra, arum, drihtscipe, drihtscipes, drihtscype, dryhtscype	dire-suffering	fyrenearfeða, fyrenearfeðe, fyrenearfeþa, fyrenearfeþe
		disable	amen, amyrde, amyrran, amyrred, lemedon, lemian
diligent	georn, georne	disappear	aslupan, geswiðrod, geswiþrod, swiðrade, swiðrian, swiðrode, swiþrade, swiþrian, swiþrode
dim	dim, dimman, dimme		
diminish	geswicað, geswicaþ, geswiðrod, geswiþrod, gewanod, lytlað, lytlaþ, lytlian, lytligan, lytlod, lytlode, swiðrade, swiðrian, swiðrode, swiþrade, swiþrian, swiþrode, wanian		
		disappearing	heononweard
		disappointed	onhlytme, unhlitme
		disassemble	tolucan
		disaster-news	weaspell, weaspelle
		disaster-story	weaspell, weaspelle
		discerning	gleawferhð, gleawferhþ, scearp, scearpe, scearpne
din	bearhtm, bearhtme, hlyn	discernment	gescad
dinner	swæsendu, swæsendum	discourse	meðel, meþel, meþle
dip	dyfan, dyfde	discover	ascian, axian, axoden, axude, geacsian, geahsod, geascodon, geaxode, onfand, onfindan, onfond, onfunde, onfunden
dire	atol, grim, grimma, grimman, grimme, grimne, grimre, sliðen, sliþen, þrealic, wælgrim, wællgrim		
direct	geriht, gestyran, rihtan, rihte, wealdan, wealden, weold, weoldon	discovery	fandung, fandunga
		discuss	eahtedon, eahtian, eahtodan, eahtode, ehtigað, ehtigaþ, geæhted
directly	gegnum		
directly-created	selfsceafte	discussion	run, rune
dire-distress	fyren-ðearf, fyren-þearf, þreanedla, þreanedlan, þreanyd, þreanydum	disdain	forhicgan, forhicge, forhogian, forhogode
		disease	adl, broc, broce, coðu, coþu, coþum, cwild
		disembarking	upganga, upgangan

Word List (English to Ænglisc)

English	Ænglisc	English	Ænglisc
disfavour	unhyldo	distant-	feorcyþðe,
disgrace	bysmor, edwitscype, sceond, sceonde	acquaintance	feorcyþðu, feorcyþþe, feorcyþþu
disgraced	æwiscmod		
disgraced-in-mind	æwiscmode	distant-current	fyrnstream, fyrnstreama
disguise	gehiwodon, hiwian		
dish	ðis, disc, discas, þis	distant-journey	feorweg, feorwegas, feorwegum, widlast, widlastum
disheartened	onhlytme, unhlitme		
dishonour	bysmeredon, bysmerian, gebysmrian, unhlisa, unhlisan	distant-past	feorran, feorren
		distant-path	widweg, widwegas
		distant-streams	fyrnstreama
dishonourable	arleas, unarlic	distant-way	feorweg, feorwegas, feorwegum
dishonourably	unarlice, unwurðlice, unwurþlice	distinct	syndrig
dismayed	acol	distinction	weorðmynd, weorðmynda, weorðmynde, weorþmynd, weorþmynda, weorþmynde
dismount	lihtan, lihte		
disordered	rædfæst, rædleas, rædlease		
dispatch	bædan, bædde, gebæded, onsend, onsendan, onsende, onsended, onsendeð, onsendeþ, onsendon	distinguished	geðungen, geþungen
		distress	hreaw, hreowan, hreoweð, hreoweþ, modsefan, modsorg, oncyð, oncyþ, oncyþðe, oncyþþe, sarnissum, sarnys, sarnysse, sorg, sorga, sorge, sorgum, sorh, sorhg, we, wea, wean, weana, wrace, wracu, wræce
dispense	brittade, brittian, brytnade, brytnian		
dispenser	brytta, bryttan		
disperse	to-faran, to-faren, to-for, to-foron		
dispirited	onhlytme, unhlitme		
display	ætæwde, æteowan, æteowde, ætywan, onwreoh, onwreon, wæfersyn, wæfersyne		
		distribute	bryttað, bryttade, bryttaþ, bryttedon, bryttian, bryttigin
displease	ofþyncan	distributor	brytta
displeasure	unhyldo, unþanc, unþances	district	scir, scire, scyppend, scyr, scyre
dispose-of	ateah, ateon		
dispute	geflit	disturb	styrede, styreþ, styrge, styrian
dissolve	gemealt, gemyltan, mealt, meltan, multon		
		disturbance	unstilnes
dissuade-from	belean	dive-or-swim-through	þurhdeaf, þurhdufan
distance	lengo, trem, trym		
distant	feor, feorres	diverse	missenlic, missenlicum

Word List (English to *Ænglisc*)

English	*Ænglisc*	English	*Ænglisc*
diversely	missenlice	do	dædon, deð, deþ, do, doð, don, doþ, dreag, dreah, dreogað, dreogan, dreogaþ, dreogeð, dreogeþ, dreoh, druge, drugon, dyde, dydest, dydon, fremed, fremeð, fremede, fremedon, fremest, fremeþ, fremmað, fremman, fremmaþ, fremme, fremmen, gæworht, gedæde, gedeð, gedeþ, gedo, gedoð, gedon, gedoþ, gedrogen, gedyde, gedydon, gefremed, gefremede, gefremeden, gefremedon, gefremman, gefremmanne, gelædað, gelædaþ, gelædde, gelæde, gelædedd, gemacod, geworht, geworhte, geworhtne, geworhton, gewyrc, gewyrcan
divert	oðwendan, oþwendan		
divide	adælan, adæled, adælede, brittade, brittian, bryttað, bryttade, bryttaþ, bryttedon, bryttian, bryttigin, dælað, dælan, dælaþ, dælde, dældon, dæle, dæleð, dæleþ, dælon, gedælan, gedælde, gedæled, gedaled, gesced, sceadan, sceadeð, sceadeþ, tobræd, tobrægd, tobredon, tobregdan, todælan, todælden, totwæman, totwæmed, totweman		
divided	ungeþeod, ungeþeode		
divine	godcund, godcunde, godcundlic, godcundlicum, godes, godlic		
division	dæl, dælas, dæle, gedal, gedale, scir		
		do-away	toscufeð, toscufeþ
		do-away-with	fornam, fornamon, forniman, fornom, fornoman, fornumen
		doctor	læce, læces
		document	gewrit, gewritu, gewrytum
		do-evil	gesyngad, syngian
		dog	hun, hund, hundum
		dominate	ricsian, rixian, rixode
		done	gedon
		donkey	esol, esolas
		do-not	ne

Word List (English to Ænglisc)

English	Ænglisc	English	Ænglisc
doom	dom, domes, meotodsceaft, meotudgesceaft, metodsceaft, metodsceafte	dragon-hoard	wyrmhord, wyrmhorda
		dragon-kind	wyrmcynn, wyrmcynnes
doomed	awyrdan, awyrded, fægan, fæge, fægean, fæges, fægne, fægum	draw	abræd, abrægd, abregd, abregdan, abregde, abroden, abrugdon, ateon, bedragan, bedrog, teon, tihte, tyhtað, tyhtan, tyhtaþ
doomed-one	fægan		
doomed-to-die	deaðfæge, deaþfæge, fromweard, fromweardum	draw-a-sword	abræd, abrægd, abregd, abregdan, abregde, abroden, abrugdon, bræd, brægd, bregdan, bregde, bregdon, broden, brogdne, brudon, brugdon, gebræd, gebroden, geteah, geteoh, getogen, teah, teon, togen
doomed-to-die-by-blows	slegefæge		
door	duru, durum, hlinduru, muð, muða, muðan, muðe, muþ, muþa, muþan, muþe		
doubt	tweo, tweode, tweon		
dove	culufran, culufre		
do-without	forþolian	draw-back	wandian, wandode
down	neoþeweard, neoþeweardne, niðer, nioðor, nioþor, niþer, nyde, nyðer, nyþer, ofdune	drawing	getugon
		drawn	gebrægd
		draw-near	nealæcan, nealæced, nealæcte
		dread	andraedan, broga, brogan, ondrædað, ondrædan, ondrædaþ, ondrædeþ, ondred, ondrede, ondredon, onegan, onsæton, onsittan
down-from-above	ufan, ufon		
downward	niðerweard, niþerweard		
downwards	neoþeweard, neoþeweardne, niðer, nioðor, nioþor, niþer, nyðer, nyþer		
drag	teon	dreaded	ondred
dragon	draca, dracan, guðfloga, guðflogan, guþfloga, guþflogan, hordweard, hringboga, hringbogan, wurman, wyrican, wyrm, wyrmas, wyrme, wyrmes, wyrmum	dreadful	atelic, forhtan
		dreadful-calamity	brohþrea
		dreadful-torment	witebroga, witebrogan
		dream	gemætte, mætan, swæfne, swefn, swefna, swefne
		dreams	dreama, dreamas
		drearily	dreorig
		dreary	dreorig, dreorigne, driorig, driorigne
dragon-body	wyrmlic, wyrmlicum		
dragon-hall	wyrmsele	dreary-hall	dreorsele

344

Word List (English to Ænglisc)

English	Ænglisc	English	Ænglisc
dreary-hall?-bloody-hall?	dreorsele	drive-out	afligde, aflygan, aflygde, asceaf, ascufan, bedraf, bedrifan, bedrifenne, flyman, flymde, geflymed, gewræc, gewrec, gewrecen, gewrecene, oðþringan, oðþringeð, oðþrong, oþþringan, oþþringeð, oþþringeþ, oþþrong, wræc, wræce, wræcon, wrec, wrecan, wrece, wrecen
drench	begeotan, begoten, beswyled, beswylian		
dress	gegærwan, gegired, gegiredan, gegyred, gegyrede, gegyrwan, gegyrwed, gierede, gierwaþ, girwan, gyrde, gyrede, gyredon, gyrla, gyrlan, gyrwað, gyrwan, gyrwaþ		
dressing	gyrde		
drill-a-hole	borian, borige		
drink	dranc, drinc, drincan		
drinker	beorscealc, beorscealca, drincend, drincendra	drove-away	adraf
		drown	besencan, besenceð, besenceþ, drencan, drencte
drinking	drenc, drence, drinc		
drinking-cup	bolla, bollan		
drinking-happiness	gytesæl, gytesalum	drowning	drenc, drence, drenceflod
drinking-vessel	dryncfæt		
drip	drype, dryppan?	drunk	druncen, druncne, medowerig, medowerige, medowerigum, symbelwerig
drip-over	begeotan, begoten		
dripping-blood	dreor		
drive	cnossian, cnossod, cnossode, cnyssan, draf, drifað, drifan, drifaþ, drife	drunken	druncnum, druncon, winsad, winsade, winsadum
drive-a-nail-through	þurhdrifan		
drive-apart	todraf, todrifan	drunken-female-slave	druncmennen
drive-away	adraf, adrifan, adrifen, adrifest, aflyman, aflymde, afysan, afysed, bedraf, bedrifan, bedrifenne, fordraf, fordrifan, forþringan, forwræc, forwrecan	drunk-on-ale	ealogal, ealogalra
		drunk-with-mead	medugal, meodugal, meodugales
		drunk-with-wine	wingal
		dry	drige, dryge
		dry-land	land, landa, lande, landes, lond, londe, londes
drive-back	forsceaf, forscufan		
driven	gebeded	dry-land-in-a-marsh	fenhop, fenhopu
driven-away	adræfed, todræfed	dubiousness	tweo, tweon
drive-off	forswapan, forswapen, forsweop	Dublin	Difelin
		dumb	dumb
		dune	sona, sondbeorg, sondbeorgum
		dung	meox, scerne

345

English	*Ænglisc*
during	*for, ofer, ofor*
during-that-time	*þenden*
dusky	*fealone, fealu, fealwe, salo, wan, wann, wanna, wanre, won, wonn, wonna, wonnan, wonne*
dust	*dust, duste, greot*
duty	*gerihte, nede, neod, neode, nyd, rightly, riht, rihte, ryht, truly*
dwarf	*dweores, dweorh*
dwell	*buað, buan, buaþ, bude, bugan, bun, buon, byne, eardast, eardian, eardod, eardode, gebun, gewunedon, gewunigen, wuna, wunað, wunade, wunaþ, wunedon, wuniað, wunian, wuniaþ, wuniende, wunod, wunode, wunodon*
dwelled	*wunode*
dweller	*buend, buendra*
dwellers-in-iniquity	*bealuwara, bealuwaras*
dwell-in	*bugan, eardian, eardigean, eardode, eardodon, weardian, weardode*
dwelling	*burg, burga, burgum, burh, byht, byrig, geard, geardas, geardum, ham, hamas, hame, hames, hof, hofe, hofu, hofum, in, inn, inne, tun, wic, wica, wicum, wicun, wunian, wuniaþ, wunung, wununge*
dwelling-place	*eardgeard, eardwica, wicstede*
dwellings	*hofu*
dwells	*wunað*
dye	*telg*
dyke	*eorðweall, eorþweall*

E, e

English	*Ænglisc*
e	*e*
each	*æghwa, æghwæðer, æghwæðre, æghwæðres, æghwæðrum, æghwæm, æghwæs, æghwæþer, æghwæþre, æghwæþres, æghwæþrum, æghwilc, æghwilcne, æghwylc, æghwylcne, æghwylcum, ægþer, ælc, ælcere, ælces, ælcon, ælcre, ælcum, eac, gehuuæs, gehwa, gehwæm, gehwæne, gehwær, gehwære, gehwæs, gehwam, gehwane, gehwelcne, gehwilc, gehwilce, gehwilces, gehwilcne, gehwilcre, gehwilcum, gehwone, gehwylc, gehwylce, gehwylces, gehwylcne, gehwylcre, gehwylcum, gihuaes, hwa, hwæne, hwam, hwan, hwon, hwone, owðer, owþer, welhwylc, welhwylcra*
each-other	*oðerne*
each-thing	*æghwæs*
Eadmund (name)	*Eadmund*

Word List (English to Ænglisc)

English	Ænglisc	English	Ænglisc
eager	*arhwate, ellorfus, ellorfuse, fus, fuse, fusne, georn, georne, þurstig*	earth	*ear, eardas, eorð, eorðan, eorðe, eorðgrap, eorþ, eorþan, eorþe, foldan, folde, greot, grund, grundas, grunde, grundes, hruse, middaneard, middangeard, middangearde, middangeardes, moldan, molde, næs, næss, terre*
eager-for-fame	*lofgeorn, lofgeornost*		
eager-for-gold	*goldhwæte*		
eager-for-good-judgement	*domgeorn, domgeorne*		
eager-for-praise	*lofgeorn, lof-georn*		
eager-for-slaughter	*wælfus*		
eagerly	*georne, geornlice, geornor, neodlice*		
eager-to-get-away	*hine, hinfus*		
eager-to-press-forward-in-battle	*forðgeorn, forþgeorn*	earth-building	*eorðe, eorðreced, eorþe, eorþreced, moldern*
eager-to-travel-by-foot	*feþegeorn*	earth-covering	*sceat, sceata, sceatas, sceate, sceatt, sceatta, sceattum, sceatum*
eagle	*earn, earne*		
eagle's	*earnes*		
Eaha (name)	*Eaha*		
ealdorman	*ealdorman, ealdormann*	earth-dweller	*eorðan, eorðbuend, eorðbuende, eorðbuendra, eorðbuendum, eorþan, eorþbuend, eorþbuende, eorþbuendra, eorþbuendum, grundbuend, grundbuendra, woruldbuend, woruldbuendra*
ear	*eare*		
earl	*eorl, eorle*		
earlier	*ær, æror, ærran, ærur, fyrn, gefyrn*		
earlier-born	*ær, ærboren*		
earlier-day	*ærdæg, ærdæge, ærdagum*		
earls	*eorla, eorlas*		
early-morning	*uhtan, uhte, uhtna, uhttid*		
early-morning-misery	*uhtceare, uhtcearu*	earth-dwellers	*eorðbuende, eorðbuendra, eorðbuendum, eorðbugende, eorthweard, foldan, foldbuend, foldbuende, foldbuendum, landbuende, landbuendum, londbuend, londbuendum*
earn	*earna, earnian, geearnaþ, geearnod*		
earnestly	*georne, geornor, neodlice*		
earning	*earnian*		
		earth-dwelling	*eorðsele, eorþsele*
		earth--dwelling-dragon	*eorðdraca, eorþdraca*
		earth-hall	*eorðsele, eorþsele*

347

Word List (English to Ænglisc)

English	Ænglisc	English	Ænglisc
earth-joy	grundwela, grundwelan	earth-surface	sceat, sceata, sceatas, sceate, sceatt, sceatta, sceattum, sceatum
earth-kingdom	eorþan, eorþrice		
earthly	eorðan, eorðcund, eorðcunde, eorþcund, eorþcunde, middaneardlic, middaneardlice	earth-ways	foldwegum
		earth-wealth	grundwela, grundwelan
		earthwork	eorðweall, eorþweall
		easily	eaðe, eaðost, eal, eall, eaþe, eaþost, swæslice, yðelice, yþelice
earthly-building	foldan, foldbold		
earthly-goods	woruldfeoh		
earthly-joy	worulddream, worulddreama		
		easily-found	eaðfynde, eaþfynde
		easily-gotten	eðbegete, eþbegete
earthly-king	eorðcyning, eorðcyninges, eorþcyning, eorþcyninges, woroldcyning, worold-cyning, woroldcyninga, woruldcyingas, woruldcyning, wyruldcyning, wyruldcyninga	easily-seen	eðgesyne, eþgesyne, yþgesene
		east	eart, east
		eastern	easterne
		eastern-land	eastland, eastlandum
		eastern-river	eaststream, eaststreamas
		eastward	eastweard, east-weard
earthly-male-relative	woruldmæg, woruldmagas	easy	eaðe, eaþe, eðe, eþe, leoht, yðe, yþe
earthly-misery	woruldyrmðo, woruldyrmþo	eat	æt, æte, byrgan, byrgde, byrgean, byrigde, byrige, ðicgean, etan, eteð, eteþ, fræt, fræton, fretan, gebyrgde, gebyrge, geþægon, geþah, geþeah, onbat, onbitan, þegon, þegun, þicgan, þicgeað, þicgean, þicgeaþ, þigeð, þigeþ
earthly-possession	eorðwela, eorðwelan, eorþwela, eorþwelan		
earthly-road-or-path	eorðweg, eorðwege, eorþweg, eorþwege		
earthly-wealth	woruldgestreon, woruldgestreona, woruldgestreonum		
earth-rind	lamrindum		
earth-root	wang, wange, wong, wongas, wonge		
earth-route	wang, wange, wong, wongas, wonge	eating-strong	metes, meteþiht, meteþihtan
earth's	eorðan	eat-through	þurhetan, þurhetone
earth's-chest	eorðscrafu	ebb	ebba, ebbade, ebban, ebbian
earth-stalking	foldhrerendra		
earth-stepper	eard-stapa	Edgar	Eadgar
		Edgar (name)	Eadgar

Word List (English to Ænglisc)

English	Ænglisc	English	Ænglisc
edge	brerd, ecg, ecga, ecge, ecgum, lærig, ofer, ofre, ora, oran	eighty seven	seofon and hundeahtatig
edge-play	ecgplega, ecgplegan	eighty seventh	seofon and hundeahtatigoþa
edge-rush	ecgbracu, ecgbræce	eighty six	siex and hundeahtatig
edge-sport	ecgplega, ecgplegan	eighty sixth	six and hundeahtatigoþa
edge-wall	ecgwal, ecgwale	eighty third	þreo and hundeahtatigoþa
Edmund (name)	Eadmund		
educate	geteah, geteoh, getogen, teah, teon, togen	eighty three	þri and hundeahtatig
		eighty two	twegen and hundeahtatig, tpegen and hundeahtatig
educated	getogene		
Edward (name)	Eadweard, Eadweardes	either	aðor, æghwæðer, æghwæðre, æghwæðres, æghwæðrum, æghwæþer, æghwæþre, æghwæþres, æghwæþrum, ægþer, ahwæðer, ahwæþer, owðer, owþer
Edward's (name)	Eadweardes		
eel	æl		
effective-drop	speddropa, speddropum		
effort	geswinc		
eight	eahta		
eighteen	eahtatine, XVIII		
eighteenth	eahtateoþa		
eighth	eahteðan, eahtoþa		
eight-hundred	eahtahund		
eightieth	hundeahtatigoþa	either...or	ge
eighty	hundeahtatig, LXXX	either-of-two	gehwæðer, gehwæðere, gehwæðrum, gehwæþer, gehwæþere, gehwæþres, gehwæþrum
eighty eight	eahta and hundeahtatig		
eighty eighth	eahta and hundeahtatigoþa		
eighty fifth	fif and hundeahtatigoþa		
eighty first	an and hundeahtatigoþa	elder	aldor, aldre, ealde, ealdor, ealdre, ealdres, yldesta, yldestan, yldra, yldre, yldrum
eighty five	fif and hundeahtatig		
eighty four	feower and hundeahtatig, feoþer and hundeahtatig		
		elders	aelda, ealda
eighty fourth	feower and hundeahtatigoþa	elders'	aelda, eorðan, eorþan
eighty nine	nigon and hundeahtatig	elegant	cyrten, cyrtenu
		elegy	wordgyd
eighty ninth	nigon and hundeahtatigoþa	elevate	gestepte, herran, ræran, rærde, rærdon, stepan, stepe, stepte, stepton
eighty one	an and hundeahtatig		
eighty second	twa and hundeahtatigoþa		

Word List (English to Ænglisc)

English	Ænglisc	English	Ænglisc
elevated	uphea	encircle	bebugan, bebugeð, bebugeþ, besæt, besittan, ymbe, ymbefeng, ymbefon
eleven	endleofan		
eleventh	endlefta		
elf	ælf, ylfa, ylfe		
Elizabeth (name)	Elizabet	enclose	beleac, belucan, beluce, bewreon, bewrigen, bewrigene, bewrigenum, biwrah, forðylman, forðylmed, forþylman, forþylmed
ell	eln, elna		
else	elles		
elsewhere	ellor, ellorfus, ellorfuse		
elves	ylfa		
Ely-in-the-Fens (place)	Eligbyrig		
embankment	Beorh		
ember	gled, gledum, yslan, ysle	enclosure	burg, burh, clustor, clustro, ederas, edor, edoras, eoderas, eodor, eodur, fæste, fæsten, fæstenne, geard, geardas, geardum, haga, hagan
embrace	beclypan, beclypte, clyppað, clyppan, clyppaþ, clyppe, clypte, fæðm, fæðme, fæðmian, fæðmie, fæðmum, fæþm, fæþme, fæþmian, fæþmie, fæþmum, ymbclyppan, ymbclypte		
		enclosure-surrounding-a-dwelling	worðig, worþig
embraces	frige, frigu	encounter	gemeted, gemeting, gemette, gemetton, gemittan, gemitte, gemitton, metan, mette, metton
embrocate	gesmyrode, smyrian		
eminently-wise	foresnotor, foresnotre		
emotion	breostwylm	encourage	aretan, areted, byldan, bylde, bylded, gebylde, hwet, hweteð, hweteþ, hwettan, hwette, hwetton, onbryrd, onbryrdan, onbryrde, trymed, trymede, trymian
emperor	caseras, casere		
empire	þeodlanda, þeodlond		
employ	neat, neotan, noden, nu, nudon		
employment	drohtað, drohtaþ, drohtoð, drohtoþ		
empowered	mægeneacen		
empty	æmettig, gerume, orfeorme, rum, rume, rumne, rumre, rumum	encouraged	hyrde
empty-handed	idelhende		
emulate	efenlæcan, geeuenlæhton		
encampment	fyrdwic, fyrdwicum		

Word List (English to Ænglisc)

English	Ænglisc	English	Ænglisc
end	agan, end, ende, endestæf, endian, geændade, geendod, getwæfan, getwæfde, getwæfed, getwæfeð, getwæfeþ, gewand, ofereode, ofereodon, ofergan	endure-the-absence-of	forþolian
		enduring	dreogeð, dreogeþ, langsum, langsumu, lansumum, longsum
		enemies	Hettend
ended	geendode	enemy	andsaca, andsacum, dædhata, feond, feonda, feondas, feonde, feondes, feondum, fionda, fynd, fyrngeflitan, gelað, gelaðe, gelaþ, gelaþe, gesaca, gesacan, gesacum, hetend, hetende, hettend, hettendra, hettendum, laþra, leodsceaða, leodsceaðan, leodsceaþa, leodsceaþan, ondsaca, scaþan, sceaða, sceaðena, sceaðona, sceaðum, sceaþa, sceaþena, sceaþona, sceaþum, wiðerbreca, wiðerbrecan, wiþerbreca, wiþerbrecan
ending	geendung, geendunge		
endless	endeleas		
end-of-life	gemearces, mearc, mearce		
endowed	eacen, eacne, eacnum, ecne		
endure	adreogan, bad, beodan, bidan, bideð, biden, bideþ, bidon, ðah, ðeon, ðolad, ðolade, ðolian, ðoliaþ, ðolode, dreag, dreah, dreogað, dreogan, dreogaþ, dreogeð, dreogeþ, dreoh, drogen, ðrowad, ðrowade, ðrowian, ðrowode, druge, drugon, forberan, gebad, gebide, gebiden, geðah, gedrogen, gelæst, gelæstan, gelæste, gelæston, geþah, geþeoh, geþeon, geþolian, geþolianne, geþolode, geþungen, læst, læstan, læste, læsten, læstes, þag, þah, þe, þeah, þeon, þolad, þolað, þolade		
		enemy-army	here
		enemy-from-hell	hellsceaða, hellsceaþa
		enemy-to-the-death	ealdorgewinna
		enforced-distress	nydwracu
		enforced-payment	nydbad, nydbade
		engage-in	dælað, dælan, dælaþ, dælde, dældon, dæle, dæleð, dæleþ, dælon, gedælan, gedælde, gedæled, gedaled
endured	dreag, gebad, þolade		
endures	gedreogeð		

351

Word List (English to Ænglisc)

English	Ænglisc	English	Ænglisc
engender	temað, teman, temaþ, tymað, tyman, tymaþ, tymdon	enrage	abealch, abelgan, abolgen, belgan, gebulge, gegremed, gegremede, gegremian, gegremod, gegremode, gremian
English (name)	Anglo-Saxon, engla		
engrave	agrafan, agrof, writan, writen		
enjoy	beneah, bræc, breac, bruc, brucað, brucan, brucaþ, bruce, bruceð, bruceþ, bryttað, bryttade, bryttaþ, bryttedon, bryttian, bryttigin, genyttod, neot, neotan, niotað, niotan, niotaþ, nyttade, nyttian	enraged	abelgan, abolgen, bolgenmod, gebolgen, gebolgne, yrremod
		enraged-from	belgan, gebolgen, gebolgne
		enriched	gewelgad
		enslaved	wælisc, wælisca
		ensnare	befangen, befon, befongen, beswican, besyred, besyrwan, bifongen
enjoyed	brucan		
enjoyment	healgamen		
enjoy-oneself	dryman, drymdon	enter-a-monastic-order	geþeodde, þeoda, þeodan
enlarge	gerymde, gerymdon, gerymed, ryman, rymde	enterprise	angin
		entertain	bewenede, bewennan, biwenede, feormian, gefeormedon, gefeormod
enmity	bealu, ecghete, fæghðe, fæghþe, fæhð, fæhða, fæhðe, fæhðo, fæhðu, fæhþ, fæhþa, fæhþe, fæhþo, fæhþu, feondscipe, hete, nið, niða, niðas, niðe, niðes, niðum, niþ, niþa, niþas, niþe, niþes, niþum, oht, wiðermedo, wighete, wiþermedo, wroht, wrohte, wrohtes	entertainment	gleo, gomen
		entertainment-wood	gleobeam, gleobeames
		entice	bedragan, bedrog, forspanan, forspeon, span, spanan, speon, speone, weman, wemde, wemed, wenede, wenian
		enticement	gespon
		enticing	hat, hatan, hate, hates, hatne, haton, hatost, hatran
enmity-act	hetenið, heteniðas, heteniþ, heteniþas		
enough	geneahe, geneahhe, genehe, genehost, geniht, genog, genoge, genoh, genohra	entire	andlang, andlong, andlongne, ondlang, ondlangne, ondlong, ondlonge

352

Word List (English to Ænglisc)

English	Ænglisc	English	Ænglisc
entirely	æghwæs, aninga, anunga, eal, eall, ealle, eallenga, ealles, eallinga, eallon, eallum, ful, full, geare, gearwe, gearwor, gearwost, genunga, gere	equip-with-armour	gesyrwed, syrede, syrwan
		era	mædæg, mældæges, mældagum
		ere	ær
		erect	gestepte, steapheah, stepan, stepe, stepte, stepton, timbran, timbred, timbrede
entirely-gilt	eallgylden		
entrance	ingang		
entrap	besyred, besyrwan		
entreat	healsian, healsode	erect-a-tent	geslægene, geslegene, gesloh, slægen, slea, sleah, slean, slog, sloge, slogon, sloh
entreating	frymdi		
entrust	alyfan, alyfde, alyfed, bebead, bebeod, bebeodan, befæstan, befæste, betæcan, betæhte, bifæstan, bifæste&th		
		Ermanaric's (name)	Eormanrices
		errand	ærenda, ærende, aerendfaest, ærendian, nede, neod, neode, nyd
envelope	befealdan, befealdest		
envy	æfestra	error	gedwild, gedwilde, gedwyld, gedwylde
enwreathe	bewand, bewindað, bewindan, bewindaþ, bewunden, biwunden	escape	ætwand, ætwindan, fealh, feall, feolan, genesan, gewindan, hwyrft, hwyrftum, losað, losade, losaþ, losian, oðwand, oðwindan, oðwunden, oðwundon, oþwand, oþwindan, oþwunden, oþwundon, swice
equal	efenlæcan, geeuenlæhton, gelica, gelican, gemæc, gemæcne		
equally-blessed	efeneadig		
equip	gearwad, gearwian, gegærwan, gegarwod, gegearewod, gegearwigean, gegearwod, gegired, gegiredan, gegyred, gegyrede, gegyrwan, gegyrwed, gierede, gierwaþ, girwan, gyrde, gyrede, gyredon, gyrwað, gyrwan, gyrwaþ	escape-from	genæs, genesen, nesan
		escort	foregenga
equipment	gearwan, gearwe, gearwor, gearwum, geatwa		

Word List (English to Ænglisc)

English	Ænglisc	English	Ænglisc
establish	gesætte, gesætton, geseted, gesett, gesettan, gesette, gesetton, gestaþelað, gestaþelade, gestaþelaþ, gestaþelod, gestaþelode, onstealde, onsteled, onstellan, sete, settan, sette, setton, staðelian, staþelian	eunuch	belisnod, belisnode, eunuch, eunuchi
		evaporate	weorne
		Eve (name)	Evan
		even	eac, efne, furðum, furþum
		even-if	ðeah ðe, þeah þe
		evening	æfen, æfenne, æfentid, æfentide, æfyn
		evening-glow	æfenscima
		evening-light	æfenleoht, æfenscima
established	astelidæ, eardfæst, gesetena, onstealde, site, siteð, siteþ, siþþan, sittað, sittaþ	evening-rest	æfenræst, æfenræste
		evening-song	æfenleoð, æfenleoht, æfenleoþ
		evening-speech	æfenspræc, æfenspræce
establishment	stol, stole	event	wyrd
estate	ham, hamas, hame, hames	ever	a, æfre, ðe, næfre, o, simle, Symle, wideferhð, wideferhþ
esteem	eahtian, eahtod, eahtode, geæhtlan, geæhtle, onman, onmunan, onmunde, onmunon, wurðode, wurþian, wurþode		
		ever-before	iofore
		everlasting	ece
		every	æfre, æghwilc, ælc, eac, ealles, ealra, gehwa, gehwæm, gehwæne, gehwær, gehwære, gehwæs, gehwam, gehwane, gehwelcne, gehwilce, gehwilces, gehwilcum, gehwone, gehwylc, gehwylce, gehwylces, gehwylcne, gehwylcre, gehwylcum, welhwylc, welhwylcra
esteemed	geæhted, geæhtlan, weorþe, weorþra, wurðe, wurðran, wurþe, wurþran, wyrðe, wyrðra, wyrþe, wyrþra		
estuary	muða, muþa		
eternal	æce, ec, eca, ecan, ece, ecea, ecean, eces, eci, ecne, ecum, forðweard, forðweardum, forþweard, forþweardum		
eternal (Latin)	æterna, eternam		
eternally	a, awa, ece, o		
eternity	aldor, aldre, aldres, aldrum, ealdor, ealdre, ealdres, ecnis, ecnisse	everyone	æghwa, æghwæm, æghwæs, gehwa, gehwæm
		every-one	gehwylc
eulogy	æftercweþend, æftercweþendra	everything	æghuuæt, æghwa, æghwæt, eghwam

Word List (English to Ænglisc)

English	Ænglisc	English	Ænglisc
everything (Latin)	omnia	evil-doers	bealuwara, bealuwaras
everywhere	æghwær, gehwær, gehwer, hwær, hwar, welhwær	evil-dragon	niðdraca, niþdraca
		evil-full	bealofull, bealofulla, bealofullan
evidence	behð, behðe, behþ, behþe	evil-grasp	inwitfeng
evident	gesene, gesiene, gesyne	evil-guest	inwitgæst
		evil-hall	niðsele, niþsele
evil	balwon, bealewa, bealo, bealu, bealuwa, bealwa, bealwe, bealwes, dyrnan, dyrne, dyrnra, dyrnum, facen, facna, facne, facnes, frecnan, frecne, frecnen, inwit, inwitniða, inwitniþ, inwitniþa, inwitniþas, lað, laþ, man, mane, manum, nið, niða, niðas, niðe, niðes, niðum, niþ, niþa, niþas, niþe, niþes, niþum, sliðen, sliþen, unhæl, unhælo, unlæd, unlædan, unræd, unræde, unrædes, wawa, wawan, woh, wom, womm, womma, womme, wommum, wora, wrað	evilly	wraðlice, wraþlice, yfele
		evil-malice	inwitsearo, inwitsorh
		evil-minded	werigmod
		evil-net	inwitnet
		evil-offspring	untydras, untydre
		evil-one	inwidda
		evil-or-criminal-deed	fyrendæd, fyrendæda, fyrendædum
		evil-roof	inwithrof
		evil-share	hearmsceare, hearmscearu
		evil-slaughter	inwitscear
		evil-sorrow	inwidsorg, inwidsorge, inwitsorge, inwitsorh
		evil-speech	womcwidas, womcwide
		evil-spirit	esa, os, scinn, scinna, scinnum
		evil-thought	inwitþancum
		evil-visitor	inwitgæst, niðgæst, niþgæst
		evil-web	inwitnet
		evil-wound	inwidhlemm, inwidhlemmas
evil-act	facenstæf, facenstafas	exactly	efne, emne, georne, geornlice, geornor
evil-affliction	bealonið, bealoniðe, bealoniþ, bealoniþe	exalt	ahæfen, ahafen, ahebban, ahof, ahofon, onhebban, onhof
evil-allotment	hearmsceare, hearmscearu		
evil-companion	weagesið, weagesiðas, weagesiþ, weagesiþas	exalted	he, hea, heagum, heah, heahne, hean, heanne, heanum, heare, heaum
evil-death	bealocwealm		
evil-deed	niþgeweorc, niþgeweorca	exalted-treasure	heahgestreon, heahgestreona
evil-doer	manfordædla, manfordædlan		

Word List (English to Ænglisc)

English	Ænglisc	English	Ænglisc
examine	fandian, fandigan, fandode, gefandod, gefondad, giondwlitan, smeagan	except-that	næfne, nefne, nemne
		excessive	þearl
		excessive-appetite	guðhafoc
		excessively	forswiðe, forswiþe, to
example	bisen, bisne		
exceedingly	swiðe, swiðor, swiðost, swiþe, swiþor, swiþost, swyðe, swyðor, swyþe, swyþor	exchange	gewrixle, gewrixled, wið, wiþ, wrixl, wrixlan, wrixle
		exchange-of-words	gewrixled, wrixlan
		excite	astyred, astyrian
excellence	cista, cyst, cystum, dugeða, dugeðe, dugeðum, dugeþa, dugeþe, dugeþum, dugoða, dugoðe, dugoþa, dugoþe, duguð, duguða, duguðe, duguðum, duguþ, duguþa, duguþe, duguþum, gumcyst, gumcyste, gumcystum, selast	exculpate	beladian
		excuse	ladigan
		exemplify	onstealde, onstealdest, onstellan
		exhausted	werig
		exhort	getrimede, getrymmed, læran, lærde, læred, manian, manod, manode, trimian, trymed, trymeð, trymede, trymedon, trymeþ, trymian, trymman
excellent	aeðða, æðela, æðelan, æðele, æðelo, æðelum, æþela, æþelan, æþele, æþelicra, æþelo, æþelu, æþelum, aeþþa, betlic, cost, gecoste, geðungen, geþungen, geþungon, god, godlecran, godlic, godlice, mæra, mæran, mære, mæres, mærne, mæro, mæron, mærost, mærra, mæru, mærum, welþungen	exhortation	tihting, tihtinge
		exile	anhaga, flema, gewræc, gewrec, gewrecen, gewrecene, nydfara, wrace, wræc, wræcca, wræce, wræces, wræcmæcgas, wræcmecg, wræcmon, wræcon, wræcsiþa, wrec, wrecan, wrecca, wreccena, wrece, wrecen
		exiled	eðelleas, eðelleasum, eþelleas, eþelleasum, wræclic, wræclicne
excellently	hlisfullice		
except	butan, buton, nemþe, nimþe, nymðe, nymþe		
except-for	buton, næfne, nefne, nemne	exiled-person	wræca, wrælla, wræcna

Word List (English to Ænglisc)

English	Ænglisc	English	Ænglisc
exile-journey	wræcsið, wræcsiðum, wræcsiþ, wræcsiþa, wræcsiþas, wræcsiþum	expedition	heaðoliðendum, heaþoliðend, heaþoliðende, heaþoliþend, heaþoliþende, heaþoliþendum, rad, rade, sið, siða, siðe, siðes, siðfæt, siðfate, siþ, siþa, siþe, siþes, siþfæt, siþfate, siþon
exile-place	wræcstow, wræcstowe		
exile-track	wræclast, wræclastas		
exist	beon, gelamp, gelimpe, gelimpeð, gelimpeþ, gelomp, gelumpe, gelumpen, gestod, gestodon, is, leofað, leofast, leofaþ, libban, lifde, lifdon, limpan, limpeð, limpeþ, lomp, lybban, lyfdon, standað, standan, standaþ, stande, standeð, standeþ, stod, stodan, stodon, stondað, stondan, stondaþ, stonde, stondeð, stondeþ, stynt		
		expeditionary-force	siðwerod, siþwerod
		expedition-messenger	siðboda, siþboda
		expel	afligde, aflygan, aflygde, asceaf, ascufan, gewræc, gewrec, gewrecen, gewrecene, sceaf, sceof, scofen, scufan, scufeð, scufeþ, scufon, scufun, wræc, wræce, wræcon, wrec, wrecan, wrece, wrecen
exit	ofeode, ofgan, uton, utsiþ	experience	bidan, cunnian, cunnod, cunnode, dreag, dreah, dreogað, dreogan, dreogaþ, dreogeð, dreogeþ, dreoh, druge, drugon, gebad, gebidan, gebidanne, gebide, gebideð, gebiden, gebidenne, gebidenra, gebideþ, gebidon, gedrogen, onbyrigan, onfand, onfindan, onfond, onfunde, onfunden
exiting	hat, hatan, hate, hates, hatne, haton, hatost, hatran		
expanse	begang, begong, bigang, gelagu		
expansive	gerume, rum, rume, rumne, rumre, rumum		
expect	bad, basnedon, basnian, beodan, bidan, bideð, bideþ, bidon, gebad, gebide, gebiden, hopian, wen, wenað, wenan, wenaþ, wende, wendon, wene, weneð, weneþ		
		experienced	frod, gebideð
		expert-in-giving-praise	gilphlæden
		expire	arinnan, aurnen
		explain	asæde, asecgan
expectation	wen, wena, wenan, wenum	explanation	swutelung, swutelunge

Word List (English to Ænglisc)

English	Ænglisc	English	Ænglisc
explore	*cunnað, cunnade, cunnaþ, cunnedon, cunnian, cunnige, cunnod, cunnode, gecunnad, rasian, rasod*	extremely	*firenum, firnum, fyrenum, fyrnum, swiðlic, swiðlice, swiþlic, swiþlice, þearle, ungemete*
extend	*astreccan, astrece, astreht, aþenedon, aþenian, geræhte, geræhton, gestod, gestodon, læg, lægon, legen, licgan, raecan, ræhte, ræhton, romigan, standað, standan, standaþ, stande, standeð, standeþ, stod, stodan, stodon, stondað, stondan, stondaþ, stonde, stondeð, stondeþ, stynt*	exult	*ahliehhan, ahlog, ahloh, feon, gealp, gefægon, gefeah, gefegon, gefeh, gielpan, gulpon, gylpe*
		exultant	*hremge, hremig, hremige*
		eye	*eagan, eage, eagena, eagum, heafodsien, heafodsiene, heafodsyne*
		eyes	*eagum*
		eyesight	*heafodsien, heafodsiene, heafodsyne*

F, f

English	Ænglisc
extended	*andlang, andlong, andlongne, ondlang, ondlangne, ondlong, ondlonge*
extensive	*brad, bradan, brade, bradnæ, bradre, sid, sidan, side, sidne, sidra, sidre, widan, widbrad, widbradne, widgil, widgillan, widscofen*
extensive-kindred	*widfolc*
extensive-land	*widland, widlond*
extensively	*sid, side, wide*
extent	*begang, begong, bigang*
extol	*hered, herede, herian*
extravagant-treasure	*ofermaðm, ofermaðmum, ofermaþm, ofermaþmum*

English	Ænglisc
face	*andwlita, andwlitan, ansien, ansyn, ansyne, heafde, hleor, onsyn*
faceplate	*beadogrima, beadogriman*
face-protection	*hleorberg, hleorbergan*
face-protector	*grima, grimhelm, grimhelmas, grimmon, hleorberg, hleorbergan*
fades-away (Latin)	*abolescit*

Word List (English to Ænglisc)

English	Ænglisc	English	Ænglisc
fail	abreoðan, abreoðe, abreoþan, abreoþe, alæg, alicgan, alicgean, dreosan, dreoseð, dreoseþ, forbærst, forberstan, forborsten, gedreas, gedreosan, gedreoseð, gedreoseþ, gedroren, gedruron, geswiceð, gewac, teorað, teoraþ, wican	faithful-to-a-lord	þeoden, þeodenhold, þeodenholde, þeodenholdra
		faithless	ortrywe, untreowa, untreowe, wærleas
		fall	afeallan, afeallen, bedreosan, bedroren, bedrorene, befeallan, befeallen, befeallene, bidroren, bidrorene, cringan, dreosan, dreoseð, dreoseþ, feallan, feallen, feallende, fealleþ, feol, feoll, feollon, fyl, fyll, fylle, gecranc, gecringan, gecrungen, gecrungon, gedreas, gedreosan, gedreoseð, gedreoseþ, gedroren, gedruron, gefealleð, gefealleþ, gefeol, gefeoll, gesigan, hreas, hreosan, hreosende, hruron, hryre, sigan, sigeð, sigeþ, sigon
failing	dreorgiað		
fail-to-fulfil	aleh, aleogan		
fainting	swima, swiman		
fair	ambyr, fæger, fægere, fægerra, fægerum, fægir, fægran, fægre, fægroste, fegere, gefægra, godlecran, godlic, godlice		
fairer	fægerra		
fairly	fæger, fægere		
fairy	ælf, esa, os, ylfa, ylfe		
fairy-bright	Ælfrices, ælfsciene, ælfscieno, ælfscinu		
faith	geleafa, geleafan, leafa, treow, treowa, treowe, treowum		
		fall-asleep	onslæpan, onslæpen, onslep, onslepon
faithful	fæle, fæsthydig, fæsthydigne, getreowra, getrywe, hold, holde, holdne, holdost, holdra, trywe, wære, wærfæst, wærfæstne, wærfæstra	fall-dead	feallan, feallende, fealleþ, feol, feoll, feollon, gefealleð, gefealleþ, gefeol, gefeoll
		fallen	gedrorene, gehrorene
		fall-in-battle	crincgan, cringan, cruncon, crunge, crungon, gecranc, gecrang, gecrong, wighryre
faithfulness	higetreow, higetreowa		
faithful-or-obedient-to-the-Lord	drihtenhold		
		falling	ðriostre

Word List (English to *Ænglisc*)

English	*Ænglisc*	English	*Ænglisc*
fall-onto	feallan, feallende, fealleþ, feol, feoll, feollon, gefealleð, gefealleþ, gefeol, gefeoll	family	cinne, cneoris, cneorisn, cneoriss, cneorissa, cneorisse, cneorissum, cnosl, cnosle, cyn, cynn, cynna, cynne, cynnes, gemagas, had, hade, hades, hired, hus, husa, huse, huses, hyrde, hyred, hyredes, mæg, mægburg, mægburge, mægburh, mægum, maga, magas, magum
fallow	fealene		
fall-to	feallan, feallende, fealleþ, feol, feoll, feollon, gefealleð, gefealleþ, gefeol, gefeoll		
fall-upon	behreosan, bihrorene		
false			
false			
false			
false			
false		family-entitlement	folcriht, folcrihta
false		family-members	him, hina, hiwan, hiwum
false			
false		family-resemblance	magwlite
false		famine	hungor
falsehood	leasung, leasunga, ligen, ligenum, lygenum	famous	blædfæst, blædfæstne, breme, folcmære, folcmæro, gefræge, gefrægen, gefrægn, mæra, mæran, mære, mæres, mærne, mæro, mæron, mærost, mærra, mæru, mærum, tireadig, tireadigra, tireadigum, tirfæst, widcuðne, widcuþ, widcuþes, widcuþne
false-land	unland, unlonde		
falsely	leaslice		
falsely-accuse	forsæcgan		
fame	mærð, mærða, mærðe, mærðo, mærðu, mærþ, mærþa, mærþe, mærþo, mærþu, tiir, tir, tire, tires, tyr		
famed	tirfæst	famous-deed	lofdæd, lofdædum
fame-seeking	domgeorn, domgeorne	famous-exploit	mærð, mærða, mærðe, mærðo, mærðu, mærþ, mærþa, mærþe, mærþo, mærþu
		famous-for-victories	sigerof, sigerofe
		far	feor, feorr, feorran, feorres, fyr, fyrr, side, widdor, wide, widost, widre
		far-and-wide	wide, widlast, widlastum

Word List (English to Ænglisc)

English	Ænglisc	English	Ænglisc
far-apart	gewidost	father-before-him	ærfæder
fare	færde, færdon, færen, feran, ferde, ferdon, fere, ferende, gefare, geferde, geferdon, gefere, gefered, geferede, geferedon, geferian	father's	fæder
		father's-land	fædergeard, fædergeardum
		fault	facen, scylde
		faultless	æfæst, æfæste
		faults	facne, gyltum
		favour	ar, est, estum, giefu, hyldo, milts, miltse, miltsum, tið, tiðe, tiþ, tiþe
fares	fareð, fareþ		
far-flying-one	widfloga, widflogan		
far-from	feorres	favourable	ambyr, este, hold, hyðelic
far-lands	feorlondum		
far-off	feorran, feorren	fear	andraedan, ege, egesa, egesan, egesum, egsa, egsan, forhtian, murn, ondrædað, ondrædan, ondrædaþ, ondrædeþ, ondred, ondrede, ondredon, onegan, onsæton, onsite, onsittan
farther	furðor, furður, furþor, furþur		
farther-away	gerumlicor		
far-wandering	widlast, widlastum		
fast	fæst, fæste, fæstne, fæstor, fæstum		
fasten	befæstan, befæste, beluce, bifæstan, bifæste&th, fæste, fæstnian, feterian, gefæstnod, gefæstnodon, gefeterode, gelocen, gespeon, locenra, lucan, lucon, spannan, spenn	feared	forht
		fearful	andrysne, andrysnum, ondrysne
		feast	gebeorscipe, gereordum, symbel, symbla, symble, symle, wist
fastened	fæste, fæstum		
fastening	gebind, gespan, gespong, gesponne	feasting	fyll, fylle, swæsendu, swæsendum
fatal	onsæge		
fate	gescipe, meotodsceaft, meotudgesceaft, metodsceaft, metodsceafte, sið, siða, siðe, siðes, siþ, siþa, siþe, siþes, siþon, wyrd, wyrda, wyrde	feast-joy	symbelwynn, symbelwynne
		feast-wary	symbelwerig
		feather	feðer, feðera, feþer, feþera, feþra, fiþrum
		feather-arrow	fæðergearwe, fæðergearwum, fæþergearwe, fæþergearwum
fated	fæge		
fated-spirit	geosceaftgast, geosceaftgasta		
fates	wyrde		
father	fæder, feder		
father (Latin)	Patri		

Word List (English to Ænglisc)

English	Ænglisc	English	Ænglisc
feather-covering	feðerhama, feðerhaman, feðerhoma, feðerhoman, feþerhama, feþerhaman, feþerhoma, feþerhoman	fellow-Christian	gebroðor, gebroðra, gebroðrum, gebroþor, gebroþra, gebroþrum
		fellow-judge	gesætla, gesætlan
		fellow-monk	gebroðor, gebroðra, gebroðrum, gebroþor, gebroþra, gebroþrum
feather-home	feðerhama, feðerhaman, feðerhoma, feðerhoman, feþerhama, feþerhaman, feþerhoma, feþerhoman	female	fæmnan, fæmne, fæmnum, femnan
		female-accuser	wrægistre
		female-relative	mæge, magan, mage, mege
		female-sea-wolf	brimwylf
		female-servant	þeowen, þinen, þinene, þinenne, wyln
feathering	fæðergearwe, fæðergearwum, fæþergearwe, fæþergearwum	female-slave	þeowe, þeowen, þeowmennen, þeowra, wale
featherless	fiþerleas	feminine-relative	mæge
feeble	lef	fen	fen, fenn, fenne
feed	afedan, fed, fedað, fedan, fedaþ, feddan, fedde, feded, fedeþ	fen-cliff	fenhleoðu, fenhleoþu, fenhlið, fenhliþ
feed-a-hawk	lepeþ, leppan	fennel	finol
feel	felan, feleþ, gefele, gefeleð, gefeleþ	fen-passage	fengelad
		fen-path	fengelad
feels	gefele, gefeleð	fen-slope	fenhleoðu, fenhleoþu, fenhlið, fenhliþ
feign	bræd, brægd, bregdan, bregde, bregdon, broden, brogdne, brudon, brugdon, gebræd, gebroden	fertility	tuddorsped
		fervent	hat, hatan, hate, hates, hatne, haton, hatost, hatran
feigned-injury	ligetorn, ligetorne	fervid	hat
fell	feollan, fylde, fyllan, gecrong, gedreas, gefyldan, gefyllan, gesæged, gesælde, helle, sægan	festivity	plega
		fetch	feccende, fetigan, fetigean, fetod, gefæccan, gefætte, gefecgan, gefetian, gefetige
felled	befælled, befyllan, befylled, feol, gefylled	fetched	gefette
fell-in-battle	crungon, gecrang		

362

Word List (English to Ænglisc)

English	Ænglisc	English	Ænglisc
fetter	bend, bendum, clammum, clom, clomm, clommas, clomme, clommum, feter, feterian, feterum, fetor, gefeterode, gehæfte, gehæfted, gesæled, hæft, hæftan, lioðobend, lioðobendum, lioþobend, lioþobendum, sælan, sælde, sældon, sima?, simon, teag, teage, wælclomm, wælclommum, wriðon, wriþan, wriþon	fiendish-enemy	hellsceaða, hellsceaþa
		fiends	feondum
		fierce	afor, aglæcwif, cene, cenoste, cenra, cenre, galgmod, grædig, grædige, grim, grimlic, grimma, grimman, grimme, grimne, grimre, hreo, hreoh, hreon, hreoum, reðe, reðemode, reþe, reþemod, reþemode, wælhreow, wællgrim, wælreow, wælreowe, welhreowan
fetter-bound	æsæled	fierce-fighter	æglæca, aglæacan, aglæca, aglæcan, aglæcean, ahlæcan
fettering-ice	isgebind, isgebinde		
feud	fæghðe, fæghþe, fæhð, fæhða, fæhðe, fæhðo, fæhðu, fæhþ, fæhþa, fæhþe, fæhþo, fæhþu	fierce-in-battle	guðreouw, guþreouw
		fiercely	grimme, grymme
		fierce-minded	ferðe, ferðgrim, ferþe, ferþgrim
fever	feofor, feofore	fiery	fyren, fyrene, fyrnum
feverfew (tanacetum parthenium)	feferfuige	fifteen	fiftena, fiftine, fiftyno, fyftyne, XVna
few	fea, feara, feaum, lyt, lythwon	fifteenth	fifteoþa
		fifth	fifta
fewer	læssa, læssan	fiftieth	fiftigoþa
fidelity	treowa	fifty	fiftig, fiftiges
field	æcer, æcera, æceras, feld, felda, feldas, wang, wange, wong, wongas, wonge	fifty eight	eahta and fiftig
		fifty eighth	eahta and fiftigoþa
		fifty fifth	fif and fiftigoþa
		fifty first	an and fiftigoþa
		fifty five	fif and fiftig
fiend	feond, feonda, feondas, feonde, feondes, feondum, fiond, fionda, fynd	fifty four	feower and fiftig, feoþer and fiftig
		fifty fourth	feower and fiftigoþa
		fifty nine	nigon and fiftig
fiend-grip	feondgrap, feondgrapum	fifty ninth	nigon and fiftigoþa
		fifty one	an and fiftig
fiendish	deofolcund, deofolcunda	fifty second	twa and fiftigoþa
		fifty seven	seofon and fiftig
		fifty seventh	seofon and fiftigoþa

Word List (English to Ænglisc)

English	Ænglisc	English	Ænglisc
fifty six	siex and fiftig	filthy	unsyfra, unsyfre
fifty sixth	six and fiftigoþa	final-day	endedæg, endedogor, endedogores
fifty third	þreo and fiftigoþa		
fifty three	þri and fiftig		
fifty two	twegen and fiftig, tpegen and fiftig	final-remains	endelaf
		final-reward	endelean
fight	feaht, feoht, feohtan, feohte, flitan, flite, flitende, fohten, fuhton, gefeoht, gefeohtan, gefeohte, gefohten, gemot, gemotes, gewegan, gewunne, gewunnen, guðe, hearmplega, sacan, strið, striðe, striþ, striþe, tohtan, tohte, wan, wann, wigan, winnað, winnan, winnaþ, winnende, won, wonn, wunne, wunnon	find	fand, findað, findan, findaþ, findeð, findest, findeþ, fond, funde, funden, fundon, metan, meted, mette, onfand, onfindan, onfond, onfunde, onfunden
		find-out	afanda, afandian, ascian, axian, axoden, axude, cnawan, cunnað, cunnade, cunnaþ, cunnedon, cunnian, cunnige, cunnode, frægn, fricgan, fricgean, fricgean, fricgen, frige, frignan, frin, frinan, frineð, frineþ, geacsian, geahsod, geascodon, geaxode, gecnawan, gecnaweð, gecnaweþ, gecunnad, gefrægen, gefrægn, gefrægnod, gefricge, gefricgeað, gefricgean, gefricgeaþ, gefrugnon, gefrunen, gefrungon, gefrunon, geneosode, neosan, neosian, niosað, niosan, niosaþ, niosian, onfindan, onfond, onfunden, onfundon
fight-against	ætfeohtan		
fighter	cempa, cempan		
fighting	feaht, feohtan, fitt, fitte, fuhton, gefohten, handplega, handplegan, plega		
fighting-hand	beadufolm, beadufolme		
fighting-speech	beadurun, beadurune		
fights-for	campað		
figure	ansien, ansyn, ansyne, onsyn		
file	fel, fela		
file-hard	feolheard, feolhearde		
fill	afyllan, afylled, fylde, fyllað, fyllan, fyllaþ, gefyldan, gefylde, gefyllan, gefylle, gefylled, replete		
filled	fylde, gefylled		
filth	meox, widl, widle, widlum		

Word List (English to Ænglisc)

English	Ænglisc	English	Ænglisc
finger	finger, fingra, fingras, fingrum	first	ærest, æresta, aerist, æror, ærost, forane, forma, forman, furðum, furþum, fyrmest
finger-or-toe-nail	nægl, nægla, næglum		
finished	geara, geare, gearo, gearone, gearowe, gearu, gearwe	first-born-child	frumbearn, frumbearne
Finnsburgh (place)	Finnsburuh	first-creation	frumsceaft, frumsceafta, frumsceafte
fire	ad, ade, æld, aelda, æled, bæl, bæle, bel, brand, brond, bronda, brondas, bronde, bryne, fyr, fyre, fyres, leg, legdraca, lege, lig, ligas, ligdraca, lige, liges, ligge, swioðol, swioðole, swioþol, swioþole	fish	brimhlæst, brimhlæste, firum, fisc, fisca, fiscas, flota, flotan, geflota, geflotan
		fitting	gedefe, gemet, gerisne, gerysne, onriht, onrihtne, riht, rihtan, rihte, rihtne, rihtum
fire-dragon	fyrdraca		
fire-flame	fyrwylm, fyrwylmum	five	fif, fife
fire-forged-band	fyrbend, fyrbendum	flame	bæl, bæle, bel, brand, brond, bronda, brondas, bronde, leg, lege, lig, ligas, lige, liges, ligge, wælm, wælmes, witelocc, witeloccas, wylm, wylmas, wylme
fire-hardened	fyrheard		
fire-light	fyrleoht		
fire-lit	æledleoma, æledleoman		
fire-made	fyren, fyrene		
fire-sound	fyrgebræc		
fire-terror	ligegesa, ligegesan		
fire-wave	ligyð, ligyðum, ligyþ, ligyþum		
		flames	sweoloð, sweoloðe, sweoloþ, sweoloþe
firm	anhydig, fæst, fæste, fæstne, fæstum, heardræd, heardrædne, me, meaglum, meagol, trum, trumne	flaming	fyren, fyrene
		flaming-hot	wylmhat, wylmhatne
		flatter	oleccan
		flattery	olecung, olecunge
		flee	fleag, fleah, fleogan, fleogeð, fleogende, fleogeþ, fleoh, fleon, fleonde, flogen, flugon, scacan, scacen, scæcen, sceacan, sceaceð, sceacen, sceaceþ, sceoc, scoc
firmament	rode, rodera, roderas, roderum, rodor, rodora, rodores		
firm-gripped	heardgripe		
firmly	eornoste, fæste, fæstlice, fæstor, hearde, stiðlice, stiþlice		
		flee-from	befleon, forbeah, forbogen, forbugan, forbugon, oferfleon
firmly-attached	fæst, fæste, fæstne, fæstum		
		fleeing	fleon

Word List (English to *Ænglisc*)

English	*Ænglisc*	English	*Ænglisc*
fleet	*flothere, flotherge, sciphere, scipherge*	flow	*feallan, feallen, feoll, feollon, feran, flowan, flowende, gang, gange, ganges, geotan, geotena, geotende, getan, ryne*
flesh	*flæsc, flæsce, flæsces, flæschoma, flæschoman, lic-homa*		
flesh (Latin)	*Carnis*		
flex-take-oneself	*gewende*	flow-about	*beflowan, beflowen*
flight	*fleam, fleame, fliht, flihte, flyht, flying*	flowing	*flowan*
		flown	*fleoh*
flightless	*fiþerleas*	flows-about	*beflowen*
flinch	*wandian, wandode*	flow-under	*underflowan, underflowen*
float	*fleat, fleotan, fleotende, gerad, rad, ridan, ride, rideð, rideþ, riodan*	fly	*fleag, fleah, fleogan, fleogeð, fleogende, fleogeþ, fleoh, flogen, flugon, gewand, lacan, laceð, lacende, laceþ, leolc, scio, scion, swang, swimmað, swimman, swimmaþ, swingan, swingeð, swingeþ, swyltit, swymman, wand, windan, wunde, wunden, wundnum, wundon*
floater	*fleotend, fleotendra, flota, flotan, geflota, geflotan*		
flocking	*wornas*		
flood	*beswyled, beswylian, drenceflod, egorhere, flod, floda, flodas, flode, flodes, heahflod, sæflod*		
flood-current	*egorstream, egorstreamas*		
flooded	*inflede*	fly-from	*fleon, fleonde*
flood-grey	*flodgræg*	flying	*fleogeð, fleogende*
floor	*flor, flore, syll, sylle*	flying-joy	*lyftwynn, lyftwynne*
floozy	*myltestre*	flying-molester	*lyftsceaþa, lyftsceaþan*
flour	*melo*		
flourish	*greow, growan, growende, growendra, wridað, wridade, wridan, wriðan, wridaþ, wriðende, wridendra, wridian, wriðian, wriþade, wriþan, wriþende, wriþian*	flying-thing	*lyftfloga*
		fly-net	*fleohnet*
		foam	*fam*
		foam-covered	*famig, famige*
		foamy	*famig, famige*
		foamy-prowed	*famigheals, famiheals*
		fodder	*fodder, fodre, fodres*
		foes	*laðra*
		fold	*befealdan, befealdest, fealdan, feoldan*
		folk	*folc, folca, folce, folces, folkes, follc*

Word List (English to Ænglisc)

English	Ænglisc	English	Ænglisc
folk-child	folcbearn, folcbearnum	food	æs, æse, æses, æt, æte, ætes, ætwist, andlifen, andlifne, anleofan, beodgereordu, feorm, feorme, fodder, foddor, fodre, fodres, mete, metes, nest, wist, wiste
folk-king	folccyning, folccyningas, folccyninge		
folk-multitude	folcdriht		
folk-queen	folccwen		
folk-ruler	folca, folcagend, folcagende		
folk-stead	folcstede		
folk-woman	folccwen	food-fill	wistfylle, wistfyllo
follow	æfterfylgan, folgedon, folgian, folgod, folgode, fylgan, fylgde, fylgean, fylian, fyligan, gelæst, gelæstan, gelæste, gelæston, læst, læstan, læste, læsten, læstes	food-full	wistfylle, wistfyllo
		food-giver	æt-gifa
		food-lack	metelist, meteliste
		food-strong	meteþiht, meteþihtan
		foolish	dol, dole, dollic, dollicra, dysig, hygeleas, hygelease, rædleas, rædlease
follow-a-scent	stincan, stonc	foolish-boast	dolgilp, dolgilpe
follower	gefara, gesið, gesiða, gesiðas, gesiððas, gesiððe, gesiðes, gesiðum, gesiþ, gesiþa, gesiþas, gesiþes, gesiþþas, gesiþþe, gesiþum, lastweard	foolishly	dollice
		foolishness	unsnyttru, unsnyttrum
		foot	fet, fot, fote, fotes, fotum
		foot-battle	feðewig, feðewiges, feþewig, feþewiges
		footless	feðeleas, feþeleas
followers	folgeras	foot-measure	fotgemearc, fotgemearces, fotmæl
following	folgað		
folly	dol, dole, gahwem, gal, galscipe, gedwild, gedwilde, gedwyld, gedwylde, hygeleast, hygeleaste, unræd, unræde, unræden, unrædes	footpath	feðelast, feðelaste, feþelast, feþelaste, feþelastum
		footprint	læste, last, lastas, laste, lastum, trode, trodu
		foot-soldier	feða, feðan, feþa, feþan
		footstep	feðelast, feðelaste, feþelast, feþelaste, feþelastum, swaðe, swaðu, swaþe, swaþu
		for	æfter, bi, for, forðan, fore, forþon, þurh, til, to, toweard

Word List (English to Ænglisc)

English	Ænglisc	English	Ænglisc
for-a-long-distance	rume, rumor	forest-streams	firgenstreamas
for-a-long-time	lange, leng, lengest, longe, rume, rumor	forest-stronghold	wudufæsten
		forest-track	waldswæþ, waldswaþum
for-a-time	hwile, þrage		
forbid	forbead, forbeodan, forbodene	forest-tree	wudubeam, wudubeame, wudubeames
force	ðrym, fysan, fysde, gefysed, genydde, genyded, geþræc, nede, niða, nydan, strengðo, strengþo, þrym, þrymm, þrymmas, wræc, wræcon, wrecan, wrecen	foretell	bodedon, bodian, bodode
		forethought	foreþanc
		forever	æfre, symle, wideferhð, wideferhþ
		for-ever	awa
		forge	geslægene, geslegene, gesloh, slægen, slea, sleah, slean, slog, sloge, slogon, sloh
forcefully	unwaclice		
ford	ford, forð, forda, forþ		
fore-arm	eln, elna		
forefather	ærfæder, ealdfæder		
foreign	elðeodig, elðeodigra, ellðeodigra, ellþeodig, ellþeodigne, ellþeodigra, elþeodig, elþeodige, elþeodigra, fremde, fremdes, fremdu, fremdum, wælisc, wælisca	forged	geþruen
		forget	forgeate, forgeton, forgietan, forgyteð, forgyteþ, ofergeaton, ofergietan
		forgetfulness	æminde
		forgive	alætan, alæte
		forgo	ðoliaþ, ðolode, geþolian, geþolianne, geþolode, þolað, þolaþ, þoledon, þoliað, þolian, þoliaþ, þolien, þoligende, þolodan, þolode
foreign-army	ælfylce, ælfylcum		
foreign-country	wealand, wealandum		
foreigner	feorbuend		
foreigners	elðeod, elðeoda, elþeod, elþeoda, elþeode		
		for-his	him
foreign-land	elland	forlorn	gesne
foreign-nation	elðeod, elðeoda, elþeod, elþeoda, elþeode	for-lose	forleos, forleosan
		form	anlicnes, anlicnesse, anlycnysse, bisen, bisne, gesceap, gesceapo, gesceapu, hiw, hiwe, wyrcan
foremost	fyrmest		
foreordination	geosceaft		
forest	holt, holte, holtes, holtwudu, wald, walde, weald, wealdas, wealde, wuda, wudu		
forest-fruit	wudubledum		

Word List (English to Ænglisc)

English	Ænglisc	English	Ænglisc
formal-utterance	meðelword, meðelwordum, meþelword, meþelwordum	fort-or-castle	burhwela, burhwelan
formed	mærra	fortress	burhfæsten, burhloca, burhlocan, ceastre
for-men	firum	fortress-gate	fæstengeat, fæstengeates
former	ærra, ærran		
former-day	geardæg, geardagum	forty	feowertig, feopertig, XL
former-days	ærdagum	forty eight	eahta and feowertig, eahta and feopertig
former-good	ærgod		
former-grace	ærglad, ærglade	forty eighth	eahta and feowertigoþa
former-lord	iuwine		
formerly	ær, æror, ærur, fyrn, geara, gefyrn, geo, gio, iogoþe, iu	forty fifth	fif and feowertigoþa
		forty first	an and feowertigoþa
		forty five	fif and feowertig, fif and feopertig
former-strife	fyrngeflit, fyrngeflitu		
former-struggle	aergewin	forty four	feower and feowertig, feoper and feopertig
former-transgression	ealdgewyrht, ealdgewyrhtum		
former-treasure	ærgestreon	forty fourth	feower and feowertigoþa
former-work	ærgeweorc		
fornication	forliger, forligre, forlygre, forlyres, hæmed, hæmede	forty nine	nigon and feowertig, nigon and feopertig
		forty ninth	nigon and feowertigoþa
forsake	forhealdan, forhealden, forhealdene, wiðsacan, wiðsace, wiþsacan, wiþsace	forty one	an and feowertig, an and feopertig
		forty second	twa and feowertigoþa
for-surrendering	forbugan	forty seven	seofon and feowertig, seofon and feopertig
fort	burg, burga, burgum, burh, burhfæsten, burhstede, byrig, ceaster, ceastra, ceastre, ceastrum		
		forty seventh	seofon and feowertigoþa
		forty six	siex and feowertig, siex and feopertig
forth	forð, forþ, fram, from, geforðad, to	forty sixth	six and feowertigoþa
		forty third	þreo and feowertigoþa
for-that	Forþon		
for-that-reason	forðam, forðan, forðon, forþam, forþan, forþon, since, þæs, þæsas, þy	forty three	þri and feowertig, þri and feopertig
		forty two	twegen and feowertig, tpegen and feopertig
for-the-sake-of	ðurh, þurh, þuruh	forward	forð
fortieth	feowertigoþa	forwards	forð, forþ, gegnum, wið, wiþ
fortified-dwelling	weallfæsten, weallfæstenna	for-what-reason	hwi, hwy

Word List (English to Ænglisc)

English	Ænglisc	English	Ænglisc
foster-child	fostercyld	frequently	gelome, oft, oftor, oftost, rume, rumor
fought	fuhton		
foul	ful, fula, fulan, fule, fullum	fresh	fersc, niowan, nitor, niwan, niwe, niwes, niwra, niwre
found	funde, gestaþelað, gestaþelade, gestaþelaþ, gestaþelode, onfond, staðelian, staþelian	friend	freond, freonda, freondas, freondum, frynd, gehola, wina, winas, wine, wines, winia, winigea, winum
found (Latin)	inuenta		
foundation	gesettest, gesteal, staðol, staðolas, staðole, staþel, staþelum, staþol, staþolas, staþole, wealsteal	friend-and-lord	winedrihten, winedrihtne, winedryhten, winedryhtnes
		friend-in-battle	guðwine, guðwinum, guþwine, guþwinum
founder	fruma, fruman	friend-kinsman	wine-mæg
found-out	geascodan	friendless	freondleas, freondleasne, wineleas, wineleasum
four	feower, feoþer, feowera		
fourteen	feowertine, feoþertine, feowertyne	friend-less	freond-leas, wineleas
fourteenth	feowerteoþa	friendliness	sybcwide
fourth	feorða, feorðan, feorðe, feorþa, feorþan, feorþe	friend-lord	wine-dryhten
		friendly	gesome, som
		friendly-advice	freondlar, freondlarum
fowl	fugla		
fragrance	stenc	friendly-lord	freawine
frailty	wace	friendly-male-relative	mægwine, mægwinum
fratricide	broðorcwealm, broðorcwealmes, broþorcwealm, broþorcwealmes	friend-needing	wineþearfende
		friends	freonda, frind, Frynd, wine
free	freo, freolic, freom, freomæg, freomægum, freomagum, freomann, freomanna, freomen, freora	friendship	freondlaþu, freondlufu, freondscipe, freondscype, siae, sib, sibb, sibbe, sibblufan, sibblufu, siblufan, siblufu, sybbe
freedom	freodom		
free-for-the-taking	lænan, læne, lænes, lænum	friendship-promise	winetreow, winetreowe
free-from-evil	unmæne	friendship-token	luftacen
free-man	ceorl, ceorlas, ceorle, ceorles		
freezing	freorig		

Word List (English to Ænglisc)

English	Ænglisc	English	Ænglisc
frighten	afyrhtan, afyrhte, egesian, egsode, ondrædað, ondrædan, ondrædaþ, ondrædeþ, ondred, ondrede, ondredon	frost-covered	hrinde
		frostiest	hrimigost
		frost-over	behriman, behrimed
		frosty	hrim-ceald
		frosty-cold	hrimceald, hrimcealde
		frugal	gneað, gneaþ
frightened	anforht, forht	fruit	æple, æppel, blado, blæd, blæda, blædæ, blædu, ofæt, ofætes, ofet, ofetes, wæstm, wæstma, wæstmas, wæstme, wæstmes, wæstmum, wæstum, westem
frightening	egeslic, egeslican		
from	a, æt, fram, from, heonan, of, þon, þurh, to, wiþ		
from (Latin)	a, ab		
from-a-distant-country	feorrancund, feorrancundum		
from-afar	feor, feorr, feorran, feorren, fyr, fyrr	fruits	wæstm
from-behind	herefleman	fulfil	dreag, dreah, dreogað, dreogan, dreogaþ, dreogeð, dreogeþ, dreoh, druge, drugon, fulgangan, fullian, fylde, fyllað, fyllan, fyllaþ, gedrogen, gefelled, gefyldan, gefylde, gefyllan, gefylle, gefylled
from-here	heolstre, heonan, heonane, heonengange, heonon, heonone		
from-here-goes	heonengange, hiniongae, hinionge		
from-kin	frumcyn		
from-nearby	nean, neon		
from-now-on	forð, forþ		
from-the-east	east, eastan, easten		
from-then-on	forð, forðwearde, forþ, forþwearde	full	ful, full, fulle, fullum, fulne
from-the-north	norð, norðan, norþ, norþan	full (Latin)	pleno
		fullness	fulle, fyll, fylle
from-there	ðanon, ðon, ðonan, ðonne, ðonon, þan, þanan, þanon, þanonne, þon, þonan, þonne, þonon	full-of-hardship	nearu
		fully	ful, fylle
		fully-born-one	fulborenum
		fumes	wælrec
		fun	gleodream
		funeral-procession	adfære
from-the-south	suð, suðan, suðon, suþ, suþan, suþon	funeral-pyre	adfære, adfaru, bæl
		furious	reoc
from-the-west	west, westan	furrow	furh
from-time-to-time	stundum		
from-where	hwanan, hwanon		
front	ord, orde		
front-of-troop-fighter	ord, orde		
front-step	stapol, stapole, stapulum		
frost	forst, forste, forstes, hrim		

Word List (English to Ænglisc)

English	Ænglisc	English	Ænglisc
further	fremeð, fremede, fremedon, fremest, fremeþ, fremmað, fremman, fremmaþ, fremme, fremmen, furðor, furður, furþor, furþur, fyrðran, fyrþran, gefremed, gefremede, gefremeden, gefremedon, gefremman, gefremmanne, gefyrðred, gefyrþred, gen	gangplank	bolca, bolcan
		gannet	ganet, ganetes, ganot, ganotes
		garden-bed	bed, bedd, bedde, beddes, beddum
		garment	hama, haman, hrægl, hrægla, hrægle, hrægles, sceat, sceata, sceatas, sceate, sceatt, sceatta, sceattum, sceatum, wæd, wæda, wædo, wædum, wedum
		garnished	gewlitegod
		garrulous-drunk	ealowosa, ealowosan
future	forðweard, forðweardum, forþweard, forþweardum, toweard, toweardan	Garulf (name)	Garulf
		gate	geat
		gate-in-a-wall	wealgat, wealgate
		gather	gaderian, gegaderie
		gave	geaf, gesealde, gyfe, sealdest
		gaze	starað, staraþ, starede, staredon, starian, starie, starige, wlat, wlitað, wlitan, wlitaþ, wliten, wlitest, wliton

G, g

English	Ænglisc	English	Ænglisc
gabled-building	hornreced		
gabled-hall	hornsele		
Gabriel (name)	Gabriel		
gain	gewunne, gewunnen, ræd, ræda, rædas, ræde, wan, wann, winnað, winnan, winnaþ, winnende, won, wonn, wunne, wunnon	gaze-at	onhawian, onhawoden
		gaze-on	locast, lociað, locian, lociaþ
		gaze-upon	behealdan, beheold, beheoldon
gallop	ærnan, ærndon, gehleop, hleapan, hleapeð, hleapeþ	gear	geare
		Geatish-man	Geatmæcgum, Geatmecga
gallows	galga, galgan, gealga, gealgan	Geats	Geates
		gem	gim, gimm, gimmas, sigel, siglu
gallows-like	galgmod		
gallows-tree	galgtreow, galgtreowum, gealgtreow, gealgtreowe	gender	had, hade, hades
		general	ealdorþegn, ealdorþegnum, gemæne, gemænra, gemænum
game-board	bleobord, bleobordes	generally	sid
gaming-table	bleobord, bleobordes	generations	cnea
		generosity	beaggyfu

372

Word List (English to Ænglisc)

English	Ænglisc	English	Ænglisc
generous	gimfæst, gimfæste, ginfæst, ginfæstan, ginfæstum, hold, holde, holdne, holdost, holdra	ghost	gæst, gæsta, gæste, gæstes, gast, gasta, gastae, gastas, gaste, gastes, scinn, scinna, scinnum
genitalia	gesceap, gesceapo, gesceapu	ghost-from-elsewhere	ellorgæst, ellorgast
genitals	sceome, scomu	ghostly	gæstlic, gastlic
gentle	milde, mildum, mildust, monðwære, monðwærust, monþwære, monþwærust	ghostly-or-magical-enemy	scynscaþa
		giant	ent, enta, eoten, eotena, eotenas, gigant, giganta, gigantas, gigantmæcg, gigantmæcgas, þyrs
gentleness	liþnes, liþnesse		
gently	seft, soðum, softe, soþum		
Germanic-pagan-god	esa, os	giant-kin	fife, fifelcynn, fifelcynnes
get	begeat, begeate, begeaton, beget, begietan, begieten, begytan, bicgan, bigeat, bycgan, gebohte, gehleat, geræcan, geræhte, geræhton, gestrynan, gestrynde, hloat, hleotan, raecan, ræhte, ræhton, strynan, strynde, stryndon	giant-made	entisc, entiscne, eotenisc, etonisc
		giants	enta, gigantas
		giants'	enta
		gift	geofena, geofian, geofum, giefu, gifa, gife, gifena, gifsceatt, gifsceattas, giftum, gifu, gifum, læn, tið, tiðe, tiþ, tiþe
		gift-dispensing-hall	gifstol
		gift-hall	gifheall, gifhealle
		Gifthas (a-Germanic-people)	Gifðum, Gifþum
get-by-calling	ofclipian, ofclypode		
get-by-fighting	geslean, geslogon, gesloh	gift-seat	giefstol, giefstolas, gifstol
get-drunk	blissian, blissigende, geblissad	gigantic	entisc, entiscne, eotenisc, etonisc
get-in-exchange	bicgan, bycgan, gebohte	gilded	geldenne, goldfag, goldfah, goldfahne, gylden, gyldenne, gyldnum
get-in-front-of	for-faran, for-faren, for-for, for-foron		
get-onto	gestah, gestigest, stah, stigan, stige, stigon	gilded-city	goldburg, goldburgum
		gilt	geldenne, gylden, gyldenne, gyldnum
get-through	ðurhfon, þurhfon		
ghastly	gæstlic, gastlic	girded	gyrdan, gyrded

Word List (English to *Ænglisc*)

English	*Ænglisc*	English	*Ænglisc*
girl	mæden, mædene, mægð, mægða, mægðum, mægeð, mægeþ, mægþ, mægþa, mægþum	given	geafon, giefe, gifeðe, gifu
		give-names-to	cende, cennað, cennan, cennaþ, cenned
give	ætbær, ætbæron, ætberan, ætgifan, ageaf, ageafe, ageafon, agiefan, agif, agifan, agifen, agyfe, agyfen, bead, beodan, beodeð, beodeþ, biodan, boden, bude, budon, forgeaf, forgeafe, forgeafon, forgefe, forgiefan, forgiefen, forgiefene, forgif, forgifan, forgifð, forgifen, forgifþ, geaf, geafon, gebad, gebead, gebeodan, geræhte, geræhton, geseald, gesealde, gesealdon, gesellan, gesylle, getiðad, getigðode, getigþode, getiþad, gief, giefað, giefaþ, gifan, gife, gifeðe, gifen, gifest, gifeþe, gifu, giofan	give-out	brytnade, brytnian
		give-property-to	gegododon, godes, godian
		giver	brytta, bryttan, gifa, sellend
		give-up	ageaf, ageafe, ageafon, agiefan, agif, agifan, agifen, agyfe, agyfen, alætan, alæte, geseald, gesealde, gesealdon, gesellan, gesylle, gife, gifeðe, gifen, gifeþe, gyf, gyfen, gyfeþe, ofgæfon, ofgeaf, ofgeafon, ofgeafun, ofgefan, ofgiefan, ofgif, ofgifan, ofgifen, ofgyfan, sealde, sealdest, sealdon, seleð, seleþ, selle, syleð, syleþ, syllað, syllan, syllaþ, sylle, syllon
		give-worthiness-to	geweorðad, geweorðan, geweorðod, geweorþad, geweorþan, geweorþod, gewurþad
give-birth-to	ac, acende, acennan, acenned, astrienan, astrynde, bær, bæran, bæron, berað, beran, beraþ, bere, bereð, beren, bereþ, beron, bireð, bireþ, byreð, byreþ, cende, cennað, cennan, cennaþ, cenned, fed, fedað, fedan, fedaþ, feddan, fedde, feded, fedeþ, gebær, geboren	giving	gifu
		glad	fægen, fægne
		gladden	aretan, areted
		glad-hearted	bliðheort, bliþheort
		gladly	georne, geornlice, geornor, lustum
		gladness	dream, dreama, dreamas, dreame, dreames, dreamum
give-counsel	rædan	gleam	blican, blicð, blicon, blicþ

Word List (English to Ænglisc)

English	Ænglisc	English	Ænglisc
glide	*glad, glidan, glidon, scriðan, scriþað, scriþan, scriþaþ*	glorious-king	*cyningwuldor, kyningwuldor, wuldorcining, wuldorcyning, wuldorcyninge, wuldorcyninges, wuldurcyninge*
glided	*glad*		
glint	*glitinian*		
gloomy	*deorc, deorcan, deorce, deorcum, dim, dimman, dimme, galgmod, sweorcendferhð, sweorcendferhðe, sweorcendferhþ, sweorcendferhþe, þeostre, þeostrum, þystre*	gloriously	*domlice, fægere, mærlice*
		gloriously-bright	*wuldortorht, wuldortorhtan*
		glorious-prosperity	*wuldorsped, wuldorspedum*
		glorious-spirit	*wuldorgast*
		glorious-success	*wuldorsped, wuldorspedum*
glories	*þrymmas*		
glorify	*dyrsian, gedyrsod, mærað, mæran, mæraþ, mærsian, mærsigende*	glory	*blæd, blæde, blædes, bledum, dom, domas, dome, domę, domes, ðrym, dugeða, dugeðe, dugeðum, dugeþa, dugeþe, dugeþum, dugoða, dugoðe, dugoþa, dugoþe, duguð, duguða, duguðe, duguðum, duguþ, duguþa, duguþe, duguþum, hehðe, hehðu, hehþe, hehþu, hreð, hreþ, lof, lofe, þrym, þrymm, þrymmas, tiir, tir, tire, tires, tyr, uuuldor, weorðmynd, weorþmynd, wuldor, wuldre, wuldres, wuldris*
glorious	*blædagande, blædfæst, blædfæstne, brema, breman, breme, domę, domeadig, freolecu, freolic, freolice, freolico, freolicu, freolucu, lofsum, mære, þrymfæst, þrymfæste, þrymfæstne, þrymlic, tireadge, tireadig, tireadigra, tireadigum, tirfæst, tirfæste, torhtmod, tyreadig, wuldorfæder, wuldorfæst, wuldorfæstan, wuldorfæstne*		
		glory (Latin)	*Gloria*
		glory-desirous	*dom-georn*
glorious-day	*blæddæg, blæddaga*	glory-fastened	*tirfæste*
glorious-dwelling	*wuldorgesteald, wuldorgestealdum*	glory-father	*uuldurfadur, uuuldorfæder, wuldorfæder, wuldurfadur*
glorious-fame	*wuldor, wuldorblæd*		
glorious-gift	*wuldorgyfa, wuldorgyfe*		

Word List (English to Ænglisc)

English	Ænglisc	English	Ænglisc
glory-king	*wuldorcining, wuldorcyning, wuldorcyninge, wuldorcyninges, wuldurcyninge*	go-blind	*forsæt, forsæton, forsiteð, forsiteþ, forsittan, forsweorcan, forsworceð, forsworceþ*
glove	*glof*		
glowing	*byrnende*	go-by	*agangan, agangen, agongen*
glowing-coal	*brand, brond, bronda, brondas, bronde, gled, gledum, yslan, ysle*	god	*ælmihtiga, god, gode*
		God (Latin)	*deum*
glowing-coals	*glædstede, gledstyde*	God (name)	*god, gode*
		goddess	*gydenan, gydene*
glowing-embers	*gledegesa*	God-heathen	*god, godas, gode, godes, godum*
gnash-one's-teeth	*gristbitian*		
go	*agangan, agangen, agongen, eode, eodon, eowde, færde, færdon, færeð, færen, færeþ, far, farað, faran, faraþ, fare, fareð, faren, fareþ, feran, ferde, ferdon, fere, fered, ferede, feredon, ferende, fergað, fergaþ, ferian, ferigeað, ferigeaþ, ferode, for, foran, foron, fundað, fundast, fundaþ, funde, fundedon, fundian, fundiaþ, fundode, fyredon, ga, gað, gæð, gæþ, gan, gang, gangænde, gangan, gange, gange, gangende, ganges, gangon, gaþ, geeode*	God-heathen's	*godes*
		godlike	*godlic*
		gods	*goda, godas*
		God's (name)	*godes*
		godson	*godsunu*
		God-the-Father	*heahfæder, heahfædere*
		Godwin (name)	*Godwine*
		goes	*ga, gad, gæð, gæst, gæsta, gæþ, gewiteþ*
		goes-to	*wendeþ*
		go-forth	*forð-feran, forð-ferde, forð-fered, forþ-feran, forþ-ferde, forþ-fered*
		going	*fare, faru, feðe, feþe, for, fore, gang, gangan, gange, ganges, gegangan, gegangeð, gegangeþ, gegongeð, gegongen, gegongeþ, geong, gewiteð, hwyrft, hwyrftum*
go-away	*togengan, togengdon*	going-away	*heononweard*
goblin	*ælf, ylfa, ylfe*	gold	*geald, gold, golde, goldes*
		gold-adorned	*goldbeorht*
		golden	*geldenne, gylden, gyldenne, gyldnum*
		golden-belongings	*goldæht*

Word List (English to Ænglisc)

English	Ænglisc	English	Ænglisc
golden-hilt	fealohilte, gyldenhilt	good-conduct	siodo
golden-treasure	goldmaðm, goldmaðmas, goldmaþm, goldmaþmas	good-doer	godes, godfremmend, godfremmendra
		good-father	godfæder
gold-friend	goldwine, gold-wine	good-from-old-times	ærgod
gold-giver	goldgiefa, goldgiefan, goldgifa, goldgifan, goldgyfa, goldgyfan	good-in-former-times	ærgod
		goodly	godlecran, godlic, godlice
gold-giving	goldwine	goodness	godnys, godnysse
gold-guardian	goldweard	good-one	goda, godan, goddre, gode, godne, godra, godum
gold-hall	goldsele		
gold-laden	goldhladen		
gold-lord	goldweard		
gold-ornament	fæt, fætt, fættum, fætum	good-or-desired-flood	willflod
gold-plate	fæt, fætt, fættum, fætum	good-renowned	dædrof
		goods	ceap, ceapas, ceape, duguðe, duguþe, feoh, feorm, feorme, god, goda, godan, gode, godes, godne, godra, godum
gold-proud	goldwlanc		
goldsmith	goldsmiþe, goldsmiþu		
good	deah, dohte, dohtest, dugan, duge, fægere, gedefe, god, goda, godaes, godan, gode, godes, godne, godra, godum, good, goodes, hælo, sel, selest, selesta, selestan, seleste, sella, sellan, selost, selra, selran, selre, syllan, til, tile, till, tilmodig, tilmodigne, tilne, tilra, tilu		
		good-sisters	willgesweostor
		good-thing	god, goda, godan, gode, godes, godne, godra, godum
		good-will	freod, freode
		goose	ganot
		go-out-of	ofeode, ofgan
		go-over	oferfaran, oferforan
		go-quickly	efstan, efste, efston, scio, scion
		gore	dreor, dreore, gewende, heolfor, heolfre
good-brothers	willgebroðor, willgebroþor		
		gory	heolfrig
good-companion	willgeðofta, willgeðoftan, willgesiðða, willgesiððas, willgesiþþa, willgesiþþas, willgestealla, willgesteallum, willgeþofta, willgeþoftan	Goth-land	Got-land
		go-through	ðurhwod, þurhwadan, þurhwod

Word List (English to *Ænglisc*)

English	*Ænglisc*	English	*Ænglisc*
go-to	æthwearf, æthweorfan, gesec, gesecan, gesecanne, gesece, gesecean, geseceð, geseceþ, gesohtan, gesohte, gesohtest, gesohton, sec, secan, sece, seceað, secean, seceaþ, seceð, secen, secest, seceþ, sohtan, sohte, sohten, sohtest, sohton	grant	ageaf, ageafe, ageafon, agiefan, agif, agifan, agifen, agyfe, agyfen, alyfan, alyfde, alyfed, an, ann, bead, beodan, beodeð, beodeþ, biodan, boden, bude, budon, forgeaf, forgeafe, forgeafon, forgefe, forgiefan, forgiefen, forgiefene, forgif, forgifan, forgifð, forgifen, forgifþ, gebad, gebead, gebeodan, geliefan, geliefde, geliefed, geteah, geteoh, getiðad, getigðode, getigþode, getiþad, getogen, geuðe, geunnan, geunne, geuþe, gife, gifeðe, gifen, gifeþe, gyf, gyfen, gyfeþe, lænan, lifan
govern	gewealdan, gewealdene, gewealdenne, geweold, geweoldum, wealdan, wealde, weold, weoldon		
governor	wealdend		
grace	are, bletsung, bletsunga, bletsunge, ðanc, est, estum, geofena, geofum, giefu, gifa, gife, gifena, gifu, gifum, hyldo, liðsa, liðsum, liss, lissa, lisse, lissum, liþsa, liþsum, þanc	granted	gifeðe, gifeþe, gyfeðe, gyfeþe, læne, onlag, onlah, onleah, onleon
		granted-for-a-long-time	langtwidig
gracious	bilwit, este, estig, glædman, hold, holde, holdne, holdost, holdra, liðe, liðost, liofwendum, liþe, liþost	grapple-with	wiðfeng, wiðfon, wiðgripan, wiþfeng, wiþfon, wiþgripan
		grappling-with	ætgræpe
grain	corn, corna		
grandfather	ealdafæder		

Word List (English to Ænglisc)

English	Ænglisc	English	Ænglisc
grasp	clammum, clom, clomm, clommas, clomme, clommum, fæðm, fæðme, fæðmum, fæng, fæþm, fæþme, fæþmum, fehð, fehþ, feng, fenge, fengon, fon, gefeng, gegrap, gegripon, grap, grape, grapian, grapode, grapum, gripan, gripe, gripeð, gripen, gripeþ, gripon, ongeat, ongeaton, ongietan, ongieten	great	great, greate, ma, maran, miccla, micel, micela, micelan, micla, miclan, mycel, rice, swiþe, unlytel, unlytle
		greater	mara, maran, mare
		great-glory	heahþrymnesse
		great-king	brytencyning, brytencyninges
		greatly	hearde, mæst, mæsta, mæste, mæstne, miccle, miccles, micclum, miceles, micelne, micle, micles, miclum, mycclum, mycelre, mycle, myclum, swiðlic, swiðlice, swiþe, swiþlic, swiþlice, þearle
grasping	ætgræpe		
grass	græs		
grass-covered	græsmoldan		
grass-covered-earth	græsmoldan, græsmolde		
gratify	cweman, gecwæman, gecwæmde	great-sorrow	aldorceare, aldorcearu, sinsorg, sinsorgna
grave	birgenne, byrgen, byrgenne, eorðscræf, eorðscrafa, eorðscrafu, eorþscræf, eorþscrafa, eorþscrafu, gebyrgenne, græf, leger, legerbedd, legerbedde, legere, moldern, styrne, wælbedd, wælbedde, wælrest, wælreste	great-treasure	eormenlaf, eormenlafe
		greedily	grædigne
		greedy	frec, frece, gifre, gifrost, grædig, grædige
		greedy-for-carrion	wælgifre, wælgifru, wælgifrum
		greedy-for-property	feohgifre
		green	grenan, grene, grenes, grenne, grenre
		greet	gegrettan, gegrette, gretan, greted, greteð, greteþ, grette, gretton
gravel	greot, greote		
graveyard	hlæw, hlæwe, hlaw, hlawe	grew	weox
graze	ettan, etted, ettede	grey	fealone, fealu, fealwe, græg, grægan, græge, har, hara, hare, hares, harne, harum, hasu, haswe

Word List (English to Ænglisc)

English	Ænglisc	English	Ænglisc
grey-coat	græghama	ground	foldan, folde, geard, geardas, geardum, grund, grundas, grunde, grundes, hrusan, hruse, næs, næss
grey-hair	blondenfeax, blondenfeaxe, blondenfeaxum, blondenfexa		
grey-haired	gamolfeax, gomelfeax, har	ground-bottom	grundwong
grey-in-colour	grægmæl	ground-down	giungne
grey-marked	grægmæl	ground-sharp	mylenscearpan
grief	brecð, brecða, brecþ, brecþa, cearu, grynn, grynna, gyrn, modceare, modsorg, murcnung, murcnunge, oncyð, oncyþ, oncyþðe, oncyþþe, sorg, trega, tregan, tregena, wea, wean, weana	ground-turf	wancgturf
		ground-up	gegrunden
		grove	bearnum, bearo, bearu, bearwas, bearwe, holtwudu
		grow	aweaxan, aweox, awox, crescite, ecan, geican, geiceað, geicean, geiceaþ, geicte, geludon, gesprang, gesprong, geweox, gewexen, greow, growan, growende, growendra, icte, icton, iecan, iecte, inweaxan, inwyxeð, inwyxeþ, leodan, liodan, liodende, ludon, sprang, springan, sprong, sprungon, weaxað, weaxan, weaxaþ, weaxeð, weaxen, weaxende, weaxendum, weaxeþ, weox, weoxon, wexað, wexan, wexaþ, wexe, wexendra, wridað, wriðade, wridan, wriðan, wridaþ, wriðende, wridendra, wridian, wriðian, wriþade, wriþan
grieve	hreaw, hreowan, hreoweð, hreoweþ, sorga, sorgedon, sorgian, sorgiende		
grieving	hreow, hreowa		
grieving-minded	hreowigmod, hreowigmode		
grievous	niþgrim, torn, torne, tornost, weorce		
grievously	sare		
grim	grim, grimlic, grimme, grymma		
grim-in-battle	searogrim		
grimly	grimme		
grind	gegrundene, grindan		
grind-away	begrindan, begrindeð, begrindeþ, begrunden		
grip	clammum, clomm, clommas, clomme, clommum		
grit	greot		
groan	þunede, þunian	grow-around	beweaxan, beweaxne

Word List (English to Ænglisc)

English	Ænglisc	English	Ænglisc
grow-dark	aswamað, aswamaþ, aswamian, genap, geswearc, gesweorce, nap, nipan, nipeð, nipen, nipende, nipeþ, nipon, sweorcan, sweorceð, sweorceþ	guest-house	gyste, gystern, gysterne
		guest-room	gyste, gystern, gysterne
		guests	gistmægen
		guest-travelling-on-foot	feðegest, feðegestum, feþegest, feþegestum
growing	aweox	guidance	steor, steore
grown	geðungen, geþungen	guide	gestyran, gestyrde, gewisade, gewissode, latteow, ræsbora, stieran, styran, styrde, wisa, wisade, wisan, wisian, wisie, wisige, wisode, wissian
grow-old	ealdað, ealdaþ, ealdian		
grow-over	beweaxan, beweaxne		
grows	groweð, inwyxð		
grows-cold	acolað, acolaþ		
grows-cold (Latin)	frigesscit	guilefully	wærlice
grows-dark	aðystrað, aþystraþ	guilt	firen, firena, fyren, fyrena, fyrene, gylt, gyltum, synn, synna, synne, synnum
grows-dark (Latin)	obtenebrescit		
grows-dirty	asolað, asolaþ		
grows-dirty (Latin)	squalescit		
grows-old	fore, forealdað, forealdaþ	guiltily	unrihte
		guiltless	unsynnig, unsynnigne
grows-old (Latin)	senescunt		
grow-strong	elnian, elniendra	guiltlessly	unsynnum
guard	warian, warod, warode, weard, weardade, weardiað, weardian, weardiaþ, weardigan, weardode, weardodon	guilty	fag, fagum, fah, fane, fara, faum, scildig, scyldfull, scyldfullum, scyldfulra, scyldi, scyldig, scyldige, synbysig, womfull, womscyldig
guardian	hyrdas, hyrde, mundbora, weard, weardas, wearde, weardes, weardum	gull	mæw, mæwes
		gullible	unwar, unware
		gulls	mæwes
		gunwale	streamweall
guardian-of-gold	goldweard	Guthere (name)	Guðere
guardianship	weard, wearde	Guthere's (name)	Guðhere
guarding	weardiað	Guthlaf (name)	Guþlaf
guest	cuma, cuman, gæst, gæstas, gastum, giestas, giestum, gist, gistas, gistum, gyst, gystas, gyste, gystum	Guthulf's (name)	Guðlafes
		guts	innoþ, innoþe
guest-hall	gestsele		

H, h

Word List (English to *Ænglisc*)

English	*Ænglisc*	English	*Ænglisc*
habit	ðeaw, ðeawum, sið, siða, siðe, siðes, siþ, siþa, siþe, siþes, siþon, þeaw, þeawas, þeawum	hall-inhabitant	healsittend, healsittendra, healsittendum
habitation	wic, wica, wicum, wicun	hall-joy	seledream, seledreamas
habituate	wenede, wenian	hall-man	selesecg, selesecgas
had	Ahte, gehet, hæfde	hallowed	halgad, halgodest, halgum
had-been	wurdun	hall-sitter	healsittend, healsittendra, healsittendum
haft	hæft, hæfte		
hafted-sword	hæftmece		
hail	hægel, hægl, hægles, hagle, hagol, haleted, halettan, halette	hall-sitters	fletsittende, fletsittendum
		hall-thane	seleþegn
		hall-troop	fletwerod
hail-storm	hæglfare, hæglfaru	hall-wandering	flettwað, flettwaðas, flettwaþ, flettwaþas
hair	fæx, feax, feaxe, fexe, hær, herum, witelocc, witeloccas	hall-warrior	healðegn, healðegnas, healðegnes, healþegn, healþegnas, healþegnes
hairy	ruh		
half	healf, healfa, healfe, healfne, healfre		
half-year	missarum, missera, missere, misserum	hall-wood	healwudu
hall	ðryþærn, flet, flett, flette, gumstol, gumstole, heal, heall, healle, sæl, sæld, sælða, sælþa, salo, sel, seld, sele, þryþærn, winærn, winærnes, winreced	hammer	hamer, hamere, homer, homera
		hammers	hamora
		hand	folm, folma, folman, folme, folmum, hand, handa, handæ, handbana, handbanan, handbona, handbonan, handon, handum, hond, honda, hondum, mund, mundum
hall-bed	selerest, selereste		
hall--building	healærn, healærna, healreced		
hall-companion	geselda, geseldan		
hall-councillor	selerædend, selerædende	hand-grasp	mundgripe
hall-cup	seleful	handgrip	grap, grape, grapum
hall-entertainment	healgamen	handiwork	handgesceaft, handgeweorc, handweorc, hondgeweorc, hondgeweorce
hall-games	healgamen		
hall-goods	fletgesteald, fletgestealdum, flettgesteald		
hall-guard	seleweard	hand-killer	handbana, handbanan, handbona, handbonan
hall-guest	selegyst		
hall-hero	sele-secg		

Word List (English to Ænglisc)

English	Ænglisc	English	Ænglisc
handle	*hellme*	happen	*agangan, agangen, agongen, alamp, alimpan, alumpen, becom, becoman, becomon, becuman, becwom, belamp, belimpan, gegangan, gegangeð, gegangenne, gegangeþ, gegongeð, gegongen, gegongeþ, gelamp, gelimpan, gelimpe, gelimpeð, gelimpeþ, gelomp, gelumpe, gelumpen, gesælde, getimode, lamp, limpan, limpeð, limpeþ, lomp, lumpen, lumpon, sælan, steallian, timian, wearð, wearþ, weorðan, weorþan, wesan, worden, wurdon*
handling	*feorm, feorme*		
hand-linked	*hondlocen*		
hand--made-wonder	*hondwundor, hondwundra*		
handmaid	*mennen, þinen, þinene, þinenne*		
hand-meeting	*hondgemot, hondgemota*		
hand-onslaught	*hondræs*		
hand-picked	*cista, cyst, cystum*		
hand-picked-troop	*handscale, handscalu, hondscole*		
hand-play	*handplega, handplegan, hondplegan*		
hand-revenge	*handlean*		
hand-thrust	*hondsweng*		
hand-to-hand-combat	*hand, handa, handæ, handon, handum, hond, honda, hondræs, hondum*		
hand-to-hand-killer	*handbana, handbanan, handbona, handbonan*	happily	*eadiglice, gesælige, glædlice, sæliglice*
hand-twisted	*handgewriþen, handgewriþene*	happiness	*bliss, ead, eades, gefea, gefean, sæl, sæla, sæles, sælum, salum, sele, sib, sibb, sibbe, wela, welan, wyn, wynn, wynna, wynne, wynnum*
hand-worm's	*handwurmes*		
hang	*ahangen, aheng, ahon, ahongen, behon, bihongen, hangað, hangaþ, hangian, hangode, ho, hon, hongað, hongaþ, hongiað, hongiaþ*		
hanging	*web*		
hanging-thing	*hangella*		
hang-round	*beheng, behengon, behon, behongen*		

Word List (English to Ænglisc)

English	Ænglisc	English	Ænglisc
happy	dreamhabbende, dreamhabbendra, eadega, eadga, eadge, eadhreðig, eadhreðige, eadhreþig, eadhreþige, eadig, eadigan, freo, freom, freora, gesælige, gesæliglic, glædmod, glædmode, sælig, woruldgesælig	hardship	earfeðe, earfeðu, earfeþa, earfeþe, earfeþo, earfeþu, earfoða, earfoþ, earfoþa, earfoþe, geswinc, yrmþu
		hardship-day	geswincdæg, geswincdagum
		hardship-since	earfoðsið, earfoðsiða, earfoðsiþ, earfoþsiþ, earfoþsiþa
happy-journey	gomenwaþ, gomenwaþe	hardship-time	earfoð-hwil, earfoðþrage, earfoþ-hwil, earfoþþrage
Harald (name)	Haraldes	hardship-while	earfoðhwil, earfoðhwile, earfoþhwil, earfoþhwile
harangue	maðelian, maðelod, maðelode, maþelian, maþelod, maþelode	hard-warrior	heardne
		harm	bealo, bealu, bealwa, bealwe, bealwes, dærede, derede, derian, gesceod, gesceþðan, gesceþþan, gescod, hearm, hearma, hearmas, hearme, hearmes, hearmstæf, hearmstafas, lað, laðes, laðscipe, laþ, laþes, laþscipe, sceaðen, sceaþen, sceððan, sceod, sceþðan, sceþede, sceþþan, sceþþe, scod, scodon, teosu, wea, wean, weana
harass	dreccan, dreht, drehte, ehtan, ehtende, ehton		
harassment	ehtnys, ehtnysse		
harbour	hyð, hydað, hydan, hydaþ, hyðe, hyþ, hyþe, port		
harbour-master	hyðweard, hyþweard		
hard	earfoðlic, earfoþlic, heard, hearda, heardan, hearde, heardes, heardlice, heardne, heardost, heardra, heardran, heardum, sliðen, sliþen, stið, stiðe, stiðra, stiðum, stiþ, stiþe, stiþra, stiþum, styrne		
		harmful-attacker	hearmscaþa
		harmful-enclosure	hearmloca, hearmlocan
hard-beaked	hyrnednebban	harmful-or-evil-experience	bealosiþ
harden	ahyrdan, ahyrded, gehyrde, gehyrdeð, gehyrdeþ, hyrdan		
		harmful-or-evil-twig	hearmtan, hearmtanas
hardened-edge	heardecg	harmful-struggle	hearmplega
hardly	fea	harm-journey	bealu-sið, bealu-siþ

Word List (English to Ænglisc)

English	Ænglisc	English	Ænglisc
harm-to-the-whole-people	leodbealewa, leodbealo	hate	feoð, feogan, feon, feoþ, hatian, hatode, hete, mnodhete
harness	gerædu		
harp	gleobeam, gleobeames, gomenwudu, hearpan, hearpe, sner, snere	hate-act	hetenið, heteniðas, heteniþ, heteniþas
		hateful	atol, hetelic, lað, laðan, laðlic, laþ, laþan, laþlic, unleof, unleofe
harry	gehergod, hergian, hergode	hateful-attack	hetenið, heteniðas, heteniþ, heteniþas
harsh	afor, biter, biteran, bitere, biteres, bitre, bitres, bitresta, bitter, geocor, hreðe, hreþe, reðan, reðe, reðre, reþan, reþe, reþre, unliðe, unliþe	hateful-enemy	laðgeteona, laðgeteonan, laþgeteona, laþgeteonan
		hatefully	laðlice, laðlicost, laþlice, laþlicost
		hateful-speech	hetespræc, hetespræce
harshly	fræcne, frecne	hateful-thought	heteþanc, heteþancum
harsh-spirited	stercedferhð, stercedferhðe, stercedferhþ, stercedferhþe	hateful-tree	laðtreow, laþtreow
		hateful-wound	laðbite, laþbite
hart	heorot, heort	hater	hetend, hetende
harvest	hærfest	hating	feogan
has	hafað, hafaþ	hatred	æfst, æfstum, mnodhete, nið, niða, niðas, niðe, niðes, niðum, niþ, niþa, niþas, niþe, niþes, niþum
haste	ofest, ofeste, ofost, ofoste, ofste		
hasten	arn, fundað, fundast, fundaþ, fundedon, fundian, fundiaþ, fundode, fyrðran, fyrþran, gefyrðred, gefyrþred, irnan, ræsan, ræsde, ræsed, scacan, scacen, scæcen, sceacan, sceaceð, sceacen, sceaceþ, sceoc, scoc, scylun, scyndan, scynded, urnon, yrnende, yrnendum		
		hatred-resulting-from-murder	morþorhete, morþorhetes
		haughty	healic, hygewlonc, mod-wlonc
hastened	þrungon		
hastily	ofestum, ofostum, ofstum		
hasty	hraðe, hræd, hraþe		
hasty-speech	hrædwyrde		
hasty-words	hrædwyrde		

Word List (English to Ænglisc)

English	Ænglisc	English	Ænglisc
have	agan, agon, ah, ahte, behabban, behæfdon, behealdan, beheold, beheoldon, habbað, habban, habbaþ, habben, hæbbað, hæbbaþ, hæbbe, hæfd, hæfð, hæfde, hæfdon, hæfst, hæfþ, hafa, hafað, hafast, hafaþ, hafo, hafu, hauest, næbbe, næbben, næfð, næfdon, næfþ, nagon, nah, nahte, nahton, ne, þe	having-a-tear-stained-face	tearighleor
		having-a-wound-or-wrapped-hilt	wreoþenhilt
		having-bound-hair	bundenheord, bundenheorde
		having-bright-garments	scirham, scirhame
		having-curly-hair	wundenfeax
		having-dewy-plumage	deawigfeðera, deawigfeðere, deawigfeþera, deawigfeþere
		having-naked-limbs	limnacod
		having-steel-edges	stylecg
		hawk	hafoc, Hafuc, heafoc, heoroswealwe
have-control	age, agen, agon, ah, ahte, ahton	hazel-feathered-ones	hasewanpadan
have-fun	blissian, blissigende, geblissad	he	ðæt, he, heo, hie, him, hine, his, hit, hym, hyne, hys, se, seo, þæt
have-mercy	gemiltsa, miltsian		
have-mercy-on	gemilsige		
have-need-of	behofað, behofaþ, behofian	head	gewitte, hafað, hafala, hafalan, hafaþ, hafelan, heafde, heafdon, heafdum, heafod, heafodmæg, heafodmægum, heafodmaga, heafola, heafolan, wite, witt
have-occasion-to	ðearf, ðonosnottorra, ðorfte, geþearfod, þearf, þearfan, þearfendre, þearft, þonosnottorra, þorfte, þorfton, þurfan		
have-power	ricsast	head-count	heafodgerim, heafodgerimes
have-sex-with	forlicgan, forlycgan, hæman	head-crown	molda, moldan
have-the-habit-of	scal, sceal, sceall, scealt, scel, sceolde, sceolden, sceoldest, sceoldon, sceole, sceolon, scile, scolde, scoldon, sculan, sculon, scyle	headland	hoe, hoh, næs, nosan, nose
		headland-slope	næshleoðum, næshleoþum, næshlið, næshliþ
		head-protection	heafodbeorg, heafodbeorge
		head-spinning	swima, swiman
have-to	sculan	headstrong	gehatheort, hatheort
having	habban, hafað	head-swimming	swima, swiman
having-a-dark-coat	salowigpada, salwigpad	head-watch	heafodweard, heafodwearde

Word List (English to Ænglisc)

English	Ænglisc	English	Ænglisc
heal	gehæl, gehæled, gehælede, hælan, hældon	hearth-companion	heorðgeneat, heorð-geneat, heorðgeneatas, heorðgeneatum, heorþgeneat, heorþ-geneat, heorþgeneatas, heorþgeneatum
healed	lacnað, lacnaþ		
healer	helend		
healing	hæle, hælo, hælu, heleða		
health	gesynta, gesynto, gesyntum, hæle, hælo, hælu	hearth-troop	heorðwerod, heorþwerod
healthy	andsund, ansund, gesund, gesunde, gesundne, gesundran, hæl, hælo, hal, halan, hale, onsund, onsundne	heart-love	modlufan, modlufu
		heart-of-love	heortlufan
		hearty	liffæst, liffæstan
		heat	hæþenra, hæto, hat, hyt, sweoloð, sweoloðe, sweoloþ, sweoloþe
heap	heap, heape, heapum	heat (Latin)	ardor
		heat?-flame?	swaþul, swaþule
heaped	geheapen	heathen	hæðen, hæðenan, hæðene, hæðenes, hæðenra, hæðne, hæðnum, hæþen, hæþena, hæþenan, hæþene, hæþenes, hæþenra, hæþne, hæþnum
hear	gehyrað, gehyraþ, gehyrde, gehyrdon, gehyre, gehyrest, gehyrst, hieran, hierde, hiered, hwæt, hyrað, hyran, hyraþ, hyrde, hyrdon, hyre		
		heathen-nation	hæðencynn, hæþencynn
heard	gehlyn, gehyrde, hyrde, hyrdon	heathenry	hæþenra
heard-of	gefrægn	heathen-shrine	hearh
hear-of	gefran, gefrinan, gefrunen, gefrunon	heathen-temple	hærgtraf, hærgtrafum
heart	breost, breosta, breost-cofa, breostum, ferð-loca, ferþ-loca, heortan, heorte, heortum, hræðre, hræþre, hreðer, hreðra, hreðre, hreþer, hreþra, hreþre, hyge, mod, mode, modes, modum, sefa	heath-walker	hæðstapa, hæþstapa
		heaven	heafena, heben, hefene, hefone, heofena, heofenas, heofenes, heofenum, heofna, heofne, heofnes, heofnum, heofon, heofona, heofonas, heofones, heofonum, hiofen, rodera, rodor, rodore, swegles, uproder, uprodor, wolcen
heart-care	breost-cearu		
hearth	heorð, heorðe, heorþ, heorþe		

Word List (English to Ænglisc)

English	Ænglisc	English	Ænglisc
heaven-above	upheofon, uproder, uprodor	heel	fiersn, fiersna, hoe, hoh
heaven-bird	heofonfugel, heofonfugla, heofonfuglas	height	hehðe, hehðu, hehþe, hehþu
heaven-bright	swegltorht, swegltorhtan	heir	afera, aforan, eafera, eaferan, eaferum, eafora, eaforan, eaforum, eafrum, eðelstæf, eðulstæfe, eðylstæf, eþelstæf, eþulstæfe, eþylstæf, yrfeweard, yrfewearda, yrfeweardas
heaven-guardian	heofonum, heofonweard, heofonweardes		
heaven-king	hefoncyninges, heofoncyning, heofoncyninge, heofoncyninges, sweglcyning		
heaven-kingdom	hefonrices, heofonrice, heofonrices	heirloom	eadgestreonum, ealdgestreon, ealdgestreona, ealdgewin, yrfelaf, yrfelafe
heaven-kingdom's	hefaenricaes, heofonrices	heir-of	afera
heaven-lord	heofonweard, heofonweardes	held	heolde, heoldon, neotan
heavenly	heofenlic, heofonlic, heofonlican, heofonlicne, hiofena, wuldorfæst, wuldorfæstan, wuldorfæstne	held-dear	ðeowa
		hell	cwicsusl, cwicsusle, helle, herg, hergum
		hell-bond	hellbend, hellbendum
		hell-burning	hellebryne
heavenly-body	leoma, leoman, leomena, rodortunglum, rodortungol, tungol	hell-door	helldor, helldora
		hell-fire-like	hellfirena
		hell-gate	heldor, heldora, helldor, helldora
heavenly-body-such-as-the-sun	tungel, tunglum, tungol	hell-inhabitant	helruna, helrunan
		hellish-enemy	hellesceaða, hellesceaþa, helsceaðan, helsceaþan
heavenly-dwelling	rodores, rodorstol, rodorstolas		
heavenly-structure	heofonrices, heofontimber	hell-lamentation	helleheaf, helleheafas
heavens	rodera, roderas, roderum, rodor, rodora, rodores	hell-misery	helltrega, helltregum
		hell-pain	hellewite, hellewites
heaven's	heofna, heofonas, heofones	hell-torment	hellewite, hellewites, helltrega, helltregum
heaven's-kingdom	hiofenrices	hell-torture	hellgeþwing
heavy	hefian, hefig, hefige, hefigran, swar, sware	hell-wailing	helleheaf, helleheafas
Hedening's (name)	Heodeninga		

Word List (English to Ænglisc)

English	Ænglisc	English	Ænglisc
helmet	grimhelm, grimhelmas, helm, helmas, helme, helmes, helmum, rof, rofes, wigheafola, wigheafolan	herbs	wyrta
		here	her, hider
		hereditary-endowment	fæderæþelu, fæderæþelum
		here-living	her, herbuende, herbuendra
helmet-crown	hrof, hrofe, hrofes	heresy	gedwild, gedwilde, gedwyld, gedwylde
helmet-of-invisibility	hæleðhelm, hæleþhelm, heoloþhelm, heoloþhelme	hermit	anhaga, anhogan
		hero	guma, hæl, hælæð, hælæþ, hæle, hæleð, hæleða, hæleðum, hæleþ, hæleþa, hæleþas, hæleþum, mægenagend, mægenagendra
helmet-wearer	helmberend		
helmet-with-a-metal-face-protector	grimhelmas		
help	fullæstan, fullæstu, fultum, fultumes, fylstan, fylste, fylston, gelæst, gelæstan, gelæste, gelæston, geo, geoc, geoce, healp, help, helpan, helpe, helpend, læst, læstan, læste, læsten, læstes, mundbora, mundbyrd, mundbyrde	heroes	hæleð, hæleþ, hæleþa
		heroic	beadurof, ellenþrist, ellenþriste
		heroic-deeds	eorlscipe
		heroic-helmet	hæleðhelm, hæleþhelm
		hero's	hæleþa
		herself	sylf
		hesitate	tweode, tweon
		he-sits	Siteð
		hew	forheawan, forheawen, forheow, forheowon, geheawe, geheawen, gescær, gescer, heawan, heawen, heow, heowon, heowun, scæron, scieran, scireð, scireþ, scyran
help-	geoce		
helper	geþafa		
hence	forð, forþ, heonan, heonane, heonon, heonone		
Hengest (name)	Hengest		
Heorrenda (name)	Heorrenda		
her	hire, hyre, self, selfa, selfe, selfes, selfne, selfra, selfre, selfum, seo, seolf, seolfa, sin, sine, sines, sinne, sinre, sinum, sylf, sylfa, sylfan, sylfe, sylfes, sylfne, sylfra, sylfre, sylfum	he-was (Latin)	fuit
		hewed	heowan
		hidden	deogol, dygel, forholen, gehydað, gehydde
herald	boda, bodan, hildecalla		
herb	wyrt, wyrte, wyrtum		

Word List (English to Ænglisc)

English	Ænglisc	English	Ænglisc
hide	behelan, beholen, bewreon, bewrigen, bewrigene, bewrigenum, biwrah, fell, fellum, gehydde, hel, helan, hydan, hyddon, hyde, hydeð, hydeþ, mid, miðan, miðendne, miþan, miþendne, wrah, wreah, wreo, wreon, wrigen, wrigon, wrihst, wrugon, wry, wryon	high-ness	heahnisse
		high-place	eðelstol, eþelstol, heahstede
		high-principal-city	heaburh
		high-seat	hæahsetle, heahsetl
		high-stemmed	heahstefn
		hill	beorg, beorgas, beorge, beorges, beorgum, beorh, berhge, biorgas, biorges, biorh, gehlið, gehliþo, hlæw, hlæwe, hlaw, hlawe, hleoðo, hleoðu, hleoþa, hleoþo, hleoþu, hlið, hliðe, hliðes, hlioðo, hlioþo, hliþ, hliþe, hliþes, stanbeorh
hiding-place	heolster, heolstor, heolstre		
high	bront, brontne, geap, geapes, geapne, geapum, he, hea, heagum, heah, heahan, heahfyr, heahne, hean, heanne, heanum, heare, heaum, steap, steape, steapes, steapne, uphea		
		hill-caves	dunscrafum
		hilly-region	mor, moras, more
		hilt	hæft, hæfte, hæfton, hylt
		hilted	hilted
		him	him, hine, hym, hyne, self, selfa, selfe, selfes, selfne, selfra, selfre, selfum, seolf, seolfa, sylf, sylfa, sylfan, sylfe, sylfes, sylfne, sylfra, sylfre, sylfum
high (Latin)	ipselos		
high-building	heahreced		
high-buildings	heahgetimbro		
high-destiny	heahgesceap		
higher-up	ufor		
highest	hehsta, hehstan, hehste, hehstne, hyhsta	himself	him, hine, sylf, sylfa, sylfne
highest-point	hehðe, hehðu, hehþe, hehþu	hinder	amyrde, amyrran, amyrred, dweleð, dweleþ, dwellan, forsæt, forsæton, forsiteð, forsiteþ, forsittan, forstandan, forstod, forstode, forstodon, gelette, getwæman, lettan, letton
high-father	heahfæder, heahfædere		
high-hall	heahsele		
high-king	heahcining, heahcininges, heahcyninc, heahcyning, heahcyninges, heahkyning	hindered	dweleð, gelette
		hinge	heorr, heorras
		hip	þeo
high-love	heahlufan, heahlufu	hipbone	hupeban
highly-regarded	unforcuð, unforcuþ	hip-carried-sax	hupseax

Word List (English to *Ænglisc*)

English	*Ænglisc*	English	*Ænglisc*
his	*him, his, hys, seo, sin, sine, sines, sinne, sinre, sinum*	hold-dear	*dyran*
		hold-firmly	*ætfealh, ætfeolan*
		holding	*gehyld, holdlice*
his-mind	*gemyndum*	hold-out	*ðolad, ðolade, ðolian, þolad, þolade, þolian*
his-self	*sylfan*		
hit	*hælon*		
hither	*hider*	holds	*hafað, þeah*
Hnaef (name)	*Hnæf, Hnæfe*	holds (Latin)	*tenet*
hoard	*hord, horde, hordes*	hole	*hol, pyt, seaþ, seaþe, þyrel*
hoard-building	*hordærn, hordærna, hordærne*		
		holy	*gæstlic, gastlic, haleg, halegu, halga, halgan, halgena, halgum, halig, haligan, halige, haliges, haligne, haligra, haligre, haligum, sancta, sanctus*
hoard-cove	*hord-cofa*		
hoard-delight	*hordwynn, hordwynne*		
hoarded-treasure	*hordwela, hordwelan*		
hoard-guardian	*hordweard*		
hoard-lock	*hordlocan*		
hoard-treasure	*hordgestreon, hordgestreona, hordgestreonum, hordmadum, hordwynn, hordwynne*		
		holy (Latin)	*sancto, sanctum*
		holy-book	*halgungboc*
		holy-judgement	*haligdomes*
		holy-spirit	*gæsthalge*
		holy-water	*haligwæter, haligwætere*
hoard-wealth	*hordwela, hordwelan*		
		home	*cyðð, cyððe, cyþþ, cyþþe, eard, eðel, eþel, eþelstol, eþelstolas, frumsceaft, frumsceafta, frumsceafte, ham, hama, hamas, hame, hames*
hoard-worthiness	*hordweorþung, hordweorþunge*		
hoard-worthy	*hordwyrðne, hordwyrþne, horwyrðe, horwyrþe*		
hoar-frost	*hrim, hrime*		
hoary	*har, hara, hare, hares, harne, harum*		
hold	*geheald, gehealdan, gehealde, gehealdeþ, gehealdon, geheold, heald, healdað, healdan, healdaþ, healde, healdeð, healdest, healdeþ, heold, heoldan, heolde, heoldon, hiold, lealden, warað, waraþ, wariað, warian, wariaþ, warigeað, warigeaþ, warode*	homeland	*eard, earda, eardas, earde, eardes, eðel, eðelstow, eðelstowe, eðelturf, eðle, eðyltyrf, ethel, eþel, eþeles, eþelstow, eþelstowe, eþelturf, eþle, eþyltyrf*
		homeland-joy	*eðeldream, eðeldreamas, eþeldream, eþeldreamas*

Word List (English to Ænglisc)

English	Ænglisc	English	Ænglisc
homeless	eðelleas, eðelleasum, eþelleas, eþelleasum	honour	ar, ara, arað, aran, araþ, are, arena, arian, arna, arra, arum, arweorðian, arweorþian, arwurðnys, arwurðnysse, arwurðode, arwurþnys, arwurþnysse, arwurþode, dom, domas, dome, domes, dyrsian, gedyrsod, geweorðad, geweorðan, geweorðod, geweorðode, geweorþad, geweorþade, geweorþan, geweorþod, geweorþode, gewurðien, gewurðnys, gewurðnysse, gewurðod, gewurþad, gewurþien, gewurþnys, gewurþnysse, gewurþod, hergan, herigean, mærað, mæran, mæraþ, tiir, tir, tire, tires, tirleas, tirleases, Treow, tyr, uuurðmynt, uuurþmynt, weorðade, weorðiað
home-of-the-winds	windgeard		
homes	hamas		
homesteads	eard		
homewards	ham		
honest	soðfæst, soðfæste, soðfæstra, soþfæst, soþfæste, soþfæstra, wær, wærum		
honey	hunig		
honey-savouring	hunigsmæccas		
		honourable	arfæst, arfæstan, arfæste, arweorþe, domfæst, wærfæst, wærfæstne, wærfæstra

Word List (English to Ænglisc)

English	Ænglisc	English	Ænglisc
honourably	arlice, arlicne, hlisfullice, unforcuðlice, unforcuþlice, weorðlic, weorðlice, weorðlicost, weorðmyndum, weorþlic, weorþlice, weorþlicost, weorþmyndum, worðmyndum, worþmyndum, wurðlice, wurðlicor, wurðmyndum, wurþlice, wurþlicor, wurþmyndum	horrific	niþgrim
		horror	egesa, egesan, egesum, egsa, egsan, gryra, gryre, gryrum
		horror-of	wigbealu
		horror-of-glowing-embers	gledegesa
		horse	eoh, hæncgest, hors, mear, meara, mearas, meare, mearg, mearh, mearum, wicg, wicga, wicge
		horseman	ridda, ridend
		horses	meara
honour-done-to-a-home	hamweorðung, hamweorðunge, hamweorþung, hamweorþunge	horse-thane	hors-þegn
		hospitality	gereorda, gereordu, giestliðnyss, giestliðnysse, giestliþnyss, giestliþnysse
honoured	brema, breman, breme, gewurðod, weorðfull, weorþe, weorþfull, weorþra, woerðfullost, woerþfullost, wurðe, wurðran, wurþe, wurþran, wyrðe, wyrðra, wyrþe, wyrþra	hospitality-for-the-night	nihtfeormung, nihtfeormunge
honoured-father	ealdfæder		
hook	angel		
hope	hiht, hopian, hyht, hyhte, wen		
hopeful	hihtlic, hyhtlic		
hope-full	hihtful, hihtfulne		
hopeless	ortrywe		
hopes	wenum		
horn	horn, hornum		
horn-bow	hornboga, hornbogan		
horns	hornas		
horny-beaked	hyrnednebba		
horrible	atelic, atol, atolan, atole, atolne, eatol, eatolne, egle, eglu		
horribly	þearle		
horribly-coloured	gryrefah, gryrefahne		
horrid	egeslic, egeslican		

Word List (English to *Ænglisc*)

English	*Ænglisc*	English	*Ænglisc*
host	ðrym, dugeða, dugeðe, dugeðum, dugeþa, dugeþe, dugeþum, dugoða, dugoðe, dugoþa, dugoþe, duguð, duguða, duguðe, duguðum, duguþ, duguþa, duguþe, duguþum, feormend, feormendra, feormynd, folcgetrum, folcgetrume, geþræc, heap, heape, heapum, here, herga, hergas, herge, herges, hergum, herige, heriges, mægen, mægene, mægenes, mægna, mægne, mægnes, mægnu, mægyn, mænego, mænige, mænigo, manigeo, menigeo, scole, scolu, sweot, sweotum, þryð, þryðum, þrym, þrymm, þrymmas, þryþ, þryþe	hostile	æfengrom, bealuhygdig, fag, fagum, fah, fane, fara, faum, gelað, gelaðe, gelaþ, gelaþe, gram, graman, grame, gramena, grames, gramum, grome, gromheort, gromhydig, gromra, heteþoncol, heteþoncolne, laðwende, laðwendne, laðwendo, laþ, laþwende, laþwendemod, laþwendne, laþwendo, wraþ
		hostile-attack	feondræs
		hostile-attacker-literally	dædhata
		hostile-blow	hetesweng, heteswengeas
		hostile-enemy	feondscaða, feondscaþa, feondsceaða, feondsceaðan, feondsceaþa, feondsceaþan
		hostile-grasp	feondgrap, feondgrapum, nidgripe, nithgripe
		hostile-hall	niðsele, niþsele
hostage	gisel, gysel	hostility	anda, fæghðe, fæghþe, fæhð, fæhða, fæhðe, fæhðo, fæhðu, fæhþ, fæhþa, fæhþe, fæhþo, fæhþu, feondscipe, higeteonan, hygeteona, hygeteonan, inwitniða, inwitniþ, inwitniþa, inwitniþas, nið, niþ

Word List (English to Ænglisc)

English	Ænglisc	English	Ænglisc
hosts	heapum, weorada, weoruda, wereda	huge	eacen, eacne, eacnum, ecne, gimfæst, gimfæste, ginfæst, ginfæstan, ginfæstum, great, greate, unmæte
hot	hat, hatan, hate, hates, hatne, haton, hatost, hatran		
hot-hearted	gehatheort, hatheort		
hotly	hat, hate	human	eorðan, eorðbuend, eorðbuende, eorðbuendra, eorðbuendum, eorþan, eorþbuend, eorþbuende, eorþbuendra, eorþbuendum, mennisc, mennisces, menniscra, menniscum
hottest	hatost		
hound	hund, hundum		
hour	tid, tida, tide		
house	bold, bolda, botl, botle, domes, hof, hofe, hofu, hofum, hus, husa, huse, huses, in, inn, inne, sele, wunung, wununge		
household	hired, hus, husa, huse, huses, hyrde, hyred, hyredes	human-being	folcwer, folcweras, mennisc, mennisces, menniscra, menniscum, reordberend, reordberendum, sawla, sawlberend, sawlberendra, searohæbbend, searohæbbendra, woruldbuend, woruldbuendra
household-contents	ingesteald		
household-counsellor	stigwita, stigwitum		
householder	boldagend, boldagendra		
household-treasure	botlgestreon, botlgestreona, botlgestreonum		
house-man	hiredmann, hiredmen		
house-walls	weallwalan		
how	hu	human-beings	fira, firas, firum, foldbuend, foldbuende, foldbuendum, fyra
however	ac, hwæðere, hwæðre, hwæþere, hwæþre, hwaþere, þe, þeah		
		human-effigy	monlica
however-not	nohwæðere, nohwæðre, nohwæþere, nohwæþre	humanity	mancyn, mancynn, mancynne, mancynnes, manncynnes, moncynn, moncynnæs, moncynne, moncynnes
how-now!	hu		
hue	hiw		
hue-bright	hiowbeorht		
hues	hiwa		
hug	beclypan, beclypte, ymbclyppan, ymbclypte	humanity's	niþþa
		human-joy	gumdream

Word List (English to Ænglisc)

English	Ænglisc	English	Ænglisc
human-kindred	wermægð, wermægða, wermægþ, wermægþa	hurriedly	ofestlice, ofostlice, ofstlice
humans	landbuende, landbuendum, londbuend, londbuendum	hurry	efstan, efste, efston, fysan, fysde, gefysed, onettan, onette, onetteð, onetteþ, onetton, snyredon, snyrian, teng, tengan
Humber (place)	Humbra		
humble	eaðmede, eaðmod, eadmoda, eaþmod, gehnægde, gehnæged, hnægan, hnag, hnagran, hnah, hnahran	hurt	gebroced, gebrocede, gebrocian, sceaðen, sceaþen
		husband	hlaford, hlaforde, hlafordes, hlafordum
humbly	eadmodlice		
humiliate	forbigan, forbigde, forbiged, gehnægde, gehnæged, hnægan, hynan, hynde, ofsceamian, ofsceamod	**I, i**	
		I	ic, me, mec
		i.e.-generous-lord	goldwine
		I-am	eom
		I-believe (Latin)	Credo
		ice	is, ise
		ice-binding	isgebinde
humiliated	arleas, arlease, arleasra, hean, heane, heanne, tirleas, tirleases	ice-cold	hrim-ceald, is, iscald, iscaldne, isceald, is-ceald, iscealdne
humiliating	heanlic	icicle	hrimgicel, hrim-gicel, hrimgicelum
humiliation	hynð, hynða, hynðo, hynðu, hynþ, hynþa, hynþo, hynþu	icy	isig
		icy-feathered	isig-feðera, isigfeþera, isig-feþera
humility	eaðmedu, eaðmedum, eadmodnes, eadmodnesse, eaþmedu, eaþmedum	idle	idel, idlu
		idle-handed	idelhende
		idol	herg, hergum, herheard, weg
hundred	hun, hund	idol-worship	wigweorðung, wigweorðunga, wigweorþung, wigweorþunga
hundred and first	hundteontigoþa and forma		
hundredth	hundteontigoþa		
hunger	hunger, hungor	if	gif, gyf
hung-over	medowerig, medowerige, medowerigum	ignoble	hnag, hnagran, hnah, hnahran
		ignominious	domleas, domleasan
hungry	hungri		
hung-up	ahengon		
hurl	sendan		

Word List (English to Ænglisc)

English	Ænglisc	English	Ænglisc
ignore	læt, lætað, lætan, lætaþ, læte, læteð, læteþ, let, lete, leton	improve	gebetan
		impure	ful, fula, fulan, fule, fullum, unsyfra, unsyfre
illiberal	hnag, hnagran, hnah, hnahran	impure-person	ful, fula, fulan, fule, fullum
illness-only-instance-is-at	sue, suht	in	æt, an, ðurh, in, inn, inna, innan, on, to
image	anlicnes	in-addition	mid
imagine	geþenc, geþencean, þencað, þencaþ, þence, þencean, þenceð, þencest, þenceþ, þohte, þohton	in-addition-to	eac
		in-a-friendly-manner	freondlice, freondlicor
		in-a-miserly-way	hneawlice
		inanimate	orsawle
immature	unweaxen	in-answer	eft
immeasurably	ungemete, unigmetes	in-an-ugly-or-unpleasant-way	unfægere, unfære
immediately	ædre, ædrum, ætrihte, aninga, anunga, hrade, hræþe, hraþe, hraþor, hreðe, hreþe, raðe, raþe, recene, rice, ricene, ricne, ricone, rycene, semninga, snude, sona	in-an-unfriendly-way	unfreondlice
		in-any-case	hwæðere, hwæðre, hwæþere, hwæþre, hwaþere
		incantation	galdor, galdre, gealdor
		incense	stor
		incite	ontyhtan, ontyhte, scurum, scyhtan, scyhte
immense-load	mægenbyrþen, mægenbyrþenne	incitement	ontendnyss, ontyndnys
immerse	dyfan, dyfde	incline	abeag, abugan
imminent	gelenge, lenge	incomparable	ænlic, ænlicu
immobility	wælrap, wælrapas		
immoderately	unmæðlice, unmæþlice		
impact	gegrind		
impel	bædan, bædde, fordraf, fordrifan, fysan, fysde, gebæded, gefysed, ontyhtan, ontyhte		
impel-by-necessity	genydde, genyded, nydan		
impelled	gebæded		
important-noble	aldorþegn		
impose	gescraf, scrifan, scrifeð, scrifeþ		
imprison	befæstan, befæste, bifæstan, bifæste&th		
improper	gedefe, ungedefe		

Word List (English to *Ænglisc*)

English	*Ænglisc*	English	*Ænglisc*
increase	betan, bete, crescite, ecan, gebetan, gebette, gebettest, geican, geiceað, geicean, geiceaþ, geicte, geweox, gewexen, icte, icton, iecan, iecte, miclade, miclian, onhebban, onhof, wæstm, wæstma, wæstmas, wæstme, wæstmes, wæstmum, wæstum, weaxað, weaxan, weaxaþ, weaxeð, weaxende, weaxendum, weaxeþ, weox, weoxon, westem, wexað, wexan, wexaþ, wexe, wexendra, ycað, ycan, ycaþ	infrequent-visit	seldcymas, seldcyme
		in-front	beforan, foran
		in-front-of	ætforan, beforan, biforan, for, toforan
		ingenious	orðanc
		in-goer	ingenga
		ingoing	ingenga
		in-going	ingang
		ingratitude	unþanc, unþances
		inhabit	gesæt, gesæton, geseten, gewunedon, gewunigen, sæt, sætan, sæte, sæton, setan, siþþan, sittan, weardade, weardiað, weardian, weardiaþ, weardigan, weardode, weardodon, wuna, wunað, wunade, wunaþ, wunedon, wuniað, wunian, wuniaþ, wuniende, wunode, wunodon
increased	eacen, eacne, eacnum, ecne		
indecently	unscomlice		
indeed	eal, eall, gegnunga, huru, hwæt, la	inhabitant	buend, buendra, landmann, landmanna
in-different-ways-or-places	missenlice	inhabited	byn
indigent	feasceaft, feasceafte, feasceaftig, feasceaftum	inhabiting	weardiað
		inhabiting-people	bufolc
		inheritance	gecynde, yrfe, yrfes
		inherited-private-property	sundoryrfe, sundoryrfes
in-distress	þreanydum		
ineffective?	ungleaw	inherited-seat-or-homeland	yrfestol, yrfestole
ineffective-labour	lambyrd, lambyrde		
ineligible-for-wergild	feohleas	inherited-sword	yrfelaf, yrfelafe
inexorable	aræd	inimical	lað, laþ
infected	geblonden	in-it	ðæron, þæron
infirm	lef, mettrum, mettrume, untrum, untrume	initiate	onstealde, onstealdest, onstellan
inflame	onhætan, onhæted		
inflicted	beslagen		
in-flooded	inflede		
inform	cyþan		
informant	melda, meldan		

Word List (English to Ænglisc)

English	Ænglisc	English	Ænglisc
injure	atæsan, atæsed, dærede, derede, derian, gegrettan, gegrette, gesceod, gesceþðan, gesceþþan, gescod, geswenced, geswencte, gretan, greted, greteð, greteþ, grette, gretton, hran, hrinan, hrine, hrinon, hynan, hynde, hyned, sceod, sceþðan, sceþede, sceþþan, sceþþe, scod, scodon, swencan, swencte, wyrdan, wyrde	in-pain	ermig
		in-perpetual-night	sinnihte
		in-placed	ingesteald
		in-poetry	fullwen, fullwona
		in-presence-of	beforan, for
		inquire	fricgan, fricgcean, fricgean, fricgen, frige, gefricge, gefricgeað, gefricgean, gefricgeaþ, gefrunen, gefrungon, gefrunon
		insane	wod, wodum
		insanity	wodnys, wodnysse
		inscribe	awritan, awrite
		in-secret	dearnenga, dearnunga, dearnunge
injury	æfðoncan, æfþanc, æfþancum, æfþonca, æfþoncan, anda, andan, bealo, bealu, bealwa, bealwe, bealwes, grynn, grynna, gyrn, hygeteona, lað, laðes, laðscipe, læðð, læðða, læððum, læþþ, læþþa, læþþum, laþ, laþes, laþscipe, teona, teonan, teonum, teosu	insensible	feleleas, sworcenferð, sworcenferþ
		inside	inn, innan, inne
		insides	innoþe
		insidiously	dearnenga, dearnunga, dearnunge
		insignificant	læs, læsest
		inspect	geneosode, neosan, neosian, niosað, niosan, niosaþ, niosian
		inspire	onbryrd, onbryrdan, onbryrde
injury-to-a-sinew-or-muscle	seonobenn, seonobennum	instead-of	fore
		institute	onstealde, onstealdest, onsteled, onstellan
injury-wreak	gyrnwræce		
ink	telg		
innards	innoþ, innoþe		
inner-thought	breostgehygd, breostgehygdum		
innocence	clænnys, clænnysse		
innocent	clæne, unsceððiga, unscildigan, unscyldig, unscyldigan		
in-no-way	nalæs		
innumerable	unrimu		
in-order-that	þæt		

Word List (English to *Ænglisc*)

English	*Ænglisc*	English	*Ænglisc*
instruct	bebead, bebeod, bebeodan, beboden, bebudon, gelæran, gelærdon, gelæred, gelærede, geræd, gerædest, getæce, getæhte, getæhton, lær, læran, lærde, lære, læren, rædað, rædan, rædaþ, rædde, tæcan, tæcaþ, tæhte	intelligent	ferhðgleaw, ferhðgleawe, ferhþgleaw, ferhþgleawe, gleawhydig, higeðoncol, higeðoncolre, higeþoncol, higeþoncolre, snotera, snoteran, snotere, snotor, snotra, snottor, snottra, snottre
instruct-by-example	bysnian, gebysnode		
instructed	læran	intend	aðohte, aþencan, aþohte, ðencan, ðoht, ðohte, gehogod, gehogodest, gemynt, gemynted, geteode, geteoh, geteohhian, geteohhod, geþenc, geþencean, geþinged, geþingod, hogedon, hogian, hogode, hogodon, myntan, mynte, mynteð, mynteþ, mynton, nele, nellað, nellaþ, nelle, noldan, nolde, noldon, teohhian, teohhode, þencað, þencan, þencaþ, þence, þencean, þenceð, þencest, þenceþ, þingade, þingian, þingode, þoht, þohte, þohton, wile, willað, willan, willaþ, wille, willende, wilt, woldan, wolde, wolden
instruction	larcwide, larcwidum, tihting, tihtinge		
instrument	galdor, galdre, gealdor		
in-such-a-way-that	swa		
insult	æfðoncan, æfþanc, æfþancum, æfþonca, æfþoncan, bysmor, hearm, hearma, hearmas, hearme, hearmes, higeteonan, hosp, hygeteona, hygeteonan, hynan, hynde, hyned, sceond, sceonde, tynan, tyndon		
intellect	gemynd, gemynda, gemynde, gemyndum		
intelligence	modgemynd, modgeþoht, modgeþohte, snytra, snytro, snytru, snyttru, snyttrum		
		intended	ætlan
		intending-evil	bealuhygdig, niðhycgende, niþhycgende

Word List (English to Ænglisc)

English	Ænglisc	English	Ænglisc
intending-evil-or-destruction	bealohycgend, bealohycgendra, bealohydig	in-wrestling-throw	oferwearp, oferweorpan
intend-to-go	geþingeð, geþingeþ, þingan	ire	yrre
		Ireland	Iraland
intense	hat, hatan, hate, hates, hatne, haton, hatost, hatran	Irish	Dinges
		iron	iren, irena, irenes, irenna, isen, isenes, isern, iserna, isernes
intent	ingehyd, ingehyde		
intention	hige, higes, higum, hyge, mine, myne	iron-armed-troop	irenþreat
		iron-bond	irenbend, irenbenda, irenbendum
intercede	mundbyrdan		
intercede-for	geþinged, geþingod, þingade, þingian, þingode	iron-coat	irenbyrnan, isernbyrnan
		iron-fetter	irenbend, irenbenda, irenbendum
intertwine	gelocen, locenra, lucan, lucon	iron-hard	irenheard
in-the-lead	beforan, biforan	iron-mail-coat	irenbyrnan, irenbyrne, isernbyrnan, isernbyrne
in-the-middle	tomiddes		
in-the-middle-of	tomiddes		
in-the-other-direction	forane		
		iron-shower	isernscur, isernscure
in-the-presence-of	fore		
in-the-shelter-of	under, undor	iron-sword	iren, irena, irenes, irenna
in-this-way	þus		
in-thousands	þusendmælum	iron-threat	irenþreat
intimate-bed-fellow	healsgebedda	irresistibly	unwearnum
intimately?-earnestly?	halsfæst	irrigate	leccan, leoht, leohte
		irritant	æfþunca
intimidate	egesian, egsode	is	byð, is, ys
into	an, in, inn, innan, into, on, to	Isaac (name)	Isace
		island	ealond, ealonde, eglond, eiglande, holme, ieg, iege, ige, iglond
intoxicated	win-gal		
intoxication	heafodswima		
introduce	onlædan, onlædde		
intruder	ingenga	island-dwelling	egbuendra
in-turn	eft	is-named	hattæ
invading-army	siðwerod, siþwerod	Israel	Israela
in-vain	holunge	it	ðæt, ðy, he, heo, heora, hi, hie, hiera, hig, hige, him, hine, hio, hiora, hira, hire, his, hit, hy, hym, hyne, hyra, hyre, hys, hyt, se, seo, þæt, þe
investigate	spyrede, spyrian		
investigation	fandung, fandunga		
invitation-to-drink-wine	winhatan, winhate		
invoke	clipige		
involuntarily	unwillum		
inward	geinnod, inneweard, innewerdne, innianfill	it-being-the-case-that	þa
inwardly	innan, innanweard	it-is	sy

Word List (English to *Ænglisc*)

English	*Ænglisc*	English	*Ænglisc*
its	*sin, sine, sines, sinne, sinre, sinum*	joy	*blis, bliss, blisse, bliþe, blysse, dream, dreama, dreamas, dreame, dreames, dreamum, gamen, gamene, gefea, gefean, gleodream, gomen, gomene, gumdream, hiht, hyht, hyhte, hyhtwynn, hyhtwynna, liðsa, liðsum, liss, lissa, lisse, lissum, liþsa, liþsum, mondream, mondreama, mondreamum, sæl, sæla, sæles, sælum, salum, sele, wyn, wynn, wynna, wynne, wynnum*
it-shall	*Se*		

J, j

Jacob (name)	*Iacob*		
jaw	*ceafl*		
jaws	*ceafl, goma, goman*		
jess-strap-for-a-falcon's-leg	*wyrpel, wyrplas*		
Jesus (name) (Latin)	*Iesum*		
jewel	*hyrst, hyrsta, hyrste, hyrstum, sigla, sigle, wræte, wrætt, wrætta, wrættum*		
jewel-kingdom	*gimmerice*		
jewels	*sinc*		
John (name)	*Iohannes*		
join	*fegan, fegeð, fegeþ, gefeg, gefeged, geþeodde, þeodan*		
Joseph (name)	*Iosep*	joyful	*Bliþe, dreamhabbende, dreamhabbendra, dreamhealdende, gamene, glædmod, glædmode, hyhtlic, wynlic, wynlicran, wynlicu*
Joseph's (name)	*Iosephes*		
journey	*ateah, ateon, fær, fære, for, fore, gelad, lad, lade, rad, rade, sið, siða, siðe, siðedon, siðes, siðfæt, siðfate, siðian, siðie, siðien, siðode, siþ, siþa, siþe, siþedon, siþes, siþfæt, siþfate, siþian, siþie, siþien, siþode, siþon*		
		joyful-day	*wyndæg, wyndagum*
		joyful-hearted	*hygebliþe, hygebliþran*
		joy-full	*hihtful, hihtfulne*
		joyfully	*lustum*
		joyless	*wynleas, wynleasne, wynleasran*
journey-elsewhere	*ellorsið, ellorsiþ*	joyous	*blið, bliðe, bliðne, bliþ, bliþe, bliþne, bliþra, fægen, fægne, hihtlic*
journey-forth	*forðsiþ, forðsiþes, forþsiþ, forþsiþes*		
journey-of-destruction	*spildsið, spildsiðe, spildsiþ, spildsiþe*	joyous-day	*dægwilla, dægwillan*
		joyously	*gliwstafum, wynnum*
		joyous-minded	*bliðemod, bliþemod*
journey-on-foot	*feðegang, feðegange, feþegang, feþegange*	joys	*dream, dreamas*
		joy-wood	*gomenwudu*
		jubilation	*hleahtor*
		Judas (name)	*Iudeas*

Word List (English to Ænglisc)

English	Ænglisc	English	Ænglisc
judge	Aðelwold, ademan, ademest, Aþelwold, dema, demað, deman, demaþ, demde, demdon, deme, demed, demend, forscrifan, forscrifen, gedemed	keep	eht, geheald, gehealdan, gehealde, gehealdeþ, geheold, gieman, gym, gyman, gymden, gymdon, gymeð, gymeþ, heald, healdað, healdan, healdaþ, healde, healdeð, healdest, healdeþ, heold, heoldan, heolde, heoldon, hiold, weardian, weardigan, weardode
judgement	dom, domas, dome, domes		
judgement-firm	domfæstne		
judging	demend		
judiciousness	foreþanc		
July (name)	Iulius		
just	efne, emne, riht, rihtan, rihte, rihtne, rihtum, soðfæst, soðfæste, soðfæstra, soþfæst, soþfæste, soþfæstra		
		keeper	hyrde, weard
		keeping	wær, ware
		keeping-in-mind	gemyndig
just (Latin)	iustus	keeping-secure	nearocræft, nearocræftum
just-as	swylce		
just-as-long	efenlang	keep-to	gieman, gym, gyman, gymden, gymdon, gymeð, gymeþ
justice	dom, domas, dome, domes, gerihte, rightly, riht, rihte, ryht, soð, soðe, soþ, soþe, truly		
		keep-watch	waca, wacan, woc, wocan, woce, wocon, wocun
justly	domlice, fægere, fægre, fægrost		
just-now	ungeara		

K, k

keen	scearp, scearpe, scearpne		
keen-edged	scirecg		

403

Word List (English to *Ænglisc*)

English	*Ænglisc*	English	*Ænglisc*
kill	abreat, abredwade, abredwian, abreot, abreotan, abreoten, abroten, acwealde, acwellan, aswefan, aswefede, breat, breotan, cwealdest, cwellan, cwellendum, forslean, forslegen, forwegan, forwegen, geotan, geotende, geslægene, geslegene, gesloh, heawan, heawen, heow, heowon, hynan, hynde, ofslagen, ofslean, ofslegene, ofsloh, slægen, slea, sleah, slean, slog, sloge, slogon, sloh, spilde, spillan, swebban, swefeð, swefeþ	kind-action	lufan, lufe, lufen, lufu, lufum
		kindle	ælað, ælan, ælaþ, on, onælan, onæled, onhætan, onhæted
		kindle-a-fire	weaht, weccað, weccan, weccaþ, weccean, wecceð, wecceþ, wehte
		kindling	ælað, ontendnyss, ontyndnys
		kindly	arlice
		kindness	arstaf, arstafum, milts, miltse, miltsum
		kind-of-tree	treocyn, treowcynn, treowcynnes, treowe
		kindred	cyðð, cyððe, cynn, cynnes, cyþþ, cyþþe, gemagas, mæg, mægða, mægðe, mæges, mægþa, mægþe, mægþum, maga, magas, magum
kill-by-shedding-the-blood-of	getan		
		kinds	cynn
killed	acwealde		
killer	aldorbana, aldorbanan, bana, banan, banena, bona, bonan, feorgbona, feorhbana, feorhbanan, feorhbona, feorhbonan, slaga, slagan		
killing	slege		
killing-spear	wælspera		
kin	cnosl, cnosle		
kind	cinne, cyn, cynn, cynna, cynne, cynnes, glædman, leoftæl, liðe, liþe, monðwære, monðwærust, monþwære, monþwærust		

Word List (English to Ænglisc)

English	Ænglisc	English	Ænglisc
king	*aldor, aldre, bregoweard, bregowearda, bregoweardas, cining, cyniges, cynincg, cyning, cyninga, cyningas, cyninge, cyninges, ðeoden, ðeodne, ðeodnes, ealdor, ealdre, ealdres, eðelweardas, eþelweard, eþelweardas, eþelwearde, fengel, frea, freadrihten, freadrihtnes, frean, goldgiefa, goldgiefan, goldgifa, goldgifan, goldgyfa, goldgyfan, kyning, kyninges, leod, leoda, leode, leodon, leodum, maþþumgyfa, ræswa, ræswan, sincgifa, sincgifan, sincgyfa, sincgyfan, þenden, þengel, þeoden, þeodnas, þeodne, þeodnes, þinum, þioden, waldend, waldende, waldendes, wealdend*	king's-councillor	*gewita, gewitan, weotena, wita, witan, witena*
		king's-seat	*cynestolum*
		kinsman	*gemagas, gesibb, gesibbra, gesibbum, mæg, mæga, mæges, maga, magas, magum*
		kinsmen	*mæcgea*
		kinswoman	*gesibb, gesibbra, gesibbum*
		kiss	*cyssan, cysse, cyston, gecyste*
		kith	*cyðð, cyððe, cyþþ, cyþþe*
		knee	*cneo*
		kneed	*cnedan, gecned*
		knew	*cunnade*
		knife	*seax, seaxe, seaxses*
		knife-wound	*sexbenn, sexbennum*
		knight	*cniht, cnihtas, cnihtum, cnyhtum*
		knit	*seowed, seowian*
		know	*can, cann, canst, cnawan, con, const, cuðe, cuðon, cunnan, cunne, cunnon, cuþe, cuþon, gecnawan, gecnaweð, gecnaweþ, gecunnad, gecunnade, gecunnian, nat, nyste, nyston, oncnawan, oncneow, oncniow, wast, wat, wat, wisse, wisson, wistan, wiste, wiston, witan, wite, witon, wyste, wytan*
kingdom	*bregorice, bregorices, cynedom, cynerice, cynerices, rice, rices*		
kingdom-of-heaven	*heofon-rice*		
kingdom's	*rices*		
king-glory	*kyningwuldor*		
kingly	*cynelic*		
kingly-brave	*cynerof, cynerofe, cyningbald, cyningbalde*		
		know-how-to	*cann, cuðe, cunnan, cunnon, cuþe*
kings	*cyningas*	knowing-man	*witiga*

Word List (English to Ænglisc)

English	Ænglisc	English	Ænglisc
knowledge	andgit, gefræge, gefrægen, gefrægn, gewitte, wite, witt	lament	begnornian, begnornod, begnornode, begnornodon, bemearn, bemurnan, bimurneð, bimurneþ, cwanian, cwiðan, cwiðe, cwiðed, cwiþan, cwiþe, cwiþed, gengword, giomorgyd, gnornað, gnornaþ, gnorngende, gnornian, gnornod, gnornode, gnornword, hiofan, hiofende, reotað, reotan, reotaþ, reoteð, reoteþ, seofad, seofade, seofedun, seofian, sorhleoð, sorhleoþ, wanigean
knowledgeable	felafricgende		
known	cuð, cuðe, cuðes, cuðra, cuþ, cuþe, cuþes, cuþra, gefrege, witod		
known-to	cuþ		
knows	wat		

L, l

English	Ænglisc	English	Ænglisc
labour	geswinc, swincan, swuncon, weorc, weorca, weorce, weorces, weorcum, worc, worca, worcum		
labourer	esne		
lack	gad, gæd, neod, niod, niode		
lacking	geasne, gesne, leas, leasan, lease, leasne, leasum, orfeorme, þearf, þearfa, þearfum, wana	lamentation	gnorn, gnornode, heaf, wop, wope
		lance	franca, francan
		land	eard, earda, eardas, earde, eardes, eardgeard, eðles, geard, geardas, geardum, land, landa, lande, landes, landscipe, lond, londe, londes, onlag, onlah, onleah, onleon, wancgturf
ladder	hlæder, hlædræ		
laden	gehladene, gehlædene, gehleod, geloden, hladan, hlade, hladen, hlodon		
ladle	hlade		
lady	frige, hlæfdian, hlæfdigan, hlæfdige, hlaf, hlafdian, hlafdige, ides, idesa, idese, idesum		
		landed	lende
		land-edge	landgemyrce, landgemyrcu
laid	legde, legdun	land-guardian	landweard
lake	mere, sæ	land-holding-king	landfruma
lake-bottom	meregrund, meregrundas	landing	upganga, upgangan
		land-layout	wang, wange, wong, wongas, wonge
lamb	lamb		
lame	lambyrd, lambyrde, lemedon, lemian	land-people	landwara
		land-right	landriht, londriht, londrihtes, londryht
lame-birth	lambyrde		

406

Word List (English to *Ænglisc*)

English	*Ænglisc*	English	*Ænglisc*
lands	æht, foldan, foldu, londes	law	aðystrað, æ, aþystraþ, gemet, gemete, gerihte, gesættnys, gesættnysse, lagu, rightly, riht, rihte, ryht, truly
land-wanderer	anstapan		
language	geþeode, hleoðor, hleoðre, hleoðrum, hleoþor, hleoþre, hleoþrum, reord, reorde, spæc, spæce		
		law-abiding	æfæst, æfæste
		law-maker	swutele
lank	hlanc, hlanca	laws	riht
lap	bearm, bearme, bearmum	lay	alecgan, alecgean, alede, aledon, alegde, alegdon, geled, læg, lægun, lecgað, lecgan, lecgaþ, lecge, leg, legde, legdon, lege, legeð, legeþ, legge, travel, wordgyd
larboard	bæc-bord		
large	great, greate, micel		
large-hearted	rumheort		
large-number	worn, worna, wornum		
large-piece-of-food	synsnæd, synsnædum		
large-wound	syndolh	lay-dead	læg, læge, lægon, lagon, leg, licgað, licgan, licgaþ, licgean, licgende, licgendre, lið, ligeð, ligeþ, ligst, liþ
lascivious	hygegal, hygegalan		
lasciviousness	galscipe		
last	gelæst, gelæstan, gelæste, gelæston, him, hindema, hindeman, læst, læstan, læste, læsten, læstes		
		lay-down	alecgan, alecgean, alede, aledon, alegde, alegdon
lasting	læstan, langtwidig	lay-hold-of	befangen, befon, befongen, bifongen
last-survivor	endelaf		
late	lata, late, sið, siðast, siðestan, siþ, siþast, siþestan	laying	gelæg
		lay-low	hynan, hynde
		lays	leg
late-birth	lætbyrde	lay-waste	yðan, yðde, yþan, yþde
later	siðestan, siþestan, siþþan, ufara, ufaran, ufera, uferan	lazy	læt, sæne, sænra
		lead	alaðaþ, alædan, alædde, alæde, alaþaþ, gelædað, gelædaþ, gelædde, gelæde, gelæded, læd, lædað, lædan, lædaþ, lædde, læddest, læddon, læde, læded
laugh	hlihende, hlihhan, hloh		
laugh-at	ahliehhan, ahlog, ahloh		
laughing	hlehhan		
laughter	hleahtor		
launch	draf, drifað, drifan, drifaþ, drife		
launching	gescot, gescotes	lead-astray	forlæd, forlædan, forlædd, forlæddan, forlædde, wemað, weman, wemaþ

Word List (English to Ænglisc)

English	Ænglisc	English	Ænglisc
leader	aldorwisa, ealdor, eorl, eorla, eorlas, eorle, eorles, eorlum, fruma, fruman, frumgar, frumgara, frumgaran, frumgaras, frumgare, frumgarum, heafde, heafdon, heafdum, heafod, hearra, heorra, herra, latteow, magoræswa, ordfruma, ordfruman, ræsbora, ræswa, ræswan, stigwita, stigwitum, wisa, wisan, yldesta, yldestan	leap-up	ahleapan, ahleop
		learn	geacsian, geahsod, geaxode, gefran, gefrinan, gefrunen, gefrunon, geleornian, geleornod, geleornode, leorna, leornian, leornode
		learned	frægn, gefran, gleaw
		learned-of	gefrugnon
		learning	lar, lara, lare, larena, larum
		leave	forlætan, forlæten, forlet, forleton, læf, læfan, læfde, læfed, ofgæfon, ofgeaf, ofgeafon, ofgeafun, ofgefan, ofgiefan, ofgif, ofgifan, ofgifen, ofgyfan
leaderless	aldorleas, aldorlease, aldorleasne	leave-behind	forlæt, forlætað, forlætan, forlætaþ, forlæte, forlæteð, forlæten, forlæteþ, forlet, forleton, oflætan, oflætest, oflet
leadership	ealdorduguð, ealdorduguðe, ealdorduguþ, ealdorduguþe, leodweard		
		leaving	laf
leading-officer	ealdorþegn, ealdorþegnum	leaving-black-tracks	sweartlast
		lecherous	galmod, galmoda, unsyfra, unsyfre
leading-warriors	aldorduguð, aldorduguðe, aldorduguþ, aldorduguþe	lechery	galnys, galnysse
		led	lædde, reducant
		led (Latin)	reducat
lead-to-destruction	forlæd, forlædan, forlædd, forlæddan, forlædde	left	lafan, Letan, wynstre
		legacy	laf, lafe
leaf	blæd, leaf, leafum	Leicester (place)	Ligoraceaster
lean	hlanc, hlanca, hyldan, hylde, læne	lend	lænan, lah, leon
		length	lengo, trem, trym
leap	gehleop, gesprang, gesprong, hleapan, hleapeð, hleapeþ, lacan, laceð, lacende, laceþ, leolc, sprang, springan, sprong, sprungon	lent	læne, onlag, onlah, onleah, onleon
		less	læs, læsest, læssa, læssan, leas
		lessen	lytlian, lytlod, lytlode
		lest	læs, læsest

Word List (English to Ænglisc)

English	Ænglisc	English	Ænglisc
let	forlæt, forlætað, forlætan, forlætaþ, forlæte, forlæteð, forlæten, forlæteþ, forlet, forleton, gelettan, læt, lætað, lætan, lætaþ, læte, læteð, læten, læteþ, let, lete, leton, Se, si	lie-dead	gelæg, læg, læge, lægon, lagon, leg, licgað, licgan, licgaþ, licgean, licgende, licgendre, lið, ligeð, ligeþ, ligst, liþ, swæf, swæfon, swæfun, swefað, swefan, swefaþ, swefeð, swefeþ
let-go	forlætan, oflætan, oflætest, oflet	lie-down	astreccan, astrece, astreht, beah, bugan, bugeð, bugeþ, bugon, gebeag, gebeah, gebogen, gebogenan
lethargic	læt		
let-Him-be-exalted	magnificat		
let-it-be-done	fiat		
letter-Scripture	gewrit, gewritu, gewrytum		
let-us	uton, wuton, wutun		
liar	wærloga, wærlogan, wærlogona, werloga, werlogan	liege-lord	mandrihten, mandrihtne, mandryhten, mandryhtne, mandryhtnes, mondrihten, mondryhten, mondryhtnes
liberally	gerumlicor, rumlice		
lichen-grey	ræghar		
lie	gelæg, geleah, læg, læge, lægon, lagon, leag, leasung, leasunga, leg, legen, leogan, leoge, licgað, licgan, licgaþ, licgean, licgende, licgendre, lið, ligeð, ligen, ligenum, ligeþ, ligst, liþ, lygenum, semian, seomade, seomedon, seomian, seomode, seomodon, siomian	lie-in-wait	semian, seomade, seomedon, seomian, seomode, seomodon, siomian
		lie-in-wait-for	sætan
		life	aldor, aldre, aldres, aldrum, blæd, ealdor, ealdre, ealdres, feora, feore, feores, feorg, feorh, feorum, ferh, fyore, leofes, leoht, leohte, leohtes, lif, life, lifes, lofe, lyfe, lyfes
lie-about	belicgan, belið, beligeð, beligeþ, beliþ, forleogan, forlugan	life (Latin)	uitam
		life-blood	sawldreor, sawldreore, sawuldrior, sawuldriore
lie-at-rest	semian, seomade, seomedon, seomian, seomode, seomodon, siomian	life-circumstance	lifgesceaft, lifgesceafta

Word List (English to Ænglisc)

English	Ænglisc	English	Ænglisc
life-day	aldordæg, aldordagum, ealderdagum	light (Latin)	lux
		light-beam	leoma, leoman, leomena
life-days	feorhdæg, feorhdaga, lifdagas, lifdagum	light-creator	leohtfruma, leohtfruman
		lightless	blind, blindum
life-destruction	aldorbealu	lightly	leohte
life-house	feorhhus, feorh-hus	light-of-battle	hildeleoma, hildeleoman
life-joy	lifwynn, lifwynna		
life-laying	feorhlege, feorhlegu	light-of-dragon-flame	hildeleoma, hildeleoman
lifeless	aldorleas, aldorleasne, ealdorleas, ealdorleasne, orsawle	lightweight	leoht
		like	an, gelic, gelica, gelican, gelice, gelicost, geuðe, geunnan, geunne, geuþe, on, uðe, unnan, uþe
lifelong	ealdorlangne		
life-lord	liffrea, Lif-frea, liffrean		
life-protection	lifwraðe, lifwraðu, lifwraþe, lifwraþu	likened	gelicade
		likeness	anlicnes, anlicnesse, anlycnysse, lic, lica, lice, lices, onlicnæs, onlicnes, onlicnesse
life-right	ferhtgereaht		
life's	lifes, lyfes		
life-saving	aldornere, aldorneru		
life's-guardian	feorhhyrde		
lifespan	tiddæg, tiddæge, tidege	like-this	þyslic, þyslicu
		likewise	also, swa, swilce, swylce
lift	ahæfen, ahafen, ahebban, ahof, ahofon, aræman, aræmde, hæfen, hafen, hebban, hefaenricaes, hefeð, hefeþ, hof	limb	leomu, leomum, leoþu, lið, liðum, lim, limum, liþ, liþu, liþum
		limb-mail-coat	leoðosyrcan, leoðosyrce, leoþosyrcan, leoþosyrce
lift-up	ahafen, ahebban, ahof, ahofon, aræran, arærde, arærdon, aræred, hafenian, hafenod, hafenode	limb-skill	leoðocræft, leoðocræftum, leoþocræft, leoþocræftum
		lime	lim, lime
light	ælað, ælan, ælaþ, beorht, beorhta, beorhtan, beorhte, beorhtne, beorhtost, beorhtra, beorhtre, beorhtum, byrhtan, leoht, leohtan, leohte, leohtes, leohtne, leohtra, leohtum, lihte, lioht	limit	gemearces, mearc, mearce
		Lincoln (place)	Lincylene
		lindens	linde

Word List (English to Ænglisc)

English	Ænglisc	English	Ænglisc
linden-wood	lindgestealla, lindhæbbend, lindhæbbende, lindhæbbendra, lindplega, lindplegan, lindwiga, lindwiggend, lindwiggende	live	bad, beodan, bidan, bideð, bideþ, bidon, buað, buan, buaþ, bude, bugan, bun, buon, byne, eardian, eardigean, eardod, eardode, eardodon, gebad, gebidan, gebidanne, gebide, gebiden, gebun, gesæt, gesæton, geseten, gewunedon, gewunigen, leofað, leofast, leofaþ, leofian, libban, lifd, lifde, lifdon, lifge, lifgende, lifgendne, lifgendum, lifiað, lifian, lifiaþ, lifigan, lifige, lifigende, lifigendum, lybban, lyfdon, sæt, sætan, sæte, sæton, setan, sittan, wuna, wunað, wunade
linden-wood-shield	lind, linde, lindum		
linden-wood-shield-bearing-army	lindwig		
lineage	æðelu, æþelo, æþelu		
link	seowed, seowian		
link-hilted-sword?	fet, fetelhilt		
link-in-a-chain-or-in-chainmail	hring, hringa, hringas, hringum		
linseed	linsetcorn		
lip	weler, weleras		
lips	weleras, welerum		
liquid	wæta, wætan		
listen	gehlyston, hlystan, hwæt		
litany	letanias, letanie		
lithe	swancor, swoncre		
litter	bær		
little	fea, hwon, litel, litla, litle, lyt, lytel, lythwon, lytle, lytlum	live-born	fulboren, fulborenum
		lived	lyfode
		lively	liffæst, liffæstan
little (Latin)	micro	livestock	æht, æhta, æhte, æhtum, fea, feo, feoh, feos, yrfe, yrfes
little-wen	wenchichenne		
		live-to-enjoy	gebad, gebidan, gebidanne, gebide, gebideð, gebiden, gebidenne, gebidenra, gebideþ
		livid	blatan, blatende

Word List (English to Ænglisc)

English	Ænglisc	English	Ænglisc
living	cucra, cwic, cwican, cwice, cwicera, cwices, cwiclifigende, cwiclifigendra, cwicne, cwico, cwicra, drohtað, drohtaþ, drohtoð, drohtoþ, feorheacen, feorheaceno, leofaþ, lifgende, lifgendne, lifgendum, lifiende, wunast	location	staðol, staðolas, staðole, staþel, staþelum, staþol, staþolas, staþole, styde
		location-for-settlement	staðolwang, staðolwangas, staþolwang, staþolwangas
		location-for-walls	wealsteal
		location-on-land	londstede
		lock	beleac, belocen, belucan, belucon, gelocen, locenra, lucan, lucon
living-at-home	hamsittende, hamsittendra, hamsittendum	locked	belocun, locen, locene
living-being	feora, feore, feores, feorg, feorh, feorhberend, feorhberendra, feorum, ferh, fyore	lock-up	beleac, belucan
		lodge	deposit, gelogodon, logian, wician, wicod, wicode
living-family	feorhcynn, feorhcynna	lodging	nihtfeormung, nihtfeormunge
		lofty	uplican, uplicne
living-lord	liffrea, liffrean	lonely	earm
living-person	lifgend, lifgenra	long	lang, langa, langað, langaþ, lange, langian, langne, langode, langre, langsum, langsumu, lansumum, leng, lengest, lengra, lengran, long, longade, longe, longsum
living-together	somwist		
living-torment	cwicsusl, cwicsusle		
load	gehladene, gehlædene, gehlæste, gehleod, geloden, hladan, hlade, hladen, hlæst, hlæstan, hlæste, hlodon		
loaded-with-boasting	gilphlæden	long-accumulated-treasure	longgestreon, longgestreona
loaf	hlaf	long-ago	ealdes, fyrn, gefyrn
loan	læn, lean, leana, leane, leanes, leanum	long-ago-craftsmanship	fyrngeweorc
		long-ago-day	fyrndaeg, fyrndagum
loaned	lænan, læne, onlag, onlah, onleah, onleon	long-ago-person	fyrnmann, fyrnmanna
		long-ago-struggle	fyrngewinn, fyrngewinnes
loathed	lað		
loathsome	lað	longer	leng
local	inlende		

412

Word List (English to Ænglisc)

English	Ænglisc	English	Ænglisc
longing	geliste, langað, langaþ, langoþe, longade, longaþ, longaþes, longung, longunge, neod, niod, niode	look-around	beseah, beseo, beseon, geondsceawað, geondsceawaþ, geondsceawian
longing-while	langunghwil, langunghwila	look-at	beseah, beseo, beseon, sceawian
long-lasting	longsum, longsumne	look-for	wlatian, wlatode
longs-for	lysteþ	look-over	geondseh, geondseon, giondwlitan
long-since	geara		
longsuffering	geþyld, geþyldig	look-upon	gesceawað, gesceawaþ, gesceawod, ofersawon, oferseon, onsegon, onseon, sceawa, sceawað, sceawaþ, sceawedon, sceawiað, sceawian, sceawiaþ, sceawigan, sceawige, sceawode, sceawodon
long-time-lord	ealdhlaford, ealdhlafordes		
look	gebide, gesawe, gesawon, gescyred, geseah, gesegan, gesegon, geseo, geseoð, geseon, geseoþ, gesihð, gesihþ, gesyhð, gesyhst, gesyhþ, locast, lociað, locian, lociaþ, locod, locode, sægon, sawon, seah, segen, seon, wlat, wlitað, wlitan, wlitaþ, wliten, wlitest, wliton		
		loom	hlifade, hlifian, hlifigan, hlifige, hlifigean, hliuade
		loose	onband, onbindan, onlysan, onlysde
look-about	besceawian, bewlat, bewlitan, bisceawað, bisceawaþ	loosen	alysan, alysed, onsæl, onsælan
		loot	herehuþ, herehuþe, noþ, noþe
look-after	beweotede, beweotode, bewitiað, bewitian, bewitiaþ, bewitigað, bewitigaþ, deah, dohte, dohtest, dugan, duge, feormian, gefeormedon, gefeormod, gieman, gym, gyman, gymden, gymdon, gymeð, gymeþ		

Word List (English to *Ænglisc*)

English	*Ænglisc*	English	*Ænglisc*
lord	aldor, aldordema, aldre, baldor, beaggyfa, beaggyfan, beahgifa, beahgifan, bealdor, brego, brytta, bryttan, ðeoden, ðeodne, ðeodnes, drihten, drihtne, drihtnes, dryctin, dryhten, dryhtne, ealdor, ealdre, ealdres, ederas, edor, edoras, eoderas, eodor, eodur, frea, freadrihten, freadrihtnes, frean, hearra, helm, helmas, helme, helmes, helmum, heorra, herra, hlaford, hlaforde, hlafordes, hlafordum, hlafurd, hleo, hleow, leod, ræswa, ræswan, sincgifa, sincgifan, sincgyfa, sincgyfan, strengel, þengel, þeoden, þeodnas	lordship	drihtscipe, drihtscipes, drihtscype, dryhtscype, ealdor, ealdordom
		lose	anforlætan, anforleten, beleas, beleosan, beloren, belorene, ðoliaþ, ðolode, ferlorene, forleas, forleosan, forloren, forworht, forworhte, forwyrcan, geþolian, geþolianne, geþolode, linnan, þolað, þolaþ, þoledon, þoliað, þolian, þoliaþ, þolien, þoligende, þolodan, þolode
		loss	forlor, forlore
		lot	dæl, dælas, dæle, gedal, gedale, gifeðe, gifeþe, hlytm, hlytme, siþ
		loud	hlud, hlude, hludne
		loudest	hludast
		loudly	hlude
lord (Latin)	dominum	love	freoð, freog, freogan, freoge, freondlufu, freoþ, frige, frigu, leof, leofa, leofan, leofe, leofes, leofestan, leofne, leofost, leofra, leofran, leofre, leofum, liðsa, liðsum, liofan, liss, lissa, lisse, lissum, liþsa, liþsum, lof, lofe, loue, lufan, lufe, lufen, lufiað, lufian, lufiaþ, lufien, lufode, lufu, lufum, mine, myne, sibblufan, sibblufu, siblufan, siblufu
lord-less	ðeodenleas, ðeodenlease, freondleas, freondleasne, þeodenleas, þeodenlease, wineleas, wineleasum		
lordly	bregorof, drihtlice		
lordly-chain	freawrasn, freawrasnum		
lordly-scion	dryhtbearn		
lordly-seat	bregostol		
lord-of	drihten, frea, waldend		
		love (Latin)	amor

Word List (English to *Ænglisc*)

English	*Ænglisc*	English	*Ænglisc*
loved	leofa, leofan, leofe, leofes, leofestan, leofne, leofost, leofra, leofran, leofre, leofum	lying-word	ligenword, ligenwordum

M, m

English	*Ænglisc*	English	*Ænglisc*
love-for-a-woman	wiflufan, wiflufu	made	gesceop, uuyrican, wyrican
lovely	fæger, fægere, fægerra, fægir, fægran, fægre, fægroste	made-famous	gemærsod
		made-great	gemærsodest
		made-iron	isern, iserna
love-of-a-wife	wifmyne	made-known	gecyþed!, swytelað
love-of-a-woman	wifmyne	madness	wodnys, wodnysse
lover	freond	Maering (place)	Mæringa
love-relationship	freondscipe, freondscype	magic	galdor, galdre, gealdor
love-token	luftacen	magician	dry, dryum
loving	lufsum	magistrate	aldordema
lower	bygan	magnificent	deal, deall, dealle, dealne, geatolic, þrymlic
lower-end	wyrtruma, wyrtruman		
lowly	hean, heane, heanne, hnag, hnagran, hnah, hnahran	maid	fæmnan, fæmne, fæmnum, femnan
		maiden	mæden, mædene, mædenman, mæg, mægða, mægðum, mægeð, mægeþ, mægþ, mægþa, mægþum, meowlan, meowle
loyal	hold, holde, holdne, holdost, holdra		
loyalty	hyldo, treow		
Luke (name)	Lucos		
luminary	leoma, leoman, leomena	maidservant	þeowmennen, wale
lure	bedragan, bedrog		
lust	gal, galnys, galnysse, lust, lustas, luste, lustum		
lustful	galferhð, galferhþ		
lustrous	brun, brune, brunne		
luxury	gal, galscipe		
lying	gelæg, læg, læge, lægon, lagon, leas, leasan, lease, leasne, leasum, leg, licgað, licgan, licgaþ, licgean, licgende, licgendre, lið, ligeð, ligeþ, ligst, liþ		
lying-place-bed	leger, legere		
lying-with	leger		

Word List (English to Ænglisc)

English	Ænglisc	English	Ænglisc
mail-coat	*beaduscrud, beaduscruda, breostgewædu, breostnet, breostweorðung, breostweorðunge, breostweorþung, breostweorþunge, byrnan, byrne, byrnhom, byrnhomas, byrnum, fyrdhrægl, guðbyrne, guþbyrne, herenet, herepad, herewæd, herewædum, hlencan, hlence, hringnet, licsyrce, searonet, syrcan, syrce, wælnet*	majesty-people	*dugeða, dugeðe, dugeðum, dugeþa, dugeþe, dugeþum, dugoða, dugoðe, dugoþa, dugoþe, duguð, duguða, duguðe, duguðum, duguþ, duguþa, duguþe, duguþum*
mail-coat-rings	*bræd, brægd, bregdan, bregde, bregdon, broden, brogdne, brudon, brugdon, gebræd, gebroden*	make	*dædon, deð, deþ, do, doð, don, doþ, dyde, dydest, dydon, fremeð, fremede, fremedon, fremest, fremeþ, fremmað, fremman, fremmaþ, fremme, fremmen, gæworht, geæfnan, gedæde, gedeð, gedeþ, gedo, gedoð, gedon, gedoþ, gedyde, gedydon, gefremed, gefremede, gefremeden, gefremedon, gefremman, gefremmanne, gemacod, gesceapen, gesceapene, gesceop, gescype, geworht, geworhte, geworhtne, geworhton, gewyrc, gewyrcan, gewyrce, gewyrcean, macian, sceop, scepen, scieppan, scop, weorcan, worhte, worhton, wyrcan, wyrce*
mail-coat-slaughter	*wælhlencan, wælhlence*		
mail-shirt	*byrne*		
mail-shirted-warrior	*byrnwiga, byrnwigena, byrnwiggend, byrnwiggende*		
main-strong	*mægenstrang, mægenstranga*		
maintain	*ahæfen, ahafen, ahebban, ahof, ahofon*		
majestic	*mære*		
majestic-building	*ðryþærn, þryþærn*		
majesty	*dom, domas, dome, domes, drihtscipe, ðrym, þrym, þrymm, þrymmas*	make-a-booming-noise	*þunede, þunian*
		make-a-din	*dynedan, dynede, dynian*

Word List (English to Ænglisc)

English	Ænglisc	English	Ænglisc
make-an-agreement	getruwedon, getruwode, getruwodest, truwian, truwode	make-known	acyþan, ameldian, ameldod, bead, beodan, beodeð, beodeþ, biodan, boden, bude, budon, cyð, cyðað, cyðan, cydde, cyðde, cyðdon, cyðed, cyþ, cyþað, cyþan, cyþaþ, cyþde, cyþdon, cyþed, gebad, gebead, gebeodan, gecyd, gecyðan, gecyðanne, gecyðde, gecyðed, gecyþan, gecyþanne, gecyþde, gecyþed, scyran, wissian
make-anew	geniwad, geniwod, niwiað, niwian, niwiaþ		
make-an-offering-or-oblation	offrian, ofrað, ofraþ		
make-a-noise	cirman		
make-a-speech	gyddian, gyddode		
make-a-track	spyrede, spyrian		
make-bare	beredon, berian		
make-beautiful	gewlitegad, wlitigað, wlitigaþ, wlitigian, wlitigigan		
make-bloody	blodigian, geblodegod		
make-by-craftsmanship	besmiþian, besmiþod		
make-clear	geswutelod, geswutelode, sweotolian	make-manifest	geswutelod, geswutelode, sweotolian
make-decisions	geræd, gerædest, rædað, rædan, rædaþ, rædde	make-more-spacious?	romigan
		make-music	hlynsian, hlynsode, swinsian, swinsigende, swynsode
make-delightful	gliwedon, gliwian		
make-greater	miclade, miclian		
make-happy	blissian, blissigende, geblissad		
		make-noise	hlydan, hlydde, swægende, swegan
make-hard	gehyrde, gehyrdeð, gehyrdeþ, hyrdan	maker	factor
make-higher	herran	maker (Latin)	factor
		make-space-for	gerymde, gerymdon, gerymed, ryman, rymde
		make-straight	gerihtlæcan, gerihtlæced
		make-too-drunk	oferdrencan, oferdrencte
		make-trial-of	gecunnad, gecunnade, gecunnian
		make-use-of	genyttod, nyttade, nyttian
		make-walk	feþað, feþan, feþaþ
		make-weary	gewergad, wergian
		make-whole	gehæled, gehælede, hælan, hældon

Word List (English to Ænglisc)

English	Ænglisc	English	Ænglisc
male	wæpned	man	æðela, æðelan, æðele, æðelo, æðelum, æþela, æþelan, æþele, æþelo, æþelu, æþelum, beorn, beorna, beornas, beorne, beornes, beornum, biorn, biorna, ceorl, ceorlas, ceorle, ceorles, ðegn, ðegna, ðegnas, drihtguma, drihtguman, drihtwer, drihtwera, drihtweras, dryhtguma, dryhtguman, dryhtgumum, eorl, eorla, eorlas, eorle, eorles, eorlum, esne, folcwer, folcweras, freca, frecan, guma, guman, gumena, gummann, gummanna, gumrinc, gumrincum, gumum, hæl, hælæð, hælæþ, hæle, hæleð, hæleða, hæleðum
male-descendant	cneowmæg, cneowmægas, cneowmagas		
male-gender	wæpnedcynn, wæpnedcynnes		
male-kinsman	cneomæg, cneomagum, maga, mago		
male-offspring	magotudor, magotudre		
male-person	wæpmonn, wæpnedmann, wæpnedmen		
male-relative	gemagas, mæg, mæges, maga, magan, magas, magorinc, magorinca, magorincas, magorince, magum		
malevolent	heteþoncol, heteþoncolne		
malice	æfðoncan, æfst, æfstum, æfþanc, æfþancum, æfþonca, æfþoncan, anda, inwitsearo, nið, niþ, teona, teonan, teonum		
malice-mindful	niðhedig, niðhedige, niþhedig, niþhedige		
malice-net	inwitnet		
malice-story	inwitspell		
malice-web	inwitnet	management	feorm, feorme
malicious	fæcna, fæcne, inwidsorg, inwitfull, inwitfulle, inwitsorge, inwitsorh, laþwendemod	man-and-paternal-uncle	suhtergefæderan
		manifest	ætywed, cuð, cuðe, cuðes, cuðra, cuþ, cuþe, cuþes, cuþra, gerymde, gerymdon, gerymed, gesene, gesiene, gesyne, ryman, rymde, sweotol, sweotolan, swutol, underne, undyrne
malicious-alien	inwitgæst		
malicious-hatred	teonhete		
malicious-slaughter	inwitscear		
malicious-stranger	niðgæst, niþgæst		
		manifestly	undyrne
		manifold	monigfealde

Word List (English to Ænglisc)

English	Ænglisc	English	Ænglisc
manipulation	*gebregd*	mark	*gemearca, gemearces, gemearcod, gemearcode, mæl, mæla, mæles, mælo, mælum, mearc, mearcað, mearcaþ, mearce, mearcian, mearcode, mercels, mercelses*
mankind	*eormencynn, eormencynnes, mancyn, mancynn, mancynne, mancynnes, manncynnes, moncynn, moncynne, moncynnes, monn-cynn, monnum*		
mankind's	*moncynnæs, moncynnes*	marked-by-death	*wælfag, wælfagne*
		Mark's (name)	*Marcus*
man-lord	*mondryhten*	married-couple	*sinhiwan, sinhiwum*
manly	*manlice*	marsh	*fen, fenn, fenne*
manner	*ðeawum, siodo, þeaw, þeawas, þeawum, wisan, wise, wisna, wisum, wysan*	martial-anthem	*guðleoð, guþleoþ*
		martial-deed	*beaduweorc, beaduweorces*
		martial-equipment	*guðsceorp, guþsceorp*
manners	*cinne, cyn, cynn, cynna, cynne, cynnes, þeawas*	martial-injurer	*guðsceaða, guþsceaþa*
		martial-song	*fyrdleoð, fyrdleoþ*
man's	*mann, mannes, monnes*	martial-sound	*heresweg*
		martial-sport	*guðplega, guþplega, wigplega, wigplegan*
mansion	*wic, wica, wicum, wicun*	martial-sports	*handplega, handplegan*
many	*fæla, feala, fealo, fela, genog, genoge, genoh, genohra, mænegum, mænig, mænigfeald, mænigfealde, mænigne, mænigo, manega, manegum, manig, manige, manigne, manigra, manigre, manigum, menegu, monegum, monge, monig, monige, moniges*	martial-vigour	*herewæsm, herewæsmun*
		martyrdom	*martyrdom*
		marvel	*hondwundor, hondwundra, searowundor, wunder, wundor, wundra, wundre, wundrian, wundrigende, wundrodon, wundur*
		marvellous	*sellic, sellice, syllic, syllicran, syllicre, wrætlic, wunderlicu, wundorlic, wundorlicran*
many-things	*worn, worna, wornum*		
marauding-army	*stæl-here*		
marital-bedroom	*brydbur, brydbure*	marvellous-death	*wundordeað, wundordeaðe, wundordeaþ, wundordeaþe*
		marvellously	*wundrum*

Word List (English to Ænglisc)

English	Ænglisc	English	Ænglisc
marvellous-sight	wundorsion, wundorsiona	mead-cup	medoful, meoduful, meoduscenc, meoduscencum
marvellous-smith	wundorsmiþ, wundorsmiþa	mead-drink	medu-drinc
marvellous-treasure	wundurmaððum, wundurmaþþum	mead-drinking	medodrinc, medodrince
Mary (name)	Marian, Marie	mead-hall	medoærn, medoheal, medoheall, medohealle, medu-heall, meduseld, meoduhealle
masculine	wærlecum, wærlices, wærlicum, werlic		
mass	mæssan, mæsse, mæssepreost, messepreost, messepreoste	mead-hall-ground	meodowong, meodowongas
massive-army	sinhere, sinherge	mead-halls	meodoheall
mass-priest	messepreost	mead-joy	medudream, meododream, meododreama
mast	mæst, mæste		
master	frea, hlaford, waldend	mead-joys	meododreama
match	efenlæcan, geeuenlæhton	mead-plain	meodowong, meodowongas
mate	gemæcca, gemæccum	mead-seat	medu-setl, meodosetl, meodosetla
material	getimbro		
Matilda (name)	Mæðhilde	mead-towns	meoduburgum
matter	andweorc	meal	melo, swæsendu, swæsendum, þegnung, þegnunge
Matthew's (name)	Matheus		
mature-men	duguþ		
may	mæg, mæge, mægen, maga, magan, mage, magon, meahte, mot, motan, mote, moton	meals	beodgereordu
		mean	gemynt, gemynted, hnag, hnagran, hnah, hnahran, myntan, mynte, mynteð, mynteþ, mynton
may-be	mæg		
me	ic, me, mec	meaning	andgit, ingehyd, ingehyde
mead	medo, medodrinc, medodrince, medu, meodo	means	gemete, sped
		meanwhile	þenden
mead-bench	medobenc, medobence, medubenc, medubence, meodubenc, meodubence	measure	eln, elna, gemet, gemete, gemette, gemetton, mæl, mæt, mæton, metan
		measured-cubit	elngemet, elngemeta
mead-city	medoburg, medobyrig, meoduburgum	measured-ell	elngemet, elngemeta
		measurement-in-miles	milgemearc, milgemearces

Word List (English to Ænglisc)

English	Ænglisc	English	Ænglisc
measure-out	gemette, gemetton, mæt, mæton, metan	men-band	magodriht
meat	mete, metes	men's	secga
meet	gemete, gemeted, gemette, gemetton, gemittan, gemitte, gemitton, metan, meted, mette, metton, motan	men-seat	gumstol, gumstole
		mental-bond	hyge, hygebend, hygebendum
		mental-distress	hreþerbealo
		mental-sorrow	higesorg, higesorga, hygesorg, hygesorga, hygesorge
meeting	ðing, ðinga, ðinges, geanoðe, geanoþe, gemeting, gemot, gemotes, þincg, þing, þinga, þinge, þinges	mental-trouble	modgewinna, modgewinnan
		mention	eahtedon, eahtian, eahtodan, eahtode, ehtigað, ehtigaþ, geæhted, gemænden, mænað, mænan, mænaþ, mænde, mændon, mæned, styrede, styreþ, styrge, styrian
meeting-place	meðelstede, meþelstede		
melody	dream, dreama, dreamas, dreame, dreames, dreamum		
melt	gemealt, gemyltan, mealt, meltan, multon		
		men-troop	eorlweorod
member	leoþu, lið, liðum, liþ, liþu, liþum	merchant	cepemann, cepemannum
member-of-tribe	leod	merchants	cepemannum
memory	gemynd, gemynda, gemynde, gemyndum, mine, modgemynd, myne	Mercia	Myrceon
		Mercia (place)	myrce
		Mercians	Myrce
		merciful	bilwit, milde, mildum, mildust
men	ælda, beorn, dryht, dryhtum, elde, eldum, eorlas, eorle, fira, firas, firum, foldbuend, foldbuende, foldbuendum, fyra, guma, guman, gumena, hæleð, mæca, man, manna, men, monnes, niða, niðas, niðða, niððas, niððum, niðþa, niþa, niþas, niþða, niþþa, niþþas, niþþum, niþum, scealcum, wera, weras, ylda, ylde, yldo, yldum	mercifulness	arfestnesse
		mercy	ar, ara, aran, are, arena, arna, arra, arum, ðanc, mildse, milts, miltse, miltsum, þanc
		mere	mere
		merit	earna, earnian, geearnaþ, geearnod, geearnung, geearnunga, geearnunge, gewyrht, gewyrhtum
		merriment	bencsweg
		message	ærenda, ærende, bodscipe, spell, spellum
menace	þreatedon, þreatian		

Word List (English to Ænglisc)

English	Ænglisc	English	Ænglisc
message-carrying	ærendian	might	abal, dom, domas, dome, domes, eafeþum, eafoð, eafoþ, eafoþes, eofoð, eofoðo, eofoþ, eofoþo, geweald, gewealde, gewealdum, maecti, mægen, mægencræft, mægene, mægenes, mægna, mægne, mægnes, mægnu, mægyn, meaht, meahte, miht, mihta, mihton, motan, mote, secgum, weald
messenger	ærendraca, ærendreca, ærendrecan, ærendsecg, ar, aras, ares, boda, bodan, spellboda, spellbodan		
messenger-spirit	ærendgast		
met	gemete, gemeted		
metal-mask	grima, grimmon		
metal-worker	smið, smiðas, smiþ, smiþa, smiþas, smiþes		
mew	mæw		
mid	midd, middum, midne, midre		
middle	midd, midde, middum, midne, midre	might-endowed	mægeneacen
		mightily	ðrymmum, þrymme, þrymmes, þrymmum
middle-earth	middaneard, middan-eard, middangeard, middangearde, middangeardes, middungeard	might-mood	mihtmod
		might-owner	mægenagend, mægenagendra
		mighty	domeadig, dryctin, ðryðlic, maegenrof, mæhtum, meahte, meahtig, meahtigra, mihta, mihtig, mihtiga, mihtigan, mihtiges, mihtigne, rica, rican, rice, ricne, ricost, ricra, ricum, swið, swiþ, swyð, swyþ, þearlmod, þryðge, þryðig, þryðlic, þrydlicost, þrymfæst, þrymfæste, þrymfæstne, þrymful, þryþge, þryþig, þryþlic
middle-world	middaneard, middangeard, middangearde, middangeardes		
middling	midde-weard		
midnight	middelniht, middelnihtum		
mid-ward	midde-weard		
		mighty-burden	mægenbyrþen, mægenbyrþenne
		mighty-company	mægencorðor, mægencorðrum, mægencorþor, mægencorþrum

Word List (English to *Ænglisc*)

English	*Ænglisc*
mighty-strength	mægenstrengo, mægenstrengu
mighty-support	mægenfultum, mægenfultuma
mighty-swing	maegenraes
mighty-warrior	þeodwiga
mild	milde, mildum, mildust, miltse
mile	mil
mile-track	milpaðas, milpæð, milpæþ, milpaþas
military-camp	fyrdwic, fyrdwicum
military-campaign	fyrd, fyrde
military-company	cista, cyst, cystum
military-encampment	herewic, herewicum
military-equipment	eoredgeatwe
military-expedition	wigsð, wigsþ
military-force	prass, prasse
military-leader	hildewisa, hildewisan
military-troop	eoredcystum, mægenheap, mægenheapum
milk	meolc, meolce, meoluc
Mimming (name)	Mimming

English	*Ænglisc*
mind	breosthord, feorð, feorþ, ferð, ferðe, ferhð, ferhðe, ferhðes, ferhðum, ferhþ, ferhþe, ferhþes, ferhþum, ferþ, ferþe, gehygd, gemynd, geþoht, geþohtas, geþohte, gewitloca, gewitlocan, hige, higes, higum, hræðre, hræþre, hreðer, hreðra, hreðre, hreþer, hreþra, hreþre, hyge, hygesceaft, hygesceaftum, mine, mod, mode, modes, modgeðance, modgeþanc, modgeþonc, modgeþonce, modsefa, mod-sefa, modsefan, modum, sefa, sefan, wenan
minded	gehugod
mindful	gemindige, gemynde, gemyndi, gemyndig
mindful-of	gemyndig
mind-plans	modgeþanc, modgidanc
minds	siofa, siofan
mind's	hyge, modes
mind-sad	modgidanc, modgiomor
mind-sadness	modceare, modcearu
mind-wearying	higemæðum, higemæþum, hygemeðe, hygemeþe
mine	me, min, mina, mine, mines, minne, minra, minre, minum
mingle	gemenged, mencgan, mengan

Word List (English to *Ænglisc*)

English	*Ænglisc*	English	*Ænglisc*
minister	ðegn, ðegna, ðegnas, þa, þægn, þægne, þegen, þegenas, þegn, þegna, þegnas, þegne, þegnes, þegnum	miserable	balwon, bealu, earfoðlic, earfoþlic, earm, earmcearig, earm-cearig, earme, earming, earmlic, earmne, earmra, earmran, earmre, feasceaft, feasceafte, feasceaftum, geomor, geomorlic, geomormod, geomorne, geomorre, geomran, geomre, geomuru, hean, heane, heanne, heard, hearda, heardan, hearde, heardes, heardne, heardost, heardra, heardran, heardum, hreowcearig, hreowig, hreowige, hygegeomor, hygegeomorne, hygegiomor, rædleas, rædlease, sorgful, sorgfulre, sorhful, sorhfull, sorhfullne, sorhfulne, torn, torne, tornost, unsælga, unsælig, wa, wealic, werge
minster-inhabitant	mynstermann, mynstermen, mynstermenn		
minster-man	mynstermann, mynstermen, mynstermenn		
minstrel	gleomann, gleomannes		
miracle	wundor		
mirth	gamen, gamene, gomen, gomene, hleahtor, mirigðe		
mirthful	gamene		
mischief	unræd, unræde, unrædes, yfel		
misdirect	forlæran, forlærde, forlæred		
		miserable-because-lacking-a-hall	seledreorig
		miserable-journey	earfoðsið, earfoðsiða, earfoðsiþ, earfoþsiþ, earfoþsiþa
		miserable--minded	geomormod, geomormode, geomormodum, giomormod
		miserable-person	earfeðmæcg, earfeðmæcgum, earfeþmæcg, earfeþmæcgum

Word List (English to Ænglisc)

English	Ænglisc	English	Ænglisc
miserable-residence	cearseld, cearselda	misty	mistig, mistige
miserable-track	wræclast, wræclastas	misty-gloom	mistglom, mistglome
		misty-slope	misthleoþum, misthliþ
miserable-with-age	geomorfrod	mitigate	gemilsa
miserably	bleate, earfoðlice, earfoþlice, earme, earmlice, geomore, geomormode, werige, werigne	mix	gemenged, mengan
		mixed	gebland, gemenged
		mixed-hair-colour	blondenfeax, blondenfeaxe, blondenfeaxum, blondenfexa
miseries	weana		
miserly	gneað, gneaþ, hneaw	mixed-in	geblonden
misery	bealewa, bealu, bealuwa, bealwa, breostceare, breostcearu, cearsorg, cearsorge, earfoþa, hearm, hearma, hearmas, hearme, hearmes, nydwracu, susl, susle, torn, torna, torne, wean, wita, wite, witum, wonn, wonsceaft, wonsceaftum, wrace, wracu, wræc, wræce, wræces, wyta, wytum, yrmða, yrmðe, yrmðu, yrmðum, yrmþa, yrmþe, yrmþu, yrmþum	mixed-with	geblonden
		mixture	bland, gemang, gemong, gemonge
		moan	mænan, mænde, mæned
		moans	monge
		mock	bysmeredon, bysmerian, gebysmrian, plegan, plegian, plegode
		mockery	bysmor
		model	bysen, bysene, bysna
		moist	wæt
		moisten	besteman, bestemed, bestyman, bestymed, wætan, wæteð, wæteþ, wætte
		moisture	steam, steame, wæta, wætan
misery-track	wræc-last	moment	fæc
misfortune	laðscipe, laþscipe	momentarily	ungeara
misinform	forlæran, forlærde, forlæred	monastery	mynster, mynstre
		monastic	mynsterlic, mynsterlicre
mislead	forlacan, forlacen, forlæd, forlædan, forlædd, forlæddan, forlædde, forlec	monastic-community	hired, hyrde, hyred, hyredes
		monastic-life	drohtnian, drohtnode, drohtnung, drohtnunge, gedrohtnunge
miss-a-target	missan, miste		
misshapen-birth	untydras, untydre		
mission	aerendfaest		
mist	gesweorc, mist, mistas		
mistress	hlæfdian, hlæfdigan, hlæfdige, hlafdian, hlafdige	monastic-rule	drohtnung, drohtnunge, gedrohtnunge

Word List (English to Ænglisc)

English	Ænglisc	English	Ænglisc
money	feoh, sceat, sceates, sceatt, sceattas, sceattes, sceattum	morning-long	morgenlong, morgenlongne
money-gift	feoh-gift	morning-noise	morgensweg
moneyless	feoh-leas	morning-slaughter	morgencolla, morgencollan
monk	mynstermann, mynstermen, mynstermenn	morning-time	morgentid
		morning--time	morgentid, undernmæl
monks	munecon	morning-twilight	uhtan, uhte, uhtna, uhttid
monster	aglæca, eoten, eotena, eotenas	morsel	giefl, gieflum
monsters	orcneas	mortal-blow	feorhsweng
monstrous	unheore, unheoru, unhiore, unhyre	mortal-enemy	feorhgeniðla, feorhgeniðlan, feorhgeniþla, feorhgeniþlan
monstrous-thing	forsceap, forsceape		
month	monað, monaþ, moncynnes, monðes, monoð, monþes	mortal-evil	cwealmbealu
		mortally-wounded	feorhseoc
		mortar	lim, lime
monument	beacen, beacna, beacne, beacnum, becn	Moses (name)	Moyses
		most	mæst, mæsta, mæste, mæstne
mood	mod, mode	most-greedy	gifrost
mood-caring	mod-cearig	most-high	hehsta, hehstan, hehste, hehstne, hyhsta
mood-love	modlufan, modlufu		
mood-mind	mod, modgemynd		
mood-proud	mod-wlonc	most-like	gelicost
moon	mona, monan, tungel, tunglum, tungol	most-recently	nehst, nehstan, next, niehstan, nyhstan
moor	fen, fenn, fenne, gesæled, hydað, hydan, hydaþ, mor, moras, more, sælan, sælde, sældon	most-similarly	gelicost
		most-widely-separated	gewidost
		moth	moððe, moþþe
		mother	mæder, meder, moder, modor, modur
mooring	hydað, hydan, hydaþ		
moor-retreat	morhop, morhopu	motionless	stille
morality	siodo	mound	beorg, hlæw, hlæwe, hlaw, hlawe
more	ma, mara, maran, mare	mounds	beorgum, hlæw
more-junior	geongra	mount	astag, astah, asteah, astigan, astigeð, astigeþ, gestah, gestigan, gestigen, gestigest, gestigon, stah, stigan, stige, stigon
moreover	eac		
more-remotely	widre		
morning	mergen, mergenne, morgen, morgena, morgne, morna		
morning-cold	morgenceald		
morning-light	morgenleoht		

Word List (English to Ænglisc)

English	Ænglisc	English	Ænglisc
mount-a-horse	gehleop, hleapan, hleapeð, hleapeþ	mourning	gnorn, gnornode
mountain	beorg, beorgas, beorge, beorges, beorgum, beorh, biorgas, biorges, biorh, dun, duna, dune, dunum, mor, moras, more	mouth	ceafl, goma, goman, muð, muðe, muþ, muþe
		mouth-bane	muðbona, muðbonan, muþbona, muþbonan
mountain-ash	cwicbeam, cwicbeame	mouthful	muð-ful, muð-fulne, muþ-ful, muþ-fulne
mountain-cave	dunscrafum	mouth-of-a-river	muða, muþa
mountain-current	firgenstream, firgenstreamum	mouths	muðe
mountainous-region	mor	move	astyred, astyrian, bræd, brægd, bregdan, bregde, bregdon, broden, brogdne, brudon, brugdon, gan, gebræd, gebroden, gehwearf, gehwyrfed, gesigan, gewaden, gewod, hreran, hrerde, hrered, hwærf, hwearf, hweorfan, hweorfeð, hweorfeþ, hworfan, hwurfe, hwurfon, hwyrfað, hwyrfan, hwyrfaþ, hwyrfde, hwyrfeð, hwyrfeþ, onbræd, onbrægd, onbregdan, onhreran, onhrered, sigan, sigeð, sigeþ, sigon, wadan, wæg, wægon, wagon, wegan, wege, wegeð, wegeþ, wegon, wigeð, wigeþ, wod, wodon
mountains	duna, dune		
mountain-slope	beorhhleoþum, beorhhlið, beorhhliþ		
mountain-stream	firgenstream, firgenstreamum, fyrgenstream		
mountain-top	fyrgenheafde, fyrgenheafod		
mountain-tree	fyrgenbeam, fyrgenbeamas		
mountain-wood	fyrgenholt		
mourn	begnornian, begnornod, begnornode, begnornodon, cwiðan, cwiðdon, cwiþan, cwiþdon, geomra, geomrian, geomrode, gnornað, gnornaþ, gnorngende, gnornian, gnornod, gnornode, mearn, murnan, murne, murnende, murnon		
mourn-about	begrornian, bemearn, bemurnan, bimurneð, bimurneþ	move-fast	scriðað
		movement	gebregd, hwyrft, hwyrftum, onwende
mourned	gnornung	movement-power	feðe, feþe
mournful	geomres, reotig, reotugu	move-quickly	arn, irnan, snyredon, snyrian, urnon, yrnende, yrnendum
mournful-word	gengword, gnornword		

Word List (English to Ænglisc)

English	Ænglisc	English	Ænglisc
move-rapidly	onettan, onette, onetteð, onetteþ, onetton	murder	cwalm, cwealdest, cwealm, cwealme, cwealmes, cwellan, cwellendum, feorhcwealm, morð, morðer, morðes, morðor, morðorbealo, morðra, morðre, morðres, morþ, morþer, morþes, morþor, morþorbealo, morþra, morþre, morþres
much	fæla, feala, fealo, fela, genog, genoge, genoh, genohra, maran, miccle, miccles, miccli, micclum, micel, miceles, micelne, micla, miclan, micle, micles, miclum, mycclum, mycel, mycele, mycelre, mycle, myclum, swiðe		
multitude	corðor, corðre, corðrum, corþor, corþre, corþrum, driht, drihta, dugeða, dugeðe, dugeðum, dugeþa, dugeþe, dugeþum, dugoða, dugoðe, dugoþa, dugoþe, duguð, duguða, duguðe, duguðum, duguþ, duguþa, duguþe, duguþum, gedræg, gedreag, gedriht, gemang, gemong, gemonge, heap, heape, heapum, here, herga, hergas, herge, herges, hergum, herige, heriges, mænegeo, mænego, mænige, mænigeo, mænigo, mæniu, manigeo, mengeo, menigeo, meniu, scole, scolu, worn, worna, wornum	murderer	aldorbana, aldorbanan, feorgbona, feorhbana, feorhbanan, feorhbona, feorhbonan, ordbana, ordbanan
		murderous-attack	wælræs, wælræse
		murderous-evil	feorhbealo, feorhbealu, morðbeala, morðbealu, morþbeala, morþbealu
		murderous-rain	wællregn
		murderous-spear	bongar
		murderous-spirit	wælgæst
		murderous-visitor	cwealmcuma, cwealmcuman
		muscle	banloca, banlocan
		muscle-fibre	seono, seonowe
		muscles	banloca
		music	dream, dreama, dreamas, dreame, dreames, dreamum, gleo, hlyn, sweg, swege
		music-wood	gleobeam, gleobeames
multitudes	mænego		

Word List (English to *Ænglisc*)

English	*Ænglisc*
must	*scal, sceal, sceall, scealt, scel, sceolde, sceolden, sceoldest, sceoldon, sceole, sceolon, scile, scolde, scoldon, sculan, sculon, scyle*
must-do	*aninga*
mutilated	*hamelode*
my	*me, mec, min, mine, mines, minre*
myself	*me*
mysteries	*gerynum*
mysterious	*deogol, dygel*

N, n

English	*Ænglisc*
nail	*nægl, nægla, næglum*
nailed	*nægled, næglede*
nailed-board	*næledbord*
nailed-knorrs	*negledcnearrum*
naked	*bær, bare, baro, baru, nacod*
name	*benemde, benemdon, benemnan, cygan, cygde, gecyged, gehate, gehaten, gehet, geheton, genemned, hat, hatað, hatan, hataþ, hate, haten, hatene, hatte, heht, het, hete, heton, nama, naman, namon, nemde, nemdon, nemed, nemnað, nemnan, nemnaþ, noma, noman*
named	*genemned, hatað, hate, nama*
name-given	*cenned*
names	*naman*
narrate	*awræc, awrecan, reccan, rehte*

English	*Ænglisc*
narrow	*ænga, ænge, enge, nearo, nearore, nearu, nearwan, nearwe, smæl*
narrow-path	*anpaðas, anpæð, anpæþ, anpaþas*
narrow-place	*nearu, nearwe*
nastily	*laðlice, laðlicost, laþlice, laþlicost*
nation	*bufolc, ðeod, ðeoda, ðeoðdaege, ðeode, ðeoþdaege, driht, drihta, drihtfolc, drihtfolca, dryht, dryhtum, eðelmearc, eðelmearce, eþelmearc, eþelmearce, folc, folca, folce, folces, folcmægð, folcmægþ, folcmægþa, folcscare, folcscaru, folcsceare, folcum, gedriht, gumþeod, gumþeoda, leod, leoda, leode, leodscipe, leodum, mæg, mægburg, mægburge, mægburh, mægþ, þeod, þeoda, þeode, þeodlanda, þeodlond, þeodscipe, þeodum, wermægð, wermægða, wermægþ, wermægþa, werþeod, werþeoda, werþeode*
national	*cynebearn, cynebearna*

Word List (English to Ænglisc)

English	Ænglisc	English	Ænglisc
national-army	folcgetrum, folcgetrume, leodmægen, leodmægenes, leodmægnes, þeodhere, þeodherga	native	ingemann, ingemen, inlende, landmann, landmanna
		native-habitation	eþelstol, eþelstolas
		native-land	cyðð, cyððe, cyþþ, cyþþe, eðel, eðeleard, eðeleardum, eðelland, eðel-land, eðle, eðyl, eþel, eþeleard, eþeleardum, eþelland, eþel-land, eþle, eþyl, oðle, oþle
national-capital	folcstede, folcstyde		
national-city	leodburg, leodbyrig		
national-companion	folcgesið, folcgesiðas, folcgesiþ, folcgesiþas		
national-disaster	þeodþrea, þeodþreaum	native-people	ingefolc, ingefolca
national-distress	þeodþrea, þeodþreaum	native-place	eðelstow, eðelstowe, eþelstow, eþelstowe
national-edifice	landgeweorc		
national-enemy	ðeodsceaða, þeodsceaða, þeodsceaþa	native-power	eðelðrym, eþelþrym
		native-soil	eðelturf, eðyltyrf, eþelturf, eþyltyrf
national-evil	leodbealewa, leodbealo	nattering	cwidol
		natural	gecynde, gecyndne
national-fortress	eðelstol, eþelstol	nature	æðelo, æðelum, æþele, æþelo, æþelu, æþelum, cynd, cynde, gecynd, had, hade, hades
national-homeland	eþelstol, eþelstolas, þeodlanda, þeodlond		
national-land	folclond, folclondes		
national-leadership	folcred		
national-territory	govern, leodgeard	naval-force	sciphere, scipherge
national-treasure	þeodgestreon, þeodgestreona, þeodgestreonum	near	æt, be, getenge, ne, neah, nean, nearwe, neh, neon, wið, wiþ
national-warrior	þeodguma	nearby	be, bi, big
national-wealth	folcgestreon, folcgestreonum	nearer	near, nior
		nearness	neawest
nation-land	folclondes	near-strength	nearocræft, nearocræftum
nation-member	drihtwer, drihtwera, drihtweras	neat	cyrten, cyrtenu
nation-of-men	wermægð, wermægða, wermægþ, wermægþa	necessarily	nede, niede, nyde
		necessity	nede, neod, neode, nyd, nyde
		neck	hals, halse, heals, healse, sweora, sweoran
nation-people	dryhten, dryhtfolc, dryhtfolca		
nations	þeoda		
nation's	þioda		
nation's-men	werðeode		

Word List (English to Ænglisc)

English	Ænglisc	English	Ænglisc
necklace	healsbeag, healsbeaga, healsbeah, healsbege, mene, sigla, sigle	nettle	netele
		never	na, næfre, næs, nalæs, nalas, nales, nallas, nalles, nealles, nefre, no, nusquam
neck-ring	healsbeag, healsbeaga, healsbeah, healsbege	never (Latin)	nusquam
		nevertheless	ac, ðeah, ðeh, hwæðere, hwæðre, hwæþere, hwæþre, hwaþere, seþeah, þe, þeah, þeh
neck-ring-wearing	hringweorðung, hringweorðunge, hringweorþung, hringweorþunge		
		never-the-less	ac
need	ðearf, ðearfe, ðorfte, gad, gæd, geþearfod, nyde, þærfe, þearf, þearfan, þearfe, þearfendre, þearft, þorfte, þorfton, þorftun, þurfan	new	niowan, niwan, niwe, niwes, niwra, niwre
		new-arrival	cuma, cuman
		news	færspel
		next	æfter, æftera, æftre, nehstan, nihgan, oðer, oþer
needed-journey	nedfere, neidfaerae	night	niht, nihta, nihte, nihtes, nihtum, nyhtes
needing	þearfa, þearfum, þorfte, þurstig		
needs	ðearf, niede, þarf, þearf	night-covering	nihthelm
		night-darkness	nihtscua, nihtscuwan
needy	þearfa, þearfum		
neglect	forgyman, forgymdon, forgymeð, forgymeþ, forlætan, læt, lætað, lætan, lætaþ, læte, læteð, læteþ, let, lete, leton	night-evil	nihtbealu, nihtbealwa
		night-long	nihtlang, nihtlangne, nihtlong, nihtlongne
		night-middle	middelniht, middelnihtum
		night-number	nihtgerim
neglected	forsewen	nights	niht, nihtum
neighbour	neahbuend, neahbuendum, ymbesittend, ymbesittendra, ymbsittend, ymbsittendra	night's-cover	nihts-cua
		night-wakefulness	nihtwaco
		night-watch	nihtwaco, niht-waco
		night-work	nihtweorc, nihtweorce
		nine	nigen, nigene, nigon
neither	ne, noðer, noþer	nine-hundred	nigenhund, nigonhund
neither...nor	na-hwæðer, na-hwæþer		
		nineteen	nigontine
nephew	nedfere, nefa, nefan, suhterga, suhtria, suhtrian, suhtriga, suhtrigan, swustersunu	nineteenth	nigonteoþa
		ninetieth	hundnigontigoþa
		ninety	hundnigontig
		ninety eight	eahta and hundnigontig

431

Word List (English to Ænglisc)

English	Ænglisc	English	Ænglisc
ninety eighth	eahta and hundnigontigoþa	nobility	æðele, æðelo, æðelum, æþele, æþelo, æþelu, æþelum, aldorduguð, aldorduguðe, aldoruguþ, aldorduguþe, ellen, elne, elnes, eorlscipe, eorlscype, indryhto
ninety fifth	fif and hundnigontigoþa		
ninety first	an and hundnigontigoþa		
ninety five	fif and hundnigontig		
ninety four	feower and hundnigontig, feoper and hundnigontig		
ninety fourth	feower and hundnigontigoþa		
ninety nine	nigon and hundnigontig	noble	æðela, æðelan, æðele, æðeling, æðelinga, æðelingas, æðelinge, æðelinges, æðelo, æðelum, æþela, æþelan, æþele, æþeling, æþelinga, æþelingas, æþelinge, æþelinges, æþellingum, æþelo, æþelu, æþelum, bregorof, brema, breman, breme, cynegod, cynegode, cynegodum, ealdorman, ealdormann, ellenrof, ellenrofe, ellenrofum, eorl, eorlic, eþel, freo, freom, freora, fus, fuse, fusne, healic, indrihten, indryhten, mæran, manlice, rof, rofan, rofe, rofne, rofra, rofum, torhtmod, unforcuð, unforcuþ
ninety ninth	nigon and hundnigontigoþa		
ninety one	an and hundnigontig		
ninety second	twa and hundnigontigoþa		
ninety seven	seofon and hundnigontig		
ninety seventh	seofon and hundnigontigoþa		
ninety six	siex and hundnigontig		
ninety sixth	six and hundnigontigoþa		
ninety third	þreo and hundnigontigoþa		
ninety three	þri and hundnigontig		
ninety two	twegen and hundnigontig, tpegen and hundnigontig		
ninth	nigoða, nigoðan, nigoþa, nigoþan		
ninth-hour	non		
Nithad (name)	Niðhad		
no	na, ne		
		noble-action	drihtscipe, drihtscipes, drihtscype, dryhtscype
		noble-birth	æþelborennyss

Word List (English to *Ænglisc*)

English	*Ænglisc*	English	*Ænglisc*
noble-born	æðelboren, æðelborennis, æþelboren, æþelborennis	noble-relative	sibæðeling, sibæðelingas, sibæþeling, sibæþelingas
noble-child	freobearn, freobearnum	nobles	dugeða, dugeðe, dugeðum, dugeþa, dugeþe, dugeþum, dugoða, dugoðe, dugoþa, dugoþe, duguð, duguða, duguðe, duguðum, duguþ, duguþa, duguþe, duguþum, eorla
noble-city	freoburh		
noble-clothing	eorlgewæde, eorlgewædum		
noble-creation	heahgesceaft, heahgesceafta		
noble-delight	eðelwyn, eþelwyn		
noble-descendant	æðeling, æþelan, æþele, æþeling, æþellingum, æþelu		
		noble-settlement	eðelseld, eðelsetl, eþelseld, eþelsetl
noble-guardian	eðelweardas, eþelweard, eþelweardas, eþelwearde	noble-soil	eðeltyrf
		noble-son	freobearn
		noblest	eðest
noble-hall	drihtsele, dryhtsele	noble-treasure	dryhtmaðm, dryhtmaðma, dryhtmaþm, dryhtmaþma
noble-kinsman	freomæg, freomægum, freomagum		
noble-land	eðelwyn, eþelwyn	nobly	æþelu, cymlice, cymlicor, ðegenlice, drihtlice, þegenlice, unforcuðlice, unforcuþlice, weorðlice, weorðlicost, weorðmyndum, weorþlice, weorþlicost, weorþmyndum, worðmyndum, worþmyndum, wurðlice, wurðlicor, wurðmyndum, wurþlice, wurþlicor, wurþmyndum
noble-lineage	æþelo		
noble-lord	freodrihten, freodryhtne, freowine		
noble-love	heahlufan, heahlufu		
nobleman	æðeling, æþeling, beorn, ðegn, ðegna, ðegnas, ealdor-monn, eorl, eorla, eorlas, eorle, eorles, eorlum, þa, þægn, þægne, þegen, þegenas, þegn, þegna, þegnas, þegne, þegnes, þegnum		
noble-man	freomann, freomanna, freomen	nocturnal-attacker	uhtsceaða, uhtsceaþa
nobleman's-treasure	eorlgestreon, eorlgestreona	no-good	cyst, cystleas, cystleasa
noble-one	æðelum, æþelum	noise	breahtm, breahtma, hream, hreame, sweg
noble-place	eðelstol, eþelstol		
noble-power	eðelðrym, eþelþrym		
nobler	æþelne	noisy	hlud, hlude, hludne
noble-race	æðelo, æþelo		

Word List (English to *Ænglisc*)

English	*Ænglisc*	English	*Ænglisc*
none	æne, ænegum, ængum, nænegum, nængum, næni, nænig, nænigne, nænigra, nænigum, nænne, Næs, nan, nanne, nenig	note	gemearca, gemearcod, gemearcode, mearcað, mearcaþ, mearcian, mearcode
non-fraudulent	unfæcne	not-emphatic	næs, nalæs, nalas, nales, nallas, nalles, nealles
non-land	unland, unlonde	not-far	unfeor
nor	na, ne, no	not-fearful	unearg, unearge
north	norð, north	not-given	ungyfeðe, ungyfeþe
northern-man	norðmann, norðmanna, norðmen, norðmonna, norðmonnum, norþmann, norþmanna, norþmen, norþmonna, norþmonnum	not-green	ungrene
		nothing	aht, awiht, awuht, nanðing, nanþing, nawiht, owiht, owihte
		notice	sinnan, sunnon
		not-ignobly	unheanlice
		not-little	unlytel, unlytle
		not-observe	forgyman, forgymdon, forgymeð, forgymeþ
north-man	Norð-mann, Norþ-mann	not-old	unfrod, unfrodum
	Norðmanna,	not-one	nænne, nan, nanne
Northmen	Norþmen	notorious	mære
Northmen (name)	Norðmannum, Norþmannum	not-painful	col, colran
		not-small	unwaclic, unwaclicne
north-of	be, be norðan, be norþan	not-smart	ungleaw
northward	norð-weard, norþ-weard	not-strongly	unswiðe, unswiðor, unswiþe, unswiþor
north-wind	norþanwind	not-timid	unearg, unearge
nose	neb	not-timidly-or-fearfully	unforhte
not	na, nat, ne, no		
not-adult	unweaxen	not-timid-or-afraid	unforht, unforhte
not-any	nænegum, nængum, nænig, nænigne, nænigra, nænigum	Nottingham (place)	Snotingaham
		not-very-much	unswiðe, unswiðor, unswiþe, unswiþor
		not-vigorous	unfrom
not-at-all	na, næs, nalæs, nalas, nales, nallas, nalles, nat, nateshwon, nealles, no	not-weak	unwaclic, unwaclicne
		not-weakly	unwaclice
		nourisher	ætgiefan, ætgifa, ætgifan
not-brave	unfrom	nourishment	andlifen, andlifne
not-by-any-means	nateshwon	now	gien, nu
not-disgracefully	unheanlice	now (Latin)	nunc
not-doomed-to-die	unfæge, unfægne		

Word List (English to Ænglisc)

English	Ænglisc	English	Ænglisc
number	gerim, getæl, getalum, rim, rime, rimes, rimgetæl, rimgetel	observe	beweotede, beweotode, bewitiað, bewitian, bewitiaþ, bewitigað, bewitigaþ, eode, eodon, eowde, fylgan, fylgde, fylgean, fyligan, ga, gað, gæð, gæþ, gan, gaþ, geeode, geeodon, gegæð, gegæþ, gegan, gegaþ, geiode, gesægon, geseah, gesegen, geseon, ofersawon, oferseon, onhawian, onhawoden, onsegon, onseon, wat, wiste, witan, witon
numbered	screoda, talade		
numbered-day	dægrim, dægrime, dægrimes		
number-reckoning	rimcræfte		
numerous	eacen, eacne, eacnum, ecne, genog, genoge, genoh, genohra, mænigfeald, mænigfealde		

O, o

English	Ænglisc	English	Ænglisc
oak	actreo		
oar	ar		
oath	að, aða, aðas, aðe, aðsweord, aðum, aþ, aþa, aþas, aþe, aþsweord, aþum	obstruct	for-faran, for-faren, for-for, for-foron, forsæt, forsæton, forsiteð, forsiteþ, forsittan, gemyrre
oath-breaker	treowloga, treowlogan	obtain	abiddan, ægnian, agnian, færde, færdon, færen, feran, ferde, ferdon, fere, ferende, geagnod, geferde, geferdon, gefere, gefered, geferede, geferedon, geferian, gehleat, geræcan, geræhte, geræhton, gewunne, gewunnen, hleat, hleotan, raecan, ræhte, ræhton, wan, wann, winnað, winnan, winnaþ, winnende, won, wonn, wunne, wunnon
oath-sworn	aðsweord, aþsweord		
obedient	eaðmod, eaþmod, edmod, edmodne, geþwære		
obey	folgian, folgod, folgode, fylgan, fylgde, fylgean, fyligan, gehyrað, gehyraþ, gehyrde, gehyrdon, gehyre, gehyrest, gehyrst, hieran, hierde, hiered, hyrað, hyran, hyraþ, hyrde, hyrdon, hyre		
obeyed	hyrdon		
obeys	hyræð	obtain-by-killing	geslean, geslogon, gesloh
obligation	gerihte, rightly, riht, rihte, ryht, truly		
obscure	nap, nipan, nipen, nipon	obtained-by-fighting	geslogon
observance	bigeng, bigengum		

435

Word List (English to Ænglisc)

English	Ænglisc	English	Ænglisc
obvious	underne, undyrne	of-a-dragon-coil	beah, bugan, bugeð, bugeþ, bugon, gebeag, gebeah, gebogen, gebogenan
occasion	cierr, mæl, sæl, sæla, sæles, sælum, salum, sele, sið, siða, siðe, siðes, siþ, siþa, siþe, siþes, siþon		
		of-all	ealra
		of-a-lord	hold, holde, holdne, holdost, holdra
occupation	bisgu		
occupied	byn, gebiesgad	of-angels	engla
occupy	bisgian, bisgodon, bysgað, bysgaþ, eardian, eardigean, eardode, eardodon, gebysgad, onsite, onsittan, warian, warod, warode	of-a-retainer	hold, holde, holdne, holdost, holdra
		of-a-ship-broad-beamed	sidfæþm, sidfæþme, sidfæþmed
		of-battle	hilde
		of-books	boca
		of-Christ (Latin)	Christi
occur	a-gan, bearn, beirnan, gelamp, gelimpe, gelimpeð, gelimpeþ, gelomp, gelumpe, gelumpen, limpan, limpeð, limpeþ, lomp	of-Christ (name)	Cristes
		of-curiosity	bræc, bræce, bræcon, brecað, brecan, brecaþ, brocen, gebræc, gebrocen
		of-enemies	laþum
occurring-in-the-Gospels	godspellic, godspellicum	off	of
		offences	inwitniðas
ocean	garsecg, garsecges, geofen, geofenes, geofon, gifen, gyfen, gyfenes, hæf, hafu, heafo, heafu, holm, holma, holmas, holme, holmes, lago, lagu, laguflod, laguflode, mere, mereflod, mereflode, seolhbaþo, wægholm	offend	abealch, abelgan, abolgen
		offer	abead, abeod, abeodan, abude, ageald, agieldan, an, bead, beodan, beodeð, beodeþ, bewægnan, bewægned, biodan, boden, bude, budon, gebad, gebead, gebeodan, geboden, gebudon, geræhte, geræhton, geuðe, geunnan, geunne, geuþe, lace, offrian, on, raecan, ræhte, ræhton, uðe, unnan, uþe
ocean-current	eagorstream		
ocean-house	geofonhus		
ocean-journey	lagu-lad		
ocean-stream	brimstream		
odour	stenc		
of	æt, oðer, of, on		
of-a-cliff-steep-as-a-wall	weallsteap, weallsteapan, weallsteape	offer-a-sacrifice	onsægde, onsecgan
		offering	gield, gielde, gild, gyld, lac, laca, lacum, tiadæ, tiber, tibre

Word List (English to Ænglisc)

English	Ænglisc	English	Ænglisc
offering-to-an-idol	wigweorðung, wigweorðunga, wigweorþung, wigweorþunga	often-in-contrast-with	dugeða, dugeðe, dugeðum, dugeþa, dugeþe, dugeþum, dugoða, dugoðe, dugoþa, dugoþe, duguð, duguða, duguðe, duguðum, duguþ, duguþa, duguþe, duguþum
offer-in-sacrifice	blotan		
office	geþingþo, had, hade, hades		
officer	ðegn, ðegna, ðegnas, ombeht, ombiht, ombihtum, þa, þægn, þægne, þegen, þegenas, þegn, þegna, þegnas, þegne, þegnes, þegnum afaran, bearn, bearna, bearne, bearnes, bearnum, cinne, cyn, cynn, cynna, cynne, cynnes, fæsl, fæsle, pregnant, tuddor, tudor, tudra, tudre, tudres, wocor, wocre	of-the	þære
		of-the-Angles	Engla
		of-the-Anglo-Saxons	angolsexna
		of-the-day	dæg
		of-the-eyes-become-dark	forsweorcan, forsworceð, forsworceþ
		of-the-north	norþerna
		of-the-saints (Latin)	Sanctorum
		of-the-same-length	efenlang
		of-time	ylda
		of-time-close	lenge
		of-times (Latin)	seculorum
		of-which	æghwæs
		of-wind-to-blow-around	bewawan, biwaune
offspring		of-worth	uueorðae, uueorþae, uueorþe, uuiorðe, uuiorþe, weorðae, weorþae, weorþe, wiorðe, wiorðeð, wiorþe, wiorþeþ
of-glad-mood	glædmod		
of-glory	wuldres		
of-good	goda		
of-heaven	heofena		
of-heavens	heofena		
of-kings	cyningc, kyninga		
of-lights	leohtes		
of-longing	oflongad	ogre	þyrs
of-lords	dryhtna	oh	æla
of-man	wera	oh!	hu
of-man's	manna	oh!-ah!-indeed!	la
of-men	bearna, dryhta, hæleða	oil	ele
		ointment	sapan, sape
of-necessity	niede		
of-old	geo, gio, iu		
of-peoples	gereordum		
of-sins (Latin)	peccatorum		
often	gelome, geneahe, geneahhe, genehe, genehost, hwilon, hwilum, oft, oftor, oftost, þewhile		

Word List (English to Ænglisc)

English	Ænglisc	English	Ænglisc
old	eald, ealda, ealdan, ealde, ealdes, ealdne, ealdum, frod, froda, frodan, frode, frodran, gamela, gamele, gamelum, gamol, gamolferhð, gamolferhþ, gomel, gomela, gomelan, gomele, gomelra, gomelum, gomol, harne	old-woman	iomeowlan, iomeowle
		old-worthy	gomelswyrd
		olive-tree	elebeam, elebeames
		on	an, bufan, getenge, in, inn, on
		on-account-of	for, fore
		once	æne, geara, geo, gio, heo, iu
		one	ænne, an, ana, ane, anes, anne, anra, anre, anum, man, mon, on, sum
old-age	eldo, ylde, yldo, yldu		
old-age-day	harungdæg, harungdagas	one (accusative feminine)	an-e
Old-descendants-of-Scyld (name)	GomelaScilding	one (accusative masculine)	an-ne
olden-days	GEARDAGUM	one (accusative neuter)	an
old-enemies	ealdhettende		
old-enemy	ealdfeond, ealdfeondum, ealdgeniðla, ealdgeniðlan, ealdgeniþla, ealdgeniþlan, ealdgewinna	one (dative feminine)	anre
		one (dative masculine)	an-um
		one (dative neuter)	an-um
		one (genitive feminine)	an-re
older-man	ealdor-monn	one (genitive masculine)	an-es
old-father	ærfæder		
old-friend	iuwine	one (genitive neuter)	an-es
old-hair	gamolfeax	one (instrumental feminine)	an-re
old-haired	gamolfeax, gomelfeax	one (instrumental masculine)	an-e
old-lord	ealdhlaford, ealdhlafordes	one (instrumental neuter)	an-e
old-man	har, hara, hare, hares, harne, harum	one (nominative feminine)	an
old-retainer	ealdgesið, ealdgesiðas, ealdgesiþ, ealdgesiþas	one (nominative masculine)	an
		one (nominative neuter)	an
old-story	ealdgesegen, ealdgesegena		
old-treasure	eadgestreonum, ealdgestreon, ealdgestreona, ealdgewin	one-come-to-do-murder	cwealmcuma, cwealmcuman
		one-day-long	andæg, andægne
		one-fold	anfeald
old-wise-man	fyrnwita, fyrnwitan	one-hundred	hundred, hundteontig, hunteontig

Word List (English to Ænglisc)

English	Ænglisc	English	Ænglisc
one-hundred-and-twenty	hundtwelftig	open	brad, onleac, onlucan, onsceotan, onsceote, ontynan, ontyneð, ontyneþ, open, opene, openian
one-lacking-protection	hleowlora		
one-like	ænlicra		
one-living-nearby	ymbesittend, ymbesittendra, ymbsittend, ymbsittendra	opened	geopenod, ontyneð
		opening	muð, muða, muðan, muðe, muþ, muþa, muþan, muþe, þyrel
one-minded	onmode		
one-of-two	oðer, oðre, oðres, oðrum, oþer, oþerne, oþerre, oþre, oþres, oþrum	openly	cuðlice, cuðlicor, cuþlice, cuþlicor, openlice, sweotole, sweotule, undyrne
one-sitting-beside	gesæt, gesætla, gesætlan	open-sea	uter-mere
		open-up	gerymde, gerymdon, gerymed, ryman, rymde
one-standing-around	ymbstandend, ymbstandendra		
one-step	angin	opponent	gesaca, gesacan, gesacum
on-every-side	gehwær		
one-who-dwells-alone	anhaga	opportunity	byre
		oppose	forwyrnan, forwyrnde, forwyrne, wiðsacan, wiðsace, wiþsacan, wiþsace
one-who-hands-out	brytta		
ongoing	forðweard, forðweardum, forþweard, forþweardum, gegangan, gegangeð, gegangeþ, gegongeð, gegongen, gegongeþ	opposite	andwærden, andweard, andweardan, andweardne, ongean, togeanes, togenes, wiðeræhtes, wiþeræhtes
on-high	upplican	opposition	wiðermedo, wiþermedo
only	æne, ænegum, ængum, ænlic, anga, angan		
only (Latin)	unicum		
onslaught	gripe, ræs, ræsum		
on-the-other-side	wiðeræhtes, wiþeræhtes		
onto	an, in, inn, on, wið, wiþ		
on-top-of	bufan		
onward-course	forðryne, forþryne		
onwards	to		

Word List (English to *Ænglisc*)

English	*Ænglisc*	English	*Ænglisc*
oppress	æsæled, asælan, dreccan, dreceð, dreceþ, drehte, geðread, gedreht, gedrehte, genearwad, genearwod, genyðerad, genyþerad, geþread, nearwað, nearwaþ, nearwian, nearwode, niðerian, niþerian, ofsættum, ofsettan, ricsian, rixian, rixode, þreagan, þyð, þyþ, þywað, þywan, þywaþ	ordain	gesætte, gesætton, gescraf, gescyred, geseted, gesett, gesette, gesetton, gestefnde, geteoð, geteoþ, getrimede, getrymmed, scirian, scrifan, scrifeð, scrifeþ, scyred, scyreð, scyrede, scyreþ, sete, settan, sette, setton, stefnan, teodan, teode, teon, tiode, trimian, trymeð, trymede, trymedon, trymeþ, trymian, trymman
oppression	nið, niða, niðas, niðe, niðes, niðum, niþ, niþa, niþas, niþe, niþes, niþum, onnied, þrea	order	bannan, endebyrdnes, gebannan, hatan, haten, heht, heton, stihtan, stihte
oppressive	hefian, hefig, hefige, hefigran, nearo, nearore, nearwan, nearwe, swar, sware, þrealic	ordered	het
		ordinance	ræd,ræda, rædas, ræde
		Ordlaf (name)	Ordlaf
oppressive-affliction	þreaweorc	or-fame	tirleas, tirleases
oppressive-misery	nearoþearf, nearoþearfe	origin	æðelo, æðelum, æþele, æþelo, æþelu, æþelum, fruma, fruman, frumsceaft, frumsceafta, frumsceafte, frymð, frymða, frymðe, frymþ, frymþa, frymþe, gebyrd, gebyrdo, gebyrdum, or, ore
or	aeðða, aeþþa, oðða, oþða, oþþe		
orator	ðyle, þyle		
		original-garment	frumhrægl, frumhrægle
		original-habitation	frumstol
		originator	heafodwisa

Word List (English to Ænglisc)

English	Ænglisc	English	Ænglisc
ornament	besettan, besette, gehyrsteð, gehyrsteþ, geren, gereno, hyrst, hyrsta, hyrstan, hyrste, hyrsted, hyrstedne, hyrstum, wræte, wrætlicra, wrætt, wrætta, wrættum	outlawed	fag, fagum, fah, fane, fara, faum
		out-of	of, op
		outside	beutan, buta, utan, utanweard, utanweardne, ute, uton
		outsider	feorbuend
		outward	ute-weard
		outwards	ut
ornamented	fæted, fætt, fættan, fætte, fag, fage, fagne, fagum, fah, fahne, fane, gewlo	outward-turned	utweard
		over	bufan, geond, ofer, ofor
		overcome	begeat, begeate, begeaton, beget, begietan, begytan, bigeat, gedigan, gedigde, gedigeð, gedigest, gedigeþ, gedygan, ofer, ofercomon, ofercuman, ofercumen, ofercwom, oferdrifan, ofereode, oferflat, oferflitan, oferswað, oferswaþ, oferswyðan, oferswyðeð, oferswyðeþ, oferswyþan, oferswyþeþ, oferwinnan, oferwunnen
ornamented-drinking-cup	drincfaet		
ornamented-gold	fætgold		
ornaments	frætewum, frætwe, hyrsta		
or-poem	soðgied, soþgied		
Oslac (name)	Oslac		
osprey	earn, earne		
other	oðer, oðre, oðres, oðrum, oþer, oþerne, oþerre, oþre, oþres, oþrum		
others	oþrum		
otherwise	elles		
ought-to	sceal, scolde, sculan, sculon		
ours	userne		
ours (Latin)	nostrum		
out	of, ussum, ut, ute		
outcast	fah, wrecca, wreccena	overcoming	ofercoman
outcry	gnyrn, gyrne, hream, hreame	overconfidence	ofermod
		overgrown	beweaxne
outer-sea	uter-mere	overhang	oferhelmað, oferhelmaþ, oferhelmian
outfight	oferwinnan, oferwunnen		
out-guarding	utweard	overlong	longsum, longsumne
outlast	oferhigian		
outlaw	awyrgan, awyrged, grundwyrgen, grundwyrgenne, werg, wergan, wergas, wergum, werig	overpowering-might	ofermægen, ofermægene, ofermægnes
		over-ride	beræddon

Word List (English to Ænglisc)

English	Ænglisc	English	Ænglisc
overrun	eode, eodon, eowde, ga, gað, gæð, gæþ, gan, gaþ, geeode, geeodon, gegæð, gegæþ, gegan, gegaþ, geiode	paganism	hæðenscype, hæþenra, hæþenscype
		pagan-people	hæðencynn, hæþencynn
		pagan-temple	herg, hergum, herheard
oversee	ofersawon, oferseon	paid	guldan
oversight	weard, wearde	pain	cwalm, cwealm, cwealme, cwealmes, hearm, hearma, hearmas, hearme, hearmes, sar, sare, sarnissum, sarnys, sarnysse, sorg, sorga, sorge, sorgum, sorh, sorhg, trega, tregan, tregena, weorc, weorca, weorce, weorces, weorcum, worc, worca, worcum
overstress	ofersecan, ofersohte		
overtake	oferhigian		
overwhelm	ofersecan, ofersohte		
own	ægnian, agan, age, agen, agene, agenes, agenre, agenum, agnian, agnum, agon, ah, ahte, ahton, geagnod, geswæse, nagon, nah, nahte, nahton, self, selfa, selfe, selfes, selfne, selfra, selfre, selfum, seolf, seolfa, swæs, swase, sylf, sylfa, sylfan, sylfe, sylfes, sylfne, sylfra, sylfre, sylfum		
		pained	sarlic, sarlicre
		painful	hefian, hefig, hefige, hefigran, sar, sare, sarig, sarigne, sarlic, sarlicre, sarost, sarra, sarum, weorce, weorcsum, weorcsumne
owner	agend, agendes, agendfrea, agendfrean, healdend		
ownership	onweald	painful-journey	bealusiþ
ox	neat	painfully	sare
		painful-or-violent-death	deaðcwealm, deaþcwealm

P, p

English	Ænglisc	English	Ænglisc
		palace	folcstede, folcstyde, ræcede, reced, receda, recede, recedes, sæld, sælða, sælþa, seld
pace	feðe, feþe		
pagan	hæðen, hæðenan, hæðene, hæðenes, hæðenra, hæðne, hæðnum, hæþen, hæþena, hæþenan, hæþene, hæþenes, hæþenra, hæþne, hæþnum		
		pale	blac, blacne, blatan, blatende
		pale-faced	blachleor
		pallid	blac, blacne
		palm	folm, folma, folman, folme, folmum
pagan-god	god		

Word List (English to Ænglisc)

English	Ænglisc	English	Ænglisc
paradise	neorxnawange, neorxnawanges, neorxnawong, neorxnawonge, neorxnawonges	paternal-uncle	fæder, fædera
paralysis	paralisyn, paralysis	path	foldu, foldweg, foldwegas, foldwege, gelad, lad, lade, pæþ, siðfæt, siðfate, siþfæt, siþfate, swaðe, swaðu, swaþe, swaþu, wæg, weg
pardon	alætan, alæte		
parent	ealdor, yldra, yldre, yldrum		
part	dæl, dælas, dæle, gedal, gedale, healf	path-for-an-army	herpað, herpaþ
		path-of-exile	wræc-last
partake-of	ðicgean, geþægon, geþah, geþeah, onbat, onbitan, þegon, þegun, þicgan, þicgeað, þicgean, þicgeaþ, þigeð, þigeþ	path-of-the-sea	brim-lad
		path-to-the-mead-hall	medostig, medostigge
		path-to-the-pyre	adfære
		patience	geþyld, geþyldum
		patient	geþyld, geþyldig
		patriarch	leodfruma, leodfruman
partaking	gemanan		
participate-in	gedælan, gedælde, gedæled, gedaled	patron	feormend, feormendra, feormynd
partly-constructed	samworht		
partner	gebeddan, gemæcca, gemæccum	patronage	mundbyrd, mundbyrde
		pattern	bisen, bisne
part-of	dæl	pattern-welder-sword	sceadenmæl
pass	a-gan, agangan, agangen, agongen, eonene, oferhigian	Paul (name)	Paulus
		pavilion	træf, træfe
passage-of-arms	wæpengewrixles	pay	geald, gieldan, golden, guldon
pass-away	agan, airnan, aurnen, forsiðian, forsiðod, forsiþian, forsiþod	pay-attention-to	geman, gemon, gemunað, gemunaþ, gemunde, gemundon, gemyne, munan, sinnan, sunnon
pass-over	ofereode, ofereodon, ofergan		
pass-through	geondhwearf, geondhweorfan, geondhweorfeð, geondhweorfeþ	pay-back	forgeald, forgieldan, forgolden, forgyldan, forgylde, forgyldon, geald, gieldan, golden, guldon, gyld, gyldan, wiþerlean
pastime	gomen		
pastor	hyrdas, hyrde		
pasture	ettan, etted, ettede		
paternal	fæderæþelu, fæderæþelum	pay-for	angeald, ongeald, ongyldan
paternal-dwelling	fædergeard, fædergeardum	payment	sceatt
paternal-male-relative	fæderenmæg, fæderenmæge		

Word List (English to Ænglisc)

English	Ænglisc	English	Ænglisc
peace	dryhtsibb, dryhtsibbe, freod, freode, freoðo, freoþo, frið, friðe, friðo, friþ, friþe, friþes, friþo, friþu, fryðo, fryþo, grið, griþ, liðsa, liðsum, liss, lissa, lisse, lissum, liþsa, liþsum, sib, sibb, sibbe	penetrate	ðurhfon, ðurhwadan, ðurhwaden, ðurhwod, ðurhwodon, fealh, feall, feolan, folen, fulgon, þurh, þurhbræc, þurhbrecan, þurhfon, þurhwadan, þurhwaden, þurhwod, þurhwodon
peaceable	gesome, som		
peace-agreement	frioðowære, frioðuwær, frioðuwære, frioþowære, frioþuwær, frioþuwære	penny	penig
		pensive	þances, þanchycgende
		people	ðeod, ðeoda, ðeode, driht, drihta, drihtfolc, drihtfolca, dryht, dryhtum, ðrymme, firas, folc, folca, folce, folces, folcmægð, folcmægþ, folcmægþa, folcum, foldbuend, foldbuende, foldbuendum, gedriht, gumþeod, gumþeoda, leod, leoda, leode, leodfruma, leodscipe, leodum, mægð, mægða, mægðe, mægþ, mægþa, mægþe, mægþum, mennisc, mennisces, menniscra, menniscum, þeod, þeoda, þeode, þeodscipe, þeodum, werþeod, werþeoda, werþeode
peace-candle	friðcandel, friþcandel		
peaceful-company	sibbegedriht, sibgedriht		
peaceful-disposition	freoþoþeaw, freoþoþeawas		
peaceful-field	freoðowong, freoþowong		
peaceful-virtue	freoþoþeaw, freoþoþeawas		
peace-marriage	friðusibb, friþusibb		
peace-minister	freoðoscealc, freoðoscealcas, freoþoscealc, freoþoscealcas		
peace-pledge	friðusibb, friþusibb		
peace-sign	friðotacen, friþotacen		
peace-treaty	freoðowær, freoðowære, freoþowær, freoþowære		
peace-weaver	freoðuwebbe, freoþuwebbe		
pediment	stapol, stapole, stapulum	people-custom	leodþeaw, leodþeawum
peerless	ænlic, ænlicu	people-destroyer	ðeodsceaða, þeodsceaða, þeodsceaþa

Word List (English to *Ænglisc*)

English	*Ænglisc*	English	*Ænglisc*
people-disaster	þeodþrea, þeodþreaum	perceive	angeat, cnawan, felan, feleþ, gecnawan, gecnaweð, gecnaweþ, gefele, gefeleð, gefeleþ, gesawe, gesawon, geseah, gesegan, gesegon, geseo, geseoð, geseon, geseoþ, gesihð, gesihþ, gesyhð, gesyhst, gesyhþ, ongæt, ongeat, ongeaton, ongietan, ongieten, ongit, ongitan, ongite, ongytan, ongyton, sægon, sawon, seah, seon
people-distress	þeodþrea, þeodþreaum		
people-enemy	leodhata, leodhatan		
people-fall	leodhryre, leodhryres		
people-following	folgað, folgaþ		
people-founder	leodfruma, leodfruman		
people-king	ðeodcyning, ðeod-cyning, ðeodkyning, ðiodcyning, leodcyning, þeodcyning, þeod-cyning, þeodcyninga, þeodcyningas, þeodcyninges, þeodkyning, þiodcyning		
		perceives	gecnaweð
		perceptible-sign	andan, andgiettacen
		perception	andgit
people-leader	leodfruma, leodfruman	perch-upon	gespearn, spornan
people-lord	folces, folcfrea, folcfrean		
people-man	leodwer, leodweras		
people-number	folcgetæl, monnum, monrim		
people-person	leodwer, leodweras		
people-protector	leodgebyrgea, leodgebyrgean		
people-ruling	leodweard		
peoples	þeoda		

Word List (English to Ænglisc)

English	Ænglisc	English	Ænglisc
perform	dædon, deð, deþ, do, doð, don, doþ, dreag, dreah, dreogað, dreogan, dreogaþ, dreogeð, dreogeþ, dreoh, druge, drugon, dyde, dydest, dydon, fremed, fremede, fremman, gedæde, gedeð, gedeþ, gedo, gedoð, gedon, gedoþ, gedrogen, gedyde, gedydon, gehedde, gehegan, gelæst, gelæstan, gelæste, gelæston, geworht, geworhte, gewyrcan, hegan, læst, læstan, læste, læsten, læstes, wæg, wægon, wagon, wegan, wege, wegeð, wegeþ, wegon, wigeð, wigeþ	perish	abreoðan, abreoðe, abreoþan, abreoþe, cringan, dreosan, dreoseð, dreoseþ, forwearð, forwearþ, forweorðan, forweorðe, forweorþan, forweorþe, gecranc, gecringan, gecrungen, gecrungon, gedreas, gedreosan, gedreoseð, gedreoseþ, gedroren, losað, losade, losaþ, losian
		perishable	lænan, læne, lænes, lænum
		perished	crungun
		perish-with	bedreosan, bedroren, bedrorene, bidroren, bidrorene
		permanently	fæstlice
		permission-word	leafnesword
		permit	alyfan
perhaps	eorthweard	permitted	geþafode
perhaps-its-fiery-breath	hildeswat	perpetrate	fremman
		perpetual	singal, singale
perhaps-poison	hildeswat	perpetually	singala, singales, syngales
perhaps-referring-to-chess	tæfl, tæfle	perpetual-night	synnihte
peril	bealu-sið, bealu-siþ, egesa, egesan, egesum, egsa, egsan, fær, fære, færes, fere, frecen, frecna, frecne, frecnes	perpetuate	fremeð, fremede, fremedon, fremest, fremeþ, fremmað, fremman, fremmaþ, fremme, fremmen, gefremed, gefremede, gefremeden, gefremedon, gefremman, gefremmanne
perilous	frecen, frecenra, frecnan, frecne, frecnen		
period	dægtid, fyrst, fyrste, þrag, þrage	persecute	afylgde, afylgean, ehtan, ehtende, ehton, hatian, hatode
period-just-before-dawn	uhta		

Word List (English to Ænglisc)

English	Ænglisc	English	Ænglisc
persecution	æhtnyss, æhtnyssa, ehtnys, ehtnysse	piece	dæl, dælas, dæle, gedal, gedale
persecutor	hettend, hettendra, hettendum	piece-of-food	giefl, gieflum
person	æðela, æðelan, æðele, æðelo, æðelum, æþela, æþelan, æþele, æþelo, æþelu, æþelum, feora, feore, feores, feorg, feorh, feorum, ferh, fyore, guma, guman, gumena, gumum, leod, leoda, leode, leodon, leodum, mann, manna, mannes, mannum, menn, monn, monna, monnes, monnum, sawlberend, sawlberendra	piece-of-land	staðolwang, staðolwangas, staþolwang, staþolwangas
		pierce	ðurhwadan, ðurhwaden, ðurhwod, ðurhwodon, þurhdrifan, þurhwadan, þurhwaden, þurhwod, þurhwodon
		Pilate (name)	Pilato, Pilatus
		pillow	bolster, bolstrum, hleorbolster
		pilot	forðweard, forþweard
		pin	staca, stacan
		pinnacles	horngestreon
personal-ruler	selfcyning	pious	æfæst, arfæst, arfæstan, arfæste
person-sitting-within	insittend, insittendra		
persuade	tihte, tyhtað, tyhtan, tyhtaþ, wemað, weman, wemaþ	pirate	wicing
		pit	pyt, seaþ, seaþe
		pitch	cnossian, cnossod, cnossode
persuasion	gespon		
perverse	depravedly, þweorh, woh, wom, wora	pitcher	orc, orcas
		pity	mildsa
perversely-twisted	wohbogen	place	aseted, asettan, asette, asetton, deposit, gelogodon, gesætte, gesætton, geseted, gesett, gesette, gesetton, logian, sete, setl, setla, setle, setles, setlum, settan, sette, setton, stæl, stælan, stæle, stede, stow, stowe, styde, wongstede
pervert	awend, awendan, awende		
perverted	gedwolen, gedwolene		
pestilence	cwild		
Peter (name)	Petrus		
petition	ben, bene		
petition-for	wilnian		
pharaoh's	farones		
philosophy	uðwytegung, uðwytegunge, uþwytegung, uþwytegunge		
		place-at-mead-drinking	meodosetl, meodosetla
physician	læce, læces	place-of	stæl
physicians	læca	place-of-sorrow	cear-seld
pick	alesan, alesen	place-to-cross-water	ford, forda

Word List (English to Ænglisc)

English	Ænglisc	English	Ænglisc
plague	cwild	pleasant	blið, bliðe, bliðne, bliþ, bliþe, bliþne, bliþra, eaðe, eaþe, eðe, eþe, fæger, fægere, fægerra, fægir, fægran, fægre, fægroste, glad, gladiað, gladiaþ, gladu, gladum, glæd, glæde, glædlic, glædne, heore, heoru, hyhtlic, liðe, liðost, liþe, liþost, wynsum, wynsuman, wynsumast, wynsume, wynsumne, wynsumra, yðe, yþe
plain	anfeald, anfealdne, feld, felda, feldas, wong		
plainly	gegnunga, sweotole		
plain-surface	wang, wange, wong, wongas, wonge		
plan	gesyrwed, geþenc, geþencean, hycgan, modgeðance, modgeþance, modgeþonc, modgeþonce, ræd, ræda, rædas, ræde, syrede, syrwan, þencað, þencaþ, þence, þencean, þenceð, þencest, þenceþ, þohte, þohton		
planets	tungel, tunglum, tungol	pleasantly	fægere, fægre, fægrost, swæslice
plank-fastening	þellfæsten, þellfæstenne, þencan	please	cweman, gecwæman, gecwæmde, gelicode, geliste, gelyste, licað, licaþ, lician, licode, licodon, lystan, lyste, lysteþ
plant	wyrt, wyrte, wyrtum		
plantain	wegbrade		
planted	wæstma		
plant-seeds	sawan, sawen, seow		
platform	scylfa, scylfan	pleased	fægen
play	gamen, gamene, gelac, gelacum, gomen, gomene, lac, lacan, laceð, lacende, laceþ, leolc, plegan, plegian, plegode	pleasing	gefæg, gefægra, wynsum
		pleasurable	luste
		pleasure	gomen, gumdream, hroðor, hroðra, hroðre, hroþor, hroþra, hroþre, hyhtwynn, hyhtwynna, lust, lustas, luste, lustum, neod, niod, niode, willa, willan, willum, wilna, wyllan
play-a-harp	gegrettan, gegrette, gretan, greted, greteð, greteþ, grette, gretton		
played	plegodan		
playful	gamene		
		pleasure-trip	gomenwaþ, gomenwaþe
		plectrum	sceacol

Word List (English to Ænglisc)

English	Ænglisc	English	Ænglisc
pledge	treow, treowa, treowe, treowum, wedd, wedde	poison	attor, attres
		poisoned	ætterne, ættren, ættrynne
pledges	wære	poisonous	attorsceaþan
plentiful	eðgesyne, eþgesyne, yþgesene	poisonous-enemy	attorsceaða, attorsceaðan, attorsceaþa, attorsceaþan
plenty	wist, wiste		
plight	drohtað, drohtaþ, drohtoð, drohtoþ	poison-twig	atertan, atertanum
		polish	bywan
plot	gesyrwed, syrede, syrwan	polish-off	feormian, gefeormedon, gefeormod
plough	ered, erede, erian, sules, sulh	pollute	besmitan, besmiten
ploughing	yrþ	pomp	onmedla, onmedlan
ploughing-implements	sulhgeteogo	pond	mere
		ponder	modlufan, þeahtian, þeahtode
plough-making	sulhgeweorc, sulhgeweorces	Pontius (name)	Pontio, pontisca
pluck-with-a-plectrum	wræstan	pool	mere
		poor	earm, earme, earmne, earmra, earmran, earmre, feasceaft, feasceafte, feasceaftig, feasceaftum, mæte, mætost, þearfa, þearfum, wædla, wædlum
plunder	ahudan, ahuðan, ahuþan, bestrudan, bestrudon, herehuþe, herereaf, hergian, hergode, huðe, huþe, hyþ, hyþe, noþ, noþe, strudan, strude, strudende, strudon		
poem	fitt, fitte, gid, gidd, gidda, giddum, gied, giedd, giedde, gyd, gydd, gyddum, leoð, leoþ, wordgyd	poor-man	niedwædla
		population	cneorim, cneowrim, monrim
		port	port
		portent	beacen, beacna, beacne, beacnum, becn
poet	sceop, scop, scopes		
poetry	leoþ, woðcræfte		
poetry-art	woðcræft, woðcræfte, woþcræft, woþcræfte	portion	dæl, dælas, dæle, gedal, gedale
		port-side	bæc-bord
		position	had, hade, hades, staðol, staðolas, staðole, stæl, stælan, stæle, staþel, staþelum, staþol, staþolas, staþole, stede
point	ord, orde		
pointer	æstel		
point-out	beacnian, gebeacnod, gewisade, gewissode, wisade, wisian, wisie, wisige, wisode, wissian		

Word List (English to Ænglisc)

English	Ænglisc	English	Ænglisc
possess	agan, age, agen, agon, ah, ahte, ahton, behealdan, beheold, beheoldon, beneah, habban, hæfd, hæfde, nagon, nah, nahte, nahton, ofsættum, ofsettan, warað, waraþ, wariað, warian, wariaþ, warigeað, warigeaþ, warode	power	abal, ðrym, geweald, gewealde, gewealdum, mægen, mægene, mægenellen, mægenes, mægna, mægne, mægnes, mægnu, mægyn, meaht, meahte, meahtum, miht, mihta, mihte, mihton, mihtum, sped, spede, þrym, þrymm, þrymmas, weald
possesses	beneah	power-emotion	mihtmod
possessing-lord	agendfrea, agendfrean	powerful	ðryðlic, maegenrof, meahtig, meahtigra, mihtig, mihtiga, mihtigan, mihtiges, mihtigne, rica, rican, rice, ricne, ricost, ricra, ricum, strang, stranga, strangan, strange, strangne, strangre, strangum, strengest, strengum, strong, strongum, þihtan, þryðge, þryðig, þryðlic, þrydlicost, þrymfæst, þrymfæste, þrymfæstne, þrymful, þryþge, þryþig, þryþlic
possession	æht, æhta, æhte, æhtum		
possessions	æht, feorm, feorme, frætwum		
possible-movement	hwyrft, hwyrftum		
post	post, poste		
posterity	cneoris, cneorisn, cneoriss, cneorissa, cneorisse, cneorissum, fromcyme		
pound	beatað, beatan, beataþ, beateð, beaten, beateþ, beot, beotan, beoton, gebeaten		
pour	geotan, geotena, geotende, getan		
pour-out	ageotan, agoten, agotene		
pout-out	ageat	powerful (Latin)	dinamis
		powerful-bellied	magaþiht, magaþihtan
		powerful-king	brytencyning, brytencyninges
		powerful-word	þryðword, þryþword
		power-inside	encratea
		power-wood	mægenwudu, þrecwudu
		practice	bigeng, bigengum, þeaw

Word List (English to *Ænglisc*)

English	*Ænglisc*	English	*Ænglisc*
praise	aherian, demað, deman, demaþ, demde, demdon, deme, demed, eahtedon, eahtian, eahtod, eahtodan, eahtode, ehtigað, ehtigaþ, geæhted, gedemed, hered, herede, heredon, herenes, herge, hergen, heriað, herian, herige, herigean, herigen, heroden, herodon, lof, lofe, lofian, mærað, mæran, mæraþ, mærsian, mærsigende, oliccan, wuldor, wuldrian	precious-possession	maððumwela, maððumwelan, maþþumwela, maþþumwelan
		precious-stone	eom, eorclanstan, eorclanstanas
		precious-stones	eorcanstan
		precious-sword	maðþumsweord, maþþumsweord
		precious-thing	maððum, madm, madma, maðma, madmas, maðmas, madme, madmum, maðmum, maðþum, maþðum, maþma, maþmas, maþme, maþmum, maþþum
		precious-treasures	syncfatum
		precipitous	neowel, neowelne, neowle
		predetermined-situation	gifeðe, gifeþe
praised	lof, mærða		
praise-giving	gilphlæden	pre-eminently-powerful	foremeahtig, foremeahtige, foremihtig
praise-rejoicing	wuldordreames		
praiseworthy	lofsum		
praiseworthy-action	lofdæd, lofdædum	prefect	geræfa, gerefa, gerefan
praiseworthy-deed	lof-dæd		
pray	abiddan, bæd, bædon, biddan, bidde, gebæd, gebiddað, gebiddan, gebiddaþ	pregnant	eacen, eacne, eacnum, ecne
		prelate	bisceop
prayer	gebed, gebede		
preach	bodedon, bodian, bodode		
precept	gebod, lar, lara, lare, larena, larum		
precious	deorwurðan, deorwurðe, deorwurþan, deorwurþe, leoflic		
precious-jewel	gim, gimm, gimmas, maððumsigla, maððumsigle, maþþumsigla, maþþumsigle		
precious-metal	wir, wira, wire, wirum		
precious-object	sincfæt, sincfato		

Word List (English to Ænglisc)

English	Ænglisc	English	Ænglisc
prepare	gearcian, gearwad, gearwian, gegærwan, gegarwod, gegearcod, gegearewod, gegearwigean, gegearwod, gegeorcode, gegired, gegiredan, gegyred, gegyrede, gegyrwan, gegyrwed, geteoð, geteoþ, getrimede, getrymmed, gierede, gierwaþ, girwan, gyrde, gyrede, gyredon, gyrwað, gyrwan, gyrwaþ, reðran, reþran, teodan, teode, teon, tiode, trimian, trymeð, trymede, trymedon, trymeþ, trymian, trymman	preserve	bearh, beorgan, burga, burgan, burgon, gebearg, gebearh, geborgen, healdan, heold, heoldon, lealden
		preserver	nergend
		press	geðrungen, geþrang, geþrungen, þrang, þreatedon, þreatian, þringan, þrong, þrungen, þrungon, þyð, þyþ, þywað, þywan, þywaþ
		pressed	cread
		press-forward	geðrungen, geþrang, geþrungen, þrang, þringan, þrong, þrungon
		pressingly	þiclice
		press-of-battle	geþrang
		pressure	geþræc
prepare-a-trick	geregnad, geregnode, gerenod, regnian, renian, renodest	pretend	bræd, brægd, bregdan, bregde, bregdon, broden, brogdne, brudon, brugdon, gebræd, gebroden
prepared	geara, geare, gearo, gearone, gearowe, gearu, gearwe	prevent	amyrde, amyrran, amyrred, forstandan, forstod, forstode, forstodon, gelette, getwæfan, getwæfde, getwæfed, getwæfeð, getwæfeþ, lettan, letton
prescribe	gescraf, scrifan, scrifeð, scrifeþ		
present	andwærden, andweard, andweardan, andweardne, eaweð, eaweþ, eowdon, eoweð, eoweþ, geeawed, gelang, gelong, geywan, iewan, iewde, iewe, lac, laca, lacum, ywan, ywde	previously	ær, giet, gieta, git, gyt, gyta
		previous-time	ærdæg, ærdæge, ærdagum
		prey	huðe, huþe, hyð, hyþe
		price	weorð, weorðan, weorðe, weorþ, weorþan, weorþe

Word List (English to Ænglisc)

English	Ænglisc	English	Ænglisc
prick	sticaþ, stician	private-conversation	runung, rununga, sundorspræc, sundorspræce
pride	bælc, gielp, gielpes, gielpsceaþan, gilp, gylp, gylpe, higeþryð, higeþryðe, higeþryþ, higeþryþe, mod, mode, modes, modum, oferhyda, oferhygd, oferhygda, oferhygde, ofermede, ofermetto, ofermod, ofermode, ofermodes, onmedla, onmedlan, wlence, wlenco, wlencu	privately	dearnenga, dearnunga, dearnunge, onsundran, onsundron
		private-thought	ingeþanc, ingeþancum
		prized	geæhted, geæhtlan, weorð, weorþ
		proceed	færeð, færeþ, far, farað, faran, faraþ, fare, fareð, fareþ, for, foran, foron, gefaran, gefaren, gefor, geforan, geforon
priest	mæssepreost, messepreost, messepreoste, preost	process	ymbeode, ymbgan
		proclaim	acyþan, bead, beodan, beodeð, beodeþ, biodan, bodedon, boden, bodian, bodode, bude, budon, gebad, gebead, gebeodan, gecyddest
prince	æðeling, æðelinga, æðelingas, æðelinge, æðelinges, æþeling, æþelinga, æþelingas, æþelinge, æþelinges, æþellingum, aldor, aldre, drihten, drihtenes, drihtna, drihtne, drihtnes, dryhtbearn, dryhten, dryhtna, dryhtne, dryhtnes, ealdor, ealdre, ealdres, fengel, landfruma, leod, leoda, leode, leodfruma, leodfruman, leodon, leodum, ord, orde, þeoden	proclaimed	cyðaþ
		proclaims	cyddest
		procreate	tyman
		produce	afedan, afeded, tiedrað, tiedran, tiedraþ, wæstmas, weaht, weccað, weccan, weccaþ, weccean, wecceð, wecceþ, wehte, wyrcan
		productive	forþbære, forþbæro
		profane	gewemde, gewemmed, wemman
prince-of	ealdor	profit	ræd, ræda, rædas, ræde
prince's	þeodnes		
princess	cwen	profound	deop, deopan
prison	cweartern, cwearterne	progenitor	fruma, fruman

Word List (English to *Ænglisc*)

English	*Ænglisc*	English	*Ænglisc*
progeny	cneorim, cneowrim, fæsl, fæsle, fromcynn, fromcynne, magotimber, magotimbre, team, teames, teamum, wocor, wocre	property	æht, æhta, æhte, æhtum, ceap, ceapas, ceape, cynd, cynde, dugeða, dugeðe, dugeðum, dugeþa, dugeþe, dugeþum, dugoða, dugoðe, dugoþa, dugoþe, duguð, duguða, duguðe, duguðum, duguþ, duguþa, duguþe, duguþum, ead, gestreon, gestreona, god, goda, godan, gode, godes, godne, godra, godum, sceat, sceates, sceatt, sceattas, sceattes, sceattum, yrfe, yrfes
prolong	yldan		
promise	foreweard, gehat, gehata, gehatað, gehate, gehaten, gehatum, gehet, geheton, hat, hatað, hatan, hataþ, hate, haten, hatene, hatte, heht, het, hete, heton, treow, treowa, treowe, treowum, wær, ware, worngehat		
promontory	hoh, nosan, nose		
propagate	temað, teman, temaþ, tiedrað, tiedran, tiedraþ, tydran	property-gift	feohgift, feohgiftum, feohgyft, feohgyfte, feohgyftum
		property-right	landriht, londriht, londrihtes, londryht
proper	agen, agene, agenes, agenre, agenum, agnum, gedefe, onriht, onrihtne	prophet	woðbora, woðboran, woþbora, woþboran
		propriety	cinne, cyn, cynn, cynna, cynne, cynnes, mæð, mæþ
properly	ariht, ryhte	prosper	ðah, ðeon, ðigen, ðigon, geðah, geþah, geþeoh, geþeon, geþigen, geþigon, geþungen, onðah, onðeon, onþah, onþeon, þag, þah, þeah, þeon, þigen, þigon
		prosperity	ar, ara, aran, are, arena, arna, arra, arum, ead, eades, eadwela, eadwelan, euthenia, sped, spede, wela, welan

Word List (English to *Ænglisc*)

English	*Ænglisc*	English	*Ænglisc*
prosperous	eadega, eadga, eadge, eadig, eadigan, eadiges, wælig, welig, weligne, woruldgesælig	protecting-city	freoðoburh, freoþoburh, hleowstol, hleowstole
prosperous-dwelling	botlwela	protecting-kinsman	hleomæg, hleomæges, hleomaga, hleomagum
prosperous-earth	sælwongas		
prosperous-ground	sælwongas	protecting-trees	beamsceade, beamsceadu
prosperously	eadiglice		
prostitute	myltestre	protecting-wall	foreweall, foreweallas
prostrate	astreccan, astrece, astreht	protecting-wing	hleowfeðer, hleowfeðrum, hleowfeþer, hleowfeþrum
protect	bebeorgan, bebeorh, beleac, belucan, beorgan, bewarigan, beweredon, bewerian, bewreon, bewrigen, bewrigene, bewrigenum, biwergan, biwrah, ealgian, ealgode, forstandan, forstod, forstode, forstodon, freoþian, freoþode, friðian, friþian, friþion, gealgean, gefriðode, gefriþod, gefriþode, genered, generede, generian, generigan, gescyld, gescylt, gewered, mundbyrdan, nere, nereð, nerede, nereþ, nergan, nergean, nerian, scyld, scyldan, scylde, warað, waraþ, wariað, warian, wariaþ, warigeað, warigeaþ, warod, warode, weardian, weardode, wered, wereð	protection	fæstnung, ferhweard, ferhwearde, freoðo, freoþo, friðo, friþo, friþu, fryðo, fryþo, gebeorg, gebeorge, gehyld, helm, helmas, helme, helmes, helmum, hleo, hleow, hyldo, mund, mundbyrd, mundbyrde, wær, wære, ware
		protection-beacon	freoðobeacen, freoþobeacen
		protection-from-storm	scursceade, scursceadu
		protection-sign	freoðobeacen, freoþobeacen, friðotacen, friþotacen
		protective-board	hleo, hleobord, hleobordum
		protective-city	hleoburh
		protective-clothing	hleosceorp, hleosceorpe
		protective-ornament	hleosceorp, hleosceorpe
protecting	hleo		

Word List (English to Ænglisc)

English	Ænglisc	English	Ænglisc
protector	ederas, edor, edoras, eoderas, eodor, eodur, gebeorh, gehola, hleo, hleow, mundbora, weard, weardas, wearde, weardes, weardum	provider	ætgiefan, ætgifa, ætgifan, feormend, feormendra, feormynd
		provide-with-benefits	geofian
		provision	wist
protector-kinsman	hleo-mæg	provisions	feorm, feorme, nest, wist, wiste
proud	collenferð, collenferhð, collenferhðe, collenferhþ, collenferhþe, collenferþ, collenferþe, deal, deall, dealle, dealne, healic, modega, modes, modgan, modge, modges, modgum, modi, modig, modiga, modigan, modige, modiges, modiglic, modiglicran, modigra, modigre, oferhidig, oferhydig, ofermod, ofermoda, wlanc, wlancan, wlance, wlances, wlancne, wlonc, wlonce, wlonces, wloncne, wloncum	prow	stefn, stefna, stefnan, stefne
		proximity	neawest
		prudence	foreþanc
		prudent	fore-snotor, gleaw, gleawferhð, gleawferhþ, þanchycgende
		publicly	openlice
		pull	tihte, tyhtað, tyhtan, tyhtaþ
		pull-apart	tolucan
		pull-down	bygan
		punish	awræce, awrecan, gewitnad, gewitnian, gewræc, gewrec, gewrecen, gewrecene, wræc, wræce, wræcon, wrec, wrecan, wrece, wrecen
		punishment	eadlean, eadleane, eðle, edlean, edleane, eþle, hearmscearu, hearmscearu, steor, steore, wergðo, wergþo, werhðo, werhþo, wita, wite, witelac, witeswinge, witeswingum, witum, wyta, wytum
proud-minded	hygewlonc, modwlonc, swiðmod, swiþmod		
proud-troop	modheap, modheapum		
proven	cost, gecoste		
proven-good-because-of-age	ærgod		
provide	abead, abeod, abeodan, abude, ætgifan	puppy	hwelp
provide-assurances-that	fæstnian, gefæstnod, gefæstnodon		

Word List (English to Ænglisc)

English	Ænglisc	English	Ænglisc
pure	beorht, beorhta, beorhtan, beorhte, beorhtne, beorhtost, beorhtra, beorhtre, beorhtum, byrhtan, clæne, cusc, cuscne, hlutor, hluttrum, smæte, smætum	put-up-with	forberan
		pyre	ad, ade, bæl, bæle, bælfyr, bel, wælfyr, wælfyra, wælfyre
		pyre-stood	bælstede
		pyre-wood	bælwudu

Q, q

English	Ænglisc
purify	fælsian, fælsode, gefælsod
quake	bifian, bifiende, bifode
purity	clænnys, clænnysse
quality	cynd, cynde
purple	brun
queen	cwen
purport	ingehyd, ingehyde
queenly	cwenlic
purpose	modgeþonc, willa, willan, willum, wilna, wyllan
quenched	adwæsce
quick	caf, cafne, cwic, fus, fuse, fusne, hraðe, hræd, hraþe, hwæt, hwætran, hwata, hwate, hwatum, snel, snella, snelle, snellic, snelra
pursue	afylgde, afylgean
pursued	fylgan
pursuer	lastweard
pursuing	ehteð
push	aþringan, aþrong
push-out	sceaf, sceof, scofen, scufan, scufeð, scufeþ, scufon, scufun
quick-beam	cwicbeam, cwicbeame
quickly	ardlice, fromlice, hraðe, hrædlice, hræþe, hraþe, hraþor, hreðe, hreþe, lengre, lungre, ofestlice, ofostlice, ofstlice, raðe, raþe, recene, ricene, ricone, rycene, snelle, snellice, sniome, sniomor, snude
put	ado, adon, dædon, deð, deþ, do, doð, don, doþ, dyde, dydest, dydon, gedæde, gedeð, gedeþ, gedo, gedoð, gedon, gedoþ, gedyde, gedydon
put-a-stop-to	onhohsnian, onhohsnode
put-back-on-feet	feþað, feþan, feþaþ
quickness	sped
put-down	alecgan, alecgean, alede, aledon, alegde, alegdon, genyðerad, genyþerad, niðerian, niþerian	quick-swimming	sundhwat, sundhwate
quick-witted	gearoþoncol, gearoþoncolre
quick-worded	hrædwyrde
quiet	stille, swige, swigra
quiver	acweccan, acweht, acwehte
put-to-flight	aflyman, aflymde, geflæmdest, geflemed
put-to-sleep	aswefan, aswefede, swebban, swefeð, swefeþ
quote	cweþe, gecwæð, gecwæde, gecwædon, gecwæþ

Word List (English to Ænglisc)

English	Ænglisc	English	Ænglisc
		raise-up	ahæfen, ahafen, ahebban, ahof, ahofon, aræman, aræmde, arær, aweahte, aweccan, awehte, hæfen, hafen, hebban, hefeð, hefeþ, hof, onhebban, onhof

R, r

English	Ænglisc	English	Ænglisc
race	cinne, cyn, cynn, cynna, cynne, cynnes, feorhcynn, feorhcynna, gebyrd, gebyrdo, gebyrdum, mægburg, mægburge, mægburh, mennisc, mennisces, menniscra, menniscum, teoche, teoh, teohh, teohha, teohhe	ram-male-sheep	rom, rommes
		rampart	weall
		rank	geþingþo
		ransack	rasian, rasod
		ransom	lysan
		rapacious	ungifre, wylfen, wylfenne
radiance	scima, sciman	rare	sellic, sellice, syllic, syllicran, syllicre
radiant	scir, scira, sciran, scire, scirne, scirum	rarer	sellicra
rage	grama, graman, grimman, grimmeð, grimmeþ, styrman, styrmde, styrmdon	rash	dollic, dollicra, gehatheort, hatheort
		rashly	dollice
		ravage	gehergod, hergian, hergode
raid	gehergod, hergian, hergode	raven	Hræfen, hrefn, hrefne, hremm, hremmas, wælceasega
rain	regn, regnas		
rainbow	scurboga, scurbogan		
rainy	renig	ravenous	grædig, grædige
raise	ahafen, ahebban, ahof, ahofon, aræran, arærde, arærdon, aræred, gestepte, hafenade, hafenian, hafenod, hafenode, ræran, rærde, rærdon, stepan, stepe, stepte, stepton	ravens	hræfn
		reach	fealh, feolan, folen, fulgon, gegangan, gegangeð, gegangenne, gegangeþ, gegongeð, gegongen, gegongeþ, geræcan, geræhte, geræhton, raecan, ræhte, ræhton
raised	ahofe	reach-an-agreement	geændade, geendod
raised-platform-for-high-seat	yppan, yppe	reach-out	astreccan, astrece, astreht
		reach-with-a-weapon	geræhte, geræhton, raecan, ræhte, ræhton
		read	rædan

Word List (English to Ænglisc)

English	Ænglisc	English	Ænglisc
readily	geare, gearwe, gearwor, gearwost, gere	recluse	anhaga, anhogan
		recognise	gecnawan
ready	arod, fuslic, fuslicu, geara, geare, gearo, gearone, gearowe, gearu, gearwe, gerad, gerade	recognize	cnawan, gecnawan, gecnaweð, gecnaweþ, oncnawan, oncneow, oncniow
		recompense	æfterlean, broðorgyld, broþorgyld, eadlean, eadleane, edlean, edleane
ready-for-a-journey	siðfrom, siðfrome, siþfrom, siþfrome		
ready-for-departure	utfus		
ready-handed	geareofolm		
readying	gefysde	reconcile	seman
realize	onfindan, onfond, onfunden, onfundon	recover	gewyrpte, wyrpan
		rectitude	soð, soðe, soþ, soþe
realm	lond		
reason	intinga	red	brun, read, reada, reade, readum, reodne
rebel-against	forhealdan, forhealden, forhealdene		
		red-coloured	teaforgeapa
rebuke	teonwordum	redden	hroden, reodan
receive	anfenge, cepan, ðicgean, geþægon, geþah, geþeah, geþegen, geþicgan, onfangen, onfeng, onfengon, onfoð, onfoh, onfon, onfoþ, þegon, þegun, þicgan, þicgead, þicgean, þicgeaþ, þigeð, þigeþ, underfænge, underfeng, underfon	red-stained	readfah
		reeve	geræfa, gerefa, gerefan
		reflex-change	wearp, weorpan, weorpaþ, wurpon
		reflex-take-oneself	wend, wendan, wende, wendeð, wenden, wendeþ, wendon
		refrain-from	ofersittan, ofersitte
		refuge	freoðiaþ, hleo, hleow
		refuge-in-the-fens	fenfreoðo, fenfreoþo
receive-by-lot	gehleat, hleat, hleotan	refusal	wearn, wearne
		refuse	forsacan, forsoc, forsocon, forweorn, forwyrnan, forwyrnde, forwyrne, wyrnan, wyrnde, wyrnest
received	onfeng		
receive-in-exchange	gewrixle		
recent	nehstan		
recently	niwes, ungeara		
recently-tarred	niwtyrwyd, niwtyrwydne	refused	forsoc, wyrndon
recipient	tiða, tiþa	regarding	be, bi, big
recite	arim, ariman, begale	region	eard, earda, eardas, earde, eardes, landscipe, mearc, sceat, scyr, scyre
recite-a-charm	ongalan		
reckless	wanhydig		
reckon	areccan, getealdon, geteled, tealde, tealdon, telge, tellan		

Word List (English to Ænglisc)

English	Ænglisc	English	Ænglisc
regret	mearn, murnan, murne, murnende, murnon	release	alynnan, bedælan, bið, bidælde, bidæled, biþ, forlæt, forlætað, forlætan, forlætaþ, forlæte, forlæteð, forlæten, forlæteþ, forlet, forleton, lysan, onband, onbindan, onlætan, onlæteð, onlæteþ, onlysan, onlysde
reign	rice		
reinforcement	eac, eaca, ecan		
reinforcing-troop	eaca, ecan		
reject	acwæð, acwæþ, acweðan, acweþan, acwið, acwiþ, acwyð, acwyþ, ahwet, ahwettan, aweorpan, aworpene, forhicgan, forhicge, forseah, forseon, wiðhogian, wiðhogode, wiþhogian, wiþhogode		
		released	alysde
		reliable	fæle
		relief	frofor
		relinquish	ageaf, ageafe, ageafon, agiefan, agif, agifan, agifen, agyfe, agyfen, alætan, alæte, alecgan, alecgean, alede, aledon, alegde, alegdon, anforlætan, anforleten, forlæt, forlætað, forlætan, forlætaþ, forlæte, forlæteð, forlæten, forlæteþ, forlet, forleton, gife, gifeðe, gifen, gifeþe, gyf, gyfen, gyfeþe, ofgæfon, ofgeaf, ofgeafon, ofgeafun, ofgefan, ofgiefan, ofgif, ofgifan, ofgifen, ofgyfan, oflætan, oflætest, oflet
rejoice	dryman, drymdon, feon, gefægon, gefeah, gefegon, gefeh, gefeoh, hyhtan		
rejoicing	dream, dreama, dreamas, dreame, dreames, dreamhabbende, dreamhabbendra, dreamum		
relate	asægd, asægde, asecgan, mænan, mænde, mæned		
related	gelenge, gesib, gesibb, gesibbra, gesibbum, lenge		
relation	cneowmæg, cneowmægas, cneowmagas		
relative	freond, freonda, freondas, freondum, frynd, gesibb, gesibbra, gesibbum, leodmæg, leodmagum		
relatives	magas		

Word List (English to Ænglisc)

English	Ænglisc	English	Ænglisc
remain	bad, bidan, biden, bidon, gebad, gebidan, gebiden, gebidon, gestod, gestodon, gewunedon, gewunian, gewunigen, standað, standan, standaþ, stande, standeð, standeþ, stod, stodan, stodon, stondað, stondan, stondaþ, stonde, stondeð, stondeþ, stynt, þurhwunade, þurhwunian, wuna, wunað, wunade, wunaþ, wunedon, wuniað, wunian, wuniaþ, wuniende, wunod, wunode, wunodon	remind	gemanode, gemoniað, gemoniaþ, gemonige, gemyndgad, man, manað, manaþ, manian, manode, monað, monaþ, myndgað, myndgaþ, myndgian, myndgiend
		remission (Latin)	Remissionem
		remnant	laf, lafe
		remorselessly	unmurnlice
		remove	abræd, abrægd, abregd, abregdan, abregde, abroden, abrugdon, aleoðode, aleoþian, aleoþode, asceaf, ascufan, astyrian, ateah, ateon, feorran, ofteah, ofteon, oftihð, oftihþ
remainder	laf, lafe	renew	geniwad, geniwod, niwiað, niwian, niwiaþ
remain-standing	ætstandan, ætstod		
remain-with	gewunian, gewunod, gewunode		
		renewed	edneowe
remark	gemearca, gemearcod, gemearcode, mearcað, mearcaþ, mearcian, mearcode	renounce	forsweran, forsworen, ofersittan, ofersitte
		renown	þrymm
		renowned	breme, cynerof, cynerofe, freamærne, geæþele
remedy	bot, bote, gebetan		
remember	geman, gemon, gemunað, gemunan, gemunaþ, gemunde, gemundon, gemunon, gemyne, munan, onman, onmunan, onmunde, onmunon		
		renowned-for-action	handrof, handrofra
		renowned-for-killing	cwyldrof
		renowned-in-battle	guðrof, guþrof
		renowned-to-peoples	folcmære, folcmæro
		repaid	forgyldan, ongildan
remembering	gemyndig	repairers	betend
remembers	gemon	repay	geald, gieldan, golden, guldon, gyld, gyldan, leanast, leanian, leanige, leanode
remembrance	gemynd		
		repayment	handlean

Word List (English to Ænglisc)

English	Ænglisc	English	Ænglisc
repeat	geniwad, geniwod, niwiað, niwian, niwiaþ	resemblance	anlicnes, anlicnesse, anlycnysse
repent	behreowsian	residence	bold, bolda, botl, botle, herg, hergum, herheard, sæld, sælða, sælþa, seld, setl, setla, setle, setles, setlum
repletion	fyll, fylle		
reply	andsware, andswarede, andswaredon, andswarian, andswarode, andswarodon, andswaru, andwyrde, gegncwida, gegncwide, ondsware, ondswarode, ondswaru	resist	forsæt, forsæton, forsiteð, forsiteþ, forsittan, wiðsacan, wiðsace, wiðstandan, wiðstanden, wiðstod, wiðstodon, wiðstondan, wiþsacan, wiþsace, wiþstandan, wiþstanden, wiþstod, wiþstodon, wiþstondan
reply-to	oncwæð, oncwædon, oncwæþ, oncweðan, oncweden, oncweþan	resistance	andwig, antwig, wiðre, wiðres, wiþre, wiþres
report	gefræge, gefrægen, gefrægn, sagona, sagu	resolute	anhydig, anmod, anmode, anræd, fæsthydig, fæsthydigne, heardhicgende, heardmod, heardmode, stiðferhð, stiðhicgende, stiðhydig, stiðmod, stiðmoda, stiþferhþ, stiþfrihþ, stiþhicgende, stiþhydig, stiþmod, stiþmoda, swiðhicgende, swiþhicgende, unearg, unearge, unforht, unforhte
reproach	ætwitan, ætwiton, edwit, hosp, lean, log, logon, lyhð, lyhþ, oðwitan, oþwitan, witan, wite		
repugnant	æfþunca		
repugnant-thing	æfþunca		
repulsive	atol		
reputable	unforcuð, unforcuþ		
reputably	hlisfullice		
reputation	lof, lofe		
request	ben, bena, benan, bene		
requirement	ðearf, þearf		
requite	forgeald, forgieldan, forgolden, forgyldan, forgylde, forgyldon		
rescue	ahrædde, ahreddan, ahredde, ahreddest, ahreded	resolutely	anmodlice, eornoste, þriste
rescuers	hrædding, hræddinge		

Word List (English to *Ænglisc*)

English	*Ænglisc*	English	*Ænglisc*
resolve	ðencan, ðoht, ðohte, gehogod, gehogodest, hogedon, hogian, hogod, hogode, hogodon, hycgan, þencan, þoht, þohte	rest-inactive	beah, bugan, bugeð, bugeþ, bugon, gebeag, gebeah, gebogen, gebogenan
		resting-place	ræst, ræste, rest, reste
resound	dynedan, dynede, dynian, hlamm, hlemmeð, hlemmeþ, hlimman, hlimmeð, hlimmeþ, hlummen, hlummon, hlumon, hlynsian, hlynsode, scralletan, sweog, sweogon, swogan, swogen, þunede, þunian	restless	wæfre
		restore	betan, bete, gebetan, gebette, gebettest
		rest-place	restestow, restestowe
		restrain	dweleð, dweleþ, dwellan, forhabban, gestyrde, stieran, styran, styrde
resounded	dynede	restrain-oneself	forhabban
respect	ar, ara, arað, aran, araþ, are, arena, arian, arna, arra, arum, gesceawað, gesceawaþ, gesceawod, sceawa, sceawað, sceawaþ, sceawedon, sceawiað, sceawian, sceawiaþ, sceawigan, sceawige, sceawode, sceawodon	result	gewand
		resurrection	ærest
		resurrection (Latin)	resurrectionem
		retain	healdan, heold, heoldon, lealden
respected	gefræge, gefrægen, gefrægn		
resplendent-with-gold	goldwlanc		
respond	andswarian, andswarod, andswarode		
response	andswaru		
responsibility	weard, wearde		
rest	gerestan, ræste, rest, restað, restan, restaþ, reste, reston		
rest-bed	hlimbed		
rested	gerestest		

Word List (English to *Ænglisc*)

English	*Ænglisc*	English	*Ænglisc*
retainer	ana, anbyhtscealc, anbyhtscealcas, ðegn, ðegna, ðegnas, drihtguma, drihtguman, dryhtguma, dryhtguman, dryhtgumum, esne, fyrdgestealla, fyrdgesteallum, geneat, geneatas, healðegn, healðegnas, healðegnes, healþegn, healþegnas, healþegnes, magoðegn, magoþegn, magoþegna, magoþegnum, maguþegn, maguþegnas, maguþegne, neat, ombihtscealc, ombihtscealcum, seldguma, selesecg, sele-secg, selesecgas, þægn, þægne, þegen, þegenas, þegn, þegna, þegnas, þegne, þegnes, þegnum	retribution	æfterlean, lean, leana, leane, leanes, leanum, wrace, wracu, wræce
		retribution-for-deeds-done	dædlean
		return	æthwearf, æthweorfan, eft, eftcyme, eftcymes, oncierran, oncirde, oncirran, oncyrreð, oncyrreþ, wiðertrod, wiþertrod
		return-journey	efter, eftsið, eftsiðas, eftsiðes, eftsiþ, eftsiþas, eftsiþes
		reveal	ætæwde, æteowan, æteowde, ætywan, ameldian, ameldod, cyð, cyðað, cyðan, cydde, cyðde, cyðdon, cyðed, cyþ, cyþan, cyþaþ, cyþde, cyþdon, cyþed, eaweð, eaweþ, eowdon, eoweð, eoweþ, gecyd, gecyðan, gecyðanne, gecyðde, gecyðed, gecyþan, gecyþanne, gecyþde, gecyþed, geeawed, geswutelod, geswutelode, geywan, iewan, iewde, iewe, onsæl, onsælan, ontynan, ontyneð, ontyneþ, onwreoh, onwreon, sweotolian, wissian, ywan, ywde
retainer-gifts	wenede, wenian		
retaining-bank	stæðweall, stæðweallas, stæþweall, stæþweallas		
retaliation	andlean, andwig, antwig, ondlean, wiþerlean		
retinue	hired, hyrde, hyred, hyredes		
retreat	wiðertrod, wiþertrod		
		revealed	ætywed
		revealing	ætywe
		revelation	swutelung, swutelunge

Word List (English to *Ænglisc*)

English	*Ænglisc*	English	*Ænglisc*
reveller	beorscealc, beorscealca	reward	æfterlean, eadlean, eadleane, edlean, edleane, forgeald, forgieldan, forgolden, forgyldan, forgylde, forgyldon, handlean, lean, leana, leanast, leane, leanes, leanian, leanige, leanode, leanum, med, meda, mede, medo, medum
revelry	breahtm, breahtma, mondream, mondreama, mondreamum		
revenge	andlean, gyrnwræce, ondlean, wrace, wracu, wræce		
revenge-for-injury	gyrnwracu, gyrnwræce		
reverence	arwurðnys, arwurðnysse, arwurþnys, arwurþnysse, eaðmedu, eaðmedum, eaþmedu, eaþmedum, weorðmynd, weorþmynd	reward-for-victory	sigorlean, sigorleanum
		reward-for-words	wordlean, wordleana
		reward-giver	beahgyfa
		rhetoric	getingnys, getingnysse
		rib	rib
		rich	godspedig, wælig, welig, weligne, wlanc, wlancan, wlance, wlances, wlancne, wlonc, wlonce, wlonces, wloncne, wloncum
reverently	arwurðlice, arwurþlice		
reversal	edhwyrft, edwenden		
reverse	edwendan, onhweorfan, onhworfen		
revile	bysmeredon, bysmerian, gebysmrian, tynan, tyndon	riches	dugeða, dugeðe, dugeðum, dugeþa, dugeþe, dugeþum, dugoða, dugoðe, dugoþa, dugoþe, duguð, duguða, duguðe, duguðum, duguþ, duguþa, duguþe, duguþum, ead, eades, eadwela, eadwelan, sinc, sinca, since, sinces, sped, wela, welan
revive	cwucra		
revolve	bewand, bewindað, bewindan, bewindaþ, bewunden, biwunden		
		rich-in-earthly-possessions	woruldgesælig
		rich-in-luxuries	sefteadig
		riddle	giedd

Word List (English to Ænglisc)

English	Ænglisc	English	Ænglisc
ride	faran, faren, for, foron, gerad, rad, rade, ridan, ride, rideð, riden, rideþ, ridon, riodan	ringed-pool	hringmere
		ring-giver	beaggyfa, beaggyfan, beahgifa, beahgifan
		ring-giving	beaggyfu, beahgifa, beahgife
rider	ridda, ridend		
ridge	hricg, hrincg, hringe, hrycg	ring--giving-hall	beahsele
		ring-hall	hringsele
right	gemet, onriht, onrihtne, riht, rihtan, rihte, rihtne, rihtum, swiðran, swiðre, swiþran, swiþre	ring-hoard	beaghord
		ring-iron	hringiren, hringloca, hringlocan
		ring-loop	hringboga, hringbogan
right-away	aninga, anunga	ring-made	hringde, hringed
righteous	æfæst, æfæste, arfæst, arfæstan, arfæste, domfæst, rædfæst, rihtwis, rihtwisra, soðfæst, soðfæste, soðfæstra, soþfæst, soþfæste, soþfæstra, tilmodig, tilmodigne	ring-net	hringnet
		ring-ornamented	hringmæl, hringmæled
		ring-prowed-ship	hringnaca
		ring-receiving	beahðege, beahðegu, beahþege, beahþegu, hringþege, hringþegu
righteousness	soð, soðe, soþ, soþe	rings	abeag, beaga, beagas, beagum, hringas
right-hand	swiðne, swiðra etc, swiðran, swiþne, swiþra etc, swiþran, swiþre	ring-stemmed-ship	hringedstefna, hringedstefnan
		rip-apart	toslitan, toslited, tosliteþ
rightly	rihte, ryhte		
right-now (Latin)	iamiamque	rise	astag, astah, asteah, astigan, astigeð, astigeþ, stah, stigan, stigen, stigon
right-thinking	reþehygdig		
right-to-a-native-land	eðelriht, eðelrihtes, eþelriht, eþelrihtes		
rim	brerd		
rime	hrim, hrime	risk	geneðde, geneðdon, geneþan, geneþde, geneþdon, neðde, neðdon, neðende, neþan, neþde, neþdon, neþeð, neþende, neþeþ
ring	beag, beaga, beagas, beage, beages, beagum, beah, beahwriða, beahwriðan, beahwriþa, beahwriþan, bega, begas, hring, hringa, hringan, hringas, hringdon, hringe, hringum, wir, wira, wire, wirum		
		rivalry	æfst, æfstum

Word List (English to Ænglisc)

English	Ænglisc	English	Ænglisc
river	ea, egstream, egstreamum, stream, streamas, streame, streames, streamum, wæter, wætera, wætere, wæteres, wætre, wætres, wætrum	roll-around	wealweode, wealwian, wealwigende
		rolling	gelac, gewealc
		rood	rod
		roof	gehlidu, hlid, hrof, þecen, þecene
river-bank	easteð, easteðe, easteþ, easteþe, stæð, stæðe, stæþ, stæþe, staþe, staþu, streamstað, streamstaðe, streamstaþ, streamstaþe	roofed-hall	hrofsele
		roofs	hrofas
		room	cofa, cofan, rum
		roomy	gerume, rum, rume, rumne, rumre, rumum
rivers	streamas	root	stefn, stefna, stefnan, stefne, wang, wyrt, wyrte, wyrtruma, wyrtruman, wyrtum
road	rad, rade, siðfæt, siðfate, siþfæt, siþfate, stig, stige, stræt, stræte, wæg, weg		
		rope	sal, sale, streng, strengum
		rotten	ful, fula, fulan, fule, fullum
roar	cirm, cyrm, hlamm, hlemmeð, hlemmeþ, hlimman, hlimmeð, hlimmeþ, hlummen, hlummon, hlumon, hlyn, hlynede, hlynian, hlynnan, hlynode, swægende, swegan, sweog, sweogon, swogan, swogen, swogende	rough	hreo, hreofum, hreoh, hreon, hreoum, ruh
		rough-in-texture	hreof, hreofum
		roughly	unsofte
		round-shield	rond, rondas
		rout	fleam, fleame
		route	gelad, lad, lade
		row	reon, rowan
		royally-brave	cyningbald, cyningbalde
		royal-treasure	þeodenmadm, þeodenmadmas
roaring	circinde, grymetende	ruckus-at-dawn	uhthlem
rob	besnyðede, besnyðian, besnyþede, besnyþian, bestrudan, bestrudon, reafað, reafaþ, reafeden, reafian, reafige, reafode	ruin	fordon, forspildan, forworht, forworhte, forwyrcan, forwyrd, hryre
		ruined	hreorge
rocky	cludig		
rode	ridan		

Word List (English to Ænglisc)

English	Ænglisc	English	Ænglisc
rule	agan, age, agen, agon, ah, ahte, ahton, bisen, bisne, bysen, bysene, bysna, geheald, gehealdan, gehealde, gehealdeþ, geheold, gemet, gemete, geræd, grædest, gerihte, gestyran, gewealdan, gewealdene, gewealdenne, geweold, geweoldum, heald, healdað, healdan, healdaþ, healde, healdeð, healdest, healdeþ, heold, heoldan, heolde, heoldon, hiold, nagon, nah, nahte, nahton, rædað, rædan, rædaþ, rædde, rice, rices, ricsian, rightly, riht, rihte, rixað, rixian, rixode, ryht, truly	rummage-through	fandian, fandigan, fandode, gefandod, gefondad
		run	ærnan, ærndon, arn, irnan, urnen, urnon, yrnan, yrnende, yrnendum
		rune	runstæf, runstafas
		runic-letter	runstæf, runstafas
		running	ryne, yrnendum
		run-out	airnan, arinnan, aurnen
		rush	ræs, ræsan, ræsde, ræsed, ræsum, sceote, swægende, swegan
		rushing	aþrong
		rusty	omig, omige

S, s

English	Ænglisc
sack	fætels, fætelse
sacramental-wafer	oflætan, oflæte
sacred	godcund, godcunde, godcundlic, godcundlicum
sacred-grove	herg, hergum, herheard
sacrifice	lac, laca, lacum, onbleot, onblotan, tiber, tibre
sacrificial-fire	bælfyr

English	Ænglisc
ruled	ahte, bregu
ruler	agend, anwealda, brego, bregoweard, bregowearda, bregoweardas, dema, deman, drihten, drihtenes, drihtna, drihtne, drihtnes, dryhten, dryhtna, dryhtne, dryhtnes, healdend, rædend, strengel, þengel, walden, waldend, waldende, waldendes, wealdend, wealdende, wealdendes
ruler-of	wealdend
ruling	wealdend

Word List (English to Ænglisc)

English	Ænglisc	English	Ænglisc
sad	dreorig, dreorigne, driorig, driorigne, geocor, geomor, geomorlic, geomormod, geomormode, geomormodum, geomorne, geomorre, geomran, geomre, geomuru, gio, giohðo, giohþo, giomormod, hreohmod, hreowig, hreowige, hygegeomor, hygegeomorne, hygegiomor, meðe, meþe, sarig, sarigne, sarlic, sarlicre, unbliðe, unbliþe, werge, wergum, werig, werige	safety	aldornere, aldorneru, freoðo, freoþo, friðo, friþo, friþu, fryðo, fryþo
		said	cwæð, cweþ, gecwæð, gecwæþ, sæde, sægde
		sail	draf, drifað, drifan, drifaþ, drife, gerad, geseglian, geseglod, geseglode, liden, liðendum, liþan, liþendum, merehrægl, merehrægla, rad, ridan, ride, rideð, rideþ, riodan, segl, seglian, seglod, seglode, swimmað, swimman, swimmaþ, swymman
saddle	hildesetl, sadol	sailing	sund, sunde, sundes
saddle-bright	sadolbeorht		
sad-experience	cearsið, cearsiðum, cearsiþ, cearsiþum		
sad-faced	dreorighleor		
sad-hearted	modcearig		
sadly	dreorig, geomore, werige, werigne		
sad-minded	dreorigmod, geomormode, hreowcearig, sarferhð, sarferhþ, sarigferð, sarigferþ, sarigmod, sarigmodum		
sadness	geomor, longung, longunge, modceare, uhtceare		
sad-of-heart	hygegeomorne		
sad-or-grieving-mind	hreowigmod		
sad-song	giomorgyd		
sae-house	merehus, merehuses		
safe	gesund, hæl, hal, halan, hale		

Word List (English to Ænglisc)

English	Ænglisc	English	Ænglisc
sailor	brimliðend, brimliðende, brimliþend, brimliþende, brimliþendra, brimman, brimmann, brimmanna, brimmen, faraðlacende, faraþlacende, fareð, fareðlacende, fareðlacendum, fareþ, fareþlacende, fareþlacendum, faroðlacend, faroðlacende, faroþlacend, faroþlacende, fleotend, fleotendra, flota, flotan, flotmonn, flotmonna, liðend, liðende, lidmann, lidmanna, lidmen, liþend, liþende, merefara, merefaran, mereliðend, mereliðende, mereliþend, mereliþende, sælida, sælidan, sæliðend, sæliþend, sæliþende, sæmann, sæmanna, sæmannum, sæmen, særinc, særinca, wægliðend, wægliðende, wægliðendum, wægliþend, wægliþende, wægliþendum faraðlacende, flotan, sæliþende, scipflotan,	saint	halegu, halga, halgan, halgena, halgum, halig, haligan, halige, haliges, haligre, sanct, sancta, sanctan, sancte, sanctus
		saints	haligra
		sake-of	þurh
		salmon	leax
		salt	sealt, sealte, sealtne
		salt-stone	sealtstan, sealtstanes
		salt-wave	sealt-yð, sealtyþ, sealt-yþ, sealtyþa
		salty	sealt, sealte, sealtne
		salty-waves	sealtyþa
		salute	haleted, halettan, halette
		salvation	aldornere, aldorneru, feorhnere, gesynta, gesynto, gesyntum, hæle, hælo, hælu
		salve	sapan, sape
		same	III, ilca, ilcan, ilce, self, yfles, ylcan
		sand	greot, greote, sand, sande, sonde
		sand-bank	sondbeorg, sondbeorgum
		sank	sah
		Sarah (name)	Saharie
		sat	sæt, sætan
		sated	sæd
		satiated	sæd, sædne
		satisfaction	frofre
sailors	wægliþende		
sail-road	seglrad, seglrade		
sail-yard	segelgyrd		

Word List (English to *Ænglisc*)

English	*Ænglisc*	English	*Ænglisc*
savage	grim, grimlic, grimma, grimman, grimme, grimne, grimre, hreo, reðemode, reoc, reþemod, reþemode, sliðe, sliðne, sliðra, sliþe, sliþen, sliþne, sliþra, wælhreow, wælreow, wælreowe, welhreowan	say	acwæð, acwæþ, acweðan, acweþan, acwið, acwiþ, acwyð, acwyþ, asægd, asægde, asecgan, awræc, awrecan, benemde, benemdon, benemnan, cwæð, cwædon, cwæþ, cweð, cweðan, cweðaþ, cweðe, cweden, cweþ, cweþan, cweþaþ, cweþe, cwið, cwiþ, cwyð, cwyþ, cyð, cyðað, cyðan, cydde, cyðe, cyðdon, cyþ, cyþan, cyþaþ, cyþde, cyþdon, gecwæð, gecwæde, gecwædon, gecwæþ, gecwedene, gecyd, gecyðan, gecyðanne, gecyðde, gecyðed, gecyþan, gecyþanne, gecyþde, gecyþed, gesæd, gesæde, gesægd
savagely	felon, fyrenlice, grimman		
savage-warrior	herewosa, herewosan		
save	ahrædde, ahreddan, ahredde, ahreddest, ahreded, bearh, beorgan, burgan, burgon, gebearg, gebearh, geborgen, gehæle, genered, generede, generian, generigan, nere, nereð, nerede, nereþ, nergan, nergean, nerian, nerion, sparedon, sparian, sparode		
saved	generede		
saving	gehælede		
saviour	hælend, hælendne, nergend, nergende, nergendes	say-before	foresædan, foresædon, foresecgan
saw	gesawe, seah	saying	cwet, cwyð, cwyde, cwyþ
sax	seax, seaxe, seaxses	say-previously	foresædan, foresædon, foresecgan
Saxons	Seaxe	scabbard	scæð, scæðum, scæþ, scæþum, sceað, sceaðe, sceaðum, sceaþ, sceaþe, sceaþum, sceððan, sceðe, sceþe, sceþþan
		scalped	hættode

Word List (English to Ænglisc)

English	Ænglisc	English	Ænglisc
scar	dolg	sea-bird	ganet, ganetes, ganot, ganotes, huilpan, hwilpe
scatter	stred, stregan, tofaran, toforan		
scent	swicce	sea-boat	sæbat
scents	swæcca	sea-booty	sælac, sælace
scheme	geþeaht	sea-bottom	grund, grundas, grunde, grundes, grundwong, meregrund, meregrundas, sægrund, sægrundas, sægrunde
scholar	boceras, bocere		
science-learned	cræftgleawe		
scop	gleomann, gleomannes, scop		
scorn	forhogian, forhogode		
Scots	Sceotta		
Scottish	Scittisc	sea-bottom-hall	grundsele
scream	begeall, begiellan, begollen, begullon, hreopon, hropan, hryman, hrymde	sea-building	holmærn, holmærna, sundreced
		sea-burden	brimhlæst, brimhlæste
screech	begeall, begiellan, begollen, begullon	sea-chest	mereciest, merecieste
scribe	boceras, bocere		
sea	bæðweg, bæþweg, brim, brimes, brimu, brymu, flot, garsecg, garsecges, geofen, geofenes, geofon, gifen, gyfen, gyfenes, hæf, hafu, heafo, heafu, hron-rad, lago, lagu, laguflod, laguflode, mere, mereflod, mereflode, sæ, sæm, særyric, sæs, sioleð, sioleða, sioleþ, sioleþa, sund, sunde, sundes, swanrad, swanrade, wada, wado, wadu, waðum, wæd, wædes, wæg, wæge, waþum, weg, wegas	sea-cliff	brimclif, brimclifu, holmclif, holmclife, holmclifu
		seacoast	sæ-rima
		sea-creature	sædeor
		sea-current	brimstream, brimstreamas, holmwylm, holmwylme, lagostreamum, lagustream, lagustreamas, sæflod, sæstream, sæstreamas, sæstreamum
		sea-dragon	sædraca, sædracan
		sea-eagle	earn, earne
		seafarer	merefara, merefaran, sælida, sælidan
		sea-fish	merefisc, merefixa, sæfisc, sæfisca
		sea-flow	mereflode
sea-animal	meredeor	sea-garment	merehrægl, merehrægla
sea-beach	sæwong, sæwongas		
seabird	brimfuglas, brimfugol	sea-goer	sægenga
		sea-gull	mæw

Word List (English to Ænglisc)

English	Ænglisc	English	Ænglisc
sea-horse	sæmearas, sæmearh, sæwudu	season	missarum, missera, missere, misserum, þrag, þrage
sea-house	mere-hus		
sea-journey	brimlad, brimlade, lagosið, lagosiða, lagosiþ, lagosiþa, sæsið, sæsiðe, sæsiþ, sæsiþe	seasoned-warrior	ealdgesið, ealdgesiðas, ealdgesiþ, ealdgesiþas
		sea-steed	sæmearas
sea-king	sæcyning, sæcyninga	sea-stream	eagor-stream, merestream, merestreamas
sea-lane	brim-lad		
seal-baths	seolhbaþo	sea-streams	merestreamas
sea-leader	brimwisa, brimwisan	sea-strength	merestrengo
sealed	gesælde, sealde	sea-surface	sæwong, sæwongas
sea-lord	mereweard	sea-surge	holmwylm, holmwylme, sæwylm, sæwylmas
seaman	brimmann, brimmanna, brimmen, sæliðend, sæliþend, sæliþende, sæmann, sæmanna, sæmannum, sæmen, særinc, særinca		
		sea-swallow	stearn
		sea-swell	gewealc
		seat	geset, gesetu, sess, sesse, setl, setla, setle, setles, setlum, stol, stole
		seated	onsite
sea-man	brim-man	seat-of-men	gumstole
sea-menace	wæþrea	sea-traveller	wægliðend, wægliðende, wægliðondum, wægliþend, wægliþende, wægliþendum
sea-mew	mæw, mæwes		
sea-might	holmmægen, holmmægne		
sea-offering	sælac, sælace		
sea-path	flodweg, flodwegas, merestræt, merestræta	sea-voyage	sæfor, sæ-for, sæfore, sælad, sælade, yðlad, yðlade, yþlad, yþlade
search-for-land	landsocn, landsocne		
sea-reeds	særyrica		
sea-road	lagustræt, lagustræte	sea-wall	sæweall, sæwealle
sea-roomy	sægeap	seaward	sænacan
sea-route	lagulad, lagulade, merelad, merelade	sea-water	merestream, merestreamas
sea-ship	sænaca, sænacan	sea-wave	flodyþ, holmwylm, holmwylme
seashore	sæ-rima, strand, strande	sea-way	flodweg, flodwegas
seaside	waroð, waroðas, waroðe, waroþ, waroþas, waroþe	sea-weary	merewerges, merewerig, mere-werig, sæmeðe, sæmeþe
seaside-headland	sænæss, sænæssas	seaweed	war, ware
		sea-wise	lagucræftig

Word List (English to Ænglisc)

English	Ænglisc	English	Ænglisc
sea-woman	merewif	see	beseah, beseo, beseon, gesægon, gesawe, gesawon, geseah, gesegan, gesegen, gesegon, geseo, geseoð, geseon, geseoþ, gesihð, gesihþ, gesyhð, gesyhst, gesyhþ, locast, lociað, locian, lociaþ, ofersawon, oferseon, sægon, sawon, sceawian, seah, segen, seon
sea-wood	sundwudu		
seax	seax, seaxe, seaxses		
Secgen (name)	Secgena		
second	æfter, æftera, æftre, oðer, oþer, ōþer		
secret	deogol, digol, digolnes, digolnesse, digolnysse, dygel, dygle, dyrnan, dyrne, dyrnra, dyrnum		
secretly	dyrne, onsundran		
secret-meditation	run	seed	corn, corna, sæd, sæda
secret-place	digle		
secular-learning	woruldwisdom, woruldwysdome	seed-bearing	sædberende, sædberendes
secular-life	weorold had	seeing	seað, seaþ, seoðan, seoþan
secure	fæstnian, gefæstnod, gefæstnodon, heore, heoru	seek	acsian, ahsian, ahsode, ahsodon, cunnian, cunnod, cunnode, friclan, geceosað, gesec, gesecan, gesecanne, gesece, gesecean, geseceð, geseceþ, gesoht, gesohtan, gesohte, gesohtest, gesohton, sec, secan, sece, seceað, secean, seceaþ, seceð, secen, secest, seceþ, soht, sohtan, sohte, sohten, sohtest, sohton
secure-homeland	eðelstaðol, eðelstaðolas, eþelstaþol, eþelstaþolas		
securely	fæste, fæstor		
securely-linked	locen, locene		
security	frið, friðe, friþ, friþe, friþes, staðol, staðolas, staðole, staþel, staþelum, staþol, staþolas, staþole		
seduce	bepæcan, bepæceð, bepæceþ		
seduction	forliger, forligre, forlygre, forlyres, olecung, olecunge	seek-after	cepan
		seeking	sohtan

Word List (English to Ænglisc)

English	Ænglisc	English	Ænglisc
seek-out	ceosan, ciosan, cure, curon, geceas, geceos, geceosað, geceosaþ, geceosenne, gecoren, gecorenan, gecorene, gecorone, geneosode, gesec, gesecan, gesecanne, gesece, gesecean, geseceð, geseceþ, gesohtan, gesohte, gesohtest, gesohton, neosan, neosian, niosað, niosan, niosaþ, niosian, sec, secan, sece, sceað, secean, seceaþ, seceð, secen, secest, seceþ, sohtan, sohte, sohten, sohtest, sohton	seize	befangen, befon, befongen, bifongen, fæng, fehð, fehþ, feng, fengon, fon, forgrap, forgripan, gefangen, gefeng, gefengon, gefon, gegrap, gegripon, genam, genamon, geniman, genumen, grap, grapian, grapode, gripan, gripe, gripeð, gripen, gripeþ, gripon, onwadan, onwod, wiðfeng, wiðfon, wiþfeng, wiþfon
		seldom	seldan
		select	alesan, alesen, ceosan, ciosan, cure, curon, geceas, geceos, geceosað, geceosaþ, geceosenne, gecoren, gecorenan, gecorene, gecorone
seeks	geseceð, seceð		
seem	ðuhte, ðyncan, geðuht, geþuht, geþuhton, þincan, þince, þinceað, þincean, þinceaþ, þinceð, þinceþ, þuhte, þuhton, þyncan, þynceð, þynceþ	selected-war-troop	herecist, hereciste, herecyste
		self	self, selfa, selfe, selfes, selfne, selfra, selfre, selfum, seolf, seolfa, sylf, sylfa, sylfan, sylfe, sylfes, sylfne, sylfra, sylfre, sylfum
seemly	gedefe		
seen	beseo, gesyne	sell	bebicgan, bebicge, bebohte, geseald, gesealde, gesealdon, gesellan, gesylle, sealde, sealdest, sealdon, seleð, seleþ, sellan, selle, syleð, syleþ, syllað, syllan, syllaþ, sylle, syllon
sees	sceawað		
seethe	weallað, weallan, weallaþ, weallende, weallendu, weallinde, weol, weoll		

Word List (English to Ænglisc)

English	Ænglisc	English	Ænglisc
send	asendan, asende, asendest, onsend, onsendan, onsende, onsended, onsendeð, onsendeþ, onsendon, sændan, sendan, sende, sended, sendeð, sendeþ, sendon, sened, sent	separation	dæl, dælas, dæle, gedal, gedale, gescad
		sequence	endebyrdnes
		Seraphim (name)	Serafhin
		serious	georn, georne
		serious-wound	bealubenn
		serpent	nædran, nædre, wyrm
		serpent-body	wyrmlic, wyrmlicum
		serpent-hall	wyrmsele
send-away	forsendan, forsended, sændan	serpent-kind	wyrmcynn, wyrmcynnes
send-forth	asendan, asende, asendest	serpent-like	wyrmfah
		serpents	wurman
sends	sendeð	servant	ambyhtsecg, anbyhtscealc, anbyhtscealcas, cniht, cnihtas, cnihtum, cnyhtum, ðegn, ðegna, ðegnas, foregenga, forewyrcend, forewyrcendum, hyredcniht, hyredcnihtas, hyredmann, hyredmen, magoðegn, magoþegn, magoþegna, magoþegnum, maguþegn, maguþegnas, maguþegne, ombeht, ombiht, ombihtscealc, ombihtscealcum, ombihtum, seldguma, þægn, þægne, þegen, þegenas, þegn, þegna, þegnas, þegne, þegnes, þegnum, þeo, þeow, þeowa, þeowan, weorctheos, weorcþeow, worcþeow
send-throughout	geondsendan, geondsended		
sense	andgit		
sense (Latin)	sensu		
sentence	fers		
sentence-to-death	fordæmed, fordeman		
sent-forth	asendne		
separate	adælan, adæled, adælede, aleoðode, aleoþian, aleoþode, gesced, gesundrod, gesundrode, getwæman, sceadan, sceadeð, sceadeþ, sundrian, syndrig, todælan, todælden, to-faran, to-faren, to-for, to-foron, tosyndrodost, totwæman, totwæmed, totweman, ungeþeod, ungeþeode		
separated	gedælde, sceadeð		
separate-from	bescierian, bescyrede, biscyred		
separate-into-piles	tohladan, tohlodon		
separately	onsundran, onsundron, sundor		

Word List (English to Ænglisc)

English	Ænglisc	English	Ænglisc
serve	cweman, ðeowian, folgian, folgod, folgode, gecwæman, gecwæmde, gelæset, gelæst, gelæstan, gelæste, gelæston, geþenod, læst, læstan, læste, læsten, læstes, þegnian, þegnode, þenian, þenode, þeowdon, þeowian, þeowige	set	aseted, asettan, asette, asetton, gesætte, gesætton, geseted, gesett, gesette, gesetton, sete, settan, sette, settest, setton
serve-food	aþecgan	set-an-example	bysnian, gebysnode
serve-liquid-to	scencan, scencte	set-a-trap	geregnad, geregnode, gerenod, regnian, renian, renodest
service	ambyht, ambyhto, geongordom, geongordome, geongordomes, giongorscipe, mæssan, mæsse, ombiht, þegnscipe, þegnscipes, þegnung, þegnunge, þeowdom, þeowdome	set-down	settan
		set-in-motion	weaht, weccað, weccan, weccaþ, weccean, wecceð, wecceþ, wehte
		setting	setle, setlgang, setlgange
		settle	buað, buan, buaþ, bugan, bun, buon, gebun, gesæt, gesæton, gesætte, gesætton, geseted, geseten, gesett, gesette, gesetton, geþinged, geþingod, sæt, sætan, sæte, sæton, seman, setan, sete, setlað, setlan, setlaþ, settan, sette, setton, sittan, teode, teodod, teon, þingade, þingian, þingode
service-tree	cwicbeam, cwicbeame		
serving	hyredmann, hyredmen		
serving-boy	hyredcniht, hyredcnihtas		
serving-man	hyredcniht, hyredcnihtas, ombihtþegn, ombihtþegne		
		settled	eardfæst, sæt
serving-person	byrelas, byrele, byreles	settlement	lufan, lufe, lufen, lufu, lufum
servitude	þegnscipe, þegnscipes, þeowdom, þeowdome	settlement-term	geþinge, geþingea, geþinges, geþingo
		settles	gesetu
		settle-upon	fæstnian, gefæstnod, gefæstnodon
		settling	setlaþ
		set-up	geriht, rihtan, rihte

Word List (English to Ænglisc)

English	Ænglisc	English	Ænglisc
seven	seofan, seofene, seofon, seofone, syfone, VII	seventy two	twegen and hundseofontig, tpegen and hundseofontig
seven-fold	seofonfeald		
seventeen	seofontine	seven-years-old	syfanwintre
seventeenth	seofonteoþa	severe	grim, grimma, grimman, grimme, grimne, grimre, þearl, þearlmod, unliðe, unliþe
seventh	seofoðan, seofoþa		
seventieth	hundseofontigoþa		
seven-times-as-large	seofonfeald		
seventy	hundseofontig	severely	fræcne, frecne, grimme, grymme, hearde, þearle
seventy eight	eahta and hundseofontig		
seventy eighth	eahta and hundseofontigoþa	sew	seowed, seowian
		sewing	saweð
seventy fifth	fif and hundseofontigoþa	sexual-intercourse	gebedscipe, hæmed, hæmede
seventy first	an and hundseofontigoþa	sexual-partner	gebædda, gebedda, gebeddan, gebeddum
seventy five	fif and hundseofontig		
		shackle	fetor
seventy four	feower and hundseofontig, feoper and hundseofontig	shadow	sceade, sceado, sceadu, þeostra, þeostru, þeostrum, þystre, þystro, þystru, þystrum
seventy fourth	feower and hundseofontigoþa	shadow-covering	scaduhelm, scaduhelma
seventy nine	nigon and hundseofontig	shadowy	þystre, þystrum
seventy ninth	nigon and hundseofontigoþa	shadowy-walker	sceadugenga
		shaft	scefte
seventy one	an and hundseofontig	shaft-of-wheat	sceaft, sceafta, sceft
		shaggy	ruh
seventy second	twa and hundseofontigoþa	shake	acweccan, acweht, acwehte, asceacan, asceoc, bifian, bifiende, bifode, cweccan, cwehte, hrysedon, hrysian, onsceacan, onsceoc, scacan, scacen, scæcen, sceacan, sceaceð, sceacen, sceaceþ, sceoc, scoc
seventy seven	seofon and hundseofontig		
seventy seventh	seofon and hundseofontigoþa		
seventy six	siex and hundseofontig		
seventy sixth	six and hundseofontigoþa		
seventy third	þreo and hundseofontigoþa		
seventy three	þri and hundseofontig		

Word List (English to *Ænglisc*)

English	*Ænglisc*	English	*Ænglisc*
shall	scal, sceal, sceall, scealt, scel, sceolan, sceolde, sceolden, sceoldest, sceoldon, sceole, sceolon, scile, scolde, scoldon, sculan, sculon, scyle	share	bryttað, bryttade, bryttaþ, bryttedon, bryttian, bryttigin, dæl, dælað, dælan, dælas, dælaþ, dælde, dældon, dæle, dæleð, dælest, dæleþ, dælon, gedælan, gedælde, gedæled, gedal, gedale, gedaled
shall-be	beoð, beoþ, sceal		
shall-we	sculon, scylun		
shall-you	scealt		
shame	bysmor, edwit, hynð, hynða, hynðo, hynðu, hynþ, hynþa, hynþo, hynþu, ofsceamian, ofsceamod, sceome, sceond, sceonde, scomu	shared	dæleð
		share-in	dælað, dælan, dælaþ, dælde, dældon, dæle, dæleð, dæleþ, dælon
		share-of	dæl
shameful	bismorlic, bismorlicum, bysmorful, bysmorfullum, fracod, fracodes, heanlic	sharer	tiða, tiþa
		sharp	bitre, scearp, scearpe, scearpne
		sharpen	gegrundene, grindan
shameful-life	edwitlif	shatter	to, tobærst, toberstan, toglad, toglidan
shamefully	fracodlice, fracoðlice, fracoþlice		
		shattered	scearde
shameless	ðrist, ðriste, gemah, þrist, þriste	shave	efne, efsian, geefsod
shamelessly	þriste, unscomlice	she	ðæt, he, heo, him, hine, his, hit, hym, hyne, hys, se, seo, þæt
shape	gesceap, gesceapen, gesceapo, gesceapu, gescieppan, gescop, gescopon		
		shear	efsian, geefsod, gescær
		sheared	sceard, scorene
shaped	sceope	sheath	scæð, scæðum, scæþ, scæþum, sceað, sceaðe, sceaðum, sceaþ, sceaþe, sceaþum, sceðe, sceþe
shaper	scepen, scieppend, scippend, scyppend, scyppende		
		shed	ageat, ageotan, agoten, agotene, scypen
		shed-blood	geotan, geotende
		sheep	sceap, sceape
		shelf	scylfa, scylfan

Word List (English to Ænglisc)

English	Ænglisc	English	Ænglisc
shelter	hleo, hleonian	shield-warrior	randwiga, randwigan, randwiggend, randwiggendra, randwigum, rondwiggend, rondwiggende, scyldwiga
shepherd	hyrdas, hyrde		
shield	bebeorgan, bebeorh, bord, borda, bordes, bordrand, bordum, cellod, gescyld, gescylt, guðbord, guðbordes, guþbord, guþbordes, helme, hildebord, hildebordum, lind, rand, randas, rande, rond, ronde, scild, scildas, scyld, scylda, scyldan, scyldas, scylde, wudu		
		shield-wood	lindgestealla
		shilling	scilling
		shimmered	bregdende
		shine	blican, blicð, blicon, blicþ, gladiað, gladian, gladiaþ, glitinian, lixan, lixte, lixton, scan, scinað, scinan, scinaþ, scineð, scineþ, scinna, scinon, scionon
shield-bearing	lindwiga, lindwiggend, lindwiggende	shines	scine, scyneð
		shining	bliceð, fag, fage, fagne, fagum, fah, fahne, fane, glad, gladiað, gladiaþ, gladu, gladum, glæd, glæde, glædlic, glædne, hwit, hwita, hwitan, hwite, hwitne, hwitost, hwitre, nitor, scan, scene, scennum, scenost, scenran, sceone, sceonost, sciene, scienost, scinan, scir, scira, sciran, scire, scirne, scirum, scyne, scynost, scynra, swegl, swegle
shield-boss	rand		
shield-crashing	lindcroda, lindcrodan		
shield-defence	randgebeorh		
shielded	scylde		
shield-man	scyldfreca		
shield-owner	rondhæbbend, rondhæbbendra		
shield-owning-persons	bordhæbbende		
shield-play	lindplega, lindplegan		
shield-possessor	lindhæbbend, lindhæbbende, lindhæbbendra		
shield-row	bordhreoða, bordhreoþa		
shields	linda		
shield-wall	bordweal, bordweall, scildburh, scildweall, scyldburh, wihaga, wihagan		
		shining-armour	wigblac
		shining-haired	hwitlocced, hwitloccedu

Word List (English to Ænglisc)

English	Ænglisc	English	Ænglisc
ship	æsc, æsca, æscum, asca, bat, bates, brenting, brentingas, ceol, ceolas, ceole, ceoles, flota, flotan, geofonhus, holmærn, holmærna, lid, lide, lides, merehus, merehuses, naca, nacan, næledbord, sæbat, sæmearas, sæmearh, sæwudu, scip, scipe, scipes, scipu, scype, scypon, sundwudu, wægþæl, wægþel, wæg-þel, wægþele, wæterþisa, wegflota, wuda, wundenstefna, yðlida, yðlidan, yðmearas, yðmearh, yþlida, yþlidan, yþmearas, yþmearh	shoot	gesceat, sceat, sceop, sceotan, sceoteð, sceoteþ, scoten
		shoot-arrows	gesceat, sceat, sceop, sceotan, sceoteð, sceoteþ, scoten
		shooting	gescot, gescotes, ofsceat, ofsceotan, ofscet, scyte
		shore	easteð, easteðe, easteþ, easteþe, faroð, faroðe, faroþ, faroþe, ofer, ofre, sand, sande, sonde, stæð, stæðe, stæþ, stæþe, staþe, staþu, streamstað, streamstaðe, streamstaþ, streamstaþe, waroð, waroðas, waroðe, waroþ, waroþas, waroþe, waroþum
ship-board	ceolþel, ceolþele	shoreline	landgemyrce, landgemyrcu, ora, oran
ship-deck	bord, borda, bordes, bordum		
ship-guardian	batweard, batwearde	shoreline-as-barrier8	stæðweall, stæðweallas, stæþweall, stæþweallas
ship-hold	bearm, bearme, bearmum, bord, borda, bordes, bordum, bosm, bosme		
		shoreline-cliff	ecgclif
		shore-wall	stæð-weall, stæþ-weall
shipman	flotmonn, flotmonna	shore-watch	ægweard, ægwearde
ship-route	flotweg		
ship's	lides	short	lytel, lytle, lytlum
ship's-deck	ceolþele	shortly	ungeara
ship-side	bord, borda, bordes, bordum	short-sword	hupseax
		short-time	winterstund, winterstunde
shire	scir, scire, scyr, scyre		
		shot	gesceat, gescot, gescotes, scoten
shiver	bifian, bifiende, bifode		
		shot-through	ðyrel
shone	lixte, scan		

Word List (English to Ænglisc)

English	Ænglisc	English	Ænglisc
should	scal, sceal, sceall, scealt, scel, sceolde, sceolden, sceoldest, sceoldon, sceole, sceolon, scile, scolde, scoldon, sculan, sculon, scyle	show	beacnian, cen, cennan, eaweð, eaweþ, eowdon, eoweð, eoweþ, gebeacnod, geeawed, gelæstan, gesceawað, gesceawaþ, gesceawod, getæce, getæhte, getæhton, gewisade, gewissode, geywan, iewan, iewde, iewe, oðiewan, oðiewde, oðiewdest, oþiewan, oþiewde, oþiewdest, sceawa, sceawað, sceawaþ, sceawedon, sceawiað, sceawian, sceawiaþ, sceawigan, sceawige, sceawode, sceawodon, tæcan, tæcaþ, tæhte, wæfersyn, wæfersyne, wisade, wisian, wisie, wisige, wisode, wissian, ywan, ywde
should-be	sceolde		
shoulder	bog, bogum, eaxl, eaxle, eaxlgestealla, eaxlgesteallan, eaxlum, exle		
shoulder-fastening	eaxlgespann, eaxlgespanne		
shout	ceallian, gylede, gylian, hlynede, hlynian, hlynnan, hlynode, hreopon, hropan		
shove	aþringan, aþrong, bescufan		
		show-by-signs	getacnod, tacnian
		show-consideration-for	gesceawað, gesceawaþ, gesceawod, sceawa, sceawað, sceawaþ, sceawedon, sceawiað, sceawian, sceawiaþ, sceawigan, sceawige, sceawode, sceawodon
		shower	scur, scuras, scurheard, scurum
		showing	gesceawað
		show-mercy	gemiltsa, miltsian

Word List (English to Ænglisc)

English	Ænglisc	English	Ænglisc
show-to-be-a-liar	gelignian, gelignod	sign	beacen, beacna, beacne, beacnum, becn, behð, behðe, behþ, behþe, mæl, mæla, mæles, mælo, mælum, myrce, myrcels, myrcelse, segen, segn, segnas, segne, tacen, tacn, tacne
shrewd	scearp, scearpe, scearpne		
shrine	scrin, scrine		
shrink	clinge		
shrivel	scring		
shut	beleac, belocen, belucan, belucon		
shut-up	forðylman, forðylmed, forþylman, forþylmed	sign-of-the-cross	segnade, segnian
sick	adlegan, adlig, adligum, seo, seoc, seoce, unhæl, unhælo, untrum, untrume	silent	dumb, swige, swigra
		silver	seolfor, seolfre, sylfor
		silver-coin	scilling
		similar	þyslic, þyslicu
sick-from-battle	heaðosioc, heaðosiocum, heaþosioc, heaþosiocum	similarly	gelice, gelicost
		similar-to	gelic, gelice, gelicost
		simple	anfeald, anfealdne, unorne
sickly	lef, wanhal, wanhalum	sin	facen, facna, facne, facnes, firen, firena, firendæd, firendæda, firene, fyren, fyrena, fyrene, gedwild, gedwilde, gedwyld, gedwylde, gesyngad, gylt, gyltum, leahtor, leahtrum, man, mandæd, mandædum, mane, manes, manscilde, morðer, morðor, morðra, morðre, morðres, morþer, morþor, morþra, morþre, morþres, senna, symle, syn, syngian, syngige, synn, synna, synne, synnum, unriht, unrihte, womm, womma, womme, wommum, wroht, wrohte, wrohtes, wrohtscipe
sickness	adl, broc, broce, coðu, coþu, coþum		
side	hand, handa, handæ, handon, handum, healf, healfa, healfe, healfre, hond, honda, hondum, sidan, side		
Sigeferth (name)	Sigeferð, Sigeferþ		
sigh	seofad, seofade, seofedun, seofian		
sight	ansien, ansyn, ansyne, gesihð, gesihðe, gesihþ, gesihþe, gesyhðe, gesyhþe, onsyn		
sight-power	gesihð, gesihðe, gesihþ, gesihþe, gesyhðe, gesyhþe, sie, sien, siene		

Word List (English to Ænglisc)

English	Ænglisc	English	Ænglisc
since	forðam, forðan, forðon, forþam, forþan, forþon, oþ, seoððan, seoþðan, seoþþan, siððan, siðestan, siþðan, siþestan, siþþan, syððan, syððon, syðþan, syþðan, syþþan	sing	agalan, agol, asingan, asinge, asungen, gæleð, gæleþ, galan, galdor, galdre, gealdor, sang, sing, singan, singeð, singende, singeþ, song, sungen, sungon, swinsian, swinsigende, swynsode
sincere	bilewit, unfæcne		
sinew	seono, seonowe		
sinew-bond	seonobend, seonobende	singer	scop, scopes
sinful	arleas, arlease, arleasra, gedwolen, gedwolene, mæne, manscyldig, manscyligne, scildig, scyldfull, scyldfullum, scyldfulra, scyldig, scyldige, synbysig, synfullum, synnig, synnigra, womfull, womscyldig	singing	sang, sanges, singað, song
		single	an
		single-minded	anmod, anmode
		sing-out	agalan, agol
		singular	synderlic, synderlicre
		singularly	ænlice
		sink	besencan, besenceð, besenceþ, besincan, besuncen, gesigan, hreas, hreosan, hreosende, hruron, sencan, sigað, sigan, sigaþ, sigeð, sigeþ, sigon, sincan, sincende
sinful-deed	firendæd, firendæda		
sinful-devil	synscaðan, synscaþan, synsceaþa, synsceaþan		
sinful-enemy	synscaðan, synscaþan, synsceaþa, synsceaþan	sink-down	hnag, hnah, hnigan, hnigon
		sink-in	dufan, gedeaf, gedeð, gedeþ
sinful-greed	scyldfrece, scyldfrecu	sinner	arleas, arlease, arleasra, mansceaða, mansceaðan, mansceaþa, mansceaþan, synnig, synnigra
sinful-host?	wrohtgeteme		
sinfully	unarlice		
sinfulness	unrihtwisnys, unrihtwisnysse		
sinful-way	monwisa, monwisan		
		sins	leahtra
		sip	gesupe, supan
		sister	gesweostor, sweostar, sweostor, swyster
		sister's-son	swustersunu

Word List (English to Ænglisc)

English	Ænglisc	English	Ænglisc
sit	gesæt, gesæton, geseten, sæt, sætan, sæte, sæton, setan, sitest, sittan, sitte	sixty seven	seofon and sixtig
		sixty seventh	seofon and sixtigoþa
		sixty six	siex and sixtig
		sixty sixth	six and sixtigoþa
		sixty third	þreo and sixtigoþa
sit-around	ymbsæton, ymbsittan	sixty three	þri and sixtig
		sixty two	twegen and sixtig, tpegen and sixtig
sit-down	beah, bugan, bugeð, bugeþ, bugon, gebeag, gebeah, gebogen, gebogenan	skilful	cræftig, gleaw, gleawan, gleawe, gleawne, gleawra, gleawum, orðonc, searoðoncol, searoþoncelra, searoþoncol, snotera, snoteran, snotere, snotor, snotra, snottor, snottra, snottre
sit-on-or-in	onsite, onsittan		
sit-round	ymbsæt, ymbsæton, ymbseten, ymbsittan		
sits	siteð		
sitting	sittan		
situated	gelæg, læg, læge, lægon, lagon, leg, licgað, licgan, licgaþ, licgean, licgende, licgendre, lið, ligeð, ligeþ, ligst, liþ	skilfully-made-jewel	searogimm, searogimma, searogimmas
		skilfully-made-jewels	searogimmas
		skill	cræft, cræfta, cræftas, cræfte, cræftum, list, lista, listas, listum, orðonc, orðoncum, orþanc, orþancum, orþonc, orþoncum, searo, searwum, snytra, snytro, snytru, snyttru, snyttrum
situation	styde, weorudes, weoruld, worold, worolde, woruld, worulde		
sit-upon	ofsæt, ofsittan		
six	siex, syx, vi		
six-hundred	siex, siex-hund, syxhund		
sixteen	siextine		
sixteenth	sixteoþa		
sixth	sixta	skilled	cræftig, gearwost
sixtieth	sixtigoþa	skilled-at-sailing	lagucræftig
sixty	siextig, sixtig, syxtig	skilled-in-metal-craft	smiðcræftega, smiþcræftega
sixty eight	eahta and sixtig		
sixty eighth	eahta and sixtigoþa	skilled-in-poetry	leoðcræftig, leoþcræftig
sixty fifth	fif and sixtigoþa		
sixty first	an and sixtigoþa	skilled-in-song	leoðcræftig, leoþcræftig
sixty five	fif and sixtig		
sixty four	feower and sixtig, feoþer and sixtig	skill-in-contrivance	searoþonc, searoþoncum
sixty fourth	feower and sixtigoþa	skill-in-war	guðcræft, guþcræft
sixty nine	nigon and sixtig	skin	fell, fellum
sixty ninth	nigon and sixtigoþa		
sixty one	an and sixtig		
sixty second	twa and sixtigoþa		

Word List (English to *Ænglisc*)

English	*Ænglisc*	English	*Ænglisc*
sky	heofon, lyft, lyfte, rodera, roderas, roderum, rodor, rodora, rodores, swegel, wolcen	slavery	hæftnyd, þeowdom, þeowdome, þeownyd
sky-crown	rof, rofes	slay	gesloh, ofslægen, ofslean, ofslogon, ofsloh
sky-enclosure	lyftedoras	slayed	ofsloh
sky-roof	hrof, hrofe, hrofes, rof, rofes	slayer	bana, slaga, slagan
		sleep	ræste, rest, reste, slæp, slæpe, swæf, swæfne, swæfon, swæfun, swefað, swefan, swefaþ, swefeð, swefeþ, swefn, swefna, swefne, sweofot, sweofote
slack	lata		
slacken	asealcan		
slag	sinder, sindrum		
slain-field	wælfelda		
slander	forsæcgan		
slaughter	guðscear, guðsceare, guþscear, guþsceare, hrafyl, morðorbealo, morþorbealo, wæl, wældeað, wældeaþ, wælsleaht, wælsleahta		
		sleeping-tent	burgeteld, burgetelde, burgeteldes
		sleeping-together	gebedscipe
		sleeps	swifeð
		slender	wac, wace, wacne, wacran
slaughter-bed	wælbedd, wælbedde, wælrest, wælreste	slice	snædan, snedeþ
		slice-to-death	forwrat, forwritan
slaughter-blood	wældreor, wældreore	slide	glad, glidan, glidon
		slip-away-from	aslupan
slaughter-full	wælfyll, wælfylla, wælfylle, wælfylles, wælfyllu	slit	slat, slitan, sliten, sliton
		slope	gehliðo, gehliþo, hleoðo, hleoðu, hleoþa, hleoþo, hleoþu, hlið, hliðe, hliðes, hlioðo, hlioþo, hliþ, hliþe, hliþes
slaughter-knife	wællseax, wællseaxe		
slaughter-mist	wælmist, wælmiste		
slaughter-net	wælnet		
slaughter-perhaps-a-spelling-of	wælfeall		
slaughter-shaft	wælsceaft, wælsceaftas	slow	læt, sleac
		slow-to-anger	gemetfæst
slaughter-spoils	wælreaf	sluggish	sleac, swær, swæran
slaughter-stained	wælfag, wælfagne		
slave	hæft, hæfton, mennen, þeo, þeow, þeowa, þeowan, wealas, wealh, weorctheos, weorcþeow, worcþeow, wyln	slumber	swefote
		slut	myltestre, scealt, sceand, sceande
		small	læs, læsest, lytel, lytle, lytlum, mæte, mætost, smæl
		smaller	læssa, læssan, lesse

Word List (English to Ænglisc)

English	Ænglisc	English	Ænglisc
small-number	lyt	solid	fæst, fæste, fæstne, fæstum
small-ship	cnear		
smell	stenc, stincan, stonc	solidly	fæste, fæstor
smite	beslægene, beslean, besloh	solitary-dweller	anhaga, anhogan
		solitary-flier	anfloga
smith	asmiðigen, asmiþigen, asmiþod, smið, smiðas, smiþ, smiþa, smiþas, smiþes	solitary-one	angenga, angengea, anhaga
		so-long-as	þenden
		some	hwylc, nagon, sum, sume, sumes, sumne, sumum
smiths	smiðas		
smoke	mist, mistas, racu, rec, recas, reccendne, rece, reocan, reocende, þrosm	some-kind	nathwylc, nathwylces, nathwylcum
		some-kind-of	hwelc, hwilc, hwilce, hwylc, hwylce, hwylcere, hwylcne, hwylcum, nathwylc, nathwylces, nathwylcum
smooth	smeðe, smeðne		
snake	nædran, nædre, wurman, wyrm, wyrmas, wyrme, wyrmes, wyrmum		
		some-of	sume
snake-body	wyrmlic, wyrmlicum	someone	hwelc, hwilc, hwilce, hwylc, hwylce, hwylcere, hwylcne, hwylcum, man, mon
snake-hall	wyrmsele		
snake-kind	wyrmcynn, wyrmcynnes		
snakes	wyrmfah	something	aht, awiht, awuht, edwihtan, edwihte, hwæs, hwæt, hwæt-hwegu, owiht, owihte
snow	snaw, sniwan, sniwde, sniwed		
snow-storm	hrið, hriþ		
snowy	hryðge, hryðig, hryþge, hryþig		
		something-or-other	nathwæt
so	ac, hwæt, sawla, se, seo, swa, swilce, swylce, þæs, to, to þæs	sometimes	hwile, hwilon, hwilum, þewhile, þragum
		sometimes-used-in-all	ealra, ealre
soap	sapan, sape		
so-as	swa, swilce, swylce	somewhat	hwene, hwon
soft	sefte	somewhere	gehwær, gehwer, hwergen
softly	seft, softe		
soil	hrusan, hruse, turf, turfa, turfon, tyrf, wancgturf	somewhere-or-other	nathwær
solace	frofor		
sold	sealde		
soldier	cniht, cnihtas, cnihtum, cnyhtum, fyrdrinc, fyrdrinces		
sole-ruler	anwalda, anwaldan, anwealda		

Word List (English to Ænglisc)

English	Ænglisc	English	Ænglisc
son	afera, aforan, bearn, bearnum, byras, byre, eafera, eaferan, eaferum, eafora, eaforan, eaforum, eafrum, mæcg, mæcga, mæcgum, maga, magan, mago, sumum, suna, suno, sunu, sunum, yrfeweard, yrfewearda, yrfeweardas	sorrow	cear, ceare, cearo, cearu, cearum, gehðo, gehþo, geomorre, gio, giohðe, giohðo, giohþe, giohþo, gnorn, gnornode, hreow, hreowa, sar, sare, sorg, sorga, sorge, sorgum, sorh, sorhg, sorhwylm, sorhwylmas, sorhwylmum
son (Latin)	filio, filium	sorrow-flame	cearwælm, cearwælmum, cearwylm, cearwylmas
song	cwidegiedd, cwidegiedda, fitt, fitte, galan, galdor, galdre, gealdor, gid, gidd, gidda, giddum, gied, giedd, giedde, gyd, gydd, gyddum, hleoðor, hleoþor, leoð, leoþ, sang, sanges, soðgied, song, soþgied, woðgiefu, wordgyd, woþgiefu	sorrow-for-followers	þegnsorg
		sorrowful	mod-cearig, sar, sarig, sorgcearig, sorgful, sorgfulre, sorhcearig, sorhful, sorhfull, sorhfullne, sorhfulne, unbliðe, unbliþe, winter-cearig
		sorrowful-expedition	cearsið, cearsiðum, cearsiþ, cearsiþum
song-of-terror	gryreleoð, gryreleoþ	sorrowful-in-mind	geomormod
songs	woþa	sorrowful-in-spirit	ferhðcearig, ferhþcearig
son-in-law-and-father-in-law	aðumsweoras, aðumsweran, aþumsweoras, aþumsweran	sorrowful-love	sorglufu
		sorrowfully	sare
		sorrowing-word	sorhword, sorhworda
sons	bearnum	sorrow-wave	sorhwylm, sorhwylmas, sorhwylmum
soon	ædre, ædrum, lengre, lungre, sona, ungeara		
sorcerer	dry, dryum	sort	cinne, cyn, cynn, cynna, cynne, cynnes
sorcery	dry, dryum, lyblac, lyblaca, lyblace		
sore	dolg, sar	so-that	ðæt, þæt, þætte
sorely	sare	sought	gesohte, gesohtun, sohtest, sohton
soreness	sara, sare		

Word List (English to *Ænglisc*)

English	*Ænglisc*	English	*Ænglisc*
soul	feorð, feorþ, ferð, ferðe, ferhð, ferhðe, ferhðes, ferhðum, ferhþ, ferhþe, ferhþes, ferhþum, ferþ, ferþe, fyrhðe, gæst, gæsta, gæste, gæstes, gast, gasta, gastas, gaste, gastes, hyge, saul, saula, saule, saulum, sawele, sawl, sawla, sawle, sawlum, sawol, sawul	south-porch	suðportice
		south-shore	suð-stæð, suþ-stæþ
		southward	suðe-weard, suþe-weard
		south-wind	suðwind, suþwind
		sow	sawan, sawen, seow
		space	rum
		spacious	geap, geapes, geapne, geapum, gerume, gimfæst, gimfæste, ginfæst, ginfæstan, ginfæstum, ginn, ginnan, ginne, gynn, gynne, rum, rume, rumne, rumre, rumum, wid, wida, widan, wide, widne, widre
soul-bearer	sawlberend, sawlberendra		
soul-hoard	sawlhord		
Soul-king	gastcyning, gastcyninge		
soul-murderer	gastbona	spaciously	rume, rumor
souls	sawla	spare	geara
sound	andsund, ansund, gesund, gesunde, gesundne, gesundran, hæl, hælo, hal, halan, hale, hleoðor, hleoþor, hlyn, onsund, onsundne, sweg, swege, Sweghleoþor	spark	ontendnyss, ontyndnys, spearca, spearcan
		sparkle	blican, blicð, blicon, blicþ
		spatter	bedraf, bedrifan, bedrifenne
sound-harmoniously	neomegende, neomian		
sound-loudly	scralletan		
source	ord, orde		
sourdough-starter	beorma, beorman		
south	suð, suþ		
southern	suþern, suþerne		
southern-direction	suðweg, suðwegum, suþweg, suþwegum		
southern-man	suðmonn, suðmonna, suþmonn, suþmonna		
southern-nation	suðfolc, suðfolcum, suþfolc, suþfolcum		
southern-people	suðfolc, suðfolcum, suþfolc, suþfolcum		

Word List (English to *Ænglisc*)

English	*Ænglisc*	English	*Ænglisc*
speak	acwæð, acwæþ, acweðan, acweþan, acwið, acwiþ, acwyð, acwyþ, asæcgan, cleopað, cleopaþ, cleopian, clypian, clypode, cwæð, cwædon, cwæþ, cweðan, cweden, cweþan, cygan, cygde, gecyged, gemælde, gereorded, gespæc, gespræc, gespræce, gespræcon, gespræconn, gesprece, geþinged, geþingod, gyddian, gyddode, hleoðrade, hleoðrian, hleoðrode, hleoþrade, hleoþrian, hleoþrode, maðelian, maðelod, maðelode, mæðlan, mælan, mælde, mæþlan, maþelade, maþelian, maþelod, maþelode, oncwæð, oncwæþ, oncweðan, oncweþan, reordade, reordian, reordigean, reordode	speak-to	gegrettan, gegrette, gespræc, gespræce, gespræcon, gespræconn, gesprece, gretan, greted, greteð, greteþ, grette, gretton, spræc, spræce, spræcon, sprecað, sprecan, sprecaþ, sprece, sprecen, spriceð, spriceþ, sprycst
		spear	æsc, æsca, æsctir, æscum, asca, cwicbeam, cwicbeame, daraða, dareðum, dareþum, daroð, daroþ, flan, flana, flane, flanes, franca, francan, gar, gara, garas, garcene, gare, gares, guðflan, guðflana, guþflan, guþflana, heresceaft, heresceafta, mægenwudu, ord, orde, spere, speru, þrecwudu, wælsceaft, wælsceaftas, wælsteng, wælstenge
speak-about	gewræc, gewrec, gewrecen, gewrecene, wræc, wræce, wræcon, wrec, wrecan, wrece, wrecen	spear-attack	garræs
		spear-battle	gargewinn, gargewinnes
		spear-bearer	æscberend, æscberendra, garberend, garberendra
speaker	woðbora, woðboran, woþbora, woþboran	spear-brandishing	dareðlacende
speaking	gespræcon, spræce, spreceð	spear-brave	æscrof, æscrofe, garcene
speak-of	mænan, mænde, mæned	spear-Danes	GAR-DENA, gar-Dene, gar-Denum
speak-out	cweþað	spear-death	garcwealm
speaks	cwæð	spear-fight	æscplega

Word List (English to *Ænglisc*)

English	*Ænglisc*	English	*Ænglisc*
spear-forest	garholt	speech	cwide, cwyde, gereord, gid, gidd, gidda, giddum, gied, giedd, giedde, gyd, gydd, gyddum, hleoðor, hleoðre, hleoðrum, hleoþor, hleoþre, hleoþrum, meðel, meðelword, meðelwordum, meþel, meþelword, meþelwordum, meþle, reorde, spæc, spæce, spel, spell, spella, spellum, spræc, spræca, spræce, woðgiefu, word, worda, worde, wordes, wordon, wordum, woþgiefu
spear-hand	garmundes		
spearman	sceotend, sceotendra, sceotendum, scotendum		
spear-meeting	garmittinge		
spear-mound	garmundes		
spears	garas, garum		
spear-shaft	deoreðsceaft, deoreðsceaftum, deoreþsceaft, deoreþsceaftum, garbeam, garbeames, sceaft, sceafta, sceft		
spear-shooting	ofsceat, ofsceotan, ofscet, scyte		
spear-sport	æscplega, æscplegan		
spear-strife	sperenið, spereniþ		
spear-throwing	scyte	speech-bearer	reordberend, reordberendum
spear-warrior	garwiga, garwigan, garwigend	speed	ofest, ofeste, ofost, ofoste, ofste, sped, spede
spear-wood	garholt, guðwudu		
special	synderlic, synderlicre, syndrig	speedily	hrædlice, ofestum, ofostum, ofstum
special-assignment	sundornytt, sundornytte	spell	galdor, galdre, gealdor
special-duty	sundornytt, sundornytte	spike	staca, stacan
species	teoche, teoh, teohh, teohha, teohhe	spin	span, spinnan
spectacle	wæfersyn, wæfersyne, wliteseon	spine	hricg, hrincg, hringe, hrycg

Word List (English to Ænglisc)

English	Ænglisc	English	Ænglisc
spirit	blæd, feora, feorð, feore, feores, feorg, feorh, feorþ, feorum, ferð, ferðe, ferh, ferhð, ferhðe, ferhðes, ferhðum, ferhþ, ferhþe, ferhþes, ferhþum, ferþ, ferþe, fyore, gæst, gæsta, gæste, gæstes, gast, gasta, gastae, gastas, gaste, gastes, gastes, gastum, hræðre, hræþre, hreðer, hreðra, hreðre, hreþer, hreþra, hreþre, mod, mode, modes, modsefa, mod-sefa, modsefan, modum, saula, saulum, sawele, sawl, sawla, sawle, sawlum, sawol, sawul, sefa	spiritual-attachment	hyge, hygebend, hygebendum
		spit	spiwan, spiwe
		spite	æfst, æfstum
		spit-out	spiwan, spiwe
		splashed-with-blood	dreorfah
		splendid	drihtlecu, drihtlic, drihtlice, drihtlicu, dryhtlic, dryhtlicestum, from, mæra, mæran, mære, mæres, mærne, mæro, mæron, mærost, mærra, mæru, mærum, wlanc, wlancan, wlance, wlances, wlancne, wlonc, wlonce, wlonces, wloncne, wloncum, wrætlic, wrætlicne, wrætlicran, wrætlicu
		splendidly	cymlice, cymlicor, lixeð, mærlice, mærne, wrætlice
spirit (Latin)	spiritui		
spirit-box	gastcofan	splendour	blæd, blæde, blædes, bledum, glæm, glæmes, gleam, gleoma, wlence, wlenco, wlencu, wlite, wuldor, wuldre, wuldres, wuldris
spirit-chamber	ferhðcofa, ferhðcofan, ferhþcofa, ferhþcofan, hreðerloca, hreðerlocan, hreþerloca, hreþerlocan		
		split	cleofan, clufon, sprengan, sprengde, toglad, toglidan
spirit-enclosure	ferðloca, ferð-loca, ferðlocan, ferhðloca, ferhðlocan, ferhþloca, ferhþlocan, ferþloca, ferþ-loca, ferþlocan	spoil	forspildan, spilde, spillan
		spoke	gereorded, hleoðrode, hleoþrode
spirit-house	feorgbold, feorhhus		
Spirit-king	gastcyning, gastcyninge	spoken	gesæd
		spoken-about	gespræconn
spirit-murderer	gastbona	spoken-of	gecweden
spirit-of	gastlice	spokesman	ðyle, þyle
spirits	gastas	spoor	spor
spiritual	gæstlic, gastlic		
spiritual-agitation	hygewælm		

Word List (English to Ænglisc)

English	Ænglisc	English	Ænglisc
sport	gamen, gamene, gelac, gelacum, gomen, gomene, plega, plegan, plegian, plegode	stag	heorot, heort
		stain	gemearca, gemearcod, gemearcode, mearcað, mearcaþ, mearcian, mearcode, womm, womma, womme, wommum
sporty	gamene		
spot	womm, womma, womme, wommum		
spouse	gebædda, gebedda, gebeddan, gebeddum, gemæc, gemæcca, gemæccum, gemæcne	stained	fag, fage, fagne, fagum, fah, fahne, fane
		stairs	hlæder, hlædræ
		stake	staca, stacan
spread	gesprang, gesprong, sprang, springan, sprong, sprungen, sprungon	Stamford (place)	Stanford
		stance	staðol, staðolas, staðole, staþel, staþelum, staþol, staþolas, staþole
spread-out	brædan, Passus		
spread-throughout	geondbrædan, geondbræded	stand	gestod, gestodon, standað, standan, standaþ, stande, standeð, standen, standeþ, stod, stodan, stodon, stondað, stondan, stondaþ, stonde, stondeð, stondeþ, stynt
sprig	blado, blæd, blæda, blædæ, blædu		
spring	ædra, ædre, ædrum, geludon, gesprang, gesprong, lencten, leodan, ludon, sprang, springan, sprong, sprungen, sprungon		
		stand-about	bestandan, bestemed, bestodon
spring-apart	tohlidan, tohlidene		
spring-up	aspringan, asprungen, liodan, liodende	standard	cumbles, cumblum, cumbol, fana, segn
		stand-by	bigstandað, bigstandan, bigstandaþ, gelæset, gelæstan, gelæste, gewunian, gewunod, gewunode
sprinkle-about	geondsprengan, geondsprengde		
sprout	sprytan		
spurt	gesprang, gesprong, sprang, springan, sprong, sprungon		
		stand-firm	stemnettan, stemnetton
spurt-out	ætspranc, ætspringan		
spy	leassceaweras, leassceawere	standing	astondeð, standeþ, stondað
stab	stang, sticaþ, stician, stingan	stand-on-either-side-of	bestandan, bestodon
stabbing-pain	færstice	standstill	bid
stability	fæstnung	stand-still	ætstandan, ætstod
staff	gyrde		

Word List (English to Ænglisc)

English	Ænglisc	English	Ænglisc
stand-tall	hlifade, hlifian, hlifigan, hlifige, hlifigean, hliuade	steam	reccendne, reocan, reocende, steam, steame
stand-up	aræman, aræmde, astandan, astod	steed	hæncgest
star	rodortunglum, rodortungol, steorra, steorrum, tungol	steel	isen, isenes, isern, isernes, style
		steep	bront, brontne, neowel, neowelne, neowle, stealc, steap, steape, steapes, steapne
starboard	steor-bord		
stare	starað, staraþ, starede, staredon, starian, starie, starige		
		steeple	styple
		steering	stirende
stars	tungel, tunglum, tungol	steersman	forðweard, forþweard
state	staðol, staðolas, staðole, staþel, staþelum, staþol, staþolas, staþole	stem	stefn
		stench	stenc
		step	gestop, stæppan, stæppe, steppan, stop, stopon, treddan, treddode, tryddode
stately	friþ, friþe		
station	staðole		
statue	monlica		
stature	wæstm, wæstma, wæstmas, wæstme, wæstmes, wæstmum, wæstum, westem	step-on	træd, træde, tredað, tredan, tredaþ, tredeð, tredeþ, treowum, triedeð, triedeþ
stave	stefn, stefna, stefnan, stefne	step-towards	ætstaeppan, ætstop
stay	bad, beodan, bidan, bideð, bideþ, bidon, gebad, gebidan, gebidanne, gebide, gebiden, semian, seomade, seomedon, seomian, seomode, seomodon, siomian	stern	galgmod, heard, heardhicgende, stefn, stefna, stefnan, stefne, stefnum, stið, stiðferhð, stiðhydig, stiþ, stiþferhþ, stiþfrihþ, stiþhydig, styrne
		sternly	styrnmode
		steward	burþen, burþene, geræfa, gerefa, gerefan
steadfast	fæsthydig, fæsthydigne, fæstræd, fæstrædne, stedefæst, stedefæste, trum, trumne	stick	sticaþ, stician
		sticking	stice
		stiff	stið, stiþ
		still	gean, gen, gena, gien, giena, giet, gieta, git, gyt, gyta, stille
steadfastly	stædefæste		
steady	unwealt		
steal-away	forstelan, forstolene		
		sting	stinge

494

Word List (English to *Ænglisc*)

English	*Ænglisc*	English	*Ænglisc*
stingily	hneawlice	stop	ætstandan, ætstod, endian, geændade, geendod, getwæfan, getwæfde, getwæfed, getwæfeð, getwæfeþ
stingy	hneaw		
stir	hreran, hrerde, hrered		
stirred	styrde		
stirred-up-water	sundgebland		
stir-up	astyred, astyrian, drefan, drefde, gedrefed, gewreged, hreran, onhreran, onhrered, styrede, styreþ, styrge, styrian, wregan	storm	gewidre, gewidru, hreoh, scur, scuras, scurum, storm, stormas, storme, styrman, styrmde, styrmdon, weder, wedera, wedres
stitch	færstice		
stolen	stolenne	storms	scurum, stormum
stomach	bearm, bearme, bearmum, innoþ, innoþe, maga	storm-shields	scurbeorge
		story	cwidegiedd, cwidegiedda, sagona, sagu, segen, segene, spel, spell, spella, spellum
stone	stænen, stænenne, stænnene, stan, stane		
stone-arch	stanboga, stanbogan		
		story-teller	scop, scopes
stone-burial-mound	stanbeorh	stout	ma
stone-city	stanburg, stanbyrig	strand	strand, strande
stone-cliff	stanbeorh, stancleofu, stanclif, stanclifu	strange	elðeodig, elþeodig, fremde, fremdes, fremdu, fremdum, uncuð, uncuðe, uncuðes, uncuðne, uncuðra, uncuþ, uncuþe, uncuþes, uncuþne, uncuþra, wunderlicu, wundorlic, wundorlicran
stone-fort	stanburg, stanbyrig		
stone-halls	stanhofu		
stone-made	stænen, stænenne, stænnene		
stone-slope	stanhliþe		
stone-slope-or-cliff	stanhleoþu, stanhlið, stanhliðo, stanhliþ, stanhliþe, stanhliþo		
		strange-command	wundorbebod, wundorbebodum
stone-tower	stantorr		
stony-cliff	stan-clif		
stood	stod, stodan, stode	strange-death	wundordeað, wundordeaðe, wundordeaþ, wundordeaþe
stoop	beah, bugan, bugeð, bugeþ, bugon, gebeag, gebeah, gebogen, gebogenan		
		strange-nature	sundorgecynd
		stranger	cuma, cuman, gæst, gæstas, gastum, giestum, gist, gistas, gistum, gyst, gystas, gyste, gystum, wrecca

Word List (English to Ænglisc)

English	Ænglisc	English	Ænglisc
strangers	elþeode	stretch-out	astreccan, astrece, astreht, aþenedon, aþenian
strange-wonder	searowundor		
stream	ædra, ædre, ædrum, burnan, burne, edrum, egstream, egstreamum, flod, floda, flodas, flode, flodes, gang, gange, ganges, stream, streame, wægstream, willeburnan, wylleburne	stretch-over	beþenede, beþenian
		strew	stred, stregan
		stride-over	wadan, waden, wod, wodon
		strife	gesacu, gewin, gewinn, gewinne, gewinnes, nið, niða, niðas, niðe, niðes, niðum, niþ, niþa, niþas, niþe, niþes, niþum, sacu, sæcc, sæce, secce, teonwit, wig, winn, wroht, wrohte, wrohtes
streams	streamas		
street	stræt, stræte		
strength	cræft, cræfta, cræftas, cræfte, cræftum, eafeþum, eafoð, eafoþ, eafoþes, ellen, eofoð, eofoðo, eofoþ, eofoþo, mægen, mægencræft, mægene, mægenes, mægna, mægne, mægnes, mægnu, mægyn, meaht, meahte, meahtum, miht, mihta, mihte, mihtum, strengðo, strenge, strengeo, strengo, strengþo, þryð, þryðum, þrymme, þryþ, þryþe, þryþum	strike	beatan, beaten, beot, beoton, beslægene, beslean, besloh, cnysed, cnysede, cnyssan, drep, drepan, drepen, dropen, geslægene, geslegene, gesloh, slægen, slea, sleah, slean, slog, sloge, slogon, sloh, swang, swingan, swingeð, swingeþ
		strike-against	beatað, beatan, beataþ, beateð, beateþ, beotan, gebeaten
		strike-down	ofslagen, ofslean, ofslegene, ofsloh
strength (Latin)	fortis	strike-off	ofaslean
strengthen	fulleode, fulleodon, fullgan, getrimede, getrymmed, gewealdon, swiðan, swiþan, trimian, trymeð, trymede, trymedon, trymeþ, trymian, trymman	striking	sloh
		string	sner, snere
		strip	ongyrede, ongyrwan
		strive-after	fundað, fundast, fundaþ, fundedon, fundian, fundiaþ, fundode
		striving	fus, fuse, fusne
strength-in-battle	wigcræft		
stretcher	bær		

Word List (English to Ænglisc)

English	Ænglisc	English	Ænglisc
stroke	drepe, heaðusweng, heaðuswenge, heaþusweng, heaþuswenge, sweng, swenge, swenges, swengum, swifan, swifeð, swifeþ		anhydig, higeþihtig, higeþihtigne, swiðhicgende, swiþhicgende
strong	bresne, cræftig, deah, dihtig, dohte, dohtest, dugan, duge, dyhttig, eacencræftig, fram, from, frome, fromne, fromum, heard, me, meaglum, meagol, rof, rofan, rofe, rofne, rofra, rofum, stið, stiðe, stiðlic, stiðmod, stiðmoda, stiðra, stiðum, stiþ, stiþe, stiþlic, stiþmod, stiþmoda, stiþra, stiþum, strang, stranga, strangan, strange, strangne, strangre, strangum, strengest, strenglic, strenglicran, strengum, strong, stronglic, stronglican, strongum, swið, swiþ, swyð, swyþ, þearl, þyhtig	strong-minded strong-soul struggle	modhwatu feohtan, feohte, gefeoht, gefeohtan, gefeohte, gewin, gewinn, gewinne, gewinnes, gewunne, gewunnen, gewyrc, sacan, strið, striðe, striþ, striþe, swincan, swuncon, wan, wann, winn, winnað, winnan, winnaþ, winnende, won, wonn, wunne, wunnon, wyrcan
		struggle-day	windæg, windagum
		struggling-for-life	lifbysig
		study	geleornian, geleornod, geleornode
		stump	stefn, stefna, stefnan, stefne
		subdue	gebræc, gebræcon, gebrecan, gebrocen
		subdued	gemæne, gemænra, gemænum
		subject	under, underðeodde, underþeodan, underþeodde
		subjected	nyde
		submerge	besencan, besenceð, besenceþ, sencan
strong-and-powerful	ðryðswyð, þryðswyð, þryþswyþ	submissive	eaðmod, eaþmod
stronger	swiþra	submit	beah, bugan, bugeð, bugeþ, bugon, gebeag, gebeah, gebogen, gebogenan, underðeodde, underþeodan, underþeodde
strongest	swiðost		
strong-hearted	stearcheort		
stronghold	burg, burh, fæsten, fæstenne, hleoburh		
strong-inclination	mihtmod		
strong-in-war	wigcræftig, wigcræftigne		
strong-mind	stiðferhþe		
		subordinate	forewyrcend, forewyrcendum

Word List (English to Ænglisc)

English	Ænglisc	English	Ænglisc
subsequent-journey	eftsið, eftsiðas, eftsiðes, eftsiþ, eftsiþas, eftsiþes	such-a-thing	swelc, swelce, swilc, swilces, swilcum, swulces, swylc, swylce, swylcne, swylcra, swylcum
subsequent-reputation	lastword, lastworda		
subservient	geongra	sudden-grasping	færgripe, færgripum
subside	drusade, drusian, ebbade, ebbian, sincan, sincende, swaðrian, swaþredon, swaþrian	sudden-horror	færgryre, færgryrum
		suddenly	færinga, færlice, semninga
		sudden-marvel	færwundra, fæwundor
		sudden-violence	færnið, færniða, færniþ, færniþa
substance	andweorc		
substitute	gewrixle, gewrixled, gield, gielde, gild, gyld, wrixlan	suffer	ðoliaþ, ðolode, dreag, dreah, dreogað, dreogan, dreogaþ, dreogeð, dreogeþ, dreoh, drogen, ðrowad, ðrowade, ðrowian, ðrowode, druge, drugon, gedrogen, geþolian, geþolianne, geþolode, þolað, þolaþ, þoledon, þoliað, þolian, þoliaþ, þolien, þoligende, þolodan, þolode, þrowad, þrowade, þrowedon, þrowian, þrowigean, þrowode, wite þrowade
subterranean-building	eorðreced, eorþreced		
succeed	gespeow, speow, spowan		
success	sped, spede		
successful	geþungen, geþungon, godspedig, sigisiþa, spedge, spedig, spedum		
successful-drop	speddropa, speddropum		
success-in-battle	wigsped, wigspeda		
success-in-maintaining-peace	freoðosped, freoþosped		
success-in-making-friends	freondsped		
success-in-offspring	tuddorsped	suffered	
success-in-war	heresped	suffering	adlegan, adlig, adligum, ðrowunga, earfeðe, earfeþe, weorc, weorca, weorce, weorces, weorcum, worc, worca, worcum
such	hwylce, Swa, swelc, swelce, swice, swilc, swilce, swilces, swilcum, swulces, swylc, swylce, swylcne, swylcra, swylcum		
		suffers	Dreogeð, werigmod
		sufficiency	geniht
such-as	swa, swelc, swelce, swilc, swilce, swilces, swilcum, swulces, swylc, swylce, swylcne, swylcra, swylcum	sufficient	genihtsum
		sufficiently	geneahe, geneahhe, genehe, genehost, genoge
		suicide	sylfan, sylfcwale, sylfcwalu

Word List (English to *Ænglisc*)

English	*Ænglisc*	English	*Ænglisc*
suit	gewearð, gewearþ, geworden, wærð, wærþ, wearð, wearþ, weorð, weorðað, weorðaþ, weorðe, weorðeð, weorðen, weorþ, weorþaþ, weorþe, weorþeð, weorþen, weorþeþ, worden, wurðað, wurðan, wurðaþ, wurde, wurðe, wurðeþ, wurdon, wurþan, wurþaþ, wurþe, wurþeþ, wyrð, wyrþ	support	arstaf, arstafum, bigstandað, bigstandan, bigstandaþ, fremeð, fremede, fremedon, fremest, fremeþ, fremmað, fremman, fremmaþ, fremme, fremmen, fulleode, fulleodon, fullgan, fultum, fultumes, fylstan, fylste, fylston, gefremed, gefremede, gefremeden, gefremedon, gefremman, gefremmanne, geoce, gestepte, staðol, staðolas, staðole, stapol, stapole, stapulum, staþel, staþelum, staþol, staþolas, staþole, stepan, stepe, stepte, stepton, swiðan, swiþan
suitable	gedefe, gelimplic		
sulphur	swefl, swefyl		
summer	sumeres, sumor		
summer-long	sumorlang, sumorlangne		
summon	abead, abeod, abeodan, abude, cigan, cigde, cigean, cigeð, cigeþ, cygan, cygde, gecyged, langað, langaþ, langian, langode, longade		
		supporter	folcgestælla, folcgestælna, folcgestealla, folcgesteallan, gehola, geholena, geþafa
sun	sunnan, sunne		
sunbeam	sunnbeam		
Sunday	sunnandæg		
sunder	gesundrod, gesundrode, sundrian		
		supreme	uplican
sun-going	sunganges	surface	gelagu, hricg, hrincg, hringe, hrycg, sceat
sunniest	sunwlitegost		
sunshine	sunnbeam		
sunwise	sunganges	surge	cearwælm, cearwælmum, cearwylm, cearwylmas, geswing, wælm, wælmes, weallan, wylm, wylmas, wylme
superior	aldor, aldre, ealdor, ealdre, ealdres, heahran, hearan, hearran, hehra, herran, hierran		
superior-strength	ofermægen, ofermægene, ofermægnes		
		surged	scyndeð, scyndeþ
supervise	ofersawon, oferseon	surging-fire	edwylm, edwylme
supple	swoncre	surging-sea	brimwylm

Word List (English to *Ænglisc*)

English	*Ænglisc*	English	*Ænglisc*
surging-water	yðgebland, yðgeblond, yþgebland, yþgeblond	swallow	forswealg, forswelgan, forswelge, forswulge, swealg, swealh, swelgað, swelgan, swelgaþ, swulge
surround	bebugan, bebugeð, bebugeþ, befangen, befon, befongen, belicgan, belið, beligeð, beligeþ, beliþ, besæt, beseald, besellan, besittan, beþeahte, beþeahton, beþeccan, bewand, beweorpan, bewindað, bewindan, bewindaþ, beworpen, bewunden, bifongen, biþeaht, biworpen, biwunden, clyppað, clyppan, clyppaþ, clyppe, clypte, ymbefeng, ymbefon, ymbsæton, ymbseald, ymbsellan, ymbsittan	swan	ilfetu, ylfete, ylfetu
		swan-road	swanrad, swanrade
		swarming	swirman
		swarthy	sweart
		swath-cut-through-opponents	herpað, herpaþ
		swear	swerian, swor
		sweat	swætan, swat, swate, swates
		sweaty	swatig, swatigne
		sweep	swifan, swifeð, swifeþ
		sweep-away	forswapan, forswapen, forsweop
		sweet	geswæse, swæs, swase, sweta, swete, swetne
		sweeter	swettra
		sweetest	wynsumast
		swell	swellan, þindan, þrindan, þrindende
		swept-away	fornam, fornom
surrounded	biþeaht, ymbseald	swift	swift, swifta, swiftne
surround-with-protection	ymbbearh, ymbbeorgan	swiftest	swiftust
		swift-flying	lyftswift, lyftswiftne
survey	geondseh, geondseon	swiftly	sneome
survive	gedigan, gedigde, gedigeð, gedigest, gedigeþ, gedygan, genæs, genesen, nesan	swim	fleat, fleotan, fleotende, reon, rowan, swimmað, swimman, swimmaþ, swymman
		swim-across	oferswam, oferswimman
suspend	ahangen, aheng, ahon, ahongen, ho, hon	swimmer	faraðlacende, faraþlacende, faroðlacend, faroðlacende, faroþlacend, faroþlacende
sustenance	ætwist	swimmers	swimmað

Word List (English to Ænglisc)

English	Ænglisc	English	Ænglisc
swimming	sund, sunde, sundes, sundnytt, sundnytte	sword-drink	hiorodrync, hiorodryncum
swimming-head	heafodswima	sword-evil	sweordbealo
swimming-strength	merestrengo	sword-giving	swyrdgifu
swim-on	fæðmian, fæðmie, fæþmian, fæþmie	sword-gleam	swurdleoma
		sword-gore	heorodreore, heorudreor, heorudreore
swine-likeness	swinlic, swinlicum	sword-hate	ecghete
swing	bræd, brægd, bregdan, bregde, bregdon, broden, brogdne, brudon, brugdon, gebræd, gebroden, onswaf, onswifan	sword-hilt	gehicgenne, gehiltum, hilt, hilte, hiltum, hylt
		sword-hooked	heorohocyht, heorohocyhtum
		sword-killer	ecgbana, ecgbanan
		sword-mail-coat	hioroserce, hiorosercean
swinging-in	seomian	sword-pale	hildeblac
swing-open	on, onarn, onirnan	sword-play	ecgplega, ecgplegan, sweordplegan
swipe	swifan, swifeð, swifeþ		
sword	beadoleoma, bil, bill, billa, bille, billes, billum, brand, brond, bronda, brondas, bronde, ecg, ecga, ecge, ecgum, guðbill, guðbilla, guþbill, guþbilla, heardecg, heorowearh, heorowulf, heoru, heoruwæpen, heoruwæpnum, hildebil, hildebill, hildebille, hildeleoma, hildeleoman, incgelaf, incgelafe, iren, irena, irenna, meca, mece, meces, mecum, secg, secge, sweord, sweorda, sweorde, sweordes, sweordum, swurd, swurde, swyrd, swyrdum	sword-rush	ecgþracu, ecgþræce mecum, sweordes,
		swords	sweordum, sword
		sword-slaying	bilgeslehtes
		sword-stroke	heorosweng, hondsweng
		sword-swinging	swyrdgeswing
		sword-warrior	sweordfreca, sweordfrecan, sweordwigend, sweordwigendra
		sword-weapon	heoruwæpen, heoruwæpnum
		sword-wearer	sweordberend, sweordberende
		sword-wounded	sweordwund
		sworn-oath	aðsweord, aþsweord

T, t

English	Ænglisc
table-companion	beodgeneat, beodgeneatas
tables—a-board-game	tæfl, tæfle
sword-brave	secgrofra
sword-cutting	swyrdgeswing
tail	tægel

Word List (English to Ænglisc)

English	Ænglisc	English	Ænglisc
take	anfenge, begeat, begeate, begeaton, beget, begietan, begytan, benam, beniman, benumen, bigeat, binom, dædon, deð, deþ, do, doð, don, doþ, dyde, dydest, dydon, fæng, fehð, fehþ, feng, fengon, fo, fon, gedæde, gedeð, gedeþ, gedo, gedoð, gedon, gedoþ, gedyde, gedydon, gefangen, gefeng, gefengon, gefon, gegrap, gegripon, gelædað, gelædaþ, gelædde, gelæde, gelæded, genam, genaman, gename, genamon, genim, geniman, genime, genimeð, genimeþ, genom, genumen	taken	genam
		take-off-armour	alysan, alysed
		take-oneself	gewendan, gewende
		take-pains-over	sorga, sorgedon, sorgian, sorgiende
		take-place	eode, eodon, eowde, ga, gað, gæð, gæþ, gan, gang, gangan, gange, ganges, gaþ, geeode, geeodon, gegæð, gegæþ, gegan, gegangan, gegangeð, gegangenne, gegangeþ, gegaþ, gegongeð, gegongen, gegongeþ, geiode, gesælde, sælan
		take-trouble	ceara, cearað, cearaþ, cearian
		take-up	anfenge, onfeng, onfengon, onfoð, onfoh, onfon, onfoþ
		take-vengeance-for	leanast, leanian, leanige, leanode
		take-warning	warnað, warnaþ, warnian
take-away	abræd, abrægd, abregd, abregdan, abregde, abroden, abrugdon, afyrran, afyrred, areafian, areafod, ateah, ateon, benæman, beslægene, beslean, besloh, feorran, fornam, fornamon, forniman, fornom, fornoman, fornumen, ofteah, ofteon, oftihð, oftihþ	taking	begeat
		talent	æðelo, æðelum, æþele, æþelo, æþelu, æþelum
		tall	heahsteap, lang, langa, lange, langne, langre, lengra, lengran, long, longe, uphea
		tame	atemian, temian, temiaþ
take-heart	hyrtan, hyrte	tapestry	web
take-heed	warnað, warnaþ, warnian	target	mercels, mercelses
		tariff	nydbad, nydbade
take-in	gehladene, gehlædene, gehleod, geloden, hladan, hlade, hladen, hlodon	taste	byrgan, byrgde, byrgean, byrigde, byrige, gebyrgde, gebyrge, onbyrigan
		tax	gafol, gafole, gofol

Word List (English to *Ænglisc*)

English	*Ænglisc*	English	*Ænglisc*
teach	gelæran, gelærdon, gelæred, gelærede, getæce, getæhte, getæhton, lær, læran, lærde, lære, læred, læren, tæcan, tæcaþ, tæhte, tihte, tyhtað, tyhtan, tyhtaþ	tell	asecgan, awræc, awrecan, bodedon, bodian, bodode, cyð, cyðað, cyðan, cydde, cyðde, cyðdon, cyþ, cyþan, cyþaþ, cyþde, cyþdon, gecyd, gecyðan, gecyðanne, gecyðde, gecyðed, gecyþan, gecyþanne, gecyþde, gecyþed, gesæd, gesæde, gesægd, gesægde, gesaga, getealdon, geteled, reccan, rehte, sæcgan, sædan, sæde, sædon, sægde, sægdest, sægdon, sæge, sægeð, sægeþ, sægst, saga, sagast, secgað, secgan, secgaþ, secge, secgeað, secgean, secgeaþ, secggende, sege, segeð, segeþ, tealde
teacher	lareow, lareowes		
teaching	lar, lara, larcwide, larcwidum, lare, larena, larum		
teachings	larum		
tear	slat, slit, slitan, slite, sliteð, sliten, sliteþ, sliton, tæsan, tæsde, tear, tearas, teran		
tear-apart	tobræd, tobrægd, tobredon, tobregdan, totær, toteran		
tease-wool	tæsan, tæsde		
		tell-about	styrede, styreþ, styrge, styrian
		tell-of	gemænden, mænað, mænan, mænaþ, mænde, mændon, mæned
		temper	gehyrde, gehyrdeð, gehyrdeþ, hyrdan
		tempered	fyrheard
		tempest	hreoh, storm
		temple	heahreced
		temporary	lænan, læne, lænes, lænum
		tempt	costigan, costode
		temptation	costunga
		ten	tene, tien, tyn, tyne

Word List (English to *Ænglisc*)

English	*Ænglisc*	English	*Ænglisc*
tent	feldhus, feldhusum, geteld, træf, træfe	test	afanda, afandian, fandian, fandigan, fandode, gecunnad, gecunnade, gecunnian, gefandod, gefondad
tenth	teoða, teoðan, teoþa, teoþan		
term	gemearces, mearc, mearce		
term-of-settlement	geþingea, geþinges, geþingo	testament	gecyddest
		tether	oncyrrapum
tern	stearn	than	ðon, ðonne, þænne, þam, þan, þe, þon, þone, þonne
terrible	andrysne, andrysnum, atol, atolan, atole, atolne, eatol, eatolne, egesful, egesfull, gryrelic, gryrelicne, hreðe, hreþe, niþgrim, ondrysne, reðan, reðe, reðre, reþan, reþe, reþre	thane	ðegn, ðegna, ðegnas, þægn, þægne, þegen, þegenas, þegn, þegna, þegnas, þegne, þegnes, þegnum
		thank	geþancie, þancast, þance, þancedon, þanciað, þancian, þanciende, þancode, þancodon
terrible-attacker	æglæca, aglæacan, aglæca, aglæcan, aglæcean, ahlæcan		
terrible-expedition	gryresið, gryresiðas, gryresiþ, gryresiþas	thanks	ðanc, geðonce, geþancum, geþonce, geþoncum, þanc, þance, þances, þonc
terribly-coloured	gryrefahne		
terrify	egsian, egsod, egsode		
terrifying	atelic, egsa		
terrifying-armour	gryregeatwe, gryregeatwum	thanksgiving	þancung
terrifying-spectacle	niðwundor, niþwundor	thanks-worthy	þoncsnotturra, þoncwyrðe, þoncwyrþe
terrifying-visitor	gryregiest, gryregieste, gryregist	thank-worthy	þoncwyrðe, þoncwyrþe
terrifying-water	wæteregesa, wæteregesan	than-that	þænne, þone, þonne
terrifying-wonder	færwundra, fæwundor	that	ða, ðæra, ðære, ðæt, ðam, ðe, ðonne, ðy, hyt, se, seo, þa, þære, þæs, þæt, þætte, þam, þam, þe, þet, þone, þonne
terror	broga, brogan, gryra, gryre, gryrebroga, gryrum		
terror-song	gryreleoð, gryreleoða, gryreleoþ, gryreleoþa	thatch	þecen, þecene

Word List (English to *Ænglisc*)

English	*Ænglisc*	English	*Ænglisc*
that-in	ða, ðæm, ðær, ðære, ðæs, ðam, ðara, ðe, ðon, se, seo, sio, þa, þæm, þæne, þær, þæra, þære, þæs, þæt, þam, þan, þara, þas, þat, þe, þon, þone, þonne, þy	the-Creator	meotod, meotodes, meotud, meotudes, metod, metode, metodes, metudæs, metudes
		the-cross (Latin)	crucem
		the-cursed-one	awyrgda
		the-Danes	Dene
		the-dark-feathered-one	salwigfeðera, salwigfeþera
that-was	þæs	the-day	dæg
that-which	hwæs, hwæt	the-dead	deadra
the	ða, ðæm, ðære, ðæs, ðæt, ðam, ðan, ðane, ðara, ðe, ðon, hi, se, seo, sio, sy, þa, þæm, þæne, þæra, þære, þæs, þæt, þam, þam, þan, þane, þara, þat, þe, þon, þone, þonne, þy	the-depths	deop, deopan
		the-devil	awyrgda, deoflum, gastbona, gram, graman, grame, gramena, grames, gramum, grome, gromra
		the-door	dura
		The-Dore (place)	Dor
the-Aesir-or-Ases	esa, os	the-dragon	dracan
the-air	lyft, lyfte, lyfthelm	the-dust	moldan
the-angels	ænglum, englum	thee	ðe, ðu, þe
the-Ark	earc, earce	the-eagle's	earnes
the-attacker	aglæcan	the-earl	eorla, eorle
the-best	cista, cyst, cystum	the-earth	eorðan, eorþan, foldan, hrusan, hruse, middaneard, middangeard, middangearde, middangeardes
the-better	syllan		
the-blade	ecg		
the-body	banloca, banlocan, hreðerloca, hreðerlocan, hreþerloca, hreþerlocan, lið		
		the-east (Latin)	oriente
		the-elder	ealdor
the-book (Latin)	biblos	the-end	finit
the-boughs	bearwe	the-English	engla
the-brave	collenferþe	the-evil-one	gram, graman, grame, gramena, grames, gramum, grome, gromra
the-chest	breostcofa, breostcofan		
the-clearest	switolost		
the-cliffs	hliþes	the-father (Latin)	patrem
the-country	edygled	the-firmament	roderum
the-created-world	gesceaft, woruldgesceaft, woruldgesceafta, woruldgesceafte	the-first (Latin)	principio
		the-fishes	fiscas
		the-floor	grundas
		the-food	metes
		the-glove	glofe
		thegn	aldorþegn
		the-Goths	Gotena

Word List (English to Ænglisc)

English	Ænglisc	English	Ænglisc
the-greatest	myccle	the-lord	brego, drihten, drihtenes, drihtna, drihtne, drihtnes, dryhten, dryhtna, dryhtne, dryhtnes, eallwealda, waldend, waldende, waldendes, wealdend, wealdende, wealdendes
the-ground	grundas, grunde		
the-hateful-one	laðan, laðe, laðere, laðes, laðestan, laðne, laðost, laðra, laðran, laðum, laþan, laþe, laþere, laþes, laþestan, laþne, laþost, laþra, laþran, laþre, laþum		
the-heath	hæðe		
the-heavens	heofenstolas, heofenum, rodores, swegl, sweglbosmas, swegle, swegles, tungla, uplyft, uproder, uprodor	the-lord's	drihtnes, waldendes
		them	ða, him, hy, þa, þam
		the-measurer	Meotod, metend
		the-measurer's	meotodes, metudæs
		the-mighty-one	mihtig, mihtiga, mihtigan, mihtiges, mihtigne
the-high-heaven	heahrodor, heahrodore	the-most-awesome	hreðeadegost
		the-mould	moldan
the-holy-one	halegu, halga, halgan, halgena, halgum, halig, haligan, halige, haliges, haligre	the-mouth	esa
		then	æfter, ða, ðonne, þa, þænne, þam, þan, þe, þon, þone, þonne
the-host	rimde	the-name	noma
the-human-race	gumcynn, gumcynne, gumcynnes, gumcynnum	thence	ðanon, ðonan, ðonne, ðonon, forð, forþ, þan, þanan, þanon, þanonne, þonan, þonne, þonon
their	heora, hira, hyra, þæ		
the-king	cyning	thenceforth	siþþan
the-king's	cinges	the-north	norðdæle, norþdæl, norþdæle
the-land	land, lande		
the-length	ondlongne	the-northern-part	norðdæle, norþdæl, norþdæle
the-living	lyfiendne		
the-loathed	laþe	the-oak	actreo
the-longest	lengest	Theodric (name)	ðeodric
		the-older	dugeða, dugeðe, dugeðum, dugeþa, dugeþe, dugeþum, dugoða, dugoðe, dugoþa, dugoþe, duguð, duguða, duguðe, duguðum, duguþ, duguþa, duguþe, duguþum
		the-order	hades

Word List (English to *Ænglisc*)

English	*Ænglisc*	English	*Ænglisc*
the-other	oþre	the-sky	lyfte, swegl, swegle, swegles, wolcen, wolcna, wolcne, wolcnu, wolcnum
the-others	oðrum		
the-panther	pandher		
the-people	folces		
the-pool	wæle	the-south	meridie
there	ðaem, ðær, ðære, ðar, þa, þaem, þær, þæra, þære, þar, þer, þider, þyder	the-spirit (Latin)	spiritum
		the-sun	friðcandel, friþcandel, sunne, woruldcandel
the-rear	hindan	the-terrible-one	aglæca
therefore	ðy, for, for þon, forðam, forðan, forðon, forþam, forþan, forþon, þi	the-third	þriddan
		the-track	last
		the-troops	eorodcistum
		the-true-king	soðcyning, soðcyninges, soþcyning, soþcyninges
therein	ðæron, þær, þær inne, þæron		
thereon	ðæron, þæron		
thereto	þær to	the-vast-earth	eormengrund
thereupon	eft	the-victorious-Lord	sigedrihten
the-Romans	Romwarum	the-wall	weal
the-same	some	the-water	wætan
the-same-time	antid	the-waves	yðum, yþa
the-Saviour	hælend, hælende, hælendes	the-weald	wealde
		the-west (Latin)	occidente
The-Scots	Sceotta	the-whale-road	hronrad, hronrade
these	ðæs, ðas, ðes, ðis, ðisne, ðisse, ðisses, ðys, ðysne, ðysse, ðyssum, ðysum, þæs, þarf, þas, þeos, þes, þis, þisne, þison, þissa, þisse, þissere, þisses, þissum, þisum, þys, þysne, þyssa, þysse, þyssere, þysses, þysson, þyssum, þysum	the-wife	wif, wifman, wifmon
		the-wolf	wulf
		the-wolf's	wolues
		the-woods	bearowe, holte, wuda
		the-world	cosmo, middaneard, middangeard, middangearde, middangeardes, moldan, weoruld, world, worold, worolde, woruld, worulde
		the-world-kingdom	woruldrice
	æra, flot, garsecges, hronrad, hronrade, hwælmere, hwælweg, laguflod, mere, seglrad, seglrade, sund, sunde, sundes	they	ða, heo, hi, Hig, him, hine, hy, hyra, syn, synd, þonne
		they (Latin)	sunt
		they-are	sind, sindon, syndan, syndon
the-sea		they-are (Latin)	sunt
the-skies	roderum, wolcna	the-year's	geres
		they-have	hafað
		the-young	geong

Word List (English to *Ænglisc*)

English	*Ænglisc*	English	*Ænglisc*
they-were	wæran	third	ðriddan, þridda, þriddan
thickly	ðicce, þicce, þiclice		
thief	þeof, þeofes	third (Latin)	Tertia
thieving-intruder	stælgiest	thirst	þurst
thigh	þeo	thirst-for	ofþyrstan, ofþyrsted
thin	swancor, swoncre	thirsty	þurstig
thin-curtain	fleohnet	thirteen	þreotine, XIII
thing	ðing, ðinga, ðinges, þincg, þing, þinga, þinge, þinges, wiht	thirteenth	þreotteoð, þreotteoða, þreotteoþ, þreotteoþa
things	þing		
think	aðohte, aþencan, aþohte, ðencan, ðoht, ðohte, ðuhte, ðyncan, geðuht, gehicgenne, gehyge, gemynt, gemynted, getealdon, geteled, geþenc, geþencan, geþencean, geþuht, hi, hicgan, hicgeaþ, hogod, hogode, hycgað, hycgan, hycgaþ, hycge, hycgendne, myntan, mynte, mynteð, mynteþ, mynton, smeagan, tealde, tealdon, telge, tellan, þencað, þencan, þencaþ, þence, þencean, þenceð, þencest, þenceþ, þoht, þohte, þohton, þuhte, þyncan, uuene, wene	thirtieth	þritigoþa
		thirty	ðrittiges, þritig, þrittig, þrittiges, XXX, XXXtiges
		thirty eight	eahta and þritig
		thirty eighth	eahta and þritigoþa
		thirty fifth	fif and þritigoþa
		thirty first	an and þritigoþa
		thirty five	fif and þritig
		thirty four	feower and þritig, feoper and þritig
		thirty fourth	feower and þritigoþa
		thirty nine	nigon and þritig
		thirty ninth	nigon and þritigoþa
		thirty one	an and þritig
		thirty second	twa and þritigoþa
		thirty seven	seofon and þritig
		thirty seventh	seofon and þritigoþa
		thirty six	siex and þritig
		thirty sixth	six and þritigoþa
		thirty third	þreo and þritigoþa
		thirty three	þri and þritig
		thirty two	twegen and þritig, tpegen and þritig
think-about	geþancmeta, geþancmetian		
thinking	þencaþ		
thinks	þinceð		
think-through	geondþencan, geondþence, geondþenceð, geondþenceþ		
think-worthy	onman, onmunan, onmunde, onmunon		

Word List (English to *Ænglisc*)

English	*Ænglisc*	English	*Ænglisc*
this	ðæs, ðas, ðeos, ðes, ðis, ðisse, ðisses, ðys, ðysne, ðysse, ðyssum, ðysum, hi, his, hit, is, se, seo, þa, þæne, þæs, þam, þas, þe, þeos, þes, þis, þisne, þison, þissa, þisse, þissere, þisses, þissum, þisum, þonne, þys, þysne, þyssa, þysse, þyssere, þysses, þysson, þyssum, þysum	thought	breosthord, geðoht, geðonce, gehygd, gemynd, gemynda, gemynde, gemyndum, geþanc, geþancum, geþeaht, geþoht, geþohtas, geþohte, geþonce, geþoncum, hige, higes, higum, hyge, hygesceaft, hygesceaftum, meoto, modgehygd, modgehygdum, modgemynd, modgeþoht, modgeþohte, þanc, þance, þances, þonc
this-was	þæs		
thither	þider, þyder		
those	ða, ðæm, ðæra, ðære, ðæs, ðam, ðara, ðe, ðon, hy, se, seo, sio, þa, þæm, þæne, þæra, þære, þæs, þæt, þam, þam, þan, þane, þara, þat, þe, þon, þone, þonne, þy	thoughtful	higeðoncol, higeðoncolre, higeþoncol, higeþoncolre, hohful, hydig, þancolmod, þoncol
		thoughtless	hygeleas, hygelease
		thoughtlessness	hygeleast, hygeleaste
		thoughts	gemind, geþoht, geþohtas, mod
thou	ðe, ðec, ðin, ðinne, ðinra, ðu, þe, þec, þin, þina, þine, þines, þinne, þinra, þinre, þinum, þu	thought-wiser	ðonosnottorra, þoncsnotturra, þonosnottorra
		thousand	þus, þusend, þusenda, þusendo
though	ðeah, ec, þe, þeah, þeh	thousands	þusend
		thrash-about	wealweode, wealwian, wealwigende
		threaten	hweop, hwopan
		threat-to-a-people	leodsceaða, leodsceaðan, leodsceaþa, leodsceaþan
		three	ðry, þreo, þreora, þri, þrie, þrim, þrio, þry, þrym
		three (accusative feminine)	þreo

Word List (English to Ænglisc)

English	Ænglisc
three (accusative masculine)	þri
three (accusative neuter)	þreo
three (dative feminine)	þrim
three (dative masculine)	þrim
three (dative neuter)	þrim
three (genitive feminine)	þreora
three (genitive masculine)	þreora
three (genitive neuter)	þreora
three (instrumental feminine)	þrim
three (instrumental masculine)	þrim
three (instrumental neuter)	þrim
three (nominative feminine)	þreo
three (nominative masculine)	þri
three (nominative neuter)	þreo
three hundred	þreo
three thousand	þreo þūsend
three-hundred	CCC, þreohund
three-nights	þreonihta
three-shadow	beamsceade, beamsceadu
three-times	III, þriwa
thrice	þriwa
thrive	ðah, ðeon, ðigen, ðigon, geðah, geþah, geþeoh, geþeon, geþigen, geþigon, geþungen, þag, þah, þeah, þeon, þigen, þigon
throne	heahsetl, setl, setla, setle, setles, setlum, stol, stole
throng	geðring, geðrungen, geþrang, geþrungen, hwearf, hwearfum, þrang, þringan, þrong, þrungen, þrungon, weorod, weoroda, weorode, weorude, wered, wereda, werede, weredes, weredum, werod, weroda, werode, werodes, werodum, werud, weruda, werudes, worude
thronging	geþring
through	æfter, ðurh, geond, mid, þurh, þuruh
throughout	geond, ofer, ofor
throw	bescufan, beweorpan, beworpen, biworpen, forweorp, sændan, sendan, sende, sended, sendeð, sendeþ, sendon, sent, wearp, weorpan, weorpaþ, wurpon
throw-a-spear	gesceat, sceat, sceotan, sceoteð, sceoteþ, scoten
throw-away	forweorpan, forwurpe
throw-down	oferweorp, wearp, weorpan, weorpaþ, wurpon
throwing	gescot, gescotes, wyrp
thrust	bescufan, sceaf, sceof, scofen, scufan, scufeð, scufeþ, scufon, scufun
thrust-down	sencan
thunder	þunar
Thureth (name)	þureð, þureþ
thus	ða, swa, swilce, þus
thus-as (Latin)	sicut

Word List (English to Ænglisc)

English	Ænglisc	English	Ænglisc
tide	sæflod	to-be	beo, beoð, beon, beoþ, bið, bio, bioð, bioþ, bist, biþ, byð, byþ, earnian, eart, eom, is, nære, næron, næs, ne, nearon, nis, nys, se, seo, si, siae, sie, sien, sig, sind, sindon, sint, sy, synd, syndon, synt, wæran, wære, wæron, wæs, waron, wes, wesan, westu, ys
tide-turning	sæcir		
tie	bindan, bond, bunden, bundon		
tightly	nearwe		
tight-place	nearo		
till	tilian, tilien, tilode		
timber	beam, beama, beaman, beamas, beame, beames, holtwudu, timber		
timbering	getimbro		
time	anes, anew, byre, cierr, fæc, fyrst, fyrste, hwil, hwile, mæl, mæla, mæles, mælo, mælum, rum, sæl, sæla, sæles, sælum, salum, sele, sið, siða, siðe, siðes, siþ, siþa, siþe, siþes, siþon, stefn, stund, þrag, þrage, tid, tida, tide, tiid	to-be-able-to	mæg, mægen, magan, magon, meaht, meahtan, meahte, meahton, mehte, miht, mihte, mihten, mihton, most, moste, mosten, moston, mot, motan, mote, moten, moton
time (Latin)	secula	to-be-allowed-to	most, moste, mosten, moston, mot, motan, mote, moten, moton
time-events	mælgesceaft, mælgesceafta		
times	tld		
time-trouble	mælceare, mælcearu	to-become-multiplied	gemæne, gemænigfealda, mænigfealdian
timid	acol, forht		
timidly	forhtlice	to-be-lost	losað, losade, losaþ, losian
tired	meðe, meþe		
tired-out-from-sailing	sæmeðe, sæmeþe	to-be-sorrowful	sorga, sorgedon, sorgian, sorgiende
tithe	getiðad, getiþad		
titled	teode, tiadæ	to-be-thirsty	ofþyrstan, ofþyrsted
	æfter, ðe, ne, Til, tilian, tilien, tilode,	to-break	tobræc
		to-bridle	bætan, gebæted
to	to, weard, wið, wiþ	to-cast-lots	gehleat, hleat, hleotan
to-acquire	begietan		
		to-come-after	æfterfylgan
		today	heodæg
		to--depart-from	feolan
		to-determine-by-discussion	berædan
		to-embolden	byldan, bylde, gebylde
		to-forsake	forlætan

Word List (English to Æglisc)

English	Æglisc	English	Æglisc
to-get	begeatan	torment	bræc, bræce, bræcon, brecað, brecan, brecaþ, brocen, cwalm, cwealm, cwealme, cwealmes, dreccan, dreceð, dreceþ, drehte, firen, firena, fyren, fyrena, fyrene, gebræc, gebrocen, gedreht, gedrehte, geswenced, geswencte, gewitnad, gewitnian, morðer, morðor, morðra, morðre, morðres, morþer, morþor, morþra, morþre, morþres, susl, susla, susle, swencan, swencte, witeswinge, witeswingum
together	ætgædere, ætgædre, ætsamne, ætsomne, geador, gesiþum, ongeador, samod, somed, somod, togædere, togædre, tosomne		
together-with	mid, samod, somed, somod		
to-go	gan		
to-god	gode		
to-halter	bætan, gebæted		
to-have	habban		
to-help	helpan		
to-her	sylfre		
to-here	hider		
to-him	him		
to-himself	sylfum		
to-hold	agan		
toil	swincan		
toil-day	windæg, windagum		
token	myrcels, myrcelse, tacen, tacn, tacne	torment-house	witehus
to-kill?	aþecgan	tormenting-lock	witelocc, witeloccas
told	secgað, secgan	torment-of-hell	suslhofe
toll	nydbad, nydbade	torments	wita
to-mark	gemearcian	torn	atæsed
to-me	me, mine	torque	beahwriða, beahwriðan, beahwriþa, beahwriþan
to-men	firum, hæleðum		
to-move	astyrian		
tongue	tun, tungan, tunge		
too	samod, to	torture	slat, slit, slitan, slite, sliteð, sliteþ, wita, wite, witum, wyta, wytum
took	feng, genam, geþah, namon		
too-many-a	formoni		
tooth	ban, bane, banum, toð, toðon, toðum, toþ, toþon, toþum	to-seek	secan
		to-send	sændan
		to-show	ætywan
tooth-power	toðmægenes	to-some-extent	hwene
top	heafde, heafdon, heafdum, heafod	toss	cnossað, cnossaþ, cnossian, cnysedan, cnyssað, cnyssan, cnyssaþ
to-petition	bena, benan		
to-plan	hycgan	toss-around	gewealcen, wealcan
torch	æledleoma, æledleoman	tossing	gewealc
		to-still-cause-to-be-still	gestilled, gestylled, stillan
		total	rim, rime, rimes

Word List (English to Ænglisc)

English	Ænglisc	English	Ænglisc
to-the-deep	garsecg	towering	heahsteap, steapheah
to-thee	ðe, þe		
to-the-east	wið, wið eastan, wiþ, wiþ eastan	towers	torras
		to-wet	wætan, wæteð, wæteþ, wætte
to-the-end	ende		
to-there	þider, þyder	to-where	hwæder, hwider, hwyder
to-the-south	wið suðan, wiþ suþan		
		town	burg, burga, burgum, burh, byrig, ceaster, ceastra, ceastre, ceastrum, tun
to-this-world	hider		
touch	Æþlmær, æthran, æthrinan, gegrettan, gegrette, grapian, grapode, gretan, greted, greteð, greteþ, grette, gretton, hran, hrepian, hrepode, hrinan, hrine, hrinon, neawest		
		to-you	ðe, þe
		trace	læste, last, lastas, laste, lastum, spor
		track	fotlast, gang, gange, ganges, læste, last, lastas, laste, lastum, spor, stig, stige, swaðe, swaðu, swaþe, swaþu, swatswaðu, swatswaþu, trode, trodu
tough	heard, hearda, heardan, hearde, heardes, heardne, heardost, heardra, heardran, heardum, niðheard, niþheard, trum		
		track-on-the-earth	foldweg, foldwegas, foldwege
toughly	unwaclice	tracks	laste
tough-minded	heardhicgende, heardmod, heardmode	track-word	lastword, lastworda
		trade	bebicgan, bebicge
		trail-of-footsteps	fotlast
to-venture	geneðde, geneðdon, geneþan, geneþde, geneþdon, neðde, neðdon, neðende, neþan, neþde, neþdon, neþeð, neþende, neþeþ	train	wenede, wenian
		traitor	treowloga, treowlogan, werloga, werlogan
		traitorous	ortrywe, wærleas
		tranquil	smylte
		tranquillity	frið, friðe, friþ, friþe, friþes
toward	toward		
towards	ongean, tilian, tilien, tilode, togeanes, togenes, toweard, weard, wið, wiþ	transform	wearp, weorpan, weorpaþ, wurpon
		transform-negatively	forsceop, forscieppan
to-warm	wrymeð, wrymeþ, wyrman	transgress	forbræcon, forbrecan, forbrocen, gebræc, gebrægd, gebrocen
tower	hlifade, hlifian, hlifigan, hlifige, hlifigean, hliuade, torr, torre		

Word List (English to Ænglisc)

English	Ænglisc	English	Ænglisc
transgress-a-commandment	bræc, bræce, brǣcon, brecað, brecan, brecaþ, brocen, gebræc, gebrocen, onwendan, onwended, onwendeð, onwendeþ, onwendon	travel	færde, færdon, færeð, færen, færeþ, far, farað, faran, faraþ, fare, fareð, faren, fareþ, feran, ferde, ferdon, fere, fered, ferende, for, foran, foron, gefaran, gefaren, geferde, geferdon, gefere, gefered, geferede, geferedon, geferian, gefor, geforan, liden, liðendum, liþan, liþendum, siðedon, siðian, siðie, siðien, siðode, siþade, siþedon, siþian, siþie, siþien, siþode, spyrede, spyrian
transitory	hwearflicra, hwilen, hwilnan, lænan, læne, lænes, lænum		
transitory-days	lændæg, lændaga, lændagas		
transitory-life	lændæg, lændaga, lændagas		
translate	wendan		
transport	ferede, feredon, fergað, fergaþ, ferian, ferigeað, ferigeaþ, ferode, fyredon, geferdon, gefere, gefered, geferede, geferedon, geferian		
		travelled	afaran, feran
		traveller	eardstapa, ferend, liðend, liðende, liþend, liþende, wreccea
transported	ferde	travellers	ferend
trap	searo, searwum	travelling	farað, wegfarende
trappings	frætewum, frætwa, frætwe, frætwum, gearwan, gearwe, gearwor, gearwum, gerædu	travelling-horrible	ferðgrim
		travelling-sailors	fareðlacendum, faroðlacende
		travelling-soldiers	heaðoliðendum, heaþoliðend, heaþoliðende, heaþoliþend, heaþoliþende, heaþoliþendum
travailed-by-the-wind	lyftgeswenced	travels	fare
		traverse	gemette, gemetton, mæt, mæton, metan, ofereode, ofereodon, oferfaran, oferferan, oferferde, oferfered, oferforan, ofergan
		treacherous	flah, wærleas

Word List (English to *Ænglisc*)

English	*Ænglisc*	English	*Ænglisc*
treachery	facen, facna, facne, facnes, searonið, searoniða, searoniðas, searoniþ, searoniþa, searoniþas, unræd, unræde, unrædes, untryoð, untryoða, untryoþ, untryoþa	treasure	beaghord, beg, frætewum, frætwa, frætwe, frætwum, gestreon, gestreona, hord, horde, hordes, hordweorþung, hordweorþunge, huðe, huþe, hyþ, hyþe, maððum, maððumwela, maððumwelan, madm, madma, maðma, maðmæhta, madmas, maðmas, madme, madmum, maðmum, maðþum, maðþumfæt, mæðmæht, mæþmæht, maþðum, maþm, maþma, maþmæhta, maþmas, maþme, maþmgestreon, maþmgestreona, maþmum, maþþum, maþþumfæt, maþþumwela, maþþumwelan, sinc, sincgestreon, sincgestreona, sincgestreonum, sincmaðþum, sincmaþþum, weorð, weorðan, weorðe, weorþ, weorþan, weorþe
tread	træd, træde, tredað, tredan, tredaþ, treddan, treddode, tredeð, tredeþ, triedeð, triedeþ, tryddode	treasure-chamber	hordcofa, hord-cofa, hordcofan
		treasure-city	hordburh
		treasure-cup	sincfæt, sincfato
		treasure-gift	maþðumgife, maþðumgifu, maþþumgife, maþþumgifu
		treasure-giver	maþþumgyfa, sincgifa, sincgifan, sincgyfa, sincgyfan

Word List (English to Ænglisc)

English	Ænglisc	English	Ænglisc
treasure-giving	maþðumgife, maððumgifu, maþþumgife, maþþumgifu	tribal-offspring	cynebearn, cynebearna
treasure-hall	hringsele	tribe	folc, folca, folce, folces, folcum, mægburg, mægburge, mægburh, mægþ, wermægð, wermægða, wermægþ, wermægþa
treasure-hoard	beahhord, beahhorda, beahhordes, beahhordum		
treasurer	hordweard		
treasure-receipt	sinc-þegu		
treasure-receiving	beahðege, beahðegu, beahþege, beahþegu, sincþege, sincþego, sincþegu	tribes	folca
		tribute	gafol, gafole, gofol, gomban, gombe, gombon, Sygegealdor
		tribute-	gomban
treasures	beag, beaga, beagas, beage, beages, beagum, beah, begas, frætwum, geatwa, hord, madma, maðma, sinc, sinca, since, sinces	trick	besyred, besyrwan, searo, searwum
		tried	Ongunnon
		tried-retainers	dugeða, dugeðe, dugeðum, dugeþa, dugeþe, dugeþum, dugoða, dugoðe, dugoþa, dugoþe, duguð, duguða, duguðe, duguðum, duguþ, duguþa, duguþe, duguþum
treasure-worthy	hordwyrðne, hordwyrþne, horwyrðe, horwyrþe		
treasury	hordærn, hordærna, hordærne, hordcofa, hordcofan	trifle	hwon
		trim	swancor, swoncre
treat	weman, wemde, wemed	trinity	ðrynes, ðrynesse, þrynes, þrynesse, triow
treat-with-hatred	hatian, hatode		
tree	beam, beama, beaman, beamas, beame, beames, treow, treowe, treowes, wudu	triumph	sigehreð, sigehreþ
		triumphant	sigefæst, sigefæstran, sigehreðig, sigehreþig
tree-dye	beamtelg, beamtelge	triumph-tough	tirfæstra
		troll-made	entisc, entiscne, eotenisc, etonisc
tree-of-victory	sigebeam		
trees	treowum		
trembling	byð, byfigynde, byþ		
tremendous-calamity	heahþrea		
tribal-member	leodmæg, leodmagum		

Word List (English to Ænglisc)

English	Ænglisc	English	Ænglisc
troop	corðor, corðre, corðrum, corþor, corþre, corþrum, ðreat, ðreatum, drihtfolc, drihtfolca, ðrym, eored, feða, feðan, feþa, feþan, gedriht, gedryht, getrum, getrume, irenþreat, mægen, mægene, mægenes, mægna, mægne, mægnes, mægnu, mægyn, ord, orde, sweot, sweotum, teoche, teoh, teohh, teohha, teohhe, þreat, þreatas, þreate, þreatum, þrym, þrymm, þrymmas, weorode, werod	troubled	hohful, hreohmod, torn, torne, tornost bysgað, earfoða,
		troubles	earfoþa
		trouble-since	earfoðsið, earfoðsiða, earfoðsiþ, earfoþsiþ, earfoþsiþa
		trouble-time	earfoðþrag, earfoþþrag
		trouble-while	earfoðhwil, earfoðhwile, earfoþhwil, earfoþhwile
		truce	grið, griþ
		true	getreowra, getrywe, riht, rihtan, rihte, rihtne, rihtum, soð, soðan, soðe, soðne, soðra, soðum, soþ, soþan, soþe, soþne, soþra, soþum, trywe, wær, wærum, wislic, wislicne
troop-lord	gumdryhten		
troop-men	gumfeþa		
troop-of-relatives	sibbegedriht, sibgedriht	true-belief	soðgeleafa, soðgeleafan, soþgeleafa, soþgeleafan
troop-of-seasoned-retainers	duguþ		
troops	uueorudes, weorudes	true-story	soðgied, soþgied
		true-tale	soð-gied, soþ-gied
troop-seat	gumstol, gumstole	truly	gewislice, gewislicost, huru, rihte, soð, soðlice, soðne, soþ, soþlice
trouble	bisgian, bisgo, bisgodon, bisgum, bisigu, bysgað, bysgaþ, bysigu, bysigum, drefan, drefde, earfeðu, earfeþa, earfeþo, earfeþu, earfoða, earfoþa, earfoþe, eglan, gebysgad, gedrefed, myrðe, myrðu, myrþe, myrþu, niþ, sorg, torn, torna, torne, weana	trumpet	bemum, byman, byme
		trumpet-call	wigleoð, wigleoþ
trouble-causing	weorcsum, weorcsumne		

Word List (English to *Ænglisc*)

English	*Ænglisc*	English	*Ænglisc*
trust	geliefan, geliefde, geliefed, gelyfan, gelyfde, gelyfe, gelyfeð, gelyfeþ, getruwedon, getruwode, getruwodest, getrywð, getrywþ, hiht, hihte, hyht, hyhte, soðfæstra, treow, treowa, treowan, treowde, treowe, treowum, truwian, truwode	try-out	cunnað, cunnade, cunnaþ, cunnedon, cunnian, cunnige, cunnode, gecunnad
trusted-friends	treowgeþofta	try-to-find-out	fricgan, fricgcean, fricgean, fricgen, frige, gefricge, gefricgeað, gefricgean, gefricgeaþ, gefrunen, gefrungon, gefrunon
trusting	getryweð		
trustworthy	getreowra, getrywe, gewis, gewiss, gewissan, soðfæst, soðfæste, soðfæstra, soþfæst, soþfæste, soþfæstra, trywe, wær, wærfæst, wærum	tumult	cirm, cyrm, gedreag, gelac, gelacum, geþrang, geþring, unstilnes, woma
		tumulus	beorg, beorgas, beorge, beorges, beorgum, beorh, biorgas, biorges, biorh
		tunic	tunece
		turf	turf, turfa, turfon, tyrf, wancgturf
truth	gerihte, rightly, riht, rihte, ryht, soð, soðe, soþ, soþe, treowa, truly	turn	anew, cierr, cirdon, cyrran, cyrreð, cyrreþ, gecyrre, gecyrred, gehwearf, gehweorfe, gewendan, gewende, hwærf, hwearf, hweorfað, hweorfan, hweorfaþ, hweorfeð, hweorfeþ, hworfan, hwurfe, hwurfon, hwyrfeð, hwyrfeþ, oncirde, oncyrreð, oncyrreþ, onhweorfan, onhworfen, onswaf, onswifan, stefn, wend, wendan, wende, wended, wendeð, wenden, wendeþ, wendon, windan, wond, wunden, wundon
truth-fastened	soðfæste		
truth-firm	soðfæst, soþfæst		
truthful	soð, soðfæstra		
truthfully	wærlice		
try	afanda, afandian, angan, costigan, costode, gecunnad, gecunnade, gecunnian, ongan, ongann, ongean, ongin, onginnað, onginnan, onginnaþ, onginneð, onginnen, onginneþ, ongon, ongunnan, ongunne, ongunnen, ongunnon, ongyn, ongynneð, ongynneþ		
		turn-against	ondhwearf, ondhweorfan

Word List (English to Ænglisc)

English	Ænglisc	English	Ænglisc
turn-aside-from	ahwearf, ahweorfan, ahwurfon	twenty three	þri and twentig, þri and tƿentig
turn-away	ahwearf, ahweorfan, ahwurfon, beah, bugan, bugeð, bugeþ, bugon, gebeag, gebeah, gebogen, gebogenan	twenty two	twegen and twentig, tƿegen and tƿentig
		twice	twa
		twig	tan, tanum, telga, telgan, telgum, twig, twige
		twilight	uhta
turn-back	cirdon, cyrran, cyrreð, cyrreþ, gecyrred	twist	gewand, span, spinnan, wand, windan, wond, wunden, wundnum, wundon
turned-outwards	utweard		
turn-from	geswyce		
turning	hwyrft, hwyrftum	twisted	woh, wom, wora
turn-to	hweorfan	twisted-prow	wundenhals
twain	tu, twa, twegen	twisted-staves	wundenstefna
twelfth	twelfta	twisted-sword	wundenmæl
twelve	twelf, tƿelf, twelfe, XII, XIIa	twixt	tweonum
twentieth	twentigoþa	two	tu, twa, twægen, twæm, twam, twega, twegen, tƿegen, twegin
twenty	twentig, tƿentig		
twenty eight	eahta and twentig, eahta and tƿentig		
twenty eighth	eahta and twentigoþa	two (accusative feminine)	twa, tƿa
twenty fifth	fif and twentigoþa	two (accusative masculine)	twegen, tƿegen
twenty first	an and tƿentigoþa	two (accusative neuter)	tū, twa, tƿa
twenty five	fif and twentig, fif and tƿentig	two (dative feminine)	twam, tƿam
twenty four	feower and twentig, feoƿer and tƿentig	two (dative masculine)	twam, tƿam
twenty fourth	feower and twentigoþa	two (dative neuter)	twam, tƿam
twenty nine	nigon and twentig, nigon and tƿentig	two (genitive feminine)	twega, tƿega
twenty ninth	nigon and twentigoþa	two (genitive masculine)	twega, tƿega
twenty one	an and twentig, an and tƿentig	two (genitive neuter)	twega, tƿega
twenty second	twa and twentigoþa	two (instrumental feminine)	twam, tƿam
twenty seven	seofon and twentig, seofon and tƿentig	two (instrumental masculine)	twam, tƿam
twenty seventh	seofon and twentigoþa	two (instrumental neuter)	twam, tƿam
twenty six	siex and twentig, siex and tƿentig	two (nominative feminine)	twa, tƿa
twenty sixth	six and twentigoþa	two (nominative masculine)	twegen, tƿegen
twenty third	þreo and twentigoþa		

Word List (English to Ænglisc)

English	Ænglisc	English	Ænglisc
two (nominative neuter)	tū, twa, tpa	understanding	andgit, gescad, gewitloca, gewitlocan, gewitte, modgeðance, modgeþance, modgeþoht, modgeþohte, modgeþonc, modgeþonce, wite, witt
two hundred	twa, tpa		
two thousand	twa þūsend, tpa þūsend		
two-things	twega		
tyrant	leodhata, leodhatan		

U, u

English	Ænglisc	English	Ænglisc
ugly	unfæger, unfæle	understood	ongieten
unadvised-act	unræden	undertake	angan, ongan, ongann, ongean, ongin, onginnað, onginnan, onginnaþ, onginneð, onginnen, onginneþ, ongon, ongunn, ongunnan, ongunne, ongunnen, ongunnon, ongyn, ongynneð, ongynneþ
unanimous	anmod, anmode		
un-asking	unfricgende, unfricgendum		
unassailed	unfliten, unflitne		
un-atoned	unþinged		
un-avenged	unwrecen		
un-baptised	ungefullod		
unbind	onband, onbindan		
un-burning	unbyrnende		
uncertainty	tweo		
unclean	ful, fula, fulan, fule, fullum, unclæne, unsyfra, unsyfre	undertaking	gahuuem, gahwem
		undertook	ongan
		underwater-creature	wægbora
unclothe	ongyrede, ongyrwan	undo	fordon
uncomplicated	anfeald, anfealdne	unfasten	onspeon, onsponnan
unconcerned-by	orsorg, orsorge		
unconscious	sworcenferð, sworcenferþ	unfinished	samworht
		unfortunate	heardsæligne, unsælga, unsælig
uncontested	unbefohten, unbefohtene	un-fought	unbefohten, unbefohtene
uncorrupted	gesund		
under	sub, under, undor	un-grown	unweaxen
under-eaten	undereotone	unguarded	orwearde
understand	angeat, forstandan, forstod, forstode, forstodon, gecnawan, oncnawan, oncneow, oncniow, ongæt, ongeat, ongeaton, ongietan, ongieten, ongit, ongitan, ongite, ongytan, ongyton	unhappiness	langoþe, longaþ, longaþes, wonsceaft, wonsceaftum
		unhappy	heardsælig, heardsæligne, sar, sare, sarferhð, sarferhþ, sarigferð, sarigferþ, sarost, sarra, sarum, unbliðe, unbliþe, wonsæli
		unhappy-love	sorglufu
		unharmed	gesund

Word List (English to *Ænglisc*)

English	*Ænglisc*	English	*Ænglisc*
unhealthy	wanhal, wanhalum	unrighteousness	unrihtwisnys, unrihtwisnysse
unheard-of	niowan, niwan, niwe, niwes, niwra, niwre	un-rightful-act	unriht, unrihte
		unrightfully	unrihte
unhurt	hal	unruly	unræd
uninhabited	weste, westne	un-secretly	undearninga
uninjured	andsund, ansund, onsund, onsundne	unsheathe	ateon
		unsound	unhæl, unhælo
unintentionally	unwillum	unspoiled	unwemme
united	ætsomne, anmod, anmode, gesome, som	un-stirring	unhror
		unsuccessful	unspedig, unspedigran
universal	gemæne, gemænra, gemænum	untamed	wilde
		untie	onsæl, onsælan, onwindan, onwindeð, onwindeþ
unknowing	uncuþ		
unknown	uncuþ		
unless	butan, bute, buton, næfne, nefne, nemne, nemþe, nymðe, nymþe	until	hwænne, hwonne, oð, oð þæt, oððæt, oðþæt, oþ, oþ þæt, oþðæt, oþþæt, tilian, tilien, tilode
unlike	ungelic, ungelice		
unlimited	ormæte	until-now	gena, giena
unliving	unlifigende, unlyfigende, unlyfigendes, unlyfigendne, unlyfigendum	untroubled-with	orsorg, orsorge
		untrue	untreowa, untreowe
		untrustworthy	swicol, swicole
		untruth	ligen, ligenum, lygenum
unlock	onleac, onlucan	untruthfulness	untryoð, untryoða, untryoþ, untryoþa
unloved	unleof, unleofe		
unlovely	unfæger	unwarily	unwærlice
unlucky	heardsælig, heardsæligne	unwary	unwar, unware
		unwaveringly	unwaclice
unmolested	sorhleas	unwelcome	lað, laþ
un-oppressed	gerume, rum, rume, rumne, rumre, rumum	unwillingly	unwillum
		unwind	onwindan, onwindeð, onwindeþ
un-peaceful	ungesibb, ungesibbum	unwise	ungleaw
		un-wise	unsnyttru, unsnyttrum
unpleasant	laðlic, laðlicu, laþlic, laþlicu, unliðe, unliþe, unswæslic, unswæslicne	unworthily	unwurðlice, unwurþlice
		unwounded	unwundod
unprofitable-thing	unfreme, unfremu	unwrap	onwriðan, onwriþan
unpromising	unspedig, unspedigran	unyielding	stedefæst, stedefæste
unprotected-from	unwered, werian	unyieldingly	stædefæste
unrelated	ungesibb, ungesibbum	up	up, upp, uppe
		up-high	uphea
un-right	unriht, unryhte	upkeep	feorm, feorme

Word List (English to Ænglisc)

English	Ænglisc	English	Ænglisc
up-keeper	feormend, feormendra, feormynd	utter	gewræc, gewrec, gewrecen, gewrecene, wræc, wræce, wræcon, wrec, wrecan, wrece, wrecen
upon	on, up, upp		
upon-us	us		
upper-air	uplyfte		
upright	uplang, uppriht	utterance	cwide, cwyde, meðel, meþel, meþle, word, worda, wordcwida, wordcwydas, wordcwyde, wordcwydum, worde, wordes, wordon, wordum
up-to	ætstaeppan, ætstop, oð, oþ		
upward	ufe-weard		
upwards	up, wið uppan, wiþ uppan		
urge	bæd, bædan, bædde, bædon, beden, biddan, forspanan, forspeon, fysan, fysde, gebæded, gefysed, span, spanan, speon, speone		
		utterly	forswiðe, forswiþe
		V, v	
		vain	forod
urge-on	afysan, afysed	valiant	deor, forðgeorn, forþgeorn, hwætt, modega, modgan, modge, modges, modgum, modi, modig, modiga, modigan, modige, modiges, modigra, modigre
us	unc, us, usic, ussum		
use	bræc, breac, bruc, brucað, brucan, brucaþ, bruce, bruceð, bruceþ, bryttað, bryttade, bryttaþ, bryttedon, bryttian, bryttigin, neat, neot, neotan, niotað, niotan, niotaþ, noden, nudon, nytt, nytte		
		valiantly	ellenlice
		valley	dæl, dala, dalo, dena, denu
		valorous	ellenmærðum, ellenmærþu, ellenmærþum
useful	gifre, nyt, nytt, nytte, nyt-wyrðe, nyt-wyrþe	valour	dryhtscipe, ellen, ellenmærðum, ellenmærþu, ellenmærþum, elne, elnes
useless	forod, idel, idlu, orfeorme, unnyt		
use-sparingly	sparedon, sparian, sparode		
us-two	inc	valour-deed	ellendæd, ellendæda, ellendædum
usual	geþywe		
usually	hordweard		
usually-maternal-uncle	eam, eame	valuable-possession	maðmæhta, mæðmæht, mæþmæht, maþmæhta
utility	nytt		

Word List (English to Ænglisc)

English	Ænglisc	English	Ænglisc
valued	weorðfull, weorþfull, woerðfullost, woerþfullost	venture	sïþ
		verbal-attack	beadurun, beadurune
vanguard	forðhere, forðherge, forþhere, forþherge, mearcþreat, mearcþreate, ord, orde	verbal-promise	wordbeot, wordbeotung, wordbeotunga
		verse	fers
		vertebra	banhring, banhringas
vanish	geswiðrod, geswiþrod, swiðrade, swiðrian, swiðrode, swiþrade, swiþrian, swiþrode	very	ful, full, geneahe, geneahhe, genehe, genehost, mæst, mæsta, mæste, mæstne, miccles, micclum, micel, miceles, micelne, micle, micles, miclum, mycclum, mycelre, mycle, myclum, swiðe, swiðor, swiðost, swiþe, swiþor, swiþost, swyðe, swyðor, swyþe, swyþor, to, ungemete
vanquish	oferswað, oferswaþ, oferswyðan, oferswyðeð, oferswyðeþ, oferswyþan, oferswyþeþ, oferwinnan, oferwunnen		
vanquished	sigeleas, sigelease, sigeleasne, tirleas, tirleases		
various	mislic, mislicum, missenlic, missenlicum		
		very-beautiful	ælfsciene, ælfscieno, ælfscinu
variously	missenlice	very-brave	felamodig, felamodigra
various-ways	mislice		
varying-words	gewrixle		
vassal	geneatas, neat	very-dear	felaleof, felaleofan
vast	unmæte	very-eager	georne, geornful
vast-heritage	eormenlaf, eormenlafe	very-faithful	welhold
		very-famous	foreldit, foremære, foremærost, formærne
vault	gehlidu, hlid, hwealf		
vaulted	hwealf, hwealfum		
vegetable	wyrt, wyrte, wyrtum	very-green	ælgrene
vein	ædra, ædre, ædrum	very-grey-haired	anhar
vein-spring	edrum	very-hard	forheard, forheardne, stedeheard, stedehearde
venerable	andrysne, andrysnum, ondrysne		
venerated	deorwurðan, deorwurðe, deorwurþan, deorwurþe	very-many	ealfela
		very-mighty	ðryðswyð, þryðswyð, þryþswyþ
vengeance	wrace, wracu, wræc, wræce, wræces		
venom	attor		

Word List (English to *Ænglisc*)

English	*Ænglisc*	English	*Ænglisc*
very-much	mæst, mæsta, mæste, mæstne, miccles, micclum, miceles, micelne, micle, micles, miclum, mycclum, mycelre, mycle, myclum, stiðe, stiþe, swiðe, swiðor, swiðost, swiþe, swiþor, swiþost, swyðe, swyðor, swyþe, swyþor	victorious-tree	sigebeam
		victorious-women	sigewif
		victory	æsctir, hreð, hreðsigor, hreðsigora, hreþ, hreþsigor, hreþsigora, sige, sigehreð, sigehreþ, sigel, sigeres, sigor, sigora, sigore, sigores, sigoro
		victory-banner	sigeþuf, sigeþufas
		victory-cross	sigebeam
very-nearly	fulneah	victory-field	sigewong
very-proud	felawlonc	victory-folk	sigefolca
very-sad	felageomor	victory-in-battle	guðhreð, guþhreþ
very-sinful	felasinnig, felasinnigne	victory-in-war	wigsigor
		victory-king	sigedrihten
very-strong	felahror	victory-lord	sigedrihten
very-sustaining	swiðe, swiðfeorm, swiþe, swiþfeorm	victory-time	sigehwil, sigehwila
		victory-tree	sigebeam
very-tough	regnheard, regnhearde	victory-warriors	sigebeorna
		victory-weapon	sigewæpen, sigewæpnum
very-wise	foresnotor, foresnotre, infrod, infrodum	view	gesihð, gesihðe, gesihþ, gesihþe, gesyhðe, gesyhþe
vessel	fær, fære, fæt, fatu, hordfate, wunderfæt, wunderfatum	vigorous	caf, cafne, hror, hroran, liffæst, liffæstan
vexation	anda, andan	vigorously	caflice, fromlice, heardlice
vexed	drefeð		
vibrate	cweccan, cwehte	vigour	strengðo, strengþo
vice	leahtor, leahtrum	viking	wicinga, wicingas, wicingum
victorious	blædagande, sigeeadig, sigefæst, sigefæstran, sigefest, sigerof, sigerofe, sigoreadig, sigorfæst, tireadig, tireadigra, tireadigum, tirfæst, tirfæste	vile	earmsceapen, fracod, fracodes
		vilely	fracodlice, fracoðlice, fracoþlice
		village	tun
		vindicate	beladian
		vineyard	wingeard
		violate	abrecan, abrocen, abrocene
victorious-cross	sigebeam		
victorious-exultant	sigehræmig		
victorious-people	sigefolc, sigefolca, sigefolce, sigeþeod, sigeþeode		
victorious-strong	sigerofra		

Word List (English to Ænglisc)

English	Ænglisc	English	Ænglisc
violence	geþræc, gryra, gryre, gryrum, guðþracu, guðþræce, guþþracu, guþþræce, hæst, hæste, morþor, sweordbealo	virgin	fæmnan, fæmne, fæmnum, femnan, mæden, mædene, unwemme
violent	hæst, hæstne, hreo, hreoh, hreon, hreoum, þearl, þearlmod	virginity	clænnys, clænnysse, mægðhad, mægðhade, mægþhad, mægþhade
violent-attack	niðgeteon, niðgeteone, niþgeteon, niþgeteone	virgins'	femnena
violent-attacker	færsceaða, færsceaðan, færsceaþa, færsceaþan	virtue	ar, ara, aran, are, arena, arna, arra, arum, cræft, ðeawum, dugeða, dugeðe, dugeðum, dugeþa, dugeþe, dugeþum, dugoða, dugoðe, dugoþa, dugoþe, duguð, duguða, duguðe, duguðum, duguþ, duguþa, duguþe, duguþum, geearnung, geearnunga, geearnunge, godnys, godnysse, gumcyst, gumcyste, gumcystum, mægena, þeaw, þeawas, þeawum
violent-battle	þræcwig, þræcwiges		
violent-death	wældeað, wældeaþ		
violent-flame	heaðofyr, heaðofyrum, heaðowelm, heaðowylm, heaðowylma, heaðowylmas, heaðufyr, heaðufyres, heaþofyr, heaþofyrum, heaþowelm, heaþowylm, heaþowylma, heaþowylmas, heaþufyr, heaþufyres	virtues	dugeþa
		virtuous	arfæst, arfæstan, arfæste, cusc, cuscne, geþungen, geþungon, halre, þeawfæst
violently	færlice, firenum, firnum, fyrenum, fyrnum, hæste, þearle	visible	open, opene
		vision	gesihð, gesihðe, gesihþ, gesihþe, gesyhðe, gesyhþe, heafodsien, heafodsiene, heafodsyne, sien, siene
violently-boil-or-surge	hioroweallan, hioroweallende		
violent-outlaw	heorowearh, heorowulf		

Word List (English to Ænglisc)

English	Ænglisc	English	Ænglisc
visit	geneosode, gesec, gesecan, gesecanne, gesece, gesecean, geseceð, geseceþ, gesohtan, gesohte, gesohtest, gesohton, neosan, neosian, niosað, niosan, niosaþ, niosian, sec, secan, sece, seceað, secean, seceaþ, seceð, secen, secest, seceþ, socn, socne, sohtan, sohte, sohten, sohtest, sohton	wagon	wæn
		wailing	heaf
		wait	bad, beodan, bidan, bideð, bideþ, bidon, gebad, gebidan, gebidanne, gebide, gebiden
		waited	gebad
		wake	waca, wacan, wæccan, wæccende, wæccendne, woc, wocan, woce, wocon, wocun
		wake-up	wreccan, wrehton
		walk	gan, gang, gangænde, gangan, gange, gangende, gangon, gegangan, gegangeð, gegangenne, gegangeþ, gegongen, genge, geong, geongon, gieng, giong, gongan, gonge, gongen
visiting-troop	gistmægen	walk-around	ymbeode, ymbgan
visitor	giestas, ingenga	walker-in-border-regions	mearcstapa, mearcstapan
visitors	gistmægen	walker-in-shadow	sceadugenga
voice	gereord, hleoðor, hleoðre, hleoðrum, hleoþor, hleoþre, hleoþrum, hlioðorcwidum, reord, reorde, stæmne, stefn, stefne, stemn, stemne	walking	feðegang, feðegange, feþegang, feþegange
		walking-warrior	feðecempa, feþecempa, feþecempan
void	idel, idlu		
vomit	aspaw, aspiwan		
voracious	ungifre		
vow	beot, beotedan, beotian, beotode, beotword, beotwordum, gebeot, gebeotedon	wall	wag, wage, wagum, weal, weall, weallas, wealle, wealles, weallum
vowed	beotedan		
vowing	beotword, beotwordum		
voyage	sið, siþ	wall-buildings	burgræced
voyage-?	eolet, eoletes	wall-cliff	weallclif
		walled-stronghold	wealfæsten

W, w

English	Ænglisc	English	Ænglisc
wade	gewaden, gewod, wadan, waden, wod, wodon	walled-town	burgtun, burgtunas, burhloca, burhlocan, weallfæsten, weallfæstenna
wages	andlifen, andlifne		

Word List (English to Ænglisc)

English	Ænglisc	English	Ænglisc
wallow	wealweode, wealwian, wealwigende	war-equipment	heaðoreaf, heaþoreaf, heregeatu, hildegeatwa, hildegeatwe
wall-steep	weallsteap, weallsteapan, weallsteape	warfare	wigrædenne
wall-stone	wealstan	war--hate	wighete
wall-stones	weallstana	war-head	wigheafola, wigheafolan
wand	sigegyrd		
wander	woriað, worian, woriaþ, worie	war-helmet	beadogrima, beadogriman
wanderer	anhaga, eard-stapa, wræcca	war-horn	guðhorn, guþhorn
		warily	wærlice
wandering	wæfre	war-king	guðcyning, guðkyning, guþcyning, guþkyning
wanders	waðol		
wane	gewanod, wanian		
waning	wanað		
want	gad, gæd, willan	war-leader	herewisa, wigfruma, wigfruman
wanting	wana		
wanton	hygegal, hygegalan	warlike	guþmod, heaþogeong, wiglic
war	beadowe, beadu, beaduwe, beadwa, beadwe, compwig, compwige, gewin, gewinn, gewinne, gewinnes, guð, guða, guðe, guðum, guþ, guþa, guþe, guþum, hild, hilde, orlegnið, orlegniþ, wig, wige, wiges, wigge, wigum, winn	warlike-attack	guðþracu, guðþræce, guþþracu, guþþræce
		warlike-enemy	guðsceaða, guþsceaþa
		warlike-stature	herewæsm, herewæsmun
		warlord	guðweard, guþweard
		war-mask	heregrima, heregriman
war-accoutrements	wiggetawe, wiggetawum	war-mongering	orlæggifre
war-arrow	guðflan, guðflana, guþflan, guþflana	warn	gemanode, gemoniað, gemoniaþ, gemonige, manað, manaþ, manian, manod, manode, monað, monaþ, warnað, warnaþ, warnian
war-band	wigheap		
war-banner	guðfana, guðfanum, guþfana, guþfanum, hildecumbor		
war-bird	herefugol, herefugolas		
war-board	guðbord, guðbordes, guþbord, guþbordes	warning	myrcels, myrcelse
		war-noise	hildesweg
war-bright	wigblac	warped	wearp
ward	uard, uueard, weard	war-play	guðplega, guþplega, wig-plega
war-dress	heresceorp		

Word List (English to *Ænglisc*)

English	*Ænglisc*	English	*Ænglisc*
warrior	æscberend, æscberendra, beadorinc, beadorinca, beadurinc, beorn, cempa, dreng, drenga, eorl, eorla, eorlas, eorle, eorles, eorlum, freca, frecan, fyrdrinc, fyrdrinces, garberend, garberendra, gram, graman, grame, gramena, grames, gramum, grome, gromra, guðbeorn, guðfreca, guðfrecan, guðfremmend, guðfremmendra, guðrinc, guðrinca, guðwiga, guþbeorn, guþfreca, guþfrecan, guþfremmend, guþfremmendra, guþrinc, guþrinca, guþwiga, hæl, hælæð, hælæþ, hæleð, hæleða, hæleðum, hæleþ, hæleþa, hæleþas, hæleþum, heaðorinc, heaðorincas, heaðorinces, heaðorincum, heard	war-shaft	heresceaft, heresceafta
		war-smith	wigsmið, wigsmiðum, wigsmiþ, wigsmiþum
		war-smiths	wigsmiþas
		war-song	guðleoð, guþleoþ, wigleoð, wigleoþ
		war-spoils	herehuþ, herehuþe, herereaf, orlegceap
		war-sword	wigbil
		war-terror	herebroga, herebrogan, wiggryre
		war-trappings	fyrdsearo, fyrdsearu, guðsearo, guþsearo, wighyrstum
		war-troop	guðþreat, guþþreat
		war-violence	wigbealu
		war-working	beaduweorca
	was	þa, wære, wæron, wæs, wearð, wes
		was (Latin)	erat
		wash	aþwean, aþwoh, ðwoh, gelafede, lafian, þwean, þwoh
		was-hidden (Latin)	abscondita
		was-not	ne
		waste	forspildan, weste, westne
		waste-away	gewanod, wanian
		wasteland	westen, westenne
		watch	onsegon, onseon
		watch-against-giants-or-trolls	eotonweard
		watch-over-the-shore	ægwearde
warrior-band	fyrdgetrum	watchtower	torr, torre
warrior-chief	magoræswa		
warrior-king	beorncyning		
warrior-number	rincgetæl		
warriors	bencsittende, bencsittendum, beorna, bordhæbbende, eorlas, fletsittende, fletsittendum, secg, wigend, wiggendra		
war-road	herestræt, herestræta		

Word List (English to *Ænglisc*)

English	*Ænglisc*	English	*Ænglisc*
water	brim, brimes, brimu, brimwylm, brymu, flod, floda, flodas, flode, flodes, holm, holma, holmas, holme, holmes, leccan, leoht, leohte, sund, sunde, sundes, wada, wado, wadu, wæd, wædes, wæg, wæge, wæter, wætera, wætere, wæteres, wætre, wætres, wætrum, weg, wegas, weter	wave-battalion	egorhere
		wave-bearer	wægbora
		wave-current	wægstream
		wave-floater	wegflota
		wave-host	wægþreat, wægþreate
		wave-in-a-circular-motion	gewand, wand, windan, wunden, wundnum, wundon
		wave-passage	wægfaru
		wave-plane	wægþæl, wægþel, wægþele
		wave-planking	wæg-þel
		waves	wegas, yða, yþa
		wave-sailor	yðlida, yðlidan, yðmearas, yðmearh, yþlida, yþlidan, yþmearas, yþmearh
water-body	flod, floda, flodas, flode, flodes		
		wave-sailors	yðmearas
water-filled	inflede	wave-sea	wægholm
water-full	inflede	wave-struggle	yðgewinn, yðgewinne, yðgewinnes, yþgewinn, yþgewinne, yþgewinnes
water-mixing	sundgebland		
water-monster	nicer, nicera, niceras, nicras		
water-monster-house	nicorhus, nicorhusa		
water-protection	sundhelm, sundhelme	wave-traveller	wæg-liðend, wæg-liþend
water-rusher	wæterþisa		
waters	lago, lagu, laguflod, laguflode	wave-tumult	yðgewinn, yðgewinne, yðgewinnes, yþgewinn, yþgewinne, yþgewinnes
water's	wædes		
water-terror	wæteregesa, wæteregesan		
water-wall	sæweall, sæwealle		
water-wave	wæteryð, wæteryðum, wæteryþ, wæteryþum	wavy[ornamented]-sword	wægsweord
		wax	Weax, weaxan, weaxen, weox, weoxon
water-way	lagu-lad		
watery	wæterþisa	waxed	weox
wave	flod, floda, flodas, flode, flodes, sæwylm, sæwylmas, waðum, wæg, wæge, waþema, waþum, weg, yð, yða, yðe, yðum, yþ, yþa, yþe, yþum	waxing	weaxeð
		way	fare, faru, foldweg, foldwegas, foldwege, gelad, lad, lade, wæg, weg, wisan, wise, wisna, wisum, wysan
		wayfaring	wegfarende

Word List (English to Ænglisc)

English	Ænglisc	English	Ænglisc
way-forth	forðweg, forðwegas, forðwege, forþweg, forþwegas, forþwege	weapon	mægenfultum, mægenfultuma, wæpen, wæpenes, wæpna, wæpne, wæpnes, wæpnum
way-from-the-south	suðweg, suðwegum, suþweg, suþwegum	weaponed	wæpned
way-of-life	drohtað, drohtaþ, drohtnian, drohtnode, drohtnung, drohtnunge, drohtoð, drohtoþ, for, fore, gedrohtnunge, weoruld, worold, worolde, woruld, worulde	weapon-fastened	gyrdan, gyrded
		weaponry	searo, searwum
		weapons	breostweorðung, breostweorðunge, breostweorþung, breostweorþunge, guðsearo, guþsearo, heaðoreaf, heaþoreaf, hildesceorp
		weapons-and-armour	heregeatu
way-out	utsiþ	weapon-storm	wæpenþracu, wæpenþræce
waypoint	ætstealle		
we	ure, ures, urne, urum, us, userne, usic, usser, usses, ussum, we, wit	wear	oboren, onberan, wæg, wægon, wagon, wegan, wege, wegeð, wegeþ, wegon, wered, werede, werian, wigeð, wigeþ
weak	mettrum, mettrume, swær, swæran, swancor, swoncre, tydre, wac, wace, wacne, wacran, wanhal, wanhalum, werge, wergum, werig, werige	wearily	werige, werigne
		wearisome	longsum, longsumne
weak-birth	swærbyrde	weary	geswence, reonigmod, reonigmode, werge, wergum, werig, werige, werigferðe, werigferhð, werigferhðe, werigferhþ, werigferhþe, werigferþe, werigmod
weaken	asealcan, onwæcan, onwæcen, wacað		
weaker	sæmra, sæmran		
wealth	beag, beaga, beagas, beage, beages, beagum, beah, begas, fea, feo, feoh, feos, gestreon, sceat, sceates, sceatt, sceattas, sceattes, sceattum		
		weary-from-combat	guðwerigne, guþwerigne
wealth-gift	feohgift, feohgiftum, feohgyft, feohgyfte, feohgyftum	weary-limbed	limwerig, limwerigne
		weary-minded	higemæðum, higemæþum, hygemeðe, hygemeþe

Word List (English to Ænglisc)

English	Ænglisc	English	Ænglisc
weather	weder, wedera, wederum, wedres	west	west
weather-beaten	lyftgeswenced	west-end	westende
weave	bræd, brægd, bregdan, bregde, bregdon, broden, brogdne, brudon, brugdon, gebræd, gebroden, gelocen, locenra, lucan, lucon, wefan	West-Saxon	Wesseaxena
		West-Saxons	Wesseaxe
		wet	besteman, bestemed, bestyman, bestymed, wæt
		we-two	unc, uncer, uncerne, uncran, uncre, uncres, us, user, usser, wit, wyt
wedding-gift	handgyft	whale	hronfisc, hronfixas, hwæl, hwæles, hwale, wæterþisa
week	wucan, wucu		
weep	weop, wepan		
weeping	reotig, reotugu, wop, wope	whale-lake	hwælmere
weigh-down	gehlæste, hlæstan	whale-path	hwælweg
weight (Latin)	pondus	whale-road	hron-rad
Weland's (name)	Welande	whale's	hwæles
welcome-guest	wihte, wilcuma, wilcuman	whale-way	hwælweg
		what	huuæt, hwa, hwæs, hwæt, hwelc, hwilc, hwilce, hwylc, hwylce, hwylcere, hwylcne, hwylcum
welfare	gesynta, gesynto, gesyntum		
well	fægere, fægre, fægrost, georne, geornor, stiðe, stiþe, teala, tela, wel, well		
		what-is-appropriate	gerisno, gerysne, gerysnu
well-adorned	gewlitegod	what-is-just-and-right	ferhtgereaht
wellbeing	godes		
well-informed	felafricgende	what-is-left	laf, lafe
welling	weallendan, wylm	what-is-right	gerihte, rightly, riht, rihte, ryht, truly
well-known	gefræge, gefrægen, gefrægn		
		what-kind-of	hwelc, hwilc, hwilce, hwylc, hwylce, hwylcere, hwylcne, hwylcum
well-spring	willeburne, wylla		
well-water	willeburnan, wylleburne		
Welsh	Wealas	what-of	huaet, huuæt, huuet, hwæt, hwet
Welund (name)	Welund		
wen	wenne	wheat	corn, corna
wend	wendan, wende, wended	wheat-crop	hwæt, hwætewæstm, hwætewæstma
went	hwearf		
went-away	oððe, oðeodon, oðgan, oþeodon, oþgan, oþþe	whelp	hwelp
went-out	gewat		
were	uuære, wæran, wære, wæron		
were-able-to	moston		

Word List (English to Ænglisc)

English	Ænglisc	English	Ænglisc
when	ða, ðonne, hwænne, hwonne, se, seoððan, seoþðan, seoþþan, siððan, siþðan, siþþan, swa, syððan, syðþan, syþðan, syþþan, þa, þænne, þonne	who	ðæt, ðe, hwa, hwæne, hwæt, hwam, hwan, hwon, hwone, hy, se, seo, þa, þæt, þe, þone
whence	hwanan, hwanon	who (Latin)	quem
where	ða, hwær, hwar, hwergen, hwyder, se, þær, þe	whole	andsund, ansund, gesund, gesunde, gesundne, gesundran, hæl, hal, halan, hale, onsund, onsundne
wherein-such-a-case-where	ðær, ðar, þær, þar	whom	þone
		whore	sceand, sceande
wherever	Gehwer	whose-name-is-known	namcuþ, namcuþre
whether	hwæðer, hwæt, hwæþer, hwæþer, sy	whosoever	swa, swa hwilc swa
which	ða, ðæt, ðe, esa, hwa, hwæne, hwam, hwan, hwelc, hwilcne, hwon, hwone, hwylc, se, seo, þæt, þætte, þætte, þe	why	hwi, hwy, to, to hwon
		wicked	arleas, flah, lyðra, mæne, unfæle, unlæd, unlædan, unsælga, unsælig, werg, wergan, wergas, wergum, werig
which (Latin)	que		
whichever	swæþer	wickedness	fyren, mane, manfæhðu, manfæhþu, yfel, yfele, yfeles, yfla, yfles
which-of-two	hwæðer, hwæþer		
while	ðenden, hwil, hwile, hwilnan, þenden, þonne		
whip	swang, swingan, swingeð, swingeþ	wick-reeve	wic-gerefa
		wide	brad, bradan, brade, bradnæ, bradre, geap, geapes, geapne, geapum, gerume, ginn, ginnan, ginne, gynn, gynne, rum, rume, rumne, rumre, rumum, sid, sidan, side, sidne, sidra, sidre, syddra, wid, wida, widan, wide, widne, widre, wyde
whispering	runung, rununga		
whit	wiht		
white	blac, blacne, huuit, hwit, hwita, hwitan, hwite, hwitne, hwitost, hwitre		
white-haired	hwitlocced, hwitloccedu		
white-horse	blanca, blancum		
whither	hwæder, hwider, hwyder		
Whitwell-Gap (place)	Hwitanwyllesgeat		

Word List (English to Ænglisc)

English	Ænglisc	English	Ænglisc
widely	brade, gerumlicor, rume, rumlice, rumor, side, widan, widdor, wide, widost, widre	will	nele, nellað, nellaþ, nelle, noldan, nolde, noldon, wile, willa, willað, willan, willaþ, wille, willende, willum, wilna, wilt, woldan, wolde, wolden, woldest, woldon, wyle, wyllað, wyllan, wyllaþ, wylle, wylt
widely-distributed	widsceope		
widely-famous	widmære		
widely-known	widcuðne, widcuþ, widcuþes, widcuþne		
wide-men	uðwitan		
wide-or-extensive-land	sidland		
		will-be	uuiorðeð, uuiorþeþ, uuiurðit, uuiurþit, uuyrþeþ, wiorðe, wiorðeð, wiorþe, wiorþeþ, wiurðit, wiurþit, wyrþeþ
widespread	widscofen		
widow	wuda, wudewan, wuduwan, wuduwe, wydewan, wydewe		
wield	gewealdan, gewealdene, gewealdenne, geweold, geweoldum, wealdan, wealde, wealden, weold, weoldon		
		willing-companion	wilgesið, wilgesiþ
		willing-follower	wilgesið, wilgesiþ
		willingly	unmurnlice
		will-not	ne
		win	gewinnan
		Winchester (place)	Wincestre
wielded	genæson, wealdan	wind	blæst, gewand, wand, weder, wedera, wedres, wind, windan, winde, wond, wunden, wundnum, wundon
wielder	wealdend		
wielding	gewealdum		
wife	bryd, bryda, bryde, cwen, mæg, wif, wifa, wife, wifes, wifum		
		wind-home	windgeard
wife-love	wifmyne	wind-mixing	windblond
wild	hreo, unheore, unheoru, unhiore, unhyre, wilda, wilde, wildne, wildra, wildu	winds	windas
		windswept	windge, windig, windige
		wind-swirling	windblond
wild-animal	deor, wilde, wildeor	windy	windge, windig, windige
wild-boar	eofer, eoferas, swin, swyn		
		wine	win, wine
wild-boar-banner	eofer, eoferas, swinlic, swinlicum	wine-building	winærn, winærnes, winreced
wild-boar-image	swinlic, swinlicum	wine-cup	lithwæge
wild-boar-sign	eofer, eoferas, swinlic, swinlicum	wine-drinking	wingedrinc, wingedrince, wingedrync
wilderness	westen, westenne	wine-drunk	wingal
		wine-gay	win-gal
		wine-hall	winsæl, winsalo, winsele

Word List (English to *Ænglisc*)

English	*Ænglisc*	English	*Ænglisc*
wing	feðer, feðera, feþer, feþera, feþra, fiþrum, ueþer	wise	felafricgende, frod, froda, frodan, frode, frodran, gewittig, gleaw, gleawan, gleawe, gleawferhð, gleawferhþ, gleawhydig, gleawne, gleawra, gleawum, higefrod, rædfæst, snotera, snoteran, snotere, snotor, snotra, snottor, snottra, snottre, snytrum, þancolmod, þoncol, wigtig, wis, wisa, wise, wisfæst, wisfæste, wishidig, wishydig, wisra, wisum, witega, witig
wings	feðerhama, feðerhaman, feðerhoma, feðerhoman, feþerhama, feþerhaman, feþerhoma, feþerhoman		
winter	winter, wintra, wintres, wintrum, wintrys		
winter-caring	winter-cearig		
winter-churlishness	wintercearig		
winter-cold	wintercealde, wintercealde		
winter-despondency	wintercearig		
winter-hour	winterstund, winterstunde	wise-fast	wisfæste
winters	wintra	wisely	snotorlice, snotorlicor, wislice
wintry-minded	wintercearig		
wire	wir, wira, wire, wirum	wise-man	gewita, gewitan, snotor, weotena, wita, witan, witena
wire-ornament	wir, wira, wire, wirum	wiser	snotera
wisdom	gleawra, snottra, snytra, snytro, snytru, snytrum, snyttru, snyttrum, wisdom, wisdome	wise-soul	higegleawe
		wisest	snoterost
		wise--thinking	wishycgende
		wish	an, geuðe, geunnan, geunne, geuþe, nele, nellað, nellaþ, nelle, noldan, nolde, noldon, on, uðe, unnan, uþe, wile, willa, willað, willan, willaþ, wille, willende, willum, wilna, wilt, wiston, woldan, wolde, wolden, woldest, woldon, wyle, wyllað, wyllan, wyllaþ, wylle, wylt, wyscan, wyscte
		wished	nolde, wolde, wyscte
		wishes	wyle

534

Word List (English to Ænglisc)

English	Ænglisc	English	Ænglisc
wish-for	fundað, fundast, fundaþ, fundedon, fundian, fundiaþ, fundode, gehogod, gehogodest, gesec, gesecan, gesecanne, gesece, gesecean, geseceð, geseceþ, gesohtan, gesohte, gesohtest, gesohton, hogedon, hogian, hogode, hogodon, sec, secan, sece, seceað, secean, seceaþ, seceð, secen, secest, seceþ, sohtan, sohte, sohten, sohtest, sohton, wilnian	wither-away	geweornie
		with-evil-consequence	wraðe, wraðlice, wraðum, wraþe, wraþlice, wraþum
		withhold	forwyrnan, forwyrnde, forwyrne, ofteah, ofteon, oftihð, oftihþ
		with-honour	arwurðlice, arwurþlice
		within	binnan, geinnod, in, innan, innanweard, inne, inneweard, innewerdne, innianfill, mid
		within-deep	innanweard, inneweard
		within-reach-of	gehende
		without	bereafod, bireafod, butan, buton, geasne, gesne, leas, leasan, lease, leasne, leasum, ofer, ofor, orfeorme, wana
wish-to	wille		
wit	gewitt, gewitte, wite, witt		
witch	hægtessan, hægtesse, wycce, wyccum	without-a-caretaker	feormendleas, feormendlease
witchcraft	lyblac, lyblaca, lyblace	without-a-lord	hlafordleas, hlafordlease
witchery	hægtessan	without-a-polisher	feormendleas, feormendlease
with	be, bi, big, mid, wið, wiþ	without-a-soul	orsawle, sawelleas, sawelleasne, sawolleas, sawolleasne, sawulleas, sawulleasne
with (Latin)	cum		
with-before	mid		
with-child	bearn		
with-darkened-mind	sworcenferð, sworcenferþ		
with-determination	styrnmode	without-cattle	feoh-leas
with-difficulty	unsofte	without-cause	holinga
with-difficulty-or-hardship	earfoðlice, earfoþlice	without-compensation	feohleas
withdraw	abræd, abrægd, abregd, abregdan, abregde, abroden, abrugdon, aferian, aferige, feorran, oðwendan, ofteah, ofteon, oftihð, oftihþ, oþwendan	without-compunction	unmurnlice
		without-end	grundlease
		without-feet	feðeleas, feþeleas
		without-glory	domleas, domleasan, tirleas, tirleases
		without-grouching	unmurnlice

Word List (English to Ænglisc)

English	Ænglisc	English	Ænglisc
without-honour	arleas, arlease, arleasra	woman	cwen, fæmnan, fæmne, fæmnum, femnan, freo, ides, idesa, idese, idesum, mæg, mægða, mægðum, mægeð, mægeþ, mægþa, mægþum, meowlan, meowle, wif, wifa, wife, wifes, wifman, wifmann, wifmon, wifum, wimman, wimmanna
without-hope	hihtleasne, hyhtlease		
without-hope-of	orwena		
without-intercession	unþinged		
without-joy	dreamleas		
without-pity	carleas, carleasan		
without-reason	holunge		
without-restraint	unmæðlice, unmæþlice		
without-sensation	feleleas		
without-sorrow	sorhleas		
with-pleasure	lustum	woman-love	wifmyne
with-respect-to	toweard	woman's	fæmnan
withstand	wiðhabban, wiðhæfde, wiðstandan, wiðstanden, wiðstod, wiðstodon, wiðstondan, wiþhabban, wiþhæfde, wiþstandan, wiþstanden, wiþstod, wiþstodon, wiþstondan	women	wif
		women's-apartment	bur, bure, burum
		wonder	uuldurfadur, uundra, uuundra, wndra, wunder, wundor, wundra, wundre, wundrian, wundrigende, wundrodon, wundrung, wundrunge, wundur
		wondered	wandrode
withstood	ofstonden	wondrous	wrætlic, wrætlice, wrætlicne, wrætlicran, wrætlicu, wuldres, wunderlicu, wundorlic, wundorlicne, wundorlicran, wundrum
with-welling-tears	wollenteare		
witness	gewita, gewitan, weotena, wita, witan, witena		
wit's-enclosure	gewitlocan		
woe	wa, wawa, wawan, wea, wean, weana		
woe!	eala	wondrous-cup	wunderfæt, wunderfatum
woe-deeds	weadæda		
woeful	wa, wealic	wondrous-gift	wundorgiefe, wundorgiefu
woeful-remnant	wealaf, wealafe		
woes	wean	wondrously	wrætlice, wundrum
woe-story	inwitspell	wondrous-success	wuldorblæd
wolf	wulf, wulfas, wulfe, wulfum	wood	bearnum, bearo, bearu, bearwas, bearwe, holt, holte, holtes, holtwudu, wald, walde, weald, wealdas, wealde, wuda, wudu
wolf--inhabited-hillside	wulfhleoþu, wulfhlið, wulfhliþ		
wolfish	wylfen, wylfenne		
		wooden-shield	bordwudu

Word List (English to Ænglisc)

English	Ænglisc	English	Ænglisc
wooden-stronghold	wudufæsten	work	beworht, beworhte, bewyrcan, earfoþ, gæworht, geweorc, geweorces, geweorkes, geworht, geworhte, geworhtne, geworhton, gewunne, gewunnen, gewyrc, gewyrcan, gewyrce, gewyrcean, wan, wann, weorc, weorca, weorce, weorces, weorcum, winnað, winnan, winnaþ, winnende, won, wonn, worc, worca, worces, worcum, worhte, worhton, wunne, wunnon, wyrce, wyrcean, wyrceð, wyrceþ
woods	Wudu		
wood-smoke	wudurec		
woodwork	hrostbeages		
wool	wull, wulle		
word	cwyde, giedd, hleoðorcwydas, hleoðorcwyde, hleoþorcwydas, hleoþorcwyde, word, worda, wordcwida, wordcwydas, wordcwyde, wordcwydum, worde, wordes, wordon, wordum		
worded	weorð, weorðað, weorðaþ, weorðe, weorðeð, weorðen, weorþ, weorþaþ, weorþe, weorþeð, weorþen, weorþeþ, worden		
word-gift	woðgiefu, woþgiefu		
word-hoard	wordhord	work (Latin)	labor, ponus
wording	wurðað, wurðan, wurðaþ, wurde, wurðe, wurðeþ, wurdon, wurþan, wurþaþ, wurþe, wurþeþ, wyrð, wyrþ	worked	geworhtest, worhtest
		work-for	tilian, tilien, tilode
		working	geweorc, worhtan
		working-slave	worcþeow, worcþeowe
word-right	wordriht, wordrihta	workman	wyrhta
words	word, worde, wordum	workmanship	geweorc, geweorces
		work-of	uerc, uueorc, weorc
words-promised	wordbeotunga	work-of-courage	ellen-weorc
word-successful	wordsige	work-of-former-times	ærgeweorc
word-treasury	wordhord		
word-vows	wordbeot	works	gehwylcre, weorc, weorcum, wyrcð
word-wise	wordsnotor	work-successful	worcsige
		world	gesceaft, middan-eard, middangeard, moldan, molde, woruld, worulde, wuldres
		world-candle	woruldcandel
		world-edge	worulde, woruldende
		world-end	woruldende

537

Word List (English to Ænglisc)

English	Ænglisc	English	Ænglisc
world-kingdom	uundra, uuoruldrice, woruldrice	worse	wyrs, wyrsa, wyrsan, wyrse
worldly	middaneardlic, middaneardlice, worulde, woruldlic, woruldlicra	worship	bigeng, bigengum, bigong, geweorðad, geweorðan, geweorðod, geweorðode, geweorþad, geweorþade, geweorþan, geweorþod, geweorþode, gewurðien, gewurðod, gewurþad, gewurþien, gewurþod, weorðade, weorðiað, weorðian, weorðode, weorþad, weorþade, weorþian, weorþiaþ, weorþode, wurðiað, wurðian, wurðode, wurþian, wurþiaþ, wurþode
worldly-benefit	woruldnytt, woruldnytte		
worldly-creation	gesceaft, woruldgesceaft, woruldgesceafta, woruldgesceafte		
worldly-excellence	worulddugeða, worulddugeðum, worulddugeþa, worulddugeþum, woruldduguð, woruldduguþ		
worldly-honour	worold-ar, woroldare, woruld, woruldar, worulddugeða, worulddugeðum, worulddugeþa, worulddugeþum, woruldduguð, woruldduguþ		
		worst	wyrstan
worldly-leadership	woroldræden, woroldrædenne	worth	wurðe, wurþe
		worthier	wurþlicor
worldly-strength	woruldrice, woruldstrenga, woruldstrengu	worthily	weorðlic, weorþlic
		worthiness	weorða, weorðlican, weorþscipe, wurðlice
worldly-wisdom	woruldwisdom, woruldwysdome	worthless	cystleas, cystleasa
worlds	worulda	worth-minded	weorðmynda, weorþmynda
worm	wurman, wyrm, wyrmas, wyrme, wyrmes, wyrmum	worthy	wearð, weorð, weorþ, weorþe, weorþra, wurðe, wurðran, wurþe, wurþran, wyrðe, wyrðig, wyrðne, wyrðra, wyrþe, wyrþne, wyrþra
worm-body	wyrmlic, wyrmlicum		
worm-hall	wyrmsele		
worm-kind	wyrmcynn, wyrmcynnes		
worn	worie		
worn-out	meðe, meþe		
worry	ceara, cearað, cearaþ, cearian	worthy-in-battle	fyrdwyrðe, fyrdwyrþe
worry-about	sorga, sorgedon, sorgian, sorgiende		

538

Word List (English to Ænglisc)

English	Ænglisc	English	Ænglisc
would	scal, sceal, sceall, scealt, scel, sceolde, sceolden, sceoldest, sceoldon, sceole, sceolon, scile, scolde, scoldon, sculan, sculon, scyle, wolde	wound-sword	wundenmæl
		wound-weary	fylwerig, fylwerigne
		woven-fabric	web
		wrack	wræce
		wrap	wry
		wrap-up	bewreon, bewrigen, bewrigene, bewrigenum, biwrah
wound	amyrran, atæsan, atæsed, benn, benne, bennum, dolg, geræhte, geræhton, gewundian, gewundod, gewundode, hiorodrync, hiorodryncum, raecan, ræhte, ræhton, tæsan, tæsde, wund, wunde, wundian, wundiaþ, wundum	wrath	wraþe
		wrathful	ondwrað, wrað, wraða, wraðan, wraðe, wraðra, wraðum, wraþ, wraþa, wraþan, wraþe, wraþra, wraþum
		wrathfully	uuraþe, wraþe
		wreak	wræc, wræcon, wrecan, wrecen
		wretch	wræca, wræcca, wræcna, wrecca
		wretched	earg, earges, eargra, earh, earmsceapen, wræclic, wræclicne
wound-badly	forwunded, forwundian, forwundod	wretched-caring	earm-cearig
wounded	dolhwund, forwundod, fylwerig, fylwerigne, heaðosioc, heaðosiocum, heaþosioc, heaþosiocum, seo, seoc, seoce, wund, wunde, wundum, wundun	wretchedly	bleate, laðlicost
		wretchedness	yrmða, yrmðe, yrmðu, yrmðum, yrmþa, yrmþe, yrmþu, yrmþum
		wring	span, spinnan
		write	awritan, awrite, writan, writen
		writer	boceras, bocere
		writing	gewrit, gewritu, gewritum, gewrytum
wounded-neck	wundenhals		
wounded-to-death	fylwerig, fylwerigne	wrong	gedefe, gedwolen, gedwolene, læðð, læðða, læððum, læþþ, læþþa, læþþum, teona, teonan, teonum, ungedefe
wound-from-a-sax	sexbenn, sexbennum		
wound-incapacitated	werge, wergum, werig, werige		
wounding-enemy	dolsceaða, dolsceaðan, dolsceaþa, dolsceaþan	wrongly	gedefe, ungedefelice, unrihte
wound-opening	bengeat, bengeato		
wounds	wunda, wunde	wroth	wrað, wraþ
wound-staves	wundenstefna		

539

Word List (English to *Ænglisc*)

English	*Ænglisc*	English	*Ænglisc*
# Y, y		yield	ageald, agieldan, cringan, crong, crungen, crungon, geald, gieldan, golden, guldon
yard	geard		
year	gear, geara, gearum, missarum, missera, missere, misserum, winter, wintra, wintres, wintrum, wintrys	yore	geara
		you	ðe, ðec, ðin, ðinne, ðinra, ðu, eow, ge, incer, se, þe, þec, þin, þina, þine, þines, þinne, þinra, þinre, þinum, þu
year-day	gear-dæg		
year-days	GEARDAGUM		
yearn-for	gyrn, gyrnan, gyrnde, langað, langaþ, langian, langode, longade	you (plural)	eow, eower, eowere, eowerne, eowic, eowra, eowre, eowrum, ge
year-number	gearrim, gearrimum	you-have	hafest
years-ago	geara	young	geong, geonga, geongan, geonge, geongne, geongum, giong, giunge, unfrod, unfrodum, unweaxen
yeast-foam-from-beer	beorma, beorman		
yell	begeall, begiellan, begollen, begullon, giellan, gielleð, gielleþ, gylede, gylian, gyllende, hryman, hrymde		
		youngest	gingæste
		young-girl	mædenman
yell-about	bigeal, bigyllan	young-man	geonga, hægsteald, hægstealdra, hagosteald, hagostealdes, maga, magan, mago
yelling	gyllende		
yellow	fealone, fealu, fealwe, geolow, geolwe		
		young-people	gioguþ
yellow-hilt	fealohilte	youngster	geogoð, geogoþ
yellow-shield	geolorand	young-warrior	hægsteald, hægstealdmann, hægstealdmen, hægstealdra, hagosteald, hagostealdes
yells	gylleð		
yelp	gealp		
yes	gyse		
yesterday	gystran		
yet	ac, ær, æt, gean, gen, gena, gien, giena, giet, gieta, git, gy, gyt, gyta, hwæðere, hwæþere, þa, þeah	young-warriors	hægstealdas
		your	ði, ðin, ðines, ðinne, ðinre, ðinum, ðyn, eowre, hit, hy, þin, þine, þinne, þinra, þinre, þinum, þyn, þyne, þynum
yet-not-at-all	nohwæðere, nohwæðre, nohwæþere, nohwæþre	yours	ðine, ðrinesse, þin, þinne, þinum
		yours (Latin)	eius
		yourself	ðe, selfne, sylf, sylfa

Word List (English to *Ænglisc*)

English	*Ænglisc*
youth	cniht, cnihtas, cnihtum, cnyhtum, geogoð, geogoðe, geogoðfeore, geogoðfeorh, geogoþ, geogoþe, geogoþfeore, geogoþfeorh, geoguðe, geoguðfeore, geoguþ, geoguþe, geoguþfeore, giogoð, giogoðe, giogoþ, giogoþe, gioguðe, gioguþ, gioguþe, hysas, hyse, hyssa, hyssas, hysses, iogoþe
youthful-warriors	hyssa
youth-hood	geogoðhad, geogoðhade, geogoþhad, geogoþhade
youth's	geonges
you-two	git, gyt, in, inc, incer, incit, incre, incrum
you-wield	Wealdest

Z, z

zealous	fus, fuse, fusne

www.ingramcontent.com/pod-product-compliance
Lightning Source LLC
Chambersburg PA
CBHW051357070526
44584CB00023B/3197